HARVEST OF DESPAIR

HARVEST
—— OF ——
DESPAIR

Life and Death in Ukraine under Nazi Rule

KAREL C. BERKHOFF

THE BELKNAP PRESS OF
HARVARD UNIVERSITY PRESS
Cambridge, Massachusetts and London, England
2004

Frontispiece reprinted with permission from Paul Robert Magocsi,
A *History of Ukraine* (Toronto: University of Toronto Press, 1996). Map produced
by the Cartography Office, Department of Geography, University of Toronto.

Library of Congress Cataloging-in-Publication Data

Berkhoff, Karel C. (Karel Cornelis), 1965–
Harvest of despair : life and death in Ukraine under Nazi rule / Karel C. Berkhoff.
p. cm.
Includes bibliographical references and index.
ISBN 0-674-01313-1 (alk. paper)
1. Ukraine—History—German occupation, 1941–1944.
2. Germany. Reichskommissariat Ukraine.   I. Title.

DK508.833.B47 2004
940.53'477—dc22   2003062870

To Iet Scheers and Egbert Berkhoff

CONTENTS

Figures   ix
Preface   xi

Introduction   1

1 Soviet Ukraine and the German Invasion   6

2 The Reichskommissariat Ukraine   35

3 The Holocaust of the Jews and Roma   59

4 Prisoners of War   89

5 Life in the Countryside   114

6 Conditions in the Cities   141

7 Famine in Kiev   164

8 Popular Culture   187

9 Ethnic Identity and Political Loyalties   205

10 Religion and Popular Piety   232

11 Deportations and Forced Migrations   253

12 Toward the End of Nazi Rule   275

Conclusion   305

Appendix: Tables   317
Abbreviations   319
Notes   321
Sources   439
Acknowledgments   445
Index   447

FIGURES

1 The Reichskommissariat Ukraine at its largest.   xvi

2 Local residents greet a German soldier on a tank.
Kremenchuk, eastern Ukraine, September 1941.   22

3 One result of Stalin's scorched-earth policy—the
burned-out center of Kiev, probably on October 5, 1941.   31

4 Martin Bormann, head of the Nazi party chancellery,
Adolf Hitler, and one of the Führer's aides listen to
Erich Koch, Reichskommissar for Ukraine, at the
Werewolf headquarters north of Vinnytsia. Central
Ukraine, summer 1942.   38

5 Office of a district commissar. Oleksandriia, southern
Ukraine, 1942.   40

6 Open mass grave with thousands of Jews. Podolian
town of Proskuriv (today Khmelnytsky), 1941 or 1942.   63

7 Jews from Lubny, a town in the Left Bank, and
surroundings, who have obeyed an order to assemble.
Lubny region, October 16, 1941.   79

8 Imprisoned Red Army men unload ammunition at
a storage site. Some of their non-German supervisors
carry batons. Berdychiv, central Ukraine, August 28, 1941.   104

9 "The Collective Farm System Has Come to an End!"
Nazi propaganda poster, February 1942.   121

10 A farm leader and his secretary doing bookkeeping
in their office. Pereiaslav, central Ukraine, August 1943.   128

11 Public hanging, witnessed by local adults, children,
and German soldiers. Kiev, probably late 1941 or
early 1942.   148

12 The Galician Market (formerly the Jewish Market)
    in Kiev, September 1942.   175
13 At the height of the Nazi campaign to starve Kiev,
    an auxiliary policeman armed with a rifle stops
    women who wish to go there. Summer 1942.   178
14 Public meeting to mark the second anniversary of
    the "liberation" of the town of Vasylkiv, west of
    Kiev. August 20, 1943.   189
15 "The Wall Has Come Down." Nazi propaganda
    poster. Probably printed in 1941.   214
16 Boys of pacifist Mennonite origin, now
    "ethnic Germans," have donned swastika brassards
    and parade past SS leader Heinrich Himmler and
    other high-ranking visitors. Halbstadt district near
    Zaporizhzhia, Sunday morning, November 1, 1942.   227
17 A festive procession with church items that people
    had hidden for years from the Soviet authorities.
    Mykolaïv, southern Ukraine, October 1941.   240
18 Young men and women who have been forced to
    leave their villages to work in Germany carry heavy
    luggage as they walk toward an assembly point.
    Nekrasov Street, Kiev, 1942.   264
19 Tymofii Strokach, deputy chief of the Soviet Ukrainian
    NKVD, and Demian Korotchenko, a Communist
    party secretary, inspect some of Sydir Kovpak's
    partisans on the eve of their daring raid toward the
    Carpathian Mountains. Partisan zone in the
    Zhytomyr region in northern Ukraine, June 1943.   277
20 The effects of the Nazi scorched-earth policy.
    North of Kremenchuk, in central Ukraine, August
    or September 1943.   301
21 Women and a child give a warm and spontaneous
    welcome to the Red Army. Melitopol, southern
    Ukraine, October 1943.   303
22 A woman looks for her husband's body among
    exhumed corpses in the former Nazi concentration
    camp Syrets. Kiev, 1944.   307

PREFACE

This book is a narrative history of everyday life in Nazi Germany's largest colony and an assessment of the effect of Nazi rule on a territory that had known Soviet rule for over two decades: the Reichskommissariat Ukraine, founded in 1941 and ultimately dissolved in 1944. As such it is the first detailed description of what life there was like for the native population.

My goal has been to write a territorial history, not a national one. Instead of a study of Ukraine as a whole, this is a study of the Reichskommissariat Ukraine, which comprised much, but not all Ukrainian territory; and rather than a study of Ukrainians, it is a study of all its natives. This approach requires some explanation. In researching and writing the book, my premise has been that the best framework for studying Europe during World War II is to consider the territories that existed during that war. The vast majority of studies of German-ruled eastern Europe and Russia do not follow this principle. Ukrainian authors often assume that one can study collectively events during World War II in any territory where Ukrainians lived (among several, ruled by various states). Western and Russian authors often suppose that one can study collectively the wartime events in all territories that had been part of the Soviet Union in the middle of 1939, or even in early 1941. Polish authors, for their part, often decide that one can study collectively events between 1939 and 1945 "in the Second Republic" or "on the territory of the Second Republic," even though there was no such republic after 1939 or 1945. This book deals only with events in the territory that ultimately became part of the Reichskommissariat Ukraine.

My focus here is what I call "natives" or "the native population." Although it is customary to consider as native only those people who have the titular nationality of the state in question, this is not the case here. (And I use the word without any derogatory intent.) Instead, natives here are all those who lived in Ukraine before the Germans arrived. I have in-cluded the experience and perceptions not only of the Ukrainians but also, as much as possible, of Jews, Roma, Russians, and ethnic Germans. In short, the goal has been a multiethnic history. Yet the Ukrainians, who constituted the vast majority of the population of the Reichs-kommissariat, still get the most attention.

The Poles of the Reichskommissariat do not take center stage. This is purely for practical reasons: this book focuses on events in the core of the Reichskommissariat, because doing so reveals best not only the nature of the Nazi regime, but also the long-time influence of the Soviet regime, which had ruled that central Ukrainian region for two decades. The Poles of the Reichskommissariat mostly inhabited western Volhynia, which had known Soviet rule for only a brief period between 1939 and 1941. To maintain the book's conceptual focus on Ukraine's central re-gion, I also devote very little attention to the adjacent entity with a large Ukrainian population that was called the General Government, which included the Polish and Ukrainian cities of Kraków and Lviv as well as four of the infamous Nazi death camps.

This book is primarily, although not exclusively, a history "from the bottom up." Only in this way, I believe, will it be possible to provide the reader with a sense of the everyday experiences of the natives under the Nazi system. Even the Reich commissar in charge of the area, Erich Koch, gets relatively little attention. Because in everyday life the popula-tion hardly ever saw the leading Nazis—Koch spent most of his time out-side the Reichskommissariat, in East Prussia—omitting most details about them provides a more realistic portrait of the people's predicament.

I identify as "German" those who were officially citizens of the Third Reich during the war. "Nazi" refers only to members of the Nazi party. For the use of the adjectives "Nazi" and "German" there has been no specific rule. In referring to the two factions of the Organization of Ukrai-nian Nationalists, I write of Banderites and Melnykites. These informal designations of its two factions date back to the war period and I, unlike Soviet or other polemicists, use them not to disparage but to avoid a sur-feit of abbreviations.

To promote consistency and readability, the transliteration of geo-graphic locations and personal names follows a modified Library of Con-gress transliteration based on Ukrainian usage. Some of these places, par-ticularly those in western Ukrainian regions, may be better known in their Polish, Russian, or German forms. But in this book it is Rivne, not Równe, Rovno, or Rowno; Zaporizhzhia, not Zaporozhe or Saporoshje; and Kryvy Rih, not Krivoi Rog or Kriwoj Rog. A few place names are exceptional in that they appear here only according to common English usage; key examples are Kiev and Babi Yar. And personal titles are usually translated into English; for example, a Stadtkommissar becomes here a city commissar.

HARVEST OF DESPAIR

1. The Reichskommissariat Ukraine at its largest.

INTRODUCTION

A dolf Hitler and his followers in the National Socialist German Workers' Party wanted to create a united Europe from the British Isles to the Ural Mountains. In this German Reich a national community of common German ancestry would reign supreme and there would be no Jews, no Russians, and no other allegedly harmful peoples. Well before World War II, in pursuit of this racial utopia, Hitler believed that unless the Germans acquired additional Lebensraum, or "living space," they would become extinct. To Hitler and his followers, eastern Europe was particularly appealing for expansion, because it held the promise of a rural Germanic lifestyle that Nazi ideology glorified but was disappearing from Germany itself, the most industrially developed country in Europe. In the "East" the German "race" would return to its agrarian roots and regenerate itself. Moreover, the raw materials from these lands would foster the economic independence of the Third Reich. Deeply frustrated by the outcome of World War I, Hitler confided to a representative of the League of Nations, just before he unleashed World War II, that Germany needed Ukraine, or else it could be "starved into submission again."[1]

Other peoples were living in the eastern Lebensraum, but that did not change Nazi plans. Germans were not to go hungry under any circumstances. Ukraine's Nazi Commissar, Erich Koch, consistently ordered his subordinates to obtain the planned agricultural deliveries at all cost and to disregard the predicament of the native population.[2] But famine among the local people was more than just a side effect. The elimination of the native peoples—with the exception of the ethnic Germans—whether in the short or the long term, was an integral part of Hitler's way to provide the German "race" with a clean slate and the German economy with a sound foundation. The task of the Ukrainian peasants was to help the Nazi state win the war through their labor; but meanwhile Germans would start settling the area as farmers, recreating an agrarian Ger-

1

many and thus strengthening the German "race." Along the way, the native population somehow had to disappear.

In order to realize his vision, the Führer went to war against the Soviet Union on June 22, 1941. As the German armed forces and their Hungarian, Italian, Romanian, and Slovak allies occupied Ukraine, they installed a military administration and presented themselves to the population as liberators from "Jewish Bolshevism" and "Muscovite" domination. Soon civilian Nazi rule arrived, in the form of the Reichskommissariat Ukraine. This entity grew steadily in size and by the fall of 1942 it was the Reich's largest colony, although it did not last long. By late 1943 the Red Army was back at the Dnieper River, across the Reichskommissariat, and by March 1944 the German armed forces had lost all of their territory. But even though the Reichskommissariat Ukraine existed only for a brief period, from the beginning Hitler and his fellow Nazis made a forceful and committed effort to realize their Germanic utopia there.

In some ways the Reichskommissariat was a remarkably mainstream political entity in Ukrainian history. All of its territory had been part of the Russian Empire and only one region, western Volhynia, had after World War I been part of the reconstituted Polish state. Most of the Ukrainians in the Reichskommissariat had been Orthodox Christians. Various regions where non-Ukrainians played a much more prominent role never joined—to its northeast and east, Russian-speaking cities such as Chernihiv, Kharkiv, and Donetsk; to its south, the Crimean peninsula, with its many Russians and Tatars; and, to its southwest, eastern Galicia, northern Bukovina, and Subcarpathian Rus (Transcarpathia), which had been part of the pre-1914 Habsburg Empire. Eastern Galicia in particular had a distinct historical tradition that included a Greek Catholic church, which recognized the Bishop of Rome as superior, and its main city of Lviv was a stronghold of Ukrainian politics, culture, and national consciousness.

The framework of this book is predominantly thematic. Each chapter deals with a particular topic and most of the chapters start with the year 1941. This approach enabled me to steer my way through the mountain of data with as few preconceived notions as possible. Although a focus on themes carries the risk of repetition and confusion, it has the benefit of making explicit any changes in particular policies and people's reactions to them. Thus each chapter shows not a static situation, but one that could and generally did change over time. Although readers will gain the most from reading the book from start to finish, the thematic structure will also allow readers to select one theme and see the data and my interpretation in a single chapter.

Chapter 1 briefly surveys the history of Ukraine from the revolutions of 1917 and devotes special attention to the Soviet republic of Ukraine and to the violent end of the Soviet regime, when Stalin's authorities, from a Western perspective, behaved as conquerors instead of as legitimate rulers. Many Soviet civilians, if only because they lacked accurate knowledge about the Nazis, were glad to see the Soviet regime go. Chapter 2 provides general information about the administration of the Reichskomissariat Ukraine as well as a view that the violent measures taken by the Nazis derived less from their circumstances than from their ethos.

The discussion of the Jews, the Roma, and the "Russian" prisoners of war in Chapters 3 and 4 illustrates most vividly the deadly consequences of the racism that pervaded the Reichskommissariat. With regard to the Holocaust, I argue that anti-Semitic attitudes and the death penalty for obstructing the Nazi campaign against the Jews and the Roma caused the vast majority of other natives to remain bystanders at best. Chapter 4 describes a genocidal massacre and argues that the lives of hundreds of thousands of Soviet prisoners of war in the Reichskommissariat would have been saved if only civilians had not been obstructed so much, and had the escorts and POW camp guards behaved more humanely. But that could not happen, for Nazis thought that the more "Russian" prisoners who died, the better.

Chapters 5, 6, and 7 focus on socioeconomic matters and show how the Nazis wanted to use Ukrainian peasants as cheap laborers and how they condemned the average city dweller to starvation. In Kiev, thousands starved to death in a famine promoted by confiscation of food imports. Even native city dwellers who had jobs and tried to use bribes or the black market could not, or only barely, make ends meet, and worked in a city that involved various hazards—including a potentially deadly commute and German or native supervisors who could abuse or threaten them. And in the countryside, although almost all of the peasants were pleased with the German arrival and many could obtain more food for themselves than before 1941, the conditions under which they labored were so bad that before long they wanted the Germans out. The physical abuse in particular made them feel like slaves.

The next three chapters shift the discussion from bread-and-butter concerns toward the less tangible issues of culture, identity, and religiosity. Chapter 8 argues that cultural events played only a minor role in the life of the native population of the Reichskommissariat. The scale of political gatherings and print media was small (and much smaller than before 1941), and the popular culture that the Nazis sponsored presupposed that their consumers could and should not think for themselves. The Nazi regime's cultural policies made clear its pride in violence, as well as its disdain and mistrust, which naturally offended the natives deeply. A certain mental "sovietization" had occurred before 1941, but, as Chapter 9 argues, most ordinary people did not believe in political ideologies. With the young generation being a significant exception, the ethnic identity as well as the political loyalties of most natives were indistinct. As for religion, Chapter 10 presents the argument that Orthodox and Protestant churches revived, but in general, if measured by popular religiosity or piety, only modestly. Many middle-aged natives, and certainly most young people, had little or no interest in or respect for the Orthodox church and indeed religion in general, and they did not develop it under the Nazis.

Chapters 11 and 12, the final two chapters, deal with the forced deportations of laborers to the Reich from 1942 and the rise of armed resistance from 1943. About a million people were deported to Germany in a "recruitment" campaign that became more violent by the month. From the standpoint of popular opinion in the Reichskommissariat Ukraine, the roundups and deportations were the Nazis' biggest mistake. They inspired resistance in various forms, such as self-mutilation (to make oneself ineligible for deportation), and they increased the ranks of the partisans. We also find that the only organized partisan army in the Reichskommissariat that supported Ukrainian independent statehood perpetrated massacres of innocent civilians, thereby following in the footsteps of its Soviet and Nazi antagonists. The Nazi regime ended in early 1944 in an orgy of violence, including, in Kiev, gassings of civilians who seemed to have been arrested at random.

In this book, "Dnieper Ukraine" refers to the territory of Soviet Ukraine before the acquisitions of 1939. The "Right Bank" refers to Dnieper Ukraine *west* of the Dnieper River; the "Left Bank" is in the east. Except in one quotation from a primary source, terms like "collaboration" and "collaborators," old favorites in studies of German-ruled Europe, do not appear here, for despite appearances, the term collaboration implies a condemnation for treason. There may be a political reason for issuing a condemnation, but here such language would inhibit the primary goal of this study: full understanding. With the same aim of giving precedence to understanding over moralism, I use the word "resistance" sparingly. There are historians who even consider people's pretending not to see Germans as "a subtle form of resistance," and resistance also often appears as an organizing principle in the historiography of prewar and postwar Soviet society.[3] I have not found it very useful here.

But of course I, like any historian, still bring along my own assumptions and morality. For one thing, I believe that neither national nor class solidarity are default identities. Thus terms like "Ukrainians" or "workers" in this book are not supposed to carry the connotation that the persons in question were imbued with a Ukrainian national consciousness or had a worker's consciousness. For another, throughout I have attempted to follow what I believe is the historian's first commandment, namely to present *all* of the relevant information that is found to be true. Finally, my central working assumption has been that most people, when finding themselves in an extreme situation, try first of all to survive, rather than to die as heroes or martyrs. Indeed, in my view most people prefer not become involved at all. Perhaps this perspective comes more naturally to me as a native of the Netherlands with no family or ethnic ties to eastern Europe; I'm not sure. In any event, it means I fully agree with the social psychologist Roy F. Baumeister when he claims that "although from a distance we imagine that people living in historically interesting times must have been caught up in the grand sweeping events, the majority probably were not. Rather, many people want to live their own lives with as little interference from the grand sociopolitical developments as possible. Getting a job, finding a place to live, falling in love, raising children, and similar concerns continue to dominate the daily lives of most people even during war and revolution . . . Regardless of the evil that is going on around you, one has one's own life to live."[4]

1

SOVIET UKRAINE AND THE GERMAN INVASION

On the eve of World War II, several states ruled Ukrainian-inhabited territories.[1] The largest of these was the Ukrainian Soviet Socialist Republic, with its Russian-speaking capital, Kiev. Soviet Ukraine was an integral part of the Union of Soviet Socialist Republics, or Soviet Union, formed in 1922 after years of revolution, civil war, and a Ukrainian struggle for independence. By early 1939, Soviet Ukraine consisted of fifteen oblasts (districts) and a Moldavian Autonomous Soviet Socialist Republic. The Crimean peninsula was an autonomous republic within the largest of the nine Soviet republics, the Russian Soviet Federated Socialist Republic.

The state with the second-largest number of Ukrainians was Poland, resurrected as an independent state after the conclusion of World War I. Most lived in the western part of historic Volhynia and in the eastern half of the former Habsburg province of Galicia. Western Volhynia, with its Polish-dominated towns of Lutsk and Rivne, had been part of the Russian Empire before the revolution of 1917. Now it was the Palatinate of Volhynia, but despite its name, this palatinate did not include eastern Volhynia, which was encompassed by the Soviet Ukrainian oblast of Zhytomyr. Eastern Galicia, after the fall of the short-lived West Ukrainian National Republic, eventually also came under Polish rule. In 1919, the victors of the Great War claimed authority over the region but recognized that the Polish state was occupying it, and in 1923 France, Great Britain, the United States, and Italy recognized that the Polish state had indeed annexed it. Its main cities were Lviv, Ternopil, and Stanislav. Whereas the Ukrainians of western Volhynia and Soviet Ukraine were almost all Orthodox, most Galician Ukrainians belonged to the Greek Catholic church, also known as the Uniate church.

All Ukrainian-inhabited territories in the 1920s and 1930s were overwhelmingly agrarian, but otherwise they differed substantially. Soviet Ukraine's nominal administration was a system of soviets, or councils, that existed at all levels: from the top—the republican Supreme Soviet—down to the level of the oblast, raion, city, town, and village, as well as a republican government called the Council of People's Commissars. But real power resided in two other organizations. One was the Communist party (Bolshevik) of Ukraine, which was itself a branch of the All-Union Communist party (Bolshevik) led by Joseph Stalin. Even more influential was the secret or political police, which succeeded the Cheka, Vladimir Lenin's weapon against Bolshevism's real and imagined enemies. Directed by Stalin's close associates, its name was the People's Commissariat of Internal Affairs, or NKVD. Most of its agents wore uniforms, and every urban place of work generally had its representatives.

From a Ukrainian perspective, there were some positive sides to living in Soviet Ukraine, particularly during the period of official Ukrainianization. Although Russians, Jews, and other non-Ukrainians continued to dominate the Communist party, from the 1920s Ukrainians gradually assumed positions of influence there, and the cities became more Ukrainian in composition and outlook. Several prominent Ukrainians returned from emigration, such as the historian and former president of the Central Rada of the revolutionary period, Mykhailo Hrushevsky. An extensive literacy campaign achieved significant success, and by the late 1920s, the presence and prestige in the media of the Ukrainian language, as compared to that of the Russian language, had risen significantly, although most city dwellers continued to speak Russian in daily life.[2]

The overall standard of living in the Soviet republic was low, however, and was to decline during the 1930s. Food rationing was pervasive. A major tragedy that affected most people took place during the implementation from 1928 of the First Five-Year Plan for the Soviet Union. The plan's main purpose was the development of heavy industry, and for Ukraine this meant industrialization in cities near the Dnieper bend such as Dnipropetrovsk, Kryvy Rih, and Zaporizhzhia, and in the Donbas, or Donets River Basin, in the east. Nevertheless, Soviet Ukraine remained a generally rural society. For Ukrainians, the most significant feature of the new policy was the collectivization (nationalization) of agriculture. Starting in 1929, all of the peasants had to join collective farms, and the authorities expelled or deported any who rose up, resisted in some other way, or merely seemed to be doing so. These peasants were labeled *kulaks* who, as Stalin put it, had to be "liquidated as a class." Assisted by poor peasants, urban workers, and the Red Army, party officials conducted a virtual civil war and confiscated grain. As a result, in 1932 and 1933 there was a Great Famine that cost the lives of at least three million peasants, or almost 10 percent of Soviet Ukraine's population. Conditions were so bad that cannibalism became common. The regime, however, kept silent about the famine. Although scholars still do not agree as to how many succumbed and the cause or causes, it is clear that the starvation was manmade—it did not have to happen.

During and after the famine there came unusually extensive "purges" of the Communist party and the whole of society. Those who had vigorously promoted the Ukrainian language were among the first to fall victim to a seemingly random—and still not fully explained—campaign to arrest "enemies of the people" and "saboteurs." In 1937 and 1938 the NKVD killed most of Soviet Ukraine's leading Communists. Yet the purge opened up possibilities for people like Nikita Khrushchev, Stalin's emissary to the republic in those years, who became its Communist leader. Most people whose lives this campaign ruined or ended were quite ordinary, however. In the Podolian border region of Vinnytsia alone, the NKVD arrested thousands of poor, mostly male peasants and told their relatives that because of the detainees' anti-Soviet views they were to perform forced labor somewhere, and were not allowed to receive or send mail. In fact, most were shot. Among the casualties were virtually all clergymen, so that church life was almost entirely rooted out. For all of these reasons, by the 1930s conditions in Soviet Ukraine were generally far worse than in any place to the west.

Meanwhile, in neighboring Poland, the country's non-Polish population in what politicians called Poland's "eastern borderlands" (kresy) became subject to a concerted campaign of cultural integration. This did not completely prevent the Ukrainians living there from advancing their status: they did so through separate cooperatives, political parties, schools, and their own Greek Catholic church. Nevertheless, dissatisfaction was rife and an underground Organization of Ukrainian Nationalists emerged. The OUN strove for an independent Ukrainian state and emphatically stated that this end justified any means. Thus it resorted to terrorism, particularly in its base in eastern Galicia. The Polish government responded with a violent campaign of its own against Ukrainian villages (1930) and, several years later, by incarcerating OUN activists in a concentration camp. From 1935, the government and the largest legal Ukrainian party, the Ukrainian National Democratic Alliance, made an attempt to normalize the Polish-Ukrainian relations in the Polish state, but without success.

In the late 1930s, new border changes took place in central and eastern Europe as a result of the political demands of Adolf Hitler. Soon after becoming chancellor of Germany in 1933, the Austrian-born Hitler had become the undisputed dictator of the Third Reich. After building up a strong, militaristic economy, he proceeded to expand the state. Thus early in 1938 Germany annexed Austria, in violation of the 1919 Treaty of Versailles. Then Hitler set his eyes on Czechoslovakia, and in particular on the German population of that state's so-called Sudetenland. In September 1938, he was able to obtain a settlement at Munich from Britain and France that transferred the Sudetenland to Germany. The federalist Czecho-Slovakia that remained had a short life. Several weeks later, Germany's ally Hungary acquired the southern regions of the provinces of Slovakia and Subcarpathian Rus. In the unannexed part of Subcarpathian Rus, Ukrainians, led by the OUN, created an autonomous entity called Carpatho-Ukraine, which they saw as the nucleus of an independent state. But on March 15, 1939, while Germany annexed the rest of Bohemia and Moravia and allowed Slovakia to proclaim its independence as a Nazi client state, Hungary annexed Carpatho-Ukraine as well.

Hitler now set his sights on Poland. In his action against that state he was even able to secure help from his archenemy, the Soviet Union. Although Stalin had been issuing a stream of propaganda against Nazi Germany and fascism in general, the Soviet leader realized that his prospects for winning a possible war with Germany were dim: in 1937 and 1938 he had "purged" the Red Army of its best and brightest leaders, and he knew that many of his subjects hated him and the system that he stood for. Both he and Hitler needed time to prepare for their inevitable clash. On August 23, 1939, the Soviet Union and the Third Reich signed a nonaggression treaty that became known as the Molotov-Ribbentrop pact. It included a secret clause that divided Poland into Soviet and German spheres in the event of war.

That war came just days later, when on September 1, 1939, Germany invaded Poland. Two days later, Britain and France declared war on Germany. On September 17 the Soviet Union invaded from the east and annexed Poland's eastern half, while proclaiming the "reunification" of "western Ukraine" and "western Belarus" with the Ukrainian and Belarusan Soviet republics. This way, western Volhynia and eastern Galicia became six oblasts of an enlarged Soviet Ukraine. Germany and the Soviet Union also formally became allies.

Over the next year, while Hitler conquered most of western Europe, Stalin started a war with Finland and annexed the Baltic states, which he turned into Soviet republics. He also added the Ukrainian-inhabited parts of Romania—northern Bukovina and southern Bessarabia—to Soviet Ukraine, and raised Ukraine's Moldavian ASSR to the status of a separate Soviet republic. The incorporation of Soviet Ukraine's new territories led to a violent sovietization that included deportations eastward of hundreds of thousands of "class enemies": Poles, Ukrainians, Belarusans, and Jews. Church life managed to survive, but the invaders replaced all independent cultural and economic life with state-run Soviet Ukrainian institutions.

Already by 1940, there were some Ukrainian-inhabited lands under Nazi German rule. These included territories to the west of the new Nazi-Soviet border (along the San and Buh rivers): the Lemko region, the Chełm region, and Podlachia. These formerly Polish-ruled territories were not formally annexed to the Reich, however, but rather to the large, so-called General Government for the Occupied Polish Territories. A German-sponsored umbrella organization based in Kraków, the Ukrainian Central Committee, supervised the Ukrainians there. The Nazis also released from Polish jails young OUN members led by Stepan Bandera, but these activists did not recognize the newly proclaimed leader of the organization, Andrii Melnyk, and created their own organization called the OUN-Independentists-Statists, unofficially known as the Banderites. The bitterness on both sides about this split stayed and was to preclude cooperation between the two factions.

The German Invasion

Throughout the 1930s, Soviet culture and propaganda had emphasized the threat of war. Some city dwellers, particularly schoolchildren, felt by 1940 that a war could be imminent, an idea reinforced by a song from a Soviet movie that frequently resounded from loudspeakers: "If there's war tomorrow, if the foe should attack, / If the forces of dark are at hand, / The Soviet people as one will strike back, / Will arise for a free motherland."[3] But even in 1941, not everybody in Soviet Ukraine—officially close to 41 million people[4]—seriously expected a war with Germany, or indeed any war. University students and members of the Komsomol, the Communist Youth League, for example, could be very apolitical.[5] And it is clear that the people of central Ukraine did not consider themselves to be *already* at war, although from a Baltic, Polish, and Romanian perspective they were.

More than three million German soldiers crossed the 1940 German-Soviet border in the early hours of Sunday, June 22, 1941. Soviet citizens heard about it first in a radio address by the deputy premier Viacheslav Molotov over the wire radio and loudspeaker system. Among other things, he said that Kiev had been bombarded. The people were stunned. Many Communist party members were dismayed or surprised, less because of the war than because the Soviet Union had not been the one to attack first.[6] In public meetings, Soviet citizens had to vow to defend their state. Males ages 19 to 22 were already in the Red Army; now there came a draft of all men ages 23 to 36, with men in the cities ages 16 to 18 required to join the organization for civilian air defense.[7]

Nazi Germany's war with Britain thus became a war on two fronts. Hitler hoped that the blitzkrieg strategy that he had employed against Poland would work against "Russia" as well. And indeed it did for most Ukrainian territories, which the German armed forces captured by November 1941. Assisted by Hungarian, Italian, Romanian, and Slovak units, the Wehrmacht's Army Group South rapidly advanced through Ukraine. The western Volhynian cities of Lutsk and Rivne fell on June 25 and 29, Lviv succumbed on June 30, and Proskuriv, present-day Khmelnytsky, the first major city in pre-1939 Soviet Ukraine, surrendered on July 8, followed quickly by Zhytomyr, Bila Tserkva, and Vinnytsia. Hereafter the Germans advanced fastest in Ukraine's south. After the battle for the central-western region near Uman ended with an encirclement early in August (capturing over 100,000 Red Army soldiers), the way was open to the cities of Kirovohrad, Kryvy Rih, Mykolaïv, and Kherson, and to Cherkasy and Dnipropetrovsk on the Dnieper River, all of which fell in that same month.

In the middle of September, the invaders encircled the Red Army's Southwestern Front, entrenched to the east of the Dnieper. Less than two weeks later, on September 26, the enormous battle was over and the German armed forces were in control of central Ukraine. Wehrmacht officers counted about 665,000 Red Army soldiers who became prisoners of war. Even before the end of that battle, on September 19, the Wehrmacht occupied Kiev, which Stalin had ordered to be kept whatever the price. Melitopol, close to the Sea of Azov, fell on October 6 and one week later, four months after the start of the German invasion, and at the cost of a great many Red Army soldier lives, the entire territory that was to constitute the Reichskommissariat Ukraine had changed hands.[8]

The question arises why the German armed forces were able to advance so quickly. One reason was that Stalin had ignored countless warnings of an imminent attack. Thus the Red Army in the western regions had hardly any maps and too few arms when they needed them most. But more important than any lack of insight or preparation was desertion and unwillingness to fight. Despite the threat of the death penalty for desertion, massive numbers of soldiers abandoned their posts. Almost all drafted Ukrainians from western Volhynia and eastern Galicia left the army, and the remaining Red Army soldiers near the Soviet border— mainly members of the Communist party and its Komsomol from central and eastern Ukraine—faced sniper fire from locals.[9] In central Ukraine, enormous numbers of reservists evaded their mobilization. Fedir Pihido, a Ukrainian native of the region and a reliable observer, wrote six years later (when he was about sixty years old) about how unpopular were both the Russo-Japanese war of 1905 and World War I, and how the German conflict compared: "Having spent three years at the front, I have a feeling for the mood of the soldiers. But never before had I seen or heard anything like this." Largely in vain, authorities tried to arrest deserters by blocking all of the roads.[10]

Pihido saw a large group of Red Army soldiers of various ethnic backgrounds who had just been captured in the Kiev encirclement. Because they were guarded by lenient Slovaks, they could talk to locals who approached them. "All of them complained about a terrible chaos in the army. The Red Army soldiers were always hungry and had to beg or steal. There was no underwear, no soap, many had lice. Footwear was mostly broken; they had to fight barefoot or with rags wrapped around. There were no blankets." Most also complained that they had been left to their own devices: only sergeants or lieutenants from the reserves were with them. Most important of all, it became apparent to Pihido and others that the Red Army soldiers did not *want* to fight. From all around came comments like "They want us to die for them—no, we are not as stupid as they think." "They sucked our blood for twenty-five years, enough already!" "They left our children without bread, to starve to death, but force us to defend Stalin and his Commissars." A soldier from Siberia said, "About two hundred of us got together. We decided to force our way back, at all cost, toward the Germans. We armed ourselves with submachine guns and grenades and moved toward the Dnieper. Twice we had to force our way through with grenades, for the [army] commissars tried to turn us back, to 'our people.' We killed them and moved on. That's how we reached the Dnieper. Here we gave our weapons to the Germans and they moved us across, to the Right Bank." Another prisoner told an even more vivid tale:

> In our regiment, the division commissar gathered the privates and commanders and started to incite the people to get going, in order to force our way east. He assured us that there were very few Germans and that it would be very easy. The Red Army soldiers frowned, saying nothing. So did the commanders. Then the commissar issued an order to line up. The Red Army soldiers became agitated. Our regiment commander called out to the privates: "Who do you obey? Away with the damned Chekist!" The commissar instantly drew his revolver and shot. The commander fell down. Our second lieutenant and a group of Red Army soldiers jumped on the commissar— in less than a minute, he was torn to pieces.

This narrator concluded with, "You see, the men of our regiment don't let themselves be deceived." "That's right," others joined in: "We killed the damned Stalin-dog," "A dog gets a dog's death!"[11]

The draft dodging and voluntary surrender did not mean that these people lacked courage. Rather, as a song written in Dnipropetrovsk put it some years later, "We threw away our rifles and fled to the Germans / And expected a better fate from them." Simply put, there was "nothing that they wanted to defend."[12] Many of the recruits had seen since 1939 the higher standard of living in the newly acquired Soviet territories and had become disgruntled with their own situation. The only Soviet citizens who wanted to fight at that time were the schoolchildren, recalls Lev Dudin, a Russian nationalist from Kiev.[13]

The "Unreliable Element"

As soon as the war with Germany started, the NKVD—or more precisely, the People's Commissariat of State Security, or NKGB, which had come about from the NKVD early in 1941 but reunited with it in July while retaining its separate name—became feverishly active. It ordered office workers to keep guard against "German spies" around the clock, in groups of at least two persons, and demanded likewise from factories and farms, where somebody always had to stay in the fields.[14] While some city dwellers organized their own vigilantes against possible neighborhood looters, from June 24 the NKVD organized extermination battalions. Each battalion had between one and two hundred armed members, mainly from the Communist party and the Komsomol, and they were supposed to guard important objects and catch parachutists and saboteurs. Within a month there were around 650 such battalions in Ukraine. German military intelligence gave a plausible explanation for their popularity among volunteers: the battalions did not move about and the only other legal alternative for men who did not enlist in the army was trench digging, away from home.[15]

As before the German invasion, the Soviet political police devoted special attention to what it called "the unreliable element." Those males deemed unreliable—often people whose relatives had been persecuted, or who merely had studied in Germany years ago—were not placed in the army or in the irregular People's Home Guard and were told to carry out other tasks or at least to stay put.[16] As for prisoners, on June 23 Vsevolod N. Merkulov, the head of the NKGB in Moscow, apparently instructed his subordinates in Kiev and other western Soviet cities to review all of the persons on record and to "compile lists of those whom you deem necessary to shoot." He wanted the lists within a month, presumably for approval, but time was too short. For the entire territory of the 1941 Ukrainian SSR, Soviet documents state that "during the evacuation," 8,789 prisoners were "executed in the prisons."[17]

As for the massacres in the territory that later constituted the Reichskommissariat Ukraine, the evidence is most conclusive for western Volhynia. Here the authorities were naturally very pressed for time. As villagers were drafted into the army, NKVD officers in Lutsk told the "unreliables" to stay home and to show up immediately when ordered to do so. During the first night of war, the organization busied itself with 120 prisoners whom it had earlier condemned to death, killing them with bayonets. On June 22, a German bomb hit the local prison. It became the signal for the at least two thousand Ukrainian, Polish, and Jewish inmates to stage a revolt, during which they managed to take control of the building. But NKVD troops with tanks and what the sources call armed

Komsomol members—evidently a precursor of an extermination battal-ion—surrounded them. On the morning of June 23 (or perhaps June 24), an NKVD lieutenant read out loud to them in Ukrainian an order, sup-posedly from Stalin, that closed the cases of those accused of political of-fenses and mobilized these people into the army. The prisoners lined up outside. Suddenly the tanks' machine guns started firing at them, and grenades hit them from the windows. After the barrage, a call went out in Russian: "Those still alive, get up! We won't shoot anymore!" The survi-vors numbered about 370, and spent the rest of the day and the day after burying the hundreds of bodies. Then, in the afternoon, their overseers fled and a German advance unit arrived.[18] Casualty estimates regarding the Lutsk massacre range between "some 1,500 Ukrainian political de-tainees" (the German Foreign Office), 2,800 "Ukrainians" of a total of 4,000 prisoners (the SS and German military intelligence), and 3,862 to 4,000 prisoners (a local priest and a survivor).[19]

The three-story prison of Dubno, somewhat more to the east, was the site of a still hastier bloodbath, amply documented by contemporary Ger-man reports based on interrogations of at least four named survivors and by postwar survivors' accounts. On the evening of June 24, the in-mates were ordered to go to sleep against the wall facing the door. Half an hour later, the guards started going from cell to cell, killing every-one with gunshots or bayonet stabs. When cells had many inmates, or only males, the guards shot through the peephole or threw in grenades. Valentyna Petrenko recalled after the war that "particularly startling were the screams of children, of whom there were many downstairs—those screams one can never forget." (Three other sources confirm the killing of children.) After at least forty and possibly as many as ninety minutes, the killers fled for a while, apparently because a local who had dressed up as one of them ran into the building and shouted that the Germans were coming. To enhance the effect, others outside shot weapons into the air. The interlude allowed for a number of escapes, although many prisoners were nonetheless shot near or on top of a wall. Inside the jail the shoot-ing resumed in the early hours of the next day.[20] In this way, altogether around 550 detainees, including about a hundred women, died at the Dubno prison.[21]

Information about other western localities is less detailed. In Volodymyr-Volynsky, the atrocities took place on the very first day of the German invasion. That day, Stepan Ianiuk, a Baptist who had been under arrest as an alleged "kulak," told a young Ukrainian (who later documented their conversation) about shootings in the city prison that morning, which he had miraculously survived when two bodies covered him. The young man then saw bodies himself and estimated that only twenty of some five hundred prisoners had survived.[22] In Sarny in northern Volhynia, hundreds of male and female prisoners died; in the southern town of Kremenets, the death toll was about 150.[23]

In central and eastern Ukraine, the NKVD had more time to evacuate its prisoners, but still it shot many in the days before fleeing. In the town of Chyhyryn just west of the Dnieper, according to a man from there, the agency rounded up ten people, including a teacher of German and the son of a priest, shot them in the back of the head, and buried the bodies.[24] A woman who apparently used to work in the local jail in Kirovohrad later told another local that the NKVD had released criminals but had shot "political" inmates, and other locals later spoke to a Ukrainian Wehrmacht interpreter of recent shootings of prisoners. At the prison of Uman there were hasty shootings of people who had been marched from Chortkiv in Galicia, and there are accounts of haphazard killings in Berdychiv and Vinnytsia. In Poltava's prison 240 people apparently were burned alive, and in Proskuriv, eleven were shot, along with thirteen German pilots; twenty-two other prisoners were abandoned and starved to death.[25] In general, in central Ukraine, more people than in the western regions may have been aware of the danger and have gone into hiding. The former Soviet camp inmate Mykola Prykhodko successfully hid for weeks. Had he been found, undoubtedly he would have received a bullet in the back of his head, like the 148 unfortunates later found in a prison in an unidentified nearby town on the lower Dnieper.[26]

In Kiev, the first arrests of "unreliables" came in early July, when the German army was still 250 kilometers away, and reached their climax in September, during the two weeks before the city's fall to the Germans.[27] Merkulov's order did allow for the possibility of evacuating prisoners, but it seems likely that many arrested Kievans were shot, either in jail or at prewar burial pits east of the city, near the hamlet of Bykivnia. A man from Lviv heard shots while under arrest in Kiev, and several other authors—not themselves survivors or eyewitnesses—have mentioned atrocities at that time. Moreover, an archivist of independent Ukraine's Security Service has written that at least 473 prisoners initially held in Kiev were shot during this period.[28]

The Nazi-Soviet pact of 1939 had brought about an exchange of tens of thousands of Ukrainians and ethnic Germans between the two states.[29] According to Soviet figures that seem valid for the eve of the German invasion, the territory of Soviet Ukraine within its pre-1939 borders held 392,000 ethnic Germans. Other than in the Odessa region and in the Donbas, they lived mainly in the oblasts of Dnipropetrovsk (26,000), Mykolaïv (42,000), Zaporizhzhia (89,000), and Zhytomyr (36,000).[30] On August 31, 1941, Stalin's Politburo decided to deport all of Ukraine's ethnic Germans to the east.[31] According to apparent NKVD documents, within a week the NKVD had arrested all of the males as "anti-Soviet elements" and deported them to forced labor sites in the Soviet hinterland. The rest were supposed to follow at the end of the month, but evidently many managed to stay behind. For instance, the authorities in the Zaporizhzhia oblast "registered" 53,566 ethnic Germans but deported only 31,032.[32]

A view from those affected comes from a woman from the Mennonite village of Gnadenfeld. First one hundred and fifty men were taken away "like criminals. They dared not so much as look back, or they were shouted at by their captors." As she describes it, it was the start of a virtual death march: They had to walk sixty kilometers per day and "those who could not keep up were left to perish on the road or were shot. For days they were deprived of a warm meal or water. They almost died of thirst. What dreadful treatment these men had to endure! Only a few escaped, and returned to tell us."[33] On October 2, the more than eight thousand remaining villagers were told to be ready to leave in two hours. NKVD-supervised militia men took them to a train station. After two days of waiting, the Mennonites were chased into a field. They were certain that a Soviet plane wanted to firebomb them, but much to their relief, German planes shot it down. Altogether, the German army prevented the total deportation of thirty of the fifty-seven Mennonite villages in this region.[34]

Scorched Earth

At least as important to Stalin as eliminating "unreliables" was material destruction. He made this clear in a secret order on June 27 to authorities of the regions where evacuation was under way: "All valuable materials, energy and agricultural stocks, and standing grain that cannot be taken away and can be used by the enemy *must*, in order to prevent such use— upon order of the Military Councils of the fronts—*be immediately made completely worthless, that is, must be destroyed, annihilated, and burned.*"[35] He and Molotov gave similar orders to all Communist party and government officials of the regions "near the front" on June 29: in case of a Soviet retreat, livestock and grain had to be taken along, but "all valuable property that cannot be removed, including nonferrous metals, grain, and fuel, must absolutely be destroyed." They added that partisan and sabotage groups would have to "create intolerable conditions for the enemy and all his accomplices, pursue and destroy them at every step, disrupt all their measures."[36] The republican party and government apparently ordered lower levels of administrators to select people who would destroy grain, sugar, and other valuables if that should become necessary.[37] The June 29 directive officially applied only to regions near the front, but in practice many more regional party organizations started removing and destroying food supplies. Their mindset is apparent in the Soviet-era memoirs of the then second secretary of the party committee of the Dnipropetrovsk oblast. The front was still far away, he writes, "but after reading such a critical and important document, it was impossible to think in a formal way." Ordinary people heard of Stalin's intentions only on July 3, when he finally spoke on the radio. From then on, Soviet radio warned that the invaders would find "nothing but desert and scorched earth."[38]

Stalin differed with the first secretary of Ukraine's Communist party about the extent of the destruction that was desirable. On July 9, Khrushchev proposed to Stalin that agricultural machinery should be destroyed in a much larger territory than Stalin had prescribed, namely in a zone of 100 to 150 kilometers to the east of the front, and to kill pigs and birds there and distribute them among the soldiers and the local peasants. Yet Khrushchev also proposed to let the farm workers have the seed grains and other collective farm property. In a telegram to Kiev, his superior rejected the proposals. "Birds, small livestock, and other food-stuffs, which are necessary for the remaining population" should not be killed at all, wrote Stalin, and demolition should only take place in a zone of seventy verst (about seventy-four kilometers) behind the front, after the removal of "all adult males, working livestock, grain, tractors, and combines."[39] It is possible that Khrushchev wanted to justify a situation that he realized was already coming about.

The effect of the scorched-earth policy varied. In the western Volhynian countryside, Soviet officials lacked the time to undertake a comprehensive evacuation and destruction. In fact, local peasants voluntarily disbanded many collective farms. In one village, they did so when they heard about a neighboring village that had decollectivized itself. Encouraged by the farm chairman ("It seems the Lord has mercy on us after all . . . But please take only what is yours"), everybody took out his or her collectivized horse, plow, and cart. Hours later all that was left of the I. V. Stalin Collective Farm were its records—as well as its grain and haystacks, which were divided over the following days.[40]

In central-western Ukraine, known as the Right Bank, the Soviet destruction was also limited. The German army reported from Ukraine in mid-July that the agricultural machines were useless because parts were missing, but that the fields were intact. Even the "sabotage" of the machines was not necessarily meant to destroy them; there were peasants who kept the missing parts for safekeeping. Farther east, many peasants ignored the government order to harvest the fields day and night.[41] Equally difficult to evaluate is the Soviet evacuation of people, livestock, horses, grain, and machines. Much of the livestock, it seems, was abandoned near or just across the Dnieper.[42]

The evacuation and destruction of livestock and machinery mostly affected villages near the main roads.[43] Cows were chased across unharvested fields and stacks were set on fire. Not surprisingly, the villagers tried to save the harvest and livestock, and thus—they were convinced—themselves. In most villages near the Dnieper, crowds of women and men removed grain, cows, horses, pigs, and birds, and thus disbanded the collective farms early in July, well before any Germans arrived.[44] Near the river shore village of Staiky, the peasants were too late to prevent the destruction of plows, harrows, and other equipment, but when Komsomol members and the farm head started to kill pigs, the alarmed population saved most of them and immediately dissolved the collective farm. Three tractors came to destroy the fields, but within half an hour many women were on the scene: some laid themselves down before the machines, while others pulled the drivers off.[45]

Such behavior, or even just complaining, carried great risks. The villagers of Ivanivka were being chased into the fields to destroy the grain when two carts with bags of grain passed by. Mariia Savchenko and Khyma Raba complained to one of the drivers, who was the head of the village council: he had ordered them to destroy the crop, they said, but now he was fleeing with a food supply. The next day an NKVD officer and a militia man arrested the women. Their fate became known only three months later, when their bodies were identified among several hundreds immured in a hidden basement in the Uman prison.[46]

Villages and small towns that did not need to worry about famine had time to think about how to receive the Germans. Veterans of World War I usually said that there was nothing to fear. In western Volhynia and western Polissia, peasants gave the incoming Germans the traditional bread-and-salt welcome as well as food and even dinners, to thank them for chasing out "the Bolsheviks."[47] Tears of joy flowed when these peasants saw posters that announced the proclamation of a Ukrainian state, which they celebrated with large parties. (Banderites had prepared the posters, after proclaiming statehood in Lviv on June 30, to the Nazis' chagrin.) The Germans did not interfere in the celebrations and in Rivne even saluted a newly created "Kholodny Iar First Battalion of the Ukrainian Army."[48]

Most people in the villages and small towns of Dnieper Ukraine were also glad to see the Germans. In one Podolian community, everyone stood by the road and "girls would offer the soldiers flowers, and people would offer bread and water," as a woman recalls. "We were all so happy to see them. They were going to save us from the Communists who had taken everything and starved us."[49] In the small and isolated village of Huta, airdropped leaflets were the first sign that the Germans were coming. The optimistic peasants welcomed the Wehrmacht with flowers and bread, and "everybody was glad that the Germans had come."[50] A German soldier described in his diary how countrypeople to the east of Kiev, just across the Dnieper, approached the invaders on September 20: "At first they hesitated, but when they saw that we were no beasts, they came closer with great joy and pointed the way to the east, where the Bolsheviks had gone. Then they brought flowers. Women carried their children and showed them to the German soldiers . . . All gave the general large bouquets. Elderly people, who still remembered the time of the tsars, bowed deep and humbly. An old woman, shedding tears and giving thanks, fell to her knees."[51] Some time after the first Germans occupied the Right Bank, garlands and other welcoming signs appeared across its main roads, usually on the initiative of traveling OUN activists from the west. In the small town of Makariv, fifty kilometers west of Kiev, the garland had swastikas painted on it and a German text read, "We Greet the German Army as Liberators from Bolshevism. Heil Hitler!"[52]

Some parents ordered their daughters to wear old clothes and not to go out to wash, just in case the newcomers might want to rape them. But most peasants did not think that the Germans would be cruel.[53] Farther east, however, the population was initially far more reserved and sometimes even fearful. In some villages, everyone stayed indoors for a long time, afraid that the Germans would hang and shoot civilians. Evidently the news of the murderous activities of the SS had traveled fast. But eventually the traditional hospitality prevailed there as well.[54]

The limited industry in the towns of western Volhynia largely remained intact.[55] The evacuation and destruction of industry and food stacks in the oblasts of Kamianets-Podilsky, Zhytomyr, and Vinnytsia also appear to have been superficial. A German Foreign Ministry official reported on his arrival that "in part, the destruction was carried out unprofessionally, so that the [German] technical battalions could quickly restore this or that electrical or water station."[56] The food supplies in the city of Zhytomyr were all demolished, however. More to the east, the retreating Red Army blew up the railway bridges across the Dnieper in Cherkasy, Kremenchuk, Dnipropetrovsk, and Zaporizhzhia. Factories in that region, according to plan, either evacuated in the nick of time, or else were destroyed. Fires raged during the night.[57]

One memoirist has left a detailed description of the town of Lubny in Left Bank Ukraine's Poltava region in those weeks. Paranoia about spies was rampant after June 1941 and extermination battalions roamed the streets. Citizen groups watched the sky after dark. Schoolchildren, students, and the intelligentsia had to dig trenches, "although there were many military in the city who did not have any work." Some schools moved east. Leading party members and officials drove off with their families and took along furniture and housewares, even plants. "Unreliables" were arrested and buildings were blown up. When, on September 13, the Germans finally arrived, this witness did not see anybody offer them bread and salt, but the people were "not sad or afraid" and scrutinized the newcomers "very favorably . . . The Germans made themselves comfortable for dinner and were happy to treat the children and the most importunate adults with heavy noodles and minced meat." They also just laughed at the locals who engaged in looting.[58]

In Kryvy Rih, after the industrial machines had been moved, an order went out to blow up the factories themselves. But workers commenced a sit-down strike to prevent this, and only engineers arriving from else-

2. Local residents greet a German soldier on a tank. Kremenchuk, eastern Ukraine, September 1941. (Photograph by military photographer Koch. Bundesarchiv, Bild 146/74/91/40.)

where were able to demolish anything—in this case a mine shaft.[59] Industrial destruction often took place without prior notice, however. In Zaporizhzhia, one of the large industrial cities on the lower Dnieper, workers—who, according to a former engineer, deliberately worked slowly—took most of the factories apart. Then the buildings were dynamited. But the city's main bread factory exploded without any warning, causing the deaths of more than three hundred male and female workers. The large adjacent bread store blew up at the same time and flying parts killed many customers waiting in line.[60]

The demolition of part of the Dnieper Hydroelectric Station, or Dniprohes, some ten kilometers upstream from Zaporizhzhia, took place while the Wehrmacht was still near Kryvy Rih, 120 kilometers away. In the afternoon of August 17, Red Army units were on the dam and in the lowlands. In the afternoon, without warning, the center of the dam exploded and thus unleashed a flood that destroyed everything and everyone in its path, including thousands of horses and livestock, dozens of ships, and all of Zaporizhzhia's southern district. Rumor had it that twenty thousand soldiers died. The local authorities blamed the premature explosion on sabotage. It seems that a small German advance unit had reached the Dnieper island of Khortytsia, only three kilometers from the dam. The two Soviet military engineers at the dam panicked and flipped the switch.[61]

Many citizens of Dnipropetrovsk were fearful, and paranoid about spies. Notices on telegraph poles warned that hoarders would be shot.[62] Here too, buildings were blown up without warning, but still people who anticipated famine started looting. When ten militia men on horseback arrived at the canteen of the Petrovsky Factory, the women who were looting it chased them away with a volley of plates.[63] According to a Banderite activist who covertly arrived, the looting continued after the occupiers arrived: "Most locals went from store to store, together with the Germans, and took whatever they needed. The Germans went by car and took valuables, especially radios. The population took food, the children pulled out toys. Unlike in the western [Ukrainian] lands, nobody was interested in weapons and ammunition."[64] According to another Banderite, the Germans destroyed the radios and beat or kicked women and children who were in their way. All of this took place as the city was still under Red Army fire from the Left Bank. That deadly shelling continued for three months more.[65]

Looting was far from exceptional: every city or town experienced it. For example, hundreds of peasant women who came to Zhytomyr and Berdychiv in search of their men took the opportunity to empty abandoned apartments, a large number of which had belonged to Jews and Communists.[66] Red Star, the large, unevacuated machine factory in Kirovohrad that had employed 13,000 people, was in ruins by the time the Germans arrived, all apparently through plunder during the one day when the city lacked an authority.[67] In the southern city of Kherson, the looting started while there were still Red Army units in town. These soldiers prevented a crowd from removing flour from the burning bread factory, but other sites they could not "protect." An emigré gave a sense of the popular anger involved:

The "Soviet citizens," who had been submissive so far, especially Jews of which very many had remained, threw themselves at the "socialist property." They destroyed, beat, burned,
robbed . . . Drunkards cried out and shook their fists at the
other side of the Dnieper. Women were eager to join: "Those
scumbags, the blood-suckers, they robbed us, exploited us, and
now they also burned everything. Why did they keep those reserves, why didn't they give us anything?!" "Neighbor, come
quickly to the harbor, melted soap is streaming from a burning
store." "Those bastards, those parasites, for how many years did
they not give us any soap, and now they set it on fire . . ." And
off they went, to get the soap, the preserves, all the things that
had been hidden in the stores, and which those ragged and
hungry people had waited for, until the day when everything
was destroyed. Brawls, fighting, shouts.[68]

As elsewhere, the Germans made their presence known through a loudspeaker wagon and locals offered them bread and salt.[69]

The Fall of Kiev

Because of Kiev's symbolic importance, Stalin ordered the Red Army to
hold on to it at all costs. The many contemporary accounts and memoirs
about the events there before, during, and immediately after the German
arrival on September 19 make it possible to provide a relatively detailed
reconstruction. First, following Molotov's radio address of June 22, blackouts became mandatory. Immediately Kievans started standing in line for
days so as to hoard anything money could buy.[70] Meanwhile, partly as a
result of Soviet news reports on spies, paranoia about spies developed.
Girls who merely asked for directions spent hours in militia jails, as did
"Germanic"-looking blond and blue-eyed males.[71] The authorities of
the Lukianivka district sent out people to smear on the sidewalks lime,
which glows faintly in the dark, in order to facilitate nighttime walking.
But because this was not announced, anxious locals apprehended a man
who came to see his wife, who worked in the area. "There he is," they
shouted—"that spy who made the signs for the enemy planes on where to
throw the bombs. Yes, it's him, in the blue shirt." At the district militia office, the man on duty exclaimed, "Again!" glanced at some documents,
and released the man. Even then the crowd remained unsatisfied: "Can

one really trust the militia chief? Now there are spies everywhere." Only after the woman leading the group, a house custodian, had made several phone calls to verify the information they were given, did the group release the visitor.[72]

In another attempt to quell subversion, phone company workers visited those few Kievans with a telephone and took the phones away. They came to Fedir Pihido's place three times when he was out, and his neighbors had to talk them out of bashing down his door.[73] The small number of people who owned a wireless radio received an order in the mail to hand them in for "temporary storage" and were warned that those who did not comply would be held "criminally responsible according to the laws of wartime."[74] Meanwhile, wire radios (radio receivers with only one station) and street loudspeakers started denouncing the Banderites and their Lviv proclamation. These broadcasts also repeated until the very end that "Kiev Was, Is, and Will Be Soviet."[75] The city was buzzing with rumors.

From July 2, the NKVD supervised the burning of government and other records older than 1940 and of nonessential current files. The result was a black snow. "The entire city was covered with ashes, which flew from all chimneys as burned shreds of paper, and landed on pedestrians and their clothes," a man recalls. "The wind carried these ashes, blowing them from street to street, like black clouds. In short, it was like Pompeii—a city under ashes."[76] Civilians also obliterated records on their own initiative. The teachers of School No. 94, for instance, destroyed lists of the schoolchildren's names and addresses.[77]

Stalin's radio address of July 3 galvanized Kiev's elite. The reaction was a massive exodus that continued until the very week before the German occupation. Many of these people panicked, but not all, as one Kievan recalls: "The commanders, with their chests well out, walked full of themselves and assumed a heroic air. They gave orders with much aplomb."[78] On July 9 the army mobilization started and the militia checked on males in their homes.[79] As the German army approached, Soviet Red Cross wagons brought in wounded from the front, but "more often one saw glimpses of other cars: lorries stacked to the hilt with goods. Sometimes, between the spring mattresses, mirrored wardrobes, and tightly rolled carpets, one could see rubber plants and palm trees."[80]

After arresting the city's "unreliables," the NKVD evacuated—forcefully, if necessary—thousands of writers, engineers, physicians, and agronomists to the east. One estimate indicates that a total of 197 business concerns left Kiev for the east. Some party activists said openly that those who would not evacuate would perish, for they would have nothing to live on. But people who did not belong to the elite had few ways of leaving. Many lower-ranking employees who tried waited in vain at the train station. School directors were all party members and had sensed correctly that their lives were in great danger; by early July they had departed, leaving behind the teachers, many of whom were also party members. A woman whose Communist husband had been shot in the 1930s considered fleeing, but an acquaintance who worked in the NKVD strongly advised against it: "You will die. You don't have the means to be able to evacuate. But no devil is as bad as people describe him, so don't worry."[81]

Memoirs tell unconfirmed horror stories about the evacuation of children. According to a Kievan who later emigrated, thousands of schoolboys (and almost all remaining men) were put on an eastward march during which they got no food or water. "The trip lasted many days, and many, especially children, died and remained lying on the road next to livestock that had fallen from exhaustion. In the last night before the city's surrender, when it became clear that was impossible to lead them through the [German] encirclement, several hundred children were driven across the minefield in the Pechersk district beyond the Monastery of the Caves, 'in order not to hand them over to the enemy.'"[82] A Ukrainian woman who later came to the city from the west asserts that "Kievans told us how the Bolsheviks had evacuated children: they simply gathered them from the schools, not even allowing them to say goodbye to their families. The children did not even know where they were going." Some of them supposedly escaped by leaping through windows.[83]

At an early stage thousands of bags with flour, sugar, and salt were thrown into the Dnieper, and large quantities of medicine and leather vanished in the same way. Other supplies were contaminated with fuel, were poured into the streets (oil), or went down the drain (liquor).[84] Paradoxically, many stores put up for sale items that they had not offered for years, such as pepper; and in the week before Kiev's fall even flour, sugar, and other products suddenly reappeared on store shelves.[85]

For about a month, as it was encircling the Red Army to the east of Kiev, the German Sixth Army waited to its west. There were few bomb shelters and many Kievans started digging holes (the radio provided instructions); the parks and gardens started to look like the habitat of giant moles.[86] But German airdropped leaflets that said Kiev would not be shelled apparently convinced most people that hiding was unnecessary. A rumor pointed to Hitler's alleged descent from a Russian princess and his supposed interest in Russian architecture.[87]

There were other tasks that busied the population, in particular trench digging and joining the army. The militia rounded up Kievans from shopping lines and movie theaters; but to evade the draft many males grew a beard that they hoped made them look too old, and more than a few even mutilated themselves. In the last weeks of Soviet rule, extermination battalions shot men in the streets whom they considered suspect. When, in the final days before the Kiev's fall, all men were ordered out, thousands, including young, unarmed deserters from the extermination battalions, hid in cellars and wardrobes.[88]

The morning of September 18, looting started. The principal plunder targets were stores and storage sites: smashing the windows, people removed everything, even dishes and furniture.[89] A witness later described to Soviet historians how he was in a streetcar that halted at the corner of the Jewish Market, in front of a bakery. The car waited and waited, and then he saw that a crowd was looting. "People were coming out, completely dirtied with flour and carrying bags full of flour. Passions flared: one pushes another, that one pushes a third. One person falls down somewhere, another is hurled to the ground. Bags are ripped apart, flour spills on the street. There was shouting, noise, and coarse language."[90]

Yet there was little panic in Kiev that day. Iryna Khoroshunova, a young woman sympathetic to the Soviet system, wrote in her diary that even on September 18 she could not believe the Red Army would lose the city. People looked "anxious" and "serious," she wrote, perhaps because they were afraid of criminal assaults. (Criminals were widely believed to have been released several days before.) But she also saw "many happy, smiling faces."[91] In the evening, the city's four Dnieper bridges, the new electric power station in the Podil district, the water tower, and the cannery blew up, and the food stacks at the train station were also dynamited. Because they considered most of those sites military objects, Kievans were not particularly angry. They did not know then that when the Wooden bridge exploded there were unsuspecting soldiers on it.[92] In the square opposite the university, Soviet shells had remained; Red Army soldiers detonated them there during the night.[93]

In the morning of Friday, September 19, German soldiers entered and at noon they raised the swastika flag above the belltower of the Monastery of the Caves. Some people had decorated the balconies of their homes with flowers for the occasion. The SS even reported that the Germans received a "happy reception."[94] More accurate, however, was what a German soldier noted in his diary: "The surprised population is in the streets. They still don't know how to behave. Here and there are a few timid greetings. Whenever German soldiers halt, they are immediately surrounded by a large crowd prepared to give friendly assistance and help." Later he wrote, "In the first days we still noticed several times just how much the Ukrainians fear a return of the Bolsheviks and therefore keep their distance from us."[95]

Accounts from Kievans who later emigrated confirm that most residents came out to watch but did little else. One author emphasizes people's curiosity after having been cut off from the outside world for so long.[96] Another provides an ambiguous image of events in the Khreshchatyk, Kiev's main street: "The soldiers tried to strike up conversations and exchange jokes with the public standing in rows on the sidewalk. Almost all the onlookers were sullenly silent while looking at the victors. I felt my spiritual state merge with the general somber and reticent, depressed mood of the crowd. One spectator shouted in broken [German]: 'Long live the victorious German army!' People looked at him with bewilderment and shrugged their shoulders."[97] Likewise, Khoroshunova saw near the telegraph office how Kievans and Germans simply looked at each other. No particular mood prevailed, she thought.[98] A former member of the Central Rada of the Ukrainian National Republic of the revolutionary years, who had suffered from the Soviet authorities, felt tremendous relief: "The devil's regime was gone and I had become a human being. I thought to myself, what a fatal tragedy for a citizen to wish the defeat in war of his own state."[99] But others could not necessarily see such relief.

In certain streets the mood was openly upbeat, with dancing, embracing, and drinking; but even there most adults apparently remained indoors for a while.[100] Anatolii Kuznetsov, then twelve years old and living in the Kurenivka district, writes in his reliable memoirs that the mood was happy, partly because of the sunny weather. It amazed him that the Germans who came down Frunze Street smiled and laughed, and that their infantry did not walk but moved about in trucks. "The pavements were quickly filling up with people rushing in from all sides. Like us, they first looked at this armada in amazement, then began to smile at the Germans in reply and to try and start up conversations with them. As for the Germans, practically all of them had little conversation-books that they were quickly looking through and called out to the girls on the pavement: 'Hey girl, miss . . . ! Bolshevik—finish. Ukraina!' 'Ukrayéena,' the girls corrected them with a laugh. 'Ja, ja. U-kray-éena! Go walk, spazieren, bitte!' The girls giggled and blushed, and all the people around were laughing and smiling." Elderly men and women wanted to offer these Germans bread and salt, but they came too late. Among those who offered bread and salt were also Jewish artisans.[101] According to one anti-Communist Ukrainian, who also writes that hundreds of draft-age males came out of hiding, even the Khreshchatyk was "filled with thousands of Kievans in festive clothes. Many women were holding bouquets of flowers, which they threw at the soldiers and officers passing by. It was a rare case in history when the defeated rejoiced about the arrival of the victors."[102]

Other Kievans were actually too busy to receive the Germans—they were looting, searching through the blown-up storage sites. In the Podil district, the streets, littered with broken glass, were full of people who carried and moved things. Germans took pictures or joined in, but neither group paid much attention to each other.[103] When it became clear that the Germans were minding their own business, a night and morning of looting followed, this time of the Khreshchatyk. First Germans tried to chase the looters away, and when this failed they joined in.[104]

The Great Fire

One reason why many German soldiers had arrived smiling was that inside Kiev there had been no battle. The sandbags, barbed wire, and anti-tank crosses (made from pieces of rail) that the Soviet authorities had placed in the streets were easily pushed aside. Moreover, the Germans entered a city that was essentially intact: while the encirclement battle nearby caused damage and inflicted casualties in the countryside and in Kiev's suburbs (hitting the airports and the plane factory in the Shuliavka district, on June 22), the German military felt no need to shell the city itself.[105] But their satisfaction did not last. On the day of their arrival there were fires in several houses, stores, and storage sites, which people living nearby extinguished. The next day, September 20, a mine ex-

ploded in the former arsenal next to the Monastery of the Caves, killing
the German artillery officers and soldiers who had put up quarters there.
Roundups of Jewish pedestrians started. Germans checked people's identity papers, which had an entry for "nationality" that indicated one's ethnicity, and anyone identified there as Jewish now faced great danger. Rumors—perhaps started by Germans—blamed the Jews for the defeat of
the Red Army.[106]

Five days later, on September 24, thousands of people were patiently
standing in line in the Khreshchatyk.[107] They were obeying orders to register at the German Field Command in a former hotel at 1 Prorizna
Street (then still Sverdlov Street), and to hand in any hunting rifles, gas
masks, and radios (many of which they had looted from NKVD supplies
the day before) at the former "Detskii Mir" toystore at 2 Prorizna Street.
Around two o'clock in the afternoon, a mine exploded on the first floor at
the toystore, quickly followed by an even louder detonation from its third
floor that blasted Germans from the vehicles in which they were passing
by, threw the top of the building on the crowd, and set off a large fire. In
the blast and the stampede that followed, both German and Kievans
died. Fifteen minutes later yet another explosion destroyed the Grand
Hotel, home to the German Main Staff, killing the Germans inside. Moments later, the Arcade blew up, and still more explosions rocked Hotel
Continental on nearby Karl Marx Street. Besides demolition and casualties, the explosions also brought about the release of more than three
hundred Jews, mostly gray-bearded men, held in a movie theater: their
guards had run off.[108]

All evening and night, and into the next day, explosions followed every
few minutes at 2 Prorizna Street and the Khreshchatyk. What emerged
was a detailed NKVD plan to destroy the entire city center. Before the
Germans came, NKVD and military engineers had skillfully placed, at
night and under the pretext of preparing bomb shelters, mines that were
timed to go off at different intervals. Some apartments even had easily de-
tectable decoys, while real bombs were behind wallpaper and had a connection with the light switch. Soviet underground agents spread the fires
created by the explosions by throwing around bottles of fuel.[109]

Extinguishing the blaze was all the more difficult because a strong
wind was blowing and there was no water supply. On the third day, a
large fire hose arrived from another city and started pumping water from
the Dnieper, but a group of youngsters ripped it apart. Shot on sight, the

3. One result of Stalin's scorched-earth policy—the burned-out center of Kiev, probably on October 5, 1941. (Bundesarchiv, Bild 141/351.)

youths were left there for two days. The Wehrmacht requested a special German emergency train, but it could not make it to Kiev. On the fourth day of the fire, the city fire brigade returned from its evacuation and joined an extinguishing effort that by then included many Kievans.[110] In an attempt to increase people's vigilance, the German authorities also shot the inhabitants of houses adjacent to those where mines exploded, and eventually themselves blew up apartments—but neither measure had much effect. In all, according to one source, around two hundred Germans lost their lives as a result of the explosions or as firefighters.[111]

The Khreshchatyk was cordoned off and loudspeakers and soldiers running door to door ordered people living in adjacent streets to leave their homes. In all, between 10,000 and 25,000 people became homeless and spent a week on the streets, squares, and in the park on Volodymyr Hill, an ordeal that many elderly did not survive. Eventually those Kievans whose apartments had been searched—and thoroughly emptied—were allowed to return.[112] The sea of fire engulfed about one square kilometer (247 acres), and for over a week night no longer seemed to exist. At home, Kievans kept their clothes on, so as to be able to flee fast; on street corners, people held icons and prayed. A large black cloud hung over the city.[113]

Kievans eagerly helped find more mines, for example in the Lenin Museum.[114] Particularly active in this way was a released prisoner of war who made himself known as an engineer who had been forced to place mines in twelve buildings.[115] Altogether, the Germans discovered and safely removed as many as 670 mines, such as in the Opera House (one metric ton of explosives), in the former building of the Central Rada (three tons), in the Red Army Home (nine tons), in the central Bank, and in the headquarters of the republican Communist party and NKVD.[116] A military intelligence officer who wrote some reliable reports about Ukraine, the Austrian Slavist Hans Koch told foreign journalists that 100,000 metric tons of explosives were found under the thirteenth-century Dormition Cathedral of the Monastery of the Caves. (But he exaggerated when he said, and also wrote, that the Germans disabled over ten thousand mines.)[117] The Germans certainly prevented many explosions. Remarkably, there were no Soviet mines in the Tsarist Palace and in Kiev's prestigious district of Lypky.[118] Late in October, the former Duma and the Supreme Soviet buildings still were to explode; the Germans kept the fire department from extinguishing the fire in the second building.[119]

Kievans and Germans alike were outraged. If only we had taken seriously the rumors about mines that had circulated even before the Germans came, many Kievans now told themselves.[120] On the very first day of the fire, an angry crowd started looking for the culprits, handing many innocents over to the new authorities, who shot them. At the same time, house searches began. Hundreds of Jews were arrested, along with NKVD agents, political officers, and partisans. A group of SS men hunting for Jews stated openly in an office that it entered that "all Jews must be shot!"[121] Ignoring the fact that Jews were among the victims of the fire, rumors tended to blame only "the Jews." For example, a Jew supposedly had delivered a radio that contained a bomb. Such rumors spread all the faster because many Kievans feared a terrible German revenge and wanted a scapegoat.[122]

The ominous atmosphere came to a head on Sunday, September 28, when a newly appointed "Ukrainian militia" posted large announcements all over town with text in Russian, Ukrainian, and German.[123] The unsigned posters said that on Monday morning, September 29, before eight o'clock, all of the Jews "of Kiev and its vicinity" had to appear "at the corner of Melnykov and Dokterivska Streets (near the cemeteries). They must take with them documents, money, and valuables, and also warm clothing, underwear, etc." These streets did not actually exist—the Nazis had Melnyk and Dehtiarivska Streets in mind. The largest text, in Russian, described the Jews as "zhidy," or Yids, and warned that those who disobeyed "will be shot." Looters of Jewish apartments, it went on, would also be shot.[124]

Jews and non-Jews alike agreed on one thing—the order had been triggered by the explosions and fire. A friend of Fedir Pihido's, Mr. Raizman, said, "This is the work of those tramps [bosiaki—a pun on bolsheviki, Bolsheviks]. They decided to play on us Jews one last trick. Without these terrible explosions the Germans would have left us alone."[125] Now the SS, and probably also the Ukrainian militia, spread the rumor that the Jews would be concentrated in a ghetto and put to work. Because the designated point of assembly was near a freight train station, many Jews seem to have thought that they would be sent to a concentration camp in the Reich. Another rumor said that the Germans would exchange the Jews for German prisoners of war.[126] But on the night before they were to assemble, many Jews committed suicide. Other Jews said openly that death awaited them. A Ukrainian woman overheard her Jewish neighbors before they left: "Khaim, why are you taking that pillow, for we are going to our death?" Karaite men later were rumored to have prayed all night in their synagogue and to have told everybody the next morning to get ready to die.[127] In the largest single Nazi shooting of Jews in Soviet territory, all who went to the designated street corner were murdered down the road, at Babi Yar, a ravine at Kiev's western outskirts. By the end of September 30, no fewer than 33,771 Jews had been slaughtered in a "reprisal" massacre decided on by the SS, the German Police, and the Sixth Army. Perhaps the Nazi figure did not include the non-Jewish spouses and other relatives who died along with the Jews.[128]

The events in the weeks or months before the German occupation of Soviet regions revealed above all that the regime that was giving way neither trusted nor cared about those citizens who were slipping from its control. From the very beginning, Stalin and his associates deceived the population about the true state of affairs at the front, committed atrocities, and pursued a scorched-earth policy. Meanwhile the local elite, unlike the general population, were in the know and had access to transportation—and started to flee east. From a "Western" perspective the Soviet authorities behaved not as a native government, but as a conqueror who had to leave. Incidentally, a scorched-earth policy that included the destruction of cities was a throwback to tsarist ways: When Napoleon entered Moscow in 1812, Cossacks set off a fire and the French emperor soon found himself in a leveled city that was entirely unfit for habitation. There are indications that had the Germans also captured Moscow in 1941, Stalin would have tried to destroy it at least as much as Ukraine's capital.[129]

The response of ordinary people to the fall of the regime they lived under, however, was perhaps unprecedented in the history of European warfare. For one thing, the paranoia about spies that ran rampant in the cities was probably greater than in any other country subject to German invasion. For another, it appears that most peasants were glad, if reserved. For their part, many (perhaps most) drafted soldiers did not want to fight; in 1941, they saw nothing worth risking their lives for. After twenty-five years of seclusion from the outside world and constant deception by the state-run media, they did not expect that under a German regime their lives would be at stake. Finally, the widespread looting during the Soviet retreat was not, as many intellectuals concluded, a sign of lack of civilization by ignorant masses, but an almost logical way to behave during the violent collapse of a economy that was nearly bereft of private property. Many Soviet citizens deemed looting necessary to avert death by starvation, but they also had a sense, in the cities as well as in the countryside, that they had a *right* to loot. After all, had not the Soviet authorities destroyed supplies that could have been distributed? When a local bystander asked Kievans why they were looting, they shouted back: "They took enough of us! We're taking from them whatever we can! It's ours anyway, our blood and sweat!"[130] These poor and exploited people did not think they were thieves. On the contrary—they believed that they were taking back what was rightfully theirs.

2

THE REICHSKOMMISSARIAT UKRAINE

In his long monologues over a shared meal at his wartime headquar-ters—the "Wolf's Lair" in East Prussia and the "Werewolf" in Ukraine, eight kilometers north of Vinnytsia—Hitler liked to muse about his loath-ing for all Slavs. He wanted Germany to rule its eastern colonies like he believed Britain had been ruling India. The Germans should bar the Slavs from any education, which they did not even want themselves. Teaching Ukrainians how to read would merely produce "semi-edu-cated" people, who consequently would be dissatisfied and anarchistic. A university in Kiev was out of the question, and the Germans should "not allow anything to be published." All the Führer would agree to was music for the masses and a religious life that was fractured and thus easy to con-trol. But the Ukrainians and other non-Russians could still be useful: they would work and fulfill Ukraine's role of a "breadbasket."[1]

Hitler tempered this contempt in the early summer of 1942, when he visited Army Group South near Poltava and saw Ukrainian women with blond hair and blue eyes. He concluded that those traits were traces of the Germanic Goths who had lived in the region in the fourth cen-tury.[2] But he never stopping hating the "Eastern" cities, all of which he dubbed "Russian." He thought these cities were hotbeds of Bolshevism and Russianness from which the Bolsheviks had removed all objects of cultural value. The Germans should never settle there; living in barracks outside them was better. During the initial advance, he insisted that the German armed forces should demolish the largest "Russian" cities. On July 8, 1941, the chief of general staff of Army Command, Franz Halder, recorded in his diary that Hitler wanted to flatten Petersburg and Moscow with the air force so as to "prevent from staying there people whom we will have to feed in the winter." Hitler foresaw a "national catastrophe that will rob both Bolshevism and Muscovy of its centers."[3] Two months later, on September 18, Hitler's secretary summarized the Führer's view:

"The destruction of the major Russian cities is a prerequisite for the permanence of our power in Russia."[4] In the evening of October 17, after pontificating to high-ranking Nazis about the importance of constructing highways in the "East," Hitler said, "No German should enter the Russian cities, including large ones, insofar as they will even survive the war. Petersburg and Moscow should not in any case. They must vegetate further in their shit along the highways!"[5] Another contemporary record quotes even stronger words: "We are not going to enter the Russian cities; they must die off." Remorse was unjustified, Hitler added, for "we are also eating Canadian wheat without thinking about the Indians."[6]

Erich Koch, Reichskommissar for Ukraine

On July 16, 1941, less than a month after the start of the invasion of the Soviet Union, Hitler appointed the fervent Nazi Erich Koch as Reich commissar for Ukraine, subordinate to Alfred Rosenberg's Reich Ministry for the Occupied Eastern Territories.[7] The Nazi entity that Koch and his subordinates were to rule, the Reichskommissariat Ukraine, came into being in Volhynia and Right Bank Ukraine six weeks later, on September 1. On October 20 and on November 15, it expanded east of the Horyn and Sluch rivers, north of the Southern Buh River, and up to the Dnieper. Early in 1942, the Nazi administration estimated that some 15 million people were living in the Reichskommissariat.[8] It bordered in the north the Reichskommissariat Ostland, which was much smaller, and in the northwest the Białystok district, which, in all respects except on paper, belonged to the Reich province of East Prussia, of which Koch had been and remained *Gauleiter*, or Nazi administrator. Koch preferred his job in Königsberg, in which he was only accountable to Hitler, and during the entire war probably spent less then six months in Ukraine; and while there, he demanded to be addressed as Gauleiter.[9]

The final expansion of the Reichskommissariat, this time across the Dnieper River, took place on September 1, 1942, and brought in sections in the Left Bank of five pre-1941 Soviet oblasts (Kiev, Poltava, Dnipropetrovsk, Zaporizhzhia, and Mykolaïv).[10] Thus the Reichskommissariat Ukraine came to comprise just under 340,000 square kilometers. The Wehrmacht estimated that before its arrival and the Red Army retreat, the territory of the Reichskommissariat at its greatest extent had been home to 20 to 25 million people. As for an official population count during its actual existence, the Nazis made one census, for January

1, 1943: it documented 16,910,008 inhabitants.[11] Most densely populated in the Reichskommissariat were the Kiev region in the center, historic Podolia in the southwest, and the Dnipropetrovsk region near the Dnieper bend. In order to secure a steady wood supply and efficient railroad and water transportation, included from the start was Belarusan Polissia, a large area to the north of the Pripet River with forests, marshes, the city of Brest-Litovsk, and the towns of Pinsk and Mazyr.[12]

Nazi plans foresaw a Reichskommissariat Ukraine that would extend all the way to the Volga River and include Stalingrad, but many regions of pre-1939 Soviet Ukraine remained outside. Among them were the former oblasts of Chernihiv, Sumy, and Kharkiv to the northeast and the industrial and densely populated Donbas to the east, all of which remained under German military administration as part of Rear Army Area South, as did the Crimea (which the German army fully controlled only after a year). Eastern Galicia, formerly under Polish rule and mainly inhabited by Ukrainians, remained outside the Reichskommissariat as well: on August 1, 1941, it became a district of what since 1940 had been called the General Government. Germany's ally Romania received back northern Bukovina and southern Bessarabia, which the Soviet Union had annexed in 1940, and was given substantial other Ukrainian lands west of the Southern Buh River (the present-day equivalent to most of the Odessa oblast, the south of the Vinnytsia oblast, and a western strip of the Mykolaïv oblast). Romania joined all of these territories to its larger acquisition called Transnistria.

Reichskommissar Koch was in his mid-forties and was one of the more left-wing Nazis: had he not met the Führer, he said once, then he would have become an ardent Communist. Even as a member of the Nazi party, in 1934, he had published a book in praise of the Soviet state, *Construction in the East*. All the same, Koch from the beginning was a proudly brutal Reichskommissar. He is said to have remarked once, "If I find a Ukrainian who is worthy of sitting at the same table with me, I must have him shot."[13] An admirer heard him deliver a speech and called it "not talking, but beating." Koch told his subordinates that he expected them to treat the population in a "hard and uncompromising" way, with the "constant threat and the use of punishment and reprisals, even when no direct provocation for such exists."[14] He ordered his staff members and general commissars never to meet with Ukrainians.[15] And he fully shared Hitler's vision for the "East." On September 18, 1941, at the Wolf's Lair,

4. Martin Bormann (far left), the head of the Nazi party chancellery, Adolf Hitler (left), and one of the Führer's aides (far right) listen to Erich Koch, Reichskommissar for Ukraine, at the Werewolf headquarters north of Vinnytsia. Central Ukraine, summer 1942. (Photograph by Heinrich Hoffmann. Bayerische Staatsbibliothek, Munich, Fotoarchiv Hoffmann, Q.150; 5240/15.)

he expressed a desire, as Hitler's secretary put it, to "smash Ukrainian industry and drive the proletariat back to the country," while adding for good measure (and falsely) that Ukrainian nationalists had been behind the assassination in 1918 of the German military commander of the Ukrainian satellite state.[16]

Koch's brutality also showed in his very first public announcement, "To the Population of Ukraine!" which he made on December 25, 1941. Although the Soviet system would never return, he said, the war was not over because Britain, the cause of the war, was still fighting. Ukraine's population—there was no word of Ukrainian or other nationalities—had to put up and shut up: "Twaddle and talk are of no use now; only the willingness of each to put all his force at [our] disposal. Now there is no place for loafers and gossipmongers. All forces of the land belong to the struggle against the enemies of mankind, well-being, and happiness! We will judge everyone only by the extent to which he actually helps the reconstruction of this land. Each of you will have the possibility to live according to your faith and views and to be happy. Only by industry and labor, by the highest production and achievement, by the best working of the land, and by breeding your livestock in an exemplary fashion will you prove your willingness to build a new happy time." Resistance would encounter the "implacable severity of the law . . . We will punish every idler and violator of the peace."[17]

Germans and Auxiliaries

The Reichskommissariat Ukraine consisted of six general districts (Generalbezirke), headed by general commissars. These were Volhynia-Podolia, under SA-Obergruppenführer Heinrich Schöne, in Lutsk; Zhytomyr, under Regierungspräsident Kurt Klemm, and from 1942 SS-Brigadeführer Ernst Leyser; Kiev, under Gauamtsleiter Waldemar Magunia; Mykolaïv, under NSFK-Obergruppenführer Ewald Oppermann; Dnipropetrovsk, under Oberbefehlshaber der NSDAP Claus Selzner; and Crimea, under Gauleiter Alfred Frauenfeld, in Melitopol. The Crimea general district was nothing but a "partial district" of Taurida without the Crimea proper.[18] Each general district consisted of districts with their own commissars (in the just-mentioned general districts, respectively, 25, 26, 24, 13, 15, and 5 of them.) The Soviet oblasts vanished completely. The Reichskommissariat's five largest cities—Kiev, Dnipropetrovsk, Kryvy Rih, Zaporizhzhia, and Kamianske (prewar Dniprodzerzhynsk)—were distinct and had city commissars.[19]

Koch's headquarters were in the Volhynian town of Rivne, and in the first year it was home to about eight hundred Germans. From mid-1942, Koch dismissed many; by March 1943, only 252 Germans remained. A general commissar's office typically had about a hundred Germans, while most district commissars had two or three German aides.[20] Thus overall not that many men in yellowish-brown uniforms were around, a situation that stayed constant due to the principle not to appoint Hungarians, Romanians, or other military allies. A significant problem for the Nazis was poor communication. Koch's office never even had phone connections with the general commissars in Mykolaïv, Dnipropetrovsk, and Melitopol.[21]

Districts consisted of between two and twelve raions, which matched those in the Soviet period. On July 29, 1941, the German army banned any native administrations above that level.[22] As a result, the "Ukrainian

5. Office of a district commissar. Oleksandriia, southern Ukraine, 1942. (Photograph by Dr. Gauss-Riehle. Bundesarchiv, Bild 137/78762.)

auxiliary administration," as it was collectively called, could only include a raion administration or a city, town, or village council, headed by an invariably male raion chief, mayor, or village elder.[23] The main authorized sources of income for the auxiliary administrations were taxes on trade and service charges.[24] Raion chiefs and mayors of large cities could impose fines of 200 rubles or, from July 1942, Reichskommissariat karbovantsi (both official equivalents of 20 reichsmarks) or two weeks of forced labor or incarceration.[25]

Officially, the raion chiefs only dealt with forest exploitation, wood delivery, and financial taxes. Landwirts, German agricultural leaders with officer ranks subordinate to economy commands, supervised all agricultural matters, even at the village level, although they were assisted by native agronomists, whose skills impressed the Germans favorably.[26] Moving about in light carriages and locally known as "commandants," the landwirts had much to do: the average raion landwirt had 108 collective farms to oversee, and there were other tasks, handed down by the district commissars. Almost all of the landwirts were certain that collective agriculture was more productive than private agriculture and put the presumed needs of Germany and themselves above those of the local population.[27]

The landwirts and the economy commands were part of a military organization called Economy Inspectorate South, which was a branch of Economy Staff East, an organization in Berlin with ill-defined limits of authority. With the coming of civilian Nazi rule, the southern Economy Inspectorate moved east, but the commands stayed behind under the new name of armament commands. The Wehrmacht in the Reichskommissariat retained its own food supply system, a special commander, a supreme field command (in Kiev), field and local commands (in the cities and raion capitals), and a Secret Field Police that supervised both Wehrmacht members and natives.[28]

Economy Staff East dominated the "Eastern" economy, but independent, private German corporations also came to Ukraine: the agricultural Central Trade Corporation East (ZHO) and various industrial "trustees" such as the Mining and Metallurgical Corporation East, which went to the Dnieper bend and the Donbas. The private firms employed thousands of natives, as well as Dutch and other foreign construction workers and artisans.[29]

Nazi terror in central Ukraine stemmed primarily from two SS agencies: the Main Office for Reich Security, and the Order Police. In Ukraine the Main Office was represented by both the Security Police and the SD, or Security Service, and comprised two *Einsatzgruppen*, or Operational Groups (each also subdivided). The Einsatzgruppen immediately started open-air massacres of Jews, Roma/Gypsies, psychiatric patients, real and imagined partisans, and any other "suspect" persons.[30] Depending on the context, this book refers to these SS men, most of whom were not members of the SD but of the Security Police, as either the Security Police or the SD. Natives and arriving OUN activists had organized militias, but the Nazis purged and then integrated them into an Order Police for the Reichskommissariat, which also had German members. The Higher SS and police chief, like his colleague of the Einsatzgruppen, resided in Kiev (first in Rivne) and also ruled in the Rear Army Area South.[31] There also were SS and police chiefs for each general district. Formally, Ukraine's police chief Hans-Adolf Prützmann answered not only to SS leader Heinrich Himmler in Berlin, but also to Koch and his general commissars; in reality, personal animosity frequently complicated matters. The five city commissariats had their own SS and police leaders even though Koch and Rosenberg did not want them there.[32]

The non-German members of the Order Police were collectively called the Schutzmannschaft—often simply Schuma—and they included firemen. Closed units constituted the largest category and existed in June 1942 as thirty-six battalions.[33] Most Schuma were Ukrainians—often from eastern Galicia, northern Bukovina, and Subcarpathian Rus—but there were also Russians and members of other nationalities. Those conscripted in 1942 mostly were between seventeen and twenty-one years old. All Schuma were on the payroll of the native administrations. At first, they wore no uniform but merely a yellow and blue armband with the word *Schutzmann*. They carried batons or clubs and—during special actions—rifles or pistols. Their political training taught them, among other things, that "the Jew must be destroyed."[34]

Although this study will use just the term Schuma or auxiliary policemen, city Schuma were formally Protective Police (Schutzpolizei), and countryside Schuma, Gendarmerie. By the end of November 1942, the cities housed about 8,700 Schuma and 2,800 German policemen (a ratio of three to one), and the countryside 42,600 Schuma and 3,700 German policemen (an eleven-to-one ratio).[35] But other Schuma also arrived in Koch's domain: eight "Latvian," three "Lithuanian," three "Cossack," and two "Ukrainian" battalions; ethnic German, Estonian, Uzbek, Azerbaijani, and Central Asian units; and, in western Volhynia from early 1943, a "Polish" battalion.[36] From the beginning there were also battalions with Reich Germans only. Those policemen from the Reich killed even more people than the Einsatzgruppen did. Finally, there were an order service of Jewish ghetto inmates and a camp police of camp inmates. Not surprisingly, ordinary people did not use all the various names. When referring in a neutral way to Germans whose job it was to arrest and possibly kill people, their standard term was the Gestapo, while the Schuma were known as "politsai."

Alongside the SS and police forces there also developed a judicial system for the native population. In May 1942, all native jurists were ordered to take up their profession. Most raions had one judge for civilian cases—the *Schlichter*, or mediator—who had a native superior at the district level. There was also a judge who handled criminal cases—the *Schöffe*, or juror, who was often the same person as the mediator—and he could impose two years of confinement or ten thousand karbovantsi (one thousand reichsmarks). As in the case of penalties imposed by raion chiefs and city mayors, one could not appeal against them. The raion administrations paid the salaries of the mediators and jurors, but the commissars kept a close watch, in particular on the jurors, and reserved the right to settle criminal cases themselves. Natives could also end up in military court-martials or SS and police courts.[37]

The Nazi Bureaucracy and Its Ethos

There is disagreement about the extent to which the administration of Nazi Germany's main colonies, the Reichskommissariat Ukraine and the Reichskommissariat Ostland, was efficient. Some historians argue that there was much infighting between German civilian bureaucrats, who also were incompetent and much less powerful than the ever-paramount SS.[38] One historian also emphasizes the destabilizing role of everyday violence, which as an almost metaphysical force dragged Germans and non-Germans along and brought total chaos ("atomization")—indeed, the collapse of society as such.[39] In contrast, another historian asserts that the German agencies cooperated smoothly, particularly at the local level, denies that most civilian Germans were incompetent, and calls Nazi-ruled Belarus neither chaotic nor an SS state. Nazi rule there, in this interpretation, was horribly coordinated, purposeful, and effective. This historian also dismisses the term "racial war of destruction," which some historians have used to characterize the events in the Nazi-ruled "East," because many other things besides killing preoccupied the authorities, in particular, economic constraints.[40]

Rather than studying Nazi decision making in detail and perhaps coming down on the side of either of these interpretations—SS-supervised chaos versus efficient criminality—this book looks at the events through the eyes of those on the receiving end. Yet the reader should keep in mind the Lebensraum (living space) ethos that lay behind it. To the Nazis, living space in the Soviet territories meant two things: space where the racially superior Germans could go, or be sent, to create prosperous Germanic farming communities, and space where non-Germans lived whom one could force to extract the local natural resources. It is useful to caution against a simplistic emphasis on racism or ideology in explaining Nazi criminality, but to present economic constraints as a factor that always carried equal weight produces another pitfall. After all, crises and constraints often are more imagined than real, and what makes people believe in them is, if not an ideology, than an least an ethos, or mental outlook. As this book shall argue, economic crises and constraints in the Reichskommissariat Ukraine usually were more apparent than real. In that fertile land, agricultural conditions were never compellingly bad and the Germans faced few problems in their food supply. Thus a Wehrmacht division reported in December 1941 from the Kiev region that "potatoes and fresh vegetables can be taken from the land in abundance."[41] There was enough food around to potentially save thousands of "Russian" prisoners of war and it was a racist ethos, not economic constraints or other circumstances, that enabled their captors to embark on their deliberate starvation.

In Koch's domain, the plans for German settlement took shape in the forced "consolidation" of the native ethnic Germans and in an indirect fashion with calls by Nazi leaders to their subordinates to "prepare" the area for German settlement by killing non-Germans immediately. The fate of the first target group, whom all Nazis called Volksdeutsche, or "national Germans," lay in the hands of Himmler, who ruled not only the SS but also the Reich Ministry for the Fortification of Germandom. First thirty special SS commands assumed authority of the villages where the ethnic Germans predominated and killed or evicted any remaining Jews or Slavs. They organized the ethnic German males into police units, which participated in the Holocaust by arresting and guarding Jews (and presumably Roma), interpreting at the shooting pits, and covering the bodies. Numerous ethnic Germans also perished, however, in accordance with guidelines from Rosenberg's East Ministry regarding "spoiled elements."[42]

In July and August 1942, Himmler informed his Nazi colleagues that he planned to "resettle" and concentrate the ethnic Germans near

Zhytomyr, Rivne, and Vinnytsia (of the total 45,000 in the Zhytomyr general district), near Mykolaïv (of the total 20,000 in the Mykolaïv general district), and near Zaporizhzhia and Dnipropetrovsk, in the Halbstadt and Khortytsia districts (thus adding to the Mennonites living there people from the Kryvy Rih region). In two decades, Himmler said, there would be German-only cities at the intersections of highways and railroads, each home to at most 20,000 people and encircled with German-only villages.[43] Implementation of these plans started during the late fall of 1942, when the authorities deported Ukrainian peasants from south of Zhytomyr to the Left Bank and replaced them with ethnic Germans from the infertile north, peasants who looked Ukrainian but spoke German. Both migrant groups apparently received only a few hours' notice. By the end of the year, a new district called Hegewald had come into being, comprising 481 square kilometers with some 8,000 people.[44] A September 15, 1942, decree by Koch granted the ethnic Germans use—*not* ownership—of land and homes equivalent to what they had owned years ago, on January 1, 1914. News of the twofold deportation spread fast and created anxiety among ethnic Germans and Slavs alike.[45]

But Hitler's plan included far more drastic measures than deportation. Indirect germanization focused on the elimination of non-Germans through famine and killing. Plans to starve people dated back to May 1941. In a meeting about the Soviet Union early that month, Nazi state secretaries had noted that "when what we need is taken out of the country, doubtless *x* millions will starve."[46] One of these officials, Herbert Backe of the Reich Ministry for Food and Agriculture, personally convinced Hitler that Ukraine's agriculture would solve all of Germany's food problems, and in guidelines that he sent to Economy Staff East later that month, Backe predicted "a dying off of industry" in the "East." Part of the to-be-conquered Soviet territory, essentially present-day Belarus, was a "deficit region" whose population, particularly city dwellers, "will have to suffer great famine . . . Many tens of millions of people will become superfluous in this region and will have to die or migrate to Siberia." Importing food there would undermine Germany and should not be allowed. With regard to the black-earth region, which included most of Ukraine and which was a "surplus zone," Backe's scheme "granted livable conditions" to the collective and state farm workers there. But *only* to them. Never before in history had there been a plan for mass murder on this scale.[47]

Although a historian has argued that within weeks after the Wehrmacht crossed the Soviet border these ruthless plans lost most of their meaning and the Nazis tried to *prevent* city dwellers from starving to death, the evidence set forth here shall contradict that argument. For the moment, let me note that Himmler emphasized the goal of German settlement as late as 1943, and that he often demanded concrete plans for the settlement of specific regions.[48] He and the other leading Nazis conceived of the settlement as a process that might take decades, but for which Germans should create favorable conditions now, by killing natives under the cover of war. The way in which "superfluous" natives were killed, with cold calculation and often after precise selection, rather than in a killing spree, does not demonstrate that these killings served "pragmatic," "economic," or military goals to a greater extent than the long-term goal, German settlement.[49] On the contrary, the killings served most of all the long-term goal, which all the Nazis knew so well that restating it was hardly necessary. One such restatement, however, did occur in August 1942, when an article in the SS magazine *Das Schwarze Korps* claimed that "our duty in the East is not germanization in the former sense of the term, that is, imposing German language and laws upon the population, but to ensure that only people of pure German blood inhabit the East."[50]

Long-term, not short-term, goals also explain why Himmler stepped up the terror in Ukraine in 1942. At that time, he wanted to murder all remaining Jews and to create a clean slate for German settlement, as propagated in the "General Plan East" he had commissioned. The former chief of the Schutzpolizei and Gendarmerie for Kiev and surroundings, Lieutenant-General Paul Albert Scheer, was to tell Soviet interrogators in 1946 how he and about 120 other Ukraine-based SS and police leaders were summoned for a meeting at Himmler's field headquarters in a forest near Zhytomyr. (This was supposedly in June 1942, but Himmler's datebook indicates July 26.)[51] Himmler said his earlier order to kill all of the Jews still needed to be carried out in full, and at once. He also ordered his SS and police organizations to—according to the summary by Scheer's Soviet interrogators—"clean the territory of Ukraine for the future settlement of Germans. For those purposes, we had to pursue the massive extermination of the Soviet citizens, the Ukrainians. The civilian Ukrainian population in the occupied territory, Himmler said, must be brought to a minimum."[52] Himmler likely used other words, but the result on the ground was not only what scholars of the Holocaust call the

Second Sweep against the Jews, but also an incremental, lesser-known assault on the Ukrainians, Russians, and the other non-Jews.

Koch also continued to propagate a hard line, although documentary records of him condoning killings of non-Jews in Ukraine have not been found. Late in August 1942, just back from a visit to Hitler, with whom he got along well, he told a conference of Ukraine-based German officials that "the very last must be extracted from the civilian population without regard for their welfare" and that Ukrainians were "inferior in every respect . . . If this people works ten hours daily, it will have to work eight hours for us. There must be no acts of sentimentality. This people must be governed by iron force, so as to help us to win the war now. We have not liberated it to bring blessings on the Ukraine but to secure for Germany the necessary living space and a source of food." Even after the German defeat at Stalingrad in February 1943, he issued instructions not to be any less "harsh." In fact, "on the contrary." He told a Nazi party conference in Kiev in March 1943 that "we are a master race that must remember that the lowliest German worker is racially and biologically a thousand times more valuable than the population here."[53]

The Search for Political Alternatives

Almost from the very beginning, there were Germans who said the Slavs should be treated less harshly. Koch's superior Alfred Rosenberg, a Baltic German, was a mainstream Nazi in many crucial respects: he wanted to preserve collective farming, to exploit the region as a colony, and to keep out emigrés eager to return.[54] But he also wanted to control the native population in a more indirect fashion, through a greater degree of popular cooperation (and while keeping the POWs alive).[55] He wanted to destroy the Soviet Union and perpetuate German rule in eastern Europe by encircling "Muscovy" with de-Russified satellite states. These were to be greater Finland, the Baltic region, greater White Ruthenia, "Idel-Ural," Turkestan, Siberia, and, most especially, greater Ukraine.[56] But Hitler and Koch decided early on that none of Rosenberg's "Ukrainian" proposals—a satellite state, a university, a political party—would come to fruition.[57] Koch and his like-minded deputy, Regierungspräsident Paul Dargel, remained consistent until the end. In April 1942 Rosenberg induced Koch to issue a ban on the widespread flogging of people, but this had no effect because his subordinates were well aware of his real view. During office hours they still often kept a whip on the table.[58]

On January 21, 1942, Rosenberg ordered the closure of all institutions of higher learning in the Reichskommissariat, except for medical, veterinary, agricultural, forestry, and technical faculties, and Koch repeated the order on February 4. In February, Koch also banned the teaching of German, again in accordance with the wishes of the East Ministry (although not of Rosenberg personally).[59] Yet on October 24, 1942, Koch took the initiative and ordered all educational institutions other than the (four-year) primary schools closed, including the craft and vocational schools in agriculture and forestry. Rosenberg ordered him to withdraw the decree, which he refused. Late in March 1943, Rosenberg asked Hitler to dismiss Koch, but on May 19, 1943, the aloof Führer at last backed Koch explicitly and reduced Rosenberg's task to issuing general guidelines.[60]

The Wehrmacht was also among the earliest to call for a change of policies in the "East." In January 1942, Field Marshall Walter von Reichenau, then commander-in-chief of Army Group South, called for land reform, food relief, and political autonomy for the population. In December 1942, other army representatives made even more radical proposals. Calls for reform came also from an army intelligence officer (Theodor Oberländer) and from certain circles in the Security Police and the SD.[61] The general commissar in Melitopol, Alfred Frauenfeld, was a convinced Nazi, but he wrote memoranda critical of Koch's treatment of the non-Jewish population, and Koch's colleague in the Reichskommissariat Ostland, Wilhelm Kube, often thought and acted more along Rosenberg's line. But Rosenberg lacked the skills to rally any of these potential allies.[62]

Some Ukrainians and Russians who were employed by the Germans during the war have written memoirs in which they call the introduction of civilian Nazi rule in Ukraine a sea change compared to the period of military rule. Thus a man who worked for the German army as a propagandist and informant recalls that the introduction of civilian rule in the Left Bank inaugurated "constant" arrests and killings of Ukrainians as well as a general fear.[63] But such testimonies pass over the prevalence of violence immediately after the arrival of the Germans. On the largest scale were SS and army murders of Jews and Roma. The army command also insisted on ruthlessness in the struggle against partisans, and as early as July 25, 1941, prescribed large-scale executions of locals whenever those directly responsible for sabotage or partisan activity were not found.[64] In the middle of September 1941, Wilhelm Keitel, chief of the Supreme Command of the Armed Forces, demanded the slaying of between fifty and a hundred "Communists" for any German killed by "Communist insurgents."[65]

General Field Marshall Walter von Reichenau of the Sixth Army not only demanded "radical action" against the Jews of Kiev, but also, on November 9, 1941, mercilessness against partisans ("murderous animals") and their accomplices. Unless there was evidence that the population had fought the partisans in question and had lost lives while doing so, all of the villages that had "hosted or taken care of" the partisans needed to be subjected to food confiscations, house burnings, hostage shootings, and the hanging of "accomplices." Early in December 1941, Army Group South reported that it had executed thousands and called the policy a total success.[66] Although Lieutenant General Karl Kitzinger, the Wehrmacht commander in the Reichskommissariat Ukraine, ordered in October 1941 that at least half of all hostages taken in such actions be Jews, within months most of the victims were non-Jewish Ukrainians.[67] Very vulnerable were refugees and migrants, whom the Nazis labeled "strangers" and considered likely to engage in subversion.[68] The military Secret Field Police also killed many people. In the Poltava region during 1942, a unit based in Kremenchuk shot, on average, one or two people per day (328 persons until August); another in Kobeliaky shot two or three people per day (610 until September); and the field police in Myrhorod shot about seven per day (1,710 until September).[69]

A remarkable case of Wehrmacht brutality seems to have taken place in Dnipropetrovsk. One day in October 1941, a car backed up in a Wehrmacht vehicle repair shop, hit a young local who worked there, and broke half of his ribs. The site supervisor gave a note to a German driver and the fellow was driven away. Later that day, an army interpreter who also worked at the site (a Jewish man who concealed his identity and who later recalled the event) asked the driver what the doctor had said. "What could he say? He got the note," came the response. "I was thinking of the boy's health!" "Health? What health? He's getting an injection . . . The boy cannot work any longer and has no family! He's *kaputt!*"[70] Other sources do not mention anything like this (although there are stories of lethal injections of psychiatric patients and Jews). But it is clear that violence against non-Jewish and non-Romani civilians came from both the SS and the Wehrmacht and was widespread.

At first the risks were greater for natives of the Dnieper area of Ukraine than for people in western Volhynia. One reason was the very poor clothing of the Dnieper-area residents. As has frequently been the case in the history of humanity, poor clothing alone often sufficed for getting bad treatment. The "rough" and non-"European" public manners of these people were another factor. According to the army intelligence officer Hans Koch:

> The clothing, also of the educated, is not only objectively ragged, but also deliberately neglected. Shaving, personal hygiene, shirt collars, polished boots, clean fingernails: until now, all were apparently considered bourgeois prejudices. The people here spit and blow their noses right on the floor. Human body odors are not regulated here, tooth cleaning is rare, and because everybody smokes nothing but the strongest tobacco (dried beech leaves rolled into thick newsprint), sessions even with learned and high-placed bodies can become an ordeal for a Western European. Gatherings of peasants are similar, even when they are in the open air.
>
> In personal conversation, each former Soviet citizen lacks the manner and courtesy that is customary among us. Hands in the pocket, the stinking smoking butt in the corner of the mouth, standing very close to the body of the person one is talking to (but only rarely looking him in the face)—that is the customary way of contact, also among the better and indisputably loyal circles. Even the returning or forcibly transported prisoners of war only take the cigarette out of their mouth for German officers when they are shouted at.[71]

These "proletarian" ways infuriated many Germans. A teacher arrived at a meeting in the village of Kuntseve (Novi Sanzhary raion) and did not lift his cap as he approached the local German commandant. The commandant threw it off and forced the man, for all to see, to arrive a second time, this time cap in hand. In Chyhyryn, Germans shouted "Jude!" and "Lenin!" at people who stood with their hands in their pockets, and even beat them in the face for it.[72]

Nazi propaganda hammered away that Stalin had been beaten. "Moscow, the Nest of Bolshevism, is in German Hands," it crowed, and in the spring of 1942 composite pictures showed Hitler taking a parade on Red

Square.[73] The village Gendarmerie spread the rumor that Moscow, Petersburg (Leningrad), and other Russian cities had fallen and deliberately did not destroy portraits of Molotov and General Timoshenko (and sometimes also General Voroshilov), who supposedly had gone over to the German side. Rumors planted with the assistance of former Red Army soldiers and village elders also worked along these lines.[74] Other planted rumors asserted that Stalin had fled to the United States, that he had shot himself, or that Voroshilov had shot him.[75] Nevertheless, most of the population, especially to the east of the pre-1939 border, continued to doubt all of this. During most of the Nazi period, Ukrainians, Russians, and other non-Germans in the Reichskommissariat Ukraine lacked any conviction that the Germans would stay.

The uncertain future did not stop some from attempting to create a national political structure. On August 31, 1941, a Ukrainian Council of Trust in Volhynia was formed. In a polite letter to Koch, its head, Stepan Skrypnyk, agreed that the formation of what he called "the Ukrainian state" could wait until Germany's victory in the war.[76] Koch allowed the council to engage in cultural activities, but emphatically denied the requested right to appoint Ukrainian administrators and judges and to run cooperatives.[77] Nor did he allow in his domain any branch of the Ukrainian Central Committee, which was based in the neighboring General Government.

Ukrainian activists in Kiev also tried to create their own institutions. Two or three days after the Germans arrived there, Melnykites who came from the west created a city administration, and after agreeing to their urgent request, the local historian Oleksander Ohloblyn became mayor. Another Kievan, Volodymyr Bahazii, was more enthusiastic, but the Melnykites feared that he might be a Soviet agent.[78] As Ohloblyn's deputy, Bahazii impressed the Germans so much that they made Bahazii mayor after all, on October 29. "All Ukrainians praise Melnyk," he told visiting foreign journalists in those days.[79] In addition, on October 5, in a building in the Podil district, Melnykites led by Oleh Kandyba (alias Olzhych) created what they hoped would be the nucleus of a national government, the Ukrainian National Council, and persuaded Mykola Velychkivsky, a local university instructor whom the NKVD had imprisoned before the war, to chair it. The preparations were hidden from general view, but once the council existed it apparently declared that it was striving for an independent Ukrainian state. Although many members were not Melnyk supporters, it was essentially a Melnykite front organization. Some council members accepted the strong advice of Hans Koch to rename the body the Civic Ukrainian Council, but the Melnykites refused to go along and got their way.[80] On October 7, representatives of a Melnykite, semi-official military unit called the Bukovinian Battalion, consisting of hundreds of OUN members and sympathizers from Bukovina, Bessarabia, and Galicia, marched to the top floor of the main building of the Academy of Sciences, the new office of the National Council. In the name of the battalion the commander pledged to serve the council, God, and the Ukrainian people.[81] The council declared in print that "Russian-Jewish-Bolshevik rule in Ukraine and over the Ukrainian people is gone once and for all." The first thing the Ukrainians should do now was to help the Germans in their anti-Bolshevik struggle, particularly in the fight against partisans and saboteurs.[82] Because nothing about the council ever appeared in the press or was heard on the radio, there is reason to doubt that many Kievans even knew it existed.

In a letter to the Reichskommissar, the council expressed the hope that it might help bring about "both the final victory over Communo-Bolshevism and the USSR as well the final victory and reconstruction of our country, which has been ruined by Jews and Russians."[83] Koch did not respond, and on November 17, the council, which had never been formally registered, was banned. Around that time the German authorities also disbanded regional bodies such as the Kiev Oblast Administration.[84] Thus started an unannounced assault on the Ukrainian nationalist activists. Late in November 1941, in Zhytomyr and in the town of Bazar, the site of a large nationalist commemoration, the Nazis executed Melnykites for the first time. More executions of Melnykites and sympathizers took place in Kiev in February 1942. Mayor Bahazii, now mistrusted by the Nazis for many reasons—for instance, he supposedly had tutored Khrushchev's children—also died in this wave. The method and location of the executions is unknown, but the bodies probably ended up at Babi Yar. As for the Banderites, the first were shot in the beginning of September 1941; and from November 25, the Einsatzgruppen had an official policy to shoot all of them, in secret and as looters.[85]

The suppression of the various councils and regional administrations within the Reichskommissariat was crucially important, for it meant that the native population would have no representation above the lowest level of administration, whether on a regional or an ethnic basis. This state of affairs invariably baffled Ukrainians visiting from the Reich or the General Government, where Ukrainians, Poles, and Jews all had such representative bodies. For instance, a Ukrainian Protestant and citizen of the Reich visited western Volhynia early in 1943 and searched but did not find Ukrainian representatives. Editors of the regional newspaper *Volyn* (Volhynia) told him that the Ukrainians had tried hard, but that the Germans simply wanted to fully control the situation themselves.[86]

Yet the Ukrainian nationalist or community activists, whether locals, former emigrés, or people from Galicia or Bukovina, not only created short-lived organizations: they also spread national symbols. Here they achieved some success. On September 19, 1941, a Melnykite hoisted a yellow-and-blue Ukrainian flag to the top of St. Sophia's Cathedral in Kiev. (Banderites turned it around, with the blue on top, two times, until a guard was placed.) The Germans never bothered to remove the flag, which faded in a few months.[87] In November 1941, yellow-and-blue flags, alongside German ones, were all over Kiev, such as on streetcars. They vanished early in 1942, along with the trident, the other symbol of Ukrainian independent statehood. (As late as June 1942, an ad hoc committee of the Kiev city administration recommended its use—to no avail.)[88] In other cities and towns these symbols stayed around still longer. In the spring of 1942, there were tridents and yellow-and-blue flags around in Polissia. Auxiliary administrations that had prepared stamps with tridents did not always replace them.[89] In the Poltava region, portraits of the nationalists Symon Petliura and Ievhen Konovalets, yellow-and-blue flags, and tridents remained on display until September 1942, when the region joined the Reichskommissariat; their removal surprised many locals.[90] In contrast, Russian national symbols from the very beginning were all but absent from the Reichskommissariat. The one exception, from 1943, was people wearing uniforms with the letters ROA on their sleeve, which stood for the German-sponsored and largely fictional Russian Liberation Army, led by the imprisoned Red Army general Andrei Vlasov.[91]

At the same time, the de-sovietization and germanization of public spaces proceeded irregularly. Locals or Germans pulled down the numerous statues of Stalin and other leaders.[92] Streets in Kiev received Germanic names such as Adolf Hitler Street, Wotan Street, Varangian Street, and (for the Khreshchatyk) Eichhorn Street.[93] Other public markers of the German claim to the land were German monuments and "Germans Only" notices that appeared near public toilets, good restaurants, and other places. But in small towns, de-sovietization often took some time. Tarashcha in the Kiev region, for example, retained its New Soviet Street and Komsomol Street until late 1942, when the district commissar named them after the Ukrainian writers Kotsiubynsky and Franko.[94]

A Culture of Denunciation

The Soviet regime left in its wake bitterness, hatred, and a desire among many to denounce real or imagined enemies. After the Germans arrived, those who had been NKVD informants, Soviet officials, or Soviet activists lived in fear. Mykhailo Podvorniak was an Evangelical Christian in western Volhynia whom the NKVD had forced to sign a promise of cooperation. His name was cleared when it was found on an official Soviet list of "unreliable elements."[95] Many others were not so lucky, however, and as in Soviet times, were denounced to the authorities. Unless a raion chief or other native official vouched for them, such "Bolsheviks" often perished, especially if their denunciation was given to a unit of the Einsatzgruppen, which was also shooting any nonlocals who could not identify themselves. Execution had not necessarily been what the denouncers intended.[96] Early denunciation perhaps was why the Communists of Poberezhka, Huta, Stari Bezradychy, and probably many more villages were shot so soon.[97] But it should also be noted that as before 1941, the denouncers were not necessarily motivated by political zealotry or personal animosity. In many cases, a callous pursuit of private gain—the desire to free up space in one's communal apartment, for example—was more important.[98]

Local military commands initially often took most denunciations seriously and punished the "offenders."[99] Then they realized, perhaps because their interpreters told them, that making denunciations often was a typically Soviet behavior and thus many of the accusations were false. The military commander in Kirovohrad even issued a warning that those who made unfounded accusations would be arrested, after which the flood momentarily dried up. When in one village in this region an elderly woman gave the local commandant a list with the names of fourteen members of the Komsomol, she was told to leave and be ashamed of herself.[100] Here and in many other localities the German military initially gave the local Communist party members the benefit of the doubt and merely kept a close watch on them.[101]

Throughout the Nazi period, for anything said or done, there was sooner or later a person who was willing to inform the authorities. A Kievan born in 1904 later spoke of "extraordinary treachery" in Kiev, and the SD there indeed received hundreds of denunciations, including many false ones (which the agency ascribed in part to deliberate NKVD sabotage.)[102] Among the reported "crimes" were acts that could be construed as Ukrainian nationalism. For example, in June 1943 the Autocephalous Orthodox bishop Nikanor (Abramovych) celebrated Pentecost in the town of Kaniv with a sermon on local, ancient Cossack graves and placed a cross on the grave of Ukraine's national bard, Taras Shevchenko. A denunciation led to the arrest of some 180 participants and thirty-seven of these were shot.[103]

The widespread tendency to denounce went hand in hand with pervasive mutual mistrust. Ever since the Great Terror of the 1930s, the Soviet Union had been a society virtually without trust. In its stead was the Communist virtue of "vigilance," or watchful suspicion.[104] The larger a city, the less its inhabitants seemed to have faith in each other. This tendency also existed in the Reichskommissariat. A Kievan later described the atmosphere among the local employees of the German-run opera and ballet theater, where he worked as a photographer. "Somebody would come in and start to curse Soviet rule. To object was impossible, for you wouldn't know him. Or, conversely, he would start to praise it. We did not know the people around us. You could not trust anyone, you could not say a word."[105] The mistrust could also work against the German interest. A German army chaplain explained that the Ukrainians feared that if the Soviet regime returned, their compatriots might denounce their actions under the Germans; that was why in 1941 natives "often and everywhere" lied to the Germans.[106]

The Soviet ways invariably struck "western" Ukrainians. The leader of the Banderite underground in Kiev wrote in a letter in October 1941 that he was encountering a Soviet heritage of "slyness, scrutinizing, and distrust."[107] A bishop from Volhynia in Kiev spoke of "some kind of persecution mania. People fear one another, everybody thinks the other is a spy and traitor, and each accuses the other of dishonesty, theft, and venality." Protestant Ukrainian missionaries in Proskuriv in July 1942 sensed that the population saw enemies all around.[108]

Not surprisingly, many natives did more than denounce. Those whom the NKVD had "repressed" often became highly motivated official German informants.[109] The Schuma included many with a thirst for revenge, even for seemingly small matters from the Soviet past such as having being reported for absenteeism. Various people have recalled after the war that the auxiliary policemen were especially cruel. In one village in the Novi Sanzhary raion in the Left Bank, the policemen reportedly started murdering Communists on their own initiative.[110]

A Banderite tells in his memoirs of two revenge killings in 1941 by locals (including a Jew) somewhere east of the Southern Buh River.[111] And in the western Volhynian countryside, a wave of lynchings of unpopular leaders of farms and of village soviets appears to have erupted. An NKVD informant managed to hide in a village in the Kremenets region, but one month later, when women whom he had harassed and whose husbands were gone found him, they beat him to death with sticks. Later there were also anonymous murders. In the small Volhynian town of Torchyn, dozens of former Soviet activists are said to have been secretly killed in 1942.[112]

The Jews of western Volhynia turned out to be particularly vulnerable to violence from locals. In at least twenty-seven towns and villages in that region, Jewish property was looted by many, including peasants from nearby villages, and some of the looters murdered the owners.[113] In the larger Volhynian towns, the discovery of the bodies of prisoners killed by the NKVD shocked everyone. (Some women in Dubno who found murdered relatives apparently were so upset that they rammed their heads into the prison cell walls.)[114] At once, the NKVD's misdeeds somehow became Jewish. There was talk among the Ukrainian (and presumably also Polish) population about murderers "known" to have been Jews. In Dubno, people talked about the exploits of a major called Vinokur, believed to have been the prison chief. He was said to have fled to the local castle and to have shot still more people there. Then he shot his driver and female assistant and moved on, until finally, so the story went, he was tracked down and killed. People just *knew* that he was Jewish.[115]

At the time, a survivor of the NKVD massacre in Dubno asked a man who had visited the local hospital and had met other survivors there,

> "What are they saying? Who murdered the prisoners?"
>
> "Everybody says that they were NKVD agents, prison guards, and some kind of civilians. Everybody saw Vinokur. He shot with a revolver; the civilians shot with semiautomatic guns. Among them was also a woman, a real vampire. She also shot people."

"A woman! Really?"

"It's true! Hanna Berenstein, you may remember her: black hair, portly, she wore an NKVD uniform? She was a prison guard."

"Oh yes, I remember now."

"They say that during her work she treated the women in a beastly manner, and that on that terrible night, she made one victim after another. She did it with great pleasure. She was the first to run to the women's cells, where she grabbed them one by one by their braids and shot them in the forehead, roaring with laughter."

"The sadist!"[116]

This poisonous atmosphere served as the prelude to large anti-Jewish pogroms that evidently occurred in Dubno and four other western Volhynian towns: Kremenets, Korets, Shumsk, and Tuchyn.[117] The largest pogrom was apparently in Kremenets, a town that fell to the Germans on July 3. Here hundreds of Jews were arrested—by a Ukrainian militia according to Jewish witnesses, by Germans according to one Ukrainian witness. In the local prison, they had to unearth the victims of the NKVD, and then, according to an SD report, their Ukrainian guards clubbed 130 of them to death, until the German army command stopped them.[118]

Although non-Germans, in particular Jews, were at risk from their compatriots, most of the violence still came from the Wehrmacht and especially the SS. Some of the episodes are hard to recreate from data available today. For example, it appears that in May 1942, there were thousands of arrests in the Kiev and Vinnytsia regions of Communist party members, followed by the execution of many—details, however, are unavailable.[119] The memoirs of Hryhorii Kariak, an emigré and former raion chief, provide some more information. The Novi Sanzhary raion was relatively loyal to the Germans and apparently did not have any partisans. Nor did it have a Jewish population. Nevertheless, early in the summer of 1942, auxiliary policemen shot four Communist party members and the former investigator of the Soviet prosecutor's office. In July 1942, some twenty "Gestapo agents"—probably Secret Field Police officers—arrived unexpectedly and began a month-long investigation of all the men ages eighteen to fifty-five. All five thousand men had to show their papers, which indicated Communist party membership. The officers arrested thirty-five party members, and invited complaints about these men from the population. A massive response produced more "suspects." In the end, thirty-two arrested locals were shot. Altogether, says Kariak, during the entire Nazi period, even disregarding casualties during the German retreat, as many as two hundred people were killed in the Novi Sanzhary raion alone.[120]

By mid-1942 at the latest, such events were common everywhere, and for the year 1943 there is even more evidence. For instance, over a nine-month period in that year, the army field command in Borodianka near Kiev apparently arrested seven hundred civilians (most likely non-Jews) and the field commander personally shot at least twenty-five.[121] In addition to these calculated murders, there were also many seemingly random killings. In the village of Stari Bezradychy in the Obukhiv raion, for example, a Civil War veteran, about fifty years old, showed his wooden arm to a German in order to explain why he was not scything like the others. The German shot him dead on the spot.[122] And many natives ended up for some reason in one of the Reichskommissariat's concentration camps, labor camps, or POW camps. Kievans, for instance, shuddered at the thought of the camp they called Babi Yar, near the ravine and murder site of the same name. (Its official name was Syrets.)[123] For all of these reasons, danger, brutality, and fear came to dominate ordinary people's lives.

3

THE HOLOCAUST OF THE JEWS AND ROMA

The term Holocaust has become a politically charged concept. In present-day usage, in all languages, most people take it to mean what the Library of Congress calls the Jewish Holocaust. The connotation is that the genocide of the Jews, or Shoáh in Hebrew, stands out from other genocides because only in this case were the victims collectively killed because of their ethnicity, and the method to murder them was more efficient than ever before. Indeed, everywhere in Europe, the Nazis were obsessed with the Jews. In practice, however, the Nazis also perpetrated genocide against the Roma, also known as Gypsies. They did so even though Nazi ideology and propaganda devoted little attention to this ethnic group and even though no order to kill them all has been found. In Ukraine, this Porajmos, or Great Devouring, as the Roma have called it, happened at the same time as the Shoáh. The Nazis destroyed the vast majority of both Jews and Roma, they did so for racist reasons, and they claimed to be acting less because of who the victims were than because of what those groups were supposedly *doing*—conspiring to enslave the world (Jews) and engaging in partisan activity (Jews), crime (Roma), and spying (Roma). In both cases not all the members of the victim group died as a result: the Shoáh bypassed thousands of western and central European Jews because their spouses were "Aryan," and the Porajmos left alone some "pure" Roma in the Reich.[1]

There is a dire lack of primary sources about the Romani Holocaust. The Nazis often did not even bother to report their massacres of Roma. In addition, there seems to be no account by a Romani survivor from Ukraine, and other personal accounts mention the Roma's tragic fate rarely and always briefly. A Kievan said in a postwar interview that the Roma of the city were shot two or three months after the Babi Yar massacre; another person recalls seeing Romani refugees in the Kaharlyk region, south of Kiev, in mid-1942.[2] A more detailed description comes from the Jewish survivor Mechel (Michael) Diment. Early in 1942, most Jews in the western Volhynian raion of Lokachi were still alive, if incarcerated in ghettoes. But for the 114 local Roma there was no such phase: the Nazis told them they would be "settled" and would get food, shelter, and land. On April 16, 1942, they were taken to an open space near a brick factory, where the Roma "danced with happiness, singing and playing their violins all through the night, along with their children, who were dressed in new clothes." Early the next morning, ten Schuma and a German police officer took thirty ghetto Jews with shovels to the site. Diment, apparently one of them, writes in his memoirs that their captors lined the Roma up and then let loose a hail of bullets. "The Gypsies could not escape; they were against the wall. Small children, trying to get away, hid under their mothers' dresses and this was how they were killed. Babies were shot by the killers, going from crib to crib. Immediately after the slaughter, the militia ransacked the bodies for valuables. We dug large holes, collected the bodies and threw them into a mass grave. Some were still alive."[3] Does the lack of sources about these horrors mean that virtually none of the Roma lived to tell of them? Might it mean that no one helped them, unlike, as we shall see, in the case of the Jews?

The literature on Jews is, by contrast, much more developed. According to the Soviet census of 1939, before the annexation of eastern Poland, there were 1,533,000 Jews in Soviet Ukraine, or just under 5 percent of the total population.[4] Jews in the countryside either spoke Ukrainian (with some even becoming peasants) or continued to speak Yiddish. The Yiddish-speaking group frequently disdained the peasants and blamed them for the pogroms of the revolutionary period. In the cities and towns, where most Jews lived, the Jews, like other city dwellers, mostly spoke Russian in their daily lives, but some Jews were officially of Ukrainian nationality and called themselves Ukrainian.[5]

During the 1930s, the Soviet media paid little attention to anti-Semitism, because it was banned and not supposed to exist. The authorities emphasized an alleged friendship among all of the Soviet nationalities.[6] Because it resembled the derogatory Russian word *zhid* (Yid), there was a ban on the traditional Ukrainian word for Jew, *zhyd*, which in fact had no negative connotations; and public use of either zhyd or zhid carried a prison term of up to a year. (Ukrainian speakers had to use a Russianism, *ievrei*.) Young Dnieper Ukrainians by and large internalized the taboo, even though they might continue to say zhyd in private. The word's comeback in 1941 was to shock them.[7]

With the Nazi-Soviet pact of 1939, public references to anti-Semitism, such as two Soviet films depicting the persecution of Jews in Germany, vanished altogether.[8] News about Nazi actions did reach the Soviet Union, however. For instance, in the small eastern Ukrainian town of Orikhiv there was talk in 1940 that Polish Jews were being killed.[9] Nevertheless, when the Germans and their allies crossed the Soviet border, they initially found most Jews still in place. One scholar has estimated that in those regions east of the pre-1939 Soviet Ukrainian border that experienced regime change within the first four weeks of the campaign, two-thirds of the Jewish population originally living there fell under Nazi rule.[10] From more eastern regions, more than half of the Jews managed to flee. Indeed, among the larger group of refugees and evacuees in the Soviet hinterland, Jews became relatively numerous compared to their share of Ukraine's population. This was not due to any preferential treatment by Soviet authorities, but because Jews were relatively numerous in the cities—more than one in four people in Soviet Kiev was Jewish—and thus in the evacuated offices and factories.[11]

Yet many Jews deliberately stayed behind. Perhaps they did not want to abandon elderly or frail family members: as an Israeli historian has noted, "The close family relations for which the Jews were legendary became a trap that prevented the escape of no few young people." Attachment to belongings also might have played a role.[12] But perhaps the main reason for staying, as in the case of non-Jews, was the hope for a better life. In this regard, the evidence about the Jews of Kiev is most persuasive. Anti-Communist sentiment was widespread among them.[13] From June 1941, the Soviet press available in the city had stopped its blackout of reporting about Nazi anti-Semitism, but few Jews believed the alarming Soviet reports. One Jewish man picked up German radio broadcasts and warned as many Jews as he could to flee, but people called him a panic-monger.[14] Many Kievan Jews even put a positive spin on what they heard about Nazi Germany: Soviet policies had made these artisans and tradespeople unemployed, and since the Soviet media described Nazism as an extreme form of capitalism, these Jews believed that under the Germans their living standard would improve, or at least stay the same. According to one emigré, they said they would not mind wearing a yellow star. This witness saw "the little Jewish people" gather at the Podil market in June 1941, where most agreed that they should not leave Kiev and that under the Germans they also would all have a job. "It can't get any worse than this," they said, and "What's going to happen to the people is also going to happen to us."[15] A Ukrainian woman who lived near the Jewish Market remembers overhearing Jews talk well about the Germans who had ruled Kiev in 1918. Such Jews stayed and some welcomed the Germans with bread and salt.[16]

These hopes began to fade as soon as the Germans arrived. While entering a town, German soldiers might shout, *Juden kaputt!*—"Down with the Jews!" High taxes, and child-level maximum food rations, were imposed on all Jews. Reichskommissar Koch also created a special penalty tax on organizations and offices that employed Jews.[17] The old Soviet passport, with its information on nationality, greatly facilitated this persecution. The German authorities also ordered the city administrations to compile lists of Jews.[18] Within days or at most weeks, the persecution became deadly. The killings were usually open-air mass shootings with machine guns by commandos of the Einsatzgruppen and, in particular, the Order Police.[19] Thus in countless towns and villages, thousands of Jews died within days. The Jewish Holocaust in Dnieper Ukraine was rather different from the Holocaust in western and central Europe, where Jews were put into ghettoes and then, sooner or later, were shipped away to be gassed to death. In Dnieper Ukraine, most Jewish men, women, and children died at the edge of or inside their graves: anti-tank ditches dating back to Soviet times or pits dug by prisoners of war, non-Jewish locals, or the victims themselves.

Survivor's accounts are very rare. One about the eastern Volhynian village of Pavlovychi near Ovruch has come from Evgeniia (Zhenia) Guralnik, née Kilikievskaia around 1928. Initially there came a massacre of a relatively small number of Jews, such as male Komsomol members. The largest massacre took place at the end of 1941, when the region also housed many Jews from Lutsk, Rivne, Berdychiv, and even Warsaw, who, like the local Jews, were put to various forced labor tasks. Early in November, all had to dig a large pit: three meters deep, 40 meters long, and 2.5 meters wide, supposedly to store beets over the winter. As they were digging, in the piercing wind, the laborers did not speak the unbearable truth. It was next to a Polish cemetery where all summer executions had taken place. Zhenia Guralnik's mother said, "Somehow I don't like this pit, it's very large, and we never used to store beets in the ground, but in a cellar or barn. This means no good." Ten days later the pit was ready and the Jews asked the Ukrainian policemen who supervised them, "Why did they bring this new ladder to the pit, are the beets really not going to be

6. Open mass grave with thousands of Jews. Podolian town of Proskuriv (today Khmelnytsky), 1941 or 1942. (Muzeum Wojska Polskiego, courtesy of United States Holocaust Memorial Museum, Photo Archives, 17881.)

thrown in there? What's the use of walking down there! When will we finally carry the beets?" "When they tell you so, you will carry them," the man said. "For now, do your thing, clean the beets!" The Jews completed that and other tasks. On November 25, around four o'clock in the afternoon, the SS drove everyone to the pit in three cars. Guralnik recalls that SS men and Ukrainian policemen had surrounded the area. Under terrible beatings and kicks, and with the use of dogs, the Jews were forced to undress. Then they were shot, usually down in the pit. "Before they died, many men cursed the butchers and spat in their faces." Zhenia somehow evaded the shots in the pit. She pretended to be dead, and climbed out in the evening.[20]

Her account is typical in two ways. First, the Jews—not surprisingly—were unable to realize what awaited them. Second, auxiliary policemen not only arrested Jews and cordoned off ghettoes, but also were present during the shootings.[21] In what was possibly an exceptional case, in the town of Radomyshl on September 6, 1941, Sonderkommando 4a of Einsatzgruppe C shot the adult Jews but ordered the Ukrainian policemen to shoot the children.[22] In at least some places, native policemen themselves started to persecute the Jews. Militia members and German military perpetrated anti-Jewish "excesses" (as the SD put it) in Uman on September 21, 1941.[23] The Polissian Sich, a unit of armed Ukrainians from western Volhynia and Polissia that until November 1941 had legal status as a police force, roamed the forests and Pripet marshes from a base in Olevsk, apprehended partisans and Jewish civilians, and if it did not kill them at least handed them over to the German authorities. A contemporary newspaper interview with a fifteen-year-old Sich member seems to confirm this: asked whether he was not afraid to be with the Sich "insurgents," the boy, said to have "evil eyes," replied that he "did everything they asked. I went everywhere, rode everywhere, fought, and shot Jews who had treated me badly."[24] At the end of the year the Sich's own periodical declared that "now the parasitical Jewish nation has been destroyed." When the German authorities destroyed the "fake commune"—Communism, supposedly represented by the Jews—the Sich had "lended a hand in its shameful death."[25]

The city administrations and the farms paid the native police their salaries, sometimes from money obtained from Jews.[26] Many non-Jews may have been dismayed that in this way they helped fund the persecution. When militia men robbed Jewish homes in the western Volhynian town of Horokhiv in July 1941, it caused, according to a Jewish survivor, "an outcry by the local Ukrainian leadership." But there was little else that such local leaders could do and often they themselves were forcibly involved. Thus a town mayor might receive a German order to force locals to dig pits.[27]

The Babi Yar Massacre

Before the chillingly well-organized Babi Yar massacre in Kiev, mentioned earlier, there appeared an anti-Jewish poster on September 28, 1941. Non-Jewish Ukrainians and Russians recalled later that upon seeing that poster, "few considered the possibility of the terrible truth: mass murder" and that nobody expressed any such thoughts.[28] Many, perhaps most, believed that the Jews "merely" awaited deportation, and hardly anyone expressed regret. "I've great news for you!" Anatolii Kuznetsov heard his Russian-speaking Ukrainian grandfather say that day. "From tomorrow there won't be a single Yid left in Kiev. It seems it's true what they said about them setting fire to the Khreshchatyk. Thank the Lord for that! That'll pay them back for getting rich at our expense, the bastards. Now they can go off to their blessed Palestine, or at any rate the Germans'll deal with 'em. They're being deported!" The young Anatolii himself, who had a good Jewish friend, thought that the Germans would send the Jews to Palestine and that this was for the best. Yet Lev Dudin recalls that hundreds of non-Jews petitioned the authorities to allow particular Jews to stay.[29]

All day Monday, September 29, Jews—men, women, and small children—along with non-Jewish husbands, wives, and other dear ones, walked to the designated street corner in Kiev's western Lukianivka district. The Russian middle-aged teacher L. Nartova described in her diary the view from her balcony: "People are moving in an endless row, overflowing the entire street and sidewalks. Women and men are walking, young girls, children, old people, and entire families. Many carry their belongings on wheelbarrows, but most of them are carrying things on their backs. They walk in silence, quietly. How awful . . . It went on like this for very long, the entire day and only in the evening did the crowd become smaller." She even adds—which other sources do not confirm but which may be true—that Jews also walked the next day "and so it went on for several days."[30] Fedir Pihido was on Lviv Street that Monday, around eleven o'clock, and saw how "many thousands of people, mainly old ones—but middle-aged people were also not lacking—were moving toward Babi Yar. And the children—my God, there were so many children! All this was moving, burdened with luggage and children. Here and there old and sick people who lacked the strength to move by themselves were being carried, probably by sons or daughters, on carts without any assistance. Some cry, others console. Most were moving in a self-absorbed way, in silence and with a doomed look. It was a terrible sight." In the early morning of the next day, when he "could not yet know about what had happened," Fedir Bohatyrchuk apparently saw many Jews walk in the same direction. They had "stony faces, paralyzed with fright. They already instinctively foresaw what was going to happen to them. Only the children did not suspect a thing and walked business-like, with bags in their hands or knapsacks on their shoulders. I remember a group of Jews who carried a gray-haired old man, apparently a rabbi, on a stretcher and were singing a sad song."[31]

Another observer, a female factory engineer, generalized later that when the Jews walked away, "it was such a weight on the hearts of all." However true this may have been for her, Nartova, Pihido, and others, by no means were all onlookers sad. "Unfortunately and to my shame," Bohatyrchuk writes, "I have to say that I saw quite a few of my co-religionists watching this exodus with a happy face. These short-sighted people, blinded by hatred, simply did not realize what was going on."[32] Walking on his own toward the Podil district, Kuznetsov found many non-Jews out on the streets, "standing in the gateways and porches, some of them watching and sighing, others jeering and hurling insults at the Jews. At one point a wicked-looking old woman in a dirty head scarf ran out on to the roadway, snatched a case from an elderly Jewess, and rushed back inside the courtyard. The Jewess screamed at her, but some tough characters stood in the gateway and stopped her getting in. She sobbed and cursed and complained, but nobody would take her side, and the crowd went on its way, with eyes averted. I peeped through a crack and saw a whole pile of stolen things lying in the yard." He overheard a story that a hired cabby had simply dashed off with the luggage of several families, and later he saw Jews hurry down empty streets to a backdrop of "whistles and shouts from the doorways." Among the onlookers were also many Germans. On Lviv Street, some apparently called out to Jewish girls, "Come do some cleaning here!"[33]

After the Jews and those accompanying them arrived at the designated corner, they continued walking west, down Melnyk Street (present-day Melnykov Street). The seventeen-year-old G. A. Batasheva came there with her family around ten o'clock. Trucks loaded with clothes drove by in the other direction, but people kept saying that they would be put on a train, because some undistinct people, not Jews, shouted things like, "Hurry, the trains are waiting!" The point of no return, according to Batasheva, was near the intersection of Melnyk and Puhachov streets, where many non-Jews were told to go home. From there on, German soldiers and two police battalions edged the people on toward the Jewish and Orthodox cemeteries and, behind those, a large ravine that was locally known as Babi Yar. Semiautomatic gunfire resounded from there.[34]

Another survivor, the then thirty-year-old Dina Pronicheva, recalled that just before the entrance to the Jewish cemetery, (Soviet-made) barbed wire and antitank hedgehogs blocked Melnyk Street. "Germans and Ukrainians" guarded the checkpoint. "One could enter freely, but nobody was let out, except for carters." As the procession passed the cemetery, it reached on the left Kahatna Street, which had a long fence on the left and a small Orthodox cemetery on the right. Into this street the people were directed, but Pronicheva walked straight to find out what was happening farther on. "I thought there would be a train standing there, but I saw that the Germans immediately took off and seized fur clothes. They took food and put it in one place, the clothes in another, while the people walked on. The Germans took out a large number of people, stopped those walking for a while, and took people out again. When it was my turn, I wanted first to get out, but they did not let me. I returned to my parents and did not tell them anything, in order not to upset them, and walked with them."[35]

The people made a right turn into a wide street that divided the small Orthodox cemetery from the large and also Orthodox Lukianivka Cemetery. "Both sides of Dorohozhytska Street were densely planted with young trees," Batasheva testifies, "and between them stood Hitlerites armed with automatic weapons and sticks. Many had dogs." After passing the two cemeteries, the terrified people entered a vicious gauntlet of German submachinegunners. "Those who tried to move aside . . . were beaten severely with sticks and attacked by dogs. People were also beaten without any reason." It led to a large even ground.[36] Pronicheva confirms this: "If someone fell, a dog was let loose which ripped things and the body, the person just had to get up and run downward, and fall into the hands of [non-German] policemen, who undressed people completely, and while doing so beat them terribly, wherever and however they could—with their hands, feet, some of the policemen had brass knuckles. The people went to execution covered with blood."[37]

A German source also confirms the presence of "Ukrainians" or *politsai*—ethnically nondefined if certainly non-German policemen near the ravine: A former member of the principal murder team at Babi Yar, Sonderkommando 4a of Einsatzgruppe C (enlarged for the occasion with members of police battalions 45 and 303), told German prosecutors years later that the Jews were received, undressed, pushed, and kicked "by the Ukrainians."[38] It is likely that these auxiliaries—as well as the Ukrainians at the checkpoint and the people who shouted about waiting trains—belonged to units created or commanded by Melnykites, namely the Bukovinian Battalion and a company of what was then called the "Ukrainian police."[39]

Batasheva recalls that at the edge of the even ground there were elevations with narrow aisles in them that led into the Yar. The winding ravine stretched for 150 meters and was thirty meters wide and fifteen meters deep.[40] Pronicheva convinced a policemen in Ukrainian that she was Ukrainian. "Sit down, wait until the evening," he told her. "When we've shot all the Jews, we will let you go." While waiting, she saw how "people were undressed and beaten, people laughed hysterically, they were visibly going insane, and turned gray within minutes. Babies were taken from their mothers and thrown upward through some kind of sandy wall. All the naked people were lined up two or three at a time and led to some kind of height, to the wall of sand, which had cuts in it. The people went there and did not return . . . After getting out of the so-called door, that cut, there was a small ledge on the left. Here all the people were lined up and shot from the other side by machine-guns."[41] At the end of the day she ended up in the ravine herself, alive. Overcoming great dangers, she lived to testify about the massacre.

Ukraine's other major cities experienced similar massacres in 1941. In Dnipropetrovsk on October 13 and 14, a police battalion assisted by auxiliary policemen shot at least ten thousand Jews and—most likely—non-Jewish spouses and children of intermarriages.[42] Unlike the "reprisal" executions that were meant to intimidate, the perpetrators did not mention these massacres to the population.

The Ghettoes

On September 5, 1941, Koch ordered the creation of ghettoes in cities where Jews made up a large percentage of the population.[43] Most Reichskommissariat ghettoes that we know about were in western Volhynia. In charge of each were Jewish councils that, if considered needed by the German authorities, had at their disposal a police force called the Order Service. In the summer of 1942, any remaining ghettoes were destroyed along with their inmates, as part of Himmler's Second Sweep against the Jews. Thus the Jewish Holocaust in the Reichskommissariat Ukraine was essentially over by the end of 1942. In that year and in 1943, the Nazis in Koch's domain murdered over 350,000 Jews.[44]

The Jewish councils in the Reichskommissariat ghettoes, like those in other European ghettoes, usually did not resist in the usual sense of the word. As one historian has put it, the Jews in the ghettoes of Europe "hoped that somehow the German drive would spend itself. This hope was founded in a 2,000-year-old experience. In exile the Jews had always been a minority, always in danger, but they had learned that they could avert or survive destruction by placating and appeasing their enemies."[45] The councils were far from uncontroversial, however. Corruption and favoritism developed, causing major disagreements among the ghetto inmates, and almost every ghetto included a minority (or even majority) of inmates who wanted open resistance. In the ghettoes of Dubrovytsia, Sarny, Sosnove, and Volodymyrets, these more militant Jews made plans to resist, but the councils forced them to stop. Thus when young Jews from Dubrovytsia who worked outside the ghetto schemed to disarm their guards and flee, the council warned them that unless they abandoned their plan, it would have them sent to a camp. Likewise, plans for armed resistance in Kovel and Dubno came to naught.[46]

The Order Service was made up of young Jewish males accompanied by Jewish strongmen. All tended to use force to fulfill the Nazi demands for money, taxes in kind, and laborers, and even to round up more laborers than the authorities demanded. Not surprisingly, many ghetto inmates hated them.[47] Diment's memoirs about Lokachi portray them vividly. When the Nazis demanded laborers, the ghetto council compiled a list, but nobody showed up. Then "the Jewish militia, holding sticks, accompanied by their Ukrainian equivalents, went looking for the people. Walking between the homes, the Jewish militiamen would point out a person to the Ukrainians, who seized him. Those who refused to go were beaten. Many hid in various places, but the Jewish militia, who knew all of those hiding spots, found them and turned them over to the Ukrainians. Loud name-calling and cursing was heard everywhere. In some cases where they could not find the one they were after, they would take anyone in the home they could, like a brother or sister." Two of these men thus got the nickname "Gestapo agents." During a major grain confiscation campaign in the countryside in July 1942, the district commissar demanded an astonishing seven tons of grain from the Lokachi ghetto. Disregarding cries and screams, the Jewish policemen collected some 1.8 tons.[48]

In general, open resistance came about only on the very eve of the ghettoes' destruction. In western Volhynia, there were Jewish uprisings in Kremenets, Tuchyn, and Mizoch in August, September, and October 1942, respectively. The ghetto of the small town of Tuchyn did not include all local Jews. When in September 1942 all remaining Jews were ordered to move there, its council, together with young men and women, somehow obtained guns, rifles, and grenades to fight for their lives. On September 22, German and native policemen surrounded the ghetto to enforce their order. In the early hours of September 24, shots were exchanged and the inmates set the ghetto on fire. About two-thirds of them, some two thousand people, escaped into the woods. Council chairman Getzel Schwarzman gave himself up on the third day of the uprising and took full responsibility.[49]

Individual and collective acts of resistance also occurred outside the ghettoes. When the district commissar visited Liubeshiv (near Kamin-Kashyrsky) in August 1942, and apparently told the local Jews that they would be killed, a dentist severely wounded him with a razor blade. A camp in Sarny at some time in mid-1942 held thousands of Jews and one hundred Roma. When murders started, Jews who had bribed a guard removed the fence and Roma set fire to the shacks. About one thousand prisoners escaped as a result.[50]

In Dnieper Ukraine, a number of Jews fled before any authority had registered them as Jews. According to Pihido, some Kievan Jews roamed the countryside as late as 1942.[51] Others fled westward during the recruit-ment for work in Germany. Kiev's city commissar found out and ordered the local administration to report any Jewish families from which mem-bers had gone to Germany. The city Department of Social Aid supplied the names of at least two families, after which the SS must have investi-gated whether they were still alive.[52] But a small number of Jews, with forged Polish identification, actually arrived *from* the west, from the Gen-eral Government, particularly in 1943. The men took jobs at firms or mil-itary construction sites. In Dnipropetrovsk a Polish man realized that they were Jews, but he continued to treat them well.[53] Between ten and fifteen Jewish men in uniforms and with forged documents spent much of their time escorting Jewish women to Kiev or Dnipropetrovsk.[54] A number of these Galician Jews moved on to Romania and survived the war there.

What did the Jews think about the non-Jewish bystanders? In many places, the issue was moot because the massacres started so soon, but ghetto inmates lived longer and remained in contact with the surround-ing, usually Ukrainian, population, who delivered letters (illegally) and paid Jewish craftsmen to do specific tasks.[55] Diment's memoirs suggest that many western Volhynian Jews tended to condemn "the Ukrainians" for not coming to the rescue, and that some even blamed them for what was happening. When the people of the Lokachi ghetto received a letter from other ghetto Jews that urged them to flee, a minority wanted to re-main in the ghetto and resist from there. One man used the argument that "the villages are the prime source of anti-Semitism" and others called the Ukrainians "collaborators" who were "largely responsible for our ominous predicament . . . The Ukrainians will make sure that no Jew survives; otherwise, they would be witnesses to the barbarism of the Ukrainians."[56] Although many Ukrainians indeed denounced Jews, there were others who did not. In this regard, it is important to look systematically at the attitudes and reactions of the non-Jewish popula-tion regarding the fate of the Jews, both in Dnieper Ukraine and in west-ern Volhynia.

Bystanders in Dnieper Ukraine

Anti-Semitic sentiments surfaced in Soviet Ukraine during the 1920s and mid-1930s, in particular in connection with the formation of collective farms.[57] Many non-Jews seem to have resented the presence of Jews, who because of their higher level of education were placed in positions of authority and prestige. Jews—like Russians—were relatively numerous in those positions. For example, whereas the official Jewish percentage of the entire population of pre-1939 Soviet Ukraine was 4.9, about 13.4 percent of the members of the republican Communist party in 1940 were officially Jewish. Non-Jews tended to conclude that the Jews had some kind of special relationship with the authorities.[58] It is not surprising, therefore, that the term "Jewish Bolshevism" *(zhydo-bolshevyzm)*, introduced by Nazi propaganda, found fertile ground. Older people had heard the term before, because it had come about in this very region, during the revolutionary period and struggle for independence. Once the new authorities were in place, many people who asked for favors used this term, or spoke of "the Jewish regime."[59]

Nazi propaganda insisted, "There is no place for Jews among us! Down with the Jews!"[60] The Ministry for the Occupied Eastern Territories reinforced this bias by distributing *Ukraine in Jewish Talons*, a brochure that noted, "Ukraine's history knows many eruptions of national and social anger against the Jews, the allies of Moscow and Warsaw. The Zaporozhians, the Haidamaks, the Ukrainian army of the recent past—all duly punished Jewry for its high-handedness in Ukraine." This "struggle" was ongoing and in due time "the Ukrainian people will stand before the Jews with a very large bill for everything. And this bill they will have to pay in full. The indictment will be long. The sentence will be short."[61] In March 1942, the press quoted Hitler as saying that his earlier prediction was "being realized": "not the Aryan peoples, but the Jews will be destroyed as a result of the present war."[62] It is hard to estimate the influence of such propaganda and even harder to estimate the extent to which it made non-Jews react in certain ways to the Holocaust. There is no conclusive answer now and there may never be one.

Contemporary German sources provide some information about the extent and nature of native anti-Semitism in Nazi-ruled Dnieper Ukraine. SS reports from the first few months of Nazi rule suggest that most non-Jews expressed anti-Semitic views, but also that they did not want the Jews killed. In July 1941, Einsatzgruppe C called the population of the Zhytomyr region "consciously anti-Semitic," with "a small number of exceptions."[63] Some weeks later, the murderers found anti-Semitic sentiment even more intense near the Dnieper bend, a region where their talk about the "Jewish question" was "always gratefully received by the population."[64] Four more weeks later the same Einsatzgruppe was less confident. In surveying the Kiev, Poltava, and Dnipropetrovsk regions, it noted that "Jewry is rejected by the Ukrainian along with Communism, since the Jews were predominant among the C[ommunist] P[arty] officials. The Ukrainians could see for themselves that the Jews were virtually the only ones who enjoyed the benefits of CP membership and particularly of the leading positions. A pronounced anti-Semitism on racial and ideological grounds is foreign to the population, however." In fact, "to persecute Jews using the Ukrainian population is not feasible, because the leaders and the spiritual drive are lacking; all still remember the harsh penalties which Bolshevism imposed on everyone who proceeded against the Jews."[65] The SS complained that unlike in eastern Galicia, here "the careful efforts once undertaken to bring about Jewish pogroms unfortunately have not produced the hoped-for success."[66]

German reports are ambiguous about the opinion of the non-Jews regarding the massacres of Jewish people. In September 1941, Einsatzgruppe C wrote that "almost nowhere could the population be moved to take active steps against the Jews," but it also alleged that "everywhere" the massacres of Jews were "understood and judged as positive." Several months later it spoke again of a popular "understanding" for "the treatment of the Jews." And yet, while taking note of "conversations of the population" of Kiev full of "hostility against Communists and Jews," the Einsatzgruppe also found cause for concern: "the Ukrainian" had "no real position on the Jewish question," considering it "only a religious conflict and not a racial problem."[67] An unidentified Nazi traversed the Reichskommissariat at the height of the Second Sweep, talking with civilian Nazi officials. Given what we know about the mood of the population, it seems wise to be skeptical of his report, in which he asserts that the people of Berdychiv felt "satisfaction" about the "evacuation" (murder) of the Jews, that the people of Vinnytsia "greeted [it] enthusiastically," and that the people of the Oleksandrivka district deemed it "basically justified."[68]

A revealing source might have been the letters that Ukrainians and others sent to relatives who went to Germany to work starting in 1942. Unfortunately, all that we have are two censor's reports based on letters that were checked between August 11 and November 10, 1942.[69] In them are supposedly representative quotes from some of the letters, but these tell us little: "The Jews are terribly persecuted. In Kremenets the Jews have been beaten already for three days"; "One day 500 Jews were killed. On August 8, the Jews were rounded up from all of the villages. Soon it will be the end of the Jews"; "About 3,000 Jews were killed." "No Jew is still alive here. The old, the young, the children, the doctors—up to the last they have been exterminated"; "And we are doing very well now, for there are no more Jews." The compiler of the first report commented that "several letter-writers express their compassion with the fate of the Jewish population in the Ukraine." The second report includes a comment that "the total extermination of the Jews is reported from a large number of cities and villages. Almost always this is done without an opinion. Only in a few cases do the writers express their satisfaction about it."

In a real sense, one has to wonder how important any feelings about the Jews, whether positive or negative, could have been in shaping people's behavior. After all, the Holocaust occurred in their home region, and in a situation of all-out terror. In Polissia, for example, an SS brigade killed 10,844 people, mostly Jewish men, women, and children, in just over two weeks from late July 1941. During their rampage, the perpetrators found that the local non-Jews "generally spoke well of the Jewish part of the population," even as they "actively aided with driving the Jews together." "Ukrainian priests were very helpful and placed themselves at the disposal of every action." Fear for their own lives probably made them do it: another SS brigade in the region reported later that "the Ukrainian population showed itself generally helpful as before regarding the tracing of partisans. As before, one finds a great fear."[70]

Yet Zhenia Guralnik tells a disturbing story about her experience in the village of Pavlovychi. One time before the November 1941 massacre, SS men forced all of the Jews to shed their clothes and walk to the village center, where people were on their way to church. Many locals there were hostile: "With a scream, a crowd of gapers ran over to see this unprecedented sight. There were laughs, giggles, and cynical jokes. Suddenly the German stopped us and ordered everybody to be silent. We cuddled up, as persecuted beings surrounded by a hostile crowd. The SS man walked up and down before us, carefully looking at the line-up, aligning our bare feet. He waited a minute and then roared out, 'Disperse!' Immediately the column turned into a naked group. We ran to our homes like crazy, egged on by yells and whistles from the crowd."[71] Whether such behavior was commonplace in the villages of Dnieper Ukraine is unknown.

Jews were also marched through cities and towns.[72] To generalize about the onlookers is hazardous, as the case of Kiev showed. Moreover, once the non-Jewish bystanders realized that something more than "mere" deportation was taking place, many of them became very scared. Thus in Zhytomyr small boys ran along the crowd, but adult onlookers were silent and "full of apocalyptic horror."[73] Others, however, were pitiless. During a march of Jews through Berdychiv in September 1941—after the Nazis had already shot hundreds of local Jews—there were people who "walked past the guards and took scarves and knitted woolen sweaters" from the Jewish marchers.[74]

When the non-Jews of Kiev found out that all of the Jews had been shot—many heard the sounds or saw the trucks with the clothes—the general reaction was horror and indignation, even among those who hated Jews. Kuznetsov's grandfather cried out: "Oh Mother of God, Queen of Heaven, what is this, why do they do that to them?"[75] From the second day of the massacre, the news was all over town, and people spoke of sixty thousand victims, or more.[76] Iryna Khoroshunova's diary shows how difficult it was for some to believe it all. On September 29 she wrote:

> We still don't know what they did to the Jews. There are terrifying rumors coming from the Lukianivka Cemetery. But they are still impossible to believe. They say that the Jews are being shot . . . Some people say that the Jews are being shot with machine guns, all of them. Others say that sixteen train wagons have been prepared and that they will be sent away. Where to? Nobody knows. Only one thing seems clear: all their documents, things, and food are confiscated. Then they are chased into Babi Yar and there . . . I don't know. I only know one thing: there is something terrible, horrible going on, something inconceivable, which cannot be understood, grasped, or explained.[77]

But several days later it was no longer possible to doubt:

> Everybody is saying now that the Jews are being murdered. No, they have been murdered already. All of them, without exception—old people, women, and children. Those who went home on Monday [September 29] have also been shot. People say it in a way that does not leave any doubt. No trains left

Lukianivka at all. People saw cars with warm shawls and other things driving away from the cemetery. German "accuracy." They already sorted the loot! A Russian girl accompanied her girlfriend to the cemetery, but crawled through the fence from the other side. She saw how naked people were taken toward Babi Yar and heard shots from a machine gun. There are more and more such rumors and accounts. They are too monstrous to believe. But we are forced to believe them, for the shooting of the Jews is a fact. A fact which is starting to drive us insane. It is impossible to live with this knowledge. The women around us are crying. And we? We also cried on September 29, when we thought they were taken to a concentration camp. But now? Can we really cry? I am writing, but my hair is standing on end.[78]

L. Nartova wrote with despair several weeks later: "I remember my comrades, excellent specialists, good workers. Why did they die? And there were so many of them!" In October she saw Schuma take away ill and disabled Jews. "How terrible it is to live here, how hard it is to look at that scene." A little girl in the street asked her whether these were Jews, and whether they would be killed. "Clearly she cannot grasp this thought. But who of us can?" The German intelligence officer Hans Koch was wrong to report that Kievans took the news of the massacre "calmly, often with satisfaction."[79]

The shock was all the greater when, as often happened, locals witnessed the shootings. Some indeed received orders to bury the dead or still-living victims.[80] Ukrainian girls in Berdiansk realized that their Jewish classmates would be killed and appealed for mercy to the city's military commander, in vain. "We embraced our Jewish girlfriends and said farewell to them," one of them recalls. Some time later, Nazis machine-gunned the Jews outside the town as the Ukrainian girls looked on in tears. Elderly people might react from a different perspective. Before the massacre, they "recalled tsarist times and accused the Jews of having served every regime and having made life impossible for our poor people. They had fleeced our people of various state taxes and had also occupied high positions under the tsars . . . But when the people saw the massive extermination of the Jews, then the old were also against it and indignant." It was like the shootings by the NKVD, one man said, with the only difference that those had been secret.[81]

Inevitably, the question arises to what extent the non-Jewish population denounced or saved Jews. It is important to note that Nazis threatened with death any form of help. It was not simply forbidden to have any relationship with Jews; anybody who kept in touch with Jews on his or her own initiative received a personal warning from the authorities that the death penalty would follow if he or she tried to save a Jew.[82] Posters and signs also stated that helping Jews escape was punishable by death. (In Kiev, these appeared on the first day of the Babi Yar massacre.) The non-Jews had good reason to take such threats very seriously. In some cases the penalty was imposed on entire families.[83]

The result was a general ostracism of all the remaining Jews. Nine elderly Jews appeared in the center of Kiev after the massacre and sat down near the former synagogue. "There they sat for days and nights," a witness recalls. "People went by and clearly felt sorry for them, but did not dare to walk up to them. For that, one would be executed. Then one of [the Jews] died from hunger. How horrible! He died from hunger while a large city looked on. After a while, a second died, and a third, and a fourth . . . They were dying and nobody removed the bodies." When just two remained alive, "some Kievan approached a German guard, who was standing at a nearby street corner. He asked him, while pointing at the bodies, to shoot those two. The guard thought for a moment and did it."[84]

In short, the threat of death was a powerful deterrent. (And one should perhaps also note that the practice of shunning victims of repression predated the Nazi period. During the Great Terror of the 1930s, almost everybody severed contact with family members of those arrested.)[85] Still, danger cannot fully explain the behavior of some non-Jews. For one thing, an unknown number of them saved Jews. For another, still more Ukrainians and other non-Jews denounced hidden Jews to the authorities. Many sources show such betrayal.[86] Frequently those denouncers were less fearful than simply greedy—eager to receive the high rewards (ten thousand rubles, a cow, or a food donation) promised for handing over Jews and other "enemies," such as Communists who did not register. Several days after the Babi Yar massacre, the SS in Kiev started a hunt for baptized Jews and non-Jewish spouses of Jews. Among them were many doctors. Many of them approached Fedir Bohatyrchuk, himself a radiologist, for help, but he urged them to get out of town, for he was sure that informers "always could be found." As a woman whose mother took care of an old Jewish man—until he too was denounced—said in a postwar interview: "There were plenty of scumbags."[87]

According to Kuznetsov, Jews in hiding usually were found, for, as he puts it, "there were many who wished to earn the money or cow." For example, a fourteen-year-old Jewish boy managed to return from Babi Yar, and as soon as they heard this, Kuznetsov's mother and grandmother told Kuznetsov to go and get him immediately, so that they might save him. But it was too late: German soldiers were taking the boy away on a cart. The denouncer was "a Russian woman who lived on her own on the collective farm, working with the cows." Women were arguing loudly in the yard. "Some were protesting, others argued: 'She did right. Finish with the lot of 'em. That's for the [destruction of the] Khreshchatyk.'"[88]

Every local massacre seems to have brought in its wake denunciations by a substantial percentage of the population. After the shooting of thousands of Jews near a village in the Lubny region (near Poltava) on October 16, 1941, the non-Jewish population needed some time to realize what had happened. Most were horrified, writes Lubny's then-resident Ivan Zhyhadlo. But then came an "epidemic of denunciations" of remaining Jews and of anybody from "mixed" marriages, however distant. According to Zhyhadlo, its driving force was the very same people who used to denounce people to the Soviet regime. If true, it was a very large phenomenon indeed. Thirst for revenge, envy, greed, anti-Semitism, and fear motivated these people. Communists in particular, Zhyhadlo writes, hoped to rehabilitate themselves by blaming others for forcing them to join the party. The denouncers of Jews in Dnieper Ukraine were a minority, but the size of this group is still unclear.[89] What does seem obvious is that anti-Semitism did not always play a major role, or even any at all, in the decision to denounce.

Still more common than denunciation was the looting of empty Jewish homes, in a macabre reprisal of the looting during and after the Soviet retreat. Many of the goods thus obtained showed up at markets.[90] In Kiev, German authorities recruited people to collect Jewish belongings near Babi Yar and at their homes. Intended or not, those workers profited a great deal and soon some were selling fur and jewelry in the streets. Other Kievans who had become homeless because of the Great Fire eventually occupied Jewish apartments.[91]

After the Jewish genocide, people still talked a lot about the Jews— not about their murder, but in anti-Semitic terms about the Jewish people. The memoirs of Jacob Gerstenfeld-Maltiel, one of the Galician Jewish refugees from the General Government, show this convincingly

7. Jews from Lubny, a town in the Left Bank, and surroundings, who have obeyed an order to assemble. Later that day the Nazi Security Police shall murder all of them. Lubny region, October 16, 1941. (Photograph by military photographer Johannes Hähle. Hamburger Institut für Sozialforschung, Fotoserie "Lubny," Bild 008,54.)

for Dnipropetrovsk. Early in 1943, he and a another Jew arrived there with forged documents. As "Polish" employees of a fictitious company, the young men rented a room in a workers' district, and during the afternoons, received many visitors, usually females, including in-laws, nieces, and friends of the landlady. "The attraction of our 'salon' was quite strong. Two young men coming from afar, from Europe." Apart from current events, the visitors mentioned the Jews, who were "an endless subject for discussion." Most considered their murder "a loathsome, provocative and inhuman crime . . . It seemed that nobody here was happy about this." The landlady was "decidedly not anti-Jewish. The Communist party had decreed that the Jews were as good as all the others, so for her it was a self-evident truth, which should not be criticized." But she was atypical.

> Others took advantage of the first opportunity to criticize the party's decisions, and had the time of their lives complaining in a hostile manner about the Jews. Their pronounced hostility to the Jews was mainly motivated by envy: these had acquired, by various stratagems, positions which were or seemed to be better, than those held by the non-Jews. The granting of equal rights to Jews was their only cause for complaint against the Soviet authorities. Their youthful years had been spent in the glow of fires from the pogroms of Petliura [sic], and this had stamped their souls for life. They had a grudge against the Jews, because they were teachers and taught Ukrainian schoolchildren, were employed in government offices, and so on. Then, a moment later, someone would remark that it was the Russians who had the ill-paid jobs of teachers and office workers, while the Jews grabbed the juiciest positions in the state grocery shops and restaurants.[92]

Indeed, regardless of their opinion of the Soviet regime, many non-Jews shared an anti-Semitic sentiment. By the time the Red Army returned in 1943, this antipathy was widespread among city dwellers. An added factor was the return of many Jews, whether as soldiers or civilians. City dwellers who had appropriated Jewish apartments and property were distressed to see so many Jews return. During the next years, talk along the lines of "These Jews are here again" and even "Beat the Yids" remained common in the cities.[93] The open complaining about Jews under the Nazi regime and in 1944–1945 was a return to the situation of

THE HOLOCAUST OF THE JEWS AND ROMA

the 1920s, but the anti-Semitism appears to have been more intense. In September 1945, after a Jewish soldier killed two men who had hurled anti-Semitic remarks at him, Kiev had a pogrom that took the lives of five Jews.[94]

In all, the evidence raises the possibility that neither Nazi propaganda nor the Holocaust itself produced any major changes in non-Jews' perceptions of Jews. It would seem that most non-Jews in Dnieper Ukraine who had been anti-Semitic before 1941 did not change their thinking, at least not in the short term. The one difference was that they no longer hid their prejudice. Once the Red Army returned, however, and with it many Jews and others who reclaimed apartments, the prevalence and ferocity of anti-Semitism seems to have reached new heights.[95]

Bystanders in Western Volhynia

According to German military intelligence, by 1940 Jews in former eastern Poland wanted the Germans to come.[96] True or not (and it seems unlikely), after the Red Army left, the Jews immediately suffered persecution, mainly at the hands of Germans, but also by locals. As noted in Chapter 2, pogroms erupted in several larger towns and villages in the region. The pogroms stemmed from a desire to avenge the deeds of the NKVD and from anti-Semitic sentiments, which nationalist agitators encouraged and which perhaps had been stronger in the Polish state than in Soviet Ukraine. Conclusive answers about the level of such sentiments among the general population of western Volhynia are elusive, but a bleak picture emerges from the recollections of Jewish survivor Barbara Baratz. After an initial massacre of Jewish men in Rivne on July 8, 1941, the remaining Jews of the city had to stand in line to hand in their gold and silverware, during which onlookers had "sinister smiles, as if it were a funny show." On November 5, the eve of the biggest massacre, a man placed his son and mother-in-law in the care of his Polish former maid, and, on the maid's advice, also gave her the valuables for safekeeping. But the woman reported her Jewish guests to the authorities. Baratz says this story was far from exceptional.[97] In the middle of 1942, even without a yellow star, she and other Jews evaded public places, for "although the Germans would not have recognized us so easily as Jews, the Ukrainians could tell the difference very well and would have handed us over to the Germans immediately." The city's Ukrainians she found "mostly very dangerous enemies of the Jews."[98]

As for the perception and treatment of Jews by locals in the Volhynian countryside, it does seem clear that many young Ukrainian peasants enjoyed mistreating Jews. When in July 1941 a group of Jews from the village of Svyniukhy (presently Pryvitne) were put to work, peasants came to watch and abuse them. From late August, as Michael Diment recalls, when all native policemen were replaced, "every evening a large crowd of young Ukrainians gathered in the club house to amuse themselves by mocking Jews." Early in November 1941, as Jews moved to Lokachi to the newly established ghetto there, peasants followed them while shouting, "We're finished with the Jews." Diment and five other ghetto inmates were sent back to Svyniukhy to work as craftsmen. Peasants again were hostile: "Every time we met them, the usual themes were insults and laughter."[99]

An unsigned article in the newspaper *Volyn* abetted the hostility by stating that "the fate of world Jewry was sealed as soon as Adolf Hitler vowed to combat it, up to final destruction, and drew the attention of the peoples of Europe to this danger."[100] By June 1942, a total of 250 inmates of the Lokachi ghetto worked on the outside during the day. Peasants arrived every day to pick up Jewish males, presumably for labor duties, but "they then took them into an empty home and ordered them to dance, kiss their behinds and do other humiliating things too shameful to describe. A refusal earned a terrible beating . . . More and more Jews returned from work beaten and bleeding." Early in September 1942, on the very eve of the Nazi murder of the last inhabitants, firefighters and other Schuma surrounded the ghetto, with gaps in their ranks filled by peasants with wooden sticks, iron bars, and pitchforks. One year later, as Diment hid in the home of a Ukrainian couple, he overheard several visiting peasants talking. "The entire discussion centered around Jews interspersed with vitriolic and anti-Semitic expressions like, 'There are still too many alive in America and in England.' They mentioned who was killed at the mass graves." Diment's saviors told him afterward that such talk was very common.[101]

Many western Volhynian Jews "could not understand why the gentiles, who, after so many generations of living together peacefully, became such hateful anti-Semites."[102] Undoubtedly, one cause was the popularity of radical nationalism. Another was that many Ukrainians of the region found a justification for the Jewish Holocaust in their religious faith. As one peasant told a Jewish acquaintance who had just escaped from a ghetto: "Hitler has conquered almost the whole world and he is going to slaughter all the Jews because they had crucified our Jesus. You think you can get away from this fate?"[103] Yet not all peasants who employed a religious interpretation did it in a such a mean-spirited way, as the memoirs of a Ukrainian woman from Podolia suggest. When she was a girl, she insisted that her mother tell her what was happening with the Jews she had seen in the woods. After some hesitation, her mother finally did: German SS men and Ukrainian policemen were forcing the men and women to bury their own children alive, and then the parents would be taken to Germany and turned into soap. To her daughter's anguished Why?, this peasant woman said, in a monotonous voice, "The Jews killed Christ." All the while, she had the same stony look as during the Great Famine, when her son perished.[104]

Non-Jewish Leaders and Saviors

In the Reichskommissariat Ukraine, there were no non-Jewish leaders who stood up against anti-Semitism. Both factions of the OUN were anti-Semitic themselves, and wartime documents with regard to leading Banderites show that during the German invasion, they wanted the Jews, or at the very least Jewish males, killed, and that they were willing to participate in the process.[105] Much remains unclear about the stance of Soviet agencies. Some airdropped Soviet leaflets seem to have told the Jews to remain in hiding (while threatening those assisting the Germans with death), but reports by Communist underground activists and Soviet partisans mention aid to Jews very rarely, in marked contrast to aid to prisoners of war and to non-Jews being threatened with deportation to Germany.[106] During the crucial years 1941 and 1942, there were still few Soviet partisans in the Reichskommissariat; but even when and where there were many of them, anti-Semitism appears to have abounded. Many indeed included Schuma deserters who had participated in the Holocaust.[107]

With regard to religious leaders, the situation was very bleak. In striking contrast to the leader of the Greek Catholic church in Galicia, Metropolitan Andrei Sheptytsky, the leaders of the revived Autocephalous Orthodox church in Ukraine condemned not the Holocaust, but "Jewish Bolshevism." Thus in June 1942 Archbishop Polikarp (Sikorsky) declared in a statement his hostility toward "Muscovite-Jewish Communism," and after the German defeat at Stalingrad, he urged Ukrainians to go work in Germany and thus help defeat the "Communist Muscovite-Jewish state."[108] On March 25, 1943, he said he knew why so many people who had relatives in the Red Army were fleeing before it: "They know that after this army comes the NKVD, led by the Jewish Communists." To his dismay, he said, many others did not flee, and he asked, "Have you forgotten what Jewry looks like, so vindictive and furious in its revenge, which destroyed our people during the twenty years of its rule in Great Ukraine and had started to destroy it in Western Ukraine? Do you really have an unnatural desire for the destruction of your own people? No, this cannot be. This is a blinding of the mind, clouded by blind leaders." He talked in the same vein to Nazi officials.[109] Several of his colleagues went on record with similar points of view. In their letter to Hitler on the first anniversary of the German invasion, the bishops Nikanor (Abramovych), Mstyslav (Skrypnyk), and Sylvestr (Haievsky) wrote that they were praying for a successful end to "the great Cause that You started: the defense of the honor of the German People and the liberation of humanity from atheist-Jewish-Communist enslavement."[110] At a funeral of NKVD victims in Vinnytsia in June 1943, Bishop Hryhorii (Ohiichuk) emphatically blamed Stalin and "his" Jews.[111]

Bishop Panteleimon (Rudyk) of the Autonomous Orthodox church, which recognized the Moscow Patriarchate, issued a highly anti-Semitic leaflet in Kiev in May 1943, on the occasion of a recent Soviet air raid. Long ago, it said, the devil took possession of "the people once chosen by God" and made them crucify the Son of God. "All fratricidal wars, all bloody power grabs, all criminal revolts are done by this very people . . . Through criminal deceit and violence and under the cover of Bolshevism, the sons of the devil seized power over our land and flooded it with the blood of millions of innocent people." Panteleimon called on the faithful to assist the Germans in "the destruction of the devil's regime."[112]

Such statements probably had a detrimental effect on the morale of Christian believers.[113] But it is important to note that those people had more contacts with clergy of lower rank, and here the available evidence is more diverse. There were Orthodox priests who publicly referred to "Jewish Bolshevism,"[114] but others who tried to save Jews. One saved Jews during the 1941 pogrom in Vysotsk in western Volhynia. And in the villages of Liakhiv and Porytsk, two priests and their families each hid a Jew. After Banderite activists murdered the Liakhiv priest and his family, however, Father Piereviezov of Porytsk quickly moved his Jewish guest to a convent.[115]

In Kiev's Podil district, Father Aleksei Glagolev and his wife, Tatiana, took an active stand to save Jews. After the Babi Yar massacre, the in-laws of a Jewish woman who had remained at home appealed to them for help. Father Aleksei turned to Mayor Ohloblyn, who knew the family, but Ohloblyn returned from Commander Eberhard troubled and pale. Then Tatiana gave the Jewish woman, Izabella Egorycheva-Minkina, her own passport and birth certificate and told her to replace the photograph. She also advised her to flee to a village where Izabella had acquaintances. This she did. During a house-to-house search for Jews in Kiev, Tatiana barely evaded arrest because she no longer had her identity papers—only statements by others saved her. Unsafe in the village, Izabella had to return to Kiev and for the next two years, she and her ten-year-old daughter lived with the Glagolevs: in their apartment, in the bell tower, and in the countryside. The Glagolevs also helped Tetiana Pasichna and her mother, Evgeniia Sheveleva, by falsifying a baptism record, hiding them, and taking them to Podolia, where they survived. Even though the Security Police threatened Tatiana with death if Mrs. Hermaize, a Christian Ukrainian of Jewish descent, would "turn out to be Jewish," she still vowed for the woman's non-Jewishness, an act that prolonged Mrs. Hermaize's life for three months.[116]

Because of anti-Semitism, the culture of denunciation, and the virtual certainty of the death penalty if one were caught hiding a Jew, the people who saved or tried to save Jews probably constituted a small minority. The wish not to put one's life and that of family members on the line needs great emphasis. It is instructive to point out that in the "Germanic" Netherlands, the people who helped Anne Frank hide were not even arrested. By contrast, in the Reichskommissariat Ukraine the Nazis could and did kill not only the "guilty ones," but also their children.[117]

People who tried to save Jews used the same tactics as the Glagolevs: "legalizing" Jews, hiding them, and taking them elsewhere. One legalizing technique was baptism. Apparently without involving the German military authorities in any way, Mayor Verkhovskoi of Kremenchuk in the Left Bank created barracks outside the city and placed over a thousand Jews there. Meanwhile, however, in Kremenchuk at least some of the thousands of Jews still remaining there were baptized under different names. At the end of the year, the Nazis arrested Verkhovskoi for this reason. His successor, Senytsia, allowed a priest called Romansky to continue the practice, for which the authorities executed the mayor early in 1942. Other non-Jews tried to give Jews a new identity by marrying them;

Olha Svitnytska in Uman was hanged for this reason. But probably the most common legalizing tactic was the adoption of Jewish babies and young adults.[118] Raisa Dashkevich, born in 1916 as Riva Kogut, lost consciousness during the Babi Yar massacre. When she came to, she found herself lying in the ravine among the corpses, but physically unhurt. An old woman in a nearby house cared for her in a cellar for three days, even though she knew that the SS was searching houses in the neighborhood. Raisa went to several acquaintances, some of whom gave her food or clothes, but none invited her to stay—except for her former colleague, Liudmyla Bondarenko, who adopted her and gave her a new identity document, thereby saving her life.[119]

Placing Jews in a hiding place was equally risky. One Vitold Fomenko thus saved thirty-six lives in Lutsk.[120] And Iasha Sukhenko, a Dnieper Ukrainian who was proud of his Cossack heritage, was able to secret away many Jews. Sukhenko had been dispatched to Rivne in 1939 as an engineer, and for some transgression had ended up in a Soviet camp, from which he escaped in 1941. After the Germans came, he took up jobs as an accountant and college teacher. The apparently single Sukhenko spent so much time in the Rivne ghetto that the Jews gave him a friendly nickname, Yankele. His tactic was to provide Jews with false passes and then take them by train to central Ukraine. Immediately after the destruction of the Rivne ghetto in July 1942, he brought Baratz and her daughter, supposedly his mother and Polish-born wife, to the border of Transnistria. The Nazis eventually arrested Sukhenko while he was rescuing other Jews and he did not survive.[121]

Whether in a city, town, or village, it was nearly impossible to prevent others from finding out that one was hiding Jews. Many saviors built underground shelters for this reason.[122] If this was not an option, it was essential to make others share responsibility, or at least to obtain their passive agreement. Occasionally, various households even systematically rotated Jews. In Bohuslav, Liza Petrusenko and her four children survived in this way.[123] Zhenia Guralnik's account illustrates how difficult it was to survive in the countryside and how vital it was for Jews to have not just people who came to the rescue, but also many others who were simply "on their side." After getting out of the pit in Pavlovychi in November 1941, she came upon a forester and his wife, who kindly took care of her. The next day, she moved on to another village, from which she had to flee very quickly, for a man—an auxiliary policeman?—wanted to kill her. Arriving in the small village of Verbivka (in Luhyny raion), Zhenia went to a house where she received help. Again she had to move on, however, for these people were themselves under surveillance. Indeed the man of the house, a Communist, was ordered to go to the raion administration the next day. He predicted that he would not come back alive, and proved to be right. Zhenia then spent several days with a young woman, until she was asked to leave, for "the people everywhere are chattering that I am hiding a Jewess at home." Zhenia spent the remainder of the winter as a homeless beggar, soliciting help from poor people, whom she found most helpful.

Recalling that her family had handed over winter clothes for safekeeping, she returned to Pavlovychi. But the woman who was holding the clothes chased her away. For a while, Zhenia joined up with two Jewish children, ages eleven and three, who were living in a hole—until Germans saw and shot the two. Back in Verbivka, Zhenia stayed with a woman until she was chased out in the summer. A family accepted her and treated her well, but again, although they told no one, the other villagers found out. At that crucial stage an elderly man came on Zhenia in a field. He invited her to live at his place and the childless Marko and Oksana adopted her. At this point the village elder promised that he would not denounce them, even though everybody in Verbivka realized what was going on. Thus Zhenia became a legal resident who went out to work in the fields with the others. Once, in the fall of 1942, Germans and Schuma drove up and asked about "Jews or partisans." The peasant women and the brigade leader did not give her away.[124]

Of the Ukrainians, the Baptists and Evangelical Christians seem to have helped Jews the most. In Volhynia alone, they apparently saved hundreds. These Protestants felt that their Christian faith allowed for nothing else. Also important was that they were a community in which mutual trust prevailed, so that they could quickly pass Jews from one locality to the next.[125] An unknown number of Volhynian Poles and Czechs also engaged in rescue efforts.[126] With regard to ethnic Germans, there are contradictory reports on their views of Jews, but evidence that any of them saved, or tried to save, a Jew has not been found.[127]

It remains hazardous to generalize about what the non-Jewish population thought about the Jews, and about their conduct toward them. Those Ukrainians and others who were anti-Semitic before the war remained so, regardless of their opinion about the Jews' murder. Nazi propaganda probably turned a number of non-Jews into anti-Semites, but in this regard perhaps more consequential was the confrontation with returning Jews in the footsteps of the Red Army. As for conduct, undoubtedly many non-Jews denounced Jews, but there is also evidence that a small number saved Jewish people. The vast majority of non-Jews, meanwhile, just stood by and watched.

In general, studying the Holocaust in this region brings out the important distinction between sentiments about Jews—whether positive or negative—and acts affecting them. In a setting where it was possible to obtain property or a reward, or to "prove" oneself to be reliable despite one's past membership of the Communist party, anti-Semitic prejudice frequently played only a minor role in shaping the behavior of non-Jews with regard to Jews. And all of this happened in a setting where any kind of "subversion" officially carried the death penalty. Indeed, although many people did nothing to help Jews, some showed them that they sympathized. When the Jews of the Vinnytsia ghetto assembled in April 1942 at the stadium, for example, many non-Jews approached them. According to a Russian witness, among them were people who had no Jewish relatives but who felt sorry for the Jews.[128]

4

PRISONERS OF WAR

In the capital of the Third Reich, Lev Dudin, former editor of Kiev's German-sponsored newspaper, *Poslednie novosti* (Latest news), often met with highly ranked Germans. One day he heard from them that during the winter of 1941–1942, "about two million" Soviet prisoners of war had died in German captivity. The Germans—whom he does not identify by name or rank—mentioned it "with complete calm, as if the topic was not human beings, but livestock."[1] Their comment shows that the Soviet POW mortality figure reported by the Wehrmacht Supreme Command in May 1944, a figure well-known to historians, was hardly a well-kept secret before then. Dudin adds to his memoirs a general observation: "Indeed most Germans, and certainly almost all party members, did look upon the Russians as livestock, undeserving of pity if a million of them died. This generally held attitude, and not the sadism and cruelty of some individuals, was the main reason for the millions of deaths."

Wehrmacht callousness toward "Russians" accompanied and facilitated the shooting and starvation of millions of German-held Soviet POWs. But that callousness in turn resulted to a large degree from racist orders by German policymakers who thought of the multiethnic Soviet prisoners as "Russians," and who tried to eliminate most of them in a chain of events that can be considered genocidal. Slavic sources enable us to learn the civilian Soviet population side of the story and reveal a little-known phenomenon: the myriad attempts by civilian bystanders to save the lives of the prisoners. These attempts usually came to naught, but they suggest, contrary to what some historians have assumed, that the mass mortality of these POWs probably could have been avoided.[2]

Historians have not adopted an all-encompassing term to designate what happened to the Soviet POWs during the war.[3] Some scholars explain the mass mortality as resulting primarily from highly unfavorable circumstances, such as the large numbers of prisoners; the fact that many were already exhausted and hungry when they fell into German hands; the bad conditions of the roads; and the unusual severity of the winter of 1941–1942.[4] Most students of the era, however, have not dismissed evil intentions this easily: they consider the POWs "victims of Nazi extermination policy" and refer to a "conscious policy of murder" against the POW camps in the "East" during the fall of 1941 and the unprecedented "state mass murder" of those POWs who were taken to the Reich.[5]

I submit that the shootings of the Red Army commissars and other Soviet POWs, along with the subsequent starvation of millions more, constituted a single process that started in the middle of 1941 and lasted until at least the end of 1942. Moreover, we may call it a genocidal massacre. It was a massacre because it was "an instance of killing of a considerable number of human beings under circumstances of atrocity or cruelty." And although this massacre was not full-blown genocide, it was genocidal—"tending toward or producing genocide."[6] Indeed, the treatment of the non-Jewish Soviet prisoners of war, identified by their overseers as "Russians," came very close to the parameters of the United Nations' definition of genocide: of being intended to destroy many or all of the members of a "national, ethnical, racial or religious group," in this case, an imaginary community of "Russians." From the Nazi perspective, the inferior Slavs could be useful, and that was why POWs identified as Ukrainian often were released, especially in 1941. As for "the Russian," however, many soldiers in the Wehrmacht evidently assumed that Bolshevism, the vicious ideology and political party created by "Jewry," had irreversibly "infected" him. In this Nazified frame of mind, "Russians" were either superfluous or positively dangerous. In short, racism drove the deliberate mission of destroying most of the "Russian" POWs.

An analysis of this kind needs to pay close attention to nomenclature. German propaganda labeled the captured Red Army soldiers and commanders "Bolsheviks," with the connotation that they were zealous adherents of the Communist ideology, and thus mortal enemies. But most members of the Wehrmacht, when writing or speaking, called them "Russian" prisoners of war or simply "Russians." Many Western historians also use the ethnic adjective, thereby imposing on the prisoners an identity that would have sounded strange to many of them. Russifying the prisoners in this way was and is no small matter, and at least as significant as labeling them "Bolsheviks." As I shall argue here, during 1941 and 1942 the very imposition of a Russian identity on the multiethnic So-viet POWs was crucially important in shaping their fate. The local popu-lation of Ukraine was the most precise in calling the Soviet POWs "Red Army soldiers" or simply "our prisoners."

Capture

The German armed forces found widespread defeatist attitudes in Ukraine, which explains in part why such huge numbers of Red Army soldiers and commanders (the word "officer" became official only in 1943) fell into their hands. German Army Group South counted 103,000 captured near Uman, south of Kiev (early August); a staggering 665,000 near Kiev (by September 26); 100,000 by Melitopol and Berdiansk, near the Sea of Azov (by October 10); and another 100,000 at Kerch in the Crimea (by November 16).[7] By the time these men—and a considerable number of women—had surrendered or were taken captive, they were hungry and under severe physical strain. Among the survivors of the Kiev encircle-ment battle were people who had become exhausted physically and emo-tionally during the preceding months; some cried all the time. The pris-oners quickly realized that things were going to be difficult. In the Right Bank, the German authorities forbade the local civilians to bury the bod-ies of fallen Red Army soldiers for weeks.[8]

The German army treated the captives ruthlessly. And for those who evaded the Germans, an operations order of July 10, 1941, stated that "sol-diers in civilian clothes, generally recognizable by their short haircut, are to be shot if it is determined that they are Red soldiers (exception: desert-ers)." Einsatzkommandos shot all fleeing soldiers they considered sus-pect, as well as prisoners who had been released elsewhere but failed to prove they had a good reason to be in the area.[9]

The Wehrmacht and the Security Police treated those Soviet military whom it formally recognized as POWs on the basis of various instruc-tions. One order on June 6, 1941, known as the Commissar Order, stated that the military commissars in the Red Army, men who reported to the NKVD and in practice often issued orders, were to be shot. Had this death verdict been limited to them, it would have—contrary to what some historians have assumed—found support among the Red Army rank and file, for many, if not most, commissars were hated.[10] In practice, however, the army and the SS killed not only commissars, but also pris-oners of many other categories, often at different times. One group comprised Jewish soldiers and commanders, simply because they were Jews. Another category consisted of the *politruks*, or "political leaders." Like the commissars, these were Communist party activists who shared command, but only within small units (companies, batteries, and squadrons), and often they were hardly strong believers in Communism. Also killed, for some time at least, were non-Jewish commanders, simply because they held such positions. Apparently this was because Einsatzgruppe C, which had orders (since the middle of July) to shoot mid-level Soviet officials, heard from one arrested official that all army commanders above the rank of first lieutenant were Communists.[11]

During the first months of the campaign, the Security Police also murdered many Muslims—because they were circumcised and thus considered Jews—and "Asiatics." The latter died while a vicious propaganda campaign raged in the German press with photographs of "Asiatic, Mongol physiognomies from the POW camps": these people were "truly subhumans."[12] The widespread shootings of these non-Slavs gradually ended after September 1941, when Nazi officials told the SS that not all should be killed. Ominously, the Russians were conspicuously missing from the list of nationalities to which this warning applied (included were North Caucasians, Armenians, and the various Turkic peoples, as well as Ukrainians and Belarusans).[13]

Another set of instructions dealing with the POWs was the "Guidelines for the Conduct of the Army in Russia" of May 1941 and a supplement of July 25, 1941. These guidelines called for "utmost reserve and the sharpest attention" toward the Red Army soldiers and "ruthless and energetic drastic measures against Bolshevik rabble-rousers, irregulars, wreckers, and Jews, and the total elimination of any active and passive resistance." "Particularly the Asiatic soldiers of the Red Army," the ruling claimed, were "devious, unpredictable, eager to ambush, and callous." The supplemental instructions ordered every German soldier to treat the POWs in ways *"that bear in mind the fierceness and the inhuman brutality of the Russian during battle*: The feeling of pride and superiority must remain visible at all times . . . Where it is necessary to overcome insubordination, revolts, etc., *armed force* must be employed *immediately*. Especially fugitive prisoners of war must be shot *immediately*, without even first calling a halt. Any delay in the use of arms can constitute a danger." For Germans who considered treating "the Russian" as a human being there was a warning that "any leniency or even chatting" would be punished severely.[14]

The Red Army veteran Leonid Volynsky wrote about his own captivity under such people. Captured in the Left Bank on September 18, 1941, he and others were beaten hard in the face and then were herded into a collective-farm yard in the village of Kovali, a provisional camp that quickly filled with around ten thousand prisoners. The next day a Security Police commando arrived. A uniformed interpreter ordered all commissars, "Communists," and Jews to step forward. This selection lasted for about an hour. Then the interpreter announced that anyone giving up a remaining commissar, Communist, or Jew could take his things. Somebody denounced Volynsky, who was a party member, but when the Ukrainian interpreter heard that he was not a commissar, he consulted with one of the Germans and sent him back. The prisoners who had been taken out, some four hundred people, were shot. As Volynsky puts it:

> They were taken away in groups of ten, past the trees. There, the first ten men dug themselves a common grave (the required amount of shovels had been arranged), and a brief volley of automatics rang out. The next ten were ordered to cover the grave with earth and to dig a new one. Thus it went on till the end. All died in silence, only one suddenly fell down with a heart-rending cry. He crawled across the ground to the legs of the soldiers [sic; SS men] who were coming to get the next ten. "Don't kill me, my mother is Ukrainian!" he screamed. They booted him hard, kicked his teeth out, and dragged him away under his arms. He fell silent, his bare feet dragging.[15]

In May 1942, Hitler agreed to lift the Commissar Order "on a trial basis." But the SS never stopped shooting Red Army prisoners whom it disliked. It simply refrained from doing so near the regular troops.[16]

The Death Marches

After the initial shootings, the prisoners were marched westward via transit camps toward permanent camps. Volynsky described the beginning of his group's trek: "Having finished what they were doing, the black-uniformed men handed us over to guards who wore ordinary gray-green uniforms. Four of them stood at the exit, shouting and brandishing sticks. Almost every person who went out received a hit on the back, head, or arms if he tried to cover himself." These marches lasted a long time. Those captured in the Kiev encirclement walked in September and October

1941 for over four hundred kilometers under the supervision of guards on horseback who brandished whips and shot into the air.[17] These were death marches, terribly similar to the better-known death marches of Jews (particularly those that took place from the middle of 1944).[18] For not only "fugitive" prisoners were shot on the way. In accordance with yet another order, by the commander of the Sixth Army, Walter von Reichenau, escorts also shot on sight any stragglers—prisoners too tired and emaciated to keep up. That was why the army was under orders not to register prisoner names before their arrival in the permanent camps.[19]

German reports of the implementation of von Reichenau's shooting order convinced one historian that in the entire "East" tens of thousands were shot in these circumstances. Otherwise, however, these sources are not very informative about the death marches. When Reich Minister Alfred Rosenberg mentioned these shootings in a February 1942 letter of protest to the chief of the Supreme Command of the Armed Forces, Field Marshal Wilhelm Keitel, he spoke simply of "many" such cases.[20] Fortunately there are many accounts in Slavic sources. Fedir Pihido has noted in his memoirs that some time in early December 1941 he saw a German escort shoot a prisoner near the Dnieper, simply "because he lagged about ten steps behind." This reliable author adds that "later, during my travels in the Kiev and Chernihiv regions, I often heard stories about mass shootings of prisoners on the march."[21] The transports brought to mind the Soviet deportations of the early 1930s and the middle of 1941, but did not shock the citizens of the Soviet Union any the less for that.

Shooting occurred not only during the marches, but also during pauses. Volynsky's marches stretched about forty kilometers, interrupted with one or two ten-minute stops during which the guards fed themselves and their horses. Then the order to move on would go out and "one had to get up quickly, in order not to incur a blow with a whip, boot, or rifle butt. But many had no strength to get up, and after every stop there were those who continued to lie. That was the easiest way to put an end to one's suffering. An exhausted person would be sitting on the side, an escort would approach on his horse and lash with his whip. The person would continue to sit, with his head down. Then the escort would take a carbine from the saddle or a pistol from the holster"—and would finish off the prisoner.[22]

Hunger and thirst exhausted the prisoners. The lack of food and drink was not due to their large number, however, but to army policy. The Wehrmacht simply refused to feed them properly and prevented the local populations from giving them food and water. All that Volynsky received during his march was a ladle of watery lentil or pea soup daily. "Along the roads stretched the abandoned autumn fields. When there was something to eat there, nothing could stop us. The escorts skirted us on the left and right, beat us with sticks, opened fire—it was all in vain. Leaving behind those killed in the . . . trampled field, the column moved on, crunching on mangle-wurzel [fodder beets], carrots, or potatoes." Once a prisoner about eighteen years old ran far into the field and came back with a pumpkin. "He was running as fast as he could to the road when an escort shot him with a pistol . . . We were ready to drink from any dirty pool, but they did not allow us to drink, not even from a river." As if this were not enough, some Germans engaged in sadistic teasing. In one village that they passed through, a Wehrmacht unit was stationed. "Half-naked Germans were splashing each other with water from wells. An officer in ironed breeches with lowered suspenders was standing in the shadow with his arms behind his back. A soldier standing next to him had taken a bundle of concentrated buckwheat from an opened case, and was throwing the package in the air, like a ball. It was our army concentrate, very tasty, soft-boiled, with fat and fried onions. Whenever somebody leaped from the column to catch the packet, the officer whacked him with a stick."[23]

The civilian population, mostly Ukrainian women and children, avidly tried to feed the prisoners. The general belief was that if everybody did this, somehow one's own relatives would be saved. And the locals had food to spare because the Ukrainian harvest of 1941 was very good, particularly in the Right Bank.[24] But it was very risky for them to get involved. "Sometimes, fearless old women brought rusks [hard biscuits] or bread to the road," writes Volynsky. "They were instantly knocked down and a scuffle would ensue. The escorts became enraged and broke into the swarming heap with their horses." Such women might also be beaten, after which some would send their children forward to throw bread, potatoes, or groats.[25] A Ukrainian-American recalls that some people in her village did not throw food, but "sticks and clumps of dirt." Such behavior was unusual, however, and even here others tried to help the prisoners.[26] German onlookers occasionally tried to help as well, but they faced ostracism. A German soldier who witnessed a transport responded to the pleas for bread ("Khleba, khleba") and gave away a loaf. The column guard "roared" at him.[27]

In these conditions, pretexts for shootings were not uncommon. One Ukrainian woman, referring to the year 1941, remembered that when civilians started giving out food, the guards "shot both those who gave and those who took." Thereafter peasant women started leaving bread, potatoes, corn, cabbage, and beets on the road. It is possible that by 1942, people who tried to help were treated less harshly.[28]

Feeding the prisoners while a convoy was at rest was hardly any easier, as Iryna Khoroshunova's reliable diary shows. While looking for a relative who had been in the Red Army, on or after September 24, 1941, east of the Dnieper, she came across some 35,000 POWs pausing on their way from Brovary to Darnytsia. "They are sitting. They look so terrible that our blood turns cold. It is very clear that they don't get food. The women bring them food, but the Germans don't allow them to approach. The women are crying. There are heartbreaking scenes at every turn. The women throw themselves toward the prisoners. The prisoners throw themselves at the offered food like animals, they grab it and rip it apart. But the Germans beat them on the head with rifle-butts. They beat them and the women too." Some time later at this site, women who saw relatives and hurled themselves toward them were chased them away and beaten. Nevertheless other German guards "allowed them to approach and even talk." Khoroshunova was able to give her relative the food she had brought. He told her that the prisoners had not eaten for nine days.[29]

To this point only events in the countryside have been described, but the same scenes took place in the middle of cities. Chasing POWs through cities was meant to intimidate the populace and to convince them that, as German radio had announced on October 3, 1941, the Soviet Union had lost the war. Early in October 1941, prisoner marches through Kiev took place almost every day. One day Gerhard Kegel, an official from the German Foreign Office, had to wait for two hours at a Kiev pontoon bridge for just one prisoner convoy to march across. Afterward, he recalls, "in the divided street, which had a green strip in the middle and along which the prisoners of war had been driven, lay dozens of dead Soviet soldiers . . . The escorts shot with their submachine guns any prisoner who displayed signs of physical weakness or wanted to answer the call of nature on the green strip. I saw for myself how the Nazi escorts approached them from behind, murdered them, and moved on without deigning another glance at the victims." This was happening all the time, the army intelligence officer Hans Koch told him. At the local command office, an officer told Kegel that this agency was responsible for collecting the bodies onto wagons. Sometimes it found out about such marches only afterward, in which case the murdered bodies of stragglers, "almost always dozens," remained in the streets for hours.[30]

In diaries, memoirs, and interviews, Kievans talk of this horror. Perhaps most chilling to them was the seeming calm with which the guards shot people in the head.[31] And as in the countryside, the guards sought to prevent onlookers from helping. Over the course of one hour on October 5, 1941, thousands of prisoners passed through the street in Kiev where Khoroshunova lived. When women brought water and rusks, "the prisoners hurled themselves toward them, knocked each other and the women over, ripped the rusks from the latters' hands, and then scuffled over them. Everybody around was crying. But the German guards with their brutal faces beat the prisoners with sticks and rubber batons . . . We stayed behind and six bodies remained." Other Kievans saw guards beat both prisoners and the city dwellers who tried to feed them.[32]

Hungarian convoy escorts appear to have behaved much like their German comrades. "Regarding the treatment of the prisoners there was no difference between the Germans and the Hungarians," a woman from Kiev recalls. "When a prisoner fell, they beat him with a rifle butt to get him up, and when he lacked the strength to do so, they shot him right there, on the spot. Both Germans and Magyars did this. When women tried to throw bread to the prisoners from the sidewalks, the soldiers— German and Hungarian—hurled themselves with rifles ready to fire toward the women, who dispersed in all directions."[33] Romanian soldiers are not known to have shot their non-Jewish POWs in Ukraine, but these POWs did complain to the German army about not getting any food and being beaten.[34]

Helping prisoners and thus "causing unrest" carried risk in other cities and towns as well. In September 1941, a major "disorder" occurred in Vinnytsia. Mayor Aleksandr Sevastianov announced in the local newspaper that thousands of prisoners would pass through town. He called on the population to feed them, because they had not eaten for days. Immediately city dwellers and villagers spread the word and prepared food. When the designated day came, they were lined up for kilometers. It was a hot day. Villagers had carts, women brought pots and pans, and there were heaps of apples and bread. When the prisoners saw the reception, they quickened their pace. The guards stopped them, however, and tried to disperse the locals. Then the prisoners broke through. On an order from the convoy officer, shots rang out. The civilians fled or tried to flee, but as a result of the shooting and the panicked crowd, several of them died as well. Some threw the food on the ground, but the guards trampled it. When it was all over, the locals concluded that the mayor and the Germans had wanted to trick them.[35]

As in the countryside, children also tried to help. Although few of them realized it, they were risking their lives. When prisoners of war marched along Zhytomyr's Khlibna Street on October 14, 1941, Ms. M. A. Iakivska sent her ten-year-old daughter, Nina, out with a piece of bread. A Soviet investigation later established that one of the guards shot the girl on the spot.[36] Even weeks later, nothing about the transports had changed. In the city of Oleksandriia, word got out in November 1941 that prisoners would be passing through. In spite of a cold rain, thousands of people went to look for and feed relatives and friends. A man saw how "the entire path of this tragic procession was paved with the bodies of murdered and dead prisoners. They were not removed. Cars drove across them, crushing extremities and squeezing out intestines."[37]

Jewish prisoners of war suffered the worst treatment. Whereas other columns had ten to twenty guards, Jews were totally surrounded. Often they walked only in underwear, their clothes having been stolen by those who had "exposed" them as Jews. An estimated three thousand Jewish POWs were marched toward Babi Yar in late September and early October 1941. Those who requested water or bread were killed for doing so, as Khoroshunova observed.[38] Equally memorable was a large group of sailors of the Dnieper flotilla who ended up at the same killing site. "It was already very cold, it was freezing, but they were chased in nothing but shorts and shirts," according to another woman's diary. "They were blue, their faces were bitter, but they were proud. Passers-by expressed their sympathy and threw bread and potatoes at them, but some of them threw these aside saying, 'Feed your deliverers, the Germans.' Then they all sang the 'International.'"[39]

It is possible that after the German defeat at Stalingrad in early 1943, the shootings during the POW marches stopped or at least decreased. According to a Ukrainian witness, the Soviet POWs who walked through Vinnytsia in the middle of 1943 may have looked like "ghosts who barely resembled human beings," but though "the Germans tried to chase along those who fell, . . . if they saw that people were really exhausted and could not walk any further, they took them on carts and drove them."[40] Further research may reveal whether such behavior was part of a general trend.

The POW Camps

The transit and permanent camps usually consisted of unheated wooden sheds in an open space surrounded by barbed wire. In the first months of the military campaign, POW camps in the Reichskommissariat Ukraine (then still without the Left Bank) probably held around 250,000 people, often penned like animals; by October 1941, ten permanent camps there held some 445,000 people. By April 1943, the Reichskommissariat had, besides smaller camps, at least twenty permanent camps, all but three west of the Dnieper.[41]

The treatment of the inmates was guided by September 8, 1941, secret orders of the Wehrmacht Supreme Command stating that the camp guards were liable for punishment if they did *not* use their weapons, or did not use them enough. As Field Marshal Keitel told army intelligence officers who raised objections, at issue was "the destruction of a weltanschauung." Camp guards, most of them reservists—men who had been trained during or even before World War I—seem to have complied. There was also a camp police (Lagerpolizei) consisting of prisoners armed with clubs and whips.[42]

Besides POWs the camps also included civilians—or to be more precise, males in civilian clothes. In the Zhytomyr camp, for example, an inmate saw many civilian "old men and teenagers."[43] Jews again were singled out; when the Security Police came to visit it took them out for shooting. With few exceptions, the military authorities cooperated and participated. Various techniques identified the Jews, such as "medical" checks for circumcision.[44]

Behind the guidelines for the POW camps was the idea that feeding those inside amounted to stealing from the German people. (In this regard, the camps were treated like the major "Russian" cities.) Any feeding had to be specifically reported, and ordinary German soldiers were warned often not to give the prisoners more than the minimal rations. On September 16, 1941, Reich Minister of the Economy Hermann Göring prescribed that the "Bolshevik" prisoners' "productivity" should determine their upkeep; the result was a further reduction of food rations. By and large, only individual lower-ranked men and officers attempted to alleviate the prisoners' misery. Under such conditions, mass starvation started at once and continued for months.[45]

One historian has argued that until then, those responsible for the starvation had underestimated the threat of famine, perhaps out of a prejudice that the "primitive Russian" would take longer to die than more "civilized" people. Such unawareness of the situation on the ground would explain why German policy changed to increase somewhat prisoners' food: On October 31 and November 7, Field Marshal Keitel and Göring each ordered that the food made available should suffice to enable prisoners to work.[46] But the evidence that follows suggests that all along, German policymakers had wanted to see most of the prisoners die, and that from November, they continued to deliberately starve the numerous POWs who could not work.

It is true that the German military faced a difficult situation and were surprised to find Red Army units that had no field kitchens.[47] But far more decisive was the view that prevailed at the top: at a meeting on November 13, 1941, some officers discussed ways of providing the nonworking POW camp inmates with at least some food, but Quartermaster General Eduard Wagner interjected bluntly that those prisoners "should starve."[48] One week later, Fritz von Manstein, commander of the Eleventh Army, banned the "release" of food to any prisoners or city dwellers "as long as they are not in the service of the German Armed Forces." Such food provision would be "wrongheaded humanity."[49] In a February 1942 letter to Keitel, Rosenberg worried about the prevalence of the attitude among German leaders that "the more prisoners who die, the better off we are."[50]

In this regard, the behavior of the local population is particularly revealing. The conduct of civilians shows that there was plenty of food available for the POW camps. Unless the Red Cross (discussed in some detail later) was involved, however, almost invariably camp guards and camp policemen rejected or confiscated this food. In July 1941, a delegation of Ukrainian women asked the commander of the POW camp in Zhytomyr to allow them to feed the inmates. As the Ukrainian who interpreted recalls, the man responded that this was impossible, for "I have to follow strict directives. The Führer has decided to exterminate Bolshevism, including the people spoiled by it." The Austrian commander, "visibly shaken," murmured "may God save you from the worst." Likewise, when in August 1941 the population of the village of Onufriïvka south of Kremenchuk brought food to the local camp, the Germans in charge rarely gave permission for its delivery.[51] Rosenberg complained about the obstruction of attempts to save lives. He had seen reports showing that civilians wanted to feed the prisoners, and wrote to Keitel, "Some reasonable camp commandants have indeed allowed this with success. In most cases, however, the camp commandants have forbidden the civilian population to provide the prisoners of war with food and have preferred to let them starve to death."[52]

Rosenberg's letter did not mention another phenomenon—that the camp guards shot at civilians who tried to help the prisoners. For example, in the western Volhynian town of Rivne, plenty of food supplies had remained intact after the Red Army's retreat. Peasant women brought some of the food to the local camps, but they were turned away by guards who fired at them.[53] Near the Darnytsia camp, formally part of Kiev in the forested Left Bank, were fields with potatoes and beets that could have been provided to the POWs. Nothing of the kind happened, however, and the camp guards stole all or almost all of the food donations. When, as a last resort, the women started trying to throw potatoes, carrots, and moldy bread over the fence, the guards shot at them.[54] Guards at the camp in Fastiv shot at least two women who threw bread over the fence, and guards of a transit camp some fifty kilometers from Bila Tserkva also fired shots at women who tried to do this. According to an unconfirmed account, the prisoners of the transit camp threw themselves at the shooter and wrestled his weapon away, whereafter, as punishment, the camp authorities quickly assembled the prisoners in the square and shot every tenth one.[55]

In 1942 camp commandants apparently received the food that civilians brought. But then the badly supervised camp police, inmates who controlled most of the turf, kept almost all of it. For example, most of Vinnytsia camp was under control of some two hundred policemen; Ukrainians, Russians, Uzbeks, and Kazakhs, hardly any older than twenty-five. Keeping all of the food donations for themselves, these men never went hungry.[56]

The camps had written and unwritten rules. Guards and policemen in the rather typical Zhytomyr camp imposed beatings every day, citing such pretexts as prisoners' relieving themselves beyond the utterly inadequate toilets. The official daily ration was millet (unground), while on Sundays there was boiled horsemeat. Only the most aggressive or lucky prisoners actually got the food, however, as an inmate who escaped wrote in 1941:

> Food is given out in the evening. We stand in line, but instead of leading us into the kitchen in an organized fashion, they shout, "To the canteen!" "Run!" The hungry people rush to the kitchen, where there are several dirty barrels with a millet slop. Everybody knows that there is not enough food and tries to get at it first. Jostling starts. Now the "order supervisors" [camp policemen] appear and start up . . . a line using sticks, rods, rubber truncheons—anything they can beat you with. The usual results are head injuries, nearly broken arms, or the murder of an emaciated and weak prisoner. The beatings go on for hours. Meanwhile, half of the prisoners no longer want to eat . . . They lie down on the damp ground—for there are not enough sheds for all—and sleep until 5 in the morning.

Each day started with a furious whistling, shouting, and barking. "This is the reveille. The hungry, tired, and still sleepy prisoners slowly start to get up. They are persuaded again by sticks, rubber truncheons, and rods. Moreover, some Germans . . . chase the prisoners into formation by setting German shepherds upon them."[57] The situation was equally bad in the Left Bank. In the transit camp in Khorol "almost every day [in 1941], and sometimes several times a day, the camp commandant came to watch the food being distributed. He would spur his horse and cut into the line. Many people were killed under the hooves of his horse."[58]

Not all of the sadism concerned food. At the Khorol camp, for example, a German shot with an automatic pistol at anyone who tried to shelter during a heavy rain.[59] In the POW camp in Poltava, imprisoned doctors told visiting Red Cross workers that one guard enjoyed setting his dog on weak prisoners and seeing them torn to death, and that another practiced rifle shooting on them. The camp police also were cruel and sadistic, even more so than the guards, according to some memoirs.[60]

The scale of the starvation is difficult to calculate. The commander of the armed forces stationed in the Reichskommissariat Ukraine, Lieutenant General Karl Kitzinger, estimated in December 1941 that in his domain, about 2,500 POWs were dying from hunger every day. Contemporary German figures for POW mortality in the Reichskommissariat during that month (then still without the Left Bank) differ substantially from the monthly total of 75,000 that Kitzinger's estimate suggests: they ranged from 33,713, or about 15 percent of the inmates, to as high as 134,000, or about 46 percent.[61] In the overcrowded camp on the outskirts of Kremenchuk, bodies were thrown into a pit every morning during the fall of 1941. According to a former inmate, sometimes still-living people ended up in the pit.[62] And every morning in early 1942, carts loaded with corpses rode out of the camps in Bila Tserkva and Kirovohrad. The inmates of these camps worked from dawn till dusk but received nothing other than a thin "balanda" (flour soup). Khorol was a particularly notorious death trap.[63]

The desperate, lice-ridden prisoners ate anything they could. In one of Rivne's camps, a German noticed early in September 1941 how a tree was stripped virtually bare. "On the top, two prisoners try to reach the last remaining bark, in order to alleviate their hunger," he wrote in his diary.[64] And cannibalism occurred. A representative of the German steel industry reported in October 1941 from the Kryvy Rih and Dnipropetrovsk regions that one night he saw how prisoners in a transit camp "roasted and ate their own comrades."[65] In the camp in Shepetivka, and probably elsewhere, aggressive prisoners overpowered enfeebled ones in order to kill and eat them.[66]

Before hunger brought on insanity, victims had time to ponder their fate. Anger against "them"—the commissars, the NKVD, and the Communists—competed with frustration and regret over having allowed oneself to be taken alive. There was also anger at the Germans, the camp police, and the OUN. In October 1941, most of the prisoners of Camp 365 in Volodymyr-Volynsky were Dnieper Ukrainian Red Army commanders. Some of them managed to ask a local about the June 30, 1941, Banderite declaration of Ukrainian statehood, which they had heard about while still in the Red Army. They called it a German trick to get them to surrender and then starve them.[67] News of the horrible treatment of the POWs quickly passed through the front, by word of mouth and through active propaganda—for example, escaped prisoners were displayed, emaciated, to the Red Army. The civilian population of Ukraine was certain that such propaganda would increase the Red Army's fighting spirit, and they were right.[68]

Unless they got out through release or escape, the prisoners' only

8. Imprisoned Red Army men unload ammunition at a storage site. Some of their non-German supervisors carry batons. Berdychiv, central Ukraine, August 28, 1941. (Photograph by "H. F." Bundesarchiv, Bild 146/2002/12/917.)

chance for survival was to be selected for some kind of daytime work outside the camp. For this, they usually had to give a watch or other bribe to the native police. It was worth it, for many civilians tried to help the prisoners they encountered outside of the camp. For instance, when the inmates left the camp in Kremenchuk, "the local population always threw food at them," a former inmate recalled. "When going out to work, the prisoners even left their bags behind [in the street]. Upon their return, they would find food in them, and nobody touched the bags, not even the most desperate rascals."[69]

There seemed to be almost no limit to the tasks to which the prisoners were assigned. Initially, many cleared mines: some 15,000 did this at the airport in Boryspil, east of Kiev. Other jobs included loading flour, cutting wood, harvesting crops, digging ditches, working in quarries or mines, carrying luggage at train stations, and cleaning horses, cars, or apartments. They also dug and covered mass graves for murdered Jews.[70] The guards often beat the laborers. At a bridge construction site in Kiev in early 1942, prisoners of war were falling over from exhaustion, hunger, and cold, a civilian who also worked there told a friend. "If a poor soul staggers under the weight of the load on his back, he immediately gets a hit with a rubber truncheon. They don't care where they beat him." Occasionally, their captors supplied meat—if they had shot a stray dog.[71] On October 8, 1942, L. Nartova saw POW laborers herself in Kiev's Korolenko Street, loading baskets with peat inside the "Gestapo" headquarters. "Next to the peat are standing policemen [politsai] with rifles and Germans with sticks. When the wretched men return with empty baskets, or [enter with] not entirely full ones, the scoundrels flog them with the sticks and force them not to walk, but to run. It is a terrible sight. Many people stood still with tears in their eyes. The policemen with the rifles chased them away, while the German beasts continued their shameless outrages. And this was happening in the city center, for all to see."[72] Fieldwork provided the best chance to meet locals. Many peasant girls married and thus saved these men; given the prevailing shortage of eligible bachelors, they attached little importance to their nationality.[73]

Conditions in the camps and places of work were so bad that many prisoners sustained injuries that precluded their further exploitation—and thus their further usefulness to the German authorities. Many were already disabled when taken captive. Where possible, the Red Cross accepted such disabled POWs at its hospitals, but no later than the fall of 1942, and probably earlier, it became standard Nazi procedure to shoot them. The origin of this policy remains obscure, but on September 22, 1942, Keitel is known to have secretly ordered that "Soviet prisoners of war who would have been released according to the previous regulations because they are unable to work" be handed over to the German police, who would "arrange forwarding or employment." This meant that virtually all of the disabled POWs would be murdered.[74]

Evidence from Camp 358 in Berdychiv confirms this policy. From October 1942, many prisoners unable to work were removed from the camp and shot. The final group's turn came on December 24. In the morning, SS men forced eight prisoners from the police prison to dig a pit near the village of Khazhyn, several kilometers down the road. In the afternoon, motor vehicles in various trips drove about seventy POWs to the site, where there were only four Germans. First came eighteen men missing legs. Following the standard procedure, they had to lie on top of those killed before them, and then were shot in the back of the head. What followed was unusual, because many prisoners escaped: in the second group that arrived were twenty-eight men with only slight disabilities. These were taken out of the vehicle in pairs. After three of them had been shot, the others grabbed a gun from one of the two German guards nearby, shot them both, and started running. Two were shot, but twenty-two got away. Local peasants did not give them up. By way of reprisal, the Order Police "checked" the political past of all previously released prisoners in the neighborhood and shot at least twenty "activists and Communist party members."[75]

Rescue and Resistance Efforts

Many POWs were released, especially in the first months of the war. Ethnic Germans usually got out quickly, and from September 1941, the highest authorities sanctioned the release of certain other categories of prisoners. On September 8, 1941 the German Supreme Command ordered that Ukrainian, Belarusan, and Baltic prisoners of war were eligible for immediate release, and on September 29, Hitler personally spoke out in favor of letting go large numbers of Ukrainians. Russians were deliberately omitted from these orders. But several weeks later (on November 7), Reich Minister Göring told a conference of officials that Hitler had ordered an end to the release of Ukrainians, though without giving Hitler's reasons, which remain unknown.[76] This did not put a complete end to their release, however, and five weeks later, Erich Koch complained that his district commissars frequently issued letters to camp commanders requesting the release of named prisoners. He reminded his subordinates that "the release of prisoners of war is presently forbidden."[77] Even then, some releases occurred, particularly in the Left Bank.

Initially, in western Volhynia, the Right Bank, and the Left Bank, releases occurred randomly on a very large scale. In the Zhytomyr camp, curt announcements such as: "Zhytomyr oblast, Cherniakhiv raion: get out" inaugurated them. People from these places received passes and were not asked questions.[78] Numerous sources state that in the Right Bank, at first a prisoner merely had to call himself "Ukrainian," or that it sufficed when a local woman called him her husband, brother, father, or son.[79] After this brief random stage, the camp authorities started demand-

ing that local Ukrainian authorities—a raion chief or at least a village elder—submit a statement vouching for the prisoner's nationality and reliability. Probably one reason for the tightening of control was that some of
those released had taken up partisan activity, or made an effort to cross
the front line and therefore seemed to be partisans.[80] If a prisoner's village
of origin was nearby, its elder might be called in to select the men he
wanted and take them after signing for their loyalty. Elders also visited
camps on their own initiative in order to identify locals. Prisoners from
more distant raions might be taken to villages under guard and shown to
the elder.[81]

The main way for prisoners to contact their relatives was the "people's
mail." Women avidly collected notes from POWs they encountered and
passed them on to the addressees. This was how Iryna Khoroshunova received a note from her relative, and she distributed eighteen such notes
herself in Kiev on September 27 and 28, 1941. Everywhere she went, she
discovered that others were also passing on notes. "All were united in surprising solidarity. Everybody felt exactly the same—we must tell and we
must help."[82]

There were also organized, semiofficial paths to a prisoner's release.
One option was to join recruitment drives for the auxiliary police. Many
Melnykites were involved in these campaigns, particularly in the camp
in Zhytomyr, where Ukrainians were invited to join what was supposed
to become a "Ukrainian national militia." Another category of former
POWs were the Free Cossacks, semiofficial units that fought partisans
and performed guard duties. A "Cossack" group that formed in March
1942 in the Vinnytsia region immediately joined the partisans.[83] But the
most common ticket to release from the camps was recruitment by the
German army as a *Hilfswilliger (Hiwi)*—a "voluntary helper." Because
Hitler hated the notion of "Russians" in army service, these Hiwis remained an open secret, without official duties or rights, until as late as
October 1942. They performed tasks ranging from carrying ammunition,
blacking boots, and cooking to driving trucks, caring for the wounded,
and interpreting. (Only a small percentage consisted of "real" volunteers,
that is, people who had not been prisoners.) In the entire "East" there
were by the spring of 1942 perhaps 200,000 Hiwis; a year later about
310,000; and thereafter an unknown but even larger number.[84]

Until early 1942, unofficial Ukrainian Red Cross societies played an important role in prisoner releases. The Red Cross in Kiev sent out pairs of

young women to establish the location of the camps and to compile lists of inmates. These emissaries, who wore arm bands and traveled by train, also questioned the prisoners about their treatment. As a result, by December 1941, this Red Cross office had 40,000 names at its disposal, and by February 1942, 60,000. It posted the lists outside the building.[85] The organization also helped relatives locate prisoners. (By January 1942, a prisoner search cost fifty rubles.)[86] If the Red Cross received a statement signed by a group of people vouching that a particular prisoner of war had not been a member of the Communist party or an NKVD informant, it tried to get the person released, presumably also for a fee. The Kiev Red Cross ran a canteen at the city administration and a twenty-four-hour shelter where released prisoners could delouse, eat, and sleep. A subsection organized fund-raising concerts two or three times per week for German soldiers.[87] Last but not least, the organization delivered food to the camps. It had large amounts of food at its disposal, all—apparently—gifts from peasants solicited by the emissaries.

The German authorities quickly developed a dislike of the Kiev Red Cross, and its chief, Fedir Bohatyrchuk, ascribed this to the successful food drives. Late in 1941, he writes in his memoirs, the camp authorities started to obstruct the Red Cross and "sometimes" to confiscate its food deliveries.[88] Then he asked Mayor Bahazii for help. Many people, he informed Bahazii, had asked the Red Cross to do something about the treatment of "the Ukrainian POWs." He asked him to demand from the Germans improved conditions; bans on random execution and theft of clothes; a transfer of all emaciated prisoners to hospitals; Red Cross access to all prisoners; a list of POW camps in Ukraine; and an order to the raion authorities to collect items for the prisoners. We do not know how the mayor responded, although there is evidence that the city administration tried to get prisoners released on its own.[89]

Desperate to obtain a change in German policy, the Red Cross visited German military leaders in late December 1941. The commander of the POWs in Ukraine in Rivne, Major General Josef Feichtmeier, apparently showed Bohyatyrchuk orders to starve the prisoners, which he claimed to be defying, and "promised to issue (which he did) an order to the camps regarding obstruction-free supply to our plenipotentiaries of any needed information, and banned the confiscation of parcels." Liudmyla Ivchenko recalls that Feichtmeier promised to allow the release of disabled and sick POWs, to allow Red Cross mediation in the delivery of food and clothes, and to order the separation in each camp of "Ukrainians" from other prisoners.[90]

The Red Cross did indeed distribute clothes, underwear, and medicines,[91] but altogether, its appeals to the authorities had little effect. In a sense, it was already too late, notes Ivchenko. By the end of 1941 the influence of the Red Cross was limited because of the cold. "During every transport of prisoners from Darnytsia or Kiev to Zhytomyr, the URC and women came to the train station with warm food, tea, and all the warm blankets they could find. But half of the prisoners had frozen to death in the unheated cargo wagons (teplushky). They were thrown out and piled up like firewood."[92] In February 1942, the Security Police disallowed any involvement with POWs.

The experience of the Ukrainian Red Cross in the Left Bank town of Poltava shows that more aid was possible in some regions, apparently because these were not yet part of the Reichskommissariat. The military authorities in the region publicly declared that they could not deal with the large number of prisoners because they had their own soldiers to worry about. Then Poltava's mayor appointed a woman to found and lead a Red Cross organization, which he, like many males, considered women's work. The person he chose was Halyna Ivanivna Viun, an energetic woman who got along well with both factions of the OUN. Early in November 1941, she set up the Ukrainian Red Cross of the Poltava region, which, unlike the Red Cross in Kiev, received official status. Besides prisoners of war, it also aided victims of Soviet persecution. Like their Kievan colleagues, the Poltavan activists visited camps and posted lists of names.[93]

Having concluded that the POWs were deliberately being starved to death, Viun and her associates issued calls for food donations. The German regional commander, one Brodowsky, allowed them to repair a school and use it as a medical ward, which proved valuable even though it was little more than a heated place where food was available. In addition, Galician Ukrainians who worked for Brodowsky secured permission to collect food in the countryside. Because the people of Poltava were going hungry themselves, it was easy to find one hundred volunteers for the trips. Peasants also brought food on their own initiative. In contrast to civilian-ruled Kiev, none of these transports were barred. With the aid of imprisoned doctors, the Red Cross activists tried hard to ensure that the food reached the prisoners, and Viun recalls that the daily mortality in the nearby camps dropped sharply, from the initial hundreds to "twenty-two."[94]

In the winter of 1941–1942 the Poltavan Red Cross was able to secure releases of Ukrainian prisoners who were disabled or sick and who also had local relatives. Some healthy prisoners who were Ukrainian and whom the organization considered "valuable and worth saving" also got out of the camps. POWs with a higher education were not supposed to be released, even if Ukrainian, but the two German doctors involved with the POWs ignored the rule (one in exchange for vodka, the other simply because he wanted to save lives). The November 1941 ban on releases merely inaugurated a semisecret buyout. The Red Cross contacted interested families, Viun recalls, and "rather many of them, especially peasants who had homemade lambskin coats, were able to buy off their sons, brothers, fathers, etc. from German captivity. The Germans asked one lambskin for each prisoner."[95] Even after the arrest of local OUN activists in the late spring of 1942, the Red Cross continued to function, thanks in large measure to two sympathizing German intelligence officers, one of whom was Hans Koch. Maintaining this relationship was a remarkable achievement, for OUN members had used the homes of Red Cross leaders to assemble and had traveled all over Ukraine with Red Cross papers. Moreover, what the Red Cross workers called Little Russians (Russophile Ukrainians) and Communist agents supposedly hated the organization "simply because it was Ukrainian," and often complained about it to the authorities. Only on August 1, 1942, one month before the official introduction of civilian rule in the Poltava region, was the organization demoted to an ineffectual city "Social Aid Department." These are just two examples of regional Red Cross organizations; there were others.[96]

Officially, no Red Cross official anywhere in Ukraine was allowed to help prisoners identified as Russian. The actual stance of the aid workers toward those people, however, is still unclear. Viun claims to have disobeyed Brodowsky's demand that she help only "Ukrainian" camp inmates, but her memoir mentions only Ukrainians among the recipients of aid, and the same German official later accused her of helping Ukrainians only.[97] At the present stage of research into the issue, it does appear that "Russians" and other non-Ukrainians could not expect Red Cross assistance if their nationality was not able to be concealed.

Flight was the only other means of escape, and flight attempts by Soviet POWs were a daily event in the "East."[98] At first, most took place during the marches, especially at night. Some soldiers planned well ahead, as one POW noticed in the Left Bank in 1942: many had stocked up on civilian clothes, and one at the front of the column "took a duffel bag from his shoulders and took out a shirt. Looking around, he started to change clothes. Last came a cap. All the military things he gave to his neighbors. At the next stop, near a well in a village, the German guard saw the civilian person among the military and immediately chased away the [fellow] . . . When we moved on, this man followed us along the street for a long time."[99]

Prisoners also attempted to escape from the camps and work sites. For example, thirty inmates of the Volodymyr-Volynsky camp were working at the cemetery in June 1942 when they killed a guard, tied up the others, and fled. Four covered for them with grenades and rifles. Still, sixteen were caught and shot. In revenge, the camp guards also shot three hundred uninvolved prisoners. Camp inmates dug tunnels, too, but those saved few lives.[100]

Many of the escapes were facilitated by outsiders. In the summer of 1942 more than two hundred Darnytsia camp inmates managed to flee from a wagon repair factory and received food and documents from civilian workers there. (Again, uninvolved remaining camp inmates likely were executed.)[101] In the camp in the Podolian town of Slavuta, the hospital director somehow helped a number of prisoners to get out and join the partisans, and apparently tried to kill native policemen who could not be bribed. He and fourteen fellow conspirators were eventually arrested and undoubtedly shot.[102] The extent to which the two political orientations claiming to represent the population—the OUN and the Communist party—helped rescue prisoners still awaits serious research.

An issue that may gain particular attention in Ukraine is whether the general population did "enough" to save the prisoners. Viun has stated that when she created the regional Red Cross, Poltavans for some time were in the grip of a "bizarre passivity" in the face of prisoner starvation. But then she found many active helpers.[103] The same pattern—passivity followed by frantic efforts to save lives—possibly prevailed elsewhere. In any case it should be kept in mind that, as in the case of helping Jews or saboteurs, helping POWs escape, or even failing to report them, led to the death penalty or at the very least, imprisonment. Public threats to this effect were made often, such as in June 1942 in a joint statement by Reichskommissar Koch and Lieutenant General Kitzinger.[104]

Whether they escaped, were released, or had never been imprisoned at all, former Red Army soldiers lived in the countryside in large numbers, particularly in the Right Bank, even as late as 1943. They worked as peasants or artisans, and sometimes started families—or rather, joined them: women with children and older couples whose husbands and sons had been drafted. Nobody thought badly of women who welcomed prisoners into their homes, for after all, there was a war going on. Among the newcomers were Ukrainians from east of the Dnieper, Siberians, other Russians, and peoples from the Caucasus, but all had notes by the village elders identifying them as locals.[105] Their credentials were checked, though, by 1942. The local command would order the raion chief to supply data about "the prisoners of war" or "the former Russian soldiers," such as the day of their arrival and whether or not they had been Communist party members.[106] The "localized" former Red Army men remained outsiders to some degree and easy targets for denunciation. Moreover, the German authorities occasionally rearrested them.[107] For all of these reasons, when early in 1942 a campaign started to take people to Germany to work, these men were among the first to leave, often voluntarily. Whereas until March 1942 only 1,200 officially left the Reichskommissariat for the Reich, in that month almost 6,000 departed, and in May 1942 almost 18,000 did.[108]

French, British, American, and Canadian military men in German captivity, even if they were of Jewish descent, were very likely to survive World War II.[109] But the eastern European theater of the war was brutal everywhere. On the German-led side, it already seems clear that many Hungarians and Romanians—as well as possibly Italians, Slovaks, and other non-German military—approached the level of callousness and cruelty toward their Soviet POWs that so many Wehrmacht members displayed. The conditions of German POWs as well, immediately after the Red Army captured them, and during their transport eastward, seem to have been horrific—many were killed.[110] Nevertheless, this should not obscure the significance of the treatment of the German-held "Russian" POWs. Those prisoners, mistreated and killed by the millions, were not simply casualties of "war." Indeed, the evidence presented here discredits still further the argument that situational factors were the main cause of their suffering and death. Not only were the prisoner transports actually death marches, but also, because the Ukrainian harvest of 1941 was excellent, the German authorities and the native population had plenty of food to spare. Had those civilians not been obstructed so much in their attempts to pass on some of this food to prisoners, and had the escorts and camp guards behaved in a more humane fashion, hundreds of thousands of lives could and would have been saved.

The starvation, abuse, and shooting of the "Russian" POWs was not solely due to racism. As historians have argued, although the Wehrmacht administrators and guards were bombarded with racist justifications for cruelty, it was also the very day-to-day experience of total war that brutalized its soldiers. Future studies will perhaps reveal in detail how both the Germans in charge of the Soviet POWs and those POWs who became camp policemen underwent the same moral degeneration as did the German and native (Ukrainian and other) policemen who implemented the Shoáh.[111] Once these lower-level perpetrators had become callous, their violence against the prisoners gained momentum. In this way, racism and hard-heartedness reinforced each other and produced a "genocidal massacre," in the sense that so many human beings of one "race" were deliberately killed. But it was a racist notion of the vaguely defined "Russians" that made it possible to embark on their abuse and murder in the first place.

5

LIFE IN THE COUNTRYSIDE

Almost all of the peasants welcomed the Germans and their allies as liberators. They shared food and lodging with them and treated those who were wounded. In most places, a cordial relationship developed, hampered only by the almost total lack of comprehension of each other's language. The Germans said things like "Russe kaputt"—Death to the Russian—and otherwise used, besides German, a few Polish words such as *jajko* (egg) and *matka* (mother). Whenever the frontline soldiers, many of whom were rather young, stayed on a bit longer, something resembling family life developed.[1] The peasants had no choice but to help, of course, because they were powerless. Moreover, tradition required them to be hospitable.

As in most wars, the incoming soldiers stole peasant property. Significant numbers of Germans, especially in the Left Bank, appropriated livestock, fowl, tools, and carts, even though their commanders banned and tried to stop such practices.[2] Much more common, however, was theft—perhaps armed robbery would be a better term—by Hungarians and Romanians, whose food was less efficiently distributed. The population despised these soldiers for stealing. And although the German army put up signs near ethnic German homes warning that robbers would be shot, it had little success in stopping its allies.[3]

Besides robbery, war also brings the violence of rape, of which there are scattered reports: a rape of a group by invaders in the Kaniv raion near the Dnieper on August 4, 1941, or a German officer shooting a teacher in Oleksandrivka, a town near Kirovohrad, who resisted his rape attempt.[4] In general, however, in 1941 the German military committed few rapes in villages and towns. In some cases, women were willing partners, but more important was that the army command saw to it that its soldiers could rape city and peasant girls and women who had been arrested and locked up in army brothels in the cities. The sex slaves in the officers' brothels were apparently between thirteen and sixteen years old.[5] Of those who raped in the countryside in 1941, the vast majority were not frontline German military but those with little or no access to the brothels: German civilians, German landwirts, Hungarians, and Romanians.[6]

From the beginning, the German army sporadically shot peasants. For example, in the village of Semenivka in the Poltava region, a woman ran crying after a German. When people gathered to see what was going on, the man, who had stolen her flour, grabbed his gun and killed the woman on the spot. Most of the early shootings of peasants concerned real or suspected partisans and saboteurs. Extreme cruelty could occur before the killing itself. On September 11, 1941, Germans assembled the population of the village of Khaniv (presently Pidhaine) and showed how they dealt with a captured partisan and the collective farm chairman: they beat them, cut off their ears and noses, and shot them. In another incident, twenty-seven Communist party and Komsomol members were shot by a German unit in the Left Bank village of Obolon. One was a sixteen-year-old, Mykola Hladun, who was first tortured in front of his mother.[7]

Great Expectations

And yet for most peasants, the thefts, rapes, and executions did not spoil their generally positive mood—if only because violence was hardly new to them. Fedir Pihido, a native of Staiky, recalled several years later that "relations between the population and the German troops immediately became benevolent, even friendly. Everywhere, the German soldier was a welcome guest. At various family occasions and parties, German soldiers were treated as good friends."[8] Almost all of the peasants supported without hesitation what they assumed was a war only on Stalin and his regime. The army intelligence officer Hans Koch, a native of Lviv who spoke Ukrainian, had a lot of sympathy for the Ukrainians. After spending a long period in the countryside, he concluded on September 30, 1941, that "the vast majority of the population of the Ukraine has turned out to be anti-Bolshevik. Almost all of them consider their political future to be on the side of the Axis powers, and first of all the Greater German Reich. In countless gatherings, people speak spontaneously of 'Adolf Hitler, our greatest leader and liberator.' Mothers instruct their children to address the German soldiers as 'uncle.' Every day, peasant men and women lay fresh flowers on the graves of German soldiers on their own initiative."[9]

That their living conditions would not improve was almost unthinkable for the peasants, whose extreme poverty impressed all foreigners. Their gardens lacked fences, and their huts were tidy but looked destitute.[10] In the fall of 1941, a Swiss journalist spent the night in the village of Stavyshche. The peasant home where he stayed consisted of a living room and a kitchen. Most of the cramped place was "very clean and tidy," but it made him think of a trapper's home in a novel by the German writer Karl May. "Everywhere on the floor lie planed boards, and upon close inspection, here and there one can see grass growing through. In the kitchen stands a self-made oven with an outlet directly through the side wall of the house. On it hang some black pans and a kettle. There is also a small chest and a large one, which I feel like opening. Straight through all of this is a line on which dark pants are hanging to dry, although it seems to me that in reality they are being smoked . . . The living room has a closet, a chest of drawers, a table with four chairs, three icons of the same color that for years, before the arrival of the Germans, used to lie under one of the chests in the kitchen, and three narrow beds . . . In a corner lies a knee-high pile of threshed grain. Under one of the three beds, I discover the rest of the salary received by the peasant from the Germans for his harvest work."[11]

Hans Koch met about six hundred village elders within two months that fall. None of them he considered better dressed than the poorest vagrant in Germany. Most "Soviet" peasants wore rags, and the lucky owners of shoes still tended to go barefoot so as to save them for the fall and winter. In general, the peasants owned almost nothing. "Over and over," Koch found, "the impoverished population visits the battle fields to look for a piece of belt, a discarded ammunition holder, a piece of cloth. The houses of Jews who fled [or were murdered] are ransacked for remaining goods or clothes as if by termites. Every single worthless scrap or utensil is very rare here." Once in a peasant family's place, Koch lit his kerosene lamp. The woman of the house whispered to her grown-up daughter, "I haven't seen such a lamp since my wedding." Peasants used what they called "Stalin's lightning": a can or exploded artillery shell filled with a piece of linen and any kind of fuel. Standing near such a lamp for more than a few minutes was rather risky.[12]

The peasants lived on a very meager diet and were undernourished. At one location, a heap of salt had remained at a train station. Soon people came from far and wide and fought for a share. At regional gatherings of elders and teachers, Koch noticed that "the only food (as a matter of course, taken from home by way of precaution) of all—and I mean all—the participants consisted of a piece of brown bread, garlic, and gherkins." Many peasants where he stayed over "could not even offer me a mug of milk. Either there was no milk, or literally no mug."[13]

Given these conditions, it is not surprising that an overwhelming majority of the peasants wanted a return to household (rather than collective) farming. According to a western Ukrainian, the peasants "talked about the collective farms and socialism with a holy rage." They did not say "privatization," for they considered their former land or livestock, now part of the *kolhosp* (collective farm), still theirs; from their perspective, one only needed to "dissolve the *kolhosp*" and "divide the land."[14] Only a minority doubted this strategy: some young peasants who had not experienced the pre-1929 lifestyle, and women with small children whose husbands were in the Red Army. These groups feared that without collective farming they would not be able to make a living.[15] Their conservatism usually disappeared when they observed the behavior of their fellow villagers, however, and especially when male relatives returned and other former Red Army men arrived to help the household be more productive.

In western Volhynia and near the Dnieper River, many collective farms were gone even before the Germans came; in many other regions, it was the German army's arrival that caused them to disband. In still other regions, the peasants waited until the Germans had passed through. Whenever decollectivization occurred, it generally restored pre-1929 property relations.[16] The transition could be violent. Banderites who came on the heels of the German army often saw peasants destroy tractors and combines, "like one's fiercest enemy." The activists tried to talk them out of such behavior, which they correctly ascribed to sheer hatred of the collectives. It was a throwback to the peasant Luddism of the years of collectivization, the difference being that now Stalin agreed with it—after all, willing or not, the vandals were implementing his orders to destroy unevacuated machinery. It was one reason why on August 15 the East Ministry banned decollectivization and threatened severe measures against transgressors.[17]

Directives and Adaptations

Well before the war, most villagers were female.[18] This situation changed little under the Germans. Although most local men were drafted into the military in 1941, many returned, as did many other males who had fled to the city during the 1930s. The village of Romashky (Rokytne raion, Bila Tserkva district) typified the Right-Bank countryside. On May 1, 1942, of the 862 persons ages fourteen to sixty-five, as many as 572 were female. Likewise, in an unidentified village in the Berdychiv district, twice as many women as men were working on the three farms.[19] Still, males held all positions of authority. Not only was this the norm that both sexes accepted;[20] it was also the wish of the Germans, who appointed the men at village meetings.

The pre-1941 chairman of the village soviet now was called the *starosta*, or elder, a prerevolutionary term. He had a secretary and perhaps other assistants. The title did not mean that he was old. In the Rokytne raion, for example, the average elder in 1942 was forty-one years of age. Turnover in elders seems to have been quite common.[21] Elders received a monthly state salary that depended on the size of the village and that (officially, at least) ranged from fifty to sixty German marks, or its official equivalent, 500 to 600 Reichskommissariat karbovantsi. Tasks included conducting censuses. In his records that were always handwritten and in Ukrainian, the elder had to add which villagers were able to work, and a note about each person's political reliability—with only those who had a family history of "repression" by the NKVD considered unambiguously reliable.[22] The elder received orders—as typed notes from the raion chief or landwirt, or orally at meetings—and transmitted them to the villagers.

All villagers kept their identification documents from the Soviet period, now with a German stamp on it. In the spring of 1942, those eighteen years of age and older received passes in the German and Ukrainian languages. Persons not from Ukraine, and Communists, officially only were eligible for residence permits, but providing the right German official with an adequate amount of chickens and eggs could overcome this hurdle. For brief trips outside of the village, permission from the elder sufficed (as had been the case with the chairman of the village soviet), but longer trips required a special permit.[23] Taking in overnight guests without permission was strictly forbidden. All villages had a curfew that depended on the season and the overall reliability, from the German point of view, of the raion. Although the Schuma could legally shoot trespassers on sight, people often still went about as necessary. Yet it was not uncommon for ordinary peasants to stand guard themselves during the night, given the German rule of collective responsibility in case of trouble.[24]

In some regions, harvesting had already started on a Soviet order and simply continued during and after the Germans arrived. Some of these harvesters dressed in black, so as to be less visible to Soviet planes that attacked the fields. But in the many localities where no Soviet order to harvest had been issued, hardly anybody took the initiative. Itinerant Banderites found that even though the crops were ripe, the peasants did not get to work. "This was the case wherever we went. The reason for this stagnation was that there was nobody to 'order.'"[25] The Germans also found that the peasants were "generally willing to work" but awaited orders.[26] This inaction indicated the influence of the Soviet system, under which nobody took responsibility for anything out of a fear of being denounced as a saboteur. Thus the harvest in Dnieper Ukraine started late in 1941 and generally only after Banderites or Germans asked for it. If the Ukrainian peasants would not get to work, the Wehrmacht told them in a posted announcement, "you and your family will go hungry." Another poster warned that "laziness" would bring "only famine and poverty."[27]

In western Volhynia, people did not depend on tractors and harvesting was relatively easy. In Dnieper Ukraine, however, there was a severe lack of equipment and pulling power, so that almost everything had to be done by hand, with sickles.[28] The peasants worked hard: They feared famine and the Germans paid well. For example, in Medvyn, a village near the town of Bohuslav south of Kiev, the harvesters received one in three sheaves as payment, which was more than they had received in years. Yet another reason for the hard work was the widespread anticipation of a return to household farming. Indeed, in some places the harvest already took place on designated household strips.[29]

In spite of all the obstacles the harvest was excellent, particularly in the Right Bank. In the village of Lytvynivka, north of Kiev, there were still no German authorities late in October 1941. The peasants "laid in stores for years ahead," a witness recalls. "The cellars were bursting with vegetables, the attics were piled high with apples and pears, and strings of dried fruits hung under the eaves." People ate their fill in a way that even old people could not recall.[30] Until the end of the year, when a severe winter started, the old men and women, the girls, and the children threshed the wheat with clanking chains, grinded it with stones, and passed the flour through hand sieves. In the Left Bank, destruction or evacuation of the crop had been more extensive and fear of famine was greater. Here the peasants continued working hard on the winter sowing, "in a harmony that is only possible when one's life is on the line."[31]

Despite the German ban on decollectivization, to the peasants it remained unclear for months whether the Germans would eventually sanction it. For right after the East Ministry issued its ban on decollectivization, the German army issued a leaflet that said that Germany had only private agriculture, while adding, "that's how it should be with you." A repeat of the ban followed. Not surprisingly, there were villages that continued to put parts of farm buildings up for sale.[32] Once in a while, rumors, dating back to Soviet propaganda (and disputed by German propaganda), claimed that large-scale landownership would return, or even that the former landlords, chased away starting in 1917, would be allowed to reclaim their former estates.[33]

On February 27, 1942, an elaborate propaganda campaign started. Its purpose was twofold: to preserve the collective farms and yet convince the peasants that Hitler—special portraits of whom made the rounds for the occasion—had decided to abolish them. Village assemblies listened to special fifteen-minute radio broadcasts and heard that "the hard-working peasant will get land of his own." The next day, all collective farms in the Reichskommissariat (as well as in the regions administered by Army Group South) were renamed "communal farms."

Propagandists and landwirts told village meetings that the "Ministry for the Liberated Eastern Territories" was introducing a new land order.[34] Eventually, they claimed, all of the farms would become cooperatives. Field cultivation would still be collective, but everything else, including the harvesting, would take place on individual strips of land. Moreover, cooperatives that were very efficient might eventually become individual farms. For now, however, the speakers said, every peasant in the village had to join the communal farm.[35] The peasants were disappointed or at the very least suspicious.[36]

Most official measures indeed suggested continuity with the pre-1941 period. The German authorities often retained Communist farm names such as "The Path to World Revolution." The new "labor units" were simply the old brigades and teams (whereby family units remained possible).[37] And worst of all for the peasants, whereas during the 1941 harvest the Germans had paid better than the Soviet authorities, now there was a return to Soviet "labor-days"—the notorious system of payments that took into account the time worked, the skill involved, and the size of the har-

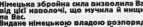

9. "The Collective Farm System Has Come to an End! (. . .) You yourselves and your work will determine whether the ultimate goal of the decree on the land order is met: 'Every Hard-Working Peasant Will Get Land of His Own!'" Colorful Nazi propaganda poster, distributed from February 1942. (Naukovo-dovidkova biblioteka tsentral'nykh derzhavnykh arkhiviv Ukraïny, 271sp.)

vest, and that ensured peasants received very little. In the Kiev region, one German labor-day paid, at best, 200 grams of leftover grain.[38]

On paper, there was the novelty of advance payment, which could amount to 500 grams of grain per day worked (and for those with large families as much as 750 grams), as well as some potatoes or beets.[39] If this really happened, it may explain why many peasants to the south of Kiev received three times more per labor-day than during the Soviet period (namely three to four kilograms) and why a local peasant remembered years later that the Germans "paid well."[40]

The main intended differences of the Nazi agricultural system concerned farm membership, attendance, and the workload. All of the changes were undesirable from a peasant perspective. For one thing, all villagers had to join the communal farm, even those who had not ever been members of a collective farm. For another, whereas before women with small children, and many other farm members, had not contributed through labor, the Germans required all members to actually work. There also came stricter regulations on the duration of labor. The official workweek in the Reichskommissariat lasted fifty-four hours. From May 1, 1942, every peasant between the ages of eighteen and sixty had to work five days a week. The only allowed exceptions were people who were disabled or chronically ill and women two months before or after childbirth. Impatient local German officials often tightened these rules still further.[41]

Because of the war, the work itself was also physically more difficult. Because of a lack of fuel, almost all of the tractors and combines stood idle, and the peasants were very reluctant to use cows as pulling power, even though German posters urged them to do so, for many thought that cows simply could not plow and might even die from it.[42] Thus almost all of the farm work was manual, with spades, plows, harrows, and other tools, homemade or obtained from released POWs-turned-artisans. And because of a shortage of seeds, only small areas were sown.[43]

The German authorities demanded large agricultural deliveries, and like the Soviet authorities before 1941, to obtain them they often used force. The most extensive food confiscation campaign took place in July 1942. It aimed to force the peasants to thresh any grain that remained from the 1941 harvest and to confiscate *all* grain, even from homes. The village police searched homes, yards, gardens, mills, and markets, and took the grain on carts to the landwirts and district commissars. In the process, many peasants lost their cows, by way of punishment for inadequate deliveries. In the Kiev general district alone, 26,570 metric tons of grain were confiscated that month. (A full 38,470 metric tons had already been taken in June.) The Germans obtained a remainder of 7,960 metric tons in early August and the special emissary from the Reichskommissariat's food and agriculture department concluded with satisfaction that the peasants of the district had no more grain.[44]

Lastly, the peasants—as before 1941—faced financial taxation. One in 1941 was for the use of land and amounted to 80 rubles per hectare. There were also personal taxes; a one-time tax of 100 rubles in May 1942 that supposedly benefited the development of the countryside, and taxes on homes, cows, horses, and dogs.[45] At first the German authorities tried to obtain these taxes from the farms, but this created so much chaos that they soon charged households. In attempting to exempt people from taxes, the elders called them disabled, old, ill, or insane, or pointed out that they were single and unable to work, very poor, a teacher, or constituted a family without an adult male.[46] (The German rules indeed allowed for exceptions for old age.) But every leniency that elders allowed but that the raion taxation committees did not sustain required the other villagers to donate more.[47]

Soviet Ukraine had 1,875 state farms, distinct from the collective farms. Peasants had never owned land there and under the Germans they did not claim that land. German landwirts personally headed each of the Reichskommissariat's 1,271 state farms, which the peasants nicknamed already in Soviet times "slave farms" and the newcomers renamed "state properties."[48] Little is known about the conditions there. Most of these farms—like the communal farms, for that matter—seem to have had a hard time finding enough money to pay even the official wages.[49] At the state farms in Irpin and Stoianka just west of Kiev, the laborers were both Kievans and local peasants who apparently worked from six o'clock in the morning to six o'clock in the evening, with a thirty-minute break and almost without tools. Twice daily there was a watery soup, half a liter of milk, and 150 grams of bread. All of their monthly salary (twenty rubles or, later, karbovantsi) went to food.[50] As for western Volhynia's 549 state farms, these at first underwent a different development: German specialists did not issue any guidelines for them and sometimes apparently left room for private peasant initiative. But during 1942 conditions started to resemble those in Dnieper Ukraine, with peasants from nearby localities forced to work there for as little as three karbovantsi per day.[51]

Work in communal and state farms lasted from the early spring to the late fall. It should be stressed, however, that peasants were also forced to carry out nonagricultural tasks. For example, men might have to work in a quarry, and during the winter thousands of men, women, and children had to shovel snow from the roads day and night.[52] In August 1942, the raion chief in Khabne (present-day Poliske) asked the district commissar to sentence eleven people who refused to work in the woods to seven years of labor camp. In June 1943, Stepan Oleksiienko of the village of Stanovyshche shirked work at a bridge construction site and generally disobeyed the village elder; the raion chief punished him with four weeks in a German labor camp.[53]

In February 1942 the German authorities had made the formation of any agricultural cooperative conditional on proper technical conditions, hard work, and fulfillment of the delivery demands. But they did not tell that they intended to allow the change for only 5 percent of Ukrainian farms, which was much less than the equally secret 20 percent they planned for the regions under control of Army Groups North and Center. Still, as time went by the 5 percent limit fell by the wayside. Of the 16,193 communal farms in the Reichskommissariat Ukraine on December 1, 1942, 1,318 were cooperatives, and an additional 370 farms were on the waiting list.[54] Late in May 1943, there were slightly more cooperatives—1,688—and during the remainder of 1943, their number increased rapidly, for Koch and his associates agreed to a target of 20 percent. On August 10, 1943, there were 2,780 cooperatives, or 16.8 percent of all farms.[55]

The formation of a cooperative involved ceremonies and parties in which raion and village authorities and hundreds of ordinary peasants participated, along with the district commissar and the landwirts. The deputy general commissar might attend the earliest conversions in his domain, such as those at selected farms in the Korostyshiv and Vasylkiv districts in September and October 1942.[56] The German officials would give a speech, translated simultaneously into Ukrainian or Russian, in which they blamed the Bolsheviks for the remaining communal farms and usually added a condescending remark, such as "In those isolated cases when peasants divided the land among themselves, without permission, this only produced chaos and dissatisfaction. Soon they came to us and asked us to restore order." Moreover, "if we would give everyone the freedom to do what he likes, many among you, after the many years of Bolshevik oppression and collective work, would prefer to work just for himself, not taking into account whether you would produce much or little." They banned permanent markers of individual strips in the cooperatives, for those would "only lead to the spreading of weeds." Except for the harvesting, all of the work would still be collective.[57] After giving their speeches, the Germans handed out certificates (hramoty) and shook hands. Often they received gifts in return, such as at the first conversion in the Zhytomyr general district, in the village of Stryzhivka.[58]

It is likely that in reality cooperatives functioned much like the communal farms. The landwirt of the Vasylkiv district, for example, demanded that even the harvest be carried out collectively.[59] The peasants certainly were skeptical of the changeover. At a conference in December 1942, Nazi agricultural officials noted that the cooperatives were "generally not welcomed, for the fixed price for agricultural produce is so low that the proceeds are by no means sufficient to live on." The SD reported in August 1943 that the populations of four districts to the south of Kiev considered the cooperatives to be collective farms in all but name.[60]

Altogether, from the perspective of Nazi agricultural planning, the first year looked good. Both the army and the Reich apparently received from Ukraine the crop amounts that specialists had calculated before the invasion.[61] But below the surface, widespread though little documented adaptations crept in that countered the Nazi vision for Ukraine. Many landwirts allowed teams, usually of family members, to limit their labor to a designated tenth of the farm land, or they allowed groups of ten households to divide the land themselves. Such informal ways, known as the "tenth" or "ten-household" systems, meant also that each team or group had its own equipment and pulling power. They received instructions from the farm leader, but the team or group leaders determined people's wages. Only the harvest was a collective affair, and thus distinct economic units evolved.[62] Even if a landwirt did not want to hear of such things, peasants often introduced them all the same, egged on by native agronomists who kept the Germans in the dark.[63] Most radically, a small number of landwirts agreed to illegally dissolve the communal farms altogether, allowing individual households to own their own plots, which they worked and harvested independently. Under such conditions, which came about in many raions in the Kiev general district, peasants worked hard.[64]

Peasant Gardens and Livestock

Gardens had been Soviet peasants' main source of subsistence, even though they did not own them and had to surrender to the Soviet state quotas of the yield and of any livestock held in them. (This rule did not apply to the plots of city workers.) Peasant gardens ranged from 0.15 to 0.6 hectares (15 to 60 *sotky*), but tended to be close to the smaller figure in the years 1939 and 1940, when the authorities shrank them so as to secure steady food exports to Germany.[65] When the Germans invaded, all peasants naturally were eager to hear what was to become of the gardens.

On August 15, 1941, Economy Staff East announced its decision to double the size of the gardens and to free them from taxation, provided that this would not impair the work on the farms. But the people who were supposed to implement the measure, the landwirts, sabotaged this directive. Koch had promised the landwirts that they would eventually own Ukraine's farms, so many landwirts were loathe to decrease the size of the farms through garden enlargements. Indeed, some stole animals and forced the peasants to labor on the landwirts' personal plots. Economy Staff East repeated the order about the gardens in January 1942.[66]

The new land order propaganda claimed unambiguously that the gardens under cultivation by farm members were their "private, tax-free property." Naturally, this went over well.[67] But as always with Nazi propaganda, there was more to it. Garden enlargement required approval by the raion administration, and peasants who had not been working particularly hard were last in line.[68] Reichskommissariat officials, acting on the spirit of statements Hitler had made after the introduction of the new land order, contemplated allowing garden enlargement only in villages that had supplied the most produce—and even then, in at most 10 percent of those villages.[69]

Nevertheless, garden increases were widespread during the spring of 1942, particularly in regions that were still under military rule. In the Right Bank, there were many regional variations. In the Zhytomyr general district, the average garden expansion in 1942 for the 75,000 affected households was 0.36 hectares. In one village in the Berdychiv district there, the gardens measured on average only 0.6 hectares in early 1943.[70] Expansions continued throughout 1942 and 1943, although there were peasants who declined because family members had been deported to the Reich.[71] When peasants disputed among themselves about encroachment on each other's gardens, the native judicial mediators often resolved the matter without informing the district commissar, even though they were supposed to do so.[72]

Most peasants' gardens initially had more livestock and fowl—a cow, a pig, some chickens—than before the Soviet retreat. Peasants had taken the animals from the collective farm or had found them abandoned. To the peasants, at least as important as the enlargement of the gardens and the increase in the number of animals there was the gardens' private status, for one reason they had kept working in the collective farm during the Soviet period had been to ensure their right to work a garden.[73] Now the danger of losing this right was gone, or so it seemed. Ironically, the result of the change was contrary to German intent—decreased work on the farm.

In spite of the propaganda, the gardens continued to be taxed. The peasants had to supply milk and milk products, eggs, meat, potatoes, and grain, in amounts that often exceeded initially stated norms.[74] The peasants might cultivate wheat or rye in the gardens (unlike in Soviet times), but to their dismay, they eventually had to surrender most or even all of these grains. If their garden harvest was bad, peasants started worrying about famine, for the German or auxiliary authorities penalized nonfulfillment of the delivery quotas with fines, confiscation of the family cow, bans on private sales that spanned entire regions, or confinement in a labor camp.[75] Therefore, peasants who had to plow with their own hands usually sowed only a part of the garden that allowed them to quickly harvest and hide the proceeds.[76]

Once in a while, the entire village had to surrender livestock, whether from gardens or the farm. This much resented measure was most severe in the months before the German retreat, but many families' last cow was taken much earlier.[77] Some peasants hid the cows in the woods. In the village of Medvyn, one family had a cow while two others each had a heifer. When the heifers were seized the families started sharing the cow, passing it on once a week. Rumors of imminent confiscation fueled waves of livestock slaughter, in contravention of rules that required the sanctioning of such slaughter by district landwirts and the delivery of half of the meat to the Germans.[78] The penalties for violating these rules varied. The raion chief in Khabne in December 1941 announced the punishment as two months' arrest (and confiscation of the meat), but that same month, the sanction announced in the Borodianka raion—and perhaps imposed on transgressors there—was death.[79] If such a case was brought before a native juror, he imposed one year of imprisonment, according to a general directive from Koch and an abstract from the German criminal code; but many district commissars considered this too lenient and threatened jurors who did not cooperate with arrest and deportation to Germany. In the Zhytomyr general district early in 1943, German courts handled illegal slaughter cases and imposed prison sentences of two or three years.[80]

The Peasants' Standard of Living

Several other factors determined the amount of grains, meat, and other food that the peasants were able to keep for themselves. Inadequate transport facilities were among them: isolated villages in the Uman region gave up all of their grain in the fall, but in the summer there was no

10. A farm leader and his secretary doing bookkeeping in their office. Pereiaslav, central Ukraine, August 1943. (Photograph by Rick. Bundesarchiv, Bild 146/2002/12/817.)

transport for the perishable fruit and vegetables and the peasants could keep them.[81] Some landwirts, too, were reasonable. In the village of Zarubyntsi (Pereiaslav raion), for instance, the farm operated according to the "tenth" principle and, as a villager recalls, the Germans "took very little because the German agronomist was not very severe. The peasants would show him the hilly and steep fields; after taking a look around, he did not demand much grain."[82]

In the villages, those best situated to cope with the high delivery quotas were the local "elite," in particular the farm and brigade leaders. The Germans simply lacked the time to supervise them: the average landwirt could speak to each farm leader at most once a week.[83] As before 1941, the village elite—all of whom were relatives or friends—did not work the land and earned the most labor-days, partly through concerted illegal action. When they caught ordinary peasants "stealing" (if that is the right word), they took the goods for themselves. As a newspaper reported, they threshed stolen grain, gathered it, "and then it starts: the storekeeper does not weigh it, the accountant does not record it, the brigade leader does not see it, the collective farm leader keeps quiet, and the elder pretends not to see."[84]

Even better off were the native officials in the raion capitals. Officially the agricultural deliveries from the farms and gardens did not involve them, for a Ukrainian (or in rare cases, a Russian) agronomist under each raion landwirt was to report to and from the farms about these matters.[85] But bad roads, particularly during the muddy season (late March to late April) and the winter, as well as the sheer lack of German personnel, gave the raion officials much leeway.[86] They took full advantage. Some raion chiefs shifted most of the responsibility for the quota to people they disliked, for example, people of another nationality. (Others even increased the quota.) Raion chiefs also influenced the local consumer cooperatives that handled the technical side of the agricultural deliveries.[87] These cooperatives were part of a large network called the All-Ukrainian Cooperative Society, the one major cooperative in the Reichskommissariat that was semilegal. It was supposed to gather agricultural produce and circulate it (to Germans or natives) in exchange for tools and consumer goods. Although Reich and ethnic Germans led its offices in the major cities, elsewhere it had thousands of representatives who were not German. The German authorities were satisfied with this system, but as a result, events on the ground often remained obscure to them.[88]

A striking example of local autonomy was the Novi Sanzhary raion in the Left Bank, inhabited by some sixty thousand people, whose native authorities successfully deceived the Germans about the size of the harvest in 1942 and 1943. Had the German norms been followed, each peasant would have received only 120 kilograms of second-rate grain for a whole year. But the raion chief, the chief agronomist, and the head of the Raion Land Administration (an entity dating back to the year of military rule) convinced the hundreds of native elders, farm leaders, and accountants to prepare two records: one real, another fake. In his proud memoir of this episode, the former raion chief asserts that in this way, the peasants received as payment more grain than they had ever obtained in the Soviet period.[89]

Altogether, the amount of food retained by ordinary peasants varied considerably from region to region, from household to household, and over time. The sources of information on this are often contradictory. In April 1942—thus still before the earlier-mentioned confiscation campaign of July 1942—the SD called the "food situation" of the native population in the Kiev general district "significantly worse" than in the Soviet period, a generalization that included the city of Kiev. At the same time, the agency called "the food possibilities" in the countryside of the Volhynia-Podolia general district "sufficient" and in Podolia even "better than in the time of the Bolsheviks." Yet later that year, Baptist evangelists found a "starving" population in Podolia.[90] In the Kirovohrad region, by 1943 gloomy sayings like the following circulated: "The German says, 'Give grain' / But where can one get it / They stripped us like an oak tree / We're going to die"; "Look how we got rich under the Germans: The Germans liberated everything, only the cat is in the hut"; and "Hitler came with a cross [swastika] and ate the cow, including its tail." Especially in the less fertile region of Polissia, many peasants lived on the brink of famine.[91] And everywhere widows, orphans, families with many small children, persons without a cow or pig, and those who did not cultivate a garden were very vulnerable.[92]

Nevertheless, the evidence still does allow for the conclusion that many—and probably most—peasants of the Reichskommissariat Ukraine had more food at their disposal than before the German occupation. The peasants of Klyntsi near Kirovohrad, a witness recalls, "lived a normal life" for "there was everything."[93] At the market in Pervomaisk on the Southern Buh River in August 1942, vegetables, fruit, milk products, and chickens were on sale for low prices. Peasants in the Zaporizhzhia region, too, had enough surplus food to feed the city. According to a local, in the fall of 1943 the markets in the region were "so full of agricultural produce that they brought to mind the years of NEP," the relative prosperity of the 1920s. Hundreds of peasants took carts loaded with produce to the very lively market in Poltava late in 1942, and in the Velyka Bahachka raion near Myrhorod, "the people lived like they had not done for a long time, perhaps since the revolution."[94]

This conclusion also held true in the Kiev region. A German informant for the German Foreign Office reported in 1942 that the violent suppression of market trade in the cities had embittered the peasants, but hiding food was easier than before 1941 so that they themselves had enough to eat.[95] Despite the July 1942 grain confiscations, the peasants of the Kiev general district did not expect food shortages during the winter to come. Peasants from Medvyn, too, have recalled in postwar interviews that they "ate well" and that "we were not hungry."[96] Fedir Pihido traveled a lot and "often heard peasants in the Kiev and Dnipropetrovsk regions say that they drank more vodka and ate more lard and fowl in the two years of German occupation than in the twenty-five years of Soviet rule." The situation was dire in some regions, he found, especially those where partisans were active. Nevertheless, as far as food was concerned, "in 1942 and 1943 the main mass of the peasantry lived rather well, especially considering the fact that there was a war going on—and, without any doubt, incomparably better than in the time of Soviet rule."[97]

Considering the near-starvation rates of the late 1930s, the rise in the peasant living standard under the Germans was not entirely surprising. But the severe state of affairs under Soviet rule does not suffice as an explanation. According to a former mediator from the Zhytomyr general district, "the standard of living seemed to rise for the majority of the peasants" because the gardens were larger.[98] Also important was that the peasants generally had more livestock than before 1941. Probably crucial, however, was that, as mentioned earlier, German supervision of the farms was less thorough than the pre-1941 Soviet control system. It had become easier to "steal." Two postwar emigrés actually consider this the one and only reason for the rising living standard.[99]

Although an extensive and informal barter system with townspeople provided the peasants with clothes, shoes, and watches,[100] the peasant accumulation of nonfood items was not substantial. Nikolai Fevr, a veteran of the Russian Civil War who visited Ukraine as a journalist for a Berlin-based Russian-language newspaper, spent several days during the fall of 1942 in a dozen villages south of Kiev. Peasants told him that they had more clothes because many Red Army soldiers had sold them their uniforms. All the same, the poor look of peasants shocked him. General Commissar Magunia also reported around this time that the countryside lacked many consumer goods, in particular shoes, clothes, housewares, and tools. By the middle of 1943, many peasants in the Reichskommissariat continued to walk barefoot and in rags.[101]

Violence and Fear

In certain regions, the peasants worked hard on the farms, but in most areas they worked as slowly and as little as possible. Brigade leaders in the village of Borodianka allowed their fellow villagers to work slowly when the landwirt was not around. One time the peasants did not see the landwirt coming while they were sitting and taking a break. "It was terri-

ble the way he started shouting at us," one women recalls. "The interpreter said, 'If you remain seated, he will kill you.'"[102] Absenteeism and
lateness were very common. Many peasants spent their time walking
about, partying, or petitioning the raion authorities about minor affairs.
That was why newspapers and posters regularly issued calls such as "Peasants, you must also provide food for your brothers in the cities!" "If you
won't sow you will go hungry," and even "Don't be lazy! The Fatherland
calls you to work!"[103]

The official punishment for work evasion was a fine of 200 rubles
(later, karbovantsi) or two weeks in a labor camp. In at least some villages, the actual penalty was several days of confinement without food or
drink. But by almost all accounts, lateness or absenteeism led to flogging
or beating, by Germans or by native officials. Peasants who did not show
up for work were likely to be summoned to the elder's office and receive
a public beating. Germans tended to use a whip; elders or farm chairmen
a birch, stick, or simply their fists. One apparently typical landwirt of a
southern district, a tall man with a crewcut nicknamed the Khan of the
Nogai Steppe, told a German who came to visit: "The fellows here understand only one language: this one!," as he raised his hand. He did not
like to beat, he added, but "one cannot function here without it. You
wouldn't believe how such a slap in the face works wonders!"[104] The
prevalence of the floggings is also evident from the several orders dealing
with them—a ban by Koch in April 1942, a request by him to the general
commissars to remind all Reich Germans of this ban in November 1942,
and a second ban in 1943.[105]

Germans abused peasants for the smallest things, such as not saying a
proper greeting, failing to do so at once, or having one's hands in one's
pockets. Some district landwirts, especially in regions with partisan activity, beat up ten to twenty peasants every day.[106] Peasants often complained in letters to relatives who were working in the Reich as Eastern
Workers. "Life is bad here," one wrote in the middle of 1942. "The Germans beat us with batons if we arrive at work late."[107] In 582 letters from
Ukraine to Germany studied between early September and early November 1942, censors cited as typical one that claimed, "They chase us to
work with anything they can beat with, batons or sticks. Yes, these people
are really civilized, literate, they are cultured . . . This is how we live: we
are beaten and are not allowed to cry. The good thing is that we are free.
All desire to live and work has been taken away from us. When there is

work, we work. Otherwise we stay home. Then the Germans come during the day and beat us hard."[108]

The longer the Germans stayed, the more vicious the beatings became. Once the entire village of Chervony Iar (near Kirovohrad) felt the brunt because work had started too late. Half of the 130 inhabitants were flogged with whips; the others tried to flee, but dogs hunted them down.[109] If village elders beat a peasant, the abused peasant sometimes filed a complaint with the regional mediator. In the courts the accused usually said that they had themselves been beaten and had received orders to do likewise to the peasants, so as to get them going. Had they not complied, they added, the peasant would not have done the work and they themselves would have been beaten to death. The mediators often acquitted such elders or imposed only a small fine.[110]

The landwirts misunderstood entirely the effect of their abusive behavior. They believed that their subjects would recall Soviet practices and would appreciate that they let them go after "only" a beating, instead of keeping them in detention. (In fact, Soviet agricultural officials had also meted out beatings, if much less often.)[111] But the floggings were public and thus especially humiliating. The people involved never forgave the perpetrators. New sayings and rhymes emerged, such as "They fleece you with leather 'cause you can't work"; "We thought the Germans would give us land, but they flog us with a whip"; and "You can't live with German laws: It's rubber on your back and a rest in the grave."[112]

Abuse was not the only danger. Death threats, overt or implied, became common. The peasants quickly realized that the new regime placed little value on their lives. In the spring of 1942, peasants from the village of Tahancha (Kaniv raion) were once feeding horses, and not working the fields, when the landwirt showed up and immediately started firing at them. And in Medvyn, a young peasant from another village came late to work and was beaten to death by the local Schuma.[113] When the Schuma and Gendarmerie publicly executed villagers, they used the gallows that eventually appeared in every village square. One day young males in Medvyn stole or sabotaged something. An eyewitness recalls: "We are all at work. Then the alarm rings in the village: 'Everybody off to a meeting at the school.' We all go, because if not, we'll be beaten terribly. We all gather. And there were these gallows, for hangings. The Germans . . . no, the Germans are just standing there—our volunteers read out loud who has done what wrong. Then they bring them up one by one and hang them. Everybody sees how they are punished."[114] And in the north of Koch's domain, collective punishment started. From the fall of 1942, entire villages in Polissia were burned down for not supplying the required produce and presumably supporting partisans. On September 2 of that year, for example, Gendarmerie officers and seventy Ukrainian Schuma killed all the inhabitants of the village of Kaminka east of Brest-Litovsk, and burned the place to the ground.[115]

Overall, peasant women were more anti-Communist and eager to own property than men. As the Germans noticed, they were also busier, probably because they felt more responsible for their children. (Some women at the age of twenty already had three or four.)[116] Under the Germans it remained not uncommon for them to work under a male brigade leader who urged them on only with a whistle.[117] But still women could be rather assertive. At a butter factory in Oleksandriia, women reportedly "rioted" in early 1942 about the demand to give up the entire milk yield. A native policeman who reminded them that at least the Bolsheviks were gone was told loudly, "We will kiss the Bolsheviks, the sooner they come back the better." Germans dispersed the crowd. For such things women could pay the ultimate price. When a woman in the town of Chyhyryn made a vulgar gesture to a German officer who demanded butter, and shouted insults at him, he reportedly hanged her from a nearby tree.[118]

Thus there came a well-founded, intense fear. Oksana Iatsenko, who was in her early twenties at the time, remembered it vividly more than fifty years later. "We had to work the fields every day. I remember, I stayed at home once: I wanted to pull out the weeds in the garden. As soon as I went to the garden to start weeding, the village chief came walking by. I saw all these people and [gasps for air]—the German. I looked and died of fear. I thought I had died. We had those plum-trees, I ran there and hid in the bushes. And they came closer and walked under the pear-tree, but didn't find me. And all the time I thought: They will kill me, they will kill me."[119]

Financial taxes, food confiscations, humiliation, and violence—most peasants concluded that their life was at least as bad as before 1941. Letters in July and August 1942 complained that "It's going to be just like under the Bolsheviks, for we have to hand in everything. It's misery"; or, "Our life used to be bad, but now . . ." Peasants in the Tarashcha region were saying by the end of that year that nothing had changed: just as before, they were giving out a lot.[120] Letter censors in late 1942 encountered complaints about the 1942 harvest, food shortages, and a threat of famine in the coming winter and spring. "It's harvest time, and yet we have no bread," one woman wrote. "The guys gather stalks, and we mill this on the hand mill, to make some bread. This is how we live up to now, and we don't know what will be next."[121]

The issue of "theft" played a major role in peasant dissatisfaction. Before 1941, the peasants survived by taking produce from the fields for themselves—using, among other things, a special pocket on the inside of their clothes—and these ways continued under the Germans.[122] In fact, it was easier to "steal" under German rule, but the abuse suffered by those caught enraged the entire peasant population. In Medvyn, for example, in a typical incident, several villagers were caught "stealing" grain and the landwirt also found bottles filled with home brewed vodka. The landwirt asked through his interpreter who owned the bottles, and when no one answered, he started lashing randomly with his whip. That evening the auxiliary police arrested several suspects and beat them all night.[123]

Collective punishment for sabotage of what the Nazis called the "food economy" received official sanction in the summer of 1942, when Koch's deputy Paul Dargel warned that a saboteur of this kind was anyone who disobeyed orders, obstructed "work that aids the food economy," failed to prevent and report "damage," or falsified data. Whenever the authorities could not find the guilty ones, they reserved the right to penalize those "responsible leaders and [farm] members" who supposedly could have prevented the mishap, or even "the entire community."[124]

Cases of wood "theft" were also punished severely. On November 11, 1942, a forester near Iakovets in the Khabne raion caught the young peasant Hrytsko Samoilenko in the act of cutting wood. Samoilenko pulled out a warrant from the elder of a nearby village, an older man called Demyd Dubodil, but it was a forgery. The Schuma in Khabne interrogated the two and on December 5 sent a report about the case to the district SS and police chief. The men were released, but on December 19 appeared in court. Raion juror M. Ivanov imposed on Samoilenko a 600 karbovantsi fine or (should he not pay up) two months' confinement, and on Dubodil a 400 karbovantsi fine or six weeks' confinement. Both also had to pay the trial costs of 100 karbovantsi each. A German translation of the verdict went to the SS.[125] The juror was following guidelines from Koch of May 1942 that called for either payment of the wood's value or confinement. Many of his subordinates, however, dismissed such verdicts as too mild, and referred the cases to another juror for another trial.[126]

Disunity

Thus although the peasants overall had more food than before 1941, they suffered abuse, lived in fear, and were pessimistic about the future. In these circumstances it is not surprising that alcoholism increased. Home brewing and conspicuous alcohol consumption at parties had already occurred in the countryside in the 1920s and 1930s,[127] but now it reached a spectacular scale. The phenomenon, one should add, was not particularly Soviet or Ukrainian—alcoholism also proliferated among Polish peasants in the General Government. (Due to high food prices, their living standard compared to the prewar period rose as well.)[128] Brewing vodka was easier than making bread, for the authorities controlled the flour mills. To make home brew, the peasants crushed the grain with small grindstones, or soaked and grounded it in pots. Also used were sugar beets, onions, horseradish, or elder.[129] The authorities repeatedly banned home brewing and warned of severe punishment, but these bans had little effect. Pihido found that at least one peasant household in every four distilled its own vodka.[130] A man who visited a village in the Left Bank in November 1941 also found that almost every household made home brew and that "even girls learned to drink" at that time.[131] By the spring of 1942, "nobody" was fighting the practice in the Novi Sanzhary raion, its former chief recalls, and hard drinking, which he correctly ascribed to low morale, was "a general phenomenon."[132]

The authorities were right to think that the practice used many resources. A teacher calculated that in his western Volhynian village alone, at least three hundred poods (about 4,900 kilograms) of grain from the 1942 harvest went to home brewing.[133] And while many people drank, others had difficulty just making ends meet. "Everybody drinks: the spiritual and secular intelligentsia, peasants, workers, and even the school youth," a Volhynian newspaper wrote. "They drink 'for an occasion' and 'without any reason.' There used to be one inn for the entire village; now there is an inn in every third hut." Peasant boys stole eggs, chickens, grain, and money from their parents to buy tobacco and drinks. Yet "often in one and the same village the poorest people have not a crumb of bread."[134]

Soon after the Germans arrived, thousands of former "kulaks" and other victims of Soviet persecution returned from the cities and industrial centers. In the first two months, over 1,500 of an estimated 5,000 former peasants residing in Zhytomyr secured permission to leave for the countryside. The Nazis, who wanted to depopulate the cities, did not block this de-urbanization and at first required only prior consent from the raion landwirt.[135] A number of German decrees, the thrust of which was that "dekulakized" peasants should get back any property confiscated in the Soviet period, came into play.[136] In rare cases nobody had taken possession of the homes of the "repressed." Then the villagers had nothing to worry about and called the "kulaks" good farmers who would return "God willing."[137] But usually the homes had been taken. If both the current and former occupants were willing to compromise, the potential problem was nipped in the bud. For example, the daughter and granddaughter of a priest who had fled the village of Klyntsi near Kirovohrad returned in 1942 and found their home occupied. The poor inhabitants immediately allowed them to settle into one room and began building their own house next to it. A former "kulak" who returned to Medvyn also got his ancestral land back easily and had no trouble even when he refused to join the communal farm.[138]

More often than not, however, the return of the "kulaks" sparked conflicts. Many village soviets had sold the houses at bargain rates to Communists and Soviet activists, and over the years the new owners had made extensive renovations and additions. It was all very well that according to German law the native authorities were to assist the victims of Soviet persecution, but in many villages, these authorities were the same people as before 1941 and often they only resumed the harassment by, for example, allotting the returnees very small gardens or imposing extra taxes and delivery quotas. Only some elders and raion officials seem to have evicted the current occupants and helped the returnees in other ways.[139] Aggrieved parties often filed a suit with the mediators. In the Novi Sanzhary raion, for instance, where there were about a thousand "dekulakized" peasants' homes, the raion landwirt allowed a special committee to sensibly decree that no current occupant of a "kulak" house should become homeless. The angry returnees then denounced the raion administration as Communist to any German who would listen, and some of those Germans unrealistically ordered their "auxiliaries" to resolve such cases within days. Thus the atmosphere became sadly similar to the "free-floating malice" that had characterized so much of prewar village life.[140]

After the Battle of Stalingrad

After the German defeat in the Battle of Stalingrad in February 1943, the predicament of the peasants improved somewhat. Some new benefits (such as the lowering of the penalty for illegal slaughter to three months in prison) existed only on paper,[141] but others were substantial. All humanitarian aid societies, including the Red Cross, had been banned in early 1942, but later that year and especially in 1943, ever more district commissars ordered the formation of regional "self-help" committees.[142] (One wonders whether the commissars must have also feared a chaotic situation because of the influx of refugees from the east.) Many of the aid committees assumed a real significance, especially after June 25, 1943, when the Reichskommissariat allowed raion administrators to raise their own taxes. The aid committee in Bohuslav reportedly served 56 meals to 378 needy people (including refugees) from early 1943 to mid-August 1943.[143]

The biggest improvement after Stalingrad, from the peasant perspective, was in land use. Despite opposition by Nazi party members, the Economy Inspectorate Center had already allowed the privatization of agriculture in its Russian and Belarusan regions, which greatly increased yields.[144] In Ukraine, however, the Nazis had barred such procedures. But on June 3, 1943, the Nazi leadership gave the go-ahead for total privatization in the entire "Eastern" countryside. The East Ministry decreed that the peasants still would have to supply Germany with produce, but any surplus would be theirs. Those few peasants who had already received land for individual use now could rightfully call it theirs. According to the propaganda, even peasants who were in the Red Army or in the Soviet hinterland could claim land in their place of origin.[145] Remarkably, even then Koch refused to distribute the announcement.

Some historians have concluded that the decree had at most a negligible effect, but the actual state of affairs was more complex.[146] In the Poltava region, an unknown proportion of farms in the Hadiach, Lokhvytsia, and Velyka Bahachka raions, and one farm in the Zinkiv raion, apparently dissolved with local German permission even before June 1943. As a result, households received six to seven hectares each.[147] In the nearby Novi Sanzhary raion, the landwirt started dividing the land after the 1942 harvest and within a year all of the 97 communal farms were gone. From early 1943 he allowed peasants to distribute the land themselves (per able-bodied person, not per farm member). The 1943 harvest was good: one hectare yielded about three hundred kilograms of grain.[148]

Privatization came later to the rest of the Kiev general district (such as near Vasylkiv) and to the Dnipropetrovsk general district.[149] On Sunday, August 22, 1943, the village of Vilna Tarasivka (Velykopolovetske raion) marked the dissolution of its two farms and of two neighboring farms. The deputy general commissar thanked those in attendance for the bread and salt, blamed the Jews for collective farming, proclaimed individual cultivation on private plots, handed out documents, and shook hands. Then a dinner started, as well as "massive merry-making of the peasants with the participation of a brass band."[150]

The peasants used such opportunities to celebrate, but they realized what was going on. As a saying had it, "The Germans are issuing land laws for the third time / That's a sure sign that they're taking to their heels." They also spoke of deceit and nonsense.[151] Some therefore refused to accept land. Had the situation at the front been otherwise, they might have taken it. Many others, however, appear to have taken land when they had the chance.[152] Shortages of people, livestock, or equipment were obstacles to private cultivation that voluntary cooperation could solve. In the Berdychiv raion (where privatization took place in August 1943), groups of ten households shared equipment and according to an overly confident German observer they worked "better than ever" and were "extremely satisfied."[153]

The improvements in working conditions actually did not take away the dissatisfaction of the vast majority of peasants, if only because in other respects things got worse. Many machinery and tractor stations became bases that supervised the farms or cooperatives. The base leaders— Germans, Dutch, and apparently also natives—who obeyed only the landwirt, tended to be ruthless and to force peasants to work even on important holidays, generally making the Nazi agricultural system more efficient.[154] The tighter control caught more "thieves" and other transgressors, and abuse by German and native officials multiplied.[155] At last the German authorities had managed to match—and indeed surpass—the Soviet system of supervising the food supply system.

In short, many peasants had on average more food during the two to three years of German rule than they used to have under Soviet rule, mainly because they worked their gardens well and because, for a long time, the German system of supervision and requisition was far less efficient than its Soviet predecessor. But collective farming remained and eventually became what the peasants considered full-blown serfdom, if only because more people then ever had to work on the farm. In years past, peasants often had referred to collective agriculture as the second serfdom—corvée without a whip.[156] And now the whip, abolished in 1861 along with tsarist serfdom, returned with a vengeance. The ever-increasing abuse and violence were why by the middle of 1942, most peasants feared for their lives in the presence of a German. More food and drink on the table meant little if one felt like one's life was expendable.

6

CONDITIONS IN THE CITIES

Studies of civilian populations during wartime should address the extent to which people looked out for each other. Did they think about and help others, or did they reserve all or most of their attention for themselves and the interests of their families? The views of historians of wartime Europe on these nearly intangible matters vary substantially. On the "community" end, there are historians who emphasize a political ideology or ethos—nationalism or patriotism (Polish, Ukrainian, Russian, Soviet, or other)—that motivated people to display solidarity. People had a sense that they belonged together and they were willing to accept the implications. Thus under foreign regimes they created, or at least supported, a resistance movement. On the other end of the interpretive spectrum are those historians who find little or no solidarity. Any unity that existed before the war, be it a "society" or a "nation," disintegrated. Social fragmentation occurred, with people living self-serving, egoistic lives, focusing on their own survival while callously disregarding their neighbors' needs. This bleak view is particularly common among German historians of Nazi Germany.[1] One intermediate interpretation acknowledges various disagreeable features of wartime life, such as demoralization, denunciation, and blackmail, but nevertheless holds that solidarity remained a defining feature of most civilians. People did care about and help each other, or at the very least thought that they were supposed to. One finds this view among, for example, a number of historians of Poland, who have found evidence of what they call an "underground society."[2]

The best way to study the issue of "solidarity" versus "atomization" may be to focus on city dwellers, who unlike peasants depend on strangers to survive. In this chapter about working conditions in the cities of the Reichskommissariat Ukraine, I will argue that life did not fully "atomize," for some acts displayed solidarity. But neither was there any underground society. If and when these city dwellers engaged in clandestine or risky pursuits, it was primarily for the benefit of themselves and their closest relatives. There were isolated efforts at creating a social security network, but those came to naught, mainly because the Nazis generally suppressed them. The city dwellers in question all had legal jobs; they were people with privilege, workers, private enterpreneurs, scientists, and scholars. But all faced at least one problem: where to live.

Housing

The people of Kiev, Dnipropetrovsk, and the other cities faced typical wartime dangers and problems. One was hostage-taking, usually of men, after acts that the new regime considered to be sabotage. For a fire or other mishap, the German authorities held all the inhabitants of a house or even street accountable and reserved the right to kill them if the perpetrators did not come forward. Many prudent Kievans therefore had a full suitcase ready and slept in their daytime clothes as early as November 1941. They wished for more police patrols and, convinced that saboteurs and criminals did not care about hostage shootings, organized vigilantes against them. They also lived in great fear of burglary or worse. Because many doorbells had been out of order for years, notes on doors indicated how many times one had to knock to see a particular person or family. Only after a response to the "Who's there?" from behind the still-closed door might the bolts and chains be lifted.[3]

One of the biggest changes in living conditions was the power given to house custodians. During the imperial and Soviet periods, custodians generally had reported any "suspicious" behavior by tenants to the authorities. As the Red Army retreated, the NKVD replaced many of these house custodians in order to streamline the hunt for deserters. After the Germans arrived, many custodians declared themselves the owners of the building, raised the rent, and told those unable to pay to move out within days. And they resumed their traditional role as informants, this time for the Nazis. Even so, the Nazis replaced many with ethnic Germans.[4]

Thousands of Kievans had to move as a result of the Great Fire and ended up in more spacious places vacated by people who had left before the German arrival or whom the Nazis had murdered.[5] Soon, however, relocating became difficult, as each city's housing department took charge and asserted the right to distribute houses according to people's backgrounds. The new bureaucrats tended to give preferential treatment to those with a history of persecution by the Soviet regime.[6] Most city dwellers remained in their prewar communal apartments, which allotted each family only one room. Nikolai Fevr, a Berlin-based journalist of Russian descent, spent two months in Kiev during the summer of 1942. He delivered letters to many people and thus saw dozens of apartments from the inside. One he himself had left in 1919 as a White Russian soldier. Now it was a typical *kommunalka:* bricks or wood blocked all of the adjacent door openings, so that the apartment had become six "cages"; four rooms had two to four people each, the former servant's room had a student, and the former bathroom housed an old woman. "In the common kitchen, the inhabitants of the place had no way of controlling the expenses for firewood. Therefore the stove had not been burning for years. On it were six ancient primus stoves, on which dinners and suppers were prepared. A corner in the kitchen was fenced off by a blanket; here the inhabitants changed clothes when they were hosting guests. The kitchen was also the place where they washed, straight from the tap above the sink. Because it was unheated, in the wintertime a virtual skating-rink formed on the floor, so that the people wore felt boots when preparing meals."[7] Such living conditions almost inevitably promoted resentment. The luckiest workers in Dnipropetrovsk had one room and a kitchen for a family of four, or two more rooms if the family was larger. Many preferred to live in shacks or barracks at the city outskirts, for there one could have chickens or geese.[8]

A minority of city dwellers lived relatively spaciously, but they knew that eviction or robbery could occur at any time. Late in 1941, General Commissar Magunia expelled all the remaining inhabitants of Lypky, Kiev's most prestigious district, on twenty-four-hours' notice, without offering other homes, and early the next year, the city commissar confiscated furniture. At the end of 1942, the city commissar decided to concentrate German civilian administrators and ethnic Germans. He therefore told many people in the center of Kiev to vacate their apartments within days, without providing a reason. The new apartments for those evicted Kievans were tiny or unfit for habitation. (And only if they had the money could they buy one—illegally—from the custodian-landlords.) There was also a ban on relocation into Kiev's Pechersk, St. Sophia, and Bohdaniv districts and, from late October 1942, a ban on moving outside one's current district. Renting a cart and driver cost around 200 reichsmarks. Not surprisingly, the SD reported an "ill feeling and nervousness" about the housing situation.[9] In Vinnytsia, the Nazis evicted people from the best quarter and demolished most buildings there so as to facilitate the city's germanization.[10]

Heat and light were scarce. New apartments had a central heating system, but this did not operate. Thus winters centered around the kitchen, which people heated with wood obtained from sheds, fences, and anything else that would burn. Fuel was a constant preoccupation, for it was important to hoard it months in advance.[11] Electricity returned to Kiev two weeks after the Germans arrived, but only Reich Germans, ethnic Germans, and high-ranking officials received it. While German homes were basking in light after sunset, the native officials with electricity were told to use it sparingly—and in September 1942 they lost it altogether.[12] Ordinary city dwellers created light with candles, long wooden chips, gas-fueled night lamps, and oil lamps: bottles of kerosene with a burning wick and a gray, trembling flame that left ceilings in profound darkness. This lack of light imposed a way of life: usually people got up around six o'clock and went to bed around nine.[13] In the middle of 1943, electricity returned to at least some homes. In Vinnytsia, for example, all inhabitants apparently received electricity by that time. But in Dnipropetrovsk there was never a time when non-Germans could use it.[14]

Going to Work

All adult city dwellers were required to have officially registered work. The authorities ordered the city populations to register at the Labor Office, an institution controlled by the city or district commissar and invariably led by a Reich or ethnic German. Communist party members who registered—and most did—usually had to repeat this at regular intervals, sometimes once per week, and in at least one city (Dnipropetrovsk) they had to wear a white brassard with a number.[15]

Having a job seemed essential for survival, but getting one was far from easy. At the end of 1941, Kiev's Labor Office apparently was "besieged by hungry people." To many it seemed that ethnic Ukrainians received preferential treatment in job placement. City dwellers "grabbed their passports and many people discovered incomprehensible things," Iryna Khoroshunova wrote in her diary. "In one and the same family, brothers and sisters were Russian and Ukrainian, for none of us had given any meaning to nationality. And many were glad to find that because of circumstances or by chance, they turned out to be Ukrainian."[16] Most city dwellers tried to register as Ukrainian and often succeeded. (This explained the very high number of Ukrainians in subsequent city censuses.)[17]

Reichskommissar Koch tightened the hiring system in March 1942. Employers who hired a person without the Labor Office's prior consent would be fined or imprisoned, he announced, unless the job took only one week to complete. By checking a labor card that every employee received, employers had to certify once a week who was working for them.[18]

At first, more than twice as many Kievans with legal work were female than were male. For various reasons, such as the return of former Red Army soldiers, this situation quickly turned around. On April 1, 1942, less then a third (101,500) of Kiev's 352,000 registered inhabitants were officially employed; two-thirds (64,300) of these, mostly "Ukrainians," were male. Over half of the about fifty thousand "Ukrainian" men with official jobs were "workers" (robitnyky). A large proportion (over 12,000 of 27,500) of "Ukrainian" females with official employment held "white-collar" jobs. Other registered "Ukrainian" occupations included handicrafts (in the case of 2,800 males), cleaning and "other kinds of day-labor" (3,800 females), and agriculture (2,000 females in the outer districts).[19]

The replacement of military with civilian Nazi rule also changed the regulations on absenteeism and lateness. Remarkably, it first made these rules less severe: The German military had preserved the harsh Soviet regulations, including the Soviet law of June 1940 that severely penalized persons with a regular job at a state firm who quit without permission (up to four months' imprisonment) or who missed all or part of the working day—for example, by arriving more than twenty minutes late (up to six months of "corrective" labor and a salary reduction of up to 25 percent).[20] But gradually the civilian authorities reimposed harsh official penalties for such matters, although—as in the case of the Soviet regulations—the degree of their implementation is another matter. It is doubtful that the German authorities always could or wanted to enforce such penalties, if only because there were not that many German supervisors, particularly in the smaller towns.[21]

The Nazis planned to pay about 10 percent more than the Soviet salaries,[22] but this was hardly an improvement since those had been well below subsistence levels. In reality, the salaries often remained the same or fell below the Soviet rates. Lower-than-Soviet rates were particularly likely to occur in small towns, where all salaries came directly from the treasury of the raion administration.[23] Female employees everywhere initially received 20 percent less then males and if unmarried 28 percent less, a discrepancy that matched the situation in the Reich but shocked Soviet citizens. Eventually, a new law for the "East" raised the female wages to those of males.[24] Wages were paid in rubles and, from July 1942, only in a currency specifically for the Reichskommissariat, the karbovanets (plural: karbovantsi). Officially it was worth ten times less than the reichsmark, which also circulated.

Getting to one's place of work posed special problems. In Kiev, the first streetcar (along the Dnieper shore) returned to service on October 11, 1941. Initially Kievans were allowed to use streetcars, provided they got on at the back. The cars circulated irregularly and from 1942, most were reserved for cargo transport and garbage collection. Natives could ride illegally if the driver accepted their money, or if they just hopped on, which carried the risk of a whipping.[25] Other reserved streetcars took the employees of specific enterprises or firms to and from work. Streetcars also ran in Mykolaïv, Vinnytsia, Zhytomyr, Dnipropetrovsk, Zaporizhzhia, and Kamianske, although in the last three cities only from February 1943.[26] There were no public buses. Because bicycles had been rare since before the war, the ricksha, such a prominent feature of city life in other parts of wartime Europe, made its appearance only in major cities. Dnieper Ukraine's most common taxi was the horse-driven cart.[27]

Given such conditions, the inhabitants of the major cities spent much of each working day walking. Some walked three kilometers, others more, on prisoner-swept streets. All cities and towns had a curfew, which started at times that depended on the season and the mood of the local German authorities. Jews had to remain inside hours longer.[28] Posted announcements warned that curfew violators would be shot on the spot. To further deter people from venturing outside at these times, the Schuma periodically fired shots into the air.[29] Other sounds that disturbed the general quiet in the streets were the great variety of cars that the Germans and their allies used and the occasional broadcasts over the loudspeaker system of German music and Ukrainian and Russian songs.[30]

Observing the curfew required some planning, for hardly anyone had a watch. A person who wanted to be sure, but lacked a working clock at home, would ask a neighbor or passerby for the time before going out.[31]

Kiev had one of the harshest curfew regimes. In mid-October 1941, the curfew suddenly—on the day that the announcement poster appeared—became the period between six o'clock in the evening and five o'clock in the morning. The next morning, there were in the streets corpses of men, women, and children.[32] Indeed, corpses in the street remained a feature of Nazi-ruled Kiev. In one story told among Kievans, a pickpocket caught in the act by local streetcar passengers was taken outside by a German and shot right then and there.[33]

But most "reprisal" shootings took place at secret locations. At first the authorities announced them. One hundred Kievans were shot on October 22, 1941; it was announced that same day. Among the victims seem to have been people randomly rounded up one morning after an explosion rocked the former Duma building on Kalinin Square. (During this roundup, in accordance with German army instructions on hostage-taking, native Ukrainians were let go.)[34] During the nights of October 29 and 30, unknown people set fire to several houses and objects at a Kiev market; on November 2, City Commander Kurt Eberhard proclaimed that earlier that day, by way of punishment for the "increasing number of cases of arson and sabotage," he had ordered the execution of three hundred "inhabitants of Kiev." Any further case, he added, would bring the execution of an even larger number.[35] Later that month, there were cases of sabotage of phone and telegraph wires; on November 29, there came the announcement that because the perpetrators had not been found, four hundred men had been shot. This was the last such announcement in Kiev, but shots continued to resound from Babi Yar and people talked about them.[36]

Passersby could be forced to watch public hangings of "saboteurs" or "Jews." German onlookers, meanwhile, often took pictures. The victims were left suspended from the balconies or lampposts—there were no public gallows in the cities—for days. In Kiev, the first public hangings, of two "arsonists," apparently took place late in September 1941.[37] They are also reported for that city in February and March 1942. On at least one of those later occasions, the ropes broke and, as a crowd looked on, the henchmen resorted to shooting the accused.[38] Inhabitants of large cities also saw gas vans (actually, one van per city) speeding by. They called this mobile gas chamber that could hold and kill fifty prisoners the *dushohubka*—the destroyer of the soul.[39]

Such sights and sounds naturally influenced people's behavior. One

11. Public hanging, witnessed by local adults, children, and German soldiers. Kiev, probably late 1941 or early 1942. (Lydia Chagoll, courtesy of United States Holocaust Memorial Museum, Photo Archives, 15544.)

response was to stay inside whenever possible, and to travel to work quickly and with caution. Many pretty women feared arrest and incarceration in the brothels. One who lived in Kiev recalls that when she or her mother left home, "we always said goodbye, for there were no guarantees that we would return . . . Whenever we saw a group of Germans, we would hide immediately, somewhere on the side or under a gate."[40]

Another precaution, dating from Soviet times, was to dress inconspicuously, which meant poorly. Males, as Nikolai Fevr noted, wore "shabby shirts belted by laces, turned double-breasted jackets, frayed ordinary trousers, and canvas shoes on bare feet, or black boots. On their heads they sometimes wore a very old, flabby hat, more often a cloth cap or an embroidered Central-Asian skull cap, or—still more often—nothing." Men also made shoes by cutting up rubber tires and stitching up the openings.[41] Women wore "bag-shaped, faded dresses, patched coats with peasant scarves on top, black, coarse stockings or no stockings at all, and worn-out shoes, often men's boots. Some wore a yellowed straw hat, but more commonly a small beret or some self-made cap from fustian. Still more common was an ordinary white shawl." In the wintertime, they wrapped their faces, leaving only space for their eyes.[42] Ukrainians who arrived from Galicia and other western regions did not wish to stand out either, but their coats, jackets, and shoes gave them away, as did the short dresses, thin stockings, and hairstyles of the women.[43] Yet other people stood out deliberately. Local males who worked at the city administrations tended to have Ukrainian embroidered shirts and long mustaches, which gave them a "patriotic" look.[44] And as the months went by, a certain fashion developed, comprising clothes purchased from German soldiers and homemade clothes based on brightly dyed potato sacks and army blankets. Girls and women wearing the homemade clothes apparently carried themselves "with the dignity and grace of big city models."[45]

German men often pretended not to see the locals in the street. When waiting for a streetcar in the company of locals, they, as one witness recalls, "as if alone, indifferently let their pants down, picked their nose, blew with two fingers, and urinated openly." People found such neglect offensive.[46] The cities also hosted an increasing number of German women, as their husbands moved them away from Allied aerial bombardments of the Reich. These women were often seen walking dogs. The only Germans who generally acknowledged the local population were children. Once a streetcar that was decorated with Hitler's portrait and swastika flags drove by Anatolii Kuznetsov. Inside were boys and girls who were obviously German or at least of German descent. They spat at him, "with a particularly cold contempt and hatred in their eyes."[47]

There are almost no eyewitness accounts of public interactions between German and local city dwellers who were not girlfriends of the Germans. A glimpse comes from Jacob Gerstenfeld-Maltiel, a man who escaped from the Lviv ghetto and reached Dnipropetrovsk early in 1943. Despite his experiences as a Jew in the General Government, the way the Germans behaved toward the Slavs of the Reichskommissariat Ukraine (all of whom he misidentifies as Russians) shocked him. It was for him "so abysmal that we, who came from the West, simply could not adjust to it. Here the Germans could really feel like the *Herrenvolk* [master race]. The Russians were put on the same level as cattle. It was inconceivable that a German would walk shoulder to shoulder with a Russian. If it happened that a German was obliged to walk with a Russian, he always strode a few paces behind him or in front. Germans sitting down with the locals in a café or a restaurant? The very idea was ridiculous! A German did not stand in line, whatever his rank was. He would commandeer the barber's chair even if ten people were waiting for a haircut. He had a free ride in the trams and always had the right to a seat. The examples could be multiplied a hundred-fold, and though these were minor irritations, they humiliated the Russian population painfully and unceasingly." Germany's allies also generally remained aloof. Like the Germans, Hungarian officers were not supposed to sit down with locals for a meal, and apparently did not to do so.[48]

People with Privilege

People who worked in German offices were better off than almost all other non-German city dwellers, for they had access to the best meals and food rations. A cleaning woman at the Railroad Administration in famine-struck Kiev might earn a below-subsistence salary, but also a daily millet soup and millet porridge that let her survive.[49] An office that processed medicinal herbs would often pay its employees in kind, such as with pumpkin seeds, and provide "luxurious" daily meals of berries, dried mushrooms, and cherry-filled millet porridge. Ukraine had known this system of employee canteens—which during the war were also common in cities like Warsaw and Paris—before the war, for most Soviet city dwellers had their main meal at work. Another important benefit of office work was the heating there during the winter. Women who cleaned German homes also could supplement their income with meals.[50]

The salaries of the people with privilege were above average, but still a pittance compared to those of their German coworkers. A specialist at the film studio in Kiev, for instance, received 2,000 karbovantsi and a steady ration, but an ordinary German technician received 22,000 karbovantsi, a better ration including cigarettes and tobacco, and access to German-only restaurants.[51] In 1942 Polish "guest workers" arrived from the General Government. Their salaries were at the German level, probably because they were registered as ethnic Germans, and once a week they also collected the German ration.[52]

German supervisors generally treated their non-native male employees worse than their non-native female employees. For instance, whereas women rarely seem to have received death threats at work, for men such threats were not uncommon. One of the few eyewitness accounts shows just how intimidating this could be. The middle-aged Mykola Kostiuk worked as an electrician and handyman in Dnipropetrovsk. Once his supervisor told him to make a key and promised to pay him for it. "But when payday came, they paid only for the electric work, not for this. I said to [the German], 'They told me that there would be a second salary.' 'A second one?' he asked. 'Isn't this enough?' I said, 'They told me so, I didn't insist on it.' 'Follow me.' And we went somewhere. He said, 'Look at that switch.' I did. 'Look at me!' I looked and he was pointing a gun at me. 'Here's your second salary! Do you want it?' Then I got scared."[53]

Although newspaper editors supposedly enjoyed privileges, they too were treated badly. The offices of Kiev's *Nove ukraïnske slovo* (The new Ukrainian word) and *Poslednie novosti* (Latest news) were in the same building as the *Deutsche Ukraine-Zeitung*, but only Germans and ethnic Germans could use the main entrance.[54] The journalists had little leeway for initiative, because their German supervisors told them to print articles supplied from German sources, and the German censors (in major cities, both the city commissar and the general commissar) often held up local news items for days if not weeks.[55] After Konstantyn Shtepa, who early in 1942 became editor of *Nove ukraïnske slovo* (apparently under threat of death), wrote in a published article that Bolshevism had equally persecuted Russians and Ukrainians and that Ukrainians could enjoy Russian literature, he had to pledge to refrain from "praising" Russian culture. Ulas Samchuk, the first editor of the Rivne newspaper *Volyn*, printed several editorials that many regarded as covert criticisms of German policy. Suspecting (wrongly) that he was the general district's leading Melnykite, the Security Police arrested him in February 1942 and kept him locked up for two months.[56]

The biggest employer in the major cities was the "auxiliary" administration. Kiev had a central *uprava*, or administration, and eleven district administrations—including the Left Bank region of Darnytsia and several villages in the south and southwest—and employed some nineteen thousand people, including teachers and the workers of the factories under its control.[57] Higher-ranking administrators had to visit regularly the Security Police and SD to talk about themselves and their colleagues. During the night of November 5, 1942, Mayor Bahazii's obedient successor, Leontii Forostivsky, was arrested along with his entire family after a supposed misunderstanding. All were released the next day.[58]

As in the Soviet period, city administrations had their own dining rooms and canteens and controlled much of the food supply in the city as a whole. But now most of the administrators still went hungry, or received no meals at all.[59] In February 1942 the German authorities annulled all "warrants" from Ukrainian offices to employees for collecting potatoes or vegetables in the countryside. Most Kievan administration employees earned less than 500 karbovantsi.[60] A woman at a registry office in Kiev in 1942 was paid 400 karbovantsi per month and a ration of sugar beets, jam, and tiny amounts of sausage and jellied meat. (Her deputy head earned three times more.) At a canteen she received—unless supplies ran out—a meager soup and a nameless substance of beets, carrots, or potatoes.[61] Likewise, one woman at the administration in Vinnytsia worked long hours for her 400 karbovantsi per month, 500 grams of grouts per week, and 200 grams of bread per day. She ate once a day and also fed her mother.[62]

Not surprisingly, in dealing with administrators, food donations and other forms of tribute were often required or at least helpful. From early 1942 Kiev had thirty inspectors who, on German orders, supposedly lowered food prices. From an emigré memoir we learn how one with experience worked: "He started out in a monotonous voice, like a sacristan in the church: 'Will you lower the prices? The prices must be lowered. The prices should not be high.' 'All right, all right, we're lowering them,' the restaurant owner said. He seated us at a table and gave each of us a plate of food."[63]

The Workers

According to the SD in September 1941, the workers of Kryvy Rih, the center of the Soviet iron industry, were "very loyal" and wanted nothing but work and a higher wage. This generalization was accurate for most of Dnieper Ukraine's workers, most of whom had been unable or unwilling to evacuate.[64] The retreating Soviet authorities had left behind as many as 80 percent of the unskilled workers who had worked in the iron industry in the Dnieper bend.[65] As noted earlier, workers in Kryvy Rih had attempted to prevent the destruction of the factories. Unlike the wait-and-see attitude so common among peasants at that time, they and the remaining engineers restored and reopened their places of work without any German signal or help.[66]

At first the Germans were in no rush to hire and demanded guarantees that job candidates were reliable and at the very least had not been in the Communist party or Komsomol. Thereafter many Germans realized that such membership often had not been based on any real conviction.[67] Although in Dnipropetrovsk Communists had to wear brassards, at the H.

Petrovsky Metallurgical Factory, whose workers the SD found "very diligent, reliable, and absolutely loyal to the enterprise," the main engineer was a man known as a former party member. Ethnicity could be more important—in one unidentified Kiev factory, Russians apparently wore the letter *R* for a while and faced discrimination.[68]

The Soviet destruction and evacuation of factory machinery posed a problem for Germans and workers alike. For example, Kirovohrad's large agricultural machine factory Red Star, which had employed thirteen thousand people, was entirely out of order and the ten factories in this city that could start functioning in 1941 employed a total of only about 1,200.[69] Of the estimated two thousand factory engines that used to be in Kryvy Rih, only fifty had remained.[70] For this reason alone, work in the metallurgical plants never amounted to much. At the Petrovsky Factory, workers and POWs first gathered leftover metal and equipment, much of which then went to the Reich, and from early 1942 they repaired German tanks and caterpillar tractors. The Comintern Metallurgical Factory in Dnipropetrovsk turned leftovers into tinplate; another factory in that city produced wagons.[71] In Kiev's large metal-processing factories—which generally retained their Soviet names—only some shops were open and tended to do repairs, such as of train wagons (at the Bolshevik) and anti-aircraft guns (at the Lenin Forge).[72] From April 1942, an ammunition industry developed and the German company Dynamit Nobel AG employed many Zaporizhzhia women there.[73]

A metal worker in Dnipropetrovsk told Fevr that his Soviet monthly salary had been 300 rubles a month, which did not even buy a pair of boots.[74] He and many such people hoped that under German rule their living standard would rise. They would be disappointed. There were bonuses (and subtractions) depending on performance, but the official hourly wage ranged from only 0.70 rubles for unschooled workers under eighteen years of age to 2.50 rubles for master workers, and the canteen meals were inadequate. Factory directors in Dnipropetrovsk tried to ease the situation by organizing the barter of nails and cutlery in the countryside.[75]

Life on the shop floor became a odd mixture of fear, resentment, and fooling around. The mutual spying and denunciations of the Soviet period remained,[76] as did the threat of harsh penalties. At the Lenin Forge there was a detention room, and the factory maintained a fifteenth shop in the Lukianivka Prison where mysterious—gruesome?—tasks awaited offenders.[77] It surprised the workers that the Germans gave hardly any directives on how to make things, or any indications of the desired quality of the produce. There were, however, insults ("Russian pig!") and widespread and official physical abuse, even for misunderstanding something or for failing to greet.[78] The German director of the Lenin Forge, one Schmidt, "would come, find somebody who was sitting and not working, and would start beating," the female engineer Nadiia Konashko recalls. "He often threw them on the floor and started to trample and batter them. These people could not get away."[79] Like the village elders, shop masters and shop heads had the right to beat, but how often they did so remains unclear. For some beatings all employees had to assemble. In the Lenin Forge this happened two or three times. On February 13, 1942, it was the turn of a skilled worker, twenty-five years old, who had taken a bottle of gasoline. Initially sentenced to death, he faced twenty blows of the birch on his naked behind. He screamed loudly on the eighth strike, however, and, possibly because no German was present, his tormentor (a former Communist party member) gave only two more.[80]

And yet, as in the countryside before 1943, many industrial workers in Kiev generally faced *less* supervision than before 1941. To them this was a very significant change. The few Germans stationed in the Lenin Forge rarely came out of their offices. "In this regard, we felt free," Konashko recalls. Likewise, to work in the Ukrainian Ship and Machine Factory (USMA) was "a blessing, for these were all our people, Russians," another worker has said. Almost all of the administrators had been there before and they "ruled as they wanted."[81] German absenteeism allowed the workers to work slowly or not at all, chatting for hours on end; to take away aluminum parts or coal; and to just leave. At the Sport Factory, one worker would hammer on a piece of iron while the others talked. And they tinkered with "all sorts of junk, mending some things, breaking others. Everybody was working for himself and went away with cigarette-lighters, buckets and pans to use in barter."[82] Work at the Lenin Forge supposedly lasted from six in the morning to four in the afternoon, but the workers left after the midday meal.[83]

The cities of Dnipropetrovsk, Kamianske, Kryvy Rih, Nikopol, and Pavlohrad (all in the same general district) all had a mining industry before 1941. By the fall of 1942, this industry again employed over thirteen thousand natives, including three thousand prisoners of war.[84] The few machines not evacuated from Kryvy Rih were repaired and transported, along with many workers, to Nikopol, the pre-1941 center of the Soviet manganese industry. (In Kryvy Rih itself, iron mining started late in 1942 and employed fewer than five thousand natives.[85]) Nikopol became the one region in the Reichskommissariat officially freed from worker round-ups for labor in Germany. Instead, locals were gathered from the countryside to work at the manganese industry site, which formally employed close to eight thousand miners, most of whom worked above ground. One in five reportedly fell ill due to a lack of nutrition and proper shoes.[86] By the end of 1942, the forced laborers at Nikopol had extracted half of the annual peacetime Soviet manganese production, and in the last half of that year alone, supplied well over Germany's total needs. As for the damaged Dniprohes dam, due to disinterest among the Nazi leadership and a lack of laborers (because of roundups for work in Germany), it resumed operation only in January 1943.[87]

Ukraine's light industry underwent a more independent development. As Fedir Pihido described the situation at the sugar refineries: "The roar of the battles had not yet faded and the Germans had barely arrived, when the factory workers and employees crept out of the holes where they had been hiding from the Bolsheviks, as deserters, and got together to reconstruct their factories. The German commissars watched and wondered where all this was coming from."[88] Many employees took out machines and parts they had hidden in wells and ponds, heaps of scrap iron, and cases in the ground, and by 1942, with little or no German assistance, most of the town-based factories were up and running. There also developed new professional associations, such as one of engineers in the Kiev region that secured for itself a ten-year lease of all the brick, cement, and ceramics factories.[89]

Various sites in Kiev produced things like spoons, nails, plows, instruments, and pocketknives: thirty-three metalworking factories supervised by the city administration, fourteen cooperatives, and seven others, including the Polytechnical Institute and a large cooperative.[90] The Kiev City Administration also supervised most food-production factories, and other food factories were operational: Mukomol (flour), Vlasna pomich (ice cream), Vilna Ukraïna (a cooperative that supplied pasties, kvass, and mineral water), and a cooperative of disabled people.[91] But many of these places apparently closed in 1942. As for the working conditions in them, Kuznetsov's experience as a pumpkin loader at a canning factory was perhaps typical. Work started at seven and officially lasted twelve hours, with one break in the canteen. Once, during the daily body search, his foreman caught him stealing and gave him a vicious beating.[92]

The significant autonomy notwithstanding, the risk of German intervention was always there. After the director of a sugar factory sent molasses to the black market, the Security Police hanged the "anti-German saboteur" in the factory yard.[93] Other Germans started confiscating and exporting the raw materials, effectively enforcing the closure of textile, soap, leather, wool, and other factories, or taking charge of the reconstructed enterprises, partly out of a disbelief in Ukrainian capabilities. Consequently, by the beginning of 1943 there were no more natives in leading positions in the light industry that remained.[94]

People did other kinds of manual labor as well. Roundups for the reconstruction of Dnieper bridges and other damaged sites took place regularly in Kiev late in 1941.[95] By 1943 the railroad employed at least 300,000 natives, probably including prisoners, mostly in manual labor positions. (Among other things, they adjusted the track to the narrower central and western European width.) They received little food and earned a pittance, sometimes only 200 karbovantsi. And tens of thousands of camp inmates built a new highway from Dnipropetrovsk through Vinnytsia to Lviv in the General Government.[96]

The New Private Sector

Bars, teahouses, and restaurants, the best of which were invariably labeled with the sign "Germans Only," constituted a legal or semilegal private sector. Many restaurants often stood empty because of the widespread poverty—early in 1942, a meal might cost 30 rubles—but the owners (usually Ukrainians or people from the Caucasus region) still became wealthy. All restaurants for a native clientele apparently had to close down in September 1942, although probably not for long.[97] There also emerged many commission stores with secondhand but often first-rate ware. One time in April 1942, the German authorities in Kiev confiscated the items on sale there and apparently sent everything to Germany.[98] Within months, Kiev's commission stores were back in business, briskly selling things acquired at bargain prices from hungry Kievans, like paintings, clergymen's vestments, Caucasian felt cloaks, ancient books, snuffboxes from the time of Catherine II, coins from the time of Tsar Peter I, manuscripts from the seventeenth century, or deluxe editions of

Kazakh poetry about Stalin. Not surprisingly, Germans and Hungarians often visited these stores, some of which became antique stores that even sold imports from cities like Warsaw and Berlin.[99] There were also private stores, which sold such things as icons, crosses, paint, doorknobs, glass jars, toys, and antiquarian books. One place in Kiev sold Ukrainian embroidered shirts, which were rather popular among Germans. (Women produced the shirts at home, for a payment that allowed them to purchase ten potatoes and a few cups of millet per shirt.)[100]

The German authorities initially gave artisans such as barbers favorable attention, or at least did not obstruct them.[101] At first even Jewish artisans could work and created a clientele with many German soldiers, which prompted Wehrmacht commander Kitzinger to ban purchases from Jews in a special directive in March 1942.[102] Non-Jewish artisans could continue, but they faced a variety of rules. Thus shoemakers in Vinnytsia by 1943 needed written permission from the district commissar to accept any job; in reality, they worked as they wanted, for payments in kind. These private entrepreneurs "did not have it that bad," as a man who processed films for a German clientele recalls. They were better off than most native city dwellers who had no *gesheft*—the germanism for a business.[103]

When the Germans arrived, many medical doctors officially started private practices; the rest of the former Soviet health care system, which had been socialized and corrupt, also became private. A visit to a public clinic cost 3, transport to a city hospital 50, and a one-day stay there 15 to 25 karbovantsi. Doctors and specialists asked at least 1,200 or 1,600 karbovantsi for their services, and could make ends meet because they also treated Germans. Ordinary hospital patients had to bring their own sheets, bandages, cotton wadding, ether for anesthesia, a heating device during winter, food, indeed even the medicines (perhaps obtained through ethnic German acquaintances). Thus not uncommonly there were outside the hospital buildings "rows of people in dressing gowns, with their hands out, asking passers-by for food."[104]

The Scientists and Scholars

Many scientists and scholars in Soviet society had found it hard to get by. Taking into account overtime pay, taxes (40 percent), compulsory and all-but-compulsory state bonds and association memberships, rent, heating, and light, the average scientist retained 770 rubles per month (if just a specialist, 534 rubles), at a time when butter cost 28 rubles per kilogram and men's shoes, 120 rubles.[105] In Kiev, the entire middle- and lower-ranking staff of the university and the research institutes found themselves under German rule.[106] If they had harbored any hope that their standard of living would rise or at least stay the same, it was quickly dashed. The new regime, typified by Hitler's casual comment once that he was opposed to "founding" a university in Kiev,[107] seemed intent on obstructing native science and scholarship in every possible way. The Nazis looted Kiev's academic, medical, and technical libraries and concentrated the books that remained at one location. The librarians, who were usually women, had to do the moving, using bags or wheelbarrows. (Although the Germans had been surprised to find women doing traditionally male physical labor, they quickly accepted it.)[108]

Any scientists besides medical specialists who retained a place to work had to demonstrate an economic use for it. Mostly agronomists, they worked in the district and raion centers and at the central Ukrainian Agricultural Office in Kiev. The city eventually housed seventeen research institutes relating to cultivation, exploitation, and animal husbandry, and there were ten others in Dnipropetrovsk, Iakymivka, Kherson, Sarny, and Uman. The working conditions were difficult, if only because of the senseless destruction by Germans.[109]

In February 1942, in accordance with a decision to shut down all institutes of higher education in the Reichskommissariat, the University of Kiev, where class teaching had not been allowed, was officially closed, and looting followed. Yet some departments were reorganized to facilitate the teaching of medical science, veterinary medicine, forestry, applied physics, and agricultural and technical subjects.[110] In Dnipropetrovsk the Wehrmacht allowed the start of an academic year, but Einsatzgruppe C then banned all lectures. Still activities there did not completely stop.[111]

The NKVD had hit hard Soviet Ukraine's academy of sciences. At the end of 1941, however, on the initiative of Mayor Bahazii and a self-proclaimed presidium headed by the chemist V. O. Plotnikov, the "Ukrainian Academy of Sciences" was renewed.[112] Creating a formal membership proved impossible, for the new regime recognized as full members only those who had been elected as such in the Soviet Union, which left only two others besides Plotnikov.[113] The staff of the academy institutes received a salary, rations, and products from the city administration until

January 1942, when the acting general commissar, SA-Brigade-Führer I. Quitzrau, proclaimed the academy closed ("conserved"), briefly arrested its secretary (the mathematician Chudinov, apparently a Ukrainian nationalist), and demanded that 75 percent of the academy staff go to Germany.[114] Officials led by City Commissar Rogausch also said that any scientific institute must have practical military significance. Although native city administrators responded that they could maintain the buildings, and that the people were working there for free, the Nazis were not convinced. Most of the scientists, however, apparently continued to show up for work.[115]

Soviet Ukraine's large polytechnical institutes, which were distinct from both the universities and the academy, generally received the same treatment. Initially the Polytechnical Institute in Kiev had two hundred professors, six hundred senior lecturers and assistants, and numerous laboratory workers, all led by Professor Mykola Velychkivsky (who also headed the short-lived Ukrainian National Council and the Academy Institute of Economics, Statistics, and Geography). Before its enforced closure in February 1942, there were no salaries. Early one morning, late in 1941, Germans drove up to the chemical faculty and proceeded to destroy the laboratories. When an assistant protested, one of the vandals grabbed her by the neck and threatened her with a revolver, while shouting that none of the onlookers could ever demand anything from a German officer.[116] In Dnipropetrovsk the Polytechnical Institute functioned for a while as the one place of work for the staffs of the city's seven institutes of higher education and research. Initially about 260 people were employed, including twelve professors and eight lecturers, but their number rapidly declined. Bans on lectures, seminars, and individual tutoring were soon imposed, and the only allowed activity became technical work.[117]

The Nazis considered the Medical Institute in Kiev useful and allowed it to open and accept students early in 1942. Over two thousand enrolled, but in the summer, most of them were sent to work in the countryside. Further, for some unknown reason the Security Police killed the director, Professor Oleksii Lazorenko.[118] A Pedagogical Institute also existed after the Germans ordered a Soviet research institute to merge with a group of university specialists. Its director spent the winter of 1941–1942 in the secretary's room, where burning Marxist-Leninist classics provided warmth. Closure of the institute came in September of 1942; the Germans suddenly arrived and told everyone to clear out within fifteen minutes.[119]

It is not surprising that scholars in the humanities only rarely found employment in their profession. Some prepared commissioned reports, mainly for a task force from the East Ministry (Einsatzstab Reichsleiter Rosenberg). The topics ranged from "Ukraine as Germany's Ancestral Homeland" (by M. Slobodianiuk) to "The Bolshevization of the Humanities of the USSR as Related to the General Development of Soviet Policy" (by K. Shtepa). The historian and short-term mayor Oleksander Ohloblyn wrote "How the Bolsheviks Ruined Ukrainian Historical Science" as well as "The German Influence on Industry in Ukraine."[120]

The Red Cross and Other Aid

Various cities had semilegal Red Cross organizations, which acted independently from each other. Early in October 1941, with ten thousand rubles of seed money donated by the city administration, a semilegal Ukrainian Red Cross began functioning in Kiev.[121] Melnykites convinced the radiologist Fedir Bohatyrchuk to take charge. The staff, mostly women, approached peasants in the region with requests for food donations to be given to prisoners of war and civilians. The number of these envoys quickly surpassed one hundred.

As a result of a visit by the Red Cross to Rivne in December 1941, several trucks with food arrived from Volhynia.[122] The food was distributed in a dining room. Most of the beneficiaries were two hundred scientists, scholars, artists, their families, and elderly people. In addition, 350 food parcels were given out each month as well as thousands of rubles each day. (As with the seed money, the provenance of these funds is unknown.) The Red Cross ran a kindergarten, a children's home, and a sewing workshop for the wives of "repressed" or evacuated men. It also opened public canteens for children.[123]

At this point, City Commissar Rogausch inaugurated an assault on the Red Cross. On December 18, 1941, he ordered all kindergartens and schools closed. Because Kiev's smallest children received meals there, their very survival thus came under threat.[124] Early in February 1942, too, the leaders of the Red Cross were briefly arrested and most of the staff members were dismissed. In their place, Rogausch appointed his own staff, including one Hulianytsky, a lecturer who worked in the city administration and who became head (under a German supervisor) of what was renamed the Ukrainian Mutual Aid Committee and then the Kiev Mutual Aid Committee.[125] Although the activities for POWs had to stop, most of the activities for civilians continued or were revived. The Aid Committee ran a dining room, workshop, children's home, daycare center (which was very important in allowing parents to hold a job), dormitory, clinics and hospitals, and, after some time, reopened about ten children's canteens. These places offered thousands of children for 1.20 karbovantsi a midday soup and 100 grams of bread; a limited number of elderly people also received this aid.[126]

From the fall of 1942, as part of an apparent tendency among civilian German administrators to attach more importance to social affairs, the working conditions of the Kiev Mutual Aid Committee and the committees in other cities began to improve. Employees received some health insurance through small percentages deducted from all salaries. Several Kiev districts freed disabled, old, or poor people from paying the rent, water, and supervisors.[127] The Kiev Mutual Aid Committee—or so it would appear from press reports—came to employ over six hundred people and provided 16,000 meals per day. The city administration was allowed to raise a tax for it and committee chair Mykhailo Nenadkevych and Mayor Forostivsky called for donations.[128] On the eve of the German retreat, in September 1943, the committee, again renamed (into an "All-Ukrainian" organization), reportedly provided 36,000 meals a day.[129]

For the purpose of distributing Soviet-style financial aid, the *pensiia*, the Kiev administration's welfare department had also created the Commission of Ukrainian Civic and Cultural Leaders, which despite its name also helped Russians. The actual amounts of aid, however, were almost always lower than promised and several city districts illegally appropriated them.[130] The commission apparently disregarded a March 1942 order from Rogausch to stop the donations,[131] and scientists in Kiev could receive meals, apparently free of charge, at the House of Scientists in the former building of the Writers' Union. Although early in 1943 an assertive Mayor Forostivsky demanded that House membership should depend in part on the degree to which a person had advanced the Ukrainians as a people, the person he appointed as the new director, a schoolteacher named M. Vovk who also brought food to people's homes, helped non-Ukrainians as well.[132]

It is instructive to compare Kiev with regions that were still under military rule. Before Poltava became part of the Reichskommissariat, its local newspaper created an arts and sciences supplement that through honorariums for articles supported scientists and scholars. The rulers of the Reichskommissariat did not allow such things and thus hit many people hard. Many educated people in Kiev are said to have committed suicide.[133]

City dwellers were lucky if they had a job; it secured their legal residence and provided a meager salary, some food, and a chance to share experiences with others and thus feel some solidarity. Most probably disliked their work; not only could it not, or only barely, make ends meet, it involved various hazards that began with the commute to the workplace, where a German or a native supervisor might abuse or threaten them.

Of course there were major differences among jobs. Those in German offices and homes were relatively well-off: they worked in heated places, had relative job security, and had some power, which opened the way to a trade in "tribute." Workers in the city administrations and in heavy industry, too, were often unemployed on the job, and quite often were under the supervision of prewar bosses and colleagues. Therefore some factories became places where it was easy to eat, steal, and then leave. At industrial sites that the new regime took more seriously, however, particularly in cities like Kryvy Rih and Dnipropetrovsk, conditions were more strict. The worst kind of job was forced labor for temporary tasks such as the construction of bridges.

A growing but still small group of city dwellers ran private or semi-private businesses: these included restaurant owners, artisans, and medical specialists. These people—presumably mostly men—earned more and had more food than before 1941. Some other city dwellers probably also saw improvement: those who had hated the NKVD's pervasive supervision and who now worked in a barely operating factory such as Kiev's Lenin Forge. But if there is such a thing as objective working conditions, it seems fair to say that for most city dwellers they deteriorated.

Particularly bleak was the fate of scholars engaged in those sciences and studies that the Nazis considered useless. These people faced famine. Although there were various social services for them and for other needy people, in essence city dwellers had to cope on their own, or with assistance from relatives and close friends. The kind of public displays of solidarity seen in other countries under Nazi rule, such as wearing a flower, boycotts, and public transport strikes, were not found in the Reichskommissariat Ukraine. This lack of overt solidarity made a strong impression on some. For example, in the fall of 1943 the eastern Ukrainian Ivan Maistrenko arrived in the capital of the Galicia district of the General Government. He noticed how streetcar passengers had a habit of paying money to the driver without asking for or getting tickets. Only when a conductor entered the car did the driver quickly hand them out. While supporting the driver, one of their own, the mostly Polish people of Lviv were boycotting "the system." It amazed the left-wing and patriotic intellectual Maistrenko. He and other "Soviet" Ukrainians, he realized with a pang, inhabited a moral universe that almost precluded such behavior. Soviet citizens would have demanded, loudly, that the driver not live off their backs.[134]

Maistrenko's account is an important reminder that the social disunity in the cities of the Reichskommissariat Ukraine was not only caused by the severity of the Nazi regime. Resisting the Nazi system was indeed dangerous, but the Soviet heritage of mistrust and enforced passivity also played a part in inhibiting solidarity.

7

FAMINE IN KIEV

The Nazis wanted to demolish "Russia's" industry and to depopulate the "Russian" cities. A direct consequence of this desire was a ruthless starvation policy against the capital of Ukraine, Kiev. It achieved significant success. The famine that ensued was less devastating than the other known famines in Nazi Europe—in Athens, from the fall of 1941 to mid-1942 (relieved by Canadian wheat imports); in the western Netherlands, from late 1944 to early 1945; and in the large Jewish ghettoes of east-central Europe, throughout the war. Nor was it as extensive as the famine in the eastern Ukrainian city of Kharkiv under its brief time of German military rule. But the Kiev famine was a major component of everyday life in central Ukraine, inflicting hunger and death and turning people into fierce opponents of the Germans.

"Kiev Must Starve"

Any discussion of this topic must start with Hitler, for much of his casual "table talk" about the "Russian" cities served as a general policy guideline. Hitler first ordered measures specifically against Kiev on August 12, 1941, when Wilhelm Keitel issued from Hitler's headquarters the directive to halt the assault on Kiev because "it is proposed to destroy the city by incendiary bombs and gunfire as soon as the supply positions allow."[1] On August 18, General Franz Halder described Hitler's order with regard to Kiev as a curt "Reduce to rubble." The air force was supposed to do half of the job.[2] In the end Kiev was not destroyed in this way, apparently because of a lack of bombs. Hitler was furious. One year later at the Werewolf, after saying that Petersburg had to be razed to the ground, he recalled how he had been "so enraged back then when the Air Force did not want to let Kiev have it. Sooner or later we must do it after all, for the inhabitants are coming back and want to govern from there."[3]

Because neither Kiev nor any other major "Eastern" city was "razed to the ground" as Hitler intended, starvation of the inhabitants quickly became the default option. Three days before Kiev's capture, on September 16, 1941, Hermann Göring, the Reich minister of economy, held a meeting with officials of the army and the Economy Staff East and with Herbert Backe, the acting minister of food and agriculture (actual minister from May 1942), who in May 1941 had secured support for a scheme to starve millions of city dwellers (see Chapter 2). Göring came out in support of Backe's scheme. The "Gypsy-like population" should not be allowed to "devour" any of the food that the Germans captured. "In the occupied territories, as a matter of principle only those who work for us must be assured of the appropriate food. Even if one wanted to feed all the inhabitants in the newly conquered territory, one would be *unable* to do so." For major cities, it was not necessary to change Hitler's general view that, as Göring put it, "from economic considerations, the occupation of large cities is not desired. It is more economical to close them off."[4]

On October 3, SS chief Heinrich Himmler visited Kiev as part of a city tour in central and southern Ukraine. Probably because the place had been granted Magdeburg rights of commerce for centuries, he considered it German and even called it "Kiroffo."[5] Afterward he went to see Hitler. The record of their conversation over dinner on October 5 does not indicate whether the Babi Yar massacre of the previous week came up, but it does show that Himmler, having seen the poorly dressed Kievans for himself, had internalized the Führer's goal that they should somehow vanish. He had seen many people in the streets and they looked awfully "proletarian." One could "easily do without eighty to ninety percent of them." SS-Obergruppenführer Friedrich Jeckeln's first impression of them was similar: they were "racially very bad." During a visit to Ukraine in the fall of 1941, the leading Nazi Fritz Sauckel heard discussions that closely matched Backe's scheme. "All German offices"—as he put it—expected "at least ten to twenty million of these people" in the region to starve to death during the coming winter.[6] Otto Bräutigam, the deputy head of the East Ministry's Main Political Department, found that "'Kiev must starve' was a saying that our agronomists put forward in cold blood during conferences."[7] These ruthless calculations seem to have complicated the issue of Kiev's status in the Reichskommissariat. As late as October 18, Hitler was still undecided, for in Kiev during the coming winter there "might easily arise food problems and, as a result, disturbances."[8] This was likely the main reason why the provincial town of Rivne, not Kiev, became the capital of the Reichskommissariat.

Most Wehrmacht leaders actively supported the starvation policy, and mentally prepared the rank-and-file by underlining an alleged need to both live off the land and supply food to the Reich, while blaming any future food problems on the former Soviet regime. Army propaganda made fully clear the Nazi view that if locals were allowed to eat this was tantamount to theft. "Each gram of bread or other food that I give to the population in the occupied territories out of good-heartedness, I am withdrawing from the German people and thus my family . . . Thus, the German soldier must stay hard in the face of hungry women and children. If he does not, he endangers the nourishment of our people. The enemy is now experiencing the fate that he had planned for us. But he alone must also answer to the world and history."[9]

The starvation policy assumed concrete shape in regulations. On September 4, 1941, Economy Staff East issued an order regarding food and city dwellers in the "East," and the next day Economy Inspectorate South released it as a top-secret regulation to its economy commands while adding a warning that the "allocation" of food to civilian city dwellers must be "limited to the essentials," payable on close supervision, and directed mainly to those in direct service of the Germans. The maximum rates per food item included a mere 300 grams of bread per person per day.[10] On November 4, Economy Staff East replaced its September order. (As before, people in the countryside, considered self-sufficient, were left out of consideration.)[11] The new guidelines granted that one goal was "to assure the feeding of the population, as far as this is possible without influencing the German interests." But great problems were supposedly unavoidable. After all, the "ruthless plundering and destruction by the Bolsheviks have very severely shaken the economic and trade life in the occupied territories. Need and misery are the unavoidable result for the native population, particularly in the major cities." Propaganda should reiterate that only the Bolsheviks were responsible. Amounts of supplied food should "be kept as low as possible in the first period, to force the population to consume its own hoarded supplies and to prevent any influencing of the needs of the Armed Forces." For now, meat or fat were not to be distributed; turnips, beets, and carrots should replace the prescribed potatoes, and buckwheat and millet the prescribed bread. The planned maximum rates should only be reached "gradually." These caps were very low. In the south, people with "useful work" would never get more per week than 2,000 grams of bread, 2,500 grams of potatoes, 100 grams of meat, and 100 grams of fat, and the directive added that at most 20 percent of the total native population could be eligible for these maximum rates. Hard laborers employed by firms that were in "the German interest" might get a little more (respectively, 2,500, 3,500, 200, and 150 grams); people not engaged in work "worthy of the name" got less (respectively, 1,500, 2,000, nothing, and 70); and children under fourteen years of age and Jews might at best get 750 grams of bread, 1,000 grams of potatoes, and 35 grams of fat. Most importantly, these rates were not targets, but maximum rates that would be acceptable in some *undefined* future. The agency expected a "real emergency situation" to "generally arise only later."

Karl von Roques, the commander of Rear Army Area South to which Kiev belonged until 1942, was born in 1880 and thus older than most Nazis. He seems to have been concerned about the food policy. Shortly after November 4, members of his staff met with representatives of Economy Inspectorate South to insist that "the nourishment of the population must be insured to a certain level, as we must enlist them for work. He who should work for us in industry and commerce should not absolutely starve. This is no humanitarian matter, but an entirely expedient measure in the German interest."[12] Yet the chief of the southern inspectorate, General Hans Stieler von Heydekampf, retorted that he needed to "proceed radically." Only Hitler could reduce the delivery quotas. "It is the population that is going to suffer," he acknowledged. "Those who work will be taken care of—to be sure only with small supplies—but not the families and nonworkers."[13]

There were also other German military who complained about the callousness toward the anticipated starvation of millions. In October, General von Reichenau, as head of the Sixth Army, had secretly banned the provision of any food from field kitchens to the population and prisoners of war. But by 1942, as the commander-in-chief of Army Group South, even this man complained that "the death by starvation or the destruction of millions of Ukrainians plays no role for the German conquerors."[14] Remarkably the sharpest criticism came from Lieutenant General Hans Leykauf, head of the food supply system for the Wehrmacht in the Reichskommissariat. Leykauf distributed in full agreement a November

29, 1941, report by an expert in army service that called the German policy in the Reichskommissariat tantamount to the "extermination" of "Jews, and the population of the large Ukrainian cities, which like Kiev do not receive any food."[15]

But other military leaders again issued supportive statements. At the height of the starvation policy toward the POWs, the new commander of the Eleventh Army, Erich von Manstein, said that food shortages in the Reich made it necessary for his army to largely feed itself and to provide as much food as possible to the Reich. "Especially in the enemy cities a large part of the population will have to go hungry. In spite of this, none of the goods that the fatherland supplies [sic] at the cost of great privation may, out of wrongheaded humanity, be distributed to prisoners and the population, if they are not employed by the German Armed Forces."[16] Göring also kept pushing for starvation. In a meeting at his Reich Aviation Ministry on November 8 with Rosenberg, Koch, and others, he clarified the actions of Economy Staff East. To him "the fate of the large cities, especially Leningrad," was "entirely alien. This war will witness the greatest starvation since the Thirty-Years' War." Any "tendencies for increasing the general standard of living" must be suppressed. City dwellers would receive only "very small amounts of food," and "with regard to large cities (Moscow, Leningrad, Kiev), for the moment nothing can be done. The resulting consequences are severe, but unavoidable."[17] Later that month he told the Italian minister of foreign affairs that "this year between twenty and thirty million persons will die in Russia of hunger. Perhaps it is well that it should be so, for certain nations must be decimated." Thus it became almost inevitable for the Rear Army Area South to pass on, finally on November 15, Economy Staff East's November 4 directive.[18]

Specialists at the Reichskommissariat's central office in Rivne also paid attention to the food supply. In their very first meeting, on October 3, 1941, all agreed that except for (ethnic) Germans, they should not allow any native to consume more than a mere 1,000 grams of bread and 10 to 50 grams of meat per week.[19] Their definitive guidelines in February 1942 regarding the cities closely resembled those of Economy Staff East. They excluded large numbers from the category of those working in "the German interest": those in army institutions, food enterprises (sugar factories, mills, bread factories, slaughterhouses, dairy farms, grain offices, and so on), sawmills, consumer goods factories (leather factories, soap factories, tanneries), and the utilities. Those who remained in that category should never get more per week than 2,000 grams of bread, 2,500 grams of potatoes, 200 grams of meat, and 500 grams of "foodstuffs." The "hardest workers" would never get more than 2,500 grams of bread, 3,500 grams of potatoes, 300 grams of meat, 500 grams of "foodstuffs," and 250 grams of sugar. The "family members" of both categories, "ordinary consumers," and children (there was no more mention of Jews) should never get more each week than 1,500 grams of bread, 2,000 grams of potatoes, and 100 grams of meat (and for now no meat at all). The provision of vegetables should "depend on available stocks." They recommended replacing the bread with inferior crops such as buckwheat and millet, and emphatically banned ration cards, for those would imply that independently of the supply there existed such a thing as a *right* to food.[20] In line with Hitler's hatred of Kiev, these policies were devastating to the capital.

A City of Beggars

Before 1939, the food supply in Kiev was relatively plentiful, but deterioration set in after the Nazi-Soviet pact and especially after June 1941. At that time the city had just under 850,000 inhabitants, about half of whom were Ukrainian, a quarter Jewish, and one in six Russian.[21] Due to the Soviet evacuation of civilians, the mobilization into the Red Army, and the massacre at Babi Yar, however, the population decreased dramatically: the city administration and the German army estimated in October 1941 that only around 400,000 people were living in Kiev.[22]

On September 24, representatives of Economy Inspectorate South in Kiev estimated that people had stored at home eight to fourteen days' worth of food.[23] On September 30, close to the estimated breaking point, the inspectorate callously banned the supply of food to Kiev.[24] Ukrainian emigré memoirs reveal that beginning in October, policemen barred people from entering the city and confiscated food that people attempted to take there. Iaroslav Haivas was a young Melnykite who arrived early in Kiev from Galicia (illegally) and who with his fellow activists appointed people to help avert a famine in the city. These people approached "economic circles, first of all former cooperators," and as a result products started to trickle into the city. Many collective farms gave up products for just a promissary note as payment, he recalls. Then, "when it seemed that things were starting to work, the German military command closed the city and blocked not only cars but also individuals from entering it."[25]

Nina Mykhalevych, another Melnykite, speaks of patrols on bridges that blocked food imports in late 1941. They "confiscated everything" and therefore a woman from Darnytsia who used to bring her milk (for her daughter) had to hide it under a large shawl.[26] The SD was patently incorrect when it reported that Kievans who attempted to buy food in the countryside and slip back into the city with it met few obstacles during that winter.[27]

One large convoy of food did arrive on October 9, 1941: peasants from the Tarashcha region, ninety kilometers to the south, brought 128 carts with forty-five tons of meal, ten thousand eggs, poultry, lard, butter, and apples, all apparently after an appeal by the Ukrainian Red Cross. According to Haivas, the German command let it in on the condition that it would be used for ill people and hospitals.[28] A Kievan close to Kiev's then mayor, Volodymyr Bahazii, has written with admiration how the leader attempted to prevent and alleviate the famine. "The population of Kiev was condemned to forced starvation, for the Germans banned any delivery of food to the stores," but Bahazii protested when, for example, in a suburb "the Gestapo police" took steps to "confiscate or destroy food that, with difficulty, had been obtained in villages for the hospitals, and food that had been delivered in a convoy of peasant carts." When these protests failed, Bahazii apparently ordered the city administration's Supply Department to distribute its stored supplies, and personally delivered food to elderly scholars, scientists, and cultural and civic activists.[29] In December 1941 he mentioned "more frequent" cases of "swelling due to famine" in a letter to City Commissar Muss. After Bahazii's arrest early in 1942, rumors circulated that the Security Police had found large caches of food at his home.[30]

Early in December 1941, Dr. von Franke, a German historian who had arrived in Kiev as part of an organization that looted the libraries (Einsatzstab Reichsleiter Rosenberg), called representatives of the scientific institutes to his office. Von Franke told his guests that "Kiev cannot support its population." All Kievans, he said, including the scientists, should disperse into the countryside. He and his colleagues would be happy to take their scientific books and equipment for safekeeping. The deputy head of the city administration's Culture and Education Department, the Galician Mykola Andrusiak, acknowledged that the Germans were not responsible for feeding the population. But he asked von Franke to at least put an end to the German confiscation of the food imports.

The political officer of the Kiev district, Reinhardt, said angrily that "the Germans haven't taken anything from the Ukrainians" and that only the Führer was in charge of the Ukrainians' fate.[31]

By that time, the staple diet of the Kievan population was bread, sold in quantities well below the official maximum rates. Even people in unoccupied but besieged and famine-struck Leningrad received more. (The daily amount of bread there ranged from 125 grams in late 1941 to 400 grams in the middle of 1942.)[32] In Kiev, the permitted rate per person, as set by the city commissar, at first was nothing. On October 10, the *weekly* rate for nonworkers became 200 grams. Increases came very slowly: to 400 grams in December; to 550 (still less than half a loaf) early the next year; to 700 in May 1942; and finally a major increase, to 1,500 grams a week—the Reichskommissariat's maximum rate for city dwellers—in August 1942. Kievans with jobs received small amounts of flour, barley, and vegetables and were authorized to buy or receive an extra loaf once or twice a month.[33]

Bread was sold on the basis of primitive bread cards, provided monthly to those on lists of names compiled by local inspectors.[34] Each bread store was supposed to serve about eleven streets, from six o'clock in the morning. In 1941, Halyna Lashchenko, another Melnykite who arrived in Kiev from the "west," often got up at five and hurried to the store, which was not far away. Even so she always found a line and sometimes hours later she still had to leave empty-handed. Anatolii Kuznetsov as a young boy used to go to the store. The prize for fighting a crowd of about two thousand people was the amount purchased with his family's four bread cards—half a loaf.[35]

The so-called bread was a surrogate made of millet. Adults called it a "brick" or, in part because of its yellow shine, "emery." Clay-like at first, the millet bread quickly fell apart in hard crumbs, and additives such as lupine, barley, and chestnut gave it a bitter taste. A lot of people at first became ill from it, but hungry children eagerly ate their "golden bread." Later the "bread" mostly consisted of grouts and husks.[36] Less frequently on the average menu were potatoes. Many Kievans bought just potato peels, put them through a meat mincer, and fried them with flour into little pancakes, or boiled them first and then minced them along with flour and vinegar. Children also found these pancakes "unbelievably nice."[37] The local newspaper, *Nove ukraïns'ke slovo*, wrote several times about the alleged benefits of chestnuts and printed regulations from the city administration about their distribution in stores in quantities of 500 grams per person per week. Kuznetsov recalls eating nothing but chestnuts for days on end.[38]

Soon large numbers of Kievans faced the prospect of death by starvation. Already on October 9, 1941, when some canteens finally reopened and sold food for rubles, long lines appeared there and people pushed and shoved at the entrance.[39] Iryna Khoroshunova wrote in her diary on October 22: "There is no bread. Many are already starting to swell up. Olia is starving, she has swollen up and has a temperature of 39.3 degrees. She will die soon. What will come of her child? He is also hungry." And the next day: "Liubov Vasilevna's legs have swollen—they cannot go any longer." According to some memoirs by Kievans, the resulting mortality was "immense."[40] Particularly vulnerable were members of the intelligentsia and the sick and elderly, for few of these people had looted during or after the change of regimes. According to one source, elderly people died "by the hundreds."[41] In a home for the disabled on the outskirts of the city, there were many days when five people died. The staff buried them in one mass grave.[42] A former official of the Kiev Communist party committee covertly traveled to Kiev in November 1941. Even in the middle of the day, he later reported, the city was "dead": "Besides Germans and policemen, one rarely met a passerby in the street. Those whom I happened to see were all mainly disabled old men and women. Emaciated or swollen from hunger, they roam the streets and walk from house to house in search of charity. Kiev has become a city of beggars . . . Walking on Kirov Street, I saw worn and dirty men, women, and children. They begged anyone getting closer to them for charity, but did not receive it. There I also came across people who were lying and sitting; they were so emaciated that they were unable to move."[43] Kirov Street (today's Mykhailo Hrushevsky Street) had been renamed Dr. Todt Street in honor of Germany's main roadbuilder; ironically, "Todt" in German means death.[44] Kuznetsov in December 1941 saw much the same:

> I hopped off [the streetcar] in the Podil and walked down the Andriïvsky Uzviz [Andrew's Hill], which was lined with beggars all the way. Some of them were whining and begging openly for money, others exposed their amputated limbs in silence. There were other, quiet, intelligent-looking elderly men and women, some with spectacles and pince-nez, standing there;

they were professors and teachers of various kinds, like our math teacher who had died. In the case of some of them who sat there you couldn't tell whether they were alive or dead. There had always been plenty of beggars about even before the war, but now there were so many it was simply frightful. They wandered all over the place, knocking on people's doors, some of them people who had lost their homes through fire, some with babies, some of them on the run, and some swollen with hunger. It was bitterly cold and the people walked down the streets with grim expressions on their faces, hunching themselves up from the wind, worried, in ragged clothes, in all sorts of strange footwear and threadbare coats. It was indeed a city of beggars.[45]

"Today is Boxing Day," the unemployed teacher L. Nartova wrote in her diary at the end of 1941. "The Germans are celebrating. They all walk full and content, all have lights in Christmas trees. But we all move about like shadows, there is total famine. People are buying food by the cup and boil a watery soup, which they eat without bread, because bread is given out only two times per week, 200 grams. And this diet is the best-case scenario. Those who have things exchange them in the countryside, but those who have nothing swell up from hunger, they are already dying. Many people have typhus."[46]

Various Germans displayed in their reports an awareness of the situation and even recognized its premeditated nature. The SD, while implicitly discounting Nazi shootings, reported an increase in mortality in the city from 58 in October 1941 to 773 in January 1942 and 1,120 in February 1942.[47] In a report about the second half of October 1941, Economy Staff East reported that since its capture, Kiev "officially has not received any grain from the outside." If true, all of the bread supplies had come in from private traders and the auxiliary city authorities. Surprisingly, the staff warned late in November that the "food situation" in Kiev and in the other cities of Ukraine and Belarus (Army Groups South and Center) was "cause for serious concern."[48] In February 1942, the supervisor of the Southern armament commands even argued that "something must be done for the maintenance of the civilian population, as it cannot go on in the present form if one does not want to lose all labor forces and achievements."[49]

But as before such calls went unheeded. The SD somewhat later reported from Kiev "a famine to which no end is in sight," but it falsely blamed logistical problems.[50] The starvation policy remained in place, and death from famine continued to threaten most Kievans. Their desperation was apparent on Hitler's birthday in April 1942. On that occasion, each bread card for once became worth 500 grams of real wheat flour. Kuznetsov showed up early in the morning and found about fifteen hundred others who were unruly even though it was well before opening time. "Near the doors people were already fighting, and a sweating, red-faced policeman barely contained the crowd." Order broke down completely around four in the afternoon when supplies started running out.[51]

The Markets

Commission stores helped out somewhat, as did the special stores of a consumer cooperative—the successor to the Soviet closed distribution centers—which sold bread, eggs, and other food below the usual price and with further reduction to members.[52] Most important for survival, however, were the markets. Since the early 1930s, Soviet markets had turned into virtual havens for private trade. Here peasants sold produce (legally, if they did not use an intermediary), and "resellers" and "speculators" sold goods on the sly.[53] Almost immediately after the Germans arrived in Kiev, livelier-than-ever trade began. Every day was market day, as countless peasants took food on their carts to the cities. As noted, in September 1941 Economy Inspectorate South ordered the economy commands to limit the food supply in cities to "the essentials" and issued a ban on food imports to Kiev. In addition, the commands were to generally allow only two market days per week.[54]

In Kiev there were the Bessarabian Covered Market at the end of the burned-out Khreshchatyk, the Hay or Grain Market in the Podil district, and the Galician Market at the western head of Shevchenko Boulevard, the main site and still known by its prewar name as the Iev-Baz, or Jewish Market. Initially events here were subdued, because people were hesitant to talk to strangers and were forbidden to stand together in groups of more than three.[55] On sale, among other things, were bread, home brewed vodka, lard, eggs, pastry, oil, garlic, matches, candles, cigarettes, clothes, dishes, books, and sometimes bread, dried carp, soap, and strawberries. Fast-food "gluttony stalls" with hot soup and pea pierogies were a wartime novelty. German, Hungarian, and other soldiers as well as native

12. The Galician Market (formerly the Jewish Market) in Kiev, September 1942. (Nederlands Instituut voor Oorlogsdocumentatie, 16709–1.)

policemen frequented the markets, paying a price that seemed right to them or simply confiscating what they desired; they also sold things themselves.[56] From 1942, some of the food (lard, sugar, flour, and so on) on sale originated from Germans who had collected it in distant regions and sold it to native traders, who were generally called speculators.[57] The nearby streets also teemed with business. Peasants sold pasties; teenagers hawked cigarettes (obtained from soldiers), matches, seeds, saccharine, sweets, and water; and soldiers sold cigarettes, flint for cigarette lighters, bread, liquor, and saccharine.[58]

The markets also existed throughout most of 1942, despite the new danger of roundups for forced labor in Germany. The civilian German authorities persistently attempted to control the trade by imposing price ceilings (amounting to significant price decreases), warning of confiscation, and banning barter. Following such decrees, the trade shifted to side streets and homes while the markets virtually disappeared—to reappear later, with even higher prices, after the authorities had removed the price ceilings.[59] Harassment was particularly intense during visits by high-ranking officials, such as that by Reich Minister Rosenberg in June 1942: then police detachments closed the sites completely.[60]

For a long time, the Soviet ruble remained legal tender, with a value of one reichsmark. The salespeople at first preferred marks, which they hoarded, and Reich credit certificates, but then refused money altogether and insisted on barter, despite bans on the practice.[61] By the end of October 1941, food was hard to get for money. Instead, for example, a Kievan could acquire 10 kilograms of potatoes for a padlock or some shoe polish; twice as many potatoes for a piece of linen (0.70 x 2.00 cm.); and about 32 kilograms of millet or barley flour for a pair of used shoes.[62] Peasants who bartered tended to demand virtually new things, and at the end of the bargain often lowered their own payment. This angered the city dwellers, some of whom thought that this was the peasants' revenge for the Great Famine of 1933.[63]

Food prices in the city rose steadily. Put another way, the ruble continued to lose value. A kilogram of bread that cost 45 rubles late in January 1942 cost 160 rubles early in May. Early in July, there came an announcement that from the sixth through the twenty-fifth of that month, there would be a currency change because "the Bolsheviks" supposedly were flooding the area with rubles.[64] Bills of five or ten rubles had to be exchanged for the equal number in a new karbovanets, and for higher ruble bills there would be only receipts.[65] People with many rubles proved unable to exchange all of them, and those who had accumulated the money in the Soviet period, especially Communist party members, now lost most of it. Some workers maliciously enjoyed this. But nobody trusted the measure and many decided not to hand in any large bills.[66]

Kievans frequently visited the countryside, to dig up potatoes, to barter, beg, or simply steal. They also frequented small-town markets, in particular the one in Bila Tserkva.[67] Although train travel to such towns was banned and those found at the station without a special permit could be arrested or, if found on the platform or track, shot on sight (as trilingual announcements warned), people still packed passenger and cargo trains. Vasyl Iablonsky, a factory worker born in 1908, recalled several years later, "You don't scare people like us. We hopped on and off we went. What's the difference how you're done for, you gotta eat." The Gendarmerie in a town once robbed him and told him to go home.[68] While returning to Kiev, Kievans used unofficial paths and brought along vodka to bribe their way through if caught. Smuggling tricks included pouring milk on top of the butter in a jar and hiding oil in a footwarmer on the body.[69]

The Noose Tightens

In June 1942, the SD signaled that Kievans had no means to live because their wages were miserable, certainly compared to the food prices, and because the Germans were taking away grain. Should nothing be done, then during the winter to come there would be a "famine."[70] Nevertheless, on July 15, at the height of the vicious "threshing and confiscation action" in the countryside, there came two decrees, one against "speculators" and one for a "just distribution of produce among those who work and their families," that threatened the lives of more Kievans than ever.[71] General Commissar Magunia and City Commissar SA Major Berndt (who had succeeded Rogausch) issued them, apparently after prompting from Rivne. Lev Dudin of Kiev's Russian-language newspaper *Poslednie novosti* was present at a meeting that summer during which Berndt apparently informed the city officials that the Reichskommissariat was demanding the immediate closure of the markets and a total ban on the transport of produce into the city by private persons. He also said that he was going to introduce food ration cards. If Dudin is to be believed, the Ukrainians persuaded Berndt not to implement these orders because the result would be famine, but one month later (probably in July), he told them that the orders had to be carried out.[72] Possibly Rosenberg had swayed him: Rosenberg had told a meeting of civilian officials and policemen at 11 Bankova Street (Magunia's office) in June to increase the exports of food and laborers and to lay the groundwork for the German colonization of Ukraine after the war.[73]

The July decrees banned unsupervised food trade at Kiev's markets and prescribed controls that led to roadblocks manned by the Schuma in the outer districts. A person checked by the Schuma might transport a standard amount—one chicken or other bird, ten eggs, 1 liter of milk, 10 kilograms of potatoes, one kilogram of bread, and one basket of vegetables. Anything more the Schuma would confiscate and pass on to the German authorities. And this was while Berndt's ration cards were weeks away from reality.[74]

Diaries by locals inform us that in the months preceding the decrees, Schuma and Germans were confiscating "everything but potatoes" and

13. At the height of the Nazi campaign to starve Kiev, an auxiliary policeman armed with a rifle stops women who wish to go there. Summer of 1942. (Photograph possibly by Scherer. Bundesarchiv, Bild 146/91/52/35.)

were "cruel when someone had been able to barter fat."[75] The July decrees worsened this situation. Along the Dymer highway leading to Kiev, Kuznetsov saw Schuma confiscate all the food that people carried, not just the standard amount, with a cynical "Do pobachennia" (See you later).[76] He and his grandfather once walked for half a day to Pushcha-Vodytsia, north of the city. On the way, distraught people coming from the opposite direction said that near the children's tuberculosis sanitarium they had been robbed of all their food. Indeed, there they saw three policemen and a pile of bags and cans. "All the roads to Kiev were blocked, it was sheer legalized robbery." Still not losing hope, he and his grandpa moved on, and obtained with some effort two bags of corn, beans, and flour. They got a ride home from a German. With only a three-minute walk left in their journey,

> We no longer had any feeling in our feet or shoulders, and we staggered along like long-distance runners at the finishing line. At that point we were stopped by two policemen. "Been carrying it far?" asked one of them ironically. We stood there in silence, because it was just unbelievable: it just couldn't happen like that. "Put it down," said the other one and proceeded briskly to help Grandpa remove his sack. "Listen, friends," said Grandpa, quite dumbfounded, in a whisper. "Listen . . ."
>
> "On your way, now, on your way," said the first policeman. "But friends, listen . . ." My grandfather was ready to fall on his knees. The police paid no attention to him, but simply took our sacks and put them down by the post where there were several others lying already. They appeared to have set up a new checkpoint here, on the approach to the market. I dragged Grandpa along by the sleeve, because he was quite beside himself and couldn't believe it had happened.[77]

Many who were robbed protested loudly or even hurled insults at the policemen. Complaining about this in *Nove ukraïns'ke slovo*, Kiev's Protective Police claimed that it was carrying out orders and dismissed the "malicious slander" that it was retaining the confiscated food for itself.[78]

Schuma also confiscated food at the outskirts of other cities and towns, with or without instructions to do so.[79] But the markets there continued to have a reasonable supply and people generally also could fall back on a garden. Many Kievans had no garden and Kiev's markets emptied dramatically. Before July 15, in the early mornings it had been possible to obtain banned goods on the sly from peasants or local traders. Now Kievans became totally dependent on the traders, for peasants stopped coming to town.[80]

The Security Police and the SD never liked the orders. Within weeks, an internal memorandum argued that "the closing off of the city has no essential economic benefits. Apart from the seizure of grain, which is presently necessary for specific reasons, one cannot see what use can be derived from the confiscation of fresh milk, vegetables, and fruit."[81] In any case, informants made it known that the closure was not total. One reason was the sheer size of Kiev and the Dnieper shore; another was the behavior of the native policemen: "While in some cases they are much too severe, in others they are said to be abstaining from regular control out of carelessness. Moreover, they are allegedly participating in a great many shady deals." In other words, they could be bribed. Third, the population had seen something like this before: "Already in Soviet times, according to sources, such closures were carried out. Then, however, it was done with a far greater deployment of controlling organs. Nevertheless, they were never able to obtain a full closure. Now the population has experience in evading such measures." This was a reference to Soviet measures taken during the Great Famine to prevent the starving peasants from entering the cities. The "speculators" were particularly experienced and had indeed become "the primary beneficiaries" of the July orders, for they simply stopped selling for a while and then resumed with a vengeance.[82] The civilian Nazi authorities realized that the decrees were failing to stop all food imports; they blamed an alleged lack of policemen. But they never went as far as some Soviet authorities during the war, who simply arrested salespeople and confiscated everything they were selling.[83]

Rationing finally came to Kiev in August. Using the rates that Rivne had set as early as February 1942, the new measure raised the weekly amount of bread sold per person more than twofold, to 1,500 grams per week. Yet fewer people than before were eligible: the weakest group could only get bread, and "family members" of the "useful" workers now could only be spouses or children younger than fourteen. The second-best-fed group had to work "in the German interest" full-time and the best-fed workers were only those who did heavy labor in weapon factories, railway factories, mines, or stone quarries. In general, persons at rest need 2,000 calories per day and hard laborers require 4,500 calories. Yet the daily supply in Kiev in September 1942 ranged from 467 calories to 2,074 calories.[84] Periods when trade in Kiev was left alone also continued to alternate with days when it was thwarted. On December 1, 1942, for example, the SD reported a "ban on trade in foodstuffs at the open markets."[85]

Morals and Attitudes

Apart from barter and smuggling, there were also less socially accepted and criminal ways in which Kievans obtained something to eat. A female student at the Medical Institute, for example, caught and ate cats.[86] And during the first days of 1943, there were rumors about cannibalism. Some said that a gang had been uncovered in the Podil that murdered people and sold their flesh. Other rumors spoke of one man who had been selling sausages for a year and had been arrested because somebody found a piece of a finger in a sausage, or because his neighbor found human body parts in his house.[87] The official press said there had been just one man, in his early fifties, who had eaten at least one sixteen-year-old girl. This Mr. Korniienko was publicly hanged on January 27 in the city center.[88]

Many Kievans survived by stealing (for lack of a neutral term) both on and off the job. It was dangerous. Vasyl Iablonsky and a friend once were caught taking salt from a train wagon, beaten up, and thrown into jail. The next day, his family came to the prison. One German guard spoke of sending them to the camps, but another, elderly German guard let the prisoners go. Homeless children often robbed other children. And a group of older teenagers got hold of hospital bedsheets by pulling them from under the patients and escaping through the window. This was while the Security Police in all of Ukraine, in little more than the first three months of 1942 alone, executed 1,009 "plunderers," or on average eleven people every day.[89]

Murder accompanied many thefts. During the month of February 1942, the Security Police heard about at least one murder in Kiev per day, and later even two or three murders per day became common. A contributing factor was that Nazis rarely investigated the killings if no German was involved.[90] General Commissar Magunia ascribed most of the crime by natives in the Kiev general district to "the poverty that is still prevalent at the moment. Remarkably great is the number of killings of children by mothers, as well as the ever-increasing number of petty and greater thefts among Ukrainians. If possible, the public prosecutor passes these cases on to the criminal jurors for further processing. Not inconsiderable is the number of serious bloody deeds among Ukrainians (murder, manslaughter, wounding causing death)."[91]

Women had two extra options to diminish the specter of death from famine (and of possible deportation to Germany). Kiev had not only prison brothels, but also secret brothels and numerous other professional prostitutes.[92] Much more common was the acquisition of a German or Hungarian boyfriend. "Often native women [in the cities] try to establish relations with Germans or allies, in order to obtain some kind of food," the SD reported.[93] Many sources—all men—claim that this was widespread in Kiev from the very beginning. Once Dudin, who was a Russian nationalist, overheard how a young woman in the street was trying to convince a German officer, who was completely unknown to her, to come to her place for some vodka or tea. The man remained silent. Then she asked, "Tell me, is it true that the German soldiers rape women?" The German smiled, saying, "As you see, it's the exact opposite."[94]

The phenomenon also existed in the other cities. German military and administrative personnel were officially not allowed to have "any relationship with the local population," with the argument that women and girls had been found to work for Soviet "gangs."[95] Clearly many ignored the ban. In 1941 a German soldier and devout Christian in Zaporizhzhia often saw German soldiers and local girls together.[96] Ulas Samchuk, a writer, journalist, and Ukrainian nationalist from western Volhynia, visited Poltava in August 1942, just before its incorporation into the Reichskommissariat. On the holiday of Spas, or Thanksgiving, he saw many young girls in the sunny street, walking "in pairs and groups, sometimes hand-in-hand with boys, sometimes with [German] soldiers. . . . They talk about dancing, courtship, and about the Germans in the sense of soldiers." Here Germans were "by no means shunned."[97] A German report from this region states likewise that German railroad employees were rarely seen in public without female company. Girls in small towns also seem to have had German boyfriends. German officials estimated during the war that Germans in the Reichskommissariat fathered ten thousand children with local women.[98]

Thus, Kiev's artificial famine was not the only force driving German-native relationships. Dudin cites as contributing factors the shortage of native men and simple curiosity. In Kirovohrad, where according to a Ukrainian it was "not shameful for a girl to have a German admirer," "there were girls and young women who said frankly that they preferred the Germans to our boys, for ours were employed in dirty work."[99] Incidentally, there is no evidence to suggest that relationships between native women and Germans were more common in Ukraine than elsewhere in Nazi-ruled Europe.

It took the German defeat at Stalingrad to change this state of affairs. In Vinnytsia in the middle of 1943, Germans apparently complained that the local women were much more aloof than those in other countries, and there were many Russian-language rhymes (chastushki) with texts such as: "Don't yell at me mother / For bombing Kiev flat / My wife was sleeping with a German / I merely woke her up."[100] Well before then, many natives seem to have believed that most young women who had relatively good jobs, such as interpreting and translating, were having sexual relations with a German—in short, that they were "German whores"—shliukh-doiche.[101] Men and women alike tended to despise these German-employed women, convinced that they were incompetent or were abusing their alleged power.[102]

How did the people of Kiev interpret the famine? During most of 1941, the SD found that they tended to blame the "speculators" and to wonder why so little action was under way to curb prices and import food.[103] In December 1941, the SD reported that the city population was disappointed, primarily because of the deteriorating economic situation, and dismayed by a rumor that marriages with Germans were not allowed. Kievans also wondered whether their treatment as an inferior people was a passing or permanent phenomenon.[104] By the beginning of 1942, however, the great majority had seen the light. "Again a ban on barter trade at the markets," the teacher L. Nartova wrote in her diary in April 1942. "What can one do, how to live? They probably want to give us a slow death. Obviously it is inconvenient to shoot everybody."[105] Iryna Khoroshunova found that it was "as if everything is being done to let the population perish sooner." Others now believed that the famine was intended to force them to go to Germany as laborers. The writer Arkadii Liubchenko had been unusually pro-German, but he found in the summer of 1942, to his own surprise, that the famine in Kiev "borders on indifference and . . . criminality."[106]

In the fall of 1942, the conversations of people in Kiev (and the rest of the Reichskommissariat) centered around the famine and the deporta-tions. Both Nartova and the SD in September and October 1942 picked up comments in lines and elsewhere such as "First they finished off the Yids, but they scoff at us for a whole year, they exterminate us every day by the dozens, they're destroying us in a slow death"; "We're supposed to die of starvation, to make place for the Germans"; and "It's better to re-volt than to starve slowly."[107] Meanwhile, some small children referred to the famine as "him," a bony, yellow, and terrifying old man with a cane and bag who took people away.[108]

The anger also came out in stares at the German men and women, who clearly were living better lives. One day in October 1942, near a German-only store on the corner of Fundukliïvka and Nesterivska streets, Germans were pushing a large cart with bread. Liubchenko wrote in his diary:

> The smell is all over the street. Passersby stop, and so do I. There are far more of us, it is a large crowd already. One would think that something special has happened here: somebody has been arrested, somebody is fighting, there has been an accident . . . No! This huge crowd is eagerly drinking the smell of fresh white bread, this crowd is hungry and emaciated. It stands si-lently and is looking gloomily. The Germans carry the bread and glance at the crowd, with suspicion and somewhat hur-riedly, like thieves. But the crowd keeps getting bigger and stands gloomily. Behind this reticence is a boiling, deep rage and fury. These people understand each other without words. Any minute, it seems, they will lash out and seize that bread, smash the cart, and thrash the store.[109]

The Final Year

On February 2, 1943, the Germans announced their defeat at Stalingrad and the food prices in Kiev soared. Three weeks later, market bread was ten times more expensive and milk five times. The salespeople declined the karbovanets and openly demanded rubles.[110] The inflation also came about because refugees from the Left Bank brought many rubles with them and because Germans for the first time started buying bread at the markets.[111] Magunia, at the urging of the Security Police, the city commissar, and the local military, apparently lifted the July 1942 decrees.[112] A Ukrainian refugee who arrived in Kiev at that time found that the only food on sale in stores was millet, millet bread, and sugar, but that the markets were lively and the prices fluctuating, if generally high. Women made buns, pierogies, potato pancakes, fritters, pastry, and ice cream, and they rarely sold these things for less than 10 rubles each. "Still others took kerchiefs, dresses, underwear, trousers, etc.—hastily sewn from painted fabrics—to the market; their little tables were the prototype of clothes stores." The streets were full of people who sold "cigarettes and matches, fruit and vegetables, homemade sweets, and certain household commodities and toys." There were still many hungry people. This witness saw, besides young people whom he considered healthy but unwilling to work, "a large number of beggars, among whom a large percentage were the so-called intelligentsia, or, in the old terminology, the 'noble' people." They asked for charity—a pickle, a cucumber, or some money—"without any shame . . . Many were sick and emaciated. Their 'requests' saved them from death by starvation."[113]

Lively as Kiev's markets had become, they remained under threat. Sometimes the German authorities, for some reason, again banned them or conducted roundups and searches there, from which some who were captured apparently bribed themselves out.[114] And until the very end, the sites continued to differ from those elsewhere in the Reichskommissariat. The markets in other locations were much more extensive operations where Germans personally bartered household commodities and clothes from Germany for eggs, butter, meat, liquor, and furs. Germans leaving or returning from holidays in the Reich transported the items or the food themselves or sent them by mail, and high-ranking German officials bribed train employees and used entire wagons for the transport of items to and from Germany. As a German report put it, Ukraine had become "the flea market of the Reich."[115]

We have some detailed information about one of those cities in the summer and fall of 1943. In Vinnytsia, peasants were allowed to bring produce for sale via carts. After bribing the local German in charge, they even sold wheat bread, while peasant women conducted a brisk trade in home brew. Refugees from Kiev, as one recalls, were overwhelmed by the "dozens of carts with quacking ducks and bristled-up hens, the sieves of eggs, fatty cottage cheese, mat lumps of lard, and magnificent onion wreaths; the long stands with freshly baked, 'real' bread, so unlike the Kievan mixture; the rows and rows of tall pitchers with fermented baked milk, mixed with tasty rosy crusts; and everywhere—on rows, on shawls on the ground, in buckets, baskets, and boxes—apples, as far as the eye could see."[116] Even roundups for forced labor in Germany no longer took place here. German soldiers paid with things like mirrors, nails, and needles. To be sure, even here prices were beyond the reach of most, and every day there were rows of hungry people, including peasants, in front of the district commissar's office who sought permission slips to buy food in the stores.[117]

On April 1, 1942, well after the first winter of famine, Kiev officially had about 352,000 inhabitants. In the middle of 1943—more than four months before the end of German rule—the city officially had about 295,600.[118] Death by starvation was not the only reason for the rapid decline in population: deportation to Germany and Nazi shootings also played their part. Nevertheless, the starvation policy was an important factor, and it much resembled the musings of Hitler and Erich Koch in 1941 about depopulating the city.

The famine was artificial and could have been avoided. Peasants were eager to visit the city to barter with the proceeds of their rich harvest, but police cordons that from July 1942 took "surplus" food—and that actually confiscated everything unless they received a large bribe—blocked them and those Kievans who ventured into the countryside. Although the blockade was not total, it took many lives. The situation was a reversal of that which had existed in 1933. In that tragic year, starving peasants had tried to enter Kiev to get some food and were arrested in and near the city. Now it was the peasants who were "privileged." The tragedy in the early 1940s caused resentment among some city dwellers who blamed the high cost of barter at the markets and in the countryside on peasants' desire to avenge their earlier suffering. Eventually, however, everyone realized who the real culprits were. Indeed, the famine policy created not only casualties, it also bred a fierce hatred of the Germans as a people. When on November 5 and 6, 1943, the Red Army pushed the Wehrmacht and the Nazis out of Kiev, the people of the capital assumed with good reason that their living conditions could only improve.

8

POPULAR CULTURE

When the writer Hryhorii Kostiuk arrived in Lviv in the fall of 1943, he found the cultural atmosphere in the Galician city very different from the one he had just left in his native Dnieper Ukraine. Lviv seemed "a real Ukrainian city" where Ukrainians controlled a publishing house, a well-funded literature and arts club, cooperatives, and trade organizations. Moreover, "all of this was infused with a strong Ukrainian patriotism that was devoid of servility or time serving. Impossible, of course, were themes openly related to anti-German resistance or anything like it—in those circumstances, that would have been foolish. But all activities had a conscious national thrust, and that in itself meant a lot. To me, after Kiev with its unenlightened atmosphere and Gestapo terror, this was a totally different and unexpected world."[1]

Indeed, in cultural affairs the Reichskommisariat Ukraine and the General Government were worlds apart. Whereas Hans Frank's domain had a distinct Ukrainian cultural scene, Erich Koch and his associates consistently opposed any vibrant cultural life for the native population. It was the Führer's wish. In speeches to fellow Nazis, Koch called the Ukrainians inferior. "As for culture," he told Nazis in Rivne in August 1942, just after a visit to Hitler's headquarters, "we have given [sic] the Ukrainians both churches. Further cultural work is out of the question."[2] Far from an empty boast, it was an accurate description of the general line of the Nazi German administration. In the Reichskommissariat, cultural activities were not impossible, but their scope was very small. It was also a very different situation from the prewar Soviet Union, when many writers, artists, and scholars had received material support from elite patrons.[3] Most importantly, Soviet Ukrainian culture had implied that people had a right to cultural experiences and might be edified by them. The official culture of the Reichskommissariat promoted a completely opposite policy.

Political Gatherings and Radio Broadcasts

For a long time, the natives who fell under Nazi rule experienced only two kinds of oral propagandists: Ukrainians of the army's Propaganda Department Ukraine, who handed out cigarettes and tobacco after movie showings and then talked about Germany according to approved texts,[4] and Ukrainians who made "tours" of Germany and on their return told gatherings that they liked what they had seen and that the Ukrainian laborers there were doing well.[5]

In western Volhynia there were large public burials of those whom the NKVD had killed during its retreat, and villages and towns created large symbolic grave mounds with a cross and texts like "To the Memory of Those Who Fell for the Freedom of Ukraine."[6] Few such ceremonies and sites are known east of the pre-1939 Soviet border. Inhabitants of the village of Medvyn south of Kiev held one: a requiem for the Ukrainians who died in 1920 in an "uprising."[7] It did seem at first that the deeds of the NKVD could be publicly remembered even after the Germans came. Soon after its arrival in Vinnytsia, a task force of the Security Police forced Jews to dig up dozens of bodies in the backyard of the NKVD building and organized an selective autopsy and identification. Thousands came to the mass funeral that followed. When an SS man started a conversation there, "hundreds" of relatives of the arrested gathered around to talk.[8] One month later, another mass grave was found in the yard. From August 15, the bodies of eighty-three men and thirteen women were reburied. But when yet another grave was found days later, the field command barred further activities, citing "the irresponsible behavior of the militia and the population" near the sites. The Vinnytsia graves became an allowed topic again only in 1943.[9] Likewise, when Kiev's auxiliary administration asked for publicity about the NKVD mass graves seven kilometers east of the city, near the hamlet of Bykivnia, the Security Police refused, disallowed memorial objects, and placed a guard to keep people away.[10]

Commemorations or celebrations of any kind in the cities remained rare. On the first anniversary of Kiev's "liberation," there were some concerts and newspaper articles, but no public speeches. The main events of this kind in the cities were May Day and, in March 1942 and March 1943, the birthday of the national bard, Taras Shevchenko.[11] Poltavans felt the transition to civilian Nazi rule strongly when, in September 1942, they organized a requiem at the grave of the father of modern Ukrainian litera-

14. Public meeting to mark the second anniversary of the "liberation" of the town of Vasylkiv, west of Kiev, August 20, 1943. Assisted by an interpreter, a German addresses Nazis (far left), choir singers, local policemen, and others. (© Bildarchiv Preußischer Kulturbesitz, Berlin 2002. B4380/02.)

ture, Ivan Kotliarevsky. People assembled by the thousands under the direction of Autocephalous Bishop Sylvestr (Haievsky), only to be informed just minutes before the start that a ban had been issued. And some Kievans commemorated the writer Lesia Ukraïnka or assembled in November 1942 through word of mouth in the cold and dark House of Scientists (where lectures on topics in the humanities, linguistics, and social sciences were allowed) to pay tribute to Ukraine's foremost historian and first president, Mykhailo Hrushevsky.[12]

One remarkable gathering in Kiev did occur, as a result of a Soviet air raid. Starting the evening of May 10, 1943, Soviet airplanes assisted by bright lamps on parachutes bombarded bridges, factories, and hospitals for three hours. They inadvertently killed at least thirty-three Kievans, and the German authorities eagerly exploited this. On May 15, a mass burial procession for the non-German casualties assembled in front of the university. In addressing the crowd, Mayor Forostivsky probably spoke along the lines of an article that he had published the day before: seeing the dead children, "we recognize the face of Jewry [*morda iudeistva*] that hates us Ukrainians so much." Bishop Nikanor (Abramovych) of the Autocephalous church spoke, a church choir sang, and clergy directed the procession to St. Sophia Square, where Autonomous clergy led by Bishop Panteleimon (Rudyk) took over and conducted the burials in a common grave at the Lukianivka Cemetery.[13]

In all, the number of political lectures, commemorations, and other meetings did not satisfy the demand. Soviet citizens had grown accustomed to such gatherings, where attendance was mandatory. Although the events often were boring, the people still felt that they kept the public up to date, created some solidarity, and gave them the sense of being taken seriously. (Some villagers indeed continued the Soviet tradition on their own, spending winter evenings at the elder's office for talks and collective readings of the newspaper.)[14] The almost total absence of German-sponsored equivalents to the countless Soviet meetings had a big effect and not one favorable to the Germans.[15]

Since 1945, psychologists have generally accepted that propaganda meetings can significantly influence both the audience and the speakers themselves; the Nazis of the Reichskommissariat Ukraine did not reap any such benefits.[16] The number of official celebrations and propaganda meetings increased only after the Battle of Stalingrad. Then also there were speeches by associates of the captured Red Army general Vlasov and his Russian Liberation Movement, by Kharkiv's former mayor, and by commissars of districts or the general district.[17]

Radio broadcasts were equally neglected. The wire radio (also broadcast over the public loudspeakers) had very little spoken Ukrainian: the Wehrmacht Command bulletin; a twice-weekly, ten-minute "Look at the Future"; and occasional talks about agriculture. Otherwise the radio station transmitted German texts read aloud and light dance music. Elaborate discussion of anything—whether Soviet history, Jews, living conditions under German rule, or the state of affairs on the Soviet side of the front—was completely absent until 1943.[18]

Reading and Writing

Had the Nazis been as interested in shaping popular opinion in Ukraine as their Soviet predecessors, they would also have used the written word more carefully. It would have been easy to create or sanction circumstances where large numbers of natives would prepare, or simply sign, written statements of belief in the new German order, and thereby create favorable conditions for subtle changes of opinions.[19] But the Nazis just were not interested: they wanted the locals to work, not think.

As for books, the German authorities tried to keep their number as small as possible, and they succeeded. Among the few published books were a novel by Ulas Samchuk, *Mariia*, published in Rivne in 1941, and some collections of poetry.[20] In Kiev, literary life barely existed after the arrests of early 1942, if only because writers who had lived under Soviet rule almost never received permission to publish. This even applied to Arkadii Liubchenko, who was anti-Communist, anti-Semitic, and pro-German. The German authorities did not import books and indeed confiscated book imports at the border if they could.[21] Nevertheless, in contrast to the state of affairs before the war, antiquarian books—often originating from the libraries of scholars and Communist party officials—were readily available at secondhand bookstores and commission stores. Imported books, particularly novels and memoirs by anti-Bolshevik authors, were in great demand and many sold at once, regardless of the price. People also borrowed them from each other through a system of waiting lists. After the libraries had been looted and purged, the remaining books could also be read there.[22]

Newspapers were easily available in towns and cities and city dwellers could subscribe to them. In the Reichskommissariat according to its January 1942 borders, there were forty-five newspapers in the Ukrainian language, each with a circulation of at most twenty thousand (thus totaling 1.5 million) and generally coming out three or four times a week. Later, with the addition of the Left Bank regions, the total came to around sixty publications.[23] No single newspaper was available in all general districts, but *Volyn* (Volhynia) and *Nove ukraïnske slovo* (The new Ukrainian word) were among the better known. In contrast, newspapers were hard to get in the countryside; often they were acquired only after a villager returned from a city with some.[24]

There was also a German-language *Deutsche Ukraine-Zeitung*. Few natives were able to read it, but when in March 1942 it discussed a plan to have German veterans colonize Ukraine, the result was great anxiety.[25] German newspapers from the Reich sold briskly at markets (they were actually supposed to be sold in kiosks only)—not as reading material, but

191

as wrapping, toilet, or cigarette paper.[26] Ukrainian-language newspapers from the General Government and the Reich, however, rarely made it through the mail. Apparently easier to obtain was a Russian-language newspaper from Berlin, *Novoe slovo* (The New Word); for some time, one could even subscribe to it at a bookstore in Kiev.[27]

After a brief period of relative editorial freedom under the German military, the newspapers shrank in size and provided almost only articles supplied by German agencies, in particular Ukraïnska Korespondentsiia, the Rivne-based branch of the German News Agency. Thus more anti-American and anti-British articles appeared than anti-Communist ones; and various articles dealt with the antecedents of "German" rule over Ukraine—the Goths, the Varangians, and Empress Catherine II. *Nove ukraïnske slovo* in addition tended to denigrate Ukraine's Cossacks and Ukrainian national consciousness. But *Volyn* from Rivne and *Podolianyn* (The Podolian) from Kamianets-Podilsky were exceptionally "Ukrainian" or at least strongly anti-Russian. Because Ukraïnska Korespondentsiia sometimes distributed these materials, these then appeared in all the newspapers of the Reichskommissariat.[28] The anti-Semitism of the press sometimes had a "national" slant. One article claimed, for example, that "Ukrainian society" was becoming more diverse because Ukrainians were "returning" to professions previously dominated by Jews and other "foreigners."[29] Articles on history were rare, however. One of the few to deal with the Great Famine remarked that only the Jews, who "lacked neither gold nor dollars," had not fallen victim to it.[30]

People at first read the newspapers with great interest. The 12,000 copies of the first issue of *Volyn* (released September 1, 1941) sold out in half a day.[31] *Ukraïnske slovo* (Kiev, 1941, initially printed in Zhytomyr), controlled by Melnykites, went on sale the day after the Germans occupied Kiev. Several weeks later, a Melnykite reported that it was "literally torn from one's hands, even though as many as fifty thousand copies are printed," and that people were standing in line for it an hour before its delivery to the kiosks.[32] Memoirs confirm that as in the case of books, the population was eager to read any newspaper that had not passed Stalin's censors; they started reading as soon as they obtained a copy. Peasants also read and circulated papers.[33]

Yet the newspapers, apart from their unsavory content, had two more serious flaws for the population. One was their lack of interaction with the readers. In the Soviet Union, people distrusted the press, but they had also gotten used to sending letters to the editor with requests or denunciations. Even if those usually did not appear in print, people had reason to believe that the editors took such letters seriously. There were also people who wrote to newspapers (as they did to institutions or political leaders) just to express their opinion about political issues. Many of these writers apparently considered such letter writing a sign of democracy. As one historian has put it, in the Soviet Union the main flow of information was not to, but *from* the readers.[34] Under the Germans, readers also sent letters and submissions to the papers, but almost no such materials appeared in them and soon there was a general conviction that sending in materials was useless, if not outright dangerous. It devalued the press enormously in the eyes of the readers.[35]

The second major flaw, from the majority perspective, was the language of the newspapers. Most city dwellers disliked reading the news in Ukrainian. *Nove ukraïnske slovo*, the Reichskommissariat's only daily paper, after a while sold poorly for that reason alone, and those who bought the Russian-language *Poslednie novosti*—the only Russian-language periodical in the entire Reichskommissariat—apparently also had to pay for a copy of *Nove ukraïnske slovo*.[36] In the cities of Dnieper Ukraine, the vast majority of the population used not Ukrainian but Russian as their daily language, as they had done for centuries. In Kiev, initially only some people with a higher education spoke Ukrainian and most other locals spoke Russian or a mixture of Russian and Ukrainian.[37] In October 1941 some in Kiev tried to speak Ukrainian in public, but this was mainly because posters from the Banderites scared them and because *Ukraïnske slovo* warned them to do so—as in the Soviet period, people assumed that the central press accurately reflected the wishes of the government.

Late in 1941 the Germans started paying attention to the press and suppressed most Ukrainian nationalists involved with it; it was then that they renamed Kiev's paper *Nove ukraïnske slovo*. That and the introduction of *Poslednie novosti* provided the signal to all but the leading officials of the city administration that they could safely revert back to Russian.[38] One year later, Ukrainian newspaper editors from military-ruled Kharkiv arrived in Kiev. Their first stop was at a barber, who was surprised that they spoke Ukrainian: "Such brave people are here no more."[39] In 1943 a man looked for a Ukrainian-language daycare center in Kiev and found only one, at the sugar factory, where many Galician Ukrainians worked. Everywhere else children spoke Russian or a mixed language, even if their supervisors spoke Ukrainian.[40]

Whereas the cities of western Volhynia experienced a marked increase in Ukrainian-language use,[41] in all of the Dnieper Ukrainian cities the language situation was similar to that of Kiev. In Uman, even non-Ukrainians initially spoke Ukrainian, but soon everybody returned to their mixed language or to Russian, which they considered more civilized.[42] One could hear some Ukrainian in Vinnytsia in mid-1943, but mostly from peasants and customers who were talking with them at the market. Young people in the village-like outskirts of Vinnytsia spoke Ukrainian to their parents but Russian to each other.[43] Likewise, schoolteachers and children in Proskuriv, and native officials in Lubny in the Left Bank, to give just two more examples, spoke Russian.[44]

City dwellers were not only unlikely to want to speak Ukrainian, it was also risky to do so, for one might therefore attract the label of "nationalist." And yet all written communication with native bureaucrats had to be in Ukrainian. The official records were in Ukrainian as well, and the courts also conducted affairs in it. This went beyond the prewar Soviet practice, when office correspondence had to be in Ukrainian but Russian often prevailed elsewhere.[45] This paradox was due to unpublished directives from Rosenberg and Koch to use Ukrainian (announced January 13 and February 2, 1942, respectively), which in turn stemmed from their deep hatred of Russians and Russian culture.[46] It is even fair to say that if one considers only the language in which the population received printed news and in which it corresponded with the authorities, the conclusion must be that Dnieper Ukraine had never before seen such a thorough and successful Ukrainianization. In 1942, in one of the very few surviving documents in which he personally wrote about Ukraine (rather than having a subordinate write and sign in his stead), Reichskommissar Koch wrote that "to me and each of my general commissars it is a self-evident political principle that the Ukrainian language and culture shall always get preferential treatment over any other Slavic language and culture. This preeminence exists in most cases, with virtually no exceptions." He equated Russian speakers with Russians: "The Ukrainian cities and also Kiev have a population that to a very great extent consists of Russians. According to the estimate of the general commissar in Kiev, in the city of Kiev about 85 percent of the population speaks Russian and 15 percent Ukrainian." He said he was supporting Ukrainian language and culture in Kiev, for instance by allowing no daily Russian-language newspaper and by allowing only the Autocephalists to use "the best church" (St. Andrew's Cathedral). But these efforts were getting "only little support from the Ukrainians themselves. For example, Ukrainian artists in

Kiev complain when they are ordered to produce themselves in the Ukrainian language, declaring that Russian is the language of the educated and Ukrainian the language of the peasants. Nevertheless," Koch concluded, "it is a matter of course that despite the conditions in Kiev, and despite the lack of cooperation from the mass of the Ukrainians, everything is being done to give Ukrainianness in Kiev and in the other Ukrainian cities a dominant position over Russianness."[47]

Ukrainian printed matter also had little success in the countryside. People with little education had trouble understanding the Ukrainian language that these used, because the Ukrainian of the Galician authors of many of the texts differed from literary Ukrainian.[48] (Most Dnieper Ukrainians had learned literary Ukrainian at school.) Koch's deputy Paul Dargel once told Ukrainian visitors from the General Government that the district commissars were concerned that the population was misunderstanding Ukrainian announcements. They understood the Russian language, he added—but it was out of the question for political reasons. He went on to muse that using only German might be best. When his guest, Volodymyr Kubiiovych, head of the Kraków-based Ukrainian Central Committee, countered that this would make it difficult for people to carry out German orders, Dargel allegedly said, "Then I'll shoot them."[49]

The several magazines that appeared were little more than newspaper supplements and rarely found their way far from the place of publication. The main ones were *Ukraïnka* (Ukrainian woman; Kostopil), *Silsky hospodar* (Agrarian master; Rivne), *Ukraïnsky khliborob* (Ukrainian farmer; Kiev, though apparently printed in Rivne), and the bulletin of the All-Ukrainian Cooperative Society.[50] For children, there were *Orlenia* (Young eagle; Rivne), *Ukraïnska dytyna* (Ukrainian child; Kostopil), and *Shkoliar* (Pupil; Vasylkiv). Their content was similar to the newspapers, although remarkably *Orlenia* referred to the Third Universal of the revolutionary period (a document that proclaimed the existence of a Ukrainian Republic) even as late as November 1942.[51] Besides locally printed leaflets, there came directly from the Reich brochures for schoolchildren about Hitler, and colorful posters. It is unclear how many of these posters reached the villages and raion centers.[52]

Schools

The treatment of the schools also provided ample evidence of the Nazis' attitude toward the culture of the people of Ukraine. In accordance with an order from Rosenberg of December 12, 1941, all grades above fourth grade were abolished (the vast majority of them were, although some district commissars did not implement the order).[53] The Reich minister also instructed Koch not to allow the population to learn German, even though he did allow it in the Reichskommissariat Ostland, a colony where thousands of boys and girls also could join a Nazi-sponsored Union of Belarusan Youth.[54]

Not infrequently, soldiers occupied or destroyed the school buildings.[55] There were hardly any textbooks, for the Soviet textbooks either were banned altogether or became useless after the prescribed removal of all references to the Soviet Union and its leaders, a process that, as an NKVD report put it, meant that "essentially nothing" remained.[56] The four-grade schools generally closed during the winter because of a lack of heat, or—more often—because the German authorities falsely proclaimed that no heat was available. Attendance during the few months of instruction was low, especially in the countryside, which prompted auxiliary authorities to impose fines on parents.[57]

At school both the children and the teachers seem to have felt very little motivation. The students in particular often vandalized Hitler's portrait, for they were "against the Germans," as a teacher recalls. "Almost all of them had their mum taken away. They were all hungry, they were all constantly afraid that the police would come and drag them away somewhere, or that their mum would be taken to 24 Lviv Street [Kiev's "recruitment" office for forced labor in Germany] and sent away. We all felt this grief."[58] Schoolchildren also refused, for example, to adopt local innovations (wearing crucifixes and answering with "Glory!" to the teacher's greeting, "Glory to Ukraine"), and argued during religious instruction. During a dictation lesson at the school in Chyhyryn, a boy was asked to write, "The workers of our city very happily greeted their liberator, the German Army." He threw the piece of chalk back at the woman teacher, shouting, "Liar!" He and his father were arrested, probably temporarily. A Communist underground activist thought that such things happened often and that the teachers were afraid to discuss outside of school the issue of anti-German unruliness.[59]

Older children, meanwhile, had no school at all and might be put to work harvesting, cleaning parks, digging up roots, or gathering chestnuts or medicinal herbs.[60] In Melitopol during the summer of 1942 even the fourth grade was canceled: these children apparently had to help tear down buildings so that the materials could be sent to Germany.[61]

Movies

Cinema was popular, if only because it seemed a way to get to know other countries. But apart from the many showings for Germans only, the numbers of films on display never came close to the prewar scale. Early in 1942, except for an unknown number of itinerant "movie wagons," the native population had access to only fifty movie theaters, mostly in the major cities.[62]

Germany's weekly newsreel preceded all films. People found this *Wochenschau*, in a Ukrainian or Russian translation, worth traveling to town for.[63] Lack of the newest edition was a persistent problem, however. For instance, in August 1942 the one Ukrainian movie theater in Dnipropetrovsk still ran newsreels from the previous winter (and thereafter a frequent lack of electricity hampered movie showings).[64] The movies in circulation tended to be German comedies and had Ukrainian or Russian subtitles or dubbing.[65] As the SD found, at first the spectators were "stunned that they completely lacked agitation" or only included the fascist salute. Apolitical Soviet movies also returned to the screen.[66] But some pure propaganda movies were shown, such as *The Life of the German Farmer and Worker and the Life of the People under Stalin's Yoke, Süß the Jew*, and *The Jews and the NKVD*.[67]

As for the provinces, a glimpse of the situation comes from a German report about the Oleksandriia district: "In the villages the film equipment is generally bad. The movies shimmer and break often, the beam is too weak. Many movies are not synchronized. *Wochenschauen* are often not supplied. Thus, a constant phenomenon is that movie visitors leave the room before the end. There should also be showings of cultural movies and movies about German crafts and German industry. The people are interested in this."[68] But because the showings often were also directed at Germans, serious movies remained rare; the German authorities assumed that their conationals preferred to watch comedies and wanted to satisfy them above all. The technical conditions deteriorated still further in 1943, resulting in frequent mismatches of image and sound or the absence of a translation.[69]

The peasants had seen musical comedies and other movies on a significant scale for the first time during the second half of the 1930s and had loved them.[70] Not surprisingly, therefore, the decreased frequency and deteriorated conditions of the movie showings caused great dissatisfaction. As a rhyme put it, "There were the Soviets / Who gave us movies and a kilogram of grain / The liberators came / And gave us a church and a hundred grams."[71]

Performances and Exhibitions

The most prestigious cultural performances were at the opera and ballet theater in Kiev, now called the Large Opera Theater. For more than a year, natives could visit it. A Kievan woman might obtain a ticket through her German boyfriend, although she had to use a separate, "non-German" cloakroom. But from late November 1942, entrance officially was only possible for Germans and allied nationalities. This policy was said to be needed to ensure soldiers a seat, but as before most visitors were German officials. Kievans felt humiliated.[72] The theater had 140 musicians, including two Jews with Ukrainian passports. Their artistic director was Wolfgang Brückner, who had conducted a radio orchestra in Königsberg and whose brother was a well-known composer. Somehow related to Erich Koch and therefore confident that he could do as he pleased, the director tended to strike the musicians physically and to generally treat them like slaves. But the staff of an astonishing one thousand received German food rations. The soloists were best off, for Germans delivered additional food to their homes.[73] To the stage came Italian variations and symphonic concerts (Beethoven, Tchaikovsky, and Brückner), ballet (such as Tchaikovsky's Queen of Spades), and opera (such as Verdi's Aïda and Wagner's Löhengrin)—with the operas in Ukrainian translation, for the singers knew no other version.[74] The theater closed altogether in January 1943. Other cities also had opera (and operetta) performances. In Vinnytsia some singers in the staging of Verdi's Rigoletto sang in Russian while others sang in Ukrainian; few people seemed to notice.[75]

Predominantly German audiences also attended "variety" shows. In Kiev, a variety theater opened in May 1942 and featured just about everything—song, dance, music, comedy, and juggling and balancing acts. Vocal parts were in Russian until September 1942, when the city commissar demanded that Ukrainian be used.[76]

"In large sections of the Ukrainian population there is a strong need for cultural activity. Teachers and intellectuals are giving new life to drama and song, even in the smallest towns." Thus read the official Reichskommissariat report for January 1942. This vitality, which surprised the Nazis, was an inheritance of the prewar Soviet campaign for "amateur art activities," which had taken root, and of the nineteenth- and early-twentieth-century Ukrainian Prosvita, or Enlightenment societies. The civilian German authorities did not ban drama, whether amateur or professional, as such, and drama theaters opened in at least twenty-four cities and towns.[77]

A guideline from Rivne stipulated that the plays had to be in Ukrainian, but implementation was not complete, because some of the necessary actors only knew a Russian text. Indeed, the Nazis did not completely eradicate Russian culture as such from the Reichskommissariat: There were also performances and broadcasts of the music of Tchaikovsky and other Russian composers.[78] But German supervision did bring about the disbandment of many of the Prosvita societies, most likely because of their too overt support of things Ukrainian.[79] According to some reports, the staff of the societies were mostly children of people with office or police jobs. They barred non-Ukrainians and adorned the Prosvita buildings with blue-and-yellow flags as well as with portraits not only of Hitler, but also of the national bard Shevchenko and the nationalist Symon Petliura.[80]

Representatives of the local city or district commissar always paid attention to which plays were in preparation and during rehearsals might demand changes, or might deny approval altogether. According to Hryhorii Kostiuk, who supervised the arts section of the city administration's Culture and Education Department in Kiev for a year, the city commissar's officials "usually" refused permission for the proposed plays.[81] It certainly happened to *Hetman Doroshenko*, which created a patriotic atmosphere during previews. This play did not pass the rehearsal stage in any city. Bans could also come later. In Vinnytsia in December 1941, the Nazis prohibited the classic play *Marusia Bohuslavka* after an actress whose brother was under arrest received an ovation for the line, "I will liberate you all!"[82]

Almost all of the permitted plays were prerevolutionary, vaudeville-like classics with titles such as *They Were Duped*—"vodka on stage," as one town mayor complained. The acting, in Ukrainian or Russian, was often melodramatic.[83] And in Vinnytsia, as well as probably in other large towns and cities, the first few performances were always for Germans only. The actors in Vinnytsia were at most second-rate and apparently made less effort after those first shows.[84] In small towns and in some cities, however, German spectators sat among the local spectators from the very beginning.[85] Because of the curfew, plays generally started no later than in the afternoon.

Western Volhynia featured quite a few small-scale vocal performances. For instance, on June 28, 1942, Rivne's movie theater was the setting for a celebration of song to mark the hundredth birthday of the Ukrainian composer Mykola Lysenko. Particularly popular in Kiev, too, were choir concerts in the city administration building.[86] But it seems that the poetry of Taras Shevchenko could not be recited legally anywhere in the Reichs-kommissariat.[87]

In the countryside there reappeared traditional blind minstrels, who traversed the land singing songs and playing a small plucked lute (kobza) or a hurdy-gurdy. They could be colorful figures. Uncle Levko, for example, born around 1860, toured the villages near Kirovohrad in a worn russet overcoat and homewoven trousers, feeling his way with a long pole. Besides his instrument he wore a large straw hat and carried a large canvas bag to receive charity donations. Locals later told a Soviet journalist that his face was stern and full of wrinkles, and that he wore a long mustache that had become yellow from tobacco. Among his songs were new compositions about contemporary life that his audiences quickly picked up. After about a year, he was denounced and hanged as a "partisan."[88] The countryside to the south of Kiev also had at least one blind minstrel, Pavlo Nosach, who apparently started singing satirical songs about Hitler when the Red Army was near.[89]

Minstrels and vagrants, old and young, also performed in cities and towns. At the market in Vinnytsia, vagrants sang Russian songs and topical chastushki (two- or four-line rhymes) that audiences really enjoyed.[90] In smaller towns there were scenes such as the following, in a place near Kryvy Rih: "With no self-consciousness at all and with their heads held high, the people danced with the verve and carefree ease of millionaires on the huge wooden stage in the center of the park where a harmoshka (accordion) quartet, accompanied by flute, guitar and violin, played waltzes, fox-trots and sentimental tangos. 'We both met in life coincidentally—thus by chance we parted. We were not aware of each others' happiness, thus by chance we parted.' A young mezzo-soprano in a fine silk gown and high-heeled shoes crooned with professional know-how and feeling to much applause from the audience."[91]

Some places in the Reichskommissariat had conditions for cultural performances that were relatively favorable. The district commissar in Kamianets-Podilsky, for instance, gave money to the local Shevchenko Theater.[92] And although Kiev's conservatory was barely functioning, there was another conservatory, in the town of Apostolove, southeast of Kryvy Rih, that had qualified instructors in song, piano, and wind and string instruments.[93] Altogether, however, after the introduction of civilian Nazi rule, hardly any "official" cultural performances were possible, and conditions for popular culture were far better almost everywhere else, whether in Lviv in the General Government, in the military zone in the east, or in Odessa in Romania's Transnistria. That is also why Kostiuk was so pleasantly surprised on his arrival in Lviv in the fall of 1943. When Ulas Samchuk came to Poltava in August 1942, a town still under military administration, the contrast with his native Volhynia and the Reichskommissariat as a whole stunned him. Along with many restaurants, bars, and movie theaters, Poltava offered a great variety of shows.[94] Indeed, the general commissar of the Reichskommissariat Ostland's district of White Ruthenia subsidized a *national* Belarusan theater.[95]

Typical for the cultural life in Koch's domain, by contrast, was what happened to the Kievan Ensemble of Bandurists, seventeen performers directed by Hryhorii Kytasty (who had done the same work in Soviet Ukraine). In June 1942 the bandurists traveled to Rivne with opera singers, gave three performances for Nazis (Koch was out of town), and received permission to tour western Volhynia for a month. But when Ukrainian audiences spontaneously burst out singing what was generally considered the Ukrainian national anthem, "Shche ne vmerla Ukraïna," the Nazis ordered the ensemble back to Kiev and then sent them to the Reich to perform for the "Eastern Workers" *(Ostarbeiter)* there.[96]

As for exhibitions, painters benefited from Germans' interest in brightly colored Ukrainian landscape portraits that preferably included a straw-covered peasant home. Kiev had a painting academy led by Fedir Krychevsky and a painters' association with some sixty members. In August 1942 painters provided work, often barely finished, for an exhibition—or more precisely, sale—that the district commissar organized in the "former" Museum of Ukrainian Art. The prices were low, on the pretext that because native workers in the Reichskommissariat earned one-fifth of what Germans earned, paintings should be sold for one-fifth of their alleged value in Germany, or only about one hundred reichsmarks per painting. Some painters therefore withdrew their work. Among those works that remained, native visitors of the exhibition were surprised not to find "socialist" themes or portraits of leaders.[97] One month later, a call for another exhibition went out, this time in "support of the best artists of the Kiev general district," to be opened in December.[98]

Besides the "former" Museum of Ukrainian Art, the only Kiev museum open to natives was the new Museum-Archive of the Transition Period. Funded by the city administration and headed by historian and former mayor Oleksander Ohloblyn, it began showing in April 1942 an exhibition about the "The Ruination by the Bolsheviks of the Cultural Treasures in the City of Kiev." When Berndt replaced Rogausch as city commissar in the middle of the year, he ordered the museum closed until further notice. It never reopened.[99]

Sports

Sports played a small role in people's lives. Initially, Melnykites in Kiev created the Sich, a sporting organization that was also used to stimulate Ukrainian nationalism. The German authorities quickly suppressed it. As for individual sports, some boxing matches are known to have taken place in Kiev in July and August 1942, but swimming in the Dnieper River in Kiev was banned from September 4, 1942.[100] The only sport that received permission to undergo some organized development was football. In one Left Bank district, there were regular football games between Ukrainians and German soldiers even though the district commissar told the local commander angrily that German-Ukrainian sporting events were not allowed.[101]

In 1942, several football teams competed in the Zenit stadium at 24 Kerosynna Street in Kiev. The team called Rukh was apparently the successor to the Sich and perhaps included Schuma. Start and Almaz, two other teams, were made up of players who worked at the bread and the jewelry factories. From June 1942, Start played four matches against German teams (antiaircraft gunners, pilots, and railroad employees) and three against Hungarian teams, thereby attracting German, Hungarian, and Kievan spectators. Natives and Hungarians paid five karbovantsi for each occasion. Start played its ninth and final match on Sunday, August 16, 1942, when it routed Rukh eight to zero. Two days later, the Security Police arrested eight Start players and accused them of being NKVD agents. The charge was not entirely groundless, for many Start players had been in Soviet Ukraine's leading soccer team, Dynamo Kiev, which Ukraine's NKVD had sponsored (other People's Commissariats sponsored other teams); and during the German invasion, at least one of the players had worked for the NKVD as a car mechanic. Twenty-four days later, all but one of the arrested were sent to the Syrets concentration camp near Babi Yar, where four of them eventually were shot. The other three Start players escaped, two thanks to police guards at a shoe factory where they were working, who deliberately looked the other way.[102]

Private Gatherings

The workload and the curfew impeded private parties and the like, but city dwellers still tried to assemble for birthdays and impromptu afternoon meetings. Indoor group activities included dancing (to an instrument, a radio, or the omnipresent record player), games (cards, dominoes, chess), and, among young people, charades.[103] At a party in Vinnytsia given by an engineer, Mykhailo Seleshko found everybody speaking Ukrainian. Moreover, the people "behaved as if in a solid bourgeois home. There was music and singing, and a sociability in an unartificial Soviet way . . . Everything was beautiful and in a form that could be the envy of any European." The scene contrasted sharply with that in the streets outside, "where everything had been dragged down to the looks and manners of the proletariat and where everything was coarse, shabby, and badly dressed."[104]

After dark, at home or perhaps during visits to neighbors, people found other simple ways to enjoy themselves. Nikolai Fevr thus describes Kiev in the early fall of 1942, after the onset of the ten o'clock curfew: "In those evening hours, Kiev's wounds [destroyed buildings] are not visible, and neither are its beggarly rags. It appears to be the beautiful city that it once was. Sitting on their balconies in the dark, the Kievans call out to each other. 'Svetlana, hi!' someone shouts from the neighboring balcony. 'Cuckoo!,' answers Svetlana from the other side of the street. 'Cuckoo, how old are you?' From the dark there comes cuckoo again, sixteen times." From open windows resonated gramophone and radio melodies, singing, and pianos; the central city blocks were almost a "gigantic conservatory."[105] It evidently annoyed the authorities, for Mayor Forostivsky at one stage ordered the Kievans to hand in all discs with "Jewish and Soviet content."[106]

In the countryside, socializing, certainly of men only, almost invariably implied—or even consisted of nothing but—bouts of hard drinking. Peasant women drank too, but they also gathered for other purposes such as spinning, weaving, and sewing, while singing new songs.[107] Not surprisingly, the young were the least satisfied with their leisure time. Dangers and rules often prevented them from socializing, and the lack of organized activities such as sports, dances, or education; the scarcity of artificial light, which impeded reading, for instance; and the difficulty of getting movie and theater tickets all left them very bored.[108]

Cultural events played a minor role in the life of the native population. Political gatherings and print media existed on a much smaller scale than before 1941, never satisfied the demand, and were considered out of step with the needs and interests of the people. In general, people missed from the Soviet period a propaganda that appeared to take them seriously and that promised them a better and "civilized" life. After many years of Soviet rule, people now expected to be addressed in a way that might be deceptive, as they often realized, but that nevertheless presupposed that they deserved something—responsible government and at least some measure of control over their lives. The Soviet regime of the 1930s had become no longer proud of its violence and often tried to hide it.[109] In contrast, the people who found themselves in Koch's domain realized soon, within months if not weeks, that the popular culture that the Nazis sponsored did not aim to edify or help them. Instead, that culture presupposed that they could and should not think for themselves. Ukrainians and others were supposed to work, and work only. The result was not lost on some Germans: the new regime issued so little propaganda, the SD of the Kiev general district reported in 1942, that one could "hardly speak of an influence over the masses."[110] The new official culture was even harder to tolerate because there were almost no alternatives available. Unlike in the General Government, there was not much of an underground press, partly because of the scarcity of both typewriters and an underground school system.

In addition to the effects of the actual brutality and violence of everyday life in the Reichskommissariat Ukraine, the Nazi regime's pride in violence and evident disdain and mistrust of the natives, so obvious from its cultural policies, offended the native population deeply. Even some ardent anti-Communists wrote in their diaries and memoirs that former Soviet citizens had come to expect any government that replaced the Nazis to improve their lives and to offer a veneer of choice.[111] In this regard, these people became nostalgic for the Soviet period; in this limited sense they were indeed "Soviet people."

9

ETHNIC IDENTITY AND POLITICAL LOYALTIES

As we have seen, many if not most natives (Ukrainians and others) had become accustomed under the Soviet system to a political culture that made them feel respected, if only in a very limited way. In this regard they conformed to the Soviet ideal. Yet they evidently by 1941 had preserved a great deal of autonomy from the ideology, or ethos, of Communism, as well as from nationalism, and the experience of Nazi rule hardly made them any more interested in either of these outlooks. In short, the totalitarian ideologies had only a minor effect on the mental outlook of ordinary people.

The focus here is on the people who before 1939 lived in the Soviet Union and who, after 1941, inhabited the territory of the Reichskommissariat. In recent years, historians have emphasized the political alternatives to the Soviet system that became available to Soviet citizens during World War II and have concluded that in wartime Ukraine, "things Ukrainian, if not Ukrainian nationalism . . . began to attract people's attention"—that is, scholars have perceived a twofold development in popular thinking that can be summed up as "peasants to Soviets, peasants to Ukrainians."[1] In studies of the outlook of populations, it is customary to study more than several years of data. The drawback of longer-term approaches, however, is that they increase the risk that evidence related to the end of the period under study will be inappropriately applied to the beginning of the period. This book attempts to circumvent the problem by placing limits on the kind of evidence considered: only those sources that concern the Reichskommissariat Ukraine during the time of Nazi rule over this territory. Thus I deliberately neglect here those natives who served in the Red Army and never lived under the Nazis (and who later, as veterans, sustained a new Soviet myth about the "Great Patriotic War"),[2] just as I ignore the complex developments in Ukraine after the Red Army returned. Such limitations should allow us to consider more clearly the influence of the Nazi regime.

Soviet Citizens and Ethnic Identity

During the 1930s, the Soviet regime sincerely and often indirectly promoted non-Russian distinctiveness among the various non-Russian speakers of the Soviet Union. Every Soviet citizen received a Russian, Kazakh, Jewish, Ukrainian, or other "nationality" and registered as such in the censuses.[3] It seems that not many ordinary citizens cared about this important measure and chose their "nationality" casually.[4] Thus when war came, the division of the population into "nationalities" had existed for some time, but few Soviet citizens had devoted much attention to it. The German occupation opened the eyes of many Soviet citizens to nationality's relevance: Jews suffered as Jews, and at first Ukrainians received, or seemed to receive, preferential treatment in job placement and in getting out of the POW camps.

All the same, many ordinary people had a hard time figuring out what ethnicity or nationality meant and hardly distinguished it from religious orientation. The average Ukrainian in Dnieper Ukraine tended to equate Catholicism (whether Roman or Greek) with Polishness,[5] and the typical peasant considered him- or herself foremost just that—*selianyn* or *khliborob*: literally, "villager" or "grain maker." By far the most popular forms of self-identification were two traditional pronouns-turned-nouns: *svoï* and *nashi*. Both words meant "our people," or literally "one's own" or "ours." For example, a Ukrainian from the town of Bohuslav was in her mid-teens in 1944 when a Red Army soldier saw her in hiding and called out, "Who's there?" She and the others answered, "My, svoï"—us, our people.[6]

In Dnieper Ukraine, "our people" tended to exclude Jews and ethnic Germans, but almost certainly included Russians. Even speakers of Ukrainian with a strong Ukrainian national consciousness considered Russians "ours." Mykhailo Seleshko, a Melnykite who interpreted for the Security Police and SD, met such Ukrainians in the Vinnytsia region in 1943 and found that they distinguished two kinds of Russians. One group, which they called *russki*, were "ours." Then when he would mention the *katsapy*, an old derogatory word for Russians, the response came that these were another, unpleasant kind—not "ours." This lack of differentiation from Russians was not new. Some peasants even still used for both the Russians and Ukrainians the traditional term Ruthenian (*ruski*).[7] In short, most Ukrainians in Dnieper Ukraine considered Ukrainians and things Ukrainian a subgroup of a larger ethnic identity, which they might call "our people" or *ruski*. Contrary to what some scholars have held, most Ukrainians in Soviet Ukraine still considered their membership in the vaguely defined group "our people" as more significant than their Ukrainianness. Being Ukrainian was not felt to be more important than, let alone incompatible with, a sense of belonging to certain non-Ukrainians.

But what kind of territorial identity, if any, did these people have? If they were patriotic, *of what* were they patriots—Ukraine, the Soviet Union, perhaps both? Were they even nationalistic in the sense of wishing for a Ukrainian state? Few historians have looked at this question.[8] In doing so here, I need to emphasize first of all that most people found the initial phase of the war with Germany profoundly humiliating. Even though many disliked the Soviet regime, they often also took personally the failures of the Soviet state's defense forces. Pavlo Negretov heard how "everyone" in the Kirovohrad region "cursed the government for the loss of the war without any glory. That it was lost nobody doubted, including myself. Old people recalled the previous war and said: at that time the Germans got here only in the fourth year of war. Now, after all our five-year-plans, in the second month." There were many Red Army deserters, but they apparently received little sympathy on their return home.[9]

Then new expectations took hold. Many people started to wait for a semi-independent Ukrainian authority. Kiev had barely changed hands when groups of people talked in the streets about its alleged members. Some mentioned Symon Petliura; others, sure that the Soviet media had not lied in 1926 when they reported his murder, identified the socialist emigré and former leader Volodymyr Vynnychenko as the premier.[10] All over Ukraine, Soviet citizens asked Galician Ukrainians and others arriving from the west about Vynnychenko (and sometimes Petliura), whether there was already a Ukrainian authority, and why Kiev did not issue any instructions. A less prevalent rumor claimed that there would also be a Ukrainian army.[11]

One source of such talk was Soviet propaganda—the prewar and wartime propaganda against the fictitious Union for the Liberation of Ukraine and the Banderites.[12] Another was Volhynian German soldiers, who told the population that there was already a Ukrainian government, mentioned names, and said that Ukraine would become a German protectorate.[13] Although the swastika flag placed next to the Ukrainian blue-and-yellow flag on St. Sophia's Cathedral on October 13, 1941 dissipated most of these expectations in Kiev, elsewhere the belief that a Ukrainian government would arrive persisted for months.[14]

Yet these rumors do not demonstrate that Ukrainian residents promoted the ultimate nationalist goal—Ukrainian statehood, whether of a semi- or fully independent kind. From the very beginning, all German agencies were concerned with any demand for independence, but while they found it among the small Ukrainian intelligentsia and the Banderites, the vast majority of the population, they discovered, neither opposed nor wanted a Ukrainian state.[15] For instance, the Ukrainophile military intelligence officer Hans Koch noted in 1941 that "the population's interest does not rise above the village, raion, and the nearest market." And in the Zhytomyr region, the SD in 1941 nowhere found "thought inclined toward the creation of an independent Ukrainian state . . . Without exception, the wish was discerned to go about the reconstruction of the country with the Germans and under German leadership."[16] In November 1941 there was evidence of self-deprecation. German agencies noted statements like, "Let the Germans stay as long as possible, to keep order," and "The Ukrainians cannot govern themselves."[17] The SD ascribed this to corruption among native administrators, but it also reported a widespread dislike of western Ukrainians and returning emigrés.[18] In the fall of 1942, the SD reiterated that any Ukrainian national consciousness in Dnieper Ukraine either was very vague or overshawed by "Communist ideals."[19]

Ukrainian-language sources generally confirm the lack of desire for Ukrainian statehood. A Banderite wrote in the beginning of 1943: "To a part of our compatriots, Moscow and the Muscovite region bit by bit have become the 'motherland,' and the Russian people and Russia—a common fatherland and a common society, that was at first Russian, then Orthodox, Slavic, proletarian, and now Soviet." They only had a "narrow, territorial feeling."[20] The wartime folklore that has been preserved is also patriotic, not ethnocentric or state-oriented: it often mentions "Ukraine," but the "Ukrainians" as a people rarely appear. Seleshko found that Ukrainians in Vinnytsia spoke of "our rich country" and thereby meant the Soviet Union, and used "Poland" when they meant Galicia (and sometimes also western Volhynia)—that is, what Ukrainian nationalists would have called "western Ukraine."[21] Evidence to the contrary is hard to find but exists: a Galician Ukrainian army interpreter recalls that people asked him whether Ukraine would become independent, and peasants apparently often asked Fedir Pihido where "our leaders" were so that they might "defend our borders with our own lives."[22]

The main reason why nationalism elicited so little interest was people's thinking about the past. Nationalism cannot exist without a sense of grievance against a real or imagined oppressor. But evidently the vast majority of Ukrainians in Nazi-ruled Dnieper Ukraine did not collectively blame "the Russians" for anything. (Complaints about Jews are not relevant here.) By far the most talked about historical event was the Great Famine of 1933—*Trydtsiat Prokliaty*, Thirty-Damned, as people called it. At last they could get the horrors they had seen then off their chests. A Volhynian evangelist recalls about his travels in central Ukraine in 1941 that every person they visited talked about it, some even all night, sometimes with details about cannibalism and about killings for the purpose of cannibalism.[23] Hans Koch saw and heard eyewitnesses address public gatherings in the countryside about the famine, where people were identified as having engaged in cannibalism, although they were not condemned for it. Peasants who had written diaries during the famine submitted them to the local newspapers (which did not publish them).[24] Not once, however, did ordinary Ukrainians go on record as blaming the Russians for the famine.

Many Ukrainians had an unself-conscious knowledge of prerevolutionary folkloric songs and customs.[25] As for the imperial period in general, older people did not denegrate it—on the contrary. In the fall of 1942, Nikolai Fevr visited a sugar factory between Bila Tserkva and Kiev and struck up a conversation. One employee said that Count Bobrinskii used to own this factory, four others, and 1,030 desiatynas (1,125 hectares or 2,781 acres) of land. Fevr said that it was not fair. "Of course it wasn't," came the answer. "But there was order! That man knew business, the enterprise really prospered! And he wasn't the only one to eat from it: thousands of people lived from this business, and how!" Another peasant added that everything had deteriorated since 1917. "The Bolsheviks chased these Bobrinskiis away, so that everything fell apart! Would you believe that [during the 1930s] we worked in the sugar industry, but often had to travel to Kiev and stand in line there for sugar? Everything up to the last particle they took away from us, and nobody knew where it went.

In Kiev there was sugar, but in Bila Tserkva there wouldn't be any for months."[26] Indeed, many, perhaps most, peasants seem to have thought that under the tsar, "things were better" in a material sense.

Some young people also made painful comparisons with the tsarist period. In August 1942 a civil engineering student in the Poltava region told a visitor what he thought of the Red Army: "They let us down. The Germans were shelling like hell, but from *nashi*, nothing! Maybe something was missing. Not enough technology. No! We have lots of technology, but there's no spirit, no culture. Under the tsar things functioned better. Then both the French and the English were against us, but they didn't reach the Volga."[27] (Incidentally, this notion was compatible with a Communist weltanschauung: Communists could reason that the "encirclement" of the USSR by capitalist enemies made the deprivations of life under socialism inevitable.[28]) As for popular recollections of the revolutionary period, these were vague and only rarely expressed. Most people considered Petliura at best one of many warlords of that time. Others talked about the persecution of Christians.[29] People's opinion or interpretation—if any—of the prewar NKVD terror is not evident from the known sources.

In short, the average Ukrainian in Dnieper Ukraine cared most of all about the undefined "our people," did not consider Soviet rule a "Russian" project, and did not consider his or her Ukrainian identity primary or even particularly relevant. Although the spread of the rumor about Vynnychenko suggests a continuing memory of the autonomous Ukrainian National Republic of the revolutionary years, there is hardly any evidence for significant popular support for an independent Ukrainian state. Neither is there any evidence for the notion that the deprivations under Nazi rule made most people attach more importance to their ethnicity. Even under the Nazi regime, ordinary people remained little interested in ethnicity, let alone nationalism. It requires effort to find even one piece of evidence of popular anti-Russian sentiment: a contemporary Banderite report that alleges strong animosity between Ukrainians and Russians in the south early in 1943.[30] From a Ukrainian nationalist point of view, the number of "genuine" Ukrainians was distressingly low.

It seems that when the Germans arrived, there were about 140,500 people with German nationality in the future territory of the Reichskommissariat.[31] In explaining their feelings under Nazi rule, it is important to note that their standard of living rose more than that of any other group, largely due to Nazi policies. They received wood, building materials, and Jewish property (such as clothes from the Auschwitz and Majdanek death camps). They paid no income tax and less of the other taxes than did other groups.[32] The peasants among them could secure permission for an agricultural cooperative or for individual cultivation (de facto, not de jure) relatively easily.[33] Yet many still migrated to the cities—in exactly the opposite direction of most non-German migrants, so that on March 4, 1942, the Nazis ruled that leaving the farm became punishable by a year of imprisonment or a fine. In the city, ethnic Germans could hold positions at many levels in the army, the civilian administration (perhaps ruling an entire district, such as Korosten), the state construction company Organisation Todt, and the Central Trade Corporation East.[34] As in the case of other natives, their salaries were usually a tenth of what Reich Germans earned and their food rations were lower, but they could use the "Germans Only" stores, and it was relatively easy for them to operate in the shadow economy, if only because they were allowed to travel by train.[35]

But it is equally important to note that the ethnic Germans did not enjoy any more religious freedom than the Slavic population. In fact, the Roman Catholics among them were rarely allowed to hold church services.[36] Schools opened just for them and had more than four grades, teaching materials arrived from Germany (although often only in May 1942), and the teachers were reeducated in Germany. Yet in the summer of 1942 Erich Koch closed the schools,[37] and later that year there was a forced migration in the Zhytomyr general district.

From the outset there was confusion as to who was *volksdeutsch*, or "national German." A 1941 Reich rule said that in order to qualify one needed at least three "purely German" grandparents, but the SS also could confer the status after a "racial review." Wehrmacht guidelines barred people of "foreign blood," but others argued that a person who had no German ancestors at all was still eligible if there were no "racial concerns" and if he or she felt and behaved as a "member of the German nation."[38] On April 29, 1942, Koch ruled that the decision was up to the SS or the local district commissar only. (The next day he banned marriages between ethnic Germans and Slavs.)[39] Early in September 1942, Himmler ordered him to introduce an official registry that already existed in the Reich, the German Nationality List, which was a stepping stone toward German citizenship. Koch complied on December 7. Koch's rules were rather broad: the list should include even "carriers of German blood" who rejected "Germanness," as well as any spouses of those on the list (except for Jewish spouses, whom he ordered killed along with their children).[40] "Alien" first names such as Jacob were summarily altered. On March 19, 1943, all on the Reichskommissariat list in one stroke became German citizens, whether they wanted to or not.[41]

Most Ukrainians and Russians in the Reichskommissariat apparently did not consider the ethnic Germans "our people." All the same, many—"everybody," as one Kievan puts it—wanted to register as ethnic Germans.[42] Many succeeded, especially in the first year. A bribe of five thousand rubles apparently did the job in Kiev.[43] The new "ethnic Germans" could include a Finnish family or a Georgian professor and his Ukrainian wife who had one ethnic German grandparent. Many civilian German administrators apparently were not aware of such dubious cases.[44] According to Pihido, most of the pseudo-Germans were "the same people who also had not done badly under Soviet rule," including even many of the flower of socialist society elite: former Communist party members and nonmember Soviet activists.[45] Those "ethnic Germans" whom Seleshko asked about ethnicity apparently answered that they were Russian. Others he actually considered Poles (local ones or wartime immigrants).[46] In western Volhynia as well, people whom Ukrainian nationalists considered Poles often became "ethnic Germans."[47]

Among the ethnic German peasants, intermarriage with non-Germans had not taken place in large numbers before 1941, least of all at the Dnieper bend, where the Germans were Catholic, Lutheran, and, in particular, Mennonite. They knew little about the Third Reich and had reservations about it or even feared it.[48] A Banderite activist in the Vinnytsia region found little German patriotism among the ethnic Germans he met.[49] According to the district commissar in Khortytsia, the local Mennonites even "cried over Russia" in 1941. He told them many times that now they were free and should be glad. But he evidently did not win over many of the older generation to the Nazi ideology. For instance, people thought it unfair that it was much harder for their non-German neighbors to receive permission to form a cooperative.[50]

Such ways among older people—as shall become evident later, the Nazis had little reason to complain about the younger generation—explained in part the abuse that many Reich Germans, to the dismay of Himmler's SS, inflicted on their alleged relatives. Ethnic German peasants got whiplashes, schoolchildren might get corporal punishment,[51] and the district commissar in Zviahel (now Novohrad-Volynsky) dispensed "harsh penalties" (presumably imprisonment) because in his view the ethnic Germans worked less hard than the Ukrainians. The German in charge of Kiev's about five thousand "ethnic Germans"—all of whom spoke little or no German—apparently was brutal to them.[52]

Encounters with "Europe"

One poster that the Nazis distributed in Ukraine was more on the mark than most. It depicted curious Soviet citizens looking out, westward, through a hole in a huge stone fence. "Stalin placed a high wall around you," the caption read. "He knew well that anyone who sees the outside world will fully grasp the pitiful state of the Bolshevik regime."[53] The German occupation did indeed (and much more than the annexation of eastern Poland in 1939 had done) provide a great opportunity to compare the Soviet way of life with that of the outside world, with what people called Europe.

Popular attitudes toward the Germans were evident already in forms of address. Ukrainian and Russian speakers addressed the males as *pan*, Sir.[54] In addition, it was striking to see how (unlike in the Red Army) German officers received the same food as the rank and file and yet somehow maintained a disciplinary distance. Equally surprising was the German soldier's standard of living, with his neat uniform, daily shave, tooth brushing, boot cleaning, and dishwashing. Compared to the Wehrmacht, it turned out, the Red Army was disorganized indeed. Just like the rapid advance of that Wehrmacht, it was a blow to people's self-esteem and cause for pity for the Red Army's rank and file.[55]

The people of Dnieper Ukraine found the first Germans incredibly naive. "Because we were used to Soviet suspiciousness, we were simply stunned by the Germans' amazing trustfulness," a woman recalls about the first days after their arrival in Kiev. "They entered completely unknown apartments without fearing booby traps. They were very sociable with the population and did not care at all about their weapons, which they just threw anywhere while unbuttoning."[56] Another woman was surprised to see how Germans caught a twelve-year-old boy with a stolen submachine gun and merely said, "Dumm, dumm!" (stupid).[57]

As noted, most peasants at first supported the Wehrmacht. The Reichskommissariat leadership reported that peasants spontaneously

15. "The Wall Has Come Down." Colorful Nazi propaganda poster showing curious Soviet citizens looking west, through a hole in a stone fence. The caption explains that "Stalin placed a high wall around you. He knew well that anyone who sees the outside world will fully grasp the pitiful state of the Bolshevik regime. Now the wall has been breached and the way to a new and better future has been opened." Probably printed in 1941. (Naukovo-dovidkova biblioteka tsentral'nykh derzhavnykh arkhiviv Ukraïny, 489sp.)

placed flowers at German graves and that during the drive for warm clothing during the first winter, "again and again the Ukrainian population generally turned out to be very willing donors" and that there were even spontaneous fund-raising actions.[58] There are also reports of old and young peasants who cried over the death of German soldiers, evidently from their "premodern" sense of compassion, which disregarded nationality. During these burials they would look on from a distance and "often a whole group of elderly men and women through loud crying and lamenting expressed their involvement," recalled a German chaplain, who also saw often how "after the closing of the grave women went to the fresh hillock and wailed with much emotion." Their laments included, "You poor one, you died in a foreign land! Now you're here and your dear ones cry for you and don't know where you are! Lord, how terrible war is! May God take you." Those whom the chaplain asked about this always referred to the general suffering of the war, which in their view united all people.[59]

Such empathy did not entirely disappear, even as suffering and deaths over time desensitized the people. (Pilgrims in the countryside south of Kiev early in 1943 prayed for the dead and the prisoners of war of both the Red and the German armies.)[60] By early 1942, however, when the deportations to Germany had started, any affection for the Germans was gone. Strangers complained to each other in the city streets about abuse simply for using "Germans Only" toilets and fumed that never before had they been beaten at the workplace.[61] The looting by many Germans, whether legal or unofficial, also created much resentment. A new saying emerged: "Among the little people, theft is called mania, among the nobles kleptomania, and among the Germans *Germaniia*."[62]

It seems clear that as early as the spring of 1942, most city dwellers hated the Germans as a people at least as much as they feared them. "I never thought I could hate this much, as I have come to hate these barbarians," L. Nartova wrote in her diary. "Everything about them is repulsive—their well-groomed mugs, so smug and arrogant, they always look at you as at something wretched, good-for-nothing, they don't care about the basic rules of decency."[63] At the end of the year, an informant wrote that about 90 percent of all Kievans were "dissatisfied" with the German administration, even though—he hastened to add—"again and again one hears very positive and favorite opinions of individual German officials and bosses."[64] Communist intelligence reported likewise early in 1943 that the overwhelming majority of Kievans "sees in every German their enslaver, robber, and murderer."[65]

By 1943, both cities and villages were seething with hatred. German (and native) policemen in Kiev felt compelled to always walk in groups and armed with rifles.[66] New expressions such as "You have a German conscience" captured the mood, as did rhymes like: "You sow, the Germans take it. You don't sow, the Germans fleece you. May the devil take them!"[67] The derogatory word *fryts* (from the German first name Fritz), long a staple in Soviet propaganda, came into popular use. Many letters to relatives working in Germany called the Germans "worse than the Bolsheviks; they made many promises, but did not keep any of them."[68] Peasant women sang songs with lyrics like: "The damned Germans have fat lips / Swollen / Yet they say we are coarse / Uncivilized." "During the day we are in the fields / At night we tend to the horses / Only the damned kraut / Plays the gramophone." "During the civil war the Ukrainians / Chased away the bourgeoisie / But the damned Germans appeared / And became the masters."[69] The hatred and fear of the Germans also explained why hardly any jokes about them appear to have been told.

A strong thirst for revenge emerged. The desire to "thrash the Germans," as it was called, found its way into stories about assassinations and, in particular, created a new folk hero. Whereas American troops during World War II invented the fictitious soldier Kilroy, in Soviet Ukraine there emerged the mythological underground fighter and partisan Kalashnikov. People believed that the partisan with the Russian name led a large partisan force, although he sometimes donned a German uniform, spoke German in cities, and left thank-you notes in German canteens with his real name. His goal was simple: to kill Germans. According to the lore, his family was arrested but quickly got out, for Kalashnikov walked into the German district commissar's office and posed an ultimatum. "All of Kiev speaks about him as a legendary hero," an informant reported in December 1942. "A year ago, he would generally have been considered a bandit." Peasants told each other that Kalashnikov supported nothing but their interests and religion and that he acted as an "international" person.[70]

At first few Soviet citizens even knew what Hitler looked like, for the Soviet media had never shown him. The Soviet newsreel on Molotov's visit to Berlin in November 1940, for example, blacked out Hitler's face.[71]

Even so, Ukrainians initially considered Hitler a great leader. His portrait, captioned "The Liberator," was in great demand and hung in homes next to the religious icon. At the official celebrations of Hitler's birthday on April 19, 1942 (a holiday), many reportedly decorated the portrait (probably with Ukrainian towels).[72] It was still on display in homes as late as August 1942, but by then it was almost devoid of meaning; as with Stalin's portrait in an earlier era, peasants were displaying it only to appear loyal. Now peasants ventured to say things like, "That 'liberator' thinks only about himself, not a word about us," or even, "Have you ever seen that a good borshch was made from a dog's tail? No, this 'liberator' is one of a kind with Stalin."[73] More and more songs and rhymes mentioned Hitler by name. Peasant women in the Kiev region sang, "The tsar in Russia abolished serfdom long ago / But here Hitler ordered slavery brought in." In Berdychiv in 1942, people said that Hitler wanted to rule the world but that he was going to "die like a dog." "Down with Hitler the liberator, long live Stalin the oppressor" was a saying in the Kamianets-Podilsky region in the summer of 1943, while people in the Dnipropetrovsk area who wanted to denigrate a person, perhaps even before the Red Army's return, used a new expression: "crazy like Hitler."[74]

The people of Dnieper Ukraine encountered various other people from "Europe." Because a significant number of them raped women in the countryside, the Romanians and Hungarians received a bad name. After the Battle of Stalingrad, about a hundred thousand Romanians and some forty thousand Hungarians again passed through Ukraine, this time in the other direction. Again many plundered, and male peasants stayed at home as much as possible to protect the women.[75] Another ally of Germany received more favorable treatment, although not at first: in Dnipropetrovsk, wearing green uniforms with white five-pointed stars, they were believed to be Whites from the revolutionary period, and encountered hostility. Soon, however, came the news that these were Italians—and thus, supposedly, womanizers with little inclination toward cruelty.[76] When they passed through Ukraine again during the summer of 1943, they looted German supplies, which the authorities refused to share with them, offered natives to work for food, sang for food (thus earning the nickname of "Running Tenors"), distributed Soviet leaflets, and even traded away their weapons. City dwellers fed them even though they had little themselves.[77]

The widespread "Soviet" suspiciousness notwithstanding, peasants received returning emigrés from the revolutionary period, whether former Ukrainian independence fighters or Whites, with traditional hospitality. In 1942, a veteran of the Ukrainian army of the revolutionary period, now working for the Organisation Todt, arrived in Bila Tserkva. People gathered around, asked questions, and pulled him by the sleeve: "Please drop by Mr. officer, have some bread and salt, you won't regret it."[78] A former White Russian who also visited this region had a hard time convincing his hosts that one week was plenty for a stay at their place.[79]

The hospitality also extended to Ukrainian natives of Galicia and western Volhynia, whether they arrived in German service or of their own accord. But those people were in for a shock: invariably, they encountered a conviction that they were *Germans* or, sometimes, Poles. In large part, this was because these Ukrainians were much better dressed. The locals seemed to believe that someone not poorly dressed could not possibly be one of "our people." Moreover, their language differed from the Ukrainian spoken in Soviet Ukraine. How could it be, the locals wondered, that these Germans could speak "Polish" or, badly to be sure, *po-nashomu*, "like us"?[80] In the Podolian town of Felshtyn, a Banderite task force in July 1941 had trouble convincing the people, as one member recalls:

"We are not Germans! We are your brothers, Ukrainians from the Western Lands—from Galicia," I add to be on the safe side. "We've come to visit you and to see if there's anything we can help you with."

"Oh, that's nice! We need to get the grain in, for otherwise it will fall to the ground and go to waste!" an older civilian of about fifty said. Although it was dark, the people, curious about the "Germans," slowly gathered around us, as if at a meeting . . .

"So there haven't been any Germans here?" I ask again.

"No, only you."

"Yes, but we are not Germans! We are just like you. Can't you tell by our language?"

"Yeah, it looks like the Germans can talk like us!" one of them answered.

"That's right," I say. "You're right, uncle! But we *are* Ukrainians!"

"Look," says friend Roman, while showing his blue-and-yellow armband. Then he points at the trident: "And that is the Ukrainian coat of arms."

"The symbol of the Ukrainian State," explains friend Halytsky, slightly shaking his head, irritated that here, so close to the Zbruch River, people do not know the national Ukrainian emblems. Only then did one of the curious people become convinced that we were not Germans. He squeezed himself toward us, saying:

"Oh yes! That's right! Remember Ivan Petrovych, that was in father Petliura's time! We had exactly the same banners. It's the same trident!"

"Just like Petliura's!" others now confirmed, while still others came closer, to see if Petliura indeed used to have that very same trident.[81]

Sources differ as to the subsequent popularity of the "westerners." Many people eventually shunned the Galicians, whom they knew the German authorities often persecuted.[82]

Visitor's tales about their lives in "Europe" were met with skepticism or amazement. Peasants frequently believed that the German officers were landlords or rich nobles, and when shown a picture of a German farmstead, they often failed to comprehend that it was a typical farmer's home.[83] Slovak soldiers, asked to tell about life "at home," "readily struck up conversations and told how workers, peasants, and the intelligentsia in their country lived; how much, and what, each of them could buy from his monthly earnings. They said that in their country, almost every peasant and worker owned a radio receiver, a bicycle, and three or four suits. Every citizen could work where he wanted, in agriculture or somewhere in the city. When something was not to his liking, he was free to go to another city or village, or take a job in another factory. The peasants were captivated," Pihido recalls, "but now and then they shook their heads in disbelief: by our Soviet standard, this life was a fairy tale."[84] Fevr rode a freight train from Bila Tserkva to Dnipropetrovsk in the fall of 1942. A large group of people asked him about ration cards in "Europe," about the darkening of cities there, the curfew times, and whether people's radios had been confiscated. When he gave a negative answer to the radio question, those listening "just could not get over their amazement."[85]

In short, the encounter with the outside world made it clear to contemporaries then, and to us now, that the mental outlook of the people of Dnieper Ukraine differed substantially from that of the newcomers. Most Soviet citizens had little or no understanding of the "Europeans," the Galician Ukrainians included. The years of isolation and indoctrination had made their mark. The question that remains is whether one should ascribe this to sovietization. The answer may become clear by considering the future that natives thought the Nazis and the Soviet regime had in store for them.

Hopes and Fears

Except in the very beginning, the vast majority of natives were never certain that the Germans would win the war and that the Soviet regime was gone forever. Reporting in the fall of 1941 after countless conversations in Ukraine, Hans Koch found peasants both passive and fearful, in particular "for the return of the Soviet system": "People are definitely impressed by the German tanks and planes. But have the rulers not changed some fifteen times within three decades, including two times the Germans? And are the Jews not whispering about the great Anglo-Saxon-Soviet coalition against Germany?" There was another problem: "People want the German victory with all their hearts, but are hundreds of thousands of Ukrainian men still not in the Soviet army, in Soviet labor battalions, concentration camps, and prisons? Are they not hostages in Moscow's hands?"[86] Iryna Khoroshunova, a Kievan who sympathized with the Soviet system, estimated in October 1941 that at least 95 percent of her acquaintances were certain that the Germans had beaten the Soviet Union, as Hitler had announced the week before. Another native recalls that many Kievans during those days "expressed satisfaction and had a radiance in their demeanor."[87] The SD thought that most Kievans had an "impatient hope for the fall of Moscow and Leningrad," which they expected to bring "an early peace . . . Here one cannot speak of a real war-weariness. Indicative of the wishes for the quick end of the war are in the first place economic considerations, and secondly the hope for the return of the exiled and conscripts."[88]

But by December doubt had taken hold: Nazi leaders noted in a report that developments at the front "partly created unrest among the population, as it fears a return of the Bolsheviks." A "considerable percentage" of the population believed that the Red Army had retreated merely for strategic reasons.[89] In February 1942, many rumors circulated about Red

Army successes and even its impending return.[90] From August to November 1942, another kind of rumor made the rounds: the Germans would soon be chased out of the Left Bank and they would give Kiev, or even the entire Right Bank, to Romania. In some versions, Romania was asking the Reich to return the *Ostarbeiter* (Eastern Workers) and prisoners of war who originated from the new "Romanian" regions. Thus the bad reputation of the Romanians temporarily took a back seat to the wish for a somewhat better life, one comparable to that in Romanian-ruled Odessa.[91] Inhabitants of Dnipropetrovsk around that time apparently believed that the Red Army had retaken Kharkiv and that the British had captured German cities. On the eve of the new year, these city dwellers even told each other that a cease-fire was drawing near.[92] When in February 1943 the German-controlled radio announced the outcome of the Battle of Stalingrad, it convinced almost everyone that the Germans would eventually leave Ukraine.[93]

Rumors about military affairs notwithstanding, people did not discuss the situation at the front very often.[94] More than anything else, people agonized about their personal fates. For this reason, the number of fortune-tellers and palm readers multiplied steadily.[95] Kievans realized that the hunger they were experiencing was designed to kill them or at least to evict them. They said, "The Germans are doing well / The Jews are done for / The Gypsies too / And the Ukrainians are next." In July and August 1942, it was rumored in the Kiev general district that the Germans would kill every person older than fifty-five.[96] Late in 1942, Kievans feared that the Germans wanted to move thousands from bombed-out German cities to homes in Kiev's Pechersk and Sophia districts and that they would kill any current inhabitant who refused to leave for Germany.[97] Given these fears, it is not surprising that the Nazis complained regularly that the Ukrainians had a very poor work ethic, and that alcoholism rose steeply.[98]

A portrayal of popular expectations in Dnieper Ukraine would be incomplete without a discussion of beliefs about events on the Soviet side of the front or, as some said, "in the Soviet Union."[99] Little is known for the years 1941 and 1942, however. A Nazi report for February 1942 states that people believed that radical reform had occurred there: Stalin had reintroduced religious freedom and had liberalized the economy.[100] In May 1942, Kievans exchanged the rumor that the United States had supplied so much flour, corn, and other products to the Soviet hinterland that there were surpluses.[101] By January 1943—if not earlier—a conviction spread of further political changes. Although Stalin and the Politburo were still in charge, the Communist ideology had been dropped; the Soviet Union had been renamed Russia, with the tsarist flag and a *Russian* army. Officers again had their prerevolutionary rights and shoulder straps that indicated rank, and Jews lost any Soviet medals and had to serve in a separate unit. Because of the return to Russian nationalism, the former persecution was now a thing of the past.[102] Another version of this widespread rumor held that Stalin had stepped down and that the new leaders were Molotov (premier), Shaposhnikov (minister of defense), and Zhukov (supreme commander).[103] Kuznetsov's Ukrainian grandfather, an anti-Communist who had become anti-German, concluded that "now the Bolsheviks have learned." It is likely that Soviet radio and other forms of propaganda contributed to the rise of such notions of radical change, as did German propaganda, which belittled actual reforms such as the introduction of rank in the Red Army.[104]

At the same time there were other rumors—frightening ones that, like the "positive" ones, often had a basis in reality. People found out that in the recaptured regions, authorities placed the note "Was in Occupied Territory" in people's passports.[105] German propaganda reported (accurately) that when the Red Army temporarily retook Kharkiv in February 1943, the NKVD set out large letter boxes, that quickly filled with denunciations, and refugees told stories of gang rapes by Red Army soldiers. Significant numbers of people feared that Stalin would simply have them hanged.[106]

The variety of the documented rumors makes it difficult to interpret popular opinion about "Soviet rule" (the phrase in Communist intelligence reports) or "the Bolsheviks" (the term in German intelligence reports and Ukrainian emigré memoirs). Moreover, the authors of generalizations about these opinions seldom consider the possibility that the people whose political "mood" they wish to describe might not equate Communist party rule with "Soviet rule." In fact, many natives, especially city dwellers, apparently made such a distinction. A Soviet partisan reported as early as January 1942 that a rumor in the Right Bank claimed that after a German retreat, there would be "Soviet rule without the Bolsheviks."[107]

The best way to approach this linguistic quandary may be to focus on the words that people themselves used to describe the Soviet regime. Just before the Germans arrived, peasants told each other that "the Soviets" were done for.[108] Once the Germans were in place, however, ordinary people rarely seem to have named the former authorities at all. They said "those," while pointing to the east, or "the former government."[109] To them, as to British and Americans at that time, the "Reds" usually meant only the Red Army.[110] This usage differs from that of smaller groups: nationally conscious Ukrainians spoke of the "Bolsheviks," fearless Russian speakers spoke of the "tramps" *(bosiaki)*, zealous anti-Semites and people requesting favors spoke of "Jewish rule" or "Yid rule," and some Christians spoke of the "devil's reign."[111]

As the violence of the Nazi regime increased in intensity and as a future victory of the Red Army became ever more likely, ordinary people gradually replaced the neutral "those" with "our people." Because people generally prefer to eschew association with a losing side, there was nothing particularly Ukrainian or Soviet about this shift. But it was controversial. A Kievan woman, about twenty-six years old, met a young friend who, having just spent months in a POW camp, could not wait for the departure of the Germans and the return of those he called *nashi*. "We could not connect," the woman recalls, for "to me, neither the Soviets nor the Germans were mine [*svoi*] anymore."[112] "Soon *nashi* will come!" some people in the Poltava region started saying during the Red Army's May 1942 offensive southeast of Kharkiv. Other locals questioned them: what good would come from those *nashi*—not the return of their sons, who had been killed in battle long ago. Instead, these objectors said, it would be "the same devil's regime that oppressed us," perhaps even another Great Famine.[113] Only when the Red Army did return were such objections no longer expressed.[114] The population continued to eschew the supposedly precise terms of "Soviet rule" and "the Bolsheviks."

Linguistic confusion aside, there can be no doubt that by 1943, the vast majority in Dnieper Ukraine longed for the arrival of the Red Army— "the Russian Army," "the Reds," *nashi*, or whatever people might call it. The SD found in the Mykolaïv region "a certain indifference of the population about a possible or suspected return of the Bolsheviks," and observed that the number of those in favor of "the Bolsheviks" had grown, "because the conviction is spreading more and more that the population could not fare worse under the Bolshevik regime."[115] Later that year, there were German reports from the Right Bank of resistance by "the broadest circles of the population" to any westward evacuation, even though there existed a "general fear of a return of the Soviets."[116] Ukraine's Communist party reported about the Right Bank that all but "the most inveterate enemies of Soviet power" wanted the Red Army to return, and that therefore the Soviet partisans were receiving support.[117] At the end of the summer, a German report estimated that about 60 percent of the population of Kryvy Rih "await[ed] the Red Army as liberators."[118]

It is one thing to say that people were eager to see the Red Army return. It is quite another to speak of a growing nostalgia for the Soviet system. Several sources mention such nostalgia, particularly among city dwellers. By 1942 the following "joke" was said to be circulating among city residents: "What was Stalin unable to achieve in twenty years that Hitler achieved in just one year? That we started to like Soviet rule."[119] A Jew from Lviv who arrived in Dnipropetrovsk early in 1943 disguised as a Polish employee of the Wehrmacht found that the locals recalled how before 1941 they could walk the streets without fear, buy things, send the children to school, and get enough to eat. Now "everybody" was calling "Soviet rule" infinitely preferable. Banderites also reported around this time from Dnipropetrovsk that "pro-Bolshevik sentiments" were "still very strong" there.[120] Lev Dudin—apparently generalizing on the basis of meetings with forced laborers in Germany—observed a "moral shift toward Soviet rule."[121]

German intelligence reports, meanwhile, preclude a conclusion that city dwellers who had been anti-Communist turned pro-"Soviet" or pro-Communist. These suggest that most city dwellers felt *both* hope and fear. "Let the Bolsheviks return," an informant heard many Kievans say. "They will shoot half of us, but the others at least will live and the misery will be over" (late 1942).[122] According to the propaganda section of the German air force, in the "eastern" territories and in Ukraine in particular, every day natives said things like, "The Red terror was followed by the German terror; if we have to be terrorized, then let it be by people who at least understand our language" (September 1943).[123] This coexistence of hope/optimism and fear/pessimism rings true. A recent study of city life in Russia during the 1930s speculates that fear of persecution perhaps even *promoted* a love of those behind it. "The more people were excluded from full citizenship or could imagine the possibility of exclusion, the more prevalent a certain type of anxious, intense, exaggerated Soviet patriotism became."[124] It is not unlikely, though impossible to demonstrate, that this phenomenon also existed in the Reichskommissariat.

The political thinking of the peasants was at least as ambiguous. They preferred to live with "our people," they said, because to them they were just that—our people in the sense of relatives. "A bad mother is still better than a step-mother who makes many promises," many said, and "It's going to be bad, but they're our people."[125] Some of the folkloric materials that were later selected for submission to the Academy of Sciences of Soviet Ukraine express a pro-"Soviet" attitude, as in aphorisms like: "Oh, oh, how can we live without Soviet power? Who has been to the Gestapo hurts all over" (Kiev region, late 1942 or early 1943);[126] "Give us the regime with the star, even if we get just rusk and water;" and "When Stalin ruled us, the collective farm knew no trouble / But when German rule came, struggle appeared in the farm" (Berdychiv and Chudniv regions, 1943).[127] Other sources suggest that the vast majority of peasants still hated and feared the Soviet system, associating it with famine and forced labor. In the Mykolaïv region after the Battle of Stalingrad, the village population "worried about the possibility of a return of the Reds and massively did not want that return," Banderites reported. Early in 1943, Banderites said that in the Uman countryside "the prevailing thought is: better the Soviets than the Germans." But the peasants had "no sympathy whatsoever for the Soviets" and feared their return.[128] Confirmation comes from a British journalist who visited the very same Uman region early in 1944, just after its recapture by the Red Army: "Many peasants were aloof and seemed indifferent to what was happening; it was clear that the Soviets—or 'the Reds,' as the peasants here called them—would have a job to develop a proper 'soviet-consciousness' among these people."[129] Thus it would seem that the Nazi period prompted at most a limited fond remembrance of "Soviet rule" and that an anxious Soviet patriotism may have existed in the cities, but such patriotism remained rare in the countryside.

Apart from a quick departure of the Germans and an end to the war, the question remains what kind of political system the peasants wanted. In recent years, historians have been suggesting that Soviet citizens did not—indeed, could not—envision any alternative between Soviet "socialism" and "capitalism" during the 1930s and during the war: most did not question the fundamentals of the Soviet system or perceive any viable alternative.[130] But it appears that the situation in wartime Ukraine was not so bleak. For one thing, peasants found at least three alternatives—a "Ukrainian authority" under German rule; Romanian rule; and an indistinct "Soviet rule without the Bolsheviks." By 1943, too, many apparently mentioned and preferred a fourth option. Some historians have recently argued that even during the revolutions of 1917, supposedly so full of hatred of tsarism, Russian peasants wanted a "good tsar" to rule over them. They did not see a contradiction between this wish and their other desire, for a republican political system.[131]

This very same sentiment also seems to have existed more than two decades later in Ukraine, or at least in its Left Bank. In June 1943, the German military authorities in Kharkiv organized an opinion survey in the Donbas and in the Kharkiv, Sumy, and Dnipropetrovsk regions. To the amazement of the native interviewers almost all of the peasant respondents said that what they really wanted was a tsar. Politicians of any kind, whether Kerenskii, Petliura, Denikin, or a Soviet leader, were liars who felt free to promise anything on their way to the top. "But a tsar—he won't deceive us," they said. "What he says, that's how is going to be." These respondents apparently believed that a monarch would consider their well-being more important than the interests of the "intelligentsia" and others.[132] A better illustration of the chasm in outlook between the peasant population and those who had ruled them since 1917 is difficult to find.

The Young Generation

There was one group in Nazi-ruled Soviet Ukraine that left behind little doubt about its views on the future and on "Soviet rule." This was the young generation; those born in the 1920s and 1930s. Young ethnic Germans—or at least the males—generally sympathized with Nazism. Strange as it may sound, even traditionally pacifist Mennonites "admired all things German uncritically and were unable to distinguish between good and bad," one of them recalls. "We had been under the Communist whip too long."[133] His generation adopted the Nazi salute ("Heil Hitler!"), and hundreds of Mennonites ranging in age from seventeen to forty volunteered for administrative, army, and police work. As a man who joined the First Ethnic German Cavalry Regiment at Gnadenfeld remembers, "the principle of non-resistance was forgotten and the men felt it their duty to assist in the struggle against the fearful oppression we had been subjected to for so long."[134] Such people acted arrogantly vis-à-

16. Boys of pacifist Mennonite origin, now "ethnic Germans," have donned swastika brassards and parade past SS leader Heinrich Himmler and other high-ranking visitors. Halbstadt district near Zaporizhzhia, Sunday morning, November 1, 1942. (Bundesarchiv, Bild 146/78/116/33.)

vis the Ukrainians, whom they called Russians. As the police veteran puts it, "We Mennonites had been suppressed for many years and our ethnic background had been made a matter of reproach. We had been called ugly names, had been oppressed in untold ways and our young people very seldom had been admitted to the institutions of higher learning. It was therefore not surprising that under the Germans our people were inclined to be somewhat domineering towards those who had for so long oppressed and rebuked them." There were "some, but very few" acts of revenge.[135]

In sharp contrast to the ethnic Germans, most other young people had a strong faith in Soviet Communism and rarely lost it under the Nazis. Pavlo Negretov, who was born in 1923, remembers that the Great Famine had not affected the loyalty of his generation to the Soviet system. "We were not bloodthirsty, but when western Ukraine and the Baltic republics were annexed, we were glad about the successes of our policy. I remember that at that time, one of my schoolmates said: 'So, now the NKVD will clean things up there . . .' And none of us took exception to him."[136] Various sources testify to a generation gap with older people. The SD, reporting in the fall of 1941 about the Kiev, Poltava, and Dnipropetrovsk regions, noted that young people were different in that they believed in Communism, although very few were "fanatics and really convinced fighters."[137] Likewise, an older Ukrainian found the youth in the Poltava region "completely on the side of the Bolsheviks." He knew two young women, both around twenty-seven years of age, from Ukrainian patriotic families. They had never joined the Komsomol, but they romanticized the Revolution and were patriots of a Soviet Ukraine as part of the Soviet Union.[138]

Most of the "Soviet generation" preferred the Soviet system and, unlike their parents, believed in the basic tenets of Communism. This did not imply sympathy for Stalin. "They praise Lenin, for they know him only from the official biographies, which render him a radiance of holiness," an Italian journalist reported about young women in Zaporizhzhia in May 1942. "But they hate Stalin with a vengeance—in a subdued voice, for they are shrouded in a permanent fear, which never leaves them."[139]

Like most older people in Dnieper Ukraine, the young were not very interested in national identity. They used the word *nashi* to describe themselves and others, not the national labels Ukrainian and Russian. The Vinnytsia region, the border area that suffered particularly severely during the 1930s, at first may have been exceptional. Here the SD found in August 1941 that "the notion of a united Soviet Russia with annexation of the Ukraine and led by Stalin could not win over the youth. Rather, up through the last years, especially among the more mature youth, the idea of a Ukraine completely separated from Russia has always been present to a certain extent, although there were no more forces actively working toward this goal." A German report in 1942 even spoke of "considerable support" for the Banderites there.[140] But Seleshko found that the many young people he spoke to in Vinnytsia in 1943 "completely lacked a feeling of national hatred and did not wish to delineate national differences . . . National ideals were foreign to them."[141]

There were two main reasons for the pro-Communist, nonnationalist attitude of most young people. One was Soviet indoctrination and isolation: to young people, Moscow was simply the center of the world.[142] They knew even less about other countries than the older generation did.

Young Kievans "did not understand a thing about either the west or the events there," returning emigrés thought.[143] A young secretary at a butter factory in Oleksandriia, for example, asked a Wehrmacht interpreter how western people like him could make butter—after all, she added, they did not have any cows. She did not believe the answer he gave, until her boss confirmed it. Much to her dismay, he also informed her that the factory machines were German imports.[144] An Italian journalist in Zaporizhzhia observed "a complete lack of knowledge about the outside, foreign world": "almost all the girls know algebra and some trigonometry, but they don't know where Rome, Berlin, or Paris are . . . They say that the steam engine was invented in year x by a Russian worker. They solve technical problems, write about machines, and can talk about the construction of the Dnieper dam—but they are starving and don't have, and never had, anything to put on. When they see a handkerchief or some piece of [Western] fabric or linen, they stare as if it's a miracle."[145] Two years later, indoctrination and isolation were still strong influences. Seleshko observed that even in the fall of 1943, the youth "generally did not consider the situation in Ukraine under the Soviet regime abnormal." Young people told him that "the old system—that is the Bolshevik one, for they did not know any other—was better than the new one." He adds that "the new system had disappointed them: fascism had turned out to be even worse than Bolshevik propaganda had presented it."[146]

Indeed, the other reason for the pro-Soviet attitude of the young was the way the Nazi regime treated them. Among their grievances were the roundups for work in Germany—which targeted them—and sheer boredom, because the schools were closed and entertainment was hard to find. Most important, they saw no future for themselves, unlike before 1941. The Germans offered them no chance to get ahead in life. "When I went to school, my biggest wish was to become a doctor," a girl said. "But now I must leave the tenth grade and try to make a living somewhere else. My life is ruined." A sixteen-year-old boy told an informant, "I sit at home and help my mother in the household. I cannot go to school because it's far away and I don't have any shoes. In the past I wanted to be an engineer."[147]

The political generation gap persisted until the very moment of the German retreat. By 1943 it was common within a single family for the older people to worry or be sad, but the young to rejoice at any Red Army advance. Late in February 1943, as diaries show, "many [Kievans] fear[ed] the coming of the Bolsheviks," but the wish for the arrival of the Red Army was steadily increasing, "especially among the youth."[148] The SD reported in May 1943 that "it is said to happen frequently that parents reject the Soviet system, while the children long for its return."[149] Seleshko noticed the same in September and October 1943 in Vinnytsia. Everyone he knew wanted the Germans out, but "the older people were all sad, while the youth made merry. There was a divide between the mood of the older and the younger ones. The older people feared the Bolsheviks, but the youth wanted them."[150]

When Germany invaded the Soviet Union in 1941, the native population wanted most of all an end to Stalin's regime and to the war. When peace failed to materialize and the new regime turned out to be unbearably oppressive, they wanted the Germans out and started to hate them. Yet throughout this period, people were and remained little interested in politics. Peasants in particular had little hope for a good life after the wished-for German retreat. They apparently wanted a tsar to rule over them but they knew he was not going to come. The younger generation, in contrast, generally wanted the Soviet system back, although they did not necessarily favor Stalin.

Because most ordinary people did not believe in political ideologies, their ethnic identity and political loyalties were vague to a degree that was very irritating, if not intolerable, for those with a clear weltanschauung—the Ukrainian nationalists and the Communists. Ordinary people never spelled out whether in saying "our people" they were including or excluding Communists and Galician Ukrainians. But it is clear that few of them considered Soviet rule a "Russian" project. Although most natives could imagine the formation of a Ukrainian administration, they did not find an independent Ukrainian state necessary. All of this was frustrating for Ukrainian nationalists. The native population was also, from a Communist point of view, insufficiently Soviet. True, as shown in Chapter 8, they expected some involvement in the political process and some respect. They were also sovietized in the sense that they disbelieved many of the things visitors told them about life in "Europe." At the same time, however, and more important, they believed little of the Communist ideology.

Until now, it seemed reasonable to assume that the Nazi period had great influence on the thinking of the people who lived through it. Some scholars who have studied World War II conclude that it unified the citizens of the Soviet Union around Stalin, whom they came to see as their one and only savior.[151] Another view holds that the Nazi experience made Ukrainians in Dnieper Ukraine more nationally conscious and more eager to create their own state.[152] The evidence presented here, however, suggests that throughout the Nazi period, prewar mental attitudes continued to exert a tremendous hold. The one proven significant change in most people's mental outlook was that the Germans, who initially were not disliked, eventually were hated as a people. But in the final analysis, the Nazi regime had nearly no effect on the mental outlook of those who survived.

In a time when a nationalist regime and a Communist regime were fighting each other to the death through military and other means, few of the civilians caught in the middle developed a more than passing interest in the ideologies that these regimes stood for. With the main exception of the young ethnic Germans, many of whom became adherents of the Nazi ideology and ethos, few natives found the mental constructs of "nation" or "class" appealing.[153] Most people's thinking was marked by what social psychologists call "nonattitudes": they had no clear preferences about the kind of government or policies they wanted, and they were inconsistent across issues.[154] In this particular case, I believe that we can take these ordinary people at their word—and the words they used were so vague as to rarely hint at underlying values, and indeed to reveal confusion about them. Oksana Iatsenko, born in 1919 in Mysailivka, was asked in 1995 when her life had been better, "during the 1930s or under the Germans." *Pry nashykh luchche zhylos,* she replied—"It was better under our people."[155] Here she meant neither the Ukrainians nor the Communists. She simply meant what she said.

10

RELIGION AND POPULAR PIETY

To further consider the mental outlook of the people of the Reichs-kommissariat, we now look at organized religion and popular religiosity, which historians of modern Europe have been studying increasingly in recent years as a topic distinct from the institutional history of religion.[1] Any study of this kind should first provide an outline of the basics of Soviet and German policies toward religion as well as the competition between the two Orthodox churches that came into being under Nazi rule, an Autonomous Orthodox church and an Autocephalous Orthodox church.

The revolutionary period that started in 1917 brought great changes to church life in Ukraine. The Russian Orthodox church there received a certain autonomy from Russia, but also lost ground against new competitors. By the 1920s, Soviet Ukraine had three Orthodox churches. The largest was the Russian Orthodox church, also called the Patriarchal church. Since 1918, the Ukraine-based part of this church had autonomous status as an exarchate, and in 1921 it received its first exarch leader. In 1920, a new, independent Ukrainian Autocephalous Orthodox church appeared on the scene and one year later, it ordained its own metropolitan, Vasyl Lypkivsky. The consecration was not in accordance with Orthodox canon law, however, but in the form of the supposedly ancient, but controversial, ritual of a "laying on of hands" by priests. The third Orthodox tendency was Renovationism, from the mid-1920s represented in Ukraine by the Orthodox Autocephalous Synodal church, which also had its own metropolitan.[2]

In 1927, the militantly atheist Soviet authorities acknowledged that the Russian Orthodox Patriarchal church had a right to exist. From then on, its two Orthodox rivals went into decline, both because the vast majority of faithful preferred the Russian Orthodox church and because of state intervention. In 1930 the regime forced the Ukrainian Autocephalous Orthodox church to declare at a synod that it no longer existed, and thereafter it arrested an estimated half of its clergy. Remnants of the church, renamed the Ukrainian Orthodox church, functioned until the mid-1930s, when its metropolitan was arrested and its parishes were closed down. Meanwhile, in 1936, the metropolitan of the Synodal church (Renovationists) was banned from holding church offices and arrested one year later, and all Synodal bishops were forced to resign. In other words, the Ukrainian Autocephalous and Synodal (Renovationist) hierarchies were eliminated and only the Russian Orthodox (Patriarchal) church remained.[3]

But eventually the Russian Orthodox church in Ukraine (Patriarchal Exarchate) suffered as much as its rivals. In 1935 and 1936 two of its bishops were arrested, and in 1937 it was the turn of the exarch. The remaining Russian Orthodox hierarchs soon shared his fate.[4] Assaults on the church were also evident at the parish level. For example, early in 1938 all priests were deported from the border region of Zhytomyr. By the end of the decade, only about a hundred Orthodox priests remained in Soviet Ukraine (besides a number of underground priests), none of whom could conduct services. The campaign against Orthodoxy was more extensive than in Soviet Russia, where hierarchies of the Renovationist and Russian Orthodox churches, while depleted, nevertheless continued to exist.[5]

During this period, there existed an Orthodox church in neighboring Poland, which the ecumenical patriarch in Istanbul recognized from 1924 as autocephalous, or independent. When Germany and the Soviet Union destroyed the Polish state in 1939, this church, led by Metropolitan Dionysii (Valedynsky), archbishop of Warsaw, received the new name of Holy Orthodox Autocephalous church in the General Government.[6] Meanwhile, in western Volhynia and eastern Galicia, under Soviet rule since 1939, most Orthodox bishops pledged allegiance to the Russian Orthodox Patriarchal locum tenens, Metropolitan Sergii (Stragorodskii) of Moscow and Kolomna. Although they did this under duress, it is conceivable that among them were those who were pleased to be rid of their "Polish" autocephaly. Barely had this new situation come about, however, when Germany invaded the Soviet Union.

German Policies and Church Leaders

As the Germans occupied Ukraine, they put up posters that announced "The Time of Stalinist Atheism Is Gone. The German Authorities Give You the Opportunity to Pray in Freedom Again."[7] In fact, in various ways, representatives of the German army were more deeply involved. Some commanders issued orders for reopening the churches, and many soldiers and officers helped clean and restore church buildings. Ukrainians who worked as army interpreters apparently told Orthodox priests that their services should be in the Ukrainian language. If they did not know it, they were allowed to use Church Slavonic if they pronounced it with a Ukrainian accent.[8]

But there were instances in which the Germans acted with caution or even with disdain. In the southern city of Kherson, the regional economy command gave the local Orthodox clergy thirty thousand rubles for the restoration of the church building, in exchange for a promise to conduct services in Church Slavonic, a written loyalty oath, and a vow to "reject all efforts to make the church a political tool of Ukrainian nationalists." There were also cases in which German soldiers turned just-restored churches into stables.[9]

These various kinds of German involvement displeased the German High Command, which quickly banned any further interference by Germans.[10] From then on, the German army at most played a mediating role. For example, in November 1941, in Boryspil east of Kiev, the local commander ordered a referendum on language use. When the pollsters disagreed about the outcome, he ordered the church building to alternate between being an "Old Slavonic church" and a "Ukrainian church."[11]

When civilian Nazi rule replaced military rule, there came a more elaborate system of control over religious life. All "Ukrainian organizations of a nonproductive and noneconomic character" had to register with the native city mayor or raion chief, and were obliged to inform him once a month about changes in their structure or personnel. On December 8, 1941, and again on July 11, 1942, Reichskommissar Koch banned all church services on weekdays, with the exception of Christmas, New Year's Day, and the two days of Easter.[12] The civilian German authorities also placed greater emphasis on the separation of church and state. Late in 1942, Koch warned that transgressing mayors or raion chiefs would be dismissed. The official ban on religious instruction at schools amounted to a radical change for western Volhynia, where such instruction had existed under Poland and even during the brief period of Soviet rule.[13]

The Nazis interfered in several other ways in church life. They allowed neither church charity nor seminaries, with the exception of one Autonomous seminary in Kremenets that was established in 1943.[14] There were also ad hoc decisions aimed at preventing the emergence of a united Orthodox church, and an almost total ban on newspaper reports about church life.[15] From mid-1942, Koch and his associates, who had come to strongly dislike the Autocephalists, started to support what had become the Autonomous Orthodox church.[16]

Most difficult to ascertain is the role of the district commissars. Many of their policies on church life appear to have depended on a personal agenda. Some used the general ban on public gatherings as an excuse to do away with local church councils or to ban celebrations.[17] Many district commissars and landwirts banned church services at certain times, especially during the harvest. As for the Security Police, it closely monitored the clergy, while banning and destroying almost anything that the Orthodox churches wanted to publish. Until the summer of 1942, these Nazis rarely intervened in disputes, but when they did, at first they tended to support the Autocephalists.[18]

In the middle of 1941, seven Orthodox bishops found themselves in German-ruled western Ukraine. On August 18, 1941, Archbishop Aleksii (Hromadsky) of Volhynia called an Oblasny Sobor, or regional synod, in the monastery of Pochaïv in far southwestern Volhynia. Here Aleksii obtained the provisional title of regional metropolitan, but the bishops in attendance still felt canonically bound to the Russian Orthodox church. They called their church by various names (the Ukrainian Orthodox church, the Orthodox Ukrainian church, the Orthodox church in Ukraine, or the Orthodox Autonomous church in Ukraine), but it became known as simply the Autonomous church.[19] Another synod on December 8 established that the best candidate for the important but vacant Archeparchy (archdiocese) of Kiev and Pereiaslav was a respected Ukrainian patriot based in the General Government, Archbishop Ilarion (Ohiienko) of Chełm and Podlachia. The synod decided to ask Ilarion's agreement to the transfer, which he gave, and—more importantly—that of his superior, Dionysii of Warsaw. The long-term plan was to convene in Kiev, with German permission, a special synod where bishops, priests, and laypersons would elevate Ilarion of Kiev and Pereiaslav to the position of metropolitan of Kiev and all Ukraine.[20]

But two hierarchs based in Ukraine did not participate in either of these synods: Bishop Polikarp (Sikorsky) of Zhytomyr and Archbishop

Oleksander (Inozemtsev) of Pinsk and Polissia. Like Aleksii and his associates, these two men did not want to submit to the "Polish" Orthodox Autocephalous church in the General Government, but they did not wish to obey "Moscow" (the Russian Orthodox Patriarchal locum tenens there) either. Under Soviet rule, they had not recognized the Moscow Patriarchate as fully as the other hierarchs had done. Polikarp made it clear that he wished to revive the original Ukrainian Autocephalous Orthodox church.[21] Laypersons in Rivne urged him to sever all ties with the Autonomists, especially when their leader Aleksii started calling himself exarch of Ukraine and metropolitan of Volhynia and Zhytomyr, and they even proceeded to call Polikarp the "administrator" of the Orthodox church in Ukraine.[22] At that stage Dionysii, heretofore shunned because he was in Warsaw and "of foreign blood" (namely Russian), became involved, apparently because he had become a Ukrainian patriot. After the Autocephalists in Ukraine had explained the situation to him, Dionysii decreed on December 24, 1941, that Polikarp was the "temporary administrator of the Orthodox Autocephalous Church in the liberated lands of Ukraine." After some time, without a specific decision, the adjective "temporary" simply disappeared.[23] The emergence of a rival Orthodox church was complete when, in February 1942, there followed the consecration of three new bishops and a separate synod that decided to accept any surviving priests of the original Ukrainian Autocephalous Orthodox church without a second consecration.[24] The new church functioned under varying names, but the most official was the Holy Orthodox Autocephalous church in the Liberated Lands of Ukraine.[25]

The Autonomists and the Autocephalists agreed that Ilarion of Chełm and Podlachia was the best candidate to lead Orthodox church life in Ukraine.[26] Thus it was not inevitable that they should fail to unite into one Orthodox church, even though there was the thorny issue of subordination to the Moscow Patriarchate. The Reichskommissariat leadership, however, refused to grant Ilarion a travel permit.[27] The Nazis, already feeling generous for allowing church life in central Ukraine to resurrect itself, did not want any Ukrainians to arrive from the General Government and speed up the resurrection. This obstruction was damaging enough, but in May 1942, Koch took one step further. Orthodox church representatives were summoned to Rivne and received notice—not from Koch, who never met any such people—that the Nazis acknowledged the existence of two Orthodox churches in the Reichskommissariat, an Autonomous church led by Aleksii and an Autocephalous church led by

Polikarp. Any polemical exchanges between them should stop, they were told.[28] Soon afterward, the five Autocephalous church hierarchs found out that consecrations of bishops would be banned. In response, they quickly consecrated seven more bishops. On May 26, there came a decree that bishop consecrations required prior permission from Koch.[29]

The Reichskommissar's next intervention came several days later, on June 1, 1942. A "Regulation of the Legal Position of Religious Organizations" proclaimed freedom of worship, but actually constrained church life. Henceforth, a general commissar could dismiss the leaders of religious organizations if he had "objections of a general political nature" against them. New denominations needed a license from Koch and he reserved the right to disband any denomination that he might deem a threat to "order and security" or that simply engaged in nonreligious activities.[30] Koch also did not want any Autocephalists in Kiev, and he ordered Polikarp to remove his bishops from there. One of the two bishops, Mstyslav (formerly Stepan Skrypnyk, the head of the Ukrainian Council of Trust in Volhynia), was even "not allowed to be in territory with a population that is mostly Ukrainian." Both bishops refused to budge.[31]

This was the setting in which both Orthodox orientations started exploring closer relations. Late in June 1942, Aleksii proposed to Polikarp that they establish "some kind of accord." When in the fall the next Autocephalous synod convened, it agreed to start negotiations. These resulted in the proclamation, on October 8, 1942, of a single Ukrainian Autocephalous Orthodox church, led by neither Aleksii nor Polikarp, but by Dionysii of Warsaw. The German authorities opposed the union, however, and forbade the press to mention it.[32] Moreover, there was internal opposition: three Autonomous hierarchs demanded that Aleksii remove his signature and relinquish his title of exarch. Aleksii eventually disavowed the union (on December 15), while holding on to his title.[33]

Along with the attempt at unification, during the fall of 1942 there emerged an outright destructive Nazi line vis-à-vis the Orthodox hierarchies. They were told that neither Orthodox orientation should have lines of authority across the borders of any general district. Moreover, each general commissar took over leadership of the churches located in his general district from the hierarchs, and bishops who did not live in the capital had to move there. From now on, each general commissar claimed the authority to select one leading bishop per church. Synods were possible, but only of bishops from a single general district. Bishop consecrations still required special permission, and the appointment of priests required consultation with the district commissars. In addition, a general commissar could dismiss any priest. All this implied that the Nazis divided the Autocephalous and Autonomous churches each into six jurisdictions. Now the Reichskommissariat Ukraine had *twelve* Orthodox churches.[34] This treatment of the Orthodox was a radical version of the divide-and-rule policies toward churches that the Nazis practiced all over Europe.[35]

The new situation inevitably caused abuses, most strikingly in the Zhytomyr general district under SS-Brigadeführer Ernst Leyser. For reasons that remain unclear, Leyser insisted on retaining two bishops who were most likely Soviet agents. The first was the Autocephalous Bishop Fotii (Tymoshchuk) of the Podolia eparchy. In August 1942, it came to light that the Polish state had convicted him as a Soviet spy before the war and that he had been stripped of the priesthood. Polikarp expelled him from the church, but Fotii stayed in Vinnytsia. He said the act of unification of October 1942 amounted to reconciliation with "Moscow," which compelled him to create "my own Ukrainian church." Leyser had a strange sympathy for the man and appointed him in early November as the highest representative of the Autocephalous church in the general district, while keeping Fotii's one potential contender, Bishop Hryhorii (Ohiichuk) of Zhytomyr, under arrest. Hryhorii was released only in mid-March 1943, after Polikarp wrote to Koch about the issue. Only at that stage did Fotii disappear—never to be seen again.[36]

The Fotii scandal was barely over when it was the turn of the Autonomous church. Early in 1943, a Russian arrived in Kiev from the Caucasus Mountains with retreating German soldiers and claimed to be Bishop Nikolai (Avtonomov) of Piatigorsk in Russia. An Autonomous bishop appointed him as a priest, but instead the man went to see Aleksii, who even created a new eparchy for him, in Mazyr in Belarusan Polissia. Soon the demeanor of "Nikolai" during mass and at German parties set off a rumor that he was an impostor. German military intelligence confirmed this and said that he was a spy for the Soviet Union, but still Leyser kept "Nikolai" in office until the very end.[37]

Besides Orthodox Christians, there were in the Reichskommissariat Ukraine Protestants and Catholics. A comparison of their status with that of Orthodox church members reveals that they were treated much differently—either significantly better (in the case of the Protestants) or much worse (in the case of the Catholics). Because the Security Police found the pacifist Baptists and Evangelical Christians harmless, it decreed that they be treated with "magnanimity." The civilian German regime took the same line, and lifted the bans on their activity that some native policemen, village elders, mayors, and raion chiefs had imposed.[38] As a result, these denominations flourished. Their missionaries even stealthily traveled about Dnieper Ukraine, preaching and distributing literature in still-illegal ways at great risk of denunciation and arrest. In Kiev and most other cities, communities were created or recreated, and some even managed to get booklets published. (The Islamic faith was also allowed. Kiev's approximately seven hundred Muslims had a mosque in the Podil district from October 1941.)[39]

In contrast, the Nazis persecuted Greek Catholic (also known as Uniate) and Roman Catholic priests. The Security Police considered the Greek Catholic church, led by Metropolitan Andrei Sheptytsky in the General Government, an "outpost" of the Vatican in the Reichskomissariat (which actually had relatively few Greek Catholics), and therefore banned it. Greek Catholic priests from Galicia who tried to move to the Reichskommissariat were turned back.[40] In the case of the Roman Catholics, Nazi hostility toward the Vatican combined with animosity toward the Poles, who in Ukraine constituted the vast majority of these Christians. Thus Roman Catholics were refused places for worship, existing churches were closed, and in some cases priests were shot—at least seventeen were killed in western Volhynia alone. The authorities even closed a Roman Catholic church in Mykolaïv where most members of the congregation were ethnic Germans.[41] An exception was the Vinnytsia district, the commissar of which allowed its one Roman Catholic church, in Hnivan, to function, apparently because most of the six thousand parishioners were Ukrainians.[42] These developments stood in marked contrast to the situation in the General Government, where the Nazis tolerated the Roman Catholic church and subsidized the Greek Catholic and most other churches.[43]

In short, the German treatment of churches in the Reichskommissariat varied considerably, depending on the denomination and the length of the German presence. As the war went on, Nazi policies became harsh and even destructive.

Popular Piety

After the Germans arrived, there were many signs of popular piety and religious life quickly revived. Peasants again dared to cross themselves in public, and some even did so when seeing the first German tanks, which

17. A festive procession with church items that people had hidden for years from the Soviet authorities. Mykolaïv, southern Ukraine, October 1941. (Nederlands Instituut voor Oorlogsdocumentatie, 34084–1.)

had white crosses painted on them. Peasant women and children started to wear crosses (sometimes even before the Germans came), and elderly peasants frequently participated in German field services.[44] The clearest sign of a revival was the restoration of churches. In villages and small towns, people assembled to paint the buildings white and install church bells, recast from pieces of iron. If the original church had been demolished before the war, ordinary buildings were used. People who had hidden icons, communion cloths, church books, utensils, and garments now brought them out. In the town of Vasylivka, south of Zaporizhzhia, a magnificent iconostasis was reassembled from parts saved by various people.[45]

The first services followed within days or at most weeks, and sometimes even before any Germans arrived. Because there were not enough

priests, villages invited priests from elsewhere to lead them.[46] "The women prayed, all the time wiping away the tears that were trickling down
their cheeks," Pihido recalls about the village of Staiky, in the Kiev
region. "People greeted each other as if it were Easter. From both sides
of the church, which was in an ordinary building, one could hear the
refrain, 'Christ has risen!' and 'The Lord wished us to live to see this
happy day.'"[47]

Soon there was a flood of people of various ages who wished to be baptized, which happened often in large crowds. Sometimes they followed
the oldest Orthodox tradition, which prescribed immersion, so that these
baptisms took place in rivers. Many people also arranged for a priest to re-
marry them. Baptisms and religious marriages were to remain a feature
of community life during the Nazi period.[48] Initially there were also
reburials, with or without a priest, in which people opened coffins to put
a cross or icon inside. This phenomenon became more rare after October 1941, however, when the Security Police began banning it. In general,
burials without the participation of a priest were illegal.[49] Particularly
noteworthy were burials of the victims of the NKVD massacres. In Lutsk
in August 1941, 3,862 prisoners who had been shot were buried in five
mass graves in a ceremony conducted by Polikarp.[50] A similar mass burial
of victims took place in Rivne, while General Karl Kitzinger, commander of the armed forces stationed in the Reichskommissariat (who
happened to arrive that day), looked on and while young nationalists carried portraits around and chanted, "Ukraine for the Ukrainians" and
"Long live Bandera, the Leader of Ukraine."[51]

One of the largest religious gatherings of the entire Nazi period was
the celebration in honor of St. Iov near the Pochaïv monastery and
church. On September 10, 1941, for the first time in twenty years, some
fifteen thousand pilgrims from the Right Bank gathered there. (During
the imperial period, tens of thousands used to gather.) The mostly female
pilgrims had been informed through word of mouth and some traveled
for days. German propagandists made good use of the event: they instructed the local authorities to put up on walls newspapers and large
portraits of Hitler, and they themselves handed out small German flags,
postcards with Hitler's portrait, and the newspaper *Volyn*. One poster was
embellished and taken along in the procession. Most of the pilgrims had
never seen a picture of Hitler before and were impressed, as the propagandists alleged. An old man smiled broadly and told others, "That's

our father, Hitler," while some women even kissed the portrait. The orderly proceedings were led by Archbishop Aleksii, who prayed for Hitler and the German army and who, in a speech to the clergy and laity, "demanded that they always remember in their prayers the Führer, the most brilliant leader of today, and the German people. The blood sacrifice of the German people should never be forgotten. He and all Ukrainians, he said, wanted the intentions and thoughts of the Führer to be realized in full."[52]

Most especially under the military authorities, but also after the introduction of civilian German rule, the auxiliary native administrations generally promoted Orthodox Christianity. A raion chief might, for example, order the village elders to repair church buildings.[53] The native administrations also brought back many traditional Orthodox holidays and made them official. Mayor Volodymyr Bahazii of Kiev, for example, reinstated fourteen holidays. And many places began celebrating these holidays according to the old-style calendar.[54] In vain, the Wehrmacht warned the native administrations against such practices and against organizing—or banning—any religious activity. Native school inspectors also "completely forgot the democratic principle of the separation of church and state."[55] As a result, Orthodox Christianity (*Zakon Bozhyi*—the Law of the Lord) was taught in many schools during the 1941–1942 school year. In one school in Kiev, which was probably typical, every class received religious instruction once a week. And in a typical village school, first-graders during the 1941–1942 school year had a subject called ethics. Among the topics were "The Creation of the Universe," "The Suffering on the Cross, the Death, and the Resurrection of Our Lord Jesus Christ," and the Lord's Prayer. Ethics also comprised secular topics such as the work ethic and the proper way to treat the elderly.[56] Any such instruction (usually by Orthodox priests) was banned everywhere by mid-1942 at the latest, with the exception of the Poltava district, where it continued due to the influential district school inspector, an ethnic German woman who lived with the regional military commander.[57]

There is still more evidence suggesting a generally pious mood. In population censuses, the vast majority of natives identified themselves as "Orthodox" and very few chose "without religion" or gave no answer.[58] Traces of a religious way of thinking also showed up in expressions that some Ukrainians, in particular peasants, used to identify the Soviet authorities; most notably, *dyiavolska vlada* or *vlada satany*—the devil's regime. In one village during the German advance, as the noises from the front became louder, a man over eighty took off his cap, crossed himself, and told his fellow villagers, "I never thought, children, that I would live to see the day, but now you see, the Lord had mercy. Pilate's Empire is coming to an end."[59]

On closer examination, however, popular attitudes toward churches, and religiosity in general, were more complex. For instance, the massive participation in the reconstruction of the churches in the countryside, even by the young generation, was perhaps less because of piety than because these buildings were the most prominent symbol of the better life that people expected—a new life that would include a labor-free Sunday. In the 1930s, it had been rare for all the members of a peasant family to have their weekly day off on the same day. Moreover, even on that day they often had to do "voluntary" work. When a German army chaplain asked male peasants in 1941 about this practice, they merely let out curses. "The women, however, tended to let out a flood of complaints. They often pointed out that the present defeat of the Bolsheviks was a just punishment by the Lord for their fight against God and the church, and in particular for the abolition of the Sunday, which made one's entire life miserable."[60] The military intelligence officer and Slavist Hans Koch was surprised at the strength of the religious revival, but he also thought that it was partly a reaction to Soviet conditions—that is, a way to celebrate the Soviet regime's expected demise.[61]

Regarding baptisms, there appears to have been a certain amount of compulsion. A Communist underground activist stated in a report about the Kiev and Kirovohrad regions that native authorities made baptism mandatory for all children up to the age of twelve and that the village elders summoned those who refused.[62] Fear also played a role. According to another Soviet source, many baptisms were preceded by rumors that unbaptized children would be shot—a clear reference to the Holocaust.[63]

The Faithful and the "Self-Consecrators"

One way to measure the extent of the religious revival is to ask whether believers actually cared about the controversy between the Autonomists and the Autocephalists. Hans Koch found that most faithful had a wait-and-see attitude and wanted the Germans to settle the matter. This over-states the indifference, however. Bishops from both orientations were besieged with requests for priests, but once people had more information, and especially once they had an option to choose because both churches had representatives in their community, the vast majority preferred the Autonomous church.[64] In the fall of 1941, the SD estimated that just under 55 percent of the Slavic population favored the Autonomous church, while 40 percent supported the Autocephalists.[65]

Hereafter the number of adherents of the Autocephalous church continued to decline, because in Kiev and beyond—in the words of the former head of the short-lived Church Council of the Autocephalous church in Ukraine—"gradually word got around that the priests of the Church of Metropolitan Vasyl Lypkivsky [that is, the church represented by Polikarp] were uncanonical and should be called 'Lypkivsky-ites' and 'self-consecrators.'"[66] The Section of Denominations of the Kiev city administration noticed likewise that the overwhelming majority of Ukraine's Orthodox faithful supported the Autonomists.[67] Indeed, one Autocephalous bishop, Nikanor, lamented to Polikarp that the parishioners of Kiev's supposedly Autocephalous Pokrov church "loathe us as 'self-consecrators' and yearn for Moscow." In the Poltava region, an estimated 80 percent of all churchgoers attended only Autonomous services, and in the Kryvy Rih region, the Autonomous church was also reportedly more influential than the Autocephalous church.[68]

To be fair, there are some reports of the continued strength of the Autocephalous orientation. According to General Commissar Magunia, by the fall of 1942 both Orthodox churches were equally represented in the Kiev general district, with the south being "strongly Autocephalous."[69] Another German, basing his ideas on conversations with Nazi officials in August 1942, found that the Autocephalists "predominated" in the central regions of Uman, Zvenyhorodka, and Kirovohrad, and in Mykolaïv in the south.[70] Presumably he was referring to the distribution of parishes.

The evidence dealing with changes of denomination by entire parishes is scarce, but it seems clear that most such changes favored the Autonomous church.[71] The main exception was western Volhynia in 1943, when parishes started to abandon the Autonomous church for the Autocephalous church. But there is reason to doubt whether this was actually done according to the wishes of most Orthodox members, for considerable pressure came from the Ukrainian Insurgent Army (UPA), the leaders of which were hostile toward the Autonomists.

Most Orthodox faithful had two problems with the Autocephalous church. One was their conviction that it was uncanonical. At least as important was the church's insistence on the use of the Ukrainian language, a rigidity that proved to be very unpopular in Dnieper Ukraine. On this matter, the Autonomous church was more flexible—Church Slavonic was its liturgical language, but a bishop could allow the use of Ukrainian if most parishioners desired. As a result, it was not unusual for Autonomous parishes in western Volhynia to have the service, in part or entirely, in Ukrainian, and to have any Church Slavonic pronounced in Ukrainian.[72] In Dnieper Ukraine, however, any priest who tried to introduce Ukrainian in the liturgy faced dissatisfaction and resistance from parishioners.[73] In Sviatoshyn, a western suburb of Kiev, an Autocephalous priest asked the choir to sing in Ukrainian. "The congregation did not want to do this," he reported. Ever since, he added, "When I hold service, the former choir singers take their position and start singing in Slavonic, and all behave as they see fit." In Kiev's Autocephalous Pokrov church, soon morning services in Church Slavonic had to be allowed. In Dnipropetrovsk, unidentified activists even placed a bomb under the cathedral, where services were in Ukrainian. The explosion caused little damage but apparently set in motion a struggle that involved vandalism against both Orthodox denominations.[74]

The resistance against Ukrainian in the church was just as great in the countryside. A glimpse comes from the record of a November 20, 1941, regional "synod" in Bucha, a village near Kiev, of forty-five faithful and priests from thirteen villages (and five parishes). Most delegates were laypersons (thirty-five), Ukrainians (forty; the rest were Russians), and (probably) women. An Autocephalous archpriest from Kiev, Ivan Potapenko, urged them to build a single Ukrainian Orthodox Autocephalous church "with one language, spirit, and administration." It was important to "liquidate all hostile leftovers of groups that were artificially created under the influence of Jewish Bolshevik propaganda." The minutes show that a vivid debate followed: "'Ukraine must be independent and the church Ukrainian,' says Synod delegate Mr. Zhovkivsky, Bucha. 'We want the divine service to be in Old Church Slavonic,' says Mrs. Borzokovskaia from the village of Bucha, a Russian woman and a very pious person who devoted her life to saving the church in Lychansk [Kyievo-Sviatoshynsky raion] from Bolshevik destruction. 'In Hostomel the divine service is in Ukrainian, that's why the people don't attend it,' say delegates who are uneducated women from the village of Shybene, Borodianka raion." The priest countered that Church Slavonic was not accessible enough. But he had to make a typical concession. Until printed Ukrainian translations of the service became available, he said, services could be in Church Slavonic, if at the very least they were pronounced with a Ukrainian accent. After some more discussion, the delegates resolved to reject all "schismatic agitation."[75]

To the Autocephalous minority, it was hard to acknowledge that most Ukrainian Orthodox churchgoers did not rally behind them, or even opposed them. Therefore they called all of the Autonomists "Russians" or "Muscovites" (moskali), an antiquated term for Russians.[76] But contrary to the belief of the Autocephalists, the popular distaste for the vernacular language in the church did not signify any commitment to a Russian national identity. Most faithful simply felt strongly that to contact the Almighty, one should use the most elevated language they knew—as one peasant put it, "the language that God spoke."[77]

The strongest basis of support for the Autocephalists was among the small Ukrainian nationalist intelligentsia.[78] But even this support was not a given. Kiev's Ukrainian Orthodox intelligentsia also frequently attended the Greek Catholic services that from January 1942 were held in the formerly Roman Catholic St. Oleksander Church. In accordance with Greek Catholic practice, these services were in Church Slavonic with Ukrainian pronunciation; only the sermon was in Ukrainian. Father Iurii Kostiuk's success aroused the envy and ire of the local Autocephalists, who knew nothing about Galician church life. The head of the short-lived Ukrainian National Council, Mykola Velychkivsky, even asked the priest to change to Latin-rite services, in exchange for a payment. The "problem" solved itself in June 1942, when Father Kostiuk received a German order to return to the General Government.[79]

Numbers of Parishes

To determine the extent of the religious revival more fully, it would be useful to refer to administrative records. Unfortunately, most have been lost or are difficult to access. For instance, the records of the Church Council and its Autocephalous successor (the Supreme Church Administration) almost certainly no longer exist.[80] The records from Polikarp's administration were taken during the emigration in 1944 and are unavailable to outside researchers. There are figures on denominations and clerics at the parish level: copies of originals that the raion chiefs sent to the district commissars. Unfortunately, these documents are "hidden" among mountains of other papers.[81] As a result, the only figures available come from published sources.

According to its fall 1942 synod, the entire Autocephalous church in both the Reichskommissariat and the regions to the east of it had a total of 513 parishes. Of these parishes, 298 were in the "Kiev region," which probably meant the Kiev eparchy.[82] A little over five hundred parishes in such a large territory is a rather small number. No such general figures are available for the Autonomous church. Friedrich Heyer, a German soldier who met many hierarchs and priests in Ukraine, estimated after the war that when parishes from both Orthodox churches are added, by the summer of 1943 about two-thirds of the pre-1917 number of parishes had been restored in the Kiev eparchy, and about half of them in the Zhytomyr eparchy. When counting only Autonomous parishes, Heyer found that a third of all pre-1917 parishes in the eparchies of Podolia and Vinnytsia were revived.[83] The available sources give numbers for six Autonomous and eight Autocephalous eparchies. Adding the highest numbers for each eparchy—which may count twice parishes that changed allegiance—results in a total of 3,500.[84] For five Autonomous and five Autocephalous eparchies (some of which small in size), there are no numbers whatsoever, but it may be estimated that these eparchies covered about a thousand parishes.[85] Thus, the total estimated number of Orthodox parishes in the Reichskommissariat, a territory that officially had 16,910,008 inhabitants on January 1, 1943, was 4,500.[86] This means that for every 3,750 natives, there was only one Autonomous or Autocephalous church. Despite the efforts to revive church life after years of Soviet persecution, then, the number of parishes remained rather low.

Figures that exist for cities support this general impression. In Kiev, churches were basically confined to the outskirts and suburbs. This was also partly because the Soviet authorities had demolished most of those located in the center, and the Germans did not allow services in St. Sophia's Cathedral (which apparently they considered a Gothic artifact). The Dormition Cathedral, partly dating back to the eleventh century and the centerpiece of the Monastery of the Caves, could not be used either, for on November 3, 1941 an explosion demolished it. (Notwithstanding widespread beliefs in independent Ukraine to the contrary, it appears that not the NKVD but the Main Office for Reich Security set off the explosion.)[87] Thus, in Kiev only one large cathedral was open for services, St. Andrew's. The Autocephalists had this church and two other church buildings at their disposal.[88] All twenty-five other churches in this city were Autonomous by the spring of 1943. The large St. Volodymyr's Cathedral had its first (Autonomous) service only on the second anniversary of the German arrival.[89] In short, there were in Kiev altogether rather few parishes. Dnipropetrovsk eventually had ten working churches, all Autonomous. But as in the case of Kiev, this was few compared to the pre-1917 situation, when the city had twenty-seven churches. Poltava also had ten Orthodox churches, while Vinnytsia had only seven (all but two Autonomous).[90]

Church Attendance

Another way to evaluate the religious revival is by studying participation in church life. There is strong evidence that many people showed up for major religious events. Large numbers of city dwellers went to the Dnieper in 1942 for the Orthodox feast of the Water Blessing. The next year, tens of thousands came for the same occasion to Dnipropetrovsk and made a long procession to the Dnieper River. Easter was a festive occasion everywhere. In 1943 it drew such a large crowd to Dnipropetrovsk that the procession around the cathedral could take place only once, instead of the prescribed three times.[91] In the countryside, almost the entire population participated in Easter services. While curfews were lifted for the occasion, the peasants enjoyed choirs, bandura music, and amateur theater. The festivity of Spas, or Thanksgiving, also returned, as did caroling by small children.[92]

One wonders, however, how much all of this participation proves more than a widespread desire to use legitimate occasions to celebrate.[93] It seems more important to focus on church attendance on regular days. According to Hans Koch, the number of churchgoers kept increasing "until 1943."[94] As for the peasants, the meager evidence does not quite confirm this trend. In a village in southern Ukraine in 1942, a German saw "old women, graybeards, but also women, young girls, and many children crowding around the entrance" of a small church. He saw no boys or young men, whom he assumed were harvesting and perhaps not interested.[95] According to Heyer, many thousands of peasants "singing and laughing on their sleds and carts" filled the enormous market of Poltava every Sunday morning. "Few of them failed to visit the market church, which, white and newly plastered, rose above the bustle."[96] A German report based on statements by Ukrainian propagandists noted that in mid-1943, church attendance in several regions was "very high."[97] But a Soviet agent reported that "usually only old people" went to church, and a man from a village in the Kiev region recalled in a postwar interview that "nobody" did.[98] Altogether, the evidence regarding the villages is ambiguous.

Regarding the major cities, the evidence on church attendance on regular days is more straightforward. In 1941 and early 1942, Kiev's St. Andrew's Cathedral, where a "state choir" sang, was generally full.[99] But after a while, as Heyer discovered, there were services here and elsewhere in the city that not a single person attended. He thought that "secularism" remained predominant in Kiev, and a local told him, "What do Kievans believe in? A piece of bread, that's all!" Likewise, according to an NKVD report from the fall of 1942, church attendance in Dnipropetrovsk was "insignificant—based on the very old."[100] In Vinnytsia, the churches in mid-1943 had bishops, clergy, and choirs, but, as the Ukrainian nationalist Mykhailo Seleshko recalls, "none had a large number of faithful, and the churches were deserted. . . . Even the oldest people rarely went to church."[101] In short, whatever the church attendance by city dwellers had been in 1941 and 1942, by 1943 it was certainly not more than modest.

There were several reasons why attendance was not as high in the countryside, and particularly in the cities, as it could have been. In the countryside, the occasional German bans during the harvest period played a role. Such local bans meant that attendance was forbidden on weekday holidays, on Saturday evening (vespers), in the middle of the day on Sunday, and sometimes even throughout the day Sunday. Germans who caught transgressors chased them out and ordered the priest to lock the building. Enraged local landwirts lashed the people with their whips or beat them with sticks. Priests were often forced to participate in the harvesting and could be beaten for ignoring bans on mid-Sunday mass. Fear of being apprehended at the church and deported to Germany also diminished attendance, as did a fear of exposing oneself as a Christian, given a possible return of the Soviet authorities.[102] This fear of exposure applied only to city dwellers, however, for villagers often already knew their neighbors' convictions.

But the main reasons why people stayed away from the church were indifference and alienation. People in Vinnytsia told Seleshko that as before 1941, people cared only about baptism.[103] They also felt alienated from their priests, whom they quickly realized were being used by "the Gestapo" for various political tasks. (All new priests had to sign a vow to spy on their communities.)[104] The priests, like all bishops, were themselves closely monitored by the Germans and their informers; among other reasons, this was to verify whether they obeyed the repeated orders from district commissars to incite the parishioners to provide every possible assistance to the Nazis. On Hitler's birthday on April 20, 1942, all priests had to pray for him in special services, and they reportedly did so "in part."[105] Such behavior of clergymen stemmed from mortal fear. There can be little doubt that the case of Father N. P. Stukalo of Oleksandriia, a town east of Kirovohrad, was typical. He is known to have received weekly instructions, and probably death threats. Another (or perhaps the same) priest in Oleksandrivka early in 1942 suggested in a homily that the Germans might leave. He was lucky to be let go after fifty blows of a birch.[106]

Popular antipathy to priests was the greatest in Dnieper Ukraine, particularly its cities. As early as October 1941, those Kievans who were still shaken by the recent massacre of the Jews at Babi Yar undoubtedly were disgusted when Autocephalous priests praised the Germans as "light-haired knights."[107] Also very important was that people's husbands, sons, and brothers had been drafted into the Red Army and were hoped to be still alive. Thus, when Father Stukalo asked his congregation to help defeat "the enemy," the parishioners got angry and attendance dropped. Old people said that he had debauched the place of worship.[108]

It is also instructive to look for differences among age groups. Anecdotal evidence provides no surprises about young females in formerly Polish western Volhynia: they were generally pious. When the Red Army returned to the region in 1944, one of its soldiers asked a local Ukrainian girl to sew a button on his clothes. It was a Sunday, so the request got a frightened reaction: "That's a sin!"[109] In Dnieper Ukraine, however, there existed a certain generational divide regarding religion. Those born in the 1920s and 1930s, the "Komsomol generation" described in Chapter 9, had little interest in going to church. In fact, the vast majority of males, and many females, from this group did not attend church at all. In the countryside they helped reconstruct the churches, but that was mainly out of solidarity and because they had never seen a mass. As early as the fall of 1941, the SD estimated that half of the young generation was atheist.[110] The young people quickly discovered that to them, masses were far less interesting than movies. They stopped attending or went "as if to a theater," as Seleshko saw. "They listened for a while how the choir sang and left. Young people said that the liturgy meant nothing to them, it was a nothing but a nice show. They complained that it was boring, for every week the performance was the same."[111] Young people also frequently behaved as if in a circus, for example, by touching the priests' gowns. Altogether, as a priest recalls, church attendance by the young was "significantly less than in the pre-Soviet period."[112]

A German chaplain who spoke Russian and spent much time in the Ukrainian countryside concluded that "religious life," as he put it, only existed "there where it had already existed before the Communist period, namely among the older generation, those older than thirty-five." The youngest of these, those up to age twenty-five, were almost all "completely alienated and indifferent."[113] But it is worth mentioning that many people over age thirty-five were also indifferent. The SD reported as early as August 1941 from the Vinnytsia countryside that it saw no outright rejection of the church but that "unambiguous support comes only from some women and elderly men. The young generation and the middle-aged appear to be indifferent on this issue, but also willing to participate once asked."[114] According to a Soviet partisan this participation actually occurred out of fear. "The middle-aged really go only in order not to attract attention," he wrote, "because the religious people take note of who does not attend church and threaten to tell the commander that 'so-and-so sympathizes with the Bolsheviks.'"[115] Although other sources do not confirm this interpretation, such a situation may well have prevailed in places. A Soviet report dealing with the end of 1941 even asserted that a "small and elderly" group was religious but that the majority of the population was "skeptical" about the opening of the churches and talked "ironically" about it. Such an attitude was particularly likely among peasants in the industrial regions, where the SD also took note of "a marked indifference."[116]

After the introduction of civilian Nazi rule and statements that the Soviet separation of church and state was still in place—or, more precisely, restored—young peasants began to object to, or otherwise disrespect, people's piety. The administration of the Autonomous Vinnytsia eparchy even complained to the German authorities about the phenomenon.[117] Baptist and Evangelical Christian missionaries held public meetings in villages and cities that were apparently well attended; a Communist report even spoke of a "large pull" in the Right Bank toward these Protestants. But their audiences invariably included people who shifted in their seats and asked each other, "Who allowed them to preach here?" There were also militant atheists, who were momentarily powerless. According to a former missionary, their faces were "contorted with malice."[118]

Only one report, based on intelligence gathered by Ukrainian propagandists, found that by the middle of 1943 young people in the Zhytomyr and Kiev regions were participating in the supposedly "abundant" church attendance.[119] But the many testimonies to the contrary cast grave doubt on this finding. Indeed, even the decision by many young males with a higher education to become priests does not mean as much as appearances might suggest. At least in part, these males had ulterior motives for joining the priesthood—a lack of other proper employment and a wish to evade manual labor.[120]

There was a religious revival in the territory of the Reichskommissariat Ukraine, but it was modest in scope. Churches reopened and bishops and priests arrived, but as time went on, the German authorities obstructed church life more and more. Most important, most young and many middle-aged natives had little or no interest in or respect for the Orthodox church and indeed religion in general. This indifference was not entirely new. To date, we know little about the nature and depth of popular piety among the Ukrainians and Russians in the late imperial and early Soviet periods, but historians tend to agree that already at that time these people were increasingly losing interest in religion or were becoming anticlerical. There also existed in those years another tendency that involved fewer people: conversion to Protestantism (specifically, to the Baptist church and Evangelical Christianity).[121] This chapter has shown that both tendencies—secularization and conversion to Protestantism—also were quite common in the Reichskommissariat Ukraine. In short, the widespread disinterest in the Orthodox church and religion in general that the tsarist and Soviet periods had bequeathed to Dnieper Ukraine changed little under the Nazi regime.

11

DEPORTATIONS AND FORCED MIGRATIONS

Early in 1942, in the wake of many mass shootings of Jews and Roma and a winter of hunger for prisoners and city dwellers, the German authorities launched a campaign to obtain laborers for factories and farms in the Reich. They had not anticipated such a campaign before the war, but now felt a need to thus alleviate the unexpected labor shortages there.[1] By June 1943, one million people had been displaced from the Reichskommissariat Ukraine in this campaign. Initially, there was some enthusiasm for going to work in the Reich, but soon the mood changed radically and most natives came to believe that going to Germany was tantamount to death. From then on, the potential *Ostarbeiter*, or Eastern Workers (their name in the Reich, though not in Ukraine), resisted in many ways. The authorities, for their part, responded with violence in order to fulfill the "recruitment" quotas. The escalating violence related to the deportations became a key factor behind the start of large-scale partisan activity.

Propaganda and Volunteers

Few workers went to the Reich during the first months of German rule in Ukraine. In December 1941, 760 miners embarked on a train to Germany from Kryvy Rih. Also that month, some 6,400 unemployed metal workers from Zaporizhzhia, fleeing famine, left voluntarily for the same destination.[2] Only from 1942 did transports westward and the propaganda supporting them become large-scale.

The propaganda for labor in the Reich appeared mainly in newspapers; leaflets; brochures; large, brightly colored posters; and an itinerant exhibition. One feature was supposedly real-life stories about people going to Germany. At workplaces and before feature film showings, *Come to Lovely Germany* was shown, a film that portrayed young people laughing and singing all the way to a German farmer's warm welcome.[3] Oral propaganda developed slowly. The radio broadcast accounts from Germany by some alleged Eastern Workers. From the end of 1942, the propaganda featured Ukrainians who pretended to be Eastern Workers on holiday. Traveling around Ukraine, they told happy tales of life in Germany in speeches at movie showings and at public meetings in market squares.[4]

The campaign stressed many supposed benefits of working in the Reich. One was simply "getting to know Germany."[5] Reichskommissar Koch promised that those working there (as well as those migrating to southern Ukraine for agricultural work) would be the first to receive land in Ukraine once the time was ripe for land distribution.[6] While in Germany, the workers would earn a good wage and receive free housing and medical care. Each month, part of their wages would be deposited in a personal savings account, which they could access on their return. Dependent relatives in Ukraine would receive financial support as well. Moreover, the workers would learn skills that would later secure them good jobs back home.[7] Because of all of these benefits, the workers would be happy. Posters depicted those abroad with captions like "Life in Germany is great! We are happy here in Germany!" "Who of us, Ukrainians," another poster asked, "would have thought that we would be asked whether we would like to work in Germany? Only now do we, who accepted that offer and are living in Germany, understand why Stalin erected a wall around us and why he did everything to prevent us from finding out what was happening over the last ten years in Germany, the land of true socialism."[8]

Besides personal gain, the propaganda emphasized—as much of prewar Soviet propaganda had done—that leaving one's native region to work elsewhere was a patriotic duty. Simply put, "While Working in Germany, You Defend Your Fatherland!" And it would "help destroy Bolshevism."[9] Working in Germany was part of an alleged cooperation between "western Europe" and "the liberated East": "the workers of the East do their best in Germany's factories, works, and fields, while the qualified German workers help to bring order to life in the East. All this is done in order to defeat Bolshevism entirely and to create a better life for all the workers in the liberated territories."[10] Later messages urged that "at a time when German youth is going to the front and won't come home until the war is over, Ukrainian youth must perform its labor duty."[11]

Orthodox church leaders, both Autonomous and Autocephalous, also had to disseminate such propaganda. In order to refute rumors about bad living conditions in the Reich, in June 1942 a statement from Metropolitan Polikarp (Sikorsky) of the Autocephalous church appeared in the press. It mentioned both the alleged benefits and the duty to go. His clergy, Polikarp said, should "explain to their congregations all the favorable conditions and rewards that surround the work of the worker in Germany, and that also take care of his family, which stays home." He also called work in Germany part of the fight against "Muscovite-Jewish Communism."[12] Bishop Veniiamyn (Novytsky) of Poltava and Lubny, of the Autonomous church, issued a call late in 1942 that was neither anti-Semitic nor anti-Russian and that merely mentioned that the Germans wanted people to go. In fact, his appeal could be taken to mean that Veniiamyn himself supported the Red Army: "Every Ukrainian worker," he said, "should understand his indebtedness to those who are sacrificing their lives at the front for everybody's well-being."[13]

At first the propaganda in 1942 met with success. Soviet citizens were used to being sent to work in distant lands, and in spite of the often difficult conditions had learned how to benefit from the experience.[14] In Kiev, the authorities demanded that volunteers first work for several weeks at the reconstruction of the Dnieper bridges. In mid-January 1942, around 1,500 young volunteers showed up at Kiev's Labor Office. They left by train to the sound of a brass band. Two more trains with Kievans departed in late February. These transports were in cars filled with straw without any sanitary provisions, but the food supply was good.[15]

The volunteers had various motives. One was a genuine curiosity about Europe's most industrialized country, a curiosity that had only increased from hearing stories told by some German soldiers. Other motives were the expectation of a good salary and the German promise of a quick return. Those who left Kiev in February generally felt that there was nothing to lose, for they were already starving.[16] In the countryside, there were even more volunteers: young people with much the same motivations (except for hunger). One woman who apparently did not really sign up herself, but merely obeyed a call-up, recalls that "we had a certain hope that in Germany we would earn something, and that we would get ourselves some decent clothes. For we saw that all the Germans wore quality clothes, made from good fabrics and well sewn."[17] Such people knew about the mistreatment, killing, and starvation of the Jews, Roma, and prisoners of war, but that did not dissuade them from going to the land of the perpetrators. "True, we still remembered the shootings of the Jews in Berdiansk," writes the same woman, "but we also recalled the good treatment on the part of Germans during our trip [in 1941] from Berdiansk to our village. We told each other, maybe it won't be that bad in Germany. The Germans are supposed to be a civilized people. Why, therefore, should they treat us cruelly?"[18]

By mid-1942, however, there were hardly any more volunteers. Statistics from the Kiev general district show a decline from 4,030 volunteers in June, to 425 in August, to a mere five in September, and none thereafter.[19] In September 1942 153,000 people, or about 7 percent of the population of this general district, and including more than 11 percent of the population of Kiev, had been sent away. By then the regional SD reported that "despite" all the propaganda, reprisal confiscations of livestock, and death threats, the native population no longer wanted to go.[20] The main reason that the number of volunteers declined was conditions in the Reich. The Dnieper Ukrainians and others working in factories and living in camps often suffered abuse, bad housing, and bad food. They resented the many humiliations—in particular, the obligation of all Eastern Workers, volunteers or not, to wear a badge with the label "OST." The marker precluded visits to theaters, moviehouses, and restaurants.[21]

Yet the overall quality of the Eastern Worker experience is not entirely clear. The few who worked for farmers were generally satisfied with their treatment and payment, and initially some even wanted to stay in Germany forever.[22] On the whole, the Eastern Workers, who were mostly females, worked much harder than either western European or Balkan foreign workers. In their native Ukraine, women generally worked harder than men. And in Germany they kept the pace and indeed worked harder than all captive males there, whichever country those came from. Even as late as 1944, these women were 90 to 100 percent as productive as German workers.[23] Why this was so requires some explanation. In a Russian survey of former Eastern Workers decades later, many described their time in Germany as the best time of their lives.[24] Does this explain why they worked so hard? Perhaps it was simply a habit that was difficult to break, or, more likely, it reflected an effort to prove oneself too valuable to be killed. But the relative satisfaction may have had less to do with the working conditions than with the workers' social life. Fedir Pihido also worked in Germany and recalls that even though he and his fellow Ukrainians were almost slaves, they *felt* free—indeed, they felt freer than ever. They talked about whatever they liked "without fearing that somebody might be eavesdropping, that we would be denounced, or that we would have to account to an NKVD investigator for some carelessly expressed thought."[25]

Back in the Reichskommissariat, Koch ordered that assistance be provided to the family members of the Eastern Workers. It usually was in the form of money, at most 130 rubles (and later karbovantsi) per month.[26] This family support, released to the native administrations by the district and city commissars, was automatically subtracted from the Eastern Worker wages—even in cases when the worker had not supported a family in the past—and the subtraction was often more than 130 rubles.[27] But although the amounts were low and much time could pass before the support was disbursed, the relatives did ask and receive these wages. Late in 1943, the amount was increased in some regions.[28]

The Great Fear

Several weeks after the departure of the volunteer trains, the authorities allowed letters to be sent. Later they urged both the Eastern Workers and their relatives in Ukraine to send postcards, which had a detachable half that could be used to acknowledge receipt.[29] Many people still had no official mail connection with their relatives in Germany, and the postcards, just like the vast majority of letters (over 80 percent) that censors did not open, could take months to arrive.[30] Nevertheless, considering the conditions of war and the huge volume of the mail, the postal system worked reasonably well, until the very eve of the German retreat.[31]

The Eastern Workers normally were allowed one letter per month. Most legally mailed letters were apparently not fully candid. As some writers stated, they could not be.[32] The Eastern Workers (and even the SD) believed that most negative letters were confiscated, but in practice the sheer volume of mail precluded this. Indeed, many sources say that the letters minced no words about beatings and other negative events and circumstances.[33] Cautious writers also somehow conveyed the truth about their living conditions and homesickness, sometimes through coded language that had been agreed on before their departure. A worker would write, for instance, that she lived "like the Shevchenkos," who would be a particularly poor family in her village. Also common was inversion of meaning, so that only a close reading would reveal that "living very well" meant the opposite.[34]

Relatives in Ukraine were permitted to send letters and also packages with clothes, food, or money, although eventually those kinds of valuables tended to get "lost" in the mail. Peasants sent their Eastern Worker children and other relatives bread, rusks, lard, even butter. Thousands of packages piled up at the post offices every day.[35] The Eastern Workers also found ways to dispatch letters illegally, usually through German soldiers based in Ukraine, with whom female Eastern Workers also corresponded. Letters to these Germans would include one or more other ones, which the man then hand-delivered. Polish guest workers also passed on letters.[36]

The most consistently truthful news about the living conditions came from the many Eastern Workers who returned starting in mid-1942. Usually these people had fallen seriously ill, had had an accident, or had become disabled during Allied bombardments. Among the returnees were also pregnant women and people over age sixty-five. All returnees were put on eastbound cargo trains without any food or medical assistance. Many women died on the way.[37] The survivors spread the word.

Hence, through these various means, news about the working conditions in the Reich quickly reached Ukraine. Real and inaccurate tales proliferated through word of mouth. A Soviet leaflet started a rumor that the laborers were put to work in northern Africa. Another rumor held that the deportations were designed to obtain workers for trench digging at the front.[38] The people in major cities were the first to know that the Eastern Workers were treated worse than any other foreign workers, and they were also the first to exchange stories of people being "sold."[39] Girls and women in Ukraine worried that they would be put into brothels, while still other rumors warned that the laborers would be sterilized.[40] People also started saying that the German deportations were not different from Siberia-bound Soviet ones. A villager in Podolia who said this at a gathering was hanged for doing so.[41]

Not surprisingly, many people became terrified of going to the Reich. Some were convinced that there they would die, either from famine or from Allied bombs. Others also believed that there was a great famine in Germany as a whole. In the Berdychiv region, one rumor in mid-1942 described the following scenario: Hitler would win the war soon and would demand that Stalin release the German prisoners of war. Stalin, however, would not do this, perhaps simply because he had already killed them all. Hitler therefore would take revenge by having all "Russians" killed, among whom he would include the Ukrainian Eastern Workers.[42] "Goodbye, dear friends," some people wrote on a wall of a deportation site. "When you see these names, speak well of us. We are going to die if we make it to Germany . . . We're here because of the *politsaï*, who are kissing the Germans' asses."[43] People also started to doubt that Germans were only murdering Jews and Roma. During at least one deportation from western Volhynia in mid-1942, there was a rumor inside the train that all would be shot and turned into soap.[44] The contemporary songs and sayings about the deportations expressed a deep sadness. These (or at least those preserved for posterity) were nonreligious and pessimistic (in marked contrast with the spirituals of African American slaves). A typical saying read: "I'm leaving school / Why study? / I must become a slave / In a foreign land."[45]

Deportation Methods

When there were no more volunteers, Fritz Sauckel, who since March 1942 was the plenipotentiary general for labor allocation, sent out commissions to conduct the deportations, which he called "recruitment." His targets in the Reichskommissariat Ukraine were high: 225,000 workers in the last three months of 1942, and another 225,000 in the first four months of 1943. Still later, Sauckel demanded that from March 15, 1943, three thousand laborers be apprehended every day, and after a while even six thousand per day.[46] His representatives told each general commissar the number of people they wanted and added that they were needed fast. Then each district and city commissar received a target number. The Labor Office, which was headed by those Germans, subdivided the quota among the raion chiefs or, in the case of the cities with a city commissar, simply passed it on to the native mayor. The districts of the major cities received additional branches of the city Labor Office. All of the native administrators were threatened with death if they could not supply the assigned total of "recruits."[47] Sometime in late 1942, the procedure changed and native officials no longer had to supply a certain number of people, but simply all people of a certain age. Hence, late in 1943 everyone born in 1926 and 1927 was supposed go to the Reich.[48]

Thus for the deportations, even more than for the Holocaust of the Jews and Roma, the Nazis needed native-born local officials to become closely involved. It is difficult to generalize about the response of these officials, but it is clear that the mayors of the large cities did not consult the population. The raion chiefs had the luxury of being able to blame subordinates, the village elders. The chief would demand from each elder that he fill a particular quota by compiling a list of names and sending it to the raion center by a certain date. Officially, the list went not to the raion chief, but to newly created labor offices at the raion level, but it appears that these offices did not amount to much. If they did constitute a separate entity, they were rarely headed by a German, as they were supposed to be, due to the shortage of German personnel by that time. At conferences in the raion center, village elders received further instructions: they had to exclude certain categories—forest workers, quarry workers, railroad workers, road builders, and employees of the machinery and tractor stations and state farms.[49] But tough decisions remained, for which the elders were not obliged to consult the other villagers. Few seem to have convened a village meeting to decide how the quota would be filled.[50]

In order to avoid being put on the list, it was essential to have the right connections. Family members of native policemen and administrators were especially protected. Others experienced much arbitrariness. From one household, two or more children might be called up, but from other homes no one.[51] Among the first draftees were the people who did not live in a given village before 1941 (usually these were former prisoners of war).[52] The first nonvolunteers also included people particularly disliked by the native authorities. In some villages, these might be Communist party members and other Soviet activists; in others they might be Ukrainian patriots or children of victims of Soviet persecution. In western Volhynia, Poles in predominantly Ukrainian villages were particularly likely to be drafted.[53] Also vulnerable were what the Reichskommissariat leadership called "adolescent, undernourished children and infirm grayhaired people of both sexes." Reportedly "randomly recruited" as early as April 1942, they apparently got little sympathy or help to prevent their deportation, although the adolescents, possibly orphans, may have volunteered to escape from hunger.[54]

Besides the auxiliary administrators, there were also other natives in positions of some authority who proposed candidates for deportation. House custodians in Kiev reported to the Labor Office "many ill people, old people unable to work, indeed even cripples, and anybody they dislike," the SD noted.[55] Many supervisors at the workplace tended to allow ill or the least productive employees to be deported. As a man who worked at the housing department in Vinnytsia puts it, "a boss merely had to point at somebody and he was sent to Germany." He remembers a native agricultural official who moved to another apartment and ordered his employees to help. One woman refused. Soon thereafter, a car took her to the Labor Office and within hours she was on a train to Germany. In addition, at least according to the SD, "formerly active" Communists in Kiev who feared their neighbors reported them for deportation, "so as to be able to continue their Communist activity."[56]

Two former raion chiefs who emigrated after the war have emphasized that they did all they could to prevent the deportations. "We" of the Novi Sanzhary raion placed young people in various offices and organizations, regardless of the needs there, Hryhorii Kariak writes, and thus protected hundreds of people.[57] Mykhailo Lebid writes that parents begged him not to send their children away. In response, the administration of the Matiïv (present-day Lukiv) raion falsified data and thus showed that many deportation candidates were needed for work that the district commissar found important—at the railroad, a sawmill, and in the fields. This was after 70 percent of the Eastern Workers' quota had been filled. Thus, the district commissar agreed to a lower quota. As a result, in two years supposedly only about two hundred people were deported.[58]

The actual situation was rather different. Not just Germans but also the raion chiefs and the city mayors, fearing for their own lives, started arresting people for deportation with aid from the German and native police. Sauckel even blamed the native administrators for the violence that inevitably ensued.[59] Although that was unfair, the fact remains that the auxiliary administrations were deeply involved in the roundups. There is some good documentation dealing with Kiev. Early in April 1942, the head of the city's Zaliznychny district became anxious. His district was more like a village than an urban area, and few people lived in communal houses. With so few custodians, it was difficult to supervise the population. These people were also rarely at home and because they had connections in the countryside, they could always flee and hide. Only about thirteen persons signed up each day as volunteers. If nothing changed, the overall daily target of fifty "recruits" would not be met. Therefore the district head asked his superior, Mayor Forostivsky, to order the district Schuma to arrest people. They could use, he said, the lists of "undesired elements" that the police and his district administration had prepared. In reply, Forostivsky issued the requested order to the district police and also authorized the district head to use it for large-scale nighttime house searches. Thus an order from City Commissar Rogausch was not needed for such searches.[60]

Raids were hardly unknown to Soviet citizens. As early as 1920, for instance, the Soviet authorities in Kiev had carried out daytime arrests of labor "deserters."[61] But those roundups had involved adults. In the spring of 1942, L. Nartova's diary captured the general mood about the deportations, which at that stage mostly involved children age fourteen: "We are stuck in a terrifying, terrible captivity and all thoughts center around one thing—who among our acquaintances and loved ones will lose their children, who will not be able to hide them. Liusia, Kostia, Galochka, Alesha . . . God, what a terrible, insane grief for parents."[62]

In massive nighttime house searches in the cities by native and German officials and policemen, everyone was apprehended, including overnight guests and mothers of small children. (Those children had to be left behind.) One woman escaped several times by running out into the street via the attic and the neighbors' house.[63] The largest operation in Kiev took place in the Podil district on July 12, 1942, between three o'clock and eleven o'clock in the morning under the direction of the Schuma and with participation by the Security Police. Squads of one German Police member, nine Schuma, one German Security Police member, one Schuma on loan to the Security Police (a Sicherheitsschutzmann), and an interpreter combed each house. Nevertheless this roundup was a failure. Not only was the timing bad—it was a Sunday, when city dwellers tended to be out of town—but the people of the Podil had received a tip-off. Several selection rounds later, the almost random arrest of 1,600 produced only about 250 deportation candidates, the vast majority women.[64]

Roundups by Germans with dogs and Schuma became a frequent phenomenon at city markets. Allegedly designed to combat speculation, the hunt really was for laborers, in particular young villagers, who had no labor cards and thus were unlikely to be rescued by employers. As the Kievan Tatiana Fesenko describes it, people during such actions "rushed about with eyes wide with horror, overturning baskets and stands, but the German policemen implacably shoved the screaming women and pale men into the large cargo vans."[65] On May 2, 1942, some 1,400 young people in Kiev were arrested this way. Their parents were then told to bring them underwear, a coat, and shoes. The roundup "astonished everyone. People are moving about like dummies," Nartova noted. "The streets are dead, even the children are in hiding." Roundups also hit parks, beaches, and movie or other theaters.[66] Eventually, post-arrest notifications to parents were no longer provided. Persons simply started to disappear without a trace until perhaps some weeks later a letter from Germany arrived.[67] Many people thought that ruses were used (although in reality they probably were not)—for example, in Rivne when a previously announced sale of consumer goods ended with a roundup.[68]

From the middle of 1942, those who attempted to escape from the roundups were shot at. One summer Sunday, German and native policemen cordoned off the market in the town of Oleksandriia. A man recalls that "the [native] policemen beat with butts and shot anybody who tried to run away. There were many wounded and people were shot dead."[69] In Kiev in October 1942, people were listening to a band at a market when they were suddenly surrounded. According to Nartova, several tried to escape but were shot.[70]

Every apprehended person in Kiev eventually arrived at 24 Lviv Street (presently Artem Street), an assembly point consisting of several houses and a yard. Despite the guards, there were escapes. Some parents were able to get their children out by bribing the policemen. (The German in charge was less placable: he usually told such parents to get lost and sometimes added a blow with his stick.) Most parents simply waited outside until their child was moved across the street into the "recruitment office" at 27 Lviv Street, where personal data were recorded and doctors (presumably Kievans) performed a superficial medical check. The "recruits" had to walk fast and the police lashed those who did not. After two or three days without any food, the prisoners were taken on foot (or sometimes by streetcar) to the train station.[71]

Peasants in a region where there was no train station nearby were also imprisoned at Lviv Street. Almost every morning, hundreds of people from all over Ukraine filled the nearby streets as Schuma chased them toward the site. Ivan Zhyhadlo has left a description: "Loaded with bags of warm clothes and carrying trunks on their shoulders, they were sweltering. Behind them was a whole string of Kievan rickshas, which the exhausted 'volunteers' had rented with their last money. They obviously had no more energy to carry everything they needed on the road

18. Young men and women who have been forced to leave their villages to work in Germany carry heavy luggage as they walk toward an assembly point. Nekrasov Street, Kiev, 1942. (Tsentral'nyi derzhavnyi kinofotofonoarkhiv Ukraïny im. H. S. Pshenychnoho, 0–17127.)

and abroad. Among them were also very young ones, and some of the women had small children in their arms." Kievans usually stopped and followed the procession with eyes "full of surprise and horror." Some said, "Ukraine is being liberated from the Ukrainians."[72]

Other Forced Migrations

There were several other kinds of forced migration. One campaign, already mentioned (in Chapter 2), took place late in 1942 in the Zhytomyr region. To create the ethnic German district of Hegewald there, the Nazis displaced many Ukrainians and ethnic Germans on very short notice. An earlier campaign focused on moving people to southern Ukraine, where there was a shortage of laborers to work the fields and harvest the crop. The plan was to move by foot 400,000 people. The first group, presumably peasants, are known to have left on March 3, 1942. It is unlikely that many went of their own accord, and they do not appear to have been promised anything substantial. Nothing more is known about this campaign.[73] Another ambitious scheme, never quite realized, entailed forcing city dwellers to work in the countryside. Enraged that not all land had been cultivated before the winter of 1941–1942, agrarian officials of the Reichskommissariat wanted to send 407,000 city dwellers, including children, to work the land in the spring of 1942. Thus 50,000 Kievans were to toil at former Soviet state farms, each digging daily a hundred square meters, supervised by Schuma and without pay. For one day's work, a laborer would get priority during supposed vegetable sales as well as permission to buy two rubles' worth of food from German outlets.[74] The district commissar in Zaporizhzhia sent city dwellers to finish the fall plowing after the deportations to Germany endangered its completion. Thousands of people were separated from their families this way, but many managed to flee back.[75]

A particularly notorious hunt for countryside workers involved the Medical Institute (Polimedykum) in Kiev, a fusion of two prewar institutes of this kind. In the spring of 1942, applications for the next fall's program were received and the number of students increased rapidly. Study, after all, meant exemption from deportation. During the summer, the district commissar sent about 1,500 medical students into the countryside to work. As one of them recalls, they actually had a good time and lots of food.[76] On their return to Kiev in the fall, however, informants warned them to go into hiding, for they would be deported to Germany. On November 13, all students were ordered to attend an informative meeting about "the guiding principles of the work of the Polimedykum." Fewer than one hundred of the 2,500 students showed up. They were told that the institute would not reopen and that all students had to report two days later at the "recruitment office." The order also was issued by General Commissar Magunia over the radio and in the press.[77] It was the start of a massive hunt. First the medical students were warned that if they disobeyed, their parents would lose their bread cards, and then they were threatened with execution. Accepting the students as employees also carried the death penalty, and those already employing any such student had to report it. In practice, the relatives of those who did not show themselves not only lost their food cards, but were taken hostage. Only then did a number of students give themselves up. Others were caught in street roundups that targeted young people. Together about a hundred medical students were deported by the end of 1942, which was far short of the German goal.[78]

During the summer of 1942, Hitler personally got involved when he ordered the "recruitment" of 400,000 women and children to work in households in the Reich, whose women were themselves often working outside the home. After personally seeing "Aryan"-looking Ukrainian peasants in August 1942, Hitler had convinced himself that Ukrainians had traces of "Germanic" blood, evidently brought to the region by the ancient Goths. He could be pragmatic and decided that Germans would benefit by assimilating some Ukrainians.[79] The press in Ukraine called on all "girls" not older than thirty-five to volunteer, citing among the benefits the availability of tap water, gas, and electricity. Whether any girls or women volunteered is unknown, but by early 1944, some 50,000 "Eastern" maids, mostly Ukrainians, were indeed working in German households. Finally, a number of scientists and technical specialists were under pressure to move to the Reich as well. Those who went seem to have worked there under tolerable conditions.[80]

Countryside Roundups

At least as brutal as the roundups in the cities were those in the countryside. The Schuma went from house to house. Late in June 1942, in a typical scenario, Ukrainian policemen arrived in the Podolian village of Pochapyntsi (Chemerivtsi raion) to collect 260 young people. They were merciless, as a woman who was then nineteen recalls: "When they arrived at our house and wanted to pick up Ivan and me, I walked back into the room, and threw myself on the pillow on my bed. I didn't want to go. I cried, 'I don't want to go! I am not going! I'm staying here!' I held the bedstead as tight as I could. A militiaman, who had walked after me into the room, grabbed me by the neck, pulled me up, placed the rifle in my side and led me away." It was peculiar to the countryside that the mothers of those rounded up cried inconsolably, as if their children had just died.[81]

The arrested peasants were locked up for the night at the local police station or village administration, or they were lined up in the square for immediate transport. Surrounding the group on all sides, the police gave the command "March!" and if a police band was present, it struck a happy tune. "Women ran along the column, screaming and sobbing, and throwing themselves on the necks of their daughters," Anatolii Kuznetsov remembers about the roundup in the village of Rykun. "The policemen pushed them away and the women fell to the ground. At the back walked the Germans, who chuckled at the scene."[82] Relatives followed the convoys from a distance. By the fall of 1942, threats and abuse of those peasants who did not go immediately—that is, those who were found in hiding—were very common and came from Schuma or Germans (who were not always present). For example, girls in the village of Stari Bezradychy in the Obukhiv raion were severely beaten, and also attacked by a bloodhound, and one who was discovered in a field was lashed with a whip by a German.[83]

The roundups greatly influenced everyday life. Teenagers and middle-aged villagers started evading the usual roads and paths.[84] In the village of Zarubyntsi near Pereiaslav, people took turns standing guard on a hilltop. If the guard left his or her spot, this indicated to the others that policemen were on their way across the Dnieper. By the time they arrived, everybody was in hiding and the village was empty. The deportations also made many people work harder; they hoped to make themselves too valuable to be deported. As in the large cities, movie theaters in the towns became unsafe, for roundups took place there.[85] Eventually, most countryside and town raids were carried out at night. Huts would be surrounded and a warning would go out that anybody who tried to escape would be shot. In response to such practices, many peasants started sleeping in the garden or in a hole somewhere else outside.[86]

The frustrated Nazi authorities demanded harsher action. On September 21, 1942, General Commissar Schöne of the Volhynia-Podolia general district ordered the burning of the homes of those who refused to go, and the arrest and transfer to labor camps of the relatives.[87] As a result, entire villages went up in flames. All of the twenty-five people in the Kremenets region village of Bilozirka (Lanivtsi raion) who received recruitment notices fled. During the night of October 1, 1942, as a local, contemporary letter describes it, "the German Gendarmerie came and set fire to the houses of those who had fled. The fire became very big, for it had not rained for two months. Moreover, there were hay stacks in the yards. You can imagine what happened. The people who rushed to the scene were not allowed to put out the fire. They were beaten and arrested. As a result six farms burned down. Meanwhile the gendarmes [also] set fire to other houses. People fell to their knees and kissed their hands, but the gendarmes went wild at them with batons and threatened to burn down the entire village." Then a villager swore that the workers would be there the next morning. As this was happening, Schuma raided the neighboring villages and "wherever they did not find workers, they locked up the parents until the children showed up." Fires actually raged "day and night" in those villages and the deportation candidates who still refused to appear were condemned to death.[88] It is very likely that other general commissars issued orders similar to Schöne's. In the Kiev general district, from August 1942 at least two district commissars engaged in hostage taking and home burnings.[89]

The boarding of the trains also produced highly emotional scenes. In the square before Kiev's train station, a brass band accompanied deportations in April 1942. Nartova wrote that "thousands of people with knapsacks on their shoulders are crying and sobbing, bitterly saying farewell to their native land."[90] Parents had to stay away from the cargo wagons; those who approached them were "shot at," according to a Communist report of early 1942. "At the station [and village] of Pisky near Lokhvytsia, there were casualties among the old men and women who ran to the station from where their arrested sons and daughters were being sent off."[91]

Resistance

Besides the violent "recruitment" measures in cities and villages, the German authorities also introduced medical exams. In Kiev, everybody was called up from October 1942 for assessment by Labor Office officials and a doctor. Such "medical" commissions sprang up everywhere.[92] Nartova was among those who went. "We suffered a good deal," she wrote—"but there were also funny moments. One of us female teachers showed up with makeup and we didn't recognize her. She had painted her hair (the Germans don't like gray), made blue spots under her eyes and elsewhere, put on large glasses, stooped, and went before the commission. The Germans were sitting at the tables, acting important and serious. She approached the table. They barely looked at her: 'Passport!' She gave the passport. '45, nein,' he said. We couldn't help but laugh to ourselves."[93] Sometimes the city commissions visited the countryside. There was often no real evaluation. Old people and fourteen-year-olds officially were ineligible but often still became "recruits."[94]

It was in connection with the medical commissions that popular resistance assumed a large scale. In order to be disqualified, many people started mutilating themselves. They provoked skin diseases, like scabies, which could occur by rubbing one's skin with garlic. The same result came from applying a yellow spring flower (molochai) to one's face, which made it swell, or caustic soda, which roughened it. Still others made sores by rubbing themselves with hard brushes and then vinegar or kerosine.[95] The most sophisticated skin afflictions were calculated to be temporary. A peasant woman in one village applied the Lylypus herb on the skin of her son and nephews, who then walked with swellings and wounds for six weeks—long enough to be discharged by the commission in Rzhyshchiv. She healed their skin with potato leaves and sugar.[96]

Another common practice was the ingestion of poison to create a sickly complexion. Young people drank a tobacco "tea" for this purpose, or smoked tea leaves. Others poured perfume or some other substance into their eyes.[97] Excessive self-mutilation included cutting one's leg and rubbing dirt in the wound, chopping off a finger or hand, burning oneself with acid or boiling water, having oneself bitten by a mad dog, or undergoing a fake appendicitis operation.[98]

Self-mutilation truly became a mass phenomenon. In the town of Znamianka (near Kirovohrad) alone, over one thousand young people injured themselves between February 1942 and July 1943. Apparently most common among female deportation candidates, self-mutilation was fraught with danger. Many afflictions became permanent and some were lethal. (There were also cases of suicide.[99]) And success was not assured. Even scabies did not always avert deportation.[100]

Doctors frequently helped to disqualify people from deportation. To many this was nothing new, as suggested by the memoirs of the medical doctor Fedir Bohatyrchuk. In 1941, during the Soviet retreat, he writes, Kievan doctors had "helped all those who wished to stay as much as they could": they had given out false prescriptions of bed rest, had reported on nonexisting tests, had used other people's x-ray pictures, had performed fake operations, and even had declared some people insane.[101] Now, under the Germans, these doctors again started issuing fictional statements and making unneeded plaster legs. There were also doctors who even induced illnesses. A medical professor who worked in the medical commission in Fastiv in 1942 produced sores in a scheme apparently arranged by Communist underground activists.[102] In Kremenchuk, almost all of the doctors tried to declare the people unfit, one of them claimed after the war: they supplied x-ray pictures as proof of tuberculosis and hid their hospital "patients" at home if they received word that a doctor from the raion health department would come to examine them.[103] In doing this, the physicians placed themselves at great risk. Six were arrested in Kamianets-Podilsky for refusing to treat people with typhus fever and for falsifying data. Their punishment is unknown. Thus it is not surprising that the doctors and nurses sought compensation for helping people in this way.[104] Yet the high rejection rate by some medical commissions was perhaps primarily due to a sincere desire to help people, without getting any payment in return.[105] Such advocates acquired a good name among the locals, which served them well after the German retreat.

There were also evasive tactics that did not involve disease. Because initially only single people were deported, many rushed into marriage, and because the mothers of children up to the age of twelve were ineligible, girls tried to become pregnant.[106] A German journalist reported in June 1943 that because pregnancy was the only legal way to avoid deportation, the birth rate in Ukraine kept rising—although some authorities forced abortion on expecting women.[107] People also eagerly adopted children from children's homes and day nurseries, or simply borrowed other people's children and went to the commission with them.[108]

At least five people were arrested in Kiev on suspicion of making a fake Labor Office stamp that declared people ineligible. Risky behavior like this was good business: a false ineligibility document sold for hundreds, if not thousands, of karbovantsi.[109] More common, although also costly, were bribes in money or in kind. The native mediators heard countless cases of parents who swore that their child's birthdate had been recorded incorrectly. Our child is really younger, they said, and they produced evidence in the form of a godfather or godmother. This method worked if all sides quickly agreed about the bribe. House custodians also accepted payment for not reporting people or for warning against upcoming roundups.[110] Suitably induced native administrators dropped cases or provided jobs that lifted the deportation threat. The payments that these officials demanded might be bottles of liquor or large sums of money—initially 1,000 rubles, eventually fifteen times as much.[111] The Schuma could be paid off as well, as could German policemen or civilian administrators, by sexual favors. At Vinnytsia's Labor Office worked a certain Kovalskaia, who as an "ethnic German" could accept bribes openly. She apparently asked for gold, foreign currency, and clothes.[112] By 1943, a new way to dodge deportation came about in the Left Bank, as it became possible to somehow join what Ukrainian sources call "the SS"—that is, the German Waffen-SS, apparently as some kind of auxiliary.[113]

The deportations became a staple of Communist and Ukrainian nationalist propaganda. In the southern harbor of Mykolaïv, for example, an illegal leaflet described them as a mass killing scheme and urged people to join the (Soviet) partisans. In Dnipropetrovsk, the German police uncovered what it called a Communist organization of people who scribbled things like, "No, no, lies!" on the recruitment posters. Twelve youngsters were arrested, and the leader committed suicide.[114] As for the OUN, some of its members initially supported the notion of going to work in Germany, but by the middle of 1942 the Banderites opposed the scheme. A leaflet posted in Nova Praha on November 4, 1942, stemming from—as the SD put it—"the Ukrainian resistance movement," warned that four days later, three hundred locals would be rounded up and "sent to their death like animals." The SD called the Banderite antideportation propaganda "not without effect."[115]

After Stalingrad

When the Germans lost the Battle of Stalingrad, the violence surrounding the deportations became more intense. Many reports for the year 1943 testify to brutality during roundups and train boardings. The police indeed acted as if they were hunting for wild animals.[116] Early in 1943 conditions at the detention site in Uman, a former school, were appalling and very likely typical. The captured males and females—probably mostly teenagers—were held in separate rooms, tightly packed together even though other rooms were empty. The only heat came from the straw on the floor, which the inmates burned. Females who had to use a toilet were accosted by the Schuma guards, but the males were not let out at all. The captives received a meager soup and some bread (one kilogram per eight persons); they also ate snow. Every day, three or four managed to escape. In those days, the Security Police shot a Ukrainian of the local labor office for failing to provide the required number of "recruits."[117]

On May 11, 1943, eight hundred young people were marched from the village of Medvyn to the town of Bohuslav. Examiners there found them suitable, and they were locked up in the local church, where they ate, played cards, and sang songs. After four days, the group, surrounded by a police cordon, was taken to the train station. "During boarding, it was horrible," a witness tells us. "The screams of the mothers, who all but threw themselves under the wagons, tore one's heart apart. The police chased them away by beating them with rifle butts."[118] A German lieutenant saw the boarding of hundreds of teenagers born in 1926—that is, they were at most seventeen years of age—in the small village of Sharivka, forty kilometers east of Kirovohrad. He was shocked and described it in a letter of protest. In the afternoon of August 21, 1943, he wrote, the children arrived from the Nova Praha raion under the tight guard of German soldiers and Schuma, all of whom held rifles, ready to fire. At the train station, they were pushed into the wagons and sometimes beaten in the process. Relatives who had waited for them wanted to pass on luggage and straw. The police kept them away, but still some parents managed to break through. Then a German labor official drew his revolver and fired into the air. "He grabbed a Ukrainian who was slower than the others, repeatedly kicked him, and shouted, 'Step back, you bastards!'" Another Nazi official hit a man on the head so hard that his 1.5-inch baton broke, even though "the Ukrainian made no movement to defend himself and calmly endured this abuse." All of this was accompanied by "terrible screaming and chasing about—the combined howling of about 800 to 1,000 persons." After about seventy-five minutes, all of the "recruits" were on the train; it left six hours later.[119] Some German soldiers who witnessed such cruelty beat up the German perpetrators. In Kiev, too, in 1943 maltreatment of both deportees and relatives occurred almost daily, and relatives usually could not hand over food or clothes.[120]

Trying to flee during such boarding meant risking one's life. In the early summer of 1943, a native policeman warned a peasant in the Podolian village of Nove Selo that his daughter had to go to Germany, for, as the daughter puts it in her memoir, the Schuma "were killing people who refused to go." Nevertheless, after consulting her parents she decided to run from the train station. She did escape, in a hail of bullets, but tripped over something in the wheat field. The obstacle turned out to be a decaying corpse. In fact, the field was full of corpses—all victims of unsuccessful flight attempts. As the girl who fell realized, the Schuma were "caught up in the Nazi madness" and one should not expect them to hesitate to shoot. Later, while hiding in a forest, she ventured out only once. Suddenly a German and a local policeman saw her. "I turned and started to dash for the forest. 'Julia! Stop, or I'll shoot you!' I stopped in my tracks. I thought of the body in the field; I didn't want Mama to find me like that. 'How did he know my name?' I thought. I turned around: The policeman was holding a pistol at arm's length, pointed right at me. I knew him, he'd gone to school with [my brother] Ivan! He was Ukrainian. He knew me, my brother, and my parents, but I somehow knew he would not hesitate to shoot me."[121] Encounters like this became very common. Reporting in September 1943 about the "recruits" at a certain train station, a German propaganda unit observed that those who fled "were shot at and a Ukrainian girl was hit in the stomach and soon died of her severe wounds."[122]

Fortunately, not all Schuma were equally likely to shoot. Realizing that Germany was losing the war, more and more of these men actually began to issue warnings of upcoming roundups.[123] Some even helped people to escape. The deportation commissions in the Mykolaïv general district, for example, complained that the Schuma were consistently trying to sabotage the "recruitment measures" by aiding and abetting flight attempts or by badly executing roundups.[124] Many "part-time" German guards seem to have acted in a similar fashion. On the train track between Kiev and Kivertsi (in Volhynia), 15,900 people were transported westward between February 2 and March 20, 1943. As many as 4,047— one in four—escaped from their guards, who included not only native or German policemen but also German soldiers and Organisation Todt employees, who were heading for a German holiday.[125] Large numbers also escaped from assembly camps and marches that year; like the escapes from trains, these probably happened because of compliance or assistance by guards.[126]

The deportations to Germany affected almost every family. In August 1942, officially half a million workers were taken out of the Reichskommissariat—a number that reached one million on June 24, 1943.[127] One in every forty inhabitants of the Reichskommissariat and the southern military zone combined was deported by August 1943. Ultimately, 1.5 million people from these two Ukrainian regions ended up in the Reich.[128] The vast majority came from the countryside, and the percentage of villagers deported was higher than the percentage of city dwellers who were deported.[129] While these figures constituted a failure by Sauckel's standards, they were still very high. Although many people stayed in the homeland by joining the partisans, even the partisans could not prevent most from being taken away. For much of the Nazi period, people were essentially on their own and had to try to disqualify themselves.

How did the deportations affect the mindset of the native population? They certainly were much talked about, invariably with indignation. By 1943 people complained openly that they were living in permanent fear of being sent away as slaves.[130] When the Germans were finally gone, the deportations remained for some time almost the sole object of conversation.[131] The conclusion should probably be that the enforced displacement of innumerable people became, as several memoirs emphasize, "the last straw" and indeed the main reason why non-Jews started to hate the Germans. The deportations "immediately severed the still weak bonds between the conquerors and the conquered," writes one memoirist. "Our people's indignation reached a climax," writes another.[132] From the standpoint of popular opinion in the Reichskommissariat Ukraine, the roundups and deportations were the Nazis' biggest mistake. And along with the growing realization that Germany would lose the war, they all but created the partisan movements.

12

TOWARD THE END OF NAZI RULE

The role of the deportations in the emergence of large numbers of partisans was all the greater because Stalin for a long time considered partisan warfare in Ukraine a low priority. This was contrary to what his public rhetoric suggested. In his radio speech of July 1941, he ordered partisan and sabotage groups to "create intolerable conditions for the enemy and all his accomplices" and to "destroy them at every step," but his known actions suggest that for over a year, he believed that partisans could not significantly influence the military struggle at the front and that in general they should save themselves. The decision to create a Central Staff for the Soviet partisans occurred only on May 30, 1942. Headed by the first secretary of the Communist party of Belarus (Panteleimon Ponomarenko), it tended to neglect Ukraine. Compared to Belarus and western Russia, which had large forests more favorable to partisan activity, the Soviet partisans in Ukraine received few supplies and other support, and relatively late in the war.[1] In addition, the Ukrainian staff of the partisan movement, under the deputy head of the republican NKVD, Tymofii Strokach, long existed only on paper.[2]

The enormous Soviet literature about the partisans we call "Soviet" is unreliable and since 1991, the topic has attracted few historians. Moreover, many key documents remain unavailable. Much, therefore, is still unclear: for instance, why Stalin, on September 5, 1942, secretly proclaimed that preconditions for the quick development everywhere of a partisan struggle "of the entire people" were in place and that therefore all existing partisan units must involve "all the wider layers of the population," even in the cities. Or why, on October 2, 1942, twelve members and candidate-members of the Central Committee of the Communist party of Ukraine and four partisan leaders created a second body to lead Ukraine's Soviet partisans, the "illegal CC CP(b)U." Or why Stalin dissolved the Central Staff (while retaining the Ukrainian and other regional staffs) early in March 1943, only to resurrect it five weeks later.[3]

Distortion and myth also largely shroud the history of the everyday life of Soviet partisans in the territory of the Reichskommissariat Ukraine. The first partisans appeared in 1941 and tended to be Red Army soldiers, members of extermination battalions, and airdropped NKVD officers.[4] The German army and the SS, using violence and threats, eliminated almost all of this first wave. German and Soviet reports late in 1941 and early in 1942 document civilians who fought the partisans or who might have supported them first but then handed them over—even though, in some cases, they were their own husbands and sons.[5] In fact, after Germans and Hungarians crushed the partisans near the Dnieper bend at the end of 1941, that southern region remained for a long time more solidly under German control than most other regions of eastern Europe. As late as December 1942, the people there still "generally opposed all attempts by Bolshevik or national Ukrainian agents to create gangs or other conspiracies," as a Nazi report put it.[6]

The relative disinterest of Soviet leaders, the unfavorable natural conditions, German violence and threats, and lack of popular support all impeded the rise of partisans in Ukraine. Yet this changed as a result of the deportations. Letters to "Eastern Workers" in the Reich, for example, convinced German letter censors that people evading deportations predominated among the partisans.[7] The partisans also included deserted auxiliary policemen, Communists, Soviet officials, former POWs, Red Army deserters, Jewish refugees, ordinary criminals, and thousands of airdropped agents.[8]

In October 1942, there were in all of Ukraine, including the military zone, just under five thousand Soviet partisans who had good contact with the Ukrainian staff. Other units had such contact irregularly or not at all.[9] By that time, Soviet partisans were most active in the Zhytomyr region and in the military zone's Chernihiv and Sumy areas. German antipartisan measures pushed them north into Belarus, but the partisans returned in November 1942 and carried out a long raid through Ukraine. Over 1,760 partisans (in four detachments) were led by Sydir Kovpak, a bearded, fifty-five-year-old Ukrainian Communist who had been under NKVD arrest at one time. Crossing the Dnieper River, they first returned to the Polissian north of the Zhytomyr general district, where they captured, among others, the district capital of Lelchitsy, killing hundreds of local Germans and "traitors."[10]

After the Battle of Stalingrad, partisan activity emerged on a truly large

19. Tymofii Strokach, deputy chief of the Soviet Ukrainian NKVD (left), and Demian Korotchenko, a Communist party secretary, inspect some of Sydir Kovpak's partisans on the eve of their daring raid toward the Carpathian Mountains. Partisan zone in the Zhytomyr region in northern Ukraine, June 1943. (Tsentral'nyi derzhavnyi kinofotofonoarkhiv Ukraïny im. H. S. Pshenychnoho, 0–43743.)

scale in Koch's domain. Letters to the Reich in April and May 1943 mentioned partisans far more often than before.[11] The partisan Kovpakites (as they came to be known) moved on to south of the Zhytomyr and Kiev general districts, in the direction of the Carpathian Mountains. In many places, partisan zones came about—regions where German authority collapsed in all but name. Indeed, by the middle of the year as much as 60 percent of the Zhytomyr general district was under the control of either Soviet partisans or Ukrainian nationalist partisans (discussed later).[12] In northern Volhynia and Polissia, the Soviet partisans resembled army regiments or, most often, battalions both in size (some eight hundred people) and in weaponry. Those elsewhere, such as in the forests of Podolia, tended to operate in groups of at most three hundred.[13] And in almost every raion, groups of fifteen to thirty-five people started partisan activity, usually as the front neared.[14]

Ukrainian staff chief Strokach claimed that in 1943 there were 100,000 Soviet partisans in all of Ukraine, and CP(b)U chief Khrushchev asserted that as many as 200,000 people would become partisans if only there were arms for them. Both exaggerated.[15] A Wehrmacht intelligence agency estimated that in June 1943 there were 30,000 Soviet partisans in "the Ukrainian SSR" (possibly excluding the Reichskommissariat's Belarusan north) and due to the advance of the Red Army this number declined to 29,000 three months later and to 24,000 in October 1943. Meanwhile, the same agency estimated the numbers of Soviet partisans in Belarus as increasing in this period from 45,000 to 76,000.[16] With regard to Ukraine west of the Dnieper River, the Communist party believed in July 1943 that there were over 16,500 Soviet partisans, which was about 1 percent of the official population of the entire Reichskommissariat at the beginning of the year.[17]

Joining an existing partisan group was never easy. Males who wanted to do so often were told to join the auxiliary police, to obtain arms and ammunition there, and then to desert. Newly recruited Red Partisans, as they often called themselves, pledged to serve "my motherland, the party, and my leader and comrade Stalin."[18] They underwent a harsh probation period. Although partisans, Soviet or not, tended to consume a lot of alcohol, all were subject to severe disciplinary rules, which were enforced with beatings and other punishments by not only the commanders, but also political commissars or (in the large units) special sections of the NKVD. Unauthorized plunder and being drunk or asleep on duty often brought the death penalty. Partisans with a serious illness that endangered the group also could be killed.[19]

Female partisans worked as cooks and cleaners. As long as they did not accept a steady boyfriend, the males considered them common property. Pregnancies were usually aborted; babies born often were given away to peasants or killed. Very few partisans had medical knowledge. In all, the partisan life was restless and often brutal, marked by semidarkness, damp cold, dirty water, disease, lice, and shortages of food, tobacco, clothing, and shoes.[20]

At Stalin's urging, the partisans (and underground activists in the cities) engaged in sabotage, mainly of the railroads (through delayed-detonation mines). To prevent these acts, from the fall of 1943 the German authorities deployed guards (military or natives) along the tracks.[21] But these assaults on railroads did indeed, as Stalin assumed, have little influence on developments at the military front. They never obstructed German transports to the front for long periods. Indeed, the main aid that the partisans gave to the Red Army was in securing good crossing points at the Dnieper in 1943.[22]

The Soviet partisans' real significance was their effect on everyday life in Nazi-ruled Ukraine. Besides engaging in sabotage, partisans distributed leaflets and newspapers. On May 1, 1943, Stalin publicly ordered them to prevent the deportations to Germany.[23] But at least as high on the partisan agenda was killing, and not just of Germans. Ukraine's NKVD had as an official aim to systematically "exterminate" the "fascist" regime, "especially [village] elders, mayors, leaders of police units, and Gestapo agents."[24] In an order on September 5, 1942, Stalin made it clear that the partisan's goals included "annihilation of the living force of the enemy." Germans and "traitors of the Motherland" alike should be either captured or killed. According to some sources, in May 1943, he even sanctioned family killings: when "traitors" were killed, their close relatives should perish with them.[25]

The partisans did indeed, in the words of a letter censor, "assault villages and small towns and kill the police, the village elders, pro-German inhabitants, and some German officials and soldiers."[26] In one of the few preserved reports about the Reichskommissariat that he actually wrote himself, Reichskommissar Koch noted correctly that "all the gangs systematically attack those natives who are in German service or sympathize with Germany." A Communist party report boasted in March 1942 that in all of Ukraine, Soviet partisans had already killed over 1,200 "spies and traitors," besides almost 240 German officers and 11,900 soldiers.[27] From April 17, 1943, to January 13, 1944, Soviet partisans in Ukraine reportedly killed close to 58,700 German military and 950 (presumably non-German) policemen.[28]

In addition, Soviet partisans and Ukrainian nationalists fought each other and their real or imagined sympathizers to the death. This struggle intensified from 1943, when there emerged the Ukrainian Insurgent Army (discussed later), which was active mostly in central and southern Volhynia.[29] Along the way, partisans of all persuasions frequently disguised their political affiliation. For instance, forty-three Schuma in the Pohrebyshche raion near Zhytomyr once in 1943 approached the Soviet partisans, whom they believed were Ukrainian nationalists and whom they wanted to join. They were told to go back and shoot their German supervisors, which they did. When they returned, they were shot themselves, which put the total body count at fifty-five.[30] In authorizing the use of auxiliary policemen as "counterpartisans," the Nazis complicated matters still further.[31]

Threats of violence were also used by partisans to enforce cooperation. In a typical case, the Shchors partisan detachment once apprehended the elder of the village of Produbiïvka near Korostyshiv and condemned him to death. The elder begged for his life and got a second chance: He should bring, the next day, 2,200 kilograms of grain. "If you don't, we will shoot you and your family," he was told. From then on, the man totally depended on the partisans, for having followed one of their orders, from the Nazi perspective he had joined them.[32] Civilians thus were stuck in the middle. To make matters worse for them, the partisans' harsh living conditions and their general isolation from civilian life fostered their resentment of those compatriots who did not choose sides. The Soviet partisans, as a historian has put it, even came to "criminalize passivity."[33]

The "Struggle against Gangs"

The Nazis again struck back hard. In September 1942, SS chief Himmler issued guidelines on what he called the "struggle against gangs." As before, he supported harsh suppression of what he called "strangers" and of the native officials who failed to report them. In more and more villages and towns, lists of the inhabitants had to be posted inside people's homes. (The elder or mayor kept a copy.) Many peasants also had to wear a tag with a personal identification number and the name of their village. The supervisory bases on the former machinery and tractor stations were reinforced with armed locals.[34]

But in practice, starting in 1942, the predominant Nazi reaction to the partisans was to kill and burn, with careful planning and horrible precision. One of the earliest casualties of these assaults in the Reichskommissariat was the village of Kortelisy near Ratne in Polissia.[35] In May 1942, a partisan unit of some fifty locals and former Red Army soldiers destroyed the local police station. In the summer, a German unit called a village meeting and shot several relatives of partisans and Eastern Worker refugees. Still deeming the village a partisan stronghold, the Nazis dealt it a final blow some months later. One September day, peasants from surrounding villages who owned carts received an order to go to Kortelisy the next day. Early that September 23, a police company and Schuma auxiliaries surrounded Kortelisy. Everybody, including all of the children, had to assemble and to bring along their money and identity papers. A man said that he needed some time, for his children were not dressed yet and it was cold. A Schuma told him not to "waste" the clothes: the meeting would be short and it would get hot, he said. Disabled villagers were taken to the square on carts. There they saw Kovel District Commissar Kassner, who told everyone through an interpreter that, because of their resistance to the German authorities, he had orders to burn them alive in their homes. But, he said, he had decided instead to shoot them. Somebody read out loud the names of those who would be spared: the village elder, the priest, the local Eastern Labor officials, the local Schuma, and the spouses and children of these villagers; all but the local Schuma were locked up in the school. Then the intruders forced the local men to dig a long and deep ditch and to undress. They started up car engines so as to muffle the sounds to come and started killing, first the men, and then the women and children. Thus nearly 2,900 people were shot with submachine guns and pistols, drowned, or bayonetted to death.

By hiding in a hay loft, Anastasiia Korneliuk, then fourteen, survived, along with her older sister Marusia. During the killings, they sat in the hay. A long time later, "at three, maybe four in the afternoon, we started to go out," she recalls. "We took a look outside and saw the butchers standing in the garden under a tree, all dressed in black. Davyd was walking toward them, his brother was a policeman. 'Davyd!' Marusia called out. 'Where *is* everybody?' 'There's no-one left. They've been killed.' 'What about you?' 'I've been chosen, I won't be killed.' . . . My sister saw that all the chosen ones wore brassards. She took off her kerchief, tore it apart, and put it around her arm and mine. It made us look like the chosen ones. We jumped out of the hay and joined the carts. We followed them closely. Near the church the bullets were still flying—they were killing those who were still breathing, and those captured by the policemen in the gardens. 'Don't you girls follow us!' the women on the carts screamed. 'We will hand you over!' My sister stepped aside and I followed her." The two girls managed to flee to family members in another village. While the chosen locals were directed to the town of Ratne, the cart owners from the nearby villages were told to remove the possessions from the homes of those killed. The next day Kortelisy was burned to the ground and ceased to exist.

In other villages, residents were burned alive. One morning in January 1943, the village of Borodianka in the Kiev region was attacked by German and auxiliary policemen. The Budnik family and several other families, a total of twenty people including women and children, were burned to death. Looking out her window, thirty meters away, one woman saw another jump out of a fire-filled hamlet, almost insane, but some auxiliaries chased and killed her and threw the body into the fire.[36] The massacres of real or imagined partisans and their accomplices in the Zhytomyr general district became ferocious: from November 1942 to mid-February 1943, "gang fighters" there shot at least 2,336 people and destroyed eighty-four villages. Only twenty-four of these villages were destroyed after consultation with district commissars, which prompted the regional SS and police leader to order his subordinates to secure the local commissar's prior permission for burning villages and meting out the "special treatment" to unarmed villagers.[37]

Young people who joined the partisans always put the lives of their families on the line. Parents of partisans were taken hostage and could be shot. At the very least they suffered abuse and lost their homes and property. In a typical sequence of events, when in April 1943 the young people from Buda near Chyhyryn joined the partisans, the district commissar leveled the village and deported all able-bodied persons, afterward overseeing the shooting of those unable to work—the old, the very young, and the ill. Such murders closely resembled the earlier massacres of the Jews and the Roma.[38] The antipartisan measures also meant more killings in the cities. For example, the Security Police announced that it had shot all the inmates of Rivne's prison on March 8, 1943, to penalize an escape attempt and the killing of a German official and a Dutch guard; in reality the hundreds perished by way of revenge for the partisan activities in the region.[39]

From the middle of 1943 the antipartisan warfare radicalized still further. On June 21, 1943, the Nazis declared all of Ukraine a "gang-fighting area,"[40] and in July, Hitler ordered Himmler to remove all people from the Belarusan and northern Ukrainian partisan zones. Able-bodied males between the ages of sixteen and fifty-five in these zones should be deported at once to Germany as prisoners of war and put into forced labor there. Younger and older males, and the able-bodied women, should be taken to camps in anticipation of deportation. As for the remaining women with small children, the SS and police were charged with "settling" or "resettling" them—language that created the option of killing them.[41] When the German authorities abandoned terrain to partisans, they apparently often shot the local native officials and Schuma, just in case. And it became their standard practice to firebomb the partisan zones from planes.[42]

The relevant orders have not been found, but the Security Police also implemented in July 1943 a secret anti-Communist campaign code-named Operation Lightning. The record of a postwar Soviet trial suggests that the Security Police and SD plenipotentiaries in the raions received an order to start an operation against all registered Communists at a specific time. In at least one raion, this source says, the Security Police and Schuma arrested the Communist party members, took them away in cars, and put them on a train to a camp in Dnipropetrovsk.[43] In reality, the Communists were shot, with their relatives, in pits outside of their villages. According to Fedir Pihido, who witnessed these arrests in the village of Staiky, those killed almost always were peasants who had joined Stalin's party in order to survive—Communists only in name. The vast majority of the more important Communists escaped, he argues, because spies and informants warned them in the nick of time, and they fled to the partisans. In this way, rather than weakening the partisans, Operation Lightning increased their number.[44] In a possibly related development, in July 1943 dozens of prominent Ukrainians were taken hostage in western Volhynia. The German authorities eventually released the women, but they shot most of the men three months later, after Nikolai Kuznetsov, an NKVD man who posed as a German officer, threw a grenade at a man who resembled Koch's deputy, Paul Dargel.[45]

German-sponsored leaflets and newspapers contained vouchers with which partisans could surrender and supposedly secure good treatment.[46] German propaganda, meanwhile, continued the death threats: one poster, for instance, informed people that the alternative to supporting "freedom and security" was that "you will destroy yourself and your family and perish along with the Red bandits."[47] Aware at last that the population feared them more than the "Jewish Bolsheviks," however, the Nazis also started producing more propaganda about the Soviet terror. From April 1943, they featured their discovery in the Katyn forest in Russia of the remains of thousands of Polish army officers shot by the NKVD in 1940. In response, several Ukrainians in Vinnytsia—a city where screams and shots resounded from the local prison on a regular basis—informed the city administration that apart from the graves of NKVD victims found in Vinnytsia in 1941, there existed many other such graves within the city limits. On May 25, 1943, the German authorities started a months-long investigation into these allegations, with the secret agenda of establishing once and for all that they were not the first to carry out mass shootings.[48] At the Polish cemetery, in the city park, and in an orchard, they found no fewer than 113 graves containing 9,439 corpses. Various commissions conducted autopsies and questioned witnesses.[49]

The newspapers wrote about the Vinnytsia graves and thousands of people from all over Ukraine came to look for lost relatives. In part because many relatives of those lost were too afraid to come, most bodies remained unidentified, but some women recognized their relatives by their belongings or by their clothes, which they had patched. Those identified included Ukrainians, Poles, Jews, and Russians, civilians and members of the military, Communists and non-Communists, and even some NKVD officers.[50] But the German-controlled radio and press referred to "ten thousand Ukrainians" killed by Stalin and the Jews. The authorities also organized trips to the graves by Ukrainian "delegates," who on their return held public talks about the experience.[51]

And yet, despite the propaganda and the overwhelming evidence, few natives believed that the bodies in the graves were indeed victims of the NKVD. In Vinnytsia many rumors made the rounds, but most said it was a German affair involving murdered Jews, western Ukrainians, people who had opposed the deportations, or Soviet POWs.[52] The denial was massive and prompted Bishop Ievlohii (Markovsky) of Vinnytsia, a former monk who had joined the Autonomous church, to call out at one of the reburials, "Ukrainians! Have you really forgotten what happened just three, four years ago, when you did not know at night what might happen to you until the morning? Have you really forgotten how the Communist party held its horrible, bloody orgies here?"[53] After the Red Army returned, most locals apparently told the new regional Soviet authorities that the corpses and belongings had looked as if they had been buried recently (not in the 1930s). Some apparently also said that the "Gestapo" had moved corpses from pit to pit so as to artificially increase their number.[54] It is possible that the Security Police had added its own victims to these graves; more likely, the NKVD had shot and buried people not only in the late 1930s, but also in 1941. Most natives, however, apparently found the NKVD shootings unbelievable, too much to take. They wanted to be *liberated*, not to see the Nazis replaced by another terrorist regime.

The "Action to Destroy the Poles"

On Sunday, August 29, 1943, the Roman Catholic faithful of Volia Ostrovetska and Ostrivky, two neighboring Polish villages in the Liuboml region, near Volhynia's border with the General Government, heard their priest say frightening things.[55] We are in mortal danger, he said. Polish activists from another region had told him that Ukrainian nationalists were about to attack the Polish population. The women and children should flee to the German garrison in Iahotyn and the men must arm themselves, he added. The anxious congregation discussed his appeal, but did little more. Later in the day, shepherds saw armed Ukrainians on dozens of carts move toward the nearby Ukrainian village of Sokil; Poles who went there did not return. Warnings came in from friendly Ukrainians. During the night, watchmen again saw armed males on the move. From Ostrivky, another Polish village could be seen going up in flames. In view of the large numbers of Ukrainians, the villagers decided not to resist whatever was in store and buried their rifles.

In the morning of August 30, flares were seen going up in the air and soon Volia Ostrovetska and Ostrivky were surrounded by Ukrainians armed with firearms, knives, axes, and pitchforks. They ordered everyone to assemble at the schools at ten o'clock for a meeting where Poles and Ukrainians would decide how to jointly fight the Germans. Some alert Poles in Volia Ostrovetska called out for resistance, but they were shot at once; some in Ostrivky issued the same call, but other Poles rebuked them. The intruders led the males away in small groups, and then the women, girls, and small children. Outside some barns, the Poles had to surrender any arms, watches, or gold, and to undress down to their underwear for "a medical check." But inside the barns they were beaten to death. When the pit in Volia Ostrovetska became full, remaining Poles were locked inside the school and either were burned alive or died from grenades.

The intruders in Ostrivky made a change of plan around noon, when German soldiers came to investigate and fired shots from afar. The aggressors hurriedly drove the women and children to a stubble field, shooting those unable to keep up. A Ukrainian on horseback read out a death verdict. His accomplices forced all to lie face down in groups of ten and shot or stabbed them to death. Finally, after the Germans had left again, armed groups roamed the area, calling out in Polish that the coast was clear and killing survivors who responded. The death toll was over a thousand, or almost 70 percent of the combined population of both villages. The others only lived because the Germans had shown up.

The premeditated massacre of these Polish villagers was far from an isolated event. Western Volhynia, less than thirty thousand square kilometers, inhabited by 1.5 million people, including 250,000 Poles, experienced in 1943 mass killings of Poles and a Polish-Ukrainian war.[56] At the very least 15,000, and possibly many thousands more, Polish men, women, and children died at the hands of Ukrainian partisans and villagers in one of the most comprehensive cases of "ethnic cleansing" in wartime eastern Europe.[57] Many Poles survived only because they fled across the Buh River to the General Government. These events involved the only Ukrainian partisan force that presented itself as an alternative to Soviet and Nazi rule, the Ukrainian Insurgent Army, or UPA.

Until the end of Communist rule in eastern Europe, the assault on the Poles of Volhynia was almost unknown beyond groups of survivors, but since then a substantial historiography has developed. Some historians explain the massacres through the concept of "provocation" by a third party (the Germans).[58] Historians sympathetic to the UPA first tend to speak of a Ukrainian struggle for survival against "the Poles," whom they say supported the German and Soviet enemies of Ukraine, and then move on to focus on the UPA's fight against the Red Army, the NKVD, and Soviet officials in the subsequent years. These authors assume and sometimes say that the Poles did not belong in Volhynia anyway and that in principle their removal was justified.[59] Other historians have applied the concept of "ethnic cleansing" to what happened to the Poles, in the sense of killings that most of all aim to remove a people from a concrete territory, rather than to kill them.[60]

A glance at memoirs and other primary sources produces a very consistent account of what happened. A Jewish woman from the town of Horokhiv who survived thanks to a Ukrainian has recalled that in the spring of 1943, the already frequent attacks by Ukrainian nationalists on Polish villagers turned into "a virtual extermination of all the Polish inhabitants who fell into their hands."[61] Taras "Bulba" Borovets, the former leader of the Polissian Sich, has recalled in North American exile that the UPA leadership's policy became to "exterminate Ukraine's national minorities," in particular the Poles.[62] Erich Koch informed Alfred

Rosenberg on June 25, 1943, that the "national Ukrainian gangs" were releasing German soldiers they had captured (but not Nazi civilian officials or policemen) and using "the opportunity to kill, often in a most brutal way, the Poles, Czechs, and ethnic Germans living in the countryside."[63] German military intelligence documented in July 1943 that the "Bandera movement" was engaged in the "extermination (*Ausrottung*) of Polish settlers in Volhynia." Late in 1944 German military intelligence again referred to deliberate extermination.[64] On April 21, 1943, using data supplied by the Soviet partisan group led by Ivan Shytov, Soviet Ukrainian partisan chief Strokach concluded that besides striving for revolution, "the Ukrainian nationalists are carrying out a beastly massacre of the defenseless Polish population, with the aim of totally destroying the Poles in Ukraine."[65] Vasyl Behma, Soviet partisan leader in the Rivne region, reported on May 28, 1943, that "in general, the activity of the nationalists until recently has been directed at the extermination of the Polish population and the Polish villages."[66] Many months later, he wrote that "the nationalists," statements in support of the freedom of all peoples notwithstanding, still were "destroying the Poles to a man." Reports of attempts at "the total destruction" or the "cleansing" of western Volhynia's Poles also came from Soviet partisans in nearby eastern Volhynia.[67]

As for UPA sources, on August 2, 1943, the leader of the Volhynia branch of the Banderite Security Service (SB), Vasyl Makar, wrote to his brother that the German Security Police had burned two hundred Ukrainian villages and had killed one thousand Ukrainian peasants with assistance from "the Polacks" (*liakhy*). In response, he added, "we destroy them mercilessly."[68] Three months later, he or another SB official spoke of a recently concluded "action to destroy the Poles" (*aktsiia nyshchennia poliakiv*)—which unfortunately had "not produced the expected results" because "most of the Polish active element has survived," an acknowledgment that most victims had been innocent civilians.[69] Findings such as these call to mind the concept of genocide, a view supported by the absence to date of evidence that leaflets ordering the Poles to cross the Buh River, and thus save themselves, circulated before the fall.[70] But whatever name we give to these events, it is clear and by now generally accepted that a murderous assault on Polish civilians took place.

Before 1939, Poles and Ukrainians in western Volhynia got along reasonably well. As war became imminent, however, more and more Ukrainians expressed anti-Polish sentiments.[71] The Soviet invader in 1939 encouraged them with his propaganda against the "Polish lords" and his deportations of the most nationally conscious Poles—settlers brought in by the Polish government during the 1920s. When the Germans arrived, the remaining anti-Ukrainian Poles usually took up jobs in the towns; fearful Poles remained in the countryside.[72]

The Ukrainians of the region, for their part, did not miss the Polish state one bit. Although most did not want a Ukrainian state just yet, nationalism was the strongest political current, especially among the young.[73] Many, if not most, young Ukrainians either joined or sympathized with the one active Ukrainian political movement, the OUN, whose Bandera faction was to play a leading role in the anti-Polish massacre. Its ideology derived from an immense frustration over the fall of Ukrainian independent statehood after World War I. But the members of the organization expected that Ukrainians would get a second chance. During the present war, they thought, the same scenario as in 1918 would unfold: Warring empires would exhaust each other, various national independence movements would step in, and the one with the strongest army would gain the upper hand. To prepare for that decisive moment, the OUN wanted all Ukrainians to obtain arms and to practice using them, if possible by joining the German police. By no means, however, should they waste their energies and resources on partisan activity.[74] Both factions had one all-powerful leader and only one moral guideline: "put the well-being of the Ukrainian Nation above everything." Anybody not with these activists was against them, they believed—a mentality that allowed them to label their victims enemies.[75]

In principle, the future independent state would include all contiguous European territory that the organization considered Ukrainian, including Chełm in the west and, in the east, Kursk, the northern Caucasus, and the eastern shores of the Sea of Azov. The task was to evict from these areas all of the "enemies and foreigners": the Poles, Russians, Romanians, Hungarians, Germans, and Jews.[76] The Jews of the past had "sucked the blood of our peasants through usury" and now they supported Communism; Banderite leaders concluded that they must be killed.[77] Russians were simply Bolsheviks, as were others who owned Russian books or were able to speak Russian.[78]

In Europe during the first half of the twentieth century, almost all nationalisms were intolerant, radical, and at least tinged with racism.

Likewise, the OUN believed that Ukrainian national consciousness was transmitted "along with the blood" and although it might lay dormant there, a national revolution would awaken it.[79] This attitude partly explains the turn to massacres of Poles in 1943. According to secret guidelines that the Bandera faction issued in May 1941, it was necessary to "destroy" Polish leaders, but to assimilate "the so-called Polish peasants."[80] The difference never meant much, however. Leaflets and posters issued in the name of Bandera in 1941 proclaimed that "Moscow, Poland, the Hungarians, Jewry are your enemies. Destroy them." Graduates from a short-lived Ukrainian military school in Lutsk marched while singing, "Death, death, death to the Polacks and the Muscovite-Jewish commune."[81] In short, killing Poles *as Poles* was part of the organization's moral dogma well before 1943.

The Galician background of most leading OUN activists in western Volhynia was also relevant, for nationalism had been the most influential ideology among Galician Ukrainians for decades and all varieties of this nationalism tended to denounce ethics as politically irrelevant. Paradoxically, the activists of the supposedly atheist OUN often were zealous Greek Catholics.[82] The Bandera faction of the OUN had its own internal security organization, the Sluzhba Bezpeky (SB). Founded by Mykola Lebed, the acting leader of the Banderites ever since Bandera's arrest in 1941, and dominated by men who like him had graduated from a German Security Police school in the Polish town of Zakopane, the SB inspired terror in civilians of all ethnicities.[83]

The first Ukrainian nationalist partisans were commanded by an outsider, Taras "Bulba" Borovets. The fighting group called the Polissian Sich that he organized in Soviet Polissia just before the German occupation impressed the German army, which made it a legal police force of about one thousand. It aspired "to kill and destroy all of Ukraine's enemies" (as its official organ put it) and members likely killed Jews in 1941 (as noted in Chapter 3). In the middle of November 1941, for reasons that remain obscure, the much enlarged Sich disbanded itself.[84] Although Borovets revived it the next year as the Ukrainian Insurgent Army (UPA), he was unsure what to do and soon sent many members home.[85]

Early in 1943, news came of the German defeat at Stalingrad. Like most western Ukrainians, the Banderites did not conclude that the Red Army was a force to be reckoned with. On the contrary, recalling the Red Army's chaotic retreat less then two years earlier, they believed that it was close to collapse.[86] After also taking note of the increasing strength and activity of the Soviet partisans, in the third week of February 1943 the Banderite leadership made the momentous decision to commence partisan warfare. The decision immediately changed the atmosphere in the region. Leon Żur, a fourteen-year-old boy from the Polish village of Borove in the Sarny region, had played with a boy from a nearby Ukrainian village for years. When early in 1943 he visited his friend again for the first time after a heavy snow, he got a much different reception.

> To my "Hello," the members of the household gave the usual answer, but Ihor, the oldest son, snapped back, "Now we say, 'Glory to Ukraine,' and we answer, 'Glory forever.'" And he started to teach it to me. "Now be sure to remember it well." Then he said, as if talking to himself, "Why is this Polack here? What's he doing here?"
>
> Andrii and I went out to the yard. Immediately Ihor came there too and started singing "Still Ukraine Is Not Dead Yet" and some song about nationalists on the march.
>
> Soon the master of the house, Sava Ieremishchuk, also came there. He walked up to me and said, "Don't come around here any more. Our young people are getting together to think about how to remove all Poles from the Ukrainian land and how to build an independent Ukraine. The Germans say they will help, but the Poles and the Communists are in the way."

Whether or not Ieremishchuk really said these words, Leon got so scared that he ran home as fast as he could.[87]

After securing an agreement with Borovets in March to merge his UPA with their "Military Units," the Banderites unilaterally renamed the units UPA and ordered all OUN members and Ukrainian Schuma to enlist. Hundreds, perhaps thousands obeyed, and hundreds of Ukrainian policemen and others arrived from the General Government to join them.[88] The German authorities recruited new Schuma, but those took to the woods as well.[89] Early in April 1943, a warning went out that any Ukrainian Schuma or employee of a German office who did not contact the OUN by April 20 would be shot as a deserter.[90] Partisans who joined the new UPA but refused to surrender their weapon immediately were shot without warning. The Melnykite leadership ordered its activists not to resist, but around 150 young Melnykite partisans in the Lutsk region started negotiations with the Security Police instead; they were to become a legal Schuma unit of the Security Police at the end of 1943.[91]

Although historians have tended to focus on Lebed, the actual commander of the new UPA for most of 1943 became Lieutenant Dmytro Kliachkivsky, alias Klym Savur, a Galician who had led the Banderites of northwestern Ukraine since late 1942. In May 1943 he created three UPA groups: a northern group near Sarny, a northwestern group near Kovel, and a southern group near Rivne and Kremenets.[92] German military intelligence estimated in October 1943 that there were 40,000 "Bandera" or "Bulba" partisans (mostly in western Volhynia but also elsewhere in "the Ukrainian SSR"). By the end of 1943, not more than 40 percent of the UPA members were OUN members or sympathizers.[93] But Banderite ways still predominated: many used the traditional greeting (raising of the right arm while saying "Glory to the heroes"), and any commander who was not a member of the OUN had a political "educator" or SB agent at his side.[94] For all the UPA's strength, civilians rarely spoke of "the UPA" or of an "army." The force was known as the Bulbovites (to Poles), the Banderites (to Poles and Ukrainians), or simply as the insurgents or our lads (to Ukrainians). Calling them lads made sense, for almost all of these partisans were teenagers or in their early twenties.[95]

It seems clear that early in 1943, the leadership of the Bandera faction decided to kill all Poles in the Ukrainian-dominated lands between the Buh River and the pre-1939 border, lands that the Polish government-in-exile and the Polish underground had continued to claim for the Polish state. According to Borovets, the Banderites (he mentions Lebed) imposed a collective death sentence on the Poles of "western Ukraine" in March 1943, sent him a list of demands in April that included their "cleansing," and instructed the UPA in June to complete the "cleansing" operation as soon as possible.[96] If this account is correct, it would explain the chronology and geography of events. The many narratives by Polish survivors indicate that in western Volhynia's eastern half, mass killings of Poles started in March 1943 and became particularly common in July (possibly partly in response to the German retreat during and after the Battle of Kursk in Russia). More to the west, the murders started and climaxed in July, while in the Liuboml region they started and climaxed in August. The peak of Volhynian massacres was from July 10 to 15, when about one hundred Polish communities came under attack.[97] The archives of

Ukraine's former KGB are said to hold documents that point at Kliachkivsky as the instigator, but outside researchers have not gained access to them.[98]

The attacks followed a pattern. During the prelude, there were Orthodox priests who blessed axes, pitchforks, and knives in their church.[99] The first bad omen to the Poles might be when Ukrainian acquaintances stopped talking to them, although Ukrainians who lived close to the targeted communities were often kept in the dark about the assault plan. In "mixed" villages, such a plan involved painting crosses on Polish homes. Flares were common attack signals, and the clothing of some attackers might suggest that they were German soldiers or Soviet partisans. One ruse was that they came to coordinate the fight against the Germans. Often there were three waves of attackers: first a walking crowd of SB officers, UPA members, and ordinary villagers, then UPA members on horseback, and finally a ring of male and female villagers who looted property and strip-searched the dead.[100] Indeed, among the killers were also ordinary Ukrainian villagers, of various ages and of both sexes.[101] If attackers doubted a potential victim's ethnicity, they demanded that he or she recite the Lord's Prayer in Ukrainian. As for Polish children, some were let go, or were taken along as servants. The attackers dynamited the Roman Catholic churches. No more than a few days after the massacre, the attackers ordered Ukrainians from nearby villages to bury the bodies.[102]

In the middle of 1943, the periodical of the Banderites, *Ideiia i chyn* (Idea and deed) placed this brief notice: "The Ukrainian population in the northwestern Ukrainian lands has started to respond to the terror and provocation by the Polish settlers, secret agents, and Communist cells with self-defense, destroying all hidden enemies of the Ukrainian people."[103] Indeed, Kliachkivsky and his followers believed they were acting in self-defense. When late in July 1943 Polish leaders in Warsaw issued a statement in support of a Ukrainian state that nevertheless reaffirmed the Polish claims to western Volhynia and eastern Galicia, the Banderite leadership spoke of "plans for the extermination of the Ukrainian people in western Ukraine."[104] Another Banderite statement, some months later, complained that the prewar Polish government had carried out a "policy of extermination" against the Ukrainians.[105] The Banderites accused the Poles of organizing "above all against us, the Ukrainians," so as to destroy or at least to subjugate them, with German and then with Soviet assistance.[106]

Most vivid of all to the Banderites in 1943 were events in several coun-
ties in the Lublin district of the General Government, known to Ukrainians, who were its majority, as the Kholm region and to Poles as the
Zamość region. Anybody in Volhynia who dared to complain to
Banderites about the murder of innocent and unarmed Poles got a furious response along these lines: "But look what the Poles did to our Ukrainian peasants in the Kholm region! Do you know that in 1942, during
March and April alone, the Poles burned down about forty Ukrainian villages and 130 churches, and killed 34,000 people! They rode horseback
on our priests and then brutally murdered them; they raped girls in front
of their parents and then killed both the girls and their parents."[107] A
young SB officer told a Ukrainian man in great detail about how he and
others murdered the Polish residents of Dominopol village on July 11,
1943. When the man, Danylo Shumuk, did not praise this act but denounced it as a black stain on the Ukrainian movement, the officer was
so offended that he got tears in his eyes. "And what if," he asked, "the
Poles had pulled your mother out of your house by the braids, murdered
her before your very eyes, and thrown her into the Buh River, as happened in 1942? If your father had been shot in front of you? If your sixteen-year-old sister had been raped, bayoneted, and then thrown into the
Buh?"[108] Social psychologists know that "violence often emerges from a
pattern in which both sides perform hostile or provoking acts."[109] Here
too, the complaints of the main aggressor had some validity. Polish underground activists *had* been murdering Ukrainian leading figures in the
Lublin district since at least May 1942, and Polish partisans (which had
grown in number after a Nazi campaign to expel peasants) assaulted police stations, which often were manned by Ukrainians. But Ukrainian policemen there had been killing Poles, and overall the events were more
complex than the Banderites wanted to admit.[110]

At first many Poles in Volhynia remained passive. Much like many
Jews earlier, these people did not consider their lives in direct danger,
even though warnings came from other Poles or sympathetic Ukrainians.
For most of these tradition-bound peasants, abandoning their places of
birth was not an option. When they realized they were in mortal danger,
many fell into a state of apathy. "We wanted an easy death," Leon Żur recalls. "People said that it would be easier to die from German hands, for
those had something to shoot with, whereas a Ukrainian bandit cut off
the head with an axe or stabbed with a pitchfork." Soviet partisans in May
1943 accused the Poles of passively waiting to be killed.[111]

The Polish partisan units that did eventually appear had a good relationship with the Soviet partisans for most of 1943. In fact, Soviet partisans created many of the Polish units and formally controlled them; other Poles joined preexisting Soviet partisan units. Thus thousands went over the Soviet side, even though that side always made clear that western Volhynia must remain part of Soviet Ukraine.[112] Other Volhynian Poles created fortified bases where Polish (and Jewish) refugees found safety. The biggest base, Pshebrazhe near Kivertsi, held some 18,000 and fended off two assaults before the Red Army's return in 1944. Polish partisans, Soviet partisans, or combinations of the two started killing Ukrainians in their villages around the bases.[113]

Polish villagers also fled to the cities and approached the Germans there for help. Rather quickly, in March and April, the Germans supplied them with weapons, in exchange for information about the UPA. In practice this meant that the armed Poles became Schuma. These young men often wanted revenge and, with or without Germans, engaged in the "struggle against gangs"—burning and looting, murdering men, women, and children.[114] The German authorities also brought in reinforcements from the Reich: Wehrmacht units with Polish-speaking "ethnic Germans" who gained notoriety for their cruelty and eagerness to burn villages.[115] From August 1943, thousands of Polish Schuma deserted and created partisan units at the fortified bases, thus turning them into strongholds of the Polish Home Army. Many other Poles were arrested in that same month. Finally, there were Poles who enlisted for work in Germany, even though the Home Army and most Polish leaders insisted that they must remain.[116]

Besides their conviction that they were defending themselves, the Ukrainian attackers shared other characteristics that facilitated the escalation of their violence. Their nationalism made them view all Poles as an entity, *the Poles*, that as such could be guilty of something. Such an outlook meant that one could not oppose the option of revenge on innocent Polish individuals. Oleksander Povshuk was a nineteen-year-old member of the Melnyk faction of the OUN and a teacher in the village of Zbytyn near Dubno. On May 15, 1943, he wrote in his diary that all of the Polish villagers were either fleeing to the cities and joining the police, or were being deported to the Reich. "Now you don't see a single Pole living in the countryside. Our partisan movement chases and destroys them."

Povshuk disapproved, but gave purely practical reasons: "The life of the peaceful Polish population won't get you independence as long as the [German] enemy remains untouched, and can oppress two captive nations. Even if you want to destroy [the Poles], now is not the time."[117]

Unfortunately, killing can become almost routine. Moreover, any sustained behavior, including killing, has a tendency to produce a conviction among those engaging in it that it is the right thing to do. The very first perpetrators of the anti-Polish massacres were desensitized from the start. Anti-Polish violence had taken place in the region ever since the Soviet occupation in 1939,[118] and more importantly, the Schuma who joined the UPA by the thousands had assisted the Nazis in the Holocaust and in the "struggle against gangs." Their brutalized state of mind also helps to explain why partisans whom Jewish, Polish, and Soviet sources identity as Ukrainians or Ukrainian nationalists perpetrated deadly assaults on Jews and on non-Jews who helped Jews.[119]

All the same, awareness of the brutalization should not obscure the presence of great agitation. Hatred emanated from many. Well before the massacres started, some Ukrainian adults and children said things like, "You stinking Polacks, we're going to cut you up," or sang songs along these lines.[120] In one village, a Polish girl with a gunshot wound went into hiding. When after one week she went to a Ukrainian neighbor and asked for food, that woman screamed, "You Polish mug, you're still alive?!" and grabbed a hoe to kill her.[121]

Some perpetrators mainly acted because they feared for their own lives. A survivor from Ostrivky recalls that when the murder of the women and children started, "all of a sudden some of the Ukrainians rebelled and refused to murder any other Poles." The Ukrainian in charge repeated the death penalty statements and added that "those who would not execute it would be shot. The threat turned out to be effective." Another woman at the stubble field heard how a Ukrainian who had refused to participate was told, "Kill; I'll kill you if you won't."[122] Ukrainians with Polish wives were ordered to kill them, along with their children; disobedience carried the death penalty. A seventeen-year-old boy, born from a Polish-Ukrainian couple in the village of Doshne near Ratne, was forced to help kill Poles; only in this way could he prove his Ukrainianness and earn his right to life.[123] There were many who were tested in this way.

The ordeal of the Autonomous Orthodox church underlined for Ukrainians the seriousness of these death threats. Early in May 1943, Metropolitan Aleksii (Hromadsky) accidentally died in a UPA ambush on the car of the local district commissar. Radical nationalists found a way to excuse the killing: Aleksii deserved to die, they said, for he had been involved in Russification.[124] His successor as Volhynian metropolitan, Bishop Damaskyn (Maliuta), publicly declared in a sermon in Rivne in June that he knew who was responsible, and bravely demanded that Ukrainians distinguish between the Polish government and the Polish population at large. "Desist from the fratricide," he urged the people of Volhynia.[125] The UPA leadership responded with further aggression against the Autonomists: their parishes were intimidated to become Autocephalous, and in June and July many Autonomous priests were killed.[126] Moreover, one night in September, three armed men who identified themselves as "Ukrainian partisans" kidnapped Bishop Manuïl (Tarnavsky) in Volodymyr-Volynsky. The Banderites probably considered the former Greek Catholic and former Autocephalous bishop a twofold traitor, and perhaps even a Soviet agent such as Fotii (Tymoshchuk) of Podolia had been; they hanged him.[127]

Fortunately, in spite of all the danger there were ordinary Ukrainians who told Polish acquaintances to flee because the Poles were going to be killed soon, or who saved Poles during or immediately after the massacres.[128] A young Polish woman in the village of Doshne near Ratne fled to a Ukrainian family. Partisans came and mentioned her name. That's not her, the man of the house said: that is a crazy person. The partisans went away. Somewhat later, he said to her, "The butchers are gone." A Polish woman in the Kovel region fled from the massacre in her village to the nearby Ukrainian village of Arsenovych, where the Pototsky family gave her shelter. Several days later, she returned to Novy Hai with a Ukrainian and his cart, to salvage food and clothes. Near her home a group of young Ukrainians saw her, but her aide averted her murder by vowing that she was a good person who had helped many Ukrainians in the past.[129] Eleven days after the massacre of the population of the Polish village of Oleksandrivka near Lutsk, Ukrainian villagers combed through the area to bury the bodies. A Polish girl lay in the field, trembling with fear as she heard them approach. "At that moment, I heard above me the voice of Herasym, a Ukrainian with whom my parents had always gotten along. Walking slowly, he said, 'Don't move, maybe they won't see you. Then I'll come for you in the evening. Your brother is at my place.'" He did and he took both youngsters to safety in Kovel.[130]

Polish survivors often mention such Ukrainian saviors, but there probably were not many of them. As in the case of the Jewish Holocaust, all
knew well that any support of the victim group put their lives (and those
of their relatives) on the line. Although there are accounts of Ukrainian
saviors of Poles who were caught but got away with a vicious beating, it
was realistic for them to expect the death penalty. The May 1941 official
guidelines for Banderite activity prescribed "terror against foreign enemies and our own traitors."[131] A Ukrainian village elder told a Polish underground activist from nearby Malyn in January 1943 that soon a Ukrainian would offer to hide him and his family. Do not accept the offer, he
said, for it is a death trap. This warning cost him his life.[132]

Early in August 1943, near the end of the anti-Polish massacres, the SB
launched a massive purge of the UPA and the Ukrainian civilian population. Again, the paranoia that drove it had a basis in reality, if an unconfirmed Soviet report can be believed: it states that as of September 1943,
there were in the OUN twenty NKVD spies, "three of whom [were] in
the OUN leadership."[133] The SB shot hundreds of UPA members or
placed them in a concentration camp near the UPA headquarters near
Velyky Stydyn in the Kostopil raion. And the agency killed Ukrainian
peasants for the slightest transgression or over the smallest grudge.[134]
Most vulnerable were the "easterners": former POWs and deserted
Schuma from east of the pre-1939 border who had been forced to join the
UPA earlier in the year. For after a small number of these (in particular
members of the UPA's Georgian, Uzbek, and other "national" subunits)
had been uncovered as Soviet spies or had gone over to the Soviet partisans, the SB found all of the "easterners" suspect. Pretending to be Soviet
partisans, SB officers visited them during the night one by one and ordered them to come along. Their obedience served to the SB as conclusive proof of treason.[135]

From August 21 to 25, immediately after the massacres and purge, the
Banderites held a special congress. Although German military intelligence noted that here the OUN made a "slide toward democratic views,"
historians have justly remarked that concrete steps toward internal democracy and individual rights were taken later, in July 1944. Above all,
the August 1943 congress stood out because it proclaimed various social
policies, evidently due to the influence of young Soviet-educated Ukrainians who had joined the organization. Perhaps it was also because of
these young Ukrainians that the conference did not commit itself to full

privatization of land, even though Kliachkivsky had announced this measure just days before.[136] After the congress, Kliachkivsky decreed that all of Ukraine must become a "single war camp." This meant the forced mobilization of all males born in the years 1914 to 1917. Once again, refusal to comply carried the death penalty.[137] The population had to store up food and start military training. The all-Ukrainian vision also ushered in a new UPA raid (after a first one in June) into central Ukraine, by some three hundred men.[138]

For much of 1943, Ukrainian villagers generally supported the UPA, if only by reporting Soviet partisan activity, for the UPA prevented round-ups for deportation to Germany and discouraged attacks by Poles and Germans.[139] Yet by the end of 1943, most were desperate for relief from the group. The partisan force not only banned wood gathering and travel to towns and ordered people to serve as mail carriers, but it also increasingly robbed civilians, and beat or even killed those who disobeyed. It was an understatement when Soviet intelligence reported that "the vast majority of the village population" did not "esteem" the "Ukrainian nationalists."[140] Mykhailo Podvorniak, a Ukrainian and Evangelical Christian recalling in particular the SB, speaks of a government that was no less "terrorist" for being, unfortunately, Ukrainian. "The terrorized people waited in silence for some kind of liberation. They were waiting to be rescued, but nobody came. Now there was a Ukraine, supposedly their own insurgents' government—but it was not any better than that of the Bolsheviks or Germans."[141]

At the end of 1943, the wave of Polish-Ukrainian massacres moved to eastern Galicia, where Kovpak's raid had exposed the weakness of German rule.[142] The job of acting leader of the Banderites somehow went from Lebed to Roman Shukhevych, alias Taras Chuprynka, a Zakopane graduate with extensive experience as a Wehrmacht soldier in Ukraine and "gang-fighting" Schuma in Belarus. Shukhevych thought more like a soldier than a politician and after joining the UPA, he quickly overshadowed Kliachkivsky. His influence showed in October 1943, when the OUN issued a communiqué in Ukrainian that condemned the Ukrainian and Polish "mutual mass murders."[143] During the next month, the OUN sponsored a conference of peoples of eastern Europe and Asia. During the remainder of the year, the UPA continued evading the Wehrmacht and releasing those members it had captured, but it stepped up its assault on German administrators and on the SS and German police.[144]

In January 1944, a UPA command headed by Shukhevych was founded that in theory comprised all Ukrainian territories and redirected the brunt of its attacks on the incoming Red Army and Soviet regime. During its offensive, it ambushed and mortally wounded, among others, General Nikolai Vatutin, commander of the Red Army's First Ukrainian Front, on February 29, 1944.[145] It was the beginning of a new, if also bloody, era.

The history of the UPA resembles the Polish uprising in Warsaw of 1944 because in both cases, the balance between heroism and recklessness will likely always remain controversial. Already early in 1943, there were nationalists such as Ulas Samchuk who thought that the Ukrainian partisan movement was unleashed too soon and produced "only a great massacre of civilians, without any results for us."[146] One Ukrainian historian has argued that better leaders would not have fought the Germans at all and thus would have saved the UPA's forces for the fight against Stalin's regime, just as the nationalists in the Baltic states did.[147] Others may think they should have fought the Germans only. Because the UPA's fight against Nazi and Soviet totalitarianism seems to be evolving into a cornerstone of a modern Ukrainian national identity, it remains to be seen whether the critical notes will find any popular resonance.

The massacre of innocent civilians is the bleakest part of the story. Just as the Nazi instigators of the genocide of the Jews and Roma, the Banderites of 1943 were responsible for launching a murderous assault on innocent men, women, and children and for forcing civilian Ukrainians to participate. Western Volhynia's anti-Polish massacre was not particularly "Ukrainian" and resembled many twentieth-century cases of ethnic cleansing and genocide.[148] On the positive side (and again as in many other cases of mass violence) there were members of the perpetrator group who objected to the killings or even tried to save lives. As noted, Bishop Damaskyn urged for an end to the massacre and various Ukrainians took concrete steps to save Poles. "Bulba" Borovets, the dislodged founder of the UPA, told the Banderites in an open letter that there were "worse enemies" than the Poles, and he called on the Ukrainians to fight the Banderites.[149] Yet none of this ultimately made much of a difference.

One can only admire survivors such as Leon Żur, who has returned to visit and campaign for reconciliation. In August 2000, inhabitants of three villages in Volhynia's Rokytne region and former inhabitants of three obliterated Polish villages gathered near a mass grave of killed

Poles, and signed a call for Polish-Ukrainian cooperation. Future generations can find a copy of this plea in one of Żur's books.[150]

The German Retreat

Energized by his victory at Stalingrad, Stalin ordered an offensive in the south. Within weeks the Red Army advanced 250 kilometers, capturing Kharkiv on February 16. That night, resistance fighters in the city of Pavlohrad, some fifty kilometers east of Dnipropetrovsk, staged a successful uprising against the local Germans and Italians, just in time to welcome the Red Army. But the Wehrmacht had used its retreat to regroup and now launched a counteroffensive that recaptured not just Pavlohrad, but almost all of the southern territory that the Red Army had regained since December 1942.[151] This dramatic turn of events also had dire consequences for some residents of Dnipropetrovsk. Returning to the city some days after having fled from it, the German authorities ordered all civilians to hand in any weapons by Sunday morning, February 21. When the result did not satisfy them, these Germans randomly arrested dozens of men and women and hanged them in the streets. Other locals were rounded up for trench digging.[152]

Many natives of ethnic German nationality tried to get their Soviet passports back during these chaotic days.[153] But from August 1943, 150,000—almost all of them—left the Reichskommissariat by train or cart. The massive exoduses were supervised by Germans, but Koch's officials still derided the ethnic German refugees as "bent on plunder and other excesses."[154] The Mennonite and other ethnic German communities in the Ukrainian countryside, which had existed since the late eighteenth century, vanished.

The finale of the Reichskommissariat began in September 1943. On the sixth and seventh days of that month, Koch ordered the evacuation from the Left Bank of all the livestock, machinery, and able-bodied people, and the destruction of everything else, producing (as he put it) "scorched earth." All of this should happen within eight weeks. The plan failed, for the Red Army reached the Dnieper shore by the end of the month.[155] Yet the role of the SS in the German retreat was true to type. Agreeing that the land should be "completely burned and destroyed" (as he told Prützmann, the higher SS and police chief for Ukraine), Himmler expressed more extreme sentiments than did Koch, who still granted that people unable to work might stay behind. German with-

20. The effects of the Nazi scorched-earth policy. After the Death's Head division of the Waffen-SS set their homes ablaze, dazed peasants walk away with children and some possessions. North of Kremenchuk, in central Ukraine, August or September 1943. (Photograph by Adendorf. Bundesarchiv, Bild 146/2002/12/717.)

drawal, Himmler told Waffen-SS division commanders in Kharkiv in April 1943, had to include *Menschenvernichtung*—"the destruction of human beings."[156]

It does seem that at least some men, women, and children who were unable or unwilling to leave were shot or died in explosions. Five days before leaving the village of Obolon in the Semenivka raion, Germans shot 122 people listed as Soviet activists, and on the final day they shot with submachine guns anyone in sight, killing forty-four. In the nearby village of Velyki Lypniahy, another unit killed 371 people in four days, including 125 children.[157] From September 20, Germans in the main nearby city, Poltava, apparently started killing anyone in sight. Nevertheless, the Left Bank was far from empty. At the very end, the Wehrmacht reported the evacuation from there of 10 percent of its population, or some 600,000 people (guards at the Dnieper bridges, however, counted only 375,000).[158]

There is some evidence of German soldiers in the fall of 1943 who were humane in their treatment of locals—apparently people who left voluntarily—allowing them on trains and feeding them from field kitchens.[159] As for the Right Bank, however, Soviet reports mention burnings and killings in the weeks or days before the German retreat. For instance, in the Podolian village of Rivno, forty males ages sixteen to fifty-seven were locked inside the church on March 22, 1944. The next morning the Red Army approached the village, but still some Germans took the time to shoot and burn their prisoners, inside a mill. Eight lived to tell of their ordeal.[160] In another incident, about seventy civilians, including a six-year-old, were shot near the prison in Uman at the very last moment. Plunder and wanton destruction proliferated, as did rape by Wehrmacht members.[161]

On September 17, 1943, the German Army Group South ordered everyone to leave the large cities on the Dnieper. Such a directive implied the separation of families, for some remained behind digging trenches or working the land. In Kiev, announcements called for trust in the military command, which would hold the city.[162] Then the inhabitants of the city center were ordered to vacate their homes within three days: the area became a forbidden zone, surrounded by barbed wire. Trespassers shall be shot on sight, it was stated, but even then locals (just as Germans and Hungarians did) dared to loot there. Many of these native burglars believed that most Germans would not harm young children and therefore took them along for protection, recalls a Kievan who remained in hiding in the city center.[163] On September 25, there was an announcement on the radio that the city districts near the Dnieper—Pechersk, Lypky, Podil, and Stare Misto—also had to be vacated, by nine o'clock the next evening. (Later, two days were added to the deadline.) Thousands of Kievans moved their belongings by foot over long distances as fast as they could. The additions to the "military zone," which now comprised half of the city, were also looted.[164] On October 21, anybody remaining anywhere in Kiev had to report to the train station. It is said that a group of people from the Kurenivka district who were directed toward the station fled and were shot when they were discovered in the Podil district.[165]

The Security Police in Kiev busied itself with eliminating all traces of its crimes. For six weeks from the middle of August, hundreds of prisoners had to dig up corpses from Babi Yar and burn them. At the end, these laborers revolted. Of the only five rebels who survived, four have estimated that over 100,000, or even 125,000, bodies were incinerated at the Yar.[166] Yet even then the SS kept on killing. In fact, its gas van operated at top speed: initially only on Tuesdays and Saturdays, then also on

21. Women and a child give a warm and spontaneous welcome to the Red Army. Melitopol, southern Ukraine, October 1943. (Tsentral'nyi derzhavnyi kinofotofonoarkhiv Ukraïny im. H. S. Pshenychnoho, 0–174917.)

other days, the van arrived at the ravine five to nine times per day. The fifty or more people inside were gassed on the way or were killed on arrival. The age and ethnicity of this group of victims varied. Among them were one hundred naked young women from a brothel.[167] To increase the victim count of these frantic gas-van murders, there were apparently indiscriminate roundups in the city. Zakhar Trubakov, one of the Jewish prisoners who had to pull the corpses out of the van and incinerate them, determined from the clothes that these were countrypeople as well as elderly men, adult women, teenagers, and young children from Kiev.[168]

The Red Army crossed the Dnieper on September 22, 1943. On November 5, German specialists dynamited Kiev's factories and power stations and set fire to some buildings.[169] In the early hours of the next day, just in time for October Revolution Day, the Red Army took control of the city. Zaporizhzhia and Dnipropetrovsk followed on October 14 and 25. Red Army soldiers entered Zhytomyr on November 12, but the Wehrmacht pushed them out again and remained in control until the last day of the year. Thereafter the Red Army captured Bila Tserkva and Kirovohrad (January 4 and 8, 1944, respectively), Rivne and Lutsk

(February 2), and, after a great battle at Korsun, Kryvy Rih (February 22), Kherson (March 13), Vinnytsia (March 20), Proskuriv (March 25), and Mykolaïv (March 28). The Reichskommissariat's Belarusan districts of Pinsk, Brest, and Kobryn now were administratively added to the Reichskommissariat Ostland and remained under German rule for several months more. Everywhere the population received the soldiers warmly. Women cried and offered them as much as they could.[170] Reports are contradictory about the reception of the "Reds" in western Volhynia, but here too relief was widespread. Khrushchev rightly reported to Stalin in March that most locals welcomed the Red Army soldiers as *nashi*—"our people."[171]

CONCLUSION

The eviction of the Germans did not immediately end the mass violence in Ukraine; instead, the Soviet authorities, moving in, suppressed the Ukrainian Insurgent Army and other nationalist groups in a very violent campaign.[1] It also did not lead to a quick or complete justice for the victims of Nazi persecution. Ukraine's former Reichskommissar, Erich Koch, for example, assumed a new identity in Hamburg. Although he was recognized by a Wehrmacht veteran in 1949, he was not taken to Ukraine. The revived Polish state received Stalin's permission to put Koch on trial for crimes committed beyond Ukraine, in the Białystok region, and he never faced Soviet judges. Sentenced to death in 1958 (and deemed mortally ill by many observers), Ukraine's tormentor instead lived on, apparently due to a Polish law that forbade the execution of ill people.[2] He died in the prison of Barczewo on November 14, 1986, at age ninety. Most of the other prominent Nazis of the Reichskommissariat Ukraine who survived the war remained at large. General Commissar Frauenfeld of Taurida wrote memoirs that appeared after his death with the title *And I Have No Regrets.*[3]

In the Soviet Union, many trials took place against "traitors" and "servants of the occupants," with little or no publicity. Along the way, Red Army veterans, former partisans, and Soviet ideologists lost no time in developing their mythical interpretation of Ukraine under the "German fascist occupants." Like many historians of western European countries, they claimed that resistance had been massive. Official interpreters also, as during the war but in contrast to their Western peers, declared passivity under the Germans a virtual criminal offense.[4] The myth reflected an apparent view that the people in Nazi-ruled Ukraine had been traitors, as a former Soviet partisan recalls being told in Moscow as early as 1942.[5] In 1946, when Petro Vershyhora, a former partisan under Sydir Kovpak, defended those who had lived their lives under the Nazis against people who attacked them merely for that reason, official critics denounced him and censors modified subsequent editions of his book.[6] The survivors of the Nazi regime received little understanding. Well into the 1980s, they had to mention on job applications and other forms whether they had "been in occupied territory," and a positive response resulted in discrimination.[7] Only the collapse of the Soviet Union gave the survivors of the Holocaust and of forced labor the chance to accept a decades-old German offer of compensation; yet post-Soviet bureaucrats illegally appropriated part of the funds and kept applicants waiting for years.[8]

The historiographical debate of European societies under Nazi and Communist regimes has centered on three issues: the overall goals and policies of the authorities; the extent of social cohesion among communities and families living under the regime; and the mental outlook and response of individuals to these extreme conditions. With regard to the first issue, I have argued here that the Nazi regime in the "East" was driven by the Nazi conviction that Ukraine was, or should become, a clean slate for the German people. When Reich Minister Rosenberg told German audiences in Kiev in June 1942 that they must prepare the land for German colonization, he was expressing the fundamental ethos of the Reichskommissariat Ukraine. This extreme German nationalism combined with anti-Bolshevism, anti-Semitism, and a racist view of the "Russians," and the results were terror, murder, massacre, and genocide.

Key targets of the Nazis were Ukraine's Jews and Roma, almost all killed in genocide; the Soviet prisoners of war, killed as "Russians" in genocidal massacre; and the people of Kiev, subjected to deliberate starvation. Most Nazi killings were not, as some contemporary Ukrainian historians believe, indiscriminate; most took place after some consideration.[9] These premeditated killings are doubly disturbing because there is no evidence that any German in the Reichskommissariat Ukraine, or anywhere else in the "East," ever lost his life for refusing to carry them out.[10]

The Nazi regime also undertook violent deportations to the Reich, committed "anti-gang" massacres, and, in the final months, implemented a violent scorched-earth policy. In Kiev, murder by the middle of 1943 continued unabated and included gassings and executions, which apparently became random. Ultimately, the total body count at Babi Yar moved far beyond the 34,000 Jews of September 1941, to perhaps as many

22. A woman looks for her husband's body among exhumed corpses in the former Nazi concentration camp Syrets. Kiev, 1944. (Tsentral'nyi derzhavnyi kinofotofonoarkhiv Ukraïny im. H. S. Pshenychnoho, 0–4220.)

as 100,000 Jews and non-Jews. We may never know for sure how many people were killed in the Reichskommissariat by the Germans and their allies and auxiliaries, or how many died at the hands of the various partisans and underground activists—if only because the perpetrators often assumed each other's identities. There are Soviet calculations, but they are highly problematic.[11] Nevertheless, it seems realistic to estimate that the Nazi regime ended the lives of at least one million civilians and prisoners of war, either in the territory of the Reichskommissariat or, after deporting them, in the Reich.

The Nazis perfected the collective farms when they forced more peasants than ever to join and systematically enforced attendance and discipline. The economic and social gains of this system for the Reich were significant. The low living standard of the average peasant increased somewhat, mainly because peasants could expand their gardens and cultivate anything they wanted there. But this improvement lost most of its meaning because of the continued forced labor imposed on the peasants on the farms, and the pervasive violence of their overseers. Meanwhile, living standards in the cities declined dramatically because the Nazis attempted, as Koch put it in one of his talks with Hitler, to "smash Ukrainian industry and drive the proletariat back to the country." City dwellers who did not migrate to the countryside were usually unemployed. They were supposed to find work or else simply starve to death. Kiev held a special place in these plans.

Unlike their colleagues in the General Government, the authorities of the Reichskommissariat allowed for hardly any Ukrainian secular cultural life. They believed that schooling and cultural activities would create restlessness. The support of universities was out of the question. Koch and his subordinates also carried out a language policy that seemed to be pro-Ukrainian, but that really stemmed from a hatred of Russians. In contrast to the Soviet regime, the Nazis both in theory and in practice allowed the Orthodox churches to operate, and they felt generous for doing so. Yet they aborted the formation of a united Ukrainian Autocephalous Orthodox church and persecuted the Roman and Greek Catholic churches, leaving alone only a minority of faithful they deemed harmless—the Baptists and Evangelical Christians.

Everyday life in the Third Reich's largest colony stood out in Nazi-ruled Europe. For most people in the Reichskommissariat Ukraine, conditions were worse than in the General Government, and incomparably worse than in western Europe. But from an "Eastern" perspective, not everything was new. The title of "commissar" that the Nazis used was identical to the Soviet usage. Physical abuse of peasants and workers had also occurred in Soviet and tsarist times, although much less frequently.[12] The Soviet regime had also shot and starved innocent civilians, and the Nazi retreat in 1943 and 1944 in its violence resembled the Soviet retreat of 1941. Yet never before in the history of Ukraine did so many social and ethnic groups suffer so much during one period. Almost everyone experienced seemingly ceaseless humiliation, most notably abuse, and lived under a cloud of danger.

Moreover, the native population had no sense that things might improve. The Soviet system had also been oppressive and lethal, but it allowed for some dignity and some involvement. Before 1941 one could complain, within strict limits, to journalists, at public meetings, and during personal visits to the superiors of harassing officials. With some effort, ordinary Soviet citizens might find a person in a position of authority who took their problems seriously. The Nazis, however, frequently barred them from even entering their offices. Likewise, Soviet propaganda at least tried to convince people of something, and the average peasant or worker had grown accustomed to being taken into account, if only in words. The Soviet authorities deceived them, but while appealing to the self-esteem, independence, and trustworthiness of ordinary people.[13] Nazi propaganda in the Reichskommissariat, by contrast, consisted of little more than warnings against laziness and threats of death.

The Reichskommissariat Ukraine had certain features in common with Nazi concentration camps such as Dachau: the pervasive terror; the obligation to witness public beatings or executions; the happy music during sad occasions; and the frequency with which captors observed their subjects with disgust or pretended not to see them at all. It is not surprising that the natives themselves often described their situation as one of captivity *(plen)* or slavery *(rabstvo)*. "We are like slaves," wrote one woman in her diary. "Often the book *Uncle Tom's Cabin* comes to mind. Once we shed tears over those Negroes; now obviously we ourselves are experiencing the same thing."[14] But the Reichskommissariat was far worse than a slaveholding society. In the vast majority of past societies for which reliable data are available, slaves were treated with some consideration. Slaveholders and other nonslaves realized that in the treatment of slaves, incentives made more sense than punishment. Slaves were supposed to be used as servants—not to be disabled, let alone killed.[15] With the exception of the ethnic Germans, the native population of the Reichskommissariat Ukraine did not even belong.

The second major point of discussion among historians of societies under Nazi and Communist regimes is the degree of social cohesion among ordinary people. Among the native population of the Reichskommissariat, we have found city dwellers who helped needy and elderly people; medical doctors, native officials, and partisans who helped POWs and deportation candidates; and people who risked their lives for Jews or endangered Poles. Life was not merely an immoral survival of the fittest, and "atomization" was not total.[16] Nevertheless, in general the balance still tilted toward social disunity. "Psychic numbing," "desensitization," "amoral familism" (living only for oneself and one's immediate relatives), or, less charitably, "brutalization" and "egoism," terms that appear in various historical and psychological studies about other people at other times or places, all adequately describe the main trend of social life.[17]

In addition, many natives in positions of authority, in particular mayors, raion chiefs, and policemen, were not only closely involved in the implementation of the Nazi policies—many also abused the limited power they had and in this way worsened the population's predicament. Further, although the oppressed in other countries under Nazi rule engaged in acts of public solidarity such as boycotts, strikes, or the donning of a symbolic flower, the people of the Reichskommissariat did not. And while there may have been what historians call an underground society in the General Government, it did not exist in the Reichskommissariat Ukraine.

Some scholars argue that the core of National Socialism, the Nazi ideal, was the rejection of the foundation of "civil society"—solidarity with strangers. In this view, to resist National Socialism required recognizing one's bonds with "others."[18] According to this definition, the vast majority of the native population did not resist Nazi rule. This was particularly evident with regard to the Jewish Holocaust. Significant numbers of bystanders were pleased to see the Jews being taken away. And when the non-Jews found out what was really happening to the Jews, although almost all were horrified and against the murders, the vast majority of them, fearing for their own lives, continued to merely watch the genocide unfold. The Communist party underground and the Organization of Ukrainian Nationalists, the two political groups that claimed to represent the population, never opposed specifically the mass murder of the Jews, not even in words. (In western Volhynia, as we learned, nationalists actually launched a deadly assault on another ethnic group, the Poles.) As for Orthodox church leaders, many talked about "Jewish Bolshevism" and the crimes of "Jewry" or "the Jews," and thus demoralized those who might have contemplated coming to the victims' aid.

Among non-Jews, resistance in the usual sense of the word only emerged in connection with the forced deportations of non-Jews to Germany. But more often than not, this fight against the deportations involved small groups acting in isolation. The partisan movements that did emerge— Ukrainian nationalist, Polish nationalist, or Communist, but invariably authoritarian and ruthless—generally could not prevent the forced deportations. And as in western Europe, this resistance only marginally supported the military struggle of Nazi Germany's opponents.[19]

It would be incorrect to explain the social disunity and lack of resistance in Nazi-ruled Ukraine only by the Nazi regime's severity or by human nature in general. The legacy of the Soviet period was equally important. Resisting the Nazi system was dangerous for oneself and one's family, but long before the German arrival there had not been any "civil society." Many Soviet citizens had internalized the Communist virtue of mistrust and what a postwar dissident would call "the outrageous small-mindedness of everyday Soviet life."[20] The Soviet system had made them self-centered, distrustful, and apathetic, so that they inhabited the "solitude of collectivism" that many observers have cited as typical for socialist societies.[21] On top of this ethos, a thirst for revenge had developed among those in Ukraine who had earlier been persecuted by the Soviet regime. In this way, the mortal dangers of Nazi rule, the conduct of many natives in positions of administrative or moral authority, human nature in general, and the legacy of socialism all combined to inhibit solidarity.

This brings us to the third historiographical issue of identities and mental outlooks. The people of Soviet Ukraine may have shared the terrible legacy of the Great Famine of 1933, a total lack of accurate knowledge about what they called Europe, and an attitude toward the Germans that started with cautious optimism and turned into hate. But the native population generally lacked a strong social or ethnic identity. Dnieper Ukrainians spoke of "our people," a vague notion that included themselves and the Russians but generally excluded Galician Ukrainians. And the Slavic majority and the Jews tended to consider each other as foreigners or even enemies. Although few of the Slavs approved of the Jews' murder, anti-Semitic grumbling was widespread. To most, the Jews were and remained "others," anything but "ours."

Regardless of how indignant the population was about the way the German authorities and their allies and auxiliaries treated the Jews, the Roma, and the POWs, the majority for a long time did not reject the regime as such. Most natives concluded that the Germans should go in early 1942, the moment they learned of the living conditions of those who had gone to work in Germany, or somewhat later, when the authorities started rounding up deportation candidates en masse. Ever more people also began to complain about the most evident (and yet easily overlooked) foreign aspect of the new regime—its language. People said, "The Bolsheviks we could at least understand."[22] Indeed, if asked in confidence, most probably would have said that they preferred to be oppressed in a familiar language, which meant Ukrainian or Russian.

In the political thinking of the vast majority, one finds no prefer-ence for either nationalism or Communism. Instead, the population held what social psychologists call "nonattitudes." Borrowing a term from the historiography of Nazi Germany, one can also speak of a widespread *Resistenz,* or immunity, to distinct ideologies. The exceptions occurred among young people, those born during the 1920s and 1930s, who tended to believe in the Soviet system—or if they were young ethnic Germans, even supposedly pacifist Mennonites, leaned toward being strong adherents of Naziism. But even the "Soviet" generation, like their older compatriots, perceived alternatives to the prewar system: a "Ukrainian authority" under German supervision; a Romanian administration; an indistinct "Soviet rule without the Bolsheviks"; or even a tsar. Although the widespread, nonnationalist notion of "our people" implied solidarity between Ukrainians and Russians, it was even more than a Soviet phenomenon a continuation of Ukraine's traditional "Little Russianism," the belief that a Ukrainian identity was fully compatible with a broader Russian identity. Indeed, the main "Soviet" trait that existed in the Reichskommissariat was not a belief but a behavioral tendency—to denounce one another to the authorities (and even here there were pre-Revolutionary antecedents).[23]

Until now, it seemed reasonable to assume that the Nazi period had a significant effect on the thinking of those who survived the Reichskommissariat Ukraine. Some historians have written that the war unified the citizens of the Soviet Union around Stalin, whom they came to see as their one and only savior.[24] Others have argued that the war "reshaped" the national consciousness of the Russians; still others, that the experience of Nazi rule made Dnieper Ukrainians more eager to create their own state.[25]

Perhaps the entire period 1941–1945 or even 1939–1945 did indeed broaden the political outlook of most Soviet citizens. The historian Amir Weiner has made a convincing case that the influence of the Red Army veterans consolidated a consciousness that was both Ukrainian and Soviet.[26] But that was after the Red Army had come back to Ukraine. The research in this study does not support the notion of important changes in mental attitudes among Ukrainians and other natives under the Nazis.

In these turbulent years, prewar mental attitudes exerted a tremendous hold. Those who fell under Nazi rule hoped for a better life, became disappointed, and then started to hate the Germans and wanted them out.

They also became used to living without Jews and Roma. Apart from these changes, however, their mental and political orientation remained profoundly stagnant. It is likely that this mental stasis served as one more factor in limiting the scale of resistance and solidarity. But it is certain that in the final analysis the Nazi regime, even as it killed and looted, had little effect on the outlook of those who survived.

APPENDIX

ABBREVIATIONS

NOTES

SOURCES

ACKNOWLEDGMENTS

INDEX

APPENDIX: TABLES

TABLE 1: OFFICIAL POPULATION FIGURES FOR THE CITY OF KIEV, 1941–1943

DATE	POPULATION
January 1, 1940[1]	846,724
January 1, 1941[2]	890,000
July 1, 1941[3]	846,300
October 1, 1941[4]	400,000 (estimate)
April 1, 1942[5]	352,139
July 1, 1942[6]	315,099 or 293,000
October 1, 1942[7]	305,366
January 1, 1943[8]	304,599 or 304,570
July 1, 1943[9]	295,639
December 1, 1943[10]	220,000 (estimate)

Note: The first three figures and the final figure are Soviet; the others are German or German-sponsored. The German figures omit most Reich Germans and ethnic Germans. In January 1942, Kiev was home to 20,000 foreign military, presumably mostly Germans. (TsDAVOV, 3206/1/78/6: Acting General Commissar Quitzrau to Koch, Kiev, January 21, 1942) In October 1942, there were 27,000 Germans, including 6,000 who were listed as ethnic Germans. (TsDAVOV, 3206/2/121/5: Hauptabteilung Ernährung und Landwirtschaft to the *Bezirksleitung* of the NSDAP, Kiev, October 17, 1942)

1. TsDAVOV, 4620/3/2a/3: Gosplan, "Pasport goroda (ekonomiko-statisticheskii spravochnik)" for Kiev. See also *Ereignismeldung UdSSR* 106 (October 7, 1941): 13.
2. Sektor informatsii Upravleniia delami Sovnarkoma USSR, *Osnovnye pokazateli narodnogo khoziaistva USSR: (Kratkii statistiko-ekonomicheskii spravochnik)* (Kiev, 1945), 139, filed at TsDAHOU, 1/23/3962.
3. TsDAHOU, 1/23/3967/5: "U.S.S.R." (booklet with typed information). Compare L. Maliuzhenko, "Kyïv za 1942 r.," *Nashe mynule*, no. 1(6) (Kiev, 1993): 157.
4. Peter Longerich, ed., *Die Ermordung der europäischen Juden: Eine umfassende Dokumentation des Holocaust 1941–1945* (Munich, 1989), 122; Paul Werner, *Ein Schweizer Journalist sieht Rußland: Auf den Spuren der deutschen Armee zwischen San und Dnjepr* (Olten, Switz., 1942), 77.
5. Maliuzhenko, "Kyïv za 1942 r.," 157, 161–162 (includes 2,797 "Germans").
6. The first figure: ibid., 161–162. The second: TsDAVOV, 3676/4/475/289: Sipo-SD report on the Kiev GB in June 1942; *Meldungen* 21 (September 18, 1942): 20.
7. Maliuzhenko, "Kyïv za 1942 r.," 161–162.
8. The first figure: ibid., 161–162. The second: TsDAVOV, 3206/2/231/46v: "Uebersicht über die Verwaltungseinteilung des Reichskommissariats Ukraine nach dem Stand vom 1. Januar 1943."
9. Leontii Forostivs'kyi, *Kyïv pid vorozhymy okupatsiiamy* (Buenos Aires, 1952), 52.
10. TsDAHOU, 1/23/555/11: Statystychne Upravlinnia URSR, "Korotka ekonomychna [*sic*] kharakterystyka vyzvolenykh oblastei URSR," n.p., 1943.

TABLE 2 OFFICIAL POPULATION FIGURES FOR SELECTED CITIES AND TOWNS
IN THE REICHSKOMMISSARIAT UKRAINE

	JANUARY 1, 1943 (German figures)	JULY 1, 1941 (Soviet figures)
Dnipropetrovsk	280,000	500,600
Kryvy Rih	125,000	(unavailable)
Zaporizhzhia	120,000	289,200
Mykolaïv	84,213	167,100
Kamianske[1]	75,000	(unavailable)
Poltava	74,821	(130,300)
Melitopol	65,054	(unavailable)
Kirovohrad	63,403	100,300
Kherson	59,210	(unavailable)
Vinnytsia	42,500	92,800
Zhytomyr	42,000	95,100
Brest-Litovsk	33,563	(unavailable)
Rivne	17,531	41,900
Lutsk	16,495	35,600
Kovel	16,233	(unavailable)
Kamianets-Podilsky	15,044	19,500
Proskuriv[2]	12,510	(unavailable)
Pinsk	12,029	(unavailable)
Zviahel/Novohrad-Volynsky[3]	12,000	(unavailable)
Pervomaisk	9,154	(unavailable)
Volodymyr-Volynsky	8,628	(unavailable)
Zdolbuniv	7,650	(unavailable)

1. The Soviet name of the city was Dniprodzerzhynsk.

2. Now Khmelnytsky.

3. In calling the place Zviahel, the Germans gave back to Novohrad-Volynsky the name it used to have before 1796.

Sources: For the German figures, TsDAVOV, 3206/2/231/45–50v: "Uebersicht über die Verwaltungseinteilung." Compare John A. Armstrong, *Ukrainian Nationalism*, 3d ed. (Englewood, Colo., 1990), 243–244. For the Soviet figures, TsDAHOU, 1/23/3967/5: "U.S.S.R." (booklet with typed information).

ABBREVIATIONS

BA-Berlin   Federal Archives of Germany, Berlin branch

BA-MA   Military Archives, Koblenz, Germany

DAKO   State Archives of the Kiev Oblast, Ukraine

HIA   Archives of the Hoover Institution on War, Revolution and Peace, Stanford University, Stanford, California

HIA-HURIP   Collection of transcripts of the Harvard University Refugee Interview Project, at the Hoover Institution Archives

IMFE   M. T. Rylsky Institute of Art Science, Folklore, and Ethnography, National Academy of Sciences of Ukraine, Kiev

Meldungen   *Meldungen aus den besetzten Ostgebieten*

NA   National Archives of the United States, Washington, D.C.

NBU   V. I. Vernadsky National Library of Ukraine, Kiev

NDB   Scholarly Reference Library of the Central State Archives of Ukraine

RGASPI   Russian State Archives of Sociopolitical History, Moscow

TsDAHOU   Central State Archives of Civic Organizations of Ukraine, Kiev

TsDAVOV   Central State Archives of the Higher Agencies of Power and Administration of Ukraine, Kiev

UCEC   Ukrainian Cultural and Educational Centre, Winnipeg, Manitoba

NOTES

Introduction

1. Ralf Bartoleit, "Die deutsche Agrarpolitik in den besetzten Gebieten der Ukraine vom Sommer 1941 bis zum Sommer 1942 unter besonderer Berücksichtigung der Einführung der 'Neuen Agrarordnung': Eine Studie über die strukturelle Durchsetzung nationalsozialistischer Programmatik," master's thesis, University of Hamburg, 1987, 24.
2. See, for example, TsDAVOV, 3676/1/232/9–10: Erich Koch to the general commissar in Dnipropetrovs'k, Rivne, November 17, 1942.
3. Tomasz Szarota, *Życie codzienne w stolicach okupowanej Europy: Szkice historyczne, Kronika wydarzeń* (Warsaw, 1995), 143 (the quotation, of the historian Henri Amouroux about Parisians in 1940). See also Jan T. Gross, "Themes for a Social History of War Experience and Collaboraton," in István Deák, Jan T. Gross, and Tony Judt, eds., *The Politics of Retribution in Europe: World War II and Its Aftermath* (Princeton, N.J., 2000), 15–35.
4. Roy F. Baumeister, *Evil: Inside Human Cruelty and Violence* (New York, 1999), 353.

1. Soviet Ukraine and the German Invasion

1. The main source for the following account of pre-1941 Ukraine is Paul Robert Magocsi, *A History of Ukraine* (Toronto, 1996), part 9.
2. See Terry Martin, *The Affirmative Action Empire: Nations and Nationalism in the Soviet Union, 1923–1939* (Ithaca, N.Y., 2001), 75–124.
3. James von Geldern and Richard Stites, eds., *Mass Culture in Soviet Russia: Tales, Poems, Songs, Movies, Plays, and Folklore, 1917–1953* (Bloomington, Ill., 1995), 317; Antonina Khelemendyk-Kokot, *Kolhospne dytynstvo i nimets'ka nevolia: Spohady* (Toronto, 1989), 122; Sheila Fitzpatrick, *Everyday Stalinism: Ordinary Life in Extraordinary Times: Soviet Russia in the 1930s* (New York, 1999), 71, 183.
4. *Osnovnye pokazateli narodnogo khoziaistva USSR: (Kratkii statistiko-ekonomicheskii spravochnik)* (Kiev, 1945), 5, a classified booklet now at TsDAHOU, 1/23/3962, mentions 40,965,600 for January 1, 1941.

5. V. P. Kravchenko, author interview.

6. F. Pihido-Pravoberezhnyi, *"Velyka Vitchyzniana viina"* (Winnipeg, 1954), 27–28; H. H. Salata, author interview; M. P. Kostiuk, author interview; HIA, B. I. Nicolaevsky collection, series no. 236, box 409, folder 19, fol. 1: Emigrant, "Nemtsy v Kieve: (Iz vospominanii ochevidtsa)," n.p., n.d.

7. On the vow, see Emigrant, "Nemtsy v Kieve," 4–5; for the draft and other requirements, see Mordechai Altshuler, "Escape and Evacuation of Soviet Jews at the Time of the Nazi Invasion," in Lucjan Dobroszycki and Jeffrey Gurock, eds., *The Holocaust in the Soviet Union: Studies and Sources on the Destruction of the Jews in the Nazi-Occupied Territories of the USSR, 1941–1945* (Armond, N.Y., 1993), 92; K. T. Turkalo, *Tortury: (Avtobiohrafiia za bol'shevyts'kykh chasiv)* (New York, 1963), 182.

8. Alexander Dallin, *German Rule in Russia, 1941–1945: A Study of Occupation Policies,* 2d ed. (Boulder, Colo., 1981), 69, n.1; G. F. Krivosheev, ed., *Grif sekretnosti sniat: Poteri vooruzhennykh sil SSSR v voinakh, boevykh deistviiakh i voennykh konfliktakh: Statisticheskoe issledovanie* (Moscow, 1993), 196.

9. TsDAHOU, 1/22/10/77: S. Oleksenko, obkom secretary, "Doklad o Kamenets-Podol'skikh partizanakh," n.p., (1943); Pihido-Pravoberezhnyi, *"Velyka Vitchyzniana viina,"* 74–75.

10. Pihido-Pravoberezhnyi, *"Velyka Vitchyzniana viina,"* 33; Nicholas Prychodko, *One of the Fifteen Million* (Toronto, 1952), 153.

11. Pihido-Pravoberezhnyi, *"Velyka Vitchyzniana viina,"* 84, 83, 85; see also Larissa Kotyeva, *Three Worlds of Larissa: A Story of Survival* (Brunswick, Me., 1993), 106.

12. IMFE, T. Krasyts'ka collection, 14–3/20/173 (song); Prychodko, *One of the Fifteen Million,* 141.

13. Vladyslav Hrynevych, "Vidlunnia holodomoru 1932–1933 rr. ta antykolhospni nastroï v Chervonii Armiï naperedodni ta pid chas 'vyzvol'nykh pokhodiv' 1939–1940 rr.," in S. Kul'chyts'kyi et al., eds., *Holod-henotsyd 1933 roku v Ukraïni: Istoryko-politolohichnyi analiz sotsial'no-demohrafichnykh ta moral'no-psykholohichnykh naslidkiv. Mizhnarodna naukovo-teoretychna konferentsiia, Kyïv, 28 lystopada 1998 r.: Materialy* (Kiev, 2000), 421–432. See also Mark von Hagen, "Soviet Soldiers and Officers on the Eve of the German invasion: Towards a Description of Social Psychology and Political Attitudes," *Soviet Union/Union Soviétique* 18, nos. 1–3 (1991): 79–101; Roger R. Reese, *Stalin's Reluctant Soldiers: A Social History of the Red Army, 1925–1941* (Lawrence, Kans., 1996). On the schoolchildren, see HIA, B. I. Nicolaevsky collection, series no. 178, box 232, folder 10, fol. 61: [Lev Vladimirovich] Dudin, "Velikii Mirazh: Sobytiia 1941–1947 godov v ponimanii sovetskogo cheloveka," n.p., 1947.

14. Arkadii Liubchenko, *Shchodennyk: Knyzhka persha* (Toronto, 1951), 150, editorial note.

15. On citizen-organized vigilante groups, see D. Karov [Dmitrii Petrovich Kandaurov], "Organy samoupravleniia v okkupirovanykh oblastiakh SSSR v gody vtoroi mirovoi voiny," *Vestnik Instituta po izuchenii istorii i kul'tury SSSR*, no. 5(12) (1954): 73; Tatiana Fesenko, *Povest' krivykh let* (New York, 1963), 68. On NKVD extermination battalions *(istrebitel'nye batal'ony)*, see V. V. Cherepanov, ed., "Shli na front dobrovol'no: O narodnom opolchenii iazykom dokumentov," *Voenno-istoricheskii zhurnal*, no. 1 (1996): 9–10; "Organizuetsia narodnoe opolchenie: Telegramma iz Kieva. 5 iiulia," *Izvestiia TsK KPSS*, no. 7 (July 1990): 198. For the response of volunteers, see NA microcopy T-501, roll 349, frame 587: Gruppe Geheime Feldpolizei 725, report about Soviet partisans in Ukraine, n.p., January 22, 1942.

16. "Organizuetsia narodnoe opolchenie," 198; Kostiuk, author interview; K. Ia. Hrynevych, author interview,. See also Fesenko, *Povest'*, 69.

17. Petro Kulakovs'kyi, comp., "Rozstriliani na pochatku viiny," *Z arkhiviv VUChK-HPU-NKVD-KHB* 1 (Kiev, 1994): 192; Krzysztof Popiński, Aleksandr Kokurin, and Aleksandr Gurjanow, *Drogi śmierci: Ewakuacja więzień sowieckich z Kresów Wschodnich II Rzeczypospolitej w czerwcu i lipcu 1941* (Warsaw, 1995), 144–145.

18. T. Prysiazhnyi, "Masovi vbyvstva v Luts'ku," *Litopys Volyni* 1 (Winnipeg, 1953): 65–70; *Zlochyny komunistychnoï Moskvy v Ukraïni vliti 1941 roku* (New York, 1960), 43–45. See also Panas Khurtovyna [Mykhailo Podvorniak], *Pid nebom Volyni: (Voienni spomyny khrystyianyna)* (Winnipeg, 1952), 83–85, 90–92; *Russian Oppression in Ukraine: Reports and Documents* (London, 1962), 190. For an account based on other sources, see Bogdan Musial, *"Konterrevolutionäre Elemente sind zu erschießen": Die Brutalisierung des deutsch-sowjetischen Krieges im Sommer 1941* (Berlin, 2000), 115–118.

19. Alfred M. De Zayas, *The Wehrmacht War Crimes Bureau, 1939–1945* (Lincoln, Neb., 1989), 211; Ernst Klee and Willi Dreßen, *"Gott mit uns": Der deutsche Vernichtungskrieg im Osten 1939–1945* (Frankfurt, 1989), 242–243, n. 13; Shmuel Spector, *The Holocaust of Volhynian Jews, 1941–1944* (Jerusalem, 1990), 75; Prysiazhnyi, "Masovi vbyvstva," 69; Leonid D—s'kyi, "Pokhoron u Luts'ku," *Litopys Volyni* 1 (1953): 72.

20. NA microcopy T-175, roll 233, frames 2721604–611: "Bericht über das sowjetrussische Staatsgefängnis Dubno und über das Blutbad vom 24. und 25. 6. 1941," a report appended to *Ereignismeldung UdSSR* 28 (July 20, 1941); Valia Petrenko, "Trahediia Dubens'koï Tiurmy (Spomyn)," *Samostiina Ukraïna* 1, nos. 5–6 (Chicago, June–July 1948): 16–19; Oleksii Satsiuk, *Smertonostsi: Opovidannia (na tli perezhytoho)* (Buenos Aires, 1947); Musial, *"Konterrevolutionäre Elemente,"* 121–122 (on children); BA-MA, RH 24–48/198: Aussenkommando GFP at Army Corps 48, "Betr.: Erschiessung von NKWD-Kommissaren und Funktionären [. . .]," n.p., July 1, 1941.

21. "Bericht über das sowjetrussische Staatsgefängnis Dubno"; De Zayas, *Wehrmacht War Crimes Bureau*, 211; Klee and Dreßen, "*Gott mit uns*," 242–243, n. 13. See also *Zlochyny komunistychnoï Moskvy*, 30–32.

22. Hryhorii Stetsiuk, *Nepostavlenyi pam"iatnyk: (Spohady)* ([Winnipeg], 1988), 34–35; T. Iakovkevych, "1939–1943 na Volodymyrshchyni (Spohady)," *Litopys Volyni* 3 (Winnipeg, 1956): 114–115.

23. De Zayas, *Wehrmacht War Crimes Bureau*, 211; *Ereignismeldung UdSSR* 28 (July 20, 1941): 7–8. Compare *Zlochyny komunistychnoï Moskvy*, 42.

24. M. Demydenko, author interview.

25. For Kirovohrad jail atrocities, see Pavel Negretov, *Vse dorogi vedut na Vorkutu* (Benson, Vt., 1985), 48; O. Horodys'kyi, "Iurii Klen—voiakom (Prodovzhennia)," *Kyïv* 4, no. 3 (Philadelphia, May–June 1953): 150. Compare Kulakovs'kyi, "Rozstriliani na pochatku viiny," 191. On the shooting of those marching from Chortkiv, see *Russian Oppression in Ukraine*, 188–189; Jan T. Gross, *Revolution from Abroad: The Soviet Conquest of Poland's Western Ukraine and Western Belorussia* (Princeton, N.J., 1988), 297–298; *Zlochyny komunistychnoï Moskvy*, 83–86. Compare Pihido-Pravoberezhnyi, "*Velyka Vitchyzniana viina*," 117; Dudin, "Velikii Mirazh," 84–85. On killings in Berdychiv and Vinnytsia, see *Russian Oppression in Ukraine*, 188–189, 196; *Zlochyny komunistychnoï Moskvy*, 23–26. For deaths in Poltava's prison, consult Dmytro Chub, *V lisakh pid Viaz'moiu: Spohady pro Druhu svitovu viinu*, exp. 2d ed. (Melbourne, 1983), 118. On killings in Proskuriv, see *Ereignismeldung UdSSR* 38 (July 30, 1941): 10; BA-MA, RW 2/149, fols. 286–287: Bericht des Wehrmachtbefehlshabers Ukraine, "Auffindung der Leichen von Wehrmacht-angehörigen," n.p., October 11, 1941.

26. Prychodko, *One of the Fifteen Million*, 142–169.

27. Fesenko, *Povest'*, 65–67; Pihido-Pravoberezhnyi, "*Velyka Vitchyzniana viina*," 49; Mykola Velychkivs'kyi, "Sumni chasy nimets'koï okupatsiï (1941–1944 roky)," *Vyzvol'nyi shliakh* 12, no. 1 (London, 1965): 43.

28. Oleksander Skotsen', *Z futbolom u svit: Spomyny* (Toronto, 1985), 279 (on shots); Velychkivs'kyi, "Sumni chasy," *Vyzvol'nyi shliakh* 12, no. 2 (1965): 152; Pihido-Pravoberezhnyi, "*Velyka Vitchyzniana viina*," 112; Oleg Chekh, "Pravda o razrushenii Kieva," *Novoe russkoe slovo* (New York), January 30, 1948, 2; Dmytro Malakov, *Oti dva roky . . .: U Kyievi pry nimtsiakh* (Kiev, 2002), 80, 82; Kulakovs'kyi, "Rozstriliani na pochatku viiny," 191 (the archivist).

29. Benjamin Pinkus and Ingeborg Fleischhauer, *Die Deutschen in der Sowjet-union: Geschichte einer nationalen Minderheit im 20. Jahrhundert* (Baden-Baden, 1987), 233.

30. O. L. Milova, comp., *Deportatsii narodov SSSR (1930-e–1950-e gody)*, vol. 2: *Deportatsiia nemtsev (sentiabr' 1941–fevral' 1942 gg.)* (Moscow, 1995), 22–23.

31. RGASPI, 17/3/1042/6: reference to Politburo resolution 21 of August 31, 1941, "O

nemtsakh, prozhivaiushchikh na territorii Ukrainskoi SSR." The resolution it-self is in an unspecified "special file" that in 2002 was still unavailable to out-side researchers.

32. V. P. Iampols'kii et al., comps., *Organy gosudarstvennoi bezopasnosti SSSR v Velikoi Otechestvennoi voine: Sbornik dokumentov*, vol. 2-2: *Nachalo: 1 sentiabria–31 dekabria 1941 goda* (Moscow, 2000), 127–128; Milova, *Deportatsii narodov SSSR*, 54.

33. Susanna Toews, *Trek to Freedom: The Escape of Two Sisters from South Russia during World War II* (Winkler, Manitoba, 1976), 17.

34. Ibid., 17–18, 20; Milova, *Deportatsii narodov SSSR*, 86 (on NKVD and militia).

35. "Iz istorii Velikoi Otechestvennoi voiny," *Izvestiia TsK KPSS*, no. 6 (June 1990): 208. Original emphasis.

36. Ibid., 217–220.

37. G. A. Kumanev, "Sovetskaia ekonomika i evakuatsiia 1941 goda," *Soviet Union/ Union Soviétique* 18 (1991): 166, without a full source reference.

38. K. S. Grushevoi, *Togda, v sorok pervom . . .* (Moscow, 1972), 31 (the quotation); William Moskoff, *The Bread of Affliction: The Food Supply in the USSR during World War II* (Cambridge, Eng., 1990), 28.

39. "Iz istorii Velikoi Otechestvennoi voiny," *Izvestiia TsK KPSS*, no. 7 (July 1990): 206–207.

40. Khurtovyna, *Pid nebom Volyni*, 87, 93.

41. For the German report, consult Klaus Segbers, *Die Sowjetunion im Zweiten Weltkrieg: Die Mobilisierung von Verwaltung, Wirtschaft und Gesellschaft im "Großen Vaterländischen Krieg" 1941–1943* (Munich, 1987), 111. See also RGASPI, 17/125/58/207: E. Vilenskii, special correspondent of *Izvestiia*, to Shcherbakov, n.p., September 8, 1941. On peasants' keeping parts, see O. M. Kutsenko, author interview. On round-the-clock harvesting, see "Komunisty Ukraïny v 1941 r.," *Ukraïns'kyi istorychnyi zhurnal*, no. 5 (1990): 101–103.

42. *Ereignismeldung UdSSR* 85 (September 16, 1941): 11; Pihido-Pravoberezhnyi, "Velyka Vitchyzniana viina," 46–47; DAKO, r-2209/1/2/28–29: list of people, n.d.

43. *Ereignismeldung UdSSR* 47 (August 9, 1941): 16–17.

44. Pihido-Pravoberezhnyi, "Velyka Vitchyzniana viina," 45.

45. Ibid., 40–44. See also Mykola S.-Chartoryis'kyi, *Vid Sianu po Krym: (Spomyny uchasnyka III Pokhidnoï Grupy-Pivden')* (New York, 1951), 182–183.

46. Pihido-Pravoberezhnyi, "Velyka Vitchyzniana viina," 117–118.

47. One example of veterans' reassurances is in Marliese Fuhrmann, *Schneebruch: Geschichte einer Verschleppung* (Landau, Ger., 1993), 48. For the peasants' wel-come, see Ulas Samchuk, *Na bilomu koni: Spomyny i vrazhennia* (Winnipeg, 1972), 146; Fritz Baade et al., comps., *Unsere Ehre heisst Treue: Kriegstagebuch des Kommandostabes Reichsführer SS. Tätigkeitsberichte der 1. und 2. SS-Inf.-*

Brigade und von Sonderkommandos der SS (Vienna, 1965), 217; Theodor Oberländer, *Der Osten und die Deutsche Wehrmacht: Sechs Denkschriften aus den Jahren 1941–43 gegen die NS-Kolonialthese* (Asendorf, Ger., 1987), 52; Walter Lahme, *Die Weisung zum Frieden* (Percha am Starnberger See, Ger., 1982), 23.

48. Khurtovyna, *Pid nebom Volyni*, 97; Ivan Vlasovs'kyi, *Narys istoriï Ukraïns'koï Pravoslavnoï Tserkvy*, vol. 9: *(XX st.)*, part 2 (New York, 1966), 201; Volodymyr Serhiichuk, [comp.], *OUN-UPA v roky viiny: Novi dokumenty i materialy* (Kiev, 1996), 262–264.

49. Julia Alexandrow with Tommy French, *Flight from Novaa Salow: Autobiography of a Ukrainian Who Escaped Starvation in the 1930s under the Russians and Then Suffered Nazi Enslavement* (Jefferson, N.C., 1995), 56. See also Josef Winkler, *Die Verschleppung: Njetoschka Iljaschenko erzählt über ihre russische Kindheit* (Frankfurt am Main, 1984), 196, 204, 211.

50. M. O. Vasylenko, author interview. See also, on the village of Onufriïvka in the Kirovohrad oblast, RGASPI, 17/125/52/37: NKVD report on Ukraine by Fitin, "O polozhenii v raionakh, okkupirovannykh protivnikom po sostoianiiu na 26.VIII-1941g.," September 3, 1941.

51. TsDAHOU, 1/23/119/6–7: NKVD of Ukraine, "Kiev. Kopiia."

52. Serhiichuk, *OUN-UPA*, 254; Werner Haupt, *Die Schlachte der Heeresgruppe Süd: Aus der Sicht der Divisionen* (Friedberg, 1985), 39. See also Walther Bienert, *Russen und Deutsche: Was für Menschen sind das? Berichte, Bilder und Folgerungen aus dem Zweiten Weltkrieg* (Stein am Rhein, Switz., 1990), 23; Pihido-Pravoberezhnyi, "*Velyka Vitchyzniana viina*," 152–153.

53. On parents' caution, see Winkler, *Die Verschleppung*, 204; Johannes Steinhoff et al., eds., *Voices from the Third Reich: An Oral History* (Washington, 1989), 136. For the general sentiment, see Kutsenko, author interview.

54. TsDAHOU, 166/3/255/38–39: essay by a third-grade student in Bilytsia, Iampil' raion, Sumy oblast; TsDAHOU, 166/3/259/9v: diary of F. K. Kusnir; Bienert, *Russen und Deutsche*, 63, 68.

55. Mykhailo Lebid', "Chasy nimets'koï okupatsiï v Matiïvs'komu raioni na Volyni (Spohady kol. holovy raionovoï upravy)," *Litopys UPA*, vol. 5 (Toronto, 1985), 199.

56. Segbers, *Die Sowjetunion*, 114. See also Otto Bräutigam, *Überblick über die besetzten Ostgebiete während des 2. Weltkrieges* (Tübingen, 1954), 44.

57. On food supplies, see *Ereignismeldung UdSSR* 27 (July 19, 1941): 5; 38 (July 30, 1941): 7. On railway bridges, see M. M. Zagorul'ko and A. F. Iudenkov, *Krakh plana "Ol'denburg": (O sryve ekonomicheskikh planov fashistskoi Germanii na vremenno okkupirovannoi territorii SSSR)*, 3d ed. (Moscow, 1980), 108. On factories, see B. Zhuk, "Pozhary v Kieve v 1941 godu," *Vestnik Instituta po izucheniiu SSSR* 2, no. 19 (1956): 106.

58. UCEC, Pavlo Ternivs'kyi [Ivan Zhyhadlo], "Spohady emigranta" (n.p., 1945), 19–23.

59. *Ereignismeldung UdSSR* 81 (September 12, 1941): 8, 10.

60. *Ereignismeldung UdSSR* 143 (December 8, 1941): 5–6; Pihido-Pravoberezhnyi, "*Velyka Vitchyzniana viina*," 50–51; HIA-HURIP, box 21, no. 65 AP, fols. 34–36: anonymous former engineer of the Zaporizhzhia Steel Works, n.p., October 22–23, 1950.

61. Pihido-Pravoberezhnyi, "*Velyka Vitchyzniana viina*," 51–53; Heinrich H. Epp, "Khortitsa 1940–43," in N. J. Kroeker, [ed.], *First Mennonite Villages in Russia, 1789–1943* (Vancouver, 1981), 121–123; Gerhard Lohrenz, *The Lost Generation and Other Stories* (Steinbach, Manitoba, 1982), 38; Grushevoi, *Togda*, 108 (on the engineers). Compare Segbers, *Die Sowjetunion*, 112–113.

62. Kostiuk, author interview. Compare Grushevoi, *Togda*, 49–50.

63. Kostiuk, author interview.

64. Orest Zovenko, *Bezimenni: Spohad uchasnyka novitnikh vyzvol'nykh zmahan'* (n.p., 1946), 73–74.

65. Zynovii Matla, *Pivdenna pokhidna hrupa* (Munich, 1952), 17–18; Kostiuk, author interview.

66. *Ereignismeldung UdSSR* 47 (August 9, 1941): 10.

67. *Ereignismeldung UdSSR* 81 (September 12, 1941): 8; Kumanev, "Sovetskaia ekonomika," 176; Negretov, *Vse dorogi*, 27–28.

68. V. Ost [pseud.], *Repatriiatsiia* (Germany, 1946), 55.

69. HIA-HURIP, box 32, no. 121 AD, fol. 11: unnamed former electrician at the power station in Kherson, n.p., November 28–29, 1950.

70. On blackouts, see Turkalo, *Tortury*, 177. On hoarding, consult Fesenko, *Povest'*, 67; Pihido-Pravoberezhnyi, "*Velyka Vitchyzniana viina*," 30.

71. Fesenko, *Povest'*, 69. See also Ost, *Repatriiatsiia*, 53.

72. Turkalo, *Tortury*, 179–182; Dudin, "Velikii Mirazh," 59.

73. Pihido-Pravoberezhnyi, "*Velyka Vitchyzniana viina*," 47.

74. Private archives of M. S. Petrovskii (Kiev): Nachal'nik Kievskogo Obl[astnogo] Upravleniia Sviazi Sviridov to M. Z. Goshon of 30/19 Levashivs'ka Street, "Izveshchenie." See also ibid., 29–30.

75. Velychkivs'kyi, "Sumni chasy," *Vyzvol'nyi shliakh* 12, no. 1 (1965): 43; Fesenko, *Povest'*, 90; Kravchenko, author interview; Anatolii Kuznetsov (A. Anatolii), *Babii iar: Roman-dokument* (New York, 1986), 144; Halyna Lashchenko, "Povorot," *Samostiina Ukraïna* [11], nos. 15–17(111–113) [sic; really nos. 3–4(111–113)] (New York, March–May 1958): 14.

76. Fesenko, *Povest'*, 67; Turkalo, *Tortury*, 179; Pihido-Pravoberezhnyi, "*Velyka Vitchyzniana viina*," 36 (the long quotation); Dudin, "Velikii Mirazh," 53.

77. TsDAHOU, 166/3/243/44: Ol'ga Sergeevna Gudzenko-Tyshkova (Ukrainian born in 1901), Kiev, March 14, 1944.

78. Evgeniia Dimer, *Ogliadivaias' nazad* (New York, 1987), 22–23 (the quotation); Dudin, "Velikii Mirazh," 51–52.

79. TsDAHOU, 166/3/244/13v: Iurii Mikhailovich Markovskii (Ukrainian born in 1904), Kiev, March 12, 1944; Emigrant, "Nemtsy v Kieve," 6.

80. Fesenko, *Povest'*, 68. See also Dudin, "Velikii Mirazh," 52.

81. On the 197 estimate, see Zagorul'ko and Iudenkov, *Krakh plana "Ol'denburg,"* 94. On the prospects for those who stayed, see Ost, *Repatriiatsiia*, 55. For the exodus of school directors, see TsDAHOU, 166/3/243/44: Gudzenko-Tyshkova. The quotation is from L. S. Khmilevs'ka, author interview, referring to her mother's conversation with an employee of the NKVD.

82. Chekh, "Pravda."

83. Halyna Lashchenko, "Povorot," *Samostiina Ukraïna* 11, no. 10(118) (Chicago, October 1958): 12. See also Emigrant, "Nemtsy v Kieve," 23.

84. Fesenko, *Povest'*, 76, 79; Pihido-Pravoberezhnyi, *"Velyka Vitchyzniana viina,"* 112; Leontii Forostivs'kyi, *Kyïv pid vorozhymy okupatsiiamy* (Buenos Aires, 1952), 22; Ost, *Repatriiatsiia*, 55; Chekh, "Pravda."

85. UCEC, [Mykola Balanchuk], "Kyïv za nimets'koï okupatsiï" (n.p., n.d.), 20; Turkalo, *Tortury*, 191.

86. Malakov, *Oti dva roky*, 43; Forostivs'kyi, *Kyïv*, 20–21; Fesenko, *Povest'*, 67; Chekh, "Pravda"; Kuznetsov, *Babii iar*, 140.

87. Fesenko, *Povest'*, 68; Ievhen Onats'kyi, "Ukraïna ochyma italiis'kykh korespondentiv u druhii svitovii viini," *Samostiina Ukraïna* 18, no. 1(191) (New York, January 1965): 33.

88. On evasion tactics, see Fesenko, *Povest'*, 67, 72; Dudin, "Velikii Mirazh," 62. On extermination battalions, see N. Iu. Pushkars'kyi, "Iak horiv Kyïv," *Ukraïns'kyi zbirnyk* 5 (Munich, 1956): 164; Chekh, "Pravda." For men in hiding, consult Pushkars'kyi, "Iak horiv Kyïv," 165; Fesenko, *Povest'*, 69, 72; Turkalo, *Tortury*, 191; Dudin, "Velikii Mirazh," 62.

89. Dudin, "Velikii Mirazh," 68; Pushkars'kyi, "Iak horiv Kyïv," 166; Kravchenko, author interview; Irina Khoroshunova, "Pervyi god voiny: Kievskie zapiski," *Iehupets'* 9 (Kiev, 2001): 46.

90. TsDAHOU, 166/3/243/16: Vladimir Mikhailovich Artobolevskii (Russian born in 1874), Kiev, February 22 and 25, 1944.

91. Khoroshunova, "Pervyi god voiny," 43, 45. On criminals, see also Dimer, *Ogliadivaias' nazad*, 23; Chekh, "Pravda."

92. Pushkars'kyi, "Iak horiv Kyïv," 164; Hrynevych, author interview; *Ereignismeldung UdSSR* 183 (March 20, 1942): 10; Dimer, *Ogliadivaias' nazad*, 23; Fesenko, *Povest'*, 71; Turkalo, *Tortury*, 192; Chekh, "Pravda"; Emigrant, "Nemtsy v Kieve," 16.

93. Emigrant, "Nemtsy v Kieve," 17; Dudin, "Velikii Mirazh," 70.

94. On the swastika flag, see Generaloberst [Franz] Halder, *Kriegstagebuch*, vol. 3,

Hans-Adolf Jacobsen, ed. (Stuttgart, 1964), 240; D. V. Malakov, ed., *Kyïv, 1941–1943: Fotoal'bom* (Kiev, 2000), 65. The flowers are mentioned in TsDAHOU, 1/22/11/10: Chepurnoi, zam. zav. orginstruktorskim otdelom TsK KP(b)U, "Informatsiia o sostoianii raboty kievskoi podpol'noi organizatsii KP(b)U," Starobil's'k, March 26, 1943. Quotation is from *Ereignismeldung UdSSR* 106 (October 7, 1941): 9.

95. TsDAHOU, 1/23/119/3, 5: "Kiev. Kopiia."
96. Fesenko, *Povest'*, 71–72.
97. Chekh, "Pravda."
98. Khoroshunova, "Pervyi god voiny," 46.
99. Turkalo, *Tortury*, 192.
100. Hrynevych, author interview.
101. A. Anatoli (Kuznetsov), *Babi Yar: A Document in the Form of a Novel* (London, 1970), 28–29. That some were Jewish is documented in Kravchenko, author interview.
102. F. P. Bogatyrchuk, *Moi zhiznennyi put' k Vlasovu i Prazhkomu manifestu* (San Francisco, 1978), 127. See also Fesenko, *Povest'*, 72.
103. Fesenko, *Povest'*, 71; Kuznetsov, *Babii iar*, 68. Compare *Ereignismeldung UdSSR* 106 (October 7, 1941): 10.
104. Kuznetsov, *Babii iar*, 78; TsDAVOV, 4620/3/243a/2: Nikolai Adrianovich Prakhov, "Chto bylo v Kieve pri nemtsakh," Kiev, May 21, 1941 [sic; prob. 1945].
105. *Ereignismeldung UdSSR* 106 (October 7, 1941): 9; Turkalo, *Tortury*, 190, 192; HIA, Alexander Dallin collection, box 8, folder 2, fol. 1: Anon., "Razrushenie goroda Kieva vo vtoruiu mirovuiu voinu," n.p., n.d.
106. On the fires, see TsDAHOU, 1/23/119/3–4: "Kiev. Kopiia"; Pushkars'kyi, "Iak horiv Kyïv," 165–166; Chekh, "Pravda." On the arsenal mine, see *Ereignismeldung UdSSR* 97 (September 28, 1941): 23, and 106 (October 7, 1941): 11; "Kiev. Kopiia," 7; A. Koshman-Kovraiskii, "Kak byl razrushen Uspenskii sobor v Kieve," *Novoe russkoe slovo*, February 10, 1948, 4. On blaming the Jews, consult Kuznetsov, *Babii iar*, 73–74; Khoroshunova, "Pervyi god voiny," 49.
107. The main sources for the paragraphs that follow are Pushkars'kyi, "Iak horiv Kyïv," and Chekh, "Pravda" (including *Novoe russkoe slovo*, January 31, 1948, 2). See also Titus D. Hewryk, *The Lost Architecture of Kiev* (New York, 1982), 38–39; Malakov, *Kyïv*, 101–139, 142.
108. On the first-floor blast, see K. Radzevych [Osyp Vynnyts'kyi], "U sorokarichchia Kyïvs'koï pokhidnoï hrupy OUN," *Kalendar-al'manakh Novoho Shliakhu*, 1982 (Toronto, n.d.), 75; Fesenko, *Povest'*, 73. On the third-floor explosion, see TsDAVOV, 4620/3/243a/53: Professor N. A. Shepelevskii, "Prebyvanie nemtsev v Kieve," n.p., n.d. On the prisoner release, see Ilya Ehrenburg and Vasily Grossman, eds., *The Black Book: The Ruthless Murder of*

Jews by German-Fascist Invaders throughout the Temporarily-Occupied Regions of the Soviet Union and in the Death Camps of Poland during the War of 1941–1945 (New York, 1981), 4.

109. Pushkars'kyi, "Iak horiv Kyïv," 165; Fesenko, *Povest'*, 73; Zhuk, "Pozhary," 107; Paul Werner, *Ein Schweizer Journalist sieht Rußland: Auf den Spuren der deutschen Armee zwischen San und Dnjepr* (Olten, Switz., 1942), 99–100; Dudin, "Velikii Mirazh," 76.

110. On the youths, see Fesenko, *Povest'*, 73; Dudin, "Velikii Mirazh," 75. Compare Zhuk, "Pozhary," 106. On the train request, consult Halder, *Kriegstagebuch*, vol. 3, 252. For the fire brigade and the Kievans, see Werner, *Ein Schweizer*, 101–102; Shepelevskii, "Prebyvanie nemtsev," 55; Pihido-Pravoberezhnyi, *"Velyka Vitchyzniana viina,"* 105.

111. On the German measures, see Lashchenko, "Povorot," *Samostiina Ukraïna* 11, no. 6(114) (New York, June 1958): 19; Emigrant, "Nemtsy v Kieve," 25. For the 200 figure, see Gerhard Kegel, *In den Stürmen unseres Jahrhunderts: Ein deutscher Kommunist über sein ungewöhnliches Leben* (Berlin, 1984), 308.

112. *Ereignismeldung UdSSR* 106 (October 7, 1941): 12–13 (mentions 25,000); BA-MA, RH 26–454/28: Abteilung VII of Security Division 454, "Betr.: Besuch bei F.K. 195 (Kiew) am 1.10.1941," n.p., October 2, 1941 (mentions 10,000); Harry Mielert, *Russische Erde: Kriegsbriefe aus Rußland* (Stuttgart, 1950), 19; Chepurnoi, "Informatsiia," 2; Kuznetsov, *Babii iar*, 82.

113. BA-MA, RH 26–454/26 (mentions one square kilometer); Zhuk, "Pozhary," 109–110; Iaroslav Haivas, "V roky nadii i beznadiï (Zustrichi i rozmovy z O. Ol'zhychem v rokakh 1939–1944)," *Kalendar-al'manakh Novoho Shliakhu*, 1977 (Toronto, n.d.), 111; Khoroshunova, "Pervyi god voiny," 55; Walter Manoschek, ed., *"Es gibt nur eines für das Judentum: Vernichtung": Das Judenbild in deutschen Soldatenbriefen 1939–1944* (Hamburg, 1995), 45; Kravchenko, author interview; TsDAHOU, 166/3/244/22v: Markovskii.

114. *Ereignismeldung UdSSR* 106 (October 7, 1941): 11, 14; TsDAVOV, 3676/1/27/ 280–282: "Zerstörung von Kulturgütern durch die Bolschewiken und Wiederherstellung durch die Deutschen."

115. *Ereignismeldung UdSSR* 119 (October 20, 1941): 10; Dudin, "Velikii Mirazh," 76.

116. Forostivs'kyi, *Kyïv*, 21; *Ereignismeldung UdSSR* 119 (October 20, 1941): 10.

117. *Trial of the Major War Criminals before the International Military Tribunal* [hereafter *TMWC*], vol. 25 (Nuremberg, 1949), 101; Onats'kyi, "Ukraïna [. . .]," *Samostiina Ukraïna* 18, no. 5(195) (New York, 1965): 27.

118. *TMWC*, vol. 25, 101; Forostivs'kyi, *Kyïv*, 31.

119. Pushkars'kyi, "Iak horiv Kyïv," 172; M. V. Koval', "Dolia ukraïns'koï kul'tury za 'novoho poriadku' (1941–1944 rr.)," *Ukraïns'kyi istorychnyi zhurnal*, nos. 11–12 (1993): 24.

120. Aleks Kristof, "Kto zheg Kiev?" *Novoe russkoe slovo,* September 25, 1951, 4.

121. *Ereignismeldung UdSSR* 97 (September 28, 1941): 24; Emigrant, "Nemtsy v Kieve," 36–37 (the quotation).

122. Pushkars'kyi, "Iak horiv Kyïv," 170; Pihido-Pravoberezhnyi, *"Velyka Vitchyzniana viina,"* 107; TsDAVOV, 4620/3/281/2: Dina Mironovna Pronicheva (Jew born in Chernihiv in 1911), stenographic report of testimony, Kiev, April 24, 1946; Khoroshunova, "Pervyi god voiny," 51; Dudin, "Velikii Mirazh," 79.

123. *Ereignismeldung UdSSR* 106 (October 7, 1941): 15.

124. Erhard Roy Wiehn, comp., *Die Schoáh von Babij Jar: Das Massaker deutscher Sonderkommandos an der jüdischen Bevölkerung von Kiew 1941 fünfzig Jahre danach zum Gedenken* (Konstanz, Ger., 1991), 144.

125. Pihido-Pravoberezhnyi, *"Velyka Vitchyzniana viina,"* 106–107.

126. On the ghetto rumor, see *Ereignismeldung UdSSR* 106 (October 7, 1941): 13; Prakhov, "Chto bylo v Kieve pri nemtsakh," 5. For the prisoner-exchange rumor, see Ehrenburg and Grossman, *Black Book,* 8.

127. On the suicides, see Khoroshunova, "Pervyi god voiny," 57. Quotation is in Moskovs'ka, author interview. For the all-night prayers, see Kuznetsov, *Babii iar,* 95.

128. *Ereignismeldung UdSSR* 101 (October 2, 1941): 2; Hartmut Rüß, "Wer war verantwortlich für das Massaker von Babij Jar?" *Militärgeschichtliche Mitteilungen* 57, no. 2 (Potsdam, 1998): 495, 499.

129. See V. K. Vinogradov et al., comps., *Lubianka v dni bitvy za Moskvu: Po rassekrechennym dokumentam FSB RF* (Moscow, 2002), 13–14, 74–80, 82–85, 100–103.

130. Chekh, "Pravda"; *Ereignismeldung UdSSR* 81 (September 12, 1941): 16.

2. The Reichskommissariat Ukraine

1. Adolf Hitler, *Monologe im Führerhauptquartier 1941–1944: Die Aufzeichnungen Heinrich Heims herausgegeben von Werner Jochmann* (Hamburg, 1980), 62–63, 311–312; Henry Picker, *Hitlers Tischgespräche im Führerhauptquartier 1941– 1942,* 2d ed. (Stuttgart, 1963), 469–470; John Connelly, "Nazis and Slavs: From Racial Theory to Racist Practice," *Central European History* 32, no. 1 (1999): 1–33.

2. Hitler, *Monologe,* 331, 334; Picker, *Hitlers Tischgespräche,* 381.

3. Gerd R. Ueberschär, comp., "Ausgewählte Dokumente," in Gerd R. Ueberschär and Wolfram Wette, eds., *"Unternehmen Barbarossa": Der deutsche Überfall auf die Sowjetunion 1941. Berichte, Analysen, Dokumente* (Paderborn, Ger., 1984), 332–333, 363; Picker, *Hitlers Tischgespräche,* 470 (on barracks).

4. NA microcopy T-84, roll 387, frame 770: Hitler's personal secretary Werner Koeppen, report of September 19, 1941, describing September 18; Timothy

Mulligan, *The Politics of Illusion and Empire: German Occupation Policy in the Soviet Union, 1942–1943* (New York, 1988), 11.

5. NA microcopy T-84, roll 387, frames 809–810: Koeppen, report of October 18, 1941.

6. Hitler, *Monologe*, 90–91.

7. Alexander Dallin, *German Rule in Russia, 1941–1945: A Study of Occupation Policies*, 2d ed. (Boulder, Colo., 1981), 84.

8. TsDAVOV, 3206/1/106/1: "Vorlaeufige Uebersicht ueber die Generalbezirke und Kreisgebiete in der Ukraine (Stand: 15.2.42) soweit das Gebiet bisher in die Zivilverwaltung uebernommen ist," Rivne, March 1, 1942.

9. Dallin, *German Rule*, 85; Gerald Reitlinger, "Last of the War Criminals: The Mystery of Erich Koch," *Commentary* 27, no. 1 (New York, January 1959): 35; Christian Gerlach, *Kalkulierte Morde: Die deutsche Wirtschafts- und Vernichtungspolitik in Weißrußland 1941 bis 1944* (Hamburg, 1999), 174–175.

10. For details, see NA microcopy T-120, roll 2533, frames E292759–760: Hitler, order of August 12, 1942, with a map; NA micropcopy T-120, roll 5, frame 827: Von Roques, Commander of Rear Army Area South, "Befehl für die Bildung des Reichskommissariats Ukraine," n.p., August 23, 1941; Norbert Müller, *Wehrmacht und Okkupation 1941–1944: Zur Rolle der Wehrmacht und ihrer Führungsorgane im Okkupationsregime des faschistischen deutschen Imperialismus auf sowjetischem Territorium* (Berlin, 1971), 76; Dallin, *German Rule*, 85, 127.

11. For the estimate, see Rolf-Dieter Müller, ed., *Die deutsche Wirtschaftspolitik in den besetzten sowjetischen Gebieten 1941–1943: Der Abschlußbericht des Wirtschaftsstabes Ost und Aufzeichnungen eines Angehörigen des Wirtschaftskommandos Kiew* (Boppard am Rhein, Ger., 1991), 519. The official census figure is in TsDAVOV, 3206/2/231/45–50: "Uebersicht über die Verwaltungseinteilung des Reichskommissariats Ukraine nach dem Stand vom 1. Januar 1943" (mentions also 339,275.83 square km). Another copy is at BA-Berlin, R 6/70, fols. 108–114.

12. For the most densely populated areas, see *Osnovnye pokazateli narodnogo khoziaistva USSR: (Kratkii statistiko-ekonomicheskii spravochnik)* (Kiev, 1945), 142, a classified booklet now at TsDAHOU, 1/23/3962. The inclusion of Belarusan Polissia is documented in Gerlach, *Kalkulierte Morde*, 179.

13. Reitlinger, "Last of the War Criminals," 32; Dallin, *German Rule*, 125–127, quotation on 167.

14. The "admirer" wrote TsDAVOV, 3206/2/71/127: Kurt Nestler, Abteilung IIa, "Die Ukraine, wie ich sie sehe," n.p., n.d. For Koch's own words, see Alex Alexiev, *Soviet Nationalities in German Wartime Strategy, 1941–1945* (Santa Monica, Calif., 1982), 12.

15. Otto Bräutigam, *Überblick über die besetzten Ostgebiete während des 2. Weltkrieges* (Tübingen, 1954), 20.

16. NA microcopy T-84, roll 387, frame 770: Koeppen, report of September 19, 1941; Mulligan, *Politics of Illusion and Empire*, 11. Compare Hitler, *Monologe*, 62–63.

17. *Volyn'* (Rivne), December 25, 1941, 1.

18. The German usage was *Generalkommissar, Generalbezirk* [GB] *Wolhynien und Podolien, Shitomir, Kiew, Nikolajew, Dnjepropetrowsk, Krim, Teilbezirk Taurien.* See Raul Hilberg, *The Destruction of the European Jews*, vol. 1, rev. ed. (New York, 1985), 348; BA-Berlin, R 6/15, fols. 1–5: Hitler, appointments of general commissars, September 30, 1941; "Uebersicht über die Verwaltungseinteilung"; NA microcopy T-84, serial 20, roll 7, frame 7252: Rosenberg's ständiger Vertreter to Ministerialrat Görnert, Berlin, September 14, 1942.

19. Original German usage: *Gebietskommissariat* or *Gebiet* (Ukr. *okruha*); *Gebietskommissar; Stadtkommissar.* See "Uebersicht über die Verwaltungseinteilung."

20. Mulligan, *Politics of Illusion and Empire*, 23, citing *Trial of the Major War Criminals before the International Military Tribunal* [TMWC], vol. 25 (Nuremberg, 1949), 257.

21. *TMWC*, vol. 25, 257.

22. NA microcopy T-501, roll 5, frames 849, 852: Rear Army Area South to Supreme Army Command, "Verwaltungsmässige Verhältnisse im rückw. Heeresgebiet Süd," n.p., September 7, 1941.

23. Original usage: *Rayonverwaltung* (Ukr. *raionova uprava*); *Stadtverwaltung* (Ukr. *mis'ka uprava*); *Dorfsverwaltung* (Ukr. *sil's'ka uprava*); and for the officials: *Rayonchef* (Ukr. *holova raionu* or *shef raionu*); *Hilfsbürgermeister* or *Bürgermeister* (Ukr. *holova mista*); *Dorfschulze, Dorfältester* or *Dorfsvorsteher* (Ukr. *starosta*). For information about salaries, see NA microcopy T-501, roll 5, frame 752: Von Roques of Rear Army Area South, "Anordnung Abt. VII, Nr. 8," n.p., August 22, 1941; NA microcopy T-175, roll 250, frames 2742638–645: "Anordnung des Reichskommissars für die Ukraine zur Regelung der Lohn- und Arbeitsbedingungen für alle von deutschen Dienststellen beschäftigten einheimischen Angestelten," Rivne, February 19, 1942.

24. TsDAVOV, 3206/5/15/203: RKU *Lagebericht* for October 1–15, 1941, Königsberg, November 4, 1941; Iaan Pennar, "Selbstverwaltung in den während des Zweiten Weltkrieges besetzten Gebieten der Sowjetunion," *Sowjetstudien* 12 (Munich, August 1962): 64.

25. TsDAVOV, 3206/1/111/36: Von Wedelstädt for Koch to all general commissars, Rivne, December 5, 1941; *Die deutsche Zivilverwaltung in den ehemaligen besetzten Ostgebieten (UdSSR)*, vol. 2 (Ludwigsburg, Ger., 1968), 179; DAKO, r-2209/1/21/82: Khabne district commissar to all raion chiefs.

26. Original usage: *Landwirtschaftsführer* or *Landwirt; Kreislandwirt; Gebietslandwirt.* Ralf Bartoleit, "Die deutsche Agrarpolitik in den besetzten

Gebieten der Ukraine vom Sommer 1941 bis zum Sommer 1942 unter
besonderer Berücksichtigung der Einführung der 'Neuen Agrarordnung': Eine
Studie über die strukturelle Durchsetzung nationalsozialistischer
Programmatik," master's thesis, Hamburg University, 1987, 56 and appendices
5a and 5b; TsDAVOV, 3206/1/11/8–9: Organisationsplan, Rivne, February 5,
1943; Mulligan, *Politics of Illusion and Empire*, 28. On the skills of native
agronomists, see *Ereignismeldung UdSSR* 52 (August 14, 1941): 13–14; Müller,
Die deutsche Wirtschaftspolitik, 133.

27. On the overseeing job, see BA-Berlin, R 6/15, fol. 70: Koenigk, head of
Hauptabteilung E of the Zhytomyr Generalbezirk, to Koch, Vinnytsia, June 17,
1943; Bartoleit, "Die deutsche Agrarpolitik," 55. For other tasks, see *Die deut-
sche Zivilverwaltung*, vol. 2, 465. For the outlook of landwirts, see Bartoleit,
"Die deutsche Agrarpolitik," 85; Siegfried Vegesack, *Als Dolmetscher im Osten:
Ein Erlebnisbericht aus den Jahren 1942–43, mit 12 Bildern nach Aufnahmen des
Verfassers* (Hannover-Döhren, Ger., 1965), 120.

28. Bartoleit, "Die deutsche Agrarpolitik," 57 (on food supply); Klaus Geßner,
"Geheime Feldpolizei—die Gestapo der Wehrmacht," in Hannes Heer and
Klaus Neumann, eds., *Vernichtungskrieg: Verbrechen der Wehrmacht 1941–1944*
(Hamburg, 1995), 343–358.

29. On the employment of natives, see Mulligan, *Politics of Illusion and Empire*,
28; Dallin, *German Rule*, 314–316; Reinhard Rürup, ed., *Der Krieg gegen die
Sowjetunion 1941–1945: Eine Dokumentation* (Berlin, 1991), 93; *Die deutsche
Zivilverwaltung*, vol. 2, 63; Mulligan, *Politics of Illusion and Empire*, 29;
Matthias Riedel, "Bergbau und Eisenhüttenindustrie in der Ukraine unter
deutscher Besatzung (1941–1944)," *Vierteljahrshefte für Zeitgeschichte* 21, no. 3
(1973): 251, 267–278 (both on corporations). For the employment of foreign
workers, see L. de Jong, *Het Koninkrijk der Nederlanden in de Tweede
Wereldoorlog*, vol. 6, part 1: *Juli '42–mei '43* (The Hague, 1975), 454, 456, 460–
462; TsDAVOV, 3206/1/78/75–76: Sonderführer Straub and Knappke, report,
Rivne, July 7, 1943; "Holiandtsi na Ukraïni," *Ukraïns'kyi visnyk* (Berlin), August
23, 1942, 5.

30. Mulligan, *Politics of Illusion and Empire*, 66; Dieter Pohl, "Die Einsatzgruppe
C," in Peter Klein, ed., *Die Einsatzgruppen in der besetzten Sowjetunion 1941/
42: Die Tätigkeits- und Lageberichte des Chefs der Sicherheitspolizei und des
SD* (Berlin, 1997), 71–87; Andrej Angrick, "Die Einsatzgruppe D," in Klein,
Die Einsatzgruppen, 88–110.

31. Ruth Bettina Birn, *Die Höheren SS- und Polizeiführer: Himmlers Vertreter im
Reich und in den besetzten Gebieten* (Düsseldorf, 1986), 74, 337, 342; Martin C.
Dean, "The German *Gendarmerie*, the Ukrainian Schutzmannschaft and the
'Second Wave' of Jewish Killings in Occupied Ukraine: German Policing at
the Local Level in the Zhitomir Region, 1941–1944," *German History* 14, no. 2

(1996): 178; Hilberg, *Destruction of the European Jews*, vol. 1, 296–297. See also Frank Golczewski, "Organe der deutschen Besatzungsmacht: Die ukrainischen Schutzmannschaften," in Wolfgang Benz, Johannes Houwink ten Cate, and Gerhard Otto, eds., *Die Bürokratie der Okkupation: Strukturen der Herrschaft und Verwaltung im besetzten Europa* (Berlin, 1998), 173–196.

32. Birn, *Die Höheren SS- und Polizeiführer*, 220–221, 223, 231 (on those who had authority over Prützmann), and 222–224 (on presence of SS and police leaders).

33. On the Schuma generally, see *Die deutsche Zivilverwaltung*, vol. 2, 142–144. For the number of battalions, see Georg Tessin, "Die Stäbe und Truppeneinheiten der Ordnungspolizei," in Hans-Joachim Neufeldt, Jürgen Huck, and Georg Tessin, [eds.], *Zur Geschichte der Ordnungspolizei 1936–1945* (Koblenz, Ger., 1957), 66–67, 104–106.

34. Dean, "German *Gendarmerie*," 178–179 (the quotation); Martin C. Dean, *Collaboration in the Holocaust: Crimes of the Local Police in Belorussia and Ukraine, 1941–44* (New York, 2000), 74; DAKO, r-2160/1/1/52–53: Field Commander, "Tymchasovyi sluzhbovyi nakaz dlia Ukraïns'koï Militsiï," Bila Tserkva, August 18, 1941; TsDAHOU, 1/23/115/18: Savchenko, VRIO NKVD USSR, to N. S. Khrushchev, "Razvedsvodka No. 32/67. O deiatel'nosti ukrainskikh natsionalistov na okkupirovannoi nemetsko-fashistskimi zakhvatchikami territorii USSR. Po sostoianiiu 1. 9. 42g.," Engel's, September 19, 1942; TsDAVOV, 3206/1/78/39–40: RKU *Lagebericht* for January 1942; Volodymyr Serhiichuk, comp., *OUN-UPA v roky viiny: Novi dokumenty i materialy* (Kiev, 1996), 20; *Die deutsche Zivilverwaltung*, vol. 2, 36–37, 144.

35. On semantics, see Dean, "German *Gendarmerie*," 178. On Schuma and police in the cities, see Tessin, "Die Stäbe," 65, whose figures include the Schuma stationed in the Crimea.

36. On the ethnic battalions, see Tessin, "Die Stäbe," 67, 101–102, 105–107; *Litopys UPA*, vol. 1, 3d, corrected ed. (Toronto, 1989), 89; *Litopys UPA*, vol. 5 (Toronto, 1984), 83; *Die deutsche Zivilverwaltung*, vol. 2, 149.

37. Mediator: *Schlichter* (Ukr. *shlikhter*); juror: *Schöffe* (Ukr. *shefen*, Russ. *sheffen*). NA microcopy T-84, roll 120, frames 419189–190: "Auszug aus dem Lagebericht des Generalkommissars," Kiev, September 1, 1942; Bräutigam, *Überblick über die besetzten Ostgebiete*, 66; Nikolas Laskovsky, "Practicing Law in the Occupied Ukraine," *American Slavic and East European Review* 10, no. 2 (1952): 123–137; V. Boldyrev, "Mestnye sudy na Ukraine v period nemetskoi okkupatsii," *Vestnik Instituta po izucheniiu SSSR*, no. 4(21) (Munich, October–December 1956): 66–72; M. Broszat, "Tätigkeit der früheren Deutschen Gerichte in der Ukraine," *Gutachten des Instituts für Zeitgeschichte*, vol. 2 (Stuttgart, 1966), 332–334; *Die deutsche Zivilverwaltung*, vol. 1, section 4 ("Das Rechtswesen") and vol. 2, 307, 310.

38. Jonathan Steinberg, "The Third Reich Reflected: German Civil Administra-

tion in the Occupied Soviet Union, 1941–4," *English Historical Review* 110, no. 437 (June 1995): 620–651.

39. Bernhard Chiari, *Alltag hinter der Front: Besatzung, Kollaboration und Widerstand im Weißrußland 1941–1944* (Düsseldorf, 1998).

40. Gerlach, *Kalkulierte Morde*, esp. 177, 195–196, 213, 1143, 1145–1146.

41. BA-MA, RH 26–454/28: Security Division 454, "Tätigkeitsbericht für die Zeit vom 21. Bis 30. September 1941," n.p., December 27, 1941.

42. On the special SS commands, see Ingeborg Fleischhauer, *Das Dritte Reich und die Deutschen in der Sowjetunion* (Stuttgart, 1983), 118, 121–122. For the participation of ethnic German males, see Fleischauer, *Das Dritte Reich*, 110–112; Dean, *Collaboration*, 66. Regarding "spoiled elements," see Meir Buchsweiler, *Volksdeutsche in der Ukraine am Vorabend und Beginn des Zweiten Weltkriegs—ein Fall doppelter Loyalität?* (Gerlingen, Ger., 1984), 315; Fleischhauer, *Das Dritte Reich*, 115, 159.

43. Fleischhauer, *Das Dritte Reich*, 170–172.

44. Ibid., 174; "Uebersicht über die Verwaltungseinteilung," 46; TsDAVOV, 4620/3/243a/103–104: professor Iu. Iu. Kramarenko, n.p., November 30, 1943. See also Wendy Lower, "A New Ordering of Space and Time: Nazi Colonial Dreams in Zhytomyr, Ukraine, 1941–1944," *German Studies Review* 25, no. 2 (May 2002): 227–254.

45. On the decree, see Buchsweiler, *Volksdeutsche*, 332. Compare Bräutigam, *Überblick über die besetzten Ostgebiete*, 79; and Fleischhauer, *Das Dritte Reich*, 174–175. For the anxiety about the deportation, see Dallin, *German Rule*, 286; NA microcopy T-84, roll 120, frames 418929–930: Sipo-SD of the Kiev GB to Dr. Thomas, Kiev, December 4, 1942.

46. Ueberschär, "Ausgewählte Dokumente," 377.

47. Rolf-Dieter Müller, "Das 'Unternehmen Barbarossa' als wirtschaftlicher Raubkrieg," in Ueberschär and Wette, "*Unternehmen Barbarossa*," 180–182; Ueberschär, "Ausgewählte Dokumente," 378–379; TMWC, vol. 36 (Nuremberg, 1949), 145–146; Gerlach, *Kalkulierte Morde*, 1128.

48. Compare Gerlach, *Kalkulierte Morde*, 111–127, 1130.

49. Compare ibid., 1002, 1147.

50. Dallin, *German Rule*, 279.

51. Peter Witte et al., eds., *Der Dienstkalender Heinrich Himmlers 1941/42* (Hamburg, 1999), 460–461, 498–500.

52. Bogdan A. Martinenko, "Tragediia Bab'ego Iara: Rassekrechennye dokumenty svidetel'stvuiut," in Erhard Roy Wiehn, comp., *Die Schoáh von Babij Jar: Das Massaker deutscher Sonderkommandos an der jüdischen Bevölkerung von Kiew 1941 fünfzig Jahre danach zum Gedenken* (Konstanz, Ger., 1991), 370–371. See also Leonid Abramenko, ed., *Kyïvs'kyi protses: Dokumenty ta materialy* (Kiev, 1995), 47; Wendy Lower, "Anticipatory Obedience and the Nazi Implementation of the Holocaust in the Ukraine: A Case Study of Central and Peripheral

Forces in the Generalbezirk Zhytomyr, 1941–1944," *Holocaust and Genocide Studies* 16, no. 1 (2002): 1–22.

53. Dallin, *German Rule*, 143, 156; Mulligan, *Politics of Illusion and Empire*, 68.

54. Dallin, *German Rule*, 54, 112–113, 668; Bartoleit, "Die deutsche Agrarpolitik," 38–39, 73–74.

55. Mulligan, *Politics of Illusion and Empire*, 71.

56. Dallin, *German Rule*, 107–111.

57. NA microcopy T-84, roll 387, frame 770: Koeppen, report of September 19, 1941.

58. NA microcopy T-120, roll 2533, frame E292728: Koch, "Betrifft: Führen und Gebrauch von Peitschen durch Angehörige der deutschen Zivilverwaltung in der Ukraine," copy, Rivne, April 18, 1942; V. Borovs'kyi, "Shist' tyzhniv na Volyni v 1943 rotsi (Iz spohadiv Ukraïns'koï Ievanhel's'ko-Reformovanoï Tserkvy)," *Litopys Volyni* 13–14 (Winnipeg, 1979–1982): 36.

59. Dallin, *German Rule*, 463, 467–468.

60. Ibid., 465; Mulligan, *Politics of Illusion and Empire*, 65–66, 68–70; Birn, *Die Höheren SS- und Polizeiführer*, 230–231.

61. Mulligan, *Politics of Illusion and Empire*, 13–14, 47–48, 50, 53, 55, 64–65, 69; Dallin, *German Rule*, 146–175, 513–514.

62. On Frauenfeld, see Mulligan, *Politics of Illusion and Empire*, 94; Dallin, *German Rule*, 264–266, 546, n. 2. See also Alfred E. Frauenfeld, *Und trage keine Reu': Vom Wiener Gauleiter zum Generalkommissar der Krim. Erinnerungen und Aufzeichnungen* (Leoni am Starnberger See, Ger., 1978). For Kube, consult Gerlach, *Kalkulierte Morde*, 162. On Rosenberg's lack of skill, see Mulligan, *Politics of Illusion and Empire*, 50, 55–56.

63. Ivan R. Kostiuk, "Kremenchuk (Z bloknota kol. voiennoho zvitodavtsia)," *Visti kombatanta*, no. 1(13) (New York, 1964): 27.

64. Müller, *Die faschistische Okkupationspolitik*, 170.

65. Hans-Adolf Jacobsen, "Kommissarbefehl und Massenexekutionen sowjetischer Kriegsgefangener," in Hans Buchheim et al., eds., *Anatomie des SS-Staates*, vol. 2 (Olten, Switz.,), 216, quoted in Christian Streit, *Keine Kameraden: Die Wehrmacht und die sowjetischen Kriegsgefangenen 1941–1945* (Stuttgart, 1978), 347, n. 158.

66. Rürup, *Der Krieg gegen die Sowjetunion*, 129–130.

67. Shmuel Spector, *The Holocaust of Volhynian Jews, 1941–1944* (Jerusalem, 1990), 157; Truman Oliver Anderson III, "The Conduct of Reprisals by the German Army of Occupation in the Southern USSR, 1941–1943," Ph.D. diss., University of Chicago, 1995, 164–165; Truman Anderson, "Incident at Baranivka: German Reprisals and the Soviet Partisan Movement in Ukraine, October–December 1941," *Journal of Modern History* 71, no. 3 (September 1999): 585–623.

68. Gerlach, *Kalkulierte Morde*, 870–884, describes the campaign against the "strangers" (*Ortsfremde*) in Belarus.

69. Calculated from GFP records at NA microcopy T-501, roll 349.

70. Private archives of V. A. Ponsov (Moscow): Iurii A. Silenchuk, "'Borot'sia i zhit" (1941–1945 g.)" (n.p., 1966), chapter 7 (manuscript).

71. TsDAVOV, 3206/2/26/6–7: Hptm. Prof. Hans Koch, "Der Sowjet-Nachlass in der Ukraine. Stimmungs- und Erfahrungsbericht. Abgeschlossen 30. 9. 1941."

72. For the Kuntseve incident, see H. Sova [Hryhorii Kariak], *Do istoriï bol'shevyts'koï diis'nosty: (25 rokiv zhyttia ukraïns'koho hromadianyna v SSSR)* (Munich, 1955), 80. On events in Chyhyryn, see M. Demydenko, author interview. See also *Ereignismeldung UdSSR* 108 (October 9, 1941): 23.

73. NDB, collection "Afishy ta plakaty okupatsiinoho periodu," 30sp: "Moskva—hnizdo bil'shovyzmu v nimets'kykh rukakh"; TsDAHOU, 1/22/391/9: Mikhail Mikh. Skirda et al., "Otchet o podpol'noi partiinoi rabote i partizanskoi bor'be v Kirovogradskoi oblasti (avgust 1941 goda–mart 1944 goda)," n.d.

74. TsDAHOU, 1/22/117/25: Balashev to Ratushnyi, deputy NKVD UkSSR, "Dokladnaia zapiska," n.p., November 9, 1941; TsDAHOU, 1/22/117/33: Anatolii Sergeevich Koziura and Vol'demar Rechevich Drolle to Kniazev, zam. nachal'nik 4-go Otdela NKVD USSR, "Kopiia," n.p., November 12, 1941; TsDAHOU, 1/22/118/140: V. I. Nichipor and V. D. Tuzlukov to Kniazev, zam. nach. 4-go Otdela NKVD USSR, "Ob"iasnitel'naia zapiska o nastroenii i polozhenii naseleniia na okkupirovannoi territorii nemtsami," n.p., December 22, 1941.

75. Irina Khoroshunova, "Pervyi god voiny. Kievskie zapiski," *Iehupets'* 9 (Kiev, 2001): 49; M. P. Kostiuk, author interview.

76. TsDAHOU, 1/23/41/42–45: St. Skrypnyk, "Satzung des Ukrainischen Vertrauensrats in Wolhynien," copy, n.p., n.d.; TsDAHOU, 1/23/41/38–41: St. Skrypnyk to the Reichskommissar, copy, Rivne, September 11, 1941.

77. TsDAHOU, 1/23/41/23–25: Koch, "An den Herrn Generalkommissar in Brest Litowsk," Königsberg, September 20, 1941.

78. Stepan Suliatyts'kyi, "Pershi dni v okupovanomu nimtsiamy Kyievi," in Kost' Mel'nyk, Oleh Lashchenko, and Vasyl' Veryha, eds., *Na zov Kyieva: Ukraïns'kyi natsionalizm u II Svitovii Viini. Zbirnyk stattei, spohadiv i dokumentiv* (Toronto, 1985), 162; Ia. Shumelda, "Pokhid OUN na skhid," in *Orhanizatsiia Ukraïns'kykh Natsionalistiv, 1929–1954: Zbirnyk stattei u 25-littia OUN* ([Paris], 1955), 262.

79. Dmytro Kyslytsia, *Svite iasnyi: Spohady. Vid r. Vovchi z Naddniprianshchyny do r. Sv. Lavrentiia na Ottavshchyni* (Ottawa, 1987), 182–183 (the date); Iehen Onats'kyi, "Ukraïna ochyma italiis'kykh korespondentiv u druhii svitovii viini," *Samostiina Ukraïna* 18, no. 3(193) (New York, 1965): 40; John A. Armstrong, *Ukrainian Nationalism*, 3d ed. (Englewood, Colo., 1990), 74, 83.

80. Mykola Velychkivs'kyi, "Sumni chasy nimets'koï okupatsiï (1941–1944 roky)," *Vyzvol'nyi shliakh* 12, no. 1 (London, 1965): esp. 42–43; Iaroslav Haivas, "V roky

nadii i beznadiï (Zustrichi i rozmovy z O. Ol'zhychem v rokakh 1939–1944),"
Kalendar-al'manakh Novoho Shliakhu, 1977 (Toronto, n.d.): 113–114; Iaroslav
Haivas, *Koly kinchalasia epokha* (n.p., 1964), 67–68; Zenon Horodys'kyi,
Ukraïns'ka Natsional'na Rada: Istorychnyi narys (Kiev, 1993), 26–27.

81. Horodys'kyi, *Ukraïns'ka Natsional'na Rada*, 35; Zenon Horodys'kyi,
"National'no-derzhavnyts'ke znachennia marshu Bukovyns'koho Kurenia do
Kyieva 1941 r. (istorychno-politychnyi ohliad)," *Kalendar'-al'manakh Novoho
Shliakhu, 1996* (Toronto, n.d.): 55.

82. TsDAVOV, 3206/1/77/6–8: "Ukrainisches Volk!" Kiev, November 1941.

83. TsDAVOV, 3206/1/77/14: [Velychkivs'kyi and secretary Antin Baranivs'kyi] to
Erich Koch, n.d., n.p.; also in Rürup, *Der Krieg gegen die Sowjetunion*, 141.

84. Armstrong, *Ukrainian Nationalism*, 78; Shumelda, "Pokhid OUN na skhid,"
264; TsDAVOV, 3206/1/78/8: acting general commissar Quitzrau to Erich
Koch, Kiev, January 21, 1942; TsDAVOV, 3206/2/27/11: RKU *Lagebericht* for December 1941.

85. Armstrong, *Ukrainian Nationalism*, 69, 77, 83–84; *TMWC*, vol. 39
(Nuremberg, 1949), 269–270.

86. Borovs'kyi, "Shist' tyzhniv na Volyni," 35.

87. Haivas, *Koly kinchalasia epokha*, 61; M. Mykhalevych, "Sorok rokiv tomu . . . ,"
in Mel'nyk, Lashchenko, and Veryha, *Na zov Kyieva*, 213; Kost' Pan'kivs'kyi,
Vid derzhavy do komitetu (New York, 1957), 106; *Shchodennyk Arkadiia
Liubchenka*, ed. Iurii Luts'kyi (L'viv, Ukr., 1999), 72.

88. On the presence of the flags in 1941, see F. H. (Fedir Haiovych), "Kyïv u
zhovtni 1941 [r.]," in Mel'nyk, Lashchenko, and Veryha, *Na zov Kyieva*, 164; A.
Kabaida, "1941," *Kalendar-al'manakh Novoho Shliakhu, 1991* (Toronto, n.d.):
50; Anatolii Kuznetsov (A. Anatolii), *Babii iar: Roman-dokument* (New York,
1986), 69. On the committee, see Ihor Verba, "Sproby vidnovlennia
Ukraïns'koï Akademiï Nauk u Kyievi (Kinets' 1941–seredyna 1942 rr.),"
Ukraïns'kyi istoryk 32, no. 1–4(124–127) (New York, 1995): 97.

89. Maksym Skorups'kyi, *U nastupakh i vidstupakh: Spohady* (Chicago, 1961), 50;
DAKO, r-2097/1/9/1: Bohuslav administration, January 1943.

90. Ulas Samchuk, *Na koni voronomu: Spomyny i vrazhennia* (Winnipeg, 1975),
220; Sova, *Do istoriï bol'shevyts'koï diis'nosty*, 85; UCEC, Pavlo Ternivs'kyi
[Ivan Zhyhadlo], "Spohady emigranta" (n.p., 1945), 25–26.

91. Pavel Negretov, *Vse dorogi vedut na Vorkutu* (Benson, Vt., 1985), 51.

92. TsDAVOV, 4620/3/243a/1: Nikolai Adrianovich Prakhov, "Chto bylo v Kieve pri
nemtsakh," Kiev, May 21, 1941 [sic; probably 1944]; Ivan Kurakh, "Tam de
prokhodyla viina (Spomyn ukraïns'koho starshyny v italiis'kii armiï)," *Visti:
Orhan Viis'kovo-politychnoï dumky Kraiovoï Upravy Bratstva kol. voiakiv 1 UD-
UNA v Nimechchyni* 15, no. 113 (Munich, March 1964): 9; O. Iaroslavs'kyi [Lev
Chaikovs'kyi?], "Vid Sianu po Dinets' (Z spohadiv perekladacha)," *Visti*

Bratstva kol. Voiakiv I UD UNA 7, nos. 7–8(69–70) (Munich, July–August 1956): 20; Mykola S.-Chartoryis'kyi, *Vid Sianu po Krym: (Spomyny uchasnyka III Pokhidnoï Grupy-Pivden')* (New York, 1951), 170.

93. D. V. Malakov, *Kyïv, 1941–1943: Fotoal'bom* (Kiev, 2000), 168; Kuznetsov, *Babii iar*, 332; Ivan Maistrenko, *Istoriia moho pokolinnia: Spohady uchasnyka revoliutsiinykh podii v Ukraïni* (Edmonton, 1985). 338; HIA-HURIP, box 22, no. 67 AD, fol. 5: anonymous informant, Munich, October 20–21 and 27, 1950.

94. On German monuments and notices, see HIA, Alexander Dallin collection, box 8, folder 2: Anonymous, "Razrushenie Goroda Kieva vo vtoruiu mirovuiu voinu," n.p., n.d. For desovietization in small towns, see *Vidrodzhennia* (Tarashcha), November 1, 1942, 4.

95. Panas Khurtovyna [Mykhailo Podvorniak], *Pid nebom Volyni: (Voienni spomyny khrystyianyna)* (Winnipeg, 1952), 92; M. P. [Mykhailo Podvorniak], "Vid smerty do zhyttia (Spohad)," *Litopys Volyni* 7 (Winnipeg, 1964): 91.

96. Examples are in Mykhailo Lebid', "Chasy nimets'koï okupatsiï v Matiïvs'kim raioni na Volyni (Spohady kol. holovy rainovoï upravy)," *Litopys UPA*, vol. 5, 201–203; and Sova, *Do istoriï bol'shevyts'koï diis'nosty*, 94. Compare *Ereignismeldung UdSSR* 86 (September 17, 1941): 12.

97. O. M. Kutsenko, M. O. Vasylenko, and Ie. M. Moskovs'ka, author interviews. See also *Ereignismeldung UdSSR* 47 (August 9, 1941): 8; *Ereignismeldung UdSSR* 81 (September 12, 1941): 15, 20–21.

98. Sheila Fitzpatrick, *Everyday Stalinism: Ordinary Life in Extraordinary Times; Soviet Russia in the 1930s* (New York, 1999), 116, 135, 207–209.

99. Ternivs'kyi, "Spohady emigranta," 31.

100. Iaroslavs'kyi, "Vid Sianu po Dinets'," 20; TsDAHOU, 166/3/244/62: I. Kuzenko (Ukrainian born in 1916), Kiev, October 29, 1946.

101. Sheila Fitzpatrick, *Stalin's Peasants: Resistance and Survival in the Russian Village after Collectivization* (New York, 1994), 177; N. S. Zozulia, author interview; Mykhailo Seleshko, *Vinnytsia: Spomyny perekladacha Komisiï doslidiv zlochyniv NKVD v 1937–1938* (New York, 1991), 55; TsDAHOU, 1/23/633/24–25: Z. Serdiuk, Kiev obkom secretary, "Politinformatsiï po Kyïvs'koï oblasti na 10.XII–1943 roku," n.p, n.d.; HIA-HURIP, box 23, no. 102 AD, fol. 6: anonymous informant from Borislav near Dnipropetrovs'k, n.p., November 17, 1950.

102. TsDAHOU, 166/3/244/19v: Iurii Mikhailovich Markovskii (Ukrainian born in 1904), Kiev, March 12, 1944; TsDAVOV, 3676/4/476/6: SD report on the Kiev GB in April 1942.

103. A. Dublians'kyi, *Ternystym shliakhom: Zhyttia Mytropolyta Nikanora Abramovycha. Do 20-littia arkhypastyrs'koho sluzhinnia, 1942–1962* (London, 1962), 50–51.

104. Fitzpatrick, *Everyday Stalinism*, 19. See also Jacob Gerstenfeld-Maltiel, *My Private War: One Man's Struggle to Survive the Soviets and the Nazis* (London,

1993), 34; *Shchodennyk Arkadiia Liubchenka*, 107–108; HIA, B. I. Nicolaevsky collection, series no. 178, box 232, folder 10, fols. 57–58: [Lev Vladimirovich] Dudin, "Velikii Mirazh: Sobytiia 1941–1947 godov v ponimanii sovetskogo cheloveka," n.p., 1947.

105. TsDAHOU, 166/3/243/42: Aleksei Mikhailovich Bashkulat (Ukrainian born in 1909), Kiev, February 28, 1944. See also [O. P. Sharandachenko], *Reiestratorka zahsu: (Iz shchodennyka kyianky)* (Kiev, 1960), 121.

106. Ernst Benz, *Die Religiöse Lage in der Ukraine: Erlebnisbericht eines Divisionspfarrers. Als Manuskript gedruckt* (Marburg, Ger., 1942), 7, 35.

107. Zena Matviichuk, "Dmytro Myron-Orlyk v lystakh pro Kyïv ta revoliutsiinu borot'bu," in Mykhailo H. Marunchak, ed., *V borot'bi za ukraïns'ku derzhavu: Eseï, spohady, svidchennia, litopysannia, dokumenty Druhoï svitovoï viiny* (Winnipeg, 1990), 843.

108. Bishop Nikanor (Abramovych), cited in Osyp Zinkevych and Oleksander Voronyn, eds., *Martyrolohiia ukraïns'kykh tserkov u chotyr'okh tomakh*, vol. 1: *Ukraïns'ka pravoslavna tserkva* (Toronto, 1987), 717; Bohdan Liubomyrenko, *Z Khrystom v Ukraïni: Zapysky viruiuchoho za roky 1941–1943* (Winnipeg, 1973), 60.

109. Kabaida, "1941," 53.

110. See, for example, TsDAHOU, 166/3/248/29: V. Tverskoi, "Dorogie druz'ia," Kiev, n.d.; HIA-HURIP, box 23, no. 548 AD, B-6, fol. 5: editor of *Vinnyts'ki visti* [Mykhailo Zerov?], n.p., April 24, 1951. On the killings in the Left Bank village, see Sova, *Do istoriï bol'shevyts'koï diis'nosty*, 78.

111. S.-Chartoryis'kyi, *Vid Sianu po Krym*, 132–133, 139. See also Seleshko, *Vinnytsia*, 141–142.

112. On the incident in the Kremenets region, see A., "Z starykh lystiv," *Litopys Volyni* 3 (Winnipeg, 1956): 104–105. For the killings in Torchyn, see Leonid D—s'kyi, "Pokhoron u Luts'ku," *Litopys Volyni* 1 (Winnipeg, 1953): 72.

113. Spector, *Holocaust of Volhynian Jews*, 64–65, 67, 71.

114. BA-MA, RH 24-48/198: GFP Aussenkommando at the 48th Army Corps, "Betr.: Erschiessung von NKWD-Kommissaren und Funktionären," n.p., July 1, 1941.

115. Valia Petrenko, "Trahediia Dubens'koï Tiurmy (Spomyn)," *Samostiina Ukraïna* 1, nos. 5–6 (Chicago, June–July 1948): 18–19.

116. Oleksii Satsiuk, *Smertonostsi: Opovidannia (Na tli perezhytoho)* (Buenos Aires, 1947), 122. Compare BA-MA, RH 24-48/198: GFP Aussenkommando at the 48th Army Corps.

117. Andrzej Zbikowski, "Local Anti-Jewish Pogroms in the Occupied Territories of Eastern Poland, June–July 1941," in Lucjan Dobroszycki and Jeffrey Gurock, eds., *The Holocaust in the Soviet Union: Studies and Sources on the Destruction of the Jews in the Nazi-Occupied Territories of the USSR, 1941–1945* (Armonk, N.Y., 1993), 177.

118. *Ereignismeldung UdSSR* 28 (July 20, 1941): 7–8; A., "Z starykh lystiv," 104; Spector, *Holocaust of Volhynian Jews*, 68.

119. Abramenko, *Kyïvs'kyi protses*, 42; TsDAHOU, 1/23/685/32: Savchenko, deputy NKVD UkSSR, to D. R. Korniets, "Spets. soob. O polozhenii v g. Vinnitsa i Vinnitskoi oblasti," Borisoglebsk, January 26, 1943.

120. Sova, *Do istoriï bol'shevyts'koï diis'nosty*, 93–96.

121. Abramenko, *Kyïvs'kyi protses*, 34–35, 38, 40. See also, for example, N. Salata and H. H. Salata, author interviews; Serhiichuk, *OUN-UPA*, 341; TsDAHOU, 1/23/633/13: Serdiuk, "Politinformatsiï"; F. Pihido-Pravoberezhnyi, *"Velyka Vitchyzniana viina"* (Winnipeg, 1954), 162.

122. Ie. M. Moskovs'ka, author interview.

123. See M. H. Dubyk, comp., *Dovidnyk pro tabory, tiurmy ta hetto na okupovanii terytoriï Ukraïny (1941–1944)/Handbuch der Lager, Gefängnisse und Ghettos auf dem besetzten Territorium der Ukraine (1941–1944)* (Kiev, 2000).

3. The Holocaust of the Jews and Roma

1. Brenda Davis Lutz and James M. Lutz, "Gypsies as Victims of the Holocaust," *Holocaust and Genocide Studies* 9, no. 3 (1995): 346–359; Robert Melson, review of Guenther Lewy, *The Nazi Persecution of the Gypsies*, *Holocaust and Genocide Studies* 16, no. 1 (2002): 109–112.

2. TsDAVOV, 4620/3/243a/14: I. Zhitov, "Prikhod nemtsev v Kiev i ikh obeshchaniia," Kiev, November 1943; V. P. Kravchenko, author interview.

3. Michael Diment, *The Lone Survivor: A Diary of the Lukacze Ghetto and Svyniukhy, Ukraine* (New York, 1992), 76–78.

4. Mordechai Altshuler, *Soviet Jewry on the Eve of the Holocaust: A Social and Demographic Profile* (Jerusalem, 1998), 2.

5. Mykhailo Seleshko, *Vinnytsia: Spomyny perekladacha Komisiï doslidiv zlochyniv NKVD v 1937–1938* (New York, 1991), 87; UCEC, Pavlo Ternivs'kyi [Ivan Zhyhadlo], "Spohady emigranta" (n.p., 1945), 33; Sofiia Parfanovych, *U Kyïevi v 1940 rotsi* (Augsburg, Ger., 1950), 60.

6. Matthias Vetter, *Antisemiten und Bolschewiki: Zum Verhältnis von Sowjetsystem und Judenfeindschaft 1917–1939* (Berlin, 1995), 319–324, 345–347.

7. Ternivs'kyi, "Spohady emigranta," 36; Vitalii Bender, *Frontovi dorohy* (Toronto, 1987), 19 (on young Ukrainians); *Ereignismeldung UdSSR* 112 (October 13, 1941): 2–3; Jacob Gerstenfeld-Maltiel, *My Private War: One Man's Struggle to Survive the Soviets and the Nazis* (London, 1993), 218 (both on imprisonment).

8. Vetter, *Antisemiten*, 347; Benjamin Pinkus and Ingeborg Fleischhauer, *Die Deutschen in der Sowjetunion: Geschichte einer nationalen Minderheit im 20. Jahrhundert* (Baden-Baden, Ger., 1987), 202; Mordechai Altshuler, "Escape and Evacuation of Soviet Jews at the Time of the Nazi Invasion: Policies and

Realities," in Lucjan Dobroszycki and Jeffrey S. Gurock, eds., *The Holocaust in the Soviet Union: Studies and Sources on the Destruction of the Jews in the Nazi-Occupied Territories of the USSR, 1941–1945* (Armonk, N.Y., 1993), 84.

9. Antonina Khelemendyk-Kokot, *Kolhospne dytynstvo i nimets'ka nevolia: Spohady* (Toronto, 1989), 123.

10. Altshuler, "Escape and Evacuation," 97, 99.

11. Ibid., 101; TsDAVOV, 4620/3/2a/3: Gosplan, "Pasport goroda" for Kiev.

12. Altshuler, "Escape and Evacuation," 91 (the quotation), 90.

13. F. Pihido-Pravoberezhnyi, *"Velyka Vitchyzniana viina"* (Winnipeg, 1954), 108; HIA, B. I. Nicolaevsky collection, series no. 178, box 232, folder 10, fols. 62, 91: [Lev Vladimirovich] Dudin, "Velikii Mirazh: Sobytiia 1941–1947 godov v ponimanii sovetskogo cheloveka," n.p., 1947; HIA, B. I. Nicolaevsky collection, series 236, box 409, folder 19, fol. 40: Emigrant, "Nemtsy v Kieve: (Iz vospominanii ochevidtsa)," n.p., n.d.

14. Ben-Cion Pinchuk, "Soviet Media on the Fate of Jews in Nazi-Occupied Territory (1939–1941)," *Yad Vashem Studies* 11 (1976): 230–231 (the quotation); Anatolii Kuznetsov (A. Anatolii), *Babii iar: Roman-dokument* (New York, 1986), 141–142; F. P. Bogatyrchuk, *Moi zhiznennyi put' k Vlasovu i Prazhkomu manifestu* (San Francisco, 1978), 122; Altshuler, "Escape and Evacuation," 90.

15. V. Marchenko, "Sovetskaia vlast' i evrei v 1941–42 g.," *Vestnik Instituta po izucheniiu istorii i kul'tury SSSR*, no. 1 (Munich, 1951): 79.

16. Kravchenko, author interview. See also HIA-HURIP, box 23, no. 441 AD, B-6, fol. 2: [Konstantyn Shtepa], n.p., February 12, 1951; HIA, Alexander Dallin collection, box 8, folder 2, fol. 10: no. 1000 B-6, anonymous Kievan, Boston, August 1950.

17. Ilya Ehrenburg and Vasily Grossman, eds., *The Black Book: The Ruthless Murder of Jews by German-Fascist Invaders throughout the Temporarily-Occupied Regions of the Soviet Union and in the Death Camps of Poland during the War of 1941–1945* (New York, 1981), 14, 28 (for the quotation); TsDAVOV, 3206/1/29/ 1–3: Erich Koch, order on taxes, October 21, 1941.

18. Oleksii Satsiuk and Iurii Shul'mins'kyi, "Nedolia zhydiv u Dubni," *Litopys Volyni* 4 (1958): 74; HIA-HURIP, box 23, no. 548 AD, B-6, fol. 2: editor of the newspaper *Vinnyts'ki visti*, n.p., April 24, 1951.

19. See Dieter Pohl, "Schauplatz Ukraine: Der Massenmord an den Juden im Militärverwaltungsgebiet und im Reichskommissariat 1941–1943," in Norbert Frei et al., eds., *Ausbeutung, Vernichtung, Öffentlichkeit: Neue Studien zur nationalsozialistischen Lagerpolitik* (Munich, 2000), 135–173.

20. [Evgeniia Gural'nik], "Iama v Pavlovychakh," in David Zil'berman, ed., *I ty eto videl* (New York, 1989), 11–14.

21. For respective examples, see Barbara Baratz, *Flucht vor dem Schicksal: Holocaust-Erinnerungen aus der Ukraine 1941–1944* (Darmstadt, Ger., 1984), 49–50,

90–91; *Ereignismeldung UdSSR* 81 (September 12, 1941): 13. See also Dieter Pohl, "Ukrainische Hilfskräfte beim Mord an den Juden," in Gerhard Paul, ed., *Die Täter der Shoah: Fanatische Nationalsozialisten oder ganz normale Deutsche?* (Göttingen, Ger., 2000), 205–234.

22. Raul Hilberg, *The Destruction of the European Jews*, rev. ed., vol. 1 (New York, 1985), 314, citing *Ereignismeldung UdSSR* 88 (September 19, 1941); Gerald Reitlinger, *The Final Solution: The Attempt to Exterminate the Jews of Europe, 1939–1945*, 2d rev. and augmented ed. (London, 1968), 246 (the date).

23. Ernst Klee and Willi Dreßen, *"Gott mit uns": Der deutsche Vernichtungskrieg im Osten 1939–1945* (Frankfurt, 1989), 8, quoting *Ereignismeldung UdSSR* 119 (October 20, 1941).

24. "Interv"iu z 'Mizhkoiu', 'piatnadtsiatylitnim povstantsem z Polis'koï Sichi'," *Volyn'*, September 21, 1941, 3. See also Fritz Baade et al., comps., *Unsere Ehre heisst Treue: Kriegstagebuch des Kommandostabes Reichsführer SS. Tätigkeitsberichte der 1. und 2. SS-Inf.-Brigade und von Sonderkommandos der SS* (Vienna, 1965), 146.

25. *Haidamaka*, no. 11 (November 22, 1941), quoted in A. V. Kentii, *Narysy istoriï Orhanizatsiï Ukraïns'kykh Natsionalistiv v 1941–1942 rr.* (Kiev, 1999), 59.

26. Volodymyr Serhiichuk, *OUN-UPA v roky viiny: Novi dokumenty i materialy* (Kiev, 1996), 20; Hilberg, *Destruction*, vol. 1, 313–314, citing *Ereignismeldung UdSSR* 80 (September 11, 1941): 11.

27. Diment, *Lone Survivor*, 19 (the quotation), 112.

28. Bogatyrchuk, *Moi zhiznennyi put'*, 130 (the quotation); Pihido-Pravoberezhnyi, *"Velyka Vitchyzniana viina,"* 106–107; Emigrant, "Nemtsy v Kieve," 38.

29. A. Anatoli (Kuznetsov), *Babi Yar: A Document in the Form of a Novel* (London, 1970), 90, 92, slightly edited. See also Dudin, "Velikii Mirazh," 80; *Ereignismeldung UdSSR* 106 (October 7, 1941): 15. On Dudin's recollections, see "Velikii Mirazh," 82.

30. "TsDAHOU, 1/22/347/1: "Iz dnevnika uchitel'nitsy gor. Kieva L. Nartovoi."

31. Pihido-Pravoberezhnyi, *"Velyka Vitchyzniana viina,"* 108; Bogatyrchuk, *Moi zhiznennyi put'*, 131.

32. TsDAHOU, 166/3/244/2: Nadezhda Petrovna Konashko (Ukrainian born in 1913), Kiev, February 22, 1944; Bogatyrchuk, *Moi zhiznennyi put'*, 131.

33. Anatoli (Kuznetsov), *Babi Yar*, 94, 96, slightly edited; Kuznetsov, *Babii iar*, 95, 101.

34. Bogdan A. Martinenko, "Tragediia Bab'ego Iara: Rassekrechennye dokumenty svidetel'stvuiut," in Erhard Roy Wiehn, comp., *Die Schoáh von Babij Jar: Das Massaker deutscher Sonderkommandos an der jüdischen Bevölkerung von Kiew 1941 fünfzig Jahre danach zum Gedenken* (Konstanz, Ger., 1991), 365; Iurii Petrashevych, "Tini Babynoho iaru: Novi fakty i svidchennia ochevydtsiv," *Kyïv* no. 1 (1994): 97 (the quotation); Hartmut Rüß, "Wer war verantwortlich für das

Massaker von Babij Jar?" *Militärgeschichtliche Mitteilungen* 57, no. 2 (1998): 483, 489–490, 495; *Ereignismeldung UdSSR* 128 (November 3, 1941): 3.

35. TsDAVOV, 4620/3/281/2: Dina Mironovna Pronicheva (Jew born in Chernihiv in 1911), stenographic report of testimony, Kiev, April 24, 1946. Kahatna Street is now called Sim"ï Khokhlovykh Street.

36. Wiehn, *Die Schoáh*, 365–366 (the quotations); Petrashevych, "Tini," 98.

37. TsDAVOV, 4620/3/281/4: Pronicheva, testimony.

38. Ernst Klee et al., comps., *"Schöne Zeiten": Judenmord aus der Sicht der Täter und Gaffer* (Frankfurt am Main, 1988), 67.

39. Andrii Duda and Volodymyr Staryk, *Bukovyns'kyi Kurin': V boiakh za ukraïns'ku derzhavnist'*, 1918, 1941, 1944 (Chernivtsi, Ukr., 1995), 84, 86; Petro Voinovs'kyi, *Moie naivyshche shchastia: Spomyny* (Kiev, 1999), 254; F. L. Levitas, "Babyn Iar (1941–1943)," in S. Ia. Ielisavets'kyi, ed., *Katastrofa i opir ukraïns'koho ievreistva (1941–1944): Narysy z istoriï Holokostu i Oporu v Ukraïni* (Kiev, 1999), 102.

40. Wiehn, *Die Schoáh*, 366; Klee, *"Schöne Zeiten,"* 63 (mentions 150, 30, and 15 meters).

41. TsDAVOV, 4620/3/281/4–5: Pronicheva, testimony.

42. *Ereignismeldung UdSSR* 135 (November 19, 1941): 22; Pohl, "Schauplatz," 148–149.

43. TsDAVOV, 3206/1/69/5v: Erich Koch to the general, "main," and district commissars of the Volhynia-Podolia GB, Königsberg, September 5, 1941. Compare the Wehrmacht instructions at NA microcopy T-501, roll 5, frame 805: v. Roques, "Anordnung Abt. VII, Nr. 12," n.p., August 28, 1941.

44. Pohl, "Schauplatz," 159–163, 170; Dean, *Collaboration in the Holocaust: Crimes of the Local Police in Belorussia and Ukraine, 1941–44* (New York, 2000), 78–104.

45. Hilberg, *Destruction*, vol. 3, 1038.

46. For an example of a disagreement, see Diment, *Lone Survivor*, 80. Compare Shmuel Spector, *The Holocaust of Volhynian Jews, 1941–1944* (Jerusalem, 1990), 159, and see 223–227, 230 for thwarted resistance plans.

47. Spector, *Holocaust*, 165, 167.

48. Diment, *Lone Survivor*, 65, 80, 85, and, on the grain confiscation campaign, 96–97.

49. Spector, *Holocaust*, 214–217.

50. Ibid., 210, 195.

51. Pihido-Pravoberezhnyi, *"Velyka Vitchyzniana viina,"* 109.

52. DAKO, r-2356/8/9/76–77: I. A. Nenadkevych, head of the Department of Social Aid, to the city commissar, Kiev, August 4, 1942.

53. Amnon Ajzensztadt, *Endurance: Chronicles of Jewish Resistance* (Oakville, N.Y., 1987), esp. 52–53, 65–66, and 98–99.

54. Gerstenfeld-Maltiel, *My Private War*, esp. 243, 271, 275, 278, and 288.

55. Diment, *Lone Survivor*, 36, 83, 98, 107.

56. Ibid., 114, 123; see also 26, 33.

57. Vetter, *Antisemiten*, 252–253; Amir Weiner, *Making Sense of War: The Second World War and the Fate of the Bolshevik Revolution* (Princeton, N.J., 2001), 273.

58. Vetter, *Antisemiten*, 230, 333, 335–336, 358; Pihido-Pravoberezhnyi, *"Velyka Vitchyzniana viina,"* 107.

59. Vetter, *Antisemiten*, 60; Examples are DAKO, r-2412/2/199/103: Kievan parishioners to the Church Council in Kiev, 1941; DAKO, r-2209/1/21/115: parishioners in Khabne to the raion chief, April 4, 1942; DAKO, r-2107/1/130/1–1v, 5–5v and 131/26–27: letters to the authorities of the Bohuslav raion, early 1942.

60. NDB, collection "Afishy ta plakaty okupatsiinoho periodu," 241sp–243sp.

61. TsDAVOV, 3833/2/74/12v: *Ukraïna v zhydivs'kykh labetakh,* also cited in Weiner, *Making Sense of War*, 258; TsDAVOV, 3206/2/68/9 (on distribution).

62. "Zhydy budut' znyshcheni: Vyslovliuvannia Adol'fa Hitlera do starykh tovaryshiv po partiï," *Dzvin voli* (Bila Tserkva), March 29, 1942, 2, cited from Gosudarstvennyi arkhiv Rossiiskoi Federatsii (State Archives of the Russian Federation, Moscow), 8114/1/942/191.

63. *Ereignismeldung UdSSR* 37 (July 29, 1941): 6.

64. Ibid. 81 (September 12, 1941): 13.

65. Ibid. 112 (October 13, 1941): 2–3. See also Mstyslav Z. Chubai, *Reid orhanizatoriv OUN vid Popradu po Chorne More: (Iz zapysnyka roiovoho)* (Munich, 1952), 41.

66. *Ereignismeldung UdSSR* 47 (August 9, 1941): 10.

67. Ibid. 81 (September 12, 1941): 13–14, 21 (see also ibid. 125 (October 26, 1941): 5); 177 (March 6, 1942): 2; 135 (November 19, 1941): 17; 142 (December 5, 1941): 3.

68. TsDAVOV, 3206/1/26/27–42: "Teilbericht Politik über die Bereisung des Reichskommissariats mit Prof. v. Grünberg in der Zeit vom 13.8. bis 3.9.1042," Rivne, September 10, 1942.

69. NA microcopy T-120, roll 2533, frames E292555, E292557, E292549/13, E292549/17: Auslandsbriefprüfstelle, "Stimmungsbericht," Berlin, September 11, 1942, and "Stimmungsbericht," Berlin, November 11, 1942.

70. Baade, *Unsere Ehre heisst Treue*, 220, 228, 146.

71. [Gural'nik], "Iama v Pavlovychakh," 10.

72. *Ereignismeldung UdSSR* 81 (September 12, 1941): 14.

73. Halyna Lashchenko, "Povorot," *Samostiina Ukraïna* 10, no. 11(107) (New York, November 1957): 21–22.

74. Vasily Grossman, "Murder of the Jews in Berdichev," in Ehrenburg and Grossman, *Black Book*, 19.

75. Anatoli (Kuznetsov), *Babi Yar*, 96; Kuznetsov, *Babii iar*, 96.

76. Pihido-Pravoberezhnyi, *"Velyka Vitchyzniana viina,"* 109; Tat'iana Fesenko, *Povest' krivykh let* (New York, 1963), 75; TsDAVOV, 4620/3/243a/7: N. A. Prakhov, "Chto bylo v Kieve pri nemtsakh," Kiev, May 21, 1941 [*sic*].

77. Irina Khoroshunova, "Pervyi god voiny: Kievskie zapiski," *Iehupets'* 9 (Kiev, 2001): 57. (Also in Wiehn, *Die Schoáh*, 292–293.)

78. Ibid., 57–58, note of October 2, 1941.

79. TsDAHOU, 1/22/347/1–2: Nartova diary, note of October 29, 1941; International Court of Justice (The Hague), Nuremberg Trial archives, document 053-PS, fol. 4: Hptm Dr. Dr. [Hans] Koch, "Bericht 10. (abgeschlossen am 5. Oktober 1941)."

80. Martin C. Dean, "The German *Gendarmerie*, the Ukrainian *Schutzmannschaft* and the 'Second Wave' of Jewish Killings in Occupied Ukraine: German Policing at the Local Level in the Zhitomir Region, 1941–1944," *German History* 14, no. 2 (1996): 182; Ehrenburg and Grossman, *Black Book*, 57.

81. Khelemendyk-Kokot, *Kolhospne dytynstvo*, 136 (on Ukrainian girls), 137–138 (on reactions of the elderly).

82. Ehrenburg and Grossman, *Black Book*, 17, 28–29.

83. Ibid., 61; Spector, *Holocaust*, 203; Panas Khurtovyna [Mykhailo Podvorniak], *Pid nebom Volyni: (Voienni spomyny khrystyianyna)* (Winnipeg, 1952), 120–121; Wiehn, *Die Schoáh*, 811.

84. Lashchenko, "Povorot," *Samostiina Ukraïna* 11, no. 10(118) (Chicago, October 1958): 12. See also Emigrant, "Nemtsy v Kieve," 39.

85. Sheila Fitzpatrick, *Everyday Stalinism: Ordinary Life in Extraordinary Times: Soviet Russia in the 1930s* (New York, 1999), 213.

86. Compare *Ereignismeldung UdSSR* 127 (October 31, 1941): 4, and 135 (November 19, 1941): 17.

87. Bogatyrchuk, *Moi zhiznennyi put'*, 131; Kravchenko, author interview (the quotation).

88. Anatoli (Kuznetsov), *Babi Yar*, 98; Kuznetsov, *Babii iar*, 98.

89. Ternivs'kyi, "Spohady emigranta," 35–36 (misplaces the event in 1942); Mordechai Altshuler, "The Unique Features of the Holocaust in the Soviet Union," in Yaacov Ro'i, ed., *Jews and Jewish Life in Russia and the Soviet Union* (Ilford, Eng., 1995), 178.

90. TsDAHOU, 166/3/244/14: Iurii Mikhailovich Markovskii (Ukrainian born in 1904), Kiev, March 12, 1944. See also TsDAVOV, 3206/2/26/5: Hptm. [Hauptmann] Prof. Hans Koch, "Der Sowjet-Nachlass in der Ukraine. Stimmungs- und Erfahrungsbericht. Abgeschlossen 30. 9. 1941," n.p., n.d.; Ehrenburg and Grossman, *Black Book*, 28–29; Mordecai Paldiel, *The Path of the Righteous: Gentile Rescuers of Jews during the Holocaust* (Hoboken, N.J., 1993), 286.

91. *Ereignismeldung UdSSR* 106 (October 7, 1941): 13 (on the homeless); Dudin, "Velikii Mirazh," 84; Fesenko, *Povest'*, 75.

92. Gerstenfeld-Maltiel, *My Private War*, 218.

93. M. Philips Price, *Russia, Red or White: A Record of a Visit to Russia after Twenty-Seven Years* (London, n.d.), 60 (the first quotation); Weiner, *Making Sense of War*, 193; Mordechai Altshuler, "Antisemitism in Ukraine toward the End of the Second World War," *Jews in Eastern Europe* 3, no. 22 (Jerusalem, Winter 1993): 40–81, especially the translation on pp. 52–62 of TsDAHOU, 1/23/1363/1–14.

94. Weiner, *Making Sense of War*, 192; TsDAHOU, 1/23/2366/1–18v: eight documents dealing with the case; Vetter, *Antisemiten*, 160 (on the 1920s).

95. See also Boris Slutskii, *Zapiski o voine: Stikhotvoreniia i ballady* (St. Petersburg, 2000), 157. For a different evaluation of the influence of Nazi rule on anti-Semitism, see Weiner, *Making Sense of War*, 287, 289–290.

96. Hilberg, *Destruction*, vol. 1, 315.

97. Baratz, *Flucht vor dem Schicksal*, 51 (the quotation), 71. See also Philip Friedman, "Ukrainian-Jewish Relations during the Nazi Occupation," *YIVO Annual of Jewish Social Science* 12 (New York, 1958–1959): 276.

98. Baratz, *Flucht vor dem Schicksal*, 84.

99. Diment, *Lone Survivor*, 13, 35, 41–42, 52.

100. "Evropa zvil'niaiet'sia vid zhydiv," *Volyn'*, March 12, 1942, 2.

101. Diment, *Lone Survivor*, 94–95 (first quotation), 128 (on peasants' involvement), 200–201 (second quotation).

102. Ibid., 52.

103. Spector, *Holocaust*, 241.

104. Julia Alexandrow with Tommy French, *Flight from Novaa Salow: Autobiography of a Ukrainian Who Escaped Starvation in the 1930s under the Russians and Then Suffered Nazi Enslavement* (Jefferson, N.C., 1995), 62–63.

105. Karel C. Berkhoff and Marco Carynnyk, "The Organization of Ukrainian Nationalists and Its Attitude toward Germans and Jews: Iaroslav Stets'ko's 1941 *Zhyttiepys*," *Harvard Ukrainian Studies* 23, nos. 3–4 (1999): 149–184.

106. *Ereignismeldung UdSSR* 187 (March 30, 1942): 7 (on leaflets); M. I. [*sic*] Koval, "The Nazi Genocide of the Jews and the Ukrainian Population, 1941–1944," in Zvi Gitelman, ed., *Bitter Legacy: Confronting the Holocaust in the USSR* (Bloomington, Ind., 1997), 54–55.

107. Friedman, "Ukrainian-Jewish Relations," 287; Kenneth Slepyan, "The Soviet Partisan Movement and the Holocaust," *Holocaust and Genocide Studies* 14, no. 1 (2000): 1–27. See also NA microcopy T-78, roll 565, frame 322, translated without a source reference in "Selected Soviet Sources on the World War II Partisan Movement," in John A. Armstrong, ed., *Soviet Partisans in World War*

II (Madison, Wisc., 1964), 668. On Belarus, compare Leo Heiman, *I Was a Soviet Guerrilla* (London, 1959), 92, 122.

108. "Sviatyi oboviazok ukraïns'koho narodu," *Ukraïns'kyi holos*, June 21, 1942, 3; *Ukraïns'kyi holos*, February 14, 1943, 3.

109. *Ukraïns'kyi holos*, May 6, 1943, 3 (the quotation); "Osvidchennia Vysokopreosviashchenishoho Administratora Sv. Pravoslavnoï Tserkvy v Ukraïni u Raikhskomisariiati," *Volyn'*, February 12, 1942, 1; Christoph Kleßmann, "Nationalsozialistische Kirchenpolitik und Nationalitätenfrage im Generalgouvernement (1939–1945)," *Jahrbücher für Geschichte Osteuropas* 18, no. 4 (1970): 596.

110. DAKO, r-2412/2/199/74: Kiev, June 22, 1942.

111. Weiner, *Making Sense of War*, 268.

112. NDB, collection "Lystivky okupatsiinoho periodu," 2602lf, 2603lf: Iepyskop Panteleimon, "Proty anarkhiï zloho dukha," n.p., n.d. (Also at TsDAHOU, 1/22/390/12–13v.)

113. I am not so certain of this as Spector, *Holocaust*, 243.

114. For an example, see DAKO, r-2329/2/2/78: "Oholoshennia," [July 1942].

115. Friedman, "Ukrainian-Jewish Relations," 294, n. 80.

116. Ehrenburg and Grossman, *Black Book*, 10–11, 373–380.

117. Yakov Suslensky, *They Were True Heroes: About the Participation of Ukrainian Citizens in the Rescuing of Jews from Nazi Genocide* (Kiev, 1995), 116. See also Frank Golczewski, "Die Revision eines Klischees: Die Rettung von verfolgten Juden im Zweiten Weltkrieg durch Ukrainer," in Wolfram Benz and Juliane Wetzel, eds., *Solidarität und Hilfe für Juden während der NS-Zeit*, vol. 2 (Berlin, 1998), 9–82.

118. On baptism, see NA microcopy T-501, roll 33, frames 391, 397–398: Feldkommandantur (V) 239, monthly reports dated October 24 and November 24, 1941; *Ereignismeldung UdSSR* 177 (March 6, 1942): 3. On hanging, see Feliks Levitas and Mark Shimanovskii, *Babii iar: Stranitsy tragedii* (Kiev, 1991), 41. For an example of an adoption, see Suslensky, *They Were True Heroes*, 80–81.

119. Wiehn, *Die Schoáh*, 810–812. See also ibid., 251.

120. Spector, *Holocaust*, 245.

121. Baratz, *Flucht vor dem Schicksal*, 82–84, 113–114, 121.

122. Ehrenburg and Grossman, *Black Book*, 355–357; Mordecai Paldiel, *The Path of the Righteous: Gentile Rescuers of Jews during the Holocaust* (Hoboken, N.J., 1993), 277–279.

123. N. F. Bondarenko, author interview. Bondarenko's family was involved.

124. [Gural'nik], "Iama v Pavlovychakh," 15–26.

125. Spector, *Holocaust*, 244; M. P. [Mykhailo Podvorniak], "Vid smerty do zhyttia

(Spohad)," *Litopys Volyni* 7 (Winnipeg, 1964): 91–96; Khurtovyna, *Pid nebom Volyni*, 111–113, 118–123; Spector, *Holocaust*, 244, 371; Friedman, "Ukrainian-Jewish Relations," 294, n. 82; Paldiel, *Path of the Righteous*, 273–277.

126. Spector, *Holocaust*, 249–250, 252. Compare Nahum Kohn and Howard Roiter, *A Voice from the Forest: Memoirs of a Jewish Partisan* (New York, 1980), 34–35.

127. On views of ethnic Germans, see Ingeborg Fleischhauer, *Das Dritte Reich und die Deutschen in der Sowjetunion* (Stuttgart, 1983), 92–93, 108; Meir Buchsweiler, *Volksdeutsche in der Ukraine am Vorabend und Beginn des Zweiten Weltkriegs—ein Fall doppelter Loyalität?* (Gerlingen, Ger., 1984), 242–243.

128. TsDAHOU, 166/3/246/32: Mikhail Ivanovich Sokolov, [Vinnytsia?], January 20, 1946.

4. Prisoners of War

1. HIA, B. I. Nicolaevsky collection, series no. 178, box 232, folder 10, fols. 168–169: [Lev Vladimirovich] Dudin, "Velikii Mirazh: Sobytiia 1941–1947 godov v ponimanii sovetskogo cheloveka," n.p., 1947.

2. Compare Christian Streit, *Die Wehrmacht und die sowjetischen Kriegsgefangenen 1941–1945* (Stuttgart, 1978), 137, 189; S. P. MacKenzie, "The Treatment of Prisoners of War in World War II," *Journal of Modern History* 66, no. 3 (1994): 507.

3. Jörg Osterloh, *Sowjetische Kriegsgefangene 1941–1945 im Spiegel nationaler and internationaler Untersuchungen: Forschungsüberblick und Bibliographie* (Dresden, 1995); Christian Streit, "Sowjetische Kriegsgefangene in deutscher Hand: Ein Forschungsüberblick," in Klaus-Dieter Müller et al., eds., *Die Tragödie der Gefangenschaft in Deutschland und in der Sowjetunion 1941–1956* (Cologne, 1998), 281–290.

4. For example, Joachim Hoffmann, *Stalins Vernichtungskrieg 1941–1945*, 2d expanded ed. (Munich, 1995), 89.

5. Christian Streit, "Soviet Prisoners of War," in Israel Gutman, ed., *Encyclopedia of the Holocaust*, vol. 3 (New York, 1990), 1192–1195; Christian Gerlach, "Die Ausweitung der deutschen Massenmorde in den besetzten sowjetischen Gebieten im Herbst 1941: Überlegungen zur Vernichtungspolitik gegen Juden und sowjetische Kriegsgefangene," in his *Krieg, Ernährung, Völkermord: Forschungen zur deutschen Vernichtungspolitk im Zweiten Weltkrieg* (Hamburg, 1998), 11, 36; Reinhard Otto, *Wehrmacht, Gestapo und sowjetische Kriegsgefangene im deutschen Reichsgebiet 1941/42* (Munich, 1998), 272. See also Christian Gerlach, *Kalkulierte Morde: Die deutsche Wirtschafts- und Vernichtungspolitik in Weißrußland 1941 bis 1944* (Hamburg, 1999), 774–859.

6. *Webster's Third New International Dictionary of the English Language, Unabridged*, vol. 2 (Chicago, 1981), 1388, and vol. 1, 947. Compare Frank Chalk

and Kurt Jonassohn, *The History and Sociology of Genocide: Analyses and Case Studies* (New Haven, Conn., 1990), 23–26.

7. Streit, *Wehrmacht*, 240.

8. Irina Khoroshunova, "Pervyi god voiny. Kievskie zapiski," *Iehupets'* 9 (Kiev, 2001): 50 (on survivors' emotional state); TsDAHOU, 1/22/123/68: Petr Timofeevich Berdnik, "Kharakteristika polozhenii na okkupirovannoi territorii" n.p., n.d.

9. Ernst Klee and Willi Dreßen, *"Gott mit uns": Der deutsche Vernichtungskrieg im Osten 1939–1945* (Frankfurt, 1989), 29; *Ereignismeldung UdSSR* 47 (August 9, 1941): 9; *Ereignismeldung UdSSR* 128 (November 3, 1941): 3, published in Norbert Müller [et al.], ed., *Die faschistische Okkupationspolitik in den zeitweilig besetzten Gebieten der Sowjetunion (1941–1944)* (Berlin, 1991), 210.

10. Examples are in F. Pihido-Pravoberezhnyi, *"Velyka Vitchyzniana viina"* (Winnipeg, 1954), 85.

11. Streit, *Wehrmacht*, 91, 100, 254.

12. Alexander Dallin, *German Rule in Russia, 1941–1945: A Study of Occupation Policies*, 2d ed. (Boulder, Colo., 1981), 69.

13. Streit, *Wehrmacht*, 98.

14. Ibid., 49–50, 106, 318, n. 128; Müller, *Die faschistische Okkupationspolitik*, 169–171. Emphasis in the original.

15. Leonid Volynskii, "Skvoz' noch': K istorii odnoi bezymiannoi mogily," *Novyi mir* 29, no. 1 (1963): 119–124.

16. Streit, *Wehrmacht*, 254. Compare Alfred Streim, *Sowjetische Gefangene in Hitlers Vernichtungskrieg: Berichte und Dokumente 1941–1945* (Heidelberg, 1982), 96, n. 49.

17. Volynskii, "Skvoz' noch'," 125; Streit, *Wehrmacht*, 164; Ilya Ehrenburg and Vasily Grossman, eds., *The Black Book: The Ruthless Murder of Jews by German-Fascist Invaders throughout the Temporarily-Occupied Regions of the Soviet Union and in the Death Camps of Poland during the War of 1941–1945* (New York, 1981), 546–547.

18. Shmuel Krakowski, "Death Marches," in *Encyclopedia of the Holocaust*, vol. 1, 348–354.

19. On the shooting of slow-marching prisoners, see Streit, *Wehrmacht*, 171; Klee and Dreßen, *"Gott mit uns,"* 140. On not registering prisoner names, see Gerlach, "Die Ausweitung der deutschen Massenmorde," 24.

20. Streit, *Wehrmacht*, 152, 167, 171, 98; the full text of Rosenberg's letter is in *Trial of the Major War Criminals before the International Military Tribunal* [TMWC], vol. 25 (Nuremberg, 1949), 156–161.

21. Pihido-Pravoberezhnyi, *"Velyka Vitchyzniana viina,"* 138. See also Panas Khurtovyna [Mykhailo Podvorniak], *Pid nebom Volyni: (Voienni spomyny khrystyianyna)* (Winnipeg, 1952), 105–106; Ulas Samchuk, *Na bilomu koni:*

Spomyny i vrazhennia (Winnipeg, 1972), 242; Halyna V"iun, *Pid znakom Chervonoho Khresta v Poltavi, 1941–42 rr.: Spohad-zvit dlia istoriï* ([Neu-Ulm, Ger.], 1973), 8.

22. Volynskii, "Skvoz' noch'," 125–126.

23. Ibid., 126–128.

24. See Chapter 5.

25. Volynskii, "Skvoz' noch'," 127; TsDAHOU, 166/3/243/114: Vera Fedorovna Bogdanova ([Russian?] born in 1911), n.p., January 20, 1946.

26. Julia Alexandrow with Tommy French, *Flight from Novaa Salow: Autobiography of a Ukrainian Who Escaped Starvation in the 1930s under the Russians and Then Suffered Nazi Enslavement* (Jefferson, N.C., 1995), 56.

27. Walther Bienert, *Russen und Deutsche: Was für Menschen sind das? Berichte, Bilder und Folgerungen aus dem Zweiten Weltkrieg* (Stein am Rhein, Switz., 1990), 57–58.

28. Halyna Lashchenko, "Povorot," *Samostiina Ukraïna* 11, no. 11(119) (Chicago, November 1958): 13. See also TsDAHOU, 166/3/243/65. For evidence of a change in treatment, see I. A. Lugin, *Polglotka svobody* (Paris, 1987), 174.

29. Khoroshunova, "Pervyi god voiny," 52.

30. Gerhard Kegel, *In den Stürmen unseres Jahrhunderts: Ein deutscher Kommunist über sein ungewöhnliches Leben* (Berlin, 1984), 302, 305–307.

31. V. P. Kravchenko and K. Ia. Hrynevych, author interviews; HIA, Alexander Dallin collection, box 8, folder 2, fol. 9: no. 1000, anonymous Kievan, Boston, August 1950; HIA, B. I. Nicolaevsky collection, series no. 236, box 409, folder 19, fol. 52: Emigrant [pseud.], "Nemtsy v Kieve: (Iz vospominanii ochevidtsa)."

32. Khroshunova, "Pervyi god voiny," 59 (quotation); TsDAHOU, 166/3/243/43v: Aleksei Mikhailovich Bashkulat (Ukrainian born in 1909), Kiev, February 28, 1944; TsDAHOU, 166/3/244/22: Iurii Mikhailovich Markovskii (Ukrainian born in 1904), Kiev, March 12, 1944.

33. Liudmyla Ivchenko, "Ukraïns'kyi Chervonyi Khrest u Kyievi (1941–1942)," in Modest Ripeckyj, ed., *Medychna opika v UPA*, which is *Litopys UPA*, vol. 23 (Toronto, 1992), 39. A pioneering study on the Hungarian military and brutality against civilians is Truman O. Anderson, "A Hungarian *Vernichtungskrieg?* Hungarian Troops and the Soviet Partisan War in Ukraine, 1942," *Militärgeschichtliche Mitteilungen* 58 (1999): 345–366.

34. NA microcopy T-501, roll 278, frames 1105–1106, 1108: German translations of letters.

35. TsDAHOU, 166/3/246/29–30: Mikhail Ivanovich Sokolov, [Vinnytsia?], January 20, 1946.

36. Klee and Dreßen, "*Gott mit uns*," 37.

37. TsDAHOU, 1/22/391/16: Mikhail Mikh. Skirda [et al.], "Otchet o podpol'noi partiinoi rabote i partizanskoi bor'be v Kirovogradskoi oblasti (avgust 1941 goda–mart 1944 goda)," n.d.

38. Khoroshunova, "Pervyi god voiny," 54, 58; Feliks Levitas and Mark Shimanovskii, *Babii iar: Stranitsy tragedii* (Kiev, 1991), 33–34.

39. TsDAHOU, 1/22/347/6: "Iz dnevnika uchitel'nitsy gor. Kieva L. Nartovoi." Compare TsDAHOU, 166/3/243/43: Bashkulat; TsDAVOV, 4620/3/243a/59: Professor N. A. Shepelevskii, "Prebyvanie nemtsev v Kieve," n.p., n.d.

40. Mykhailo Seleshko, *Vinnytsia: Spomyny perekladacha Komisiï doslidiv zlochyniv NKVD v 1937–1938* (New York, 1991), 113.

41. Gerlach, "Die Ausweitung der deutschen Massenmorde," 45; Wolodymyr Kosyk, *L'Allemagne national-socialiste et l'Ukraine* (Paris, 1986), 161; Leonid Abramenko, ed., *Kyïvs'kyi protses: Dokumenty i materialy* (Kiev, 1995), map between pp. 176 and 177.

42. On the special orders and reaction of camp police, see Reinhard Rürup, ed., *Der Krieg gegen die Sowjetunion: Eine Dokumentation* (Berlin, 1991), 110–111; Streim, *Sowjetische Gefangene*, 16, 32, 34, 145; Iaroslav Haivas, *Koly kinchalasia epokha* (n.p., 1964), 54. For more on the camp police, consult Streit, *Wehrmacht*, 181; Streim, *Sowjetische Gefangene*, 145.

43. TsDAHOU, 1/22/122/84: Motel'e, "O moem partizanskom otriade 'Pobeda ili smert'," [after October 16, 1941]. Compare *Ereignismeldung UdSSR* 37 (July 29, 1941): 7.

44. Motel'e, "O moem partizanskom otriade," 81–82. On an exception, in the Vinnytsia camp, see Streit, *Wehrmacht*, 101–103.

45. Streit, *Wehrmacht*, 143–144, 161.

46. Ibid., 145, 154.

47. Ibid., 150.

48. Gerd R. Ueberschär, comp., "Ausgewählte Dokumente," in Gerd R. Ueberschär and Wolfgang Wette, eds., *"Unternehmen Barbarossa": Der deutsche Überfall auf die Sowjetunion 1941: Berichte, Analysen, Dokumente* (Paderborn, Ger., 1984), 362; Gerlach, "Die Ausweitung der deutschen Massenmorde," 41–42.

49. Streit, *Wehrmacht*, 161–162.

50. *TMWC*, vol. 25, 156–161; Ueberschär, "Ausgewählte Dokumente," 399–400; Klee and Dreßen, *"Gott mit uns,"* 142–147.

51. Borys Lewytzkyj, *Die Sowjetukraine 1944–1963* (Cologne, 1964), 398, n. 9 (quotation); TsDAHOU, 166/3/244/56: I. Kuzenko (Ukrainian born in 1916), Kiev, October 29, 1946.

52. *TMWC*, vol. 25, 156–161; Ueberschär, "Ausgewählte Dokumente," 399–400; Klee and Dreßen, *"Gott mit uns,"* 142–147.

53. Natalia Iakhnenko, *Vid biura do Brygidok: Trokhy spohadiv z 1939–1941 rokiv, L'viv* (Munich, 1986), 249.

54. Anatolii Kuznetsov (A. Anatolii), *Babii iar: Roman-dokument* (New York, 1986), 179–180.

55. For the Fastiv camp incident, see RGASPI, 17/125/52/84: Fitin of the 1st

upravlenie of the NKVD to Shcherbakov, "O polozhenii v raionakh, okkupirovannykh protivnikom," Moscow, September 24, 1941. On the transit camp, see Lashchenko, "Povorot," 13.

56. Arigon Iron, "V nimets'kim poloni (Spohady)," *Visti Bratstva kol. Voiakiv 1 UD UNA*, 5, nos. 1–2 (Munich, 1954): 12–14, and nos. 3–4 (1954): 19–21.

57. Motel'e, "O moem partizanskom otriade," 83.

58. Ehrenburg and Grossman, *Black Book*, 386.

59. Volynskii, "Skvoz' noch'," 128.

60. V"iun, *Pid znakom Chervonoho Khresta*, 17 (German guards); Iron, "V nimets'kim poloni"; Kuznetsov, *Babii iar*, 182 (camp police).

61. Streit, *Wehrmacht*, 133; Gerlach, "Die Ausweitung der deutschen Massenmorde," 45.

62. TsDAHOU, 166/3/243/114, 116: Bogdanova.

63. TsDAHOU, 1/22/123/68: Berdnik; Pihido-Pravoberezhnyi, "Velyka Vitchyzniana viina," 141; and on Khorol, see, for example, Danylo Shumuk, *Life Sentence: Memoirs of a Ukrainian Political Prisoner* (Edmonton, 1984), 43–50.

64. Klee and Dreßen, "Gott mit uns," 141.

65. Streit, *Wehrmacht*, 152. See also, on the camps in Rivne, Klee and Dreßen, "Gott mit uns," 139; BA-MA, RW 2/149, fols. 441–473.

66. Klee and Dreßen, "Gott mit uns," 142.

67. Hryhorii Stetsiuk, *Nepostavlenyi pam"iatnyk: (Spohady)* ([Winnipeg], 1988), 33.

68. See, for example, Pihido-Pravoberezhnyi, "Velyka Vitchyzniana viina," 141. See also *Meldungen* 47 (March 29, 1943): 12, 19.

69. TsDAHOU, 166/3/243/115: Bogdanova. See also HIA-HURIP, box 22, no. 32 AD, B-6, fol. 8: anonymous informant, n.p., October 7, 1950.

70. TsDAHOU, 166/3/246/9–14: Mikhail Nikolaevich Sviridovskii (born in 1908), Kiev, March 3, 1944 (on Boryspil'); TsDAVOV, 3206/2/27/26: RKU *Lagebericht* for December 1941; Motel'e, "O moem partizanskom otriade," 83; Iron, "V nimets'kim poloni," 20 (on graves); *Meldungen* 43 (February 26, 1943): 17.

71. TsDAHOU, 1/22/347/6: Nartova diary, note of March 19, 1942. For similar comments see TsDAHOU, 166/3/248/31: V. Tverskoi, "Dorogie druz'ia," Kiev, n.d.

72. TsDAHOU, 1/22/347/17: Nartova diary. See also, on Zhytomyr, Motel'e, "O moem partizanskom otriade," 84.

73. TsDAVOV, 3206/5/15/489: RKU *Lagebericht* for September and October 1942; TsDAVOV, 3206/4/6/40: Dr. Ackermann for Wirtschaftsinspektion Süd, Chefgruppe La, to the Wirtschaftkommandos, September 27, 1941; S. Slavko, "Het' z 'internatsionalizmom' v pytanniakh shliubu," *Ukraïns'kyi holos* (Proskuriv), December 21, 1941, 2.

74. Streit, *Wehrmacht*, 185.

75. Streim, *Sowjetische Gefangene*, 119–128.

76. Raul Hilberg, *The Destruction of the European Jews*, vol. 3, rev. ed. (New York, 1985), 898, n. 23; Müller, *Die faschistische Okkupationspolitik*, 200, 216; Ueberschär, "Ausgewählte Dokumente," 385.

77. TsDAVOV, 3206/1/111/53: Der Reichskommissar fuer die Ukraine, II c 4, Im Auftrag gez. Schreiber, "Betrifft: Entlassung von Ukrainern aus der Kriegsgefangenschaft," Rivne, December 15, 1941.

78. Motel'e, "O moem partizanskom otriade," 84.

79. Pihido-Pravoberezhnyi, "*Velyka Vitchyzniana viina*," 83, 123, 129; M. Demydenko, author interview; HIA-HURIP, box 32, no. 121 AD, B-6, fol. 16: electrician from Kherson, n.p., November 28–29, 1950.

80. See, for example, DAKO, r-2209/1/2/119–120: woman from the village of Stebly to a camp commandant, December 15, 1941, and statement by the elder and five others; Motel'e, "O moem partizanskom otriade," 84; F. P. Bogatyrchuk, *Moi zhiznennyi put' k Vlasovu i Prazhkomu manifestu* (San Francisco, 1978), 132.

81. Motel'e, "O moem partizanskom otriade," 84; UCEC: Pavlo Ternivs'kyi [Ivan Zhyhadlo], "Spohady emigranta" (n.p., 1945), 24; TsDAHOU, 1/22/117/33: A. S. Koziura and V. R. Drolle, "Kopiia. Zam. nachal'niku 4-go Otdela NKVD USSR maioru tov. Kniazevu," November 12, 1941; Ehrenburg and Grossman, *Black Book*, 387–388.

82. Khoroshunova, "Pervyi god voiny," 53, 56. See also Kuznetsov, *Babii iar*, 182–183.

83. On the auxiliary police, see John A. Armstrong, *Ukrainian Nationalism*, 3d ed. (Englewood, Colo., 1990), 67; Vasyl' Veryha, *Vtraty OUN v chasi Druhoï Svitovoï viiny abo "Zdobudesh ukraïns'ku derzhavu abo zhynesh u borot'bi za neï"* (Toronto, 1991), 149; Motel'e, "O moem partizanskom otriade," 82–83. On the Free Cossacks, see TsDAHOU, 1/23/115/28 and 1/23/124/27–28, 76–77: three NKVD reports to N. S. Khrushchev, September and October 1942; Volodymyr Serhiichuk, [comp.], *OUN-UPA v roky viiny: Novi dokumenty i materialy* (Kiev, 1996), 349; Aleksandr Reent and Aleksandr Lysenko, "Ukrainians in Armed Formations of the Warring Sides during World War II," *Journal of Slavic Military Studies* 10, no. 1 (1997): 226.

84. Dallin, *German Rule in Russia*, 535–536; Timothy Mulligan, *The Politics of Illusion and Empire: German Occupation Policy in the Soviet Union, 1942–1943* (New York, 1988), 148.

85. Ivchenko, "Ukraïns'kyi Chervonyi Khrest," 43, 45; *Ereignismeldung UdSSR* 191 (April 10, 1942): 39.

86. DAKO, r-2209/1/22/132: Red Cross leader Fedir Bohatyrchuk to a district commissar, January 16, 1942; DAKO, r-2209/1/22/131: raion chief Okhrimenko to all village elders of the Khabne raion, January 29, 1942. Compare Bogatyrchuk, *Moi zhiznennyi put'*, 132.

87. DAKO, r-2356/1/58/33–34: Bohatyrchuk to Mayor Bahazii, November 26, 1941; DAKO, r-2356/15/21/1: anonymous "Dopovidna Zapyska," March 15, 1942; Lashchenko, "Povorot," 13.

88. Bogatyrchuk, *Moi zhiznennyi put'*, 132–134; Ivchenko, "Ukraïns'kyi Chervonyi Khrest," 41; DAKO, r-2679/1/1/26 and r-2145/1/1/17: letters by raion chiefs.

89. DAKO, r-2356/1/58/33–34: Bohatyrchuk to Mayor Bahazii, November 26, 1941; DAKO, r-2356/17/1: letters.

90. Bogatyrchuk, *Moi zhiznennyi put'*, 134–135; Ivchenko, "Ukraïns'kyi Chervonyi Khrest," 47–49.

91. DAKO, r-2356/15/21/1: "Dopovidna Zapyska."

92. Ivchenko, "Ukraïns'kyi Chervonyi Khrest," 47.

93. V"iun, *Pid znakom Chervonoho Khresta*, 9–10, 12–15. See also TsDAHOU, 1/23/527/9–10: NKVD to D. S. Korotchenko, "Dokladnaia zapiska," Kharkiv, October 26, 1943, also in Serhiichuk, *OUN-UPA*, 99–101.

94. V"iun, *Pid znakom Chervonoho Khresta*, 16, 18, 20–25.

95. Ibid., 17, 26–27, 28.

96. Ibid., 15, 32–36, 41. For the Red Cross organization in Rivne, see Samchuk, *Na bilomu koni*, 206–207; Khurtovyna, *Pid nebom Volyni*, 106.

97. V"iun, *Pid znakom Chervonoho Khresta*, 14, 26, 36. Compare Ivchenko, "Ukraïns'kyi Chervonyi Khrest," 44.

98. Streim, *Sowjetische Gefangene*, 161.

99. Khurtovyna, *Pid nebom Volyni*, 106; Lugin, *Polglotka svobody*, 173 (the quotation).

100. M. V. Koval' and N. M. Lemeshchuk, "Soprotivlenie sovetskikh voennoplennykh fashizmu na vremenno okkupirovannoi territorii Ukrainy," *Istoriia SSSR*, no. 3 (1971): 116–117.

101. Ibid., 118, citing TsDAHOU, 166/2/221/214–215.

102. *Meldungen* 19 (September 4, 1942): 6.

103. V"iun, *Pid znakom Chervonoho Khresta*, 9.

104. *Ukraïns'kyi holos*, July 2, 1942, 1; Ulas Samchuk, *Na koni voronomu: Spomyny i vrazhennia* (Winnipeg, 1975), 196; *Die deutsche Zivilverwaltung in den ehemaligen besetzten Ostgebieten (UdSSR)*, vol. 2 (Ludwigsburg, Ger., 1968), 289, 306, 327, 336.

105. Volynskii, "Skvoz' noch'," 137; Pihido-Pravoberezhnyi, "*Velyka Vitchyzniana viina*," 155; O. M. Kutsenko, author interview.

106. See, for example, DAKO, r-2145/1/1/16: Liashchenko, chief of the Borodianka raion, to a village elder, December 23, 1941.

107. Pihido-Pravoberezhnyi, "*Velyka Vitchyzniana viina*," 155; TsDAHOU, 166/3/246/92: Nikolai Makarovich Kharchenko (born in 1906), [Melitopol'?], January 22, 1946.

108. TsDAVOV, 3206/5/15/268–269, 319: RKU *Lageberichte* for February 1942 and

March 1942; Kosyk, *L'Allemagne national-socialiste*, 162. I have rounded the figures.

109. Shmuel Krakowski and Yoav Gelber, "Jewish Prisoners of War," in *Encyclopedia of the Holocaust*, vol. 3, 1189.

110. MacKenzie, "Treatment of Prisoners of War," 510–511.

111. Streit, *Wehrmacht*, 161, 169–170, 240; Omer Bartov, *Hitler's Army: Soldiers, Nazis, and War in the Third Reich* (New York, 1991), 86–89; Christopher R. Browning, *Ordinary Men: Reserve Police Battalion 101 and the Final Solution in Poland* (New York, 1993).

5. Life in the Countryside

1. Wilhelm Tieke, *Ein ruheloser Marsch war unser Leben: Kriegsfreiwillig 1940–1945* (Osnabrück, Ger., 1977), 52; Walther Bienert, *Russen und Deutsche: Was für Menschen sind das? Berichte, Bilder und Folgerungen aus dem Zweiten Weltkrieg* (Stein am Rhein, Switz., 1990), 24.

2. Volodymyr Serhiichuk, [comp.], *OUN-UPA v roky viiny: Novi dokumenty i materialy* (Kiev, 1996), 252–253; NA microcopy T-501, roll 33, frame 389: Feldkommandantur (V)239, Abt. VII Az. 029, "Monatsbericht der Abteilung VII für die Zeit vom 15.9.–15.10.41," [Kremenchuk], October 24, 1941.

3. NA microcopy T-501, roll 5, frame 849: Bfh.rückw.H.Geb.Süd, Abt. VII/174/41 to OKH, "Verwaltungsmässige Verhältnisse im rückw. Heeresgebiet Süd," Headquarters, September 7, 1941; NA microcopy T-501, roll 33, frame 1099: [Commander of Rear Army Area South,] "Tätigkeitsbericht der Abt. VI vom 1.–30.10.1941," n.p., n.d.

4. RGASPI, 17/125/52/48, 51: Fitin, nachal'nik 1 upravleniia NKVD SSSR to Shcherbakov, "Spetsoobshchenie o polozhenii v raionakh, ekkupirovannykh [sic] protivnikom," Moscow, September 6, 1941.

5. On willing women, see HIA, B. I. Nicolaevsky collection, series no. 236, box 409, folder 19: Emigrant, "Nemtsy v Kieve: (Iz vospominanii ochevidtsa)," n.p., n.d., fol. 21. Compare TsDAVOV, 3206/2/26/10–11: Hptm. Prof. Hans Koch, "Der Sowjet-Nachlass in der Ukraine. Stimmungs- und Erfahrungsbericht. Abgeschlossen 30. 9. 1941." On army brothels, consult TsDAHOU, 1/22/123/15: "Razvedyvatel'naia svodka Ukrainskogo shtaba partizan. dvizheniia n. 12 po sostoianiiu na 14.IX-1942 g.," n.p., September 16, 1942 (on age); HIA-HURIP, box 22, no. 67AD, fols. 4, 6: anonymous informant, Munich, October 20–21, 27, 1950; HIA-HURIP, box 22, no. 96AD, B-6, fol. 2: anonymous Orthodox priest, n.p., November 15, 1950; HIA-HURIP, box 23, no. 102 AD, B-6, fol. 11: anonymous informant, n.p., November 17, 1950; O. Iaroslavs'kyi [Lev Chaikovs'kyi?], "Vid Sianu po Dinets' (Z spohadiv perekladacha)," *Visti Bratstva kol. Voiakiv I UD UNA*, 7, nos. 7–8 (69–70) (Munich, July–August 1956): 19; Siegfried von

Vegesack, *Als Dolmetscher im Osten: Ein Erlebnisbericht aus den Jahren 1942–43* (Hannover, 1965), 88, 262.

6. On Germans, see Alexander Werth, *Russia at War, 1941–1945* (New York, 1965), 722; Ivan Maistrenko, *Istoriia moho pokolinnia: Spohady uchasnyka revoliutsiinykh podii v Ukraïni* (Edmonton, 1985), 337; Serhiichuk, *OUN-UPA*, 335. On Hungarians and Romanians, see *Ereignismeldung UdSSR* 81 (September 12, 1941): 18–19, and 133 (November 14, 1941): 32; Mykola S.-Chartoryis'kyi, *Vid Sianu po Krym: (Spomyny uchasnyka III Pokhidnoï Grupy-Pivden')* (New York, 1951), 154, 158, 171–172, 197; Zynovii Matla, *Pivdenna pokhidna hrupa* (Munich, 1952), 28; NA microcopy T-501, roll 278, frames 1121–1122: Wirtschaftskommando Ostrowo, Staffel 15 to D.V.K. 1 (3.rum.Armee), n.p., September 12, 1941.

7. For the flour-stealing incident, see TsDAHOU, 1/22/177/92: Mikh. Stepanovich Kolesikin, "Ob"iasnenie," November 25, 1941. On suspected partisans and saboteurs, see F. Pihido-Pravoberezhnyi, *"Velyka Vitchyzniana viina"* (Winnipeg, 1954), 121–122. On the torture and killing in Khaniv, consult TsDAHOU, 1/22/118/65: E. A. Sidorenko to Political Department of the 21st Army, n.p., December 13, 1941. For the atrocities in Obolon', see TsDAHOU, 1/23/599/29: "Akt," Obolon', October 3, 1943.

8. Pihido-Pravoberezhnyi, *"Velyka Vitchyzniana viina,"* 122.

9. Koch, "Der Sowjet-Nachlass," 1 (verso).

10. Mykhailo Hartymiv, "Zemleiu ukraïns'koiu . . . ," in Kost' Mel'nyk, Oleh Lashchenko, and Vasyl' Veryha, eds., *Na zov Kyieva: Ukraïns'kyi natsionalizm u II Svitovii Viini. Zbirnyk stattei, spohadiv i dokumentiv* (Toronto, 1985), 119; Ia. Shumelda, "Pokhid OUN na skhid," in *Orhanizatsiia Ukraïns'kykh Natsionalistiv, 1929–1954: Zbirnyk stattei u 25-littia OUN* ([Paris], 1955), 259.

11. Paul Werner, *Ein Schweizer Journalist sieht Rußland: Auf den Spuren der deutschen Armee zwischen San und Dnjepr* (Olten, Switz., 1942), 127–128.

12. Koch, "Der Sowjet-Nachlass," 4–5; for "Stalin's lightning," see Fedor Belov, *The History of a Soviet Collective Farm* (London, 1956), 168–169; Werner, *Ein Schweizer Journalist*, 128.

13. Koch, "Der Sowjet-Nachlass," 4–5.

14. Mstyslav Z. Chubai, *Reid orhanizatoriv OUN vid Popradu po Chorne More: (Iz zapysnyka roiovoho)* (Munich, 1952), 40 (on rage); *Ereignismeldung UdSSR* 100 (October 1, 1941): 2, and 191 (April 10, 1942): 22; *Meldungen* 7 (June 12, 1942): 10; Kost' Pan'kivs'kyi, *Vid derzhavy do komitetu* (New York, 1957), 69–70, 104; BA-MA, RH 26–454/28: Security Division 454, report from the Zhytomyr region, October 4, 1941; NA microcopy T-501, roll 33, frame 1098; TsDAVOV, 3676/4/161/48, 55: report based on Ukrainian propagandists, Berlin, November 30, 1943; DAKO, r-2215/1/1/3–4: Maksymovychy administration, protocols 3 and 4, September 12 and 14, 1941; Ralf Bartoleit, "Die deutsche Agrarpolitik in den

besetzten Gebieten der Ukraine vom Sommer 1941 bis zum Sommer 1942 unter besonderer Berücksichtigung der Einführung der 'Neuen Agrarordnung': Eine Studie über die strukturelle Durchsetzung nationalsozialistischer Programmatik," master's thesis, Hamburg University, 1987, 65, 80–81.

15. TsDAHOU, 1/22/123/65: Petr Timofeevich Berdnik, "Kharakteristika polozhenii na okkupirovannoi territorii," n.p., n.d. Compare the more political interpretation in Amir Weiner, *Making Sense of War: The Second World War and the Fate of the Bolshevik Revolution* (Princeton, N.J., 2001), 306.

16. On decollectivization generally see Ortwin Buchbender and Reinhold Sterz, eds., *Das andere Gesicht des Krieges: Deutsche Feldpostbriefe 1939–1945* (Munich, 1982), 45; Serhiichuk, *OUN-UPA*, 260. For restoration of pre-1929 property relations, see *Ereignismeldung UdSSR* 107 (October 8, 1941): 14.

17. S.-Chartoryis'kyi, *Vid Sianu*, 118, 174–175; Bartoleit, "Die deutsche Agrarpolitik," 68; Lynne Viola, *Peasant Rebels under Stalin: Collectivization and the Culture of Peasant Resistance* (New York, 1996), 77–78.

18. Sheila Fitzpatrick, *Stalin's Peasants: Resistance and Survival in the Russian Village after Collectivization* (New York, 1994), 218.

19. For the proportion of women in Romashky, see DAKO, r-2294/1/1/3: "Oblik naselennia s. Romashki 1942 r."; for the village near Berdychiv, see "Suchasne ukraïns'ke selo (Vid vlasnoho korespondenta)," *Ukraïns'kyi visnyk* (Berlin), April 4, 1943, 6–7.

20. Fitzpatrick, *Stalin's Peasants*, 182.

21. DAKO, r-2292/1/4/1–4.

22. On wages, see H. Sova [Hryhorii Kariak], *Do istoriï bol'shevyts'koï diis'nosty: (25 rokiv zhyttia ukraïns'koho hromadianyna v SSSR)* (Munich, 1955), 89. For the detailed censuses, see TsDAHOU, 166/3/249/26v: Ivan Levkovych Tubolets' (Ukrainian, age 42), village of Lukavytsia [Pereiaslav-Khmel'nyts'kyi raion, Kiev oblast], August 10, 1946; DAKO, r-2292/1/3/9 and r-2292/1/4/5, 8, 10–11: name lists.

23. Sova, *Do istoriï*, 91; TsDAHOU, 1/23/685/30: Savchenko, Zam. NKVD USSR, to D. R. Korniets, "Spets. soob. O polozhenii v g. Vinnitsa i Vinnitskoi oblasti," Borisoglebsk, January 26, 1943. A permit is archived at TsDAVOV, 3206/2/139/16.

24. TsDAHOU, 1/23/124/29–30; *Ukraïns'kyi holos* (Proskuriv), October 15, 1942, 1, and January 7, 1943, 4; N. S. Zozulia and Ie. M. Moskovs'ka, author interviews (on overnight guests); O. Sarapuka and M. Prylipko, author interviews (on curfews); M. Kh. Hohulia, author interview; DAKO, r-2215/1/1/5: administration of Maksymovychy, protokol 4, September 14, 1941 (on peasants standing guard).

25. Pihido-Pravoberezhnyi, "*Velyka Vitchyzniana viina*," 56, 77–79; S.-Chartoryis'kyi, *Vid Sianu*, 116, quotation on 159.

26. *Ereignismeldung UdSSR* 26 (July 18, 1941): 6. See also Bartoleit, "Die deutsche Agrarpolitik," 72–73; Koch, "Der Sowjet-Nachlass," 9.

27. On the role of Banderites, see NA microcopy T-501, roll 33, frame 571: Security Division 444, "Lagebericht," n.p., August 28, 1941; *Ereignismeldung UdSSR* 52 (August 14, 1941): 10, 107 (October 8, 1941): 12–13, and 129 (November 5, 1941): 15; S.-Chartoryis'kyi, *Vid Sianu*, 159; Orest Zovenko, *Bezimenni: Spohad uchasnyka novitnykh vyzvol'nykh zmahan'* (n.p., 1946), 66. On the role of Germans, see Sarapuka, author interview; *Ereignismeldung UdSSR* 40 (August 1, 1941): 19, 47 (August 9, 1941): 8, 107 (October 8, 1941): 11; and 128 (November 3, 1941): 2.

28. Pan'kivs'kyi, *Vid derzhavy*, 104; Hohulia, author interview.

29. On fear of famine, see *Ereignismeldung UdSSR* 107 (October 8, 1941): 12, and 112 (October 13, 1941): 6. On payment, see Hohulia, Moskovs'ka, Sarapuka, and Zozulia, author interviews; *Ereignismeldung UdSSR* 85 (September 16, 1941): 13; Pihido-Pravoberezhnyi, *"Velyka Vitchyzniana viina,"* 120. On household strips, consult Belov, *History of a Soviet Collective Farm*, 20.

30. A. Anatoli (Kuznetsov) [Anatolii Kuznetsov], *Babi Yar: A Document in the Form of a Novel* (London, 1970), 192 (the quotation); Anatolii Kuznetsov (A. Anatolii), *Babii iar: Roman-dokument* (New York, 1986), 192–193; Maistrenko, *Istoriia moho pokolinnia*, 337; Koch, "Der Sowjet-Nachlass," 11.

31. Anatoli (Kuznetsov), *Babi Yar*, 193; Sova, *Do istoriï*, 77 (the quotation).

32. Bartoleit, "Die deutsche Agrarpolitik," 74–75; DAKO, r-2160/1/1/2: "NAKAZ no. Do raioniv Kyïvs'koï Okruhy," October 24, 1941. On farm buildings still being sold, see DAKO, r-2209/1/17/74–77: Steshchyna adminstration protocol, July 19, 1942; DAKO, r-2209/1/49/4–4v: "Vytiah z protokolu n 26. Zasidannia Sil's'koï Upravy s. Buda-Radyns'ka," September 1942.

33. *Ukraïns'kyi holos*, March 26, 1942, 2; TsDAVOV, 4620/3/243a/15: Ivan Nikolaevich Zhitov, "Komissii po rassledovaniiu nemetskikh zverstv na Ukraine," Kiev, November 1943; Ortwin Buchbender, *Das tönende Erz: Deutsche Propaganda gegen die Rote Armee im Zweiten Weltkrieg* (Stuttgart, 1978), 309.

34. Original usage: *hromads'ke hospodarstvo (hromhosp)*, *Gemeinwirtschaft*. Buchbender, *Das tönende Erz*, 134, 136; Katrin Boeckh, "Die deutsche Propaganda im 'Reichskommissariat Ukraine'," *Studien zu deutsch-ukrainischen Beziehungen* 2 (Munich, 1996), 16–18.

35. TsDAHOU, 1/23/601/114: Dr. Shiller [Otto Schiller] of the Nadzvychaina komisiia dlia poriadkuvannia zemel'noho pytannia v Ukraïni, "Do ostatochnoho uporiadkuvannia ustaliuiet'sia taki napriamni shcho do ustroiu i zahospodariuvannia hromads'kykh hospodarstv (tymchasovi postanovy pro pratsiu)," translation from the German, n.p., n.d.

36. *Meldungen* 7 (June 12, 1942): 6, 9; Bartoleit, "Die deutsche Agrarpolitik," 99–100; TsDAHOU, 1/22/123/67: Berdnik, "Kharakteristika polozhenii."

37. On farm names see, for example, Vegesack, *Als Dolmetscher im Osten*, 108. For new "labor units," see TsDAHOU, 1/23/601/115: Shiller, "Do ostatochnoho uporiadkuvannia."

38. On "labor-days," see Fitzpatrick, *Stalin's Peasants*, 145, 192, 197; *Ereignismeldung UdSSR* 28 (July 20, 1941): 10, and 45 (August 7, 1941): 4. On the situation in the Kiev region, consult TsDAHOU, 1/23/633/14: Z. Serdiuk, Kiev obkom secretary, "Politinformatsiï po Kyïvs'koï oblasti na 10.XII–1943 roku," n.p., n.d. See also DAKO, r-2160/1/4/8: chief of the Borodianka raion to a village elder, March 5, 1943; TsDAHOU, 166/3/245/71: Tetiana Ivanivna Pyskovets' (Ukrainian, peasant from Borodianka), Borodianka, January 22, 1946.

39. TsDAHOU, 1/23/601/116–117: Shiller, "Do ostatochnoho uporiadkuvannia."

40. Pihido-Pravoberezhnyi, *"Velyka Vitchyzniana viina,"* 158–159; H. H. Salata, author interview.

41. For the mandate to join, see Mykhailo Seleshko, *Vinnytsia: Spomyny perekladacha Komisiï doslidiv zlochyniv NKVD v 1937–1938* (New York, 1991), 99, 104. On the prewar situation, see Fitzpatrick, *Stalin's Peasants*, 172. On having to work, see TsDAHOU, 1/22/122/31: Iakov Fedorovich Nosenko, komissar partizanskogo otriada Kanevskogo raiona Kievskoi oblasti to Zam. nach. 4-go Otdela NKVD USSR, "Dokladnaia zapiska," n.p., January 3, 1942; TsDAHOU, 1/23/601/115: Shiller, "Do ostatochnoho uporiadkuvannia"; TsDAVOV, 3206/5/15/492: RKU *Lagebericht* for September and October 1942. For further restrictions, see, for example, *Ukraïns'kyi holos*, April 12, 1942, 1.

42. TsDAHOU, 1/22/123/89: Informatsiia tov. Matsko o polozhenii na territorii, vremenno okkupirovannoi nemetskimi voiskami, n.p., n.d. (on machinery); Vegesack, *Als Dolmetscher im Osten*, 114, 119. See also NA microcopy T-84, roll 120, frame 418946: Sipo-SD of Kiev GB to Ukraine Sipo-SD, Kiev, September 28, 1942; NBU, Filiia 1, Viddil starodrukiv, poster 1495: "Zapriahaite Vashykh koriv."

43. On manual farm work, see Pihido-Pravoberezhnyi, *"Velyka Vitchyzniana viina,"* 159. On seed shortages and areas sown, see TsDAHOU, 1/23/124/16: Savchenko, VRIO NKVD USSR to Khrushchev, "Razvedsvodka No. 11: O polozhenii v okkupirovannoi protivnikom Vinnitsoi oblast po sostoianiiu na 30. 9. 42g.," Engel's, October 16, 1942; TsDAHOU, 1/23/685/31: Savchenko to Korniets, "Spets. soob."

44. NA microcopy T-84, roll 120, frames 418845–849: Sipo-SD of Kiev GB to Ukraine Sipo-SD, Kiev, August 10, 1942. See also NA microcopy T-120, roll 2533, frame E292557: "Stimmungsbericht" by Auslandbriefprüfstelle, September 11, 1942; Kuznetsov, *Babii iar*, 270, 273; Sova, *Do istoriï*, 86; Nikolas

Laskovsky, "Practicing Law in the Occupied Ukraine," *American Slavic and East European Review* 10, no. 2 (1952): 123; TsDAVOV, 3206/1/26/30, 31v: "Teilbericht Politik über die Bereisung des Reichskommissariats mit Prof. v. Grünberg in der Zeit vom 13.8. bis 3.9.1942," Rivne, September 20, 1942.

45. On land taxation, see DAKO, r-2457/1/16/3: Ivankiv raion chief, decree, Ivankiv, December 19, 1941. For the other taxes, consult TsDAVOV, 3206/2/139/2–3: elder of Liuten'ka (Hadiach raion), notes, September 1942; TsDAHOU, 1/23/633/ 14: Serdiuk, "Politinformatsiï."

46. DAKO, r-2107/1/13/2–3v, 6–7v: elder of Vil'khovets' (Bohuslav raion), name lists, May 25 and June 5, 1942; DAKO, r-2107/1/12/9: elder of Dybenets' (Bohuslav raion), name list, June 6, 1942; DAKO, r-2457/1/16/11–12: elder of Blidcha (Ivankiv raion), name list, August 12, 1942.

47. TsDAHOU, 1/23/601/116: Shiller, "Do ostatochnoho uporiadkuvannia"; DAKO, r-2209/1/18/9v: "Zasidannia Raiopodatkovoi komisiï Khabens'koho raionu pry Raifinviddili," February 16, 1942.

48. Original usage: *rabhospy* (a pun on *radhospy*); *Staatsgut, derzhavnyi maietok*; *Betriebslandwirt*. Timothy Mulligan, *The Politics of Illusion and Empire: German Occupation Policy in the Soviet Union, 1942–1943* (New York, 1988), 94; Anatol' Halan, *Budni soviets'koho zhurnalista* (Buenos Aires, 1956), 37–38; Otto Bräutigam, *Überblick über die besetzten Ostgebiete während des 2. Weltkrieges* (Tübingen, 1954), 37; Chubai, *Reid orhanizatoriv*, 38.

49. Rolf-Dieter Müller, ed., *Die deutsche Wirtschaftspolitik in den besetzten sowjetischen Gebieten 1941–1943: Der Abschlußbericht des Wirtschaftsstabes Ost und Aufzeichnungen eines Angehörigen des Wirtschaftskommandos Kiew* (Boppard am Rhein, Ger., 1991), 433; NA microcopy T-84, roll 120, frame 418930: Sipo-SD of the Kiev GB to Ukraine Sipo-SD, Kiev, December 14, 1942.

50. TsDAHOU, 166/3/244/82–83: Vera Filippovna Kal'nitskaia, n.p., n.d.

51. Müller, *Die deutsche Wirtschaftspolitik*, 433; Bräutigam, *Überblick*, 52; TsDAVOV, 3206/5/15/267: RKU *Lagebericht* for February 1942, Rivne, March 15, 1942; *Litopys UPA*, vol. 5 (Toronto, 1984), 28, 274.

52. On quarry work, see *Vidrodzhennia* (Tarashcha), October 1, 1942, 4. On snow shoveling, see TsDAVOV, 3206/5/15/300: RKU *Lagebericht* for February 1942; *Shchodennyk Arkadiia Liubchenka*, ed. Iurii Luts'kyi (Lviv, Ukr., 1999), 125.

53. On events in Khabne, see DAKO, r-2209/1/21/202: raion chief, August 6, 1942. For the Oleksiienko incident, see DAKO, r-2215/1/15/54: raion chief Halushko, June 25, 1943.

54. Original usage: *kliborobs'ka spilka, Landbau-Genossenschaft*. Bartoleit, "Die deutsche Agrarpolitik," appendix 17b. Compare Müller, *Die deutsche Wirtschaftspolitik*, 434.

55. Mulligan, *Politics of Illusion*, 97.

56. *Vidrodzhennia*, October 1, 1942, 3, October 4, 1942, 4, and October 11, 1942, 4.

57. DAKO, r-2209/1/85/38–43: "Zrazok promovy do selian pry zasnuvanni khliborobs'koï spilky," and Russian version, Kiev, August 14, 1942; DAKO, r-2209/1/85/143–145: Dr. Miller, note in Russian translation, n.p., n.d. (on harvesting).

58. *Vidrodzhennia*, October 4, 1942, 4.

59. *Vidrodzhennia*, October 11, 1942, 4; Bartoleit, "Die deutsche Agrarpolitik," 121.

60. NA microcopy T-84, roll 120, frames 418928–931: Sipo-SD of Kiev GB to Ukraine Sipo-SD, Kiev, December 14, 1942 (the quotation); NA microcopy T-84, roll 120, frames 418932–935: Sipo-SD of Kiev GB to Ukraine Sipo-SD, Kiev, August 7, 1943.

61. Bartoleit, "Die deutsche Agrarpolitik," 111, 122.

62. Original usage: *desiatky; desiatykhatky.* TsDAHOU, 1/23/633/12: Serdiuk, "Politinformatsiï"; TsDAHOU, 166/3/249/4v–5: Roman Ober"ianiv Shevchenko (Ukrainian), village of Zarubyntsi, Kiev oblast, August 7, 1946; HIA, Alexander Dallin collection, box 8, folder 2, fol. 8: no. 1000 B-6, anonymous informant, Boston, August 1950; Serhiichuk, *OUN-UPA*, 340.

63. Alexander Dallin, *German Rule in Russia, 1941–1945: A Study of Occupation Policies*, 2d ed. (London, 1981), 354; HIA-HURIP, box 32, no. 121AD, fols. 11–12: anonymous informant from Kherson, n.p., November 28–29, 1950; HIA, Alexander Dallin collection, box 4, folder 7, fols. 5–6: no. G-2 AD, Otto Schiller, Stuttgart, February 17 and 19, 1951.

64. Pihido-Pravoberezhnyi, *"Velyka Vitchyzniana viina,"* 157, 159; HIA, Alexander Dallin collection, box 4, folder 7, fol. 6: Schiller.

65. Fitzpatrick, *Stalin's Peasants*, 135–136, 149; *Ereignismeldung UdSSR* 45 (August 7, 1941): 4.

66. Official usage: *Hofland, prysadybna zemlia*. On the reluctance of landwirts, see Bartoleit, "Die deutsche Agrarpolitik," 72, 115; Dallin, *German Rule*, 327, 339; Bräutigam, *Überblick*, 52. On stolen animals and forced labor, consult Dallin, *German Rule,* 346. For the repeated order, see Bartoleit, "Die deutsche Agrarpolitik," 91.

67. TsDAVOV, 3206/1/34/1–2v: brochure, *Seliany!*; TsDAVOV, 3206/1/26/32: "Teilbericht Politik"; *Meldungen* 7 (June 12, 1942): 10.

68. Bartoleit, "Die deutsche Agrarpolitik," appendix 18.

69. TsDAVOV, 3206/5/15/337: RKU *Lagebericht* for March 1942, Rivne, April 15, 1942; Bartoleit, "Die deutsche Agrarpolitik," 112–113.

70. TsDAHOU, 1/23/601/49: Soviet report, "Sil's'ke hospodarstvo" [not older than October 12, 1943]; TsDAVOV, 3206/1/26/33: "Teilbericht Politik" (both on garden increases); BA-Berlin, R 6/15, fol. 67: Hauptabteilungsleiter Koenigk, leader of Hauptabteilung E at the Zhytomyr GB, text of oral report to

Rosenberg and Erich Koch, Vinnytsia, June 17, 1943 (on the situation in Zhytomyr general district); *Ukraïns'kyi visnyk*, April 4, 1943, 6–7 (on the size of plots in village near Berdychiv).

71. TsDAHOU, 1/22/10/1–3: Burchenko, Komissar soedineniia, report, August 31, 1943.

72. Laskovsky, "Practicing Law," 136; V. Boldyrev, "Mestnye sudy na Ukraine v period nemetskoi okkupatsii," *Vestnik Instituta po izucheniiu SSSR*, no. 4(21) (Munich, October–December 1956): 70–71.

73. Belov, *History of a Soviet Collective Farm*, 176.

74. TsDAHOU, 1/23/601/116: Shiller, "Do ostatochnoho uporiadkuvannia"; *Meldungen* 7 (June 12, 1942): 10; TsDAHOU, 1/23/633/14–15: Serdiuk, "Politinformatsiï."

75. Norbert Müller [et al.], ed., *Die faschistische Okkupationspolitik in den zeitweilig besetzten Gebieten der Sowjetunion (1941–1944)* (Berlin, 1991), 344 (on fear); TsDAVOV, 3206/2/17/4, 6: Khorol raion administration, resolutions, January 15 and February 13, 1943; *Vidrodzhennia*, September 20, 1942, 4; TsDAHOU, 1/22/391/15: Mikhail Mikh. Skirda [et al.], "Otchet o podpol'noi partiinoi rabote i partizanskoi bor'be v Kirovogradskoi oblasti (avgust 1941 goda–mart 1944 goda)," n.p., n.d.; TsDAHOU, 1/23/633/15: Serdiuk, "Politinformatsiï" (both on camps).

76. TsDAHOU, 1/22/6/26–28: D. S. Korotchenko to N. S. Khrushchev, "O sostoianii partizanskogo dvizheniia na pravoberezhnoi Ukraine," n.p., July 22, 1943.

77. Sova, *Do istoriï*, 88; *Meldungen* 32 (December 4, 1942): 23, and 43 (February 26, 1943): 10.

78. On cow sharing, see Sarapuka, author interview. On the slaughter of livestock, consult *Meldungen* 43 (February 26, 1943): 8–9; NA microcopy T-84, roll 120, frame 419241: district commissar Dr. Edelmann to the general commissar, "Lagebericht für die Zeit vom 20.2.43 bis 20.4.43," Boryspil', April 16, 1943.

79. DAKO, r-2210/1/3/23: raion chief Okhrimenko to the elders, December 2, 1941; DAKO, r-2145/1/1/15, Borodianka raion chief Tyshchenko and the German commander (*Komendant raionu*) to all elders, December 19, 1941.

80. Boldyrev, "Mestnye sudy," 69 (on district commissars' threats); Laskovsky, "Practicing Law," 131 (on German courts in Zhytomyr general district).

81. Werth, *Russia at War*, 727.

82. TsDAHOU, 166/3/249/20–20v: Serhii Romanovych Rudenko (Ukrainian born in 1900), village of Zarubyntsi, August 9, 1946.

83. Bartoleit, "Die deutsche Agrarpolitik," 55.

84. TsDAHOU, 166/3/249/26v: Tubolets'; *Ukraïns'kyi visnyk*, April 4, 1943, 6–7 (the quotation).

85. DAKO, r-2209/1/21/209: *Kreislandwirt* to Khabne raion agronomist, order, July 25, 1942, DAKO, r-2209/1/85/28–29.

86. TsDAVOV, 3206/2/27/10: RKU *Lagebericht* for December 1941, Rivne, January 14, 1942; TsDAVOV, 3676/4/474/167: Sipo-SD report on Kiev GB, September 15, 1942.

87. On manipulation of quotas, see TsDAVOV, 3676/1/232/9–10: Erich Koch to the general commissar in Dnipropetrovs'k, November 17, 1942. For raion chiefs' influence on consumer cooperatives, see Sova, *Do istoriï*, 88; Pihido-Pravoberezhnyi, "*Velyka Vitchyzniana viina*," 160; DAKO, r-2209/1/21/131.

88. Bräutigam, *Überblick*, 41–43; TsDAVOV, 3676/4/474/581 and 3676/4/476/53–56: Sipo-SD reports on the Kiev GB in March and April 1942; John A. Armstrong, *Ukrainian Nationalism*, 3d ed. (Englewood, Colo.), 169; Illia Vytanovych, *Istoriia ukraïns'koho kooperatyvnoho rukhu* (New York, 1964), 510–515.

89. Sova, *Do istoriï*, 86.

90. *Ereignismeldung UdSSR* 191 (April 10, 1942): 24, 29; Bohdan Liubomyrenko, *Z Khrystom v Ukraïni: Zapysky viruiuchoho za roky 1941–1943* (Winnipeg, 1973), 42 (on findings of Baptist evangelists).

91. TsDAHOU, 1/22/391/15: M. M. Skirda, "Otchet" (sayings); DAKO, r-2209/1/21/99: raion chief, list, March 18, 1942 (on the situation in Polissia).

92. Prylipko, author interview; *Ukraïns'kyi visnyk*, April 4, 1943, 6–7.

93. K. Ia. Hrynevych, author interview.

94. Barbara Baratz, *Flucht vor dem Schicksal: Holocaust-Erinnerungen aus der Ukraine 1941–1944* (Darmstadt, 1984), 106 (Pervomais'k); H. Nazhyvanenko, quoted in Iaan Pennar, "Selbstverwaltung in den während des Zweiten Weltkrieges besetzten Gebieten der Sowjetunion," *Sowjetstudien*, no. 12 (Munich, August 1962): 64 (Zaporizhzhia region); TsDAVOV, 3676/1/307/112: "Auszug aus dem Lagebericht der A-Stelle Poltava," n.p., November 28, 1942 (Poltava); Oleksander Bykovets', quoted in James E. Mace and Leonid Heretz, eds., *Oral History Project of the Commission on the Ukraine Famine*, vol. 1 (Washington, 1990), 410. See also Pennar, "Selbstverwaltung," 68 (Velyka Bahachka raion).

95. NA microcopy T-120, roll 2533, frame E292536: Foreign Office report to von Saucken, the representative of the Foreign Office at the RKU, Berlin, December 31, 1942.

96. TsDAVOV, 3676/4/475/574: Sipo-SD report on Kiev GB in October 1942, Kiev, November 1, 1942 (Kiev general district); Hohulia and Ia. N. Vasylenko, author interviews (Medvyn).

97. Pihido-Pravoberezhnyi, "*Velyka Vitchyzniana viina*," 157–158. See also HIA, Alexander Dallin collection, box 4, folder 7, fol. 12: Schiller; HIA-HURIP, box 22, no. 64AD, B-6, fol. 2: anonymous informant, n.p., November 1, 1950; HIA-

HURIP, box 23, no. 314AD, B-6, fol. 6: anonymous informant, Salzburg, December 18, 1950.

98. Laskovsky, "Practicing Law," 123.

99. HIA-HURIP, no. 548AD, B-6, fols. 1–2; HIA, B. I. Nicolaevsky collection, series no. 178, box 232, folder 10, fol. 112: [Lev Vladimirovich] Dudin, "Velikii Mirazh: Sobytiia 1941–1947 godov v ponimanii sovetskogo cheloveka," n.p., 1947.

100. Pihido-Pravoberezhnyi, "*Velyka Vitchyzniana viina*," 159–160.

101. Nikolai Fevr, *Solntse voskhodit na zapade* (Buenos Aires, 1950), 166; NA microcopy T-84, roll 120, frame 419196: "Auszug aus dem Lagebericht des Generalkommissars," Kiev, September 1, 1942 (Magunia's report); Seleshko, *Vinnytsia*, 21–22, 24; TsDAHOU, 1/22/6/26–28: Korotchenko to Khrushchev, "O sostoianii" (both on barefoot peasants).

102. TsDAHOU, 166/3/245/71: Pyskovets'.

103. DAKO, r-2209/1/13/21: Khabne raion chief to all elders (on absenteeism and lateness); *Ukraïns'kyi holos*, April 26, 1942, 3, and April 30, 1942, 3; NDB, collection "Afishy ta plakaty okupatsiinoho periodu," 147sp: "Ne ledariui!"

104. On the official punishment, see DAKO, r-2209/1/13/14: Khabne raion chief, April 21, 1942; DAKO, r-2209/1/22/402: district commissar in the Kiev GB, verdict, August 14, 1942. On actual penalties, see TsDAHOU, 1/22/122/31: Nosenko, "Dokladnaia zapiska." On public beatings, consult Gerhard Lohrenz, *The Lost Generation and Other Stories* (Steinbach, Manitoba, 1982), 56; TsDAHOU, 1/23/124/16: Savchenko to Khrushchev, "Razvedsvodka No. 11: O polozhenii." For the quotation, see Vegesack, *Als Dolmetscher im Osten*, 108, 114–115.

105. TsDAVOV, 3676/1/232/9: Erich Koch to the general commissar in Dnipropetrovs'k, November 17, 1942; Laskovsky, "Practicing Law," 133.

106. TsDAHOU, 1/22/391/14–16: Skirda, "Otchet."

107. NA microcopy T-120, roll 2533, frame E292556: Auslandsbriefprüfstelle.

108. Müller, *Die faschistische Okkupationspolitik*, 361.

109. TsDAHOU, 1/22/391/32: Skirda, "Otchet."

110. Laskovsky, "Practicing Law," 133–134.

111. Ibid., 134; Fitzpatrick, *Stalin's Peasants*, 180, 302 (on Soviet practice).

112. In the original: "Za nevminnia derut' reminniam"; "Dumaly, shcho nimets' dast' pole, a vin nahaikoiu pore"; "Nimets'ki zakony / Zhyttiu perepony / Rezyna na horbu / Vidpochynok v hrobu." IMFE, Krasyts'ka collection, 14–3/20/39, 46, 222; IMFE, 14–3/56: "Fol'klor Velykoï Vitchyznianoï viiny" (Kiev, 1945), ed. M. T. Ryl's'kyi, here folio 488 (based on IMFE, Ie. I. Prytula collection, 14–3/24/71).

113. On the Tahancha incident, see TsDAHOU, 1/22/22/24: "Doklad pribyvshego iz tyla protivnika CHEREVIK Sergeia Maksimovicha," n.p., March 25, 1943. For the situation in Medvyn, see Prylipko, author interview.

114. Hohulia, author interview. See also TsDAHOU, 1/22/117/88: "Materialy, vyshedshego iz okruzheniia polkovogo komissara Ostapenko F. P.," n.p., November 23, 1941.

115. *Ideia i chyn: Orhan Provodu OUN, 1942–1946. Peredruk pidpil'noho zhurnalu,* ed. Iurii Maïvs'kyi and Ievhen Shtendera, which is *Litopys UPA,* vol. 24 (Toronto, 1995), 122–123.

116. Koch, "Der Sowjet-Nachlass," 7; TsDAVOV, 3206/1/26/39: "Teilbericht Politik"; *Ereignismeldung UdSSR* 40 (August 1, 1941): 18 (for the number of children). See also *Ivankivs'ki visti,* January 28, 1943, 1–2.

117. Vegesack, *Als Dolmetscher im Osten,* 110.

118. TsDAHOU, 1/22/123/74: Berdnik, "Kharakteristika polozhenii."

119. O. Iatsenko, author interview.

120. NA microcopy T-120, roll 2533, frame E292557: Auslandbriefprüfstelle (letters); *Vidrodzhennia,* November 12, 1942, 3 (on complaints from Tarashcha peasants).

121. Müller, *Die faschistische Okkupationspolitik,* 359, 361. See also *Meldungen* 24 (October 9, 1942): 9.

122. *Ukraïns'kyi visnyk,* April 4, 1943, 6–7; Viola, *Peasant Rebels,* 221–223, 238–239.

123. Sarapuka, author interview. See also Hohulia, Prylipko, and H. H. Salata, author interviews.

124. NBU, Filiia 1, Viddil starodrukiv, poster 912: "Rozporiadzhennia dlia zakhystu sil's'kohospodars'kykh produktiv," July 30, 1942; German version at TsDAVOV, 3676/4/474/275–276.

125. DAKO, r-2209/1/19/1–20.

126. Boldyrev, "Mestnye sudy," 70.

127. Fitzpatrick, *Stalin's Peasants,* 208, 271.

128. Jan Tomasz Gross, *Polish Society under German Occupation: The Generalgovernement, 1939–1944* (Princeton, N.J., 1979), 103–105.

129. Hartymiv, "Zemleiu ukraïns'koiu," 132; "Suchasne ukraïns'ke selo."

130. See, for example, *Zvil'nena Ukraïna* (Bohuslav), October 16, 1941: announcement by the German commander in Bohuslav; DAKO, r-2145/1/1/34: raion chief A. Tyshchenko to all villages in the Borodianka raion, November 11, 1941; Pihido-Pravoberezhnyi, "*Velyka Vitchyzniana viina,*" 158. For more on the prevalence of home brewing, see Maistrenko, *Istoriia moho pokolinnia,* 337; Pennar, "Selbstverwaltung," 68.

131. Leonid Volynskii, "Skvoz' noch': k istorii odnoi bezymiannoi mogily," *Novyi mir* 29, no. 1 (1963): 134. See also HIA-HURIP, box 23, no. 440 AD, B-6, fol. 7: anonymous informant, n.p., February 10, 1951.

132. Sova, *Do istoriï,* 91.

133. *Ukraïnka: zhinochyi dvotyzhnevyk* (Kostopil') 2, no. 21 (November 5, 1942): 7–8.

134. *Volyn',* February 15, 1942, 2.

135. On the exodus from Zhytomyr, see *Ereignismeldung UdSSR* 87 (September 18,

1941): 9. See also Pihido-Pravoberezhnyi, *"Velyka Vitchyzniana viina,"* 39. On the Nazi response, see TsDAHOU, 1/23/601/113: Shiller, "Do ostatochnoho uporiadkuvannia."

136. Sova, *Do istoriï*, 91.

137. Fevr, *Solntse*, 167.

138. Hrynevych, author interview; Ia. N. Vasylenko, author interview (Medvyn case).

139. Seleshko, *Vinnytsia*, 99; *Ukraïns'kyi visnyk*, April 4, 1943, 6–7; TsDAHOU, 1/22/123/66: Berdnik, "Kharakteristika polozhenii." On the more helpful authorities, see Laskovsky, "Practicing Law," 135.

140. Sova, *Do istoriï*, 92. "Free-floating malice" is from Fitzpatrick, *Stalin's Peasants*, 233.

141. TsDAVOV, 3676/1/232/9: Erich Koch to the general commissar in Dnipropetrovs'k, November 17, 1942; Laskovsky, "Practicing Law," 131.

142. See, for example, DAKO, r-2215/1/15/55–56: raion chief Halushko to all elders, letter, July 6, 1943, and statutes.

143. "Samofinansuvannia raionnykh upravlin'," *Ukraïns'kyi holos*, August 25, 1943, 4; DAKO, r-2107/1/35/20: Bohuslav raion administration, note, August 16, 1943 (on the Bohuslav aid committee).

144. Bartoleit, "Die deutsche Agrarpolitik," 78–79; Vegesack, *Als Dolmetscher im Osten*, 215.

145. TsDAVOV, 3206/1/44/1: poster, "V imeny Nimets'koho Uriadu. Raikhsminister ROZENBERH, 'Dekliaratsiia Nimets'koho Uriadu pro pryvatnu vlasnist' selian na zemliu v zvil'nenykh oblastiakh."

146. Mulligan, *Politics of Illusion*, 98–101; Dallin, *German Rule*, 361.

147. TsDAHOU, 1/23/601/49: Soviet document, "Sil's'ke hospodarstvo"; Bykovets', quoted in Mace and Heretz, *Oral History Project*, 409.

148. Sova, *Do istoriï*, 97.

149. TsDAVOV, 3676/4/161/52: report, 1943; Pihido-Pravoberezhnyi, *"Velyka Vitchyzniana viina,"* 157; TsDAHOU, 1/23/633/12: Serdiuk, "Politinformatsiï."

150. L. N., "Khliborobs'ke sviato," *Dzvin voli*, August 29, 1943, 4. See also the picture in *Ukraïns'kyi holos*, August 12, 1943, 3.

151. "Vzhe nimtsi tretii raz zakony pro zemliu vypuskaiut' / Tse virnyi znak, shcho p"iatamy makhaiut'." IMFE, Ie. I. Prytula collection, 14–3/24/81, based on V. A. Kazmiruk in Berdychiv in 1943.

152. DAKO, r-2209/1/91/30–37: requests to the Khabne raion administration for registration as peasant *(khliborob)*, July 1943; Serhiichuk, *OUN-UPA*, 340; Sova, *Do istoriï*, 97.

153. TsDAVOV, 3676/4/161/50: Der Sonderbeauftragte f.d. Arbeitskräfte aus den besetzten Ostgebieten, "Betrifft: vertrauliche Aussagen von in ihre Heimat auf

Urlaub entsandter ukrainischer Propagandisten," Berlin, November 30, 1943. See also Lohrenz, *Lost Generation*, 58.

154. Original usage: *Stützpunkt, shtutspunkt, kushch*. Müller, *Die deutsche Wirtschaftspolitik*, 140; Christian Gerlach, "Die deutsche Agrarreform und die Bevölkerungspolitik in den besetzten sowjetischen Gebieten," in Christian Gerlach et al., *Besatzung und Bündnis: Deutsche Herrschaftsstrategien in Ost- und Südosteuropa* (Berlin, 1995), 32; HIA, Alexander Dallin collection, box 4, folder 7, fol. 11: Schiller; HIA-HURIP, box 23, no. 102AD, fol. 8: anonymous informant, n.p., November 17, 1950; Pihido-Pravoberezhnyi, "*Velyka Vitchyzniana viina*," 162; TsDAHOU, 1/22/391/41: Skirda, "Otchet"; DAKO, r-2160/1/4/38: Borodianka raion chief to the *hromhosp* and *Stützpunkt* leaders, November 26, 1942.

155. NA microcopy T-501, roll 28, frame 46: Graf Stolberg, Der Kommandierende General der Sicherungstruppen und Befehlshaber im Heeresgeb. Süd, to Army Group South, "Monatsbericht (1.–30.9.43)," n.p., October 6, 1943. See also Serhiichuk, *OUN-UPA*, 329, 334, 340, 344, 350.

156. Fitzpatrick, *Stalin's Peasants*, 67–69.

6. Conditions in the Cities

1. Examples are Detlev J. K. Peukert, *Inside Nazi Germany: Conformity, Opposition and Racism in Everyday Life* (Harmondsworth, Eng., 1987); Bernhard Chiari, *Alltag hinter der Front: Besatzung, Kollaboration und Widerstand im Weißrußland 1941–1944* (Düsseldorf, 1998).

2. See, for example, Jan Tomasz Gross, *Polish Society under German Occupation: The Generalgouvernement, 1939–1944* (Princeton, N.J., 1979); Richard C. Lukas, *The Forgotten Holocaust: The Poles under German Occupation, 1939–1944* (New York, 1990); Tomasz Szarota, *Życie codzienne w stolicach okupowanej Europy: Szkice historyczne, Kronika wydarzeń* (Warsaw, 1995), 55.

3. *Ereignismeldung UdSSR* 135 (November 19, 1941): 18; TsDAHOU, 1/22/347/3: "Iz dnevnika uchitel'nitsy gor. Kieva L. Nartovoi" (hereafter Nartova diary); Nikolai Fevr, *Solntse voskhodit na zapade* (Buenos Aires, 1950), 145.

4. *Ereignismeldung UdSSR* 125 (October 26, 1941): 7–8; K. T. Turkalo, *Tortury: (Avtobiohrafiia za bol'shevyts'kykh chasiv)* (New York, 1963), 184–185; Sheila Fitzpatrick, *Everyday Stalinism: Ordinary Life in Extraordinary Times. Soviet Russia in the 1930s* (New York, 1999), 46; "Dramatychna storinka istorii chekists'koho pidpillia v Kyievi (1941–1942 rr.): Stenohrama besidy z Hruzdovoiu M. I. v UShPR, 6 travnia 1943 r.," *Ukraïns'kyi istorychnyi zhurnal*, no. 5 (1991): 126.

5. Fevr, *Solntse*, 144; Tat'iana Fesenko, *Povest' krivykh let* (New York, 1963), 83.

6. Ivan Maistrenko, *Istoriia moho pokolinnia: Spohady uchasnyka revoliutsiinykh podii v Ukraïni* (Edmonton, 1985), 338.

7. Fevr, *Solntse*, 118; A. Kabaida, "1941," *Kalendar-al'manakh Novoho Shliakhu, 1991* (Toronto, n.d.): 49–50; Fitzpatrick, *Everyday Stalinism*, 47–48 (on resentment).

8. Fevr, *Solntse*, 190.

9. HIA, B. I. Nicolaevsky collection, series no. 178, box 232, folder 10, fol. 102: [Lev Vladimirovich] Dudin, "Velikii Mirazh: Sobytiia 1941–1947 godov v ponimanii sovetskogo cheloveka," n.p., 1947; NA microcopy T-84, roll 120, frames 419079–084: "Misstände und Schwierigkeiten in der Wohnungsfrage in Kiew. Lagebericht Material"; DAKO, r-2356/1/108/14–14v: Professor S. M. Drahomanov to Mayor Forostivs'kyi, Kiev, October 20, 1942; *Shchodennyk Arkadiia Liubchenka*, ed. Iurii Luts'kyi (Lviv, Ukr., 1999), 74, 81–82, 87; TsDAVOV, 3676/4/476/7: Sipo-SD report on the Kiev GB in April 1942.

10. TsDAHOU, 166/3/246/39–40: Mikhail Ivanovich Sokolov, [Vinnytsia?], January 20, 1946.

11. Kabaida, "1941," 49; TsDAHOU, 1/23/124/89: Savchenko, VRIO NKVD USSR, to N. S. Khrushchev, "Razvedsvodka No 33/68 o polozhenii v okkupirovannom protivnikom g. Dnepropetrovske. Po sostoianiiu na 20. 10. 42g.," Engel's, October 21, 1942; Jacob Gerstenfeld-Maltiel, *My Private War: One Man's Struggle to Survive the Soviets and the Nazis* (London, 1993), 219; O. Dniprova, "O. Ol'zhych u Kyievi: Spohad," in Kost' Mel'nyk, Oleh Lashchenko, and Vasyl' Veryha, eds., *Na zov Kyieva: Ukraïns'kyi natsionalizm u II Svitovii Viini. Zbirnyk stattei, spohadiv i dokumentiv* (Toronto, 1985), 166; *Meldungen* 32 (December 4, 1942): 8.

12. O. Zhdanovych, "Na zov Kyieva," in Mel'nyk, Lashchenko, and Veryha, *Na zov Kyieva*, 183; Halyna Lashchenko, "Povorot," *Samostiina Ukraïna* 11, no. 11(119) (Chicago, November 1958): 11; Ulas Samchuk, *Na koni voronomu: Spomyny i vrazhennia* (Winnipeg, 1975), 16; F. P. Bogatyrchuk, *Moi zhiznennyi put' k Vlasovu i Prazhkomu manifestu* (San Francisco, 1978), 136; TsDAVOV, 3676/4/475/617: Sipo-SD report on the Kiev GB in October 1942, Kiev, November 1, 1942.

13. Nataliia Vasylenko-Polons'ka, "Storinky spohadiv: Ukraïns'kyi Vil'nyi Universytet," *Ukraïns'kyi istoryk* 2, nos. 3–4(7–8) (New York, 1965): 40; Anatolii Kuznetsov (A. Anatolii), *Babii iar: Roman-dokument* (New York, 1986), 160; *Shchodennyk Arkadiia Liubchenka*, 63, 65; Nina Mykhalevych, "Do Kyieva! Fragment zi spohadu," in Mel'nyk, Lashchenko, and Veryha, *Na zov Kyieva*, 224; Kabaida, "1941," 49; Maistrenko, *Istoriia moho pokolinnia*, 338; Samchuk, *Na koni voronomu*, 5; Gerstenfeld-Maltiel, *My Private War*, 220.

14. Fesenko, *Povest'*, 87; TsDAHOU, 1/23/685/30: Savchenko, Zam. NKVD USSR,

to D. R. Korniets, "Spets. soob. O polozhenii v g. Vinnitsa i Vinnitskoi oblasti," Borisoglebsk, January 26, 1943; Gerstenfeld-Maltiel, *My Private War*, 220.

15. Original usage: *Arbeitsamt, Birzha pratsi*. M. P. Kostiuk, author interview; TsDAHOU, 1/23/124/72: Savchenko to Khrushchev, "Razvedsvodka No 33/68"; TsDAVOV, 3206/2/193/2: Stadtkommandant Eberhard, "Ob"iava pro obov"iazku iavku bezrobitnykh," Kiev, October 7, 1941.

16. Nartova diary, 4, note of December 26, 1941 ("besieged"); Irina Khoroshunova, "Pervyi god voiny: Kievskie zapiski," *Iehupets'* 9 (Kiev, 2001): 48.

17. TsDAHOU, 166/3/243/44v: Ol'ga Sergeevna Gudzenko-Tyshkova (Ukrainian born in 1901), Kiev, March 14, 1944 (text signed on June 5, 1944); Fesenko, *Povest'*, 76.

18. NBU, Filiia 1, Viddil starodrukiv, poster 919: "Rozporiadzhennia pro vvedennia trudovoï kartky," Kiev, February 13, 1942; D. V. Malakov, comp., *Kyïv, 1941–1943: Fotoal'bom* (Kiev, 2000), 220. On a verification in Kiev in July 1942, see DAKO, r-2356/17/7/1: newspaper clipping with July 8, 1942 order from Mayor Forostivs'kyi; *Shchodennyk Arkadiia Liubchenka*, 50; [O. P. Sharandachenko], *Reiestratorka zahsu: (Iz shchodennyka kyianky)* (Kiev, 1960), 155.

19. TsDAVOV, 3206/5/15/212: RKU *Lagebericht* for October 1–15, 1941, Königsberg, November 4, 1941 (initial proportion of males and females); L. Maliuzhenko, "Kyïv za 1942 r.," *Nashe mynule*, no. 1(6) (Kiev, 1993): 165–165.

20. Peter H. Solomon, Jr., *Soviet Criminal Justice under Stalin* (Cambridge, Eng., 1996), 301; *Ereignismeldung UdSSR* 81 (September 12, 1941): 9–10; F. Pihido-Pravoberezhnyi, "*Velyka Vitchyzniana viina*" (Winnipeg, 1954), 14; N. Polons'ka-Vasylenko, *Ukraïns'ka Akademiia Nauk: (Narys istoriï)*, vol. 2: (1931–1941) (Munich, 1958), 88.

21. *Vidrodzhennia* (Tarashcha), December 3, 1942, 4.

22. TsDAVOV, 3206/5/15/157: "Bericht über die Referentenbesprechung," copy, Rivne, October 3, 1941.

23. An example is at DAKO, r-2209/1/22/31.

24. *Ukraïns'kyi holos* (Proskuriv), November 5, 1941, 4; TsDAHOU, 166/3/244/8–11v: Mariia Alekseevna Novitskaia (Ukrainian born in 1896), Kiev, February 22, 1944; Viktor Karmazin, *Nash khleb: Dokumental'noe povestvovanie o khlebe* (Moscow, 1986), 217.

25. Khoroshunova, "Pervyi god voiny," 61; *Shchodennyk Arkadiia Liubchenka*, 47, 54, 63; Nartova diary, 2, 9; Kuznetsov, *Babii iar*, 173, 222, 225, 227, 350; *Ukraïns'kyi holos*, February 28, 1943, 4; Dmytro Kyslytsia, *Svite iasnyi: Spohady. Vid r. Vovchi z Naddniprianshchyny do r. Sv. Lavrentiia na Ottavshchyni* (Ottawa, 1987), 201.

26. TsDAVOV, 3206/2/207/17: Energieversorgung Ukraine G.m.b.H. to Wirtschaftsstab Ost, "Betr.: Straßenbahnen in den besetzten Ostgebieten,"

Rivne, January 19, 1943; TsDAVOV, 3206/2/207/20: general commissar to RKU, "Betr.: Inbetriebsetzung der elektrischen Bahnen für die örtliche Versorgung," Dnipropetrovs'k, February 15, 1943; TsDAVOV, 3206/2/207/36–37: I. A. R. Sohner at general commissar in Kiev to RKU Abt. WI, "Betr.: Einsatz der Strassenbahn in Kiew," Kiev, March 26, 1943.

27. Kuznetsov, *Babii iar,* 343.

28. Mykola Velychkivs'kyi, "Sumni chasy nimets'koï okupatsiï (1941–1944 roky)," *Vyzvol'nyi shliakh* 12, no. 2 (London, 1965): 154 and 12, no. 3 (1965): 303; *Meldungen* 43 (February 26, 1943): 20; *Shchodennyk Arkadiia Liubchenka,* 37; Gerstenfeld-Maltiel, *My Private War,* 212 (both on cleanliness of streets); TsDAHOU, 166/3/245/57: Vera Vasil'evna Ponomareva, [Pervomais'k?], January 20, 1946 (on the curfew).

29. Mykhailo Seleshko, *Vinnytsia: Spomyny perekladacha Komisiï doslidiv zlochyniv NKVD v 1937–1938* (New York, 1991), 31, 33, 46; Kuznetsov, *Babii iar,* 154; Samchuk, *Na koni voronomu,* 60; Halyna Lashchenko, "Povorot," *Samostiina Ukraïna* 11, no. 6(114) (New York, June 1958): 18.

30. Dmytro Malakov, *Oti dva roky . . . : U Kyievi pry nimtsiakh* (Kiev, 2002), 226 (on cars); [Sharandachenko], *Reiestratorka zahsu,* 44, 221; Bohdan Liubomyrenko, *Z Khrystom v Ukraïni: Zapysky viruiuchoho za roky 1941–1943* (Winnipeg, 1973), 80; TsDAVOV, 3676/4/307/43: II/III B Mü, "Die deutsche Propaganda in der Ukraine," n.p., n.d.

31. Kuznetsov, *Babii iar,* 220.

32. TsDAHOU, 1/23/121/6: announcement, "Iak represyvni zakhody [. . .]"; Velychkivs'kyi, "Sumni chasy [. . .]," *Vyzvol'nyi shliakh* 12, no. 2 (1965): 160.

33. TsDAHOU, 166/3/243/5v: Nikolai Kuz'mich Grun'skii [*sic*] (Ukrainian born in 1872), Kiev, February 19, 1944; Velychkivs'kyi, "Sumni chasy [. . .]," *Vyzvol'nyi shliakh,* 12, no. 1 (1965): 47; Leonid Abramenko, ed., *Kyïvs'kyi protses: Dokumenty i materialy* (Kiev, 1995), 42 (both on corpses in the street); Malakov, *Oti dva roky,* 152 (pickpocket story).

34. TsDAHOU, 1/23/121/4: "Oholoshennia"; Kuznetsov, *Babii iar,* 152; Dudin, "Velikii Mirazh," 130–131; John A. Armstrong, *Ukrainian Nationalism,* 3d ed., (Englewood, Colo., 1990), 167, n. 18.

35. TsDAHOU, 1/23/121/8: "Oholoshennia"; Hanna Luk"ianova, "Zi shchodennyka viiny 1941–1945 rokiv," *Rozbudova derzhavy,* no. 4 (April 1995): 58.

36. International Court of Justice, The Hague, Nuremberg Trial papers, document USSR-291 (on Nov. 29 announcement); Kuznetsov, *Babii iar,* 220. See also Abramenko, *Kyïvs'kyi protses,* 42.

37. TsDAVOV, 4620/3/243a/10: Nikolai Andrianovich Prakhov, "Chto bylo v Kieve pri nemtsakh," Kiev, May 21, 1941 [*sic*]; Iaroslav Haivas, "V roky nadiï i beznadiï (Zustrichi i rozmovy z O. Ol'zhychem v rokakh 1939–1944)," *Kalendar-*

al'manakh Novoho Shliakhu, 1977 (Toronto, n.d.), 119; Liubomyrenko, *Z Khrystom v Ukraïni*, 80. On the first public hangings in Kiev, see Luk"ianova, "Zi shchodennyka," 56.

38. *Poslednie novosti* (Kiev), March 30, 1942, 1; TsDAVOV, 3206/5/15/260: RKU *Lagebericht* for February 1942; Luk"ianova, "Zi shchodennyka," 61; Karmazin, *Nash khleb*, 218; Khoroshunova, "Pervyi god voiny," 94; TsDAHOU, 1/70/22/31: P. P. Gudzenko of Upravlenie gos. Arkhivami NKVD USSR, "O zverstvakh nemetskikh vlastei v okkupirovannykh raionakh Ukrainy 1941–1942 g.," n.p., June 1942; Nartova diary, 6.

39. K. Ia. Hrynevych, author interview. See also Eugen Kogon, Hermann Langbein, and Adalbert Rückerl, eds., *Nazi Mass Murder: A Documentary History of the Use of Poison Gas* (New Haven, Conn., 1993), 62.

40. L. S. Khmilevs'ka, author interview.

41. Fevr, *Solntse*, 123; Amnon Ajzensztadt, *Endurance: Chronicles of Jewish Resistance* (Oakville, N.Y., 1987), 62 (on shoes made from tires).

42. Fevr, *Solntse*, 123 (the quotation); Mykhailo Hartymiv, "Zemleiu ukraïns'koiu . . . ," in Mel'nyk, Lashchenko, and Veryha, *Na zov Kyieva*, 122.

43. Lashchenko, "Povorot," *Samostiina Ukraïna* 11, no. 10(118) (Chicago, October 1958): 9.

44. Ibid., 11, no. 11(119) (November 1958): 12; Kuznetsov, *Babii iar*, 287.

45. Ajzensztadt, *Endurance*, 61 (the quotation); Gerstenfeld-Maltiel, *My Private War*, 269–270.

46. Kuznetsov, *Babii iar*, 225 (the quotation); Nartova diary, 23; TsDAHOU, 166/3/246/2: Vasilii Ivanovich Iablonskii (Ukrainian born in 1908), [Kiev?], February 22, 1944; Valerii Haidabura, *Teatr, zakhovanyi v arkhivakh: Stsenichne mystetstvo v Ukraïni periodu nimets'ko-fashysts'koï okupatsiï (1941–1944)* (Kiev, 1998), 74.

47. On German women, see Kuznetsov, *Babii iar*, 228; Nartova diary, 14, 20; UCEC, Pavlo Ternivs'kyi [Ivan Zhyhadlo], "Spohady emigranta" (n.p., 1945), 38. For the quotation on children, see Kuznetsov, *Babii iar*, 254.

48. Gerstenfeld-Maltiel, *My Private War*, 218–219. On Hungarian officers, see HIA-HURIP, box 23, no. 441 AD, B-6, fol. 7: [Konstantyn Shtepa], n.p., February 12, 1951.

49. V. P. Kravchenko, author interview.

50. Szarota, *Życie codzienne*, 59; Fitzpatrick, *Everyday Stalinism*, 97 (this book is also the source of the term "people with privilege"). On heat at work, see Fesenko, *Povest'*, 86. For the situation of housecleaners, see Khmilev'ska, author interview.

51. *Shchodennyk Arkadiia Liubchenka*, 72.

52. Gerstenfeld-Maltiel, *My Private War*, 249; Ajzensztadt, *Endurance*, 55, 63.

53. Kostiuk, author interview.

54. NA microcopy T-120, roll 2533, frame E292537.

55. TsDAVOV, 3676/4/307/68–71: L. Dudin, "O propagande" (report for the Sipo-SD), n.p., October 1, 1942, with a German translation.

56. On Shtepa's situation, see Shtepa, HURIP interview, 5–6; Dudin, "Velikii Mirazh," 134; Velychkivs'kyi, "Sumni chasy [. . .]," *Vyzvol'nyi shliakh* 12, no. 3 (1965): 298. For Samchuk, see Samchuk, *Na koni voronomu*, 113, 140, 149–155, 177; *Ereignismeldung UdSSR* 191 (April 10, 1942): 36.

57. Armstrong, *Ukrainian Nationalism*, 165; Maliuzhenko, "Kyïv za 1942 r.," 178–181.

58. Kyslytsia, *Svite iasnyi*, 203; Arkadii Liubchenko, *Shchodennyk: Knyzhka persha* (Toronto, 1951), 148–149, editorial note. On Forostivs'kyi's arrest, see *Shchodennyk Arkadiia Liubchenka*, 90–91.

59. See, for example, Lashchenko, "Povorot," *Samostiina Ukraïna* 11, no. 11(119) (November 1958): 12–13.

60. On the annulling of warrants, see [Sharandachenko], *Reiestratorka zahsu*, 23, 37, 41, 48, 74, 82. For the salaries of administration employees, see Maliuzhenko, "Kyïv za 1942 r.," 178–181.

61. [Sharandachenko], *Reiestratorka zahsu*, 38, 71, 76, 87–88.

62. Seleshko, *Vinnytsia*, 84–85.

63. Maistrenko, *Istoriia moho pokolinnia*, 339; TsDAVOV, 3676/4/474/571: Sipo-SD report on the Kiev GB in March and April 1942. See also *Ereignismeldung UdSSR* 163 (February 2, 1942): 9.

64. *Ereignismeldung UdSSR* 81 (September 12, 1941): 10 (the quotation), Pihido-Pravoberezhnyi, "Velyka Vitchyzniana viina," 37; Fevr, *Solntse*, 196.

65. Matthias Riedel, "Bergbau und Eisenhüttenindustrie in der Ukraine unter deutscher Besatzung (1941–1944)," *Vierteljahrshefte für Zeitgeschichte* 21, no. 3 (1973): 252.

66. Alexander Dallin, *German Rule in Russia, 1941–1945: A Study of Occupation Policies*, 2d ed. (Boulder, Colo., 1981), 377, n. 2.

67. *Ereignismeldung UdSSR* 81 (September 12, 1941): 9; TsDAHOU, 166/3/244/4–7v: Vladimir Grigor'evich Koniushevskii ([Pole?] born in 1907), Kiev, February 22, 1944.

68. *Ereignismeldung UdSSR* 118 (October 19, 1941), 3; TsDAHOU, 1/23/124/80: Savchenko to Khrushchev, "Razvedvodka No 33/68" (on the engineer). Compare Riedel, "Bergbau und Eisenhüttenindustrie," 252. On Russians wearing identification, see TsDAVOV, 4620/3/281/13–14: Dina Mironovna Pronicheva (Jew born in Chernihiv in 1911), stenographic report of testimony, Kiev, April 24, 1946.

69. *Ereignismeldung UdSSR* 81 (September 12, 1941): 8.

70. Norbert Müller [et al.], eds., *Die faschistische Okkupationspolitik in den*

zeitweilig besetzten Gebieten der Sowjetunion (1941–1944) (Berlin, 1991), 234–235.

71. TsDAHOU, 1/23/124/81: Savchenko to Khrushchev, "Razvedsvodka No 33/68"; Siegfried von Vegesack, *Als Dolmetscher im Osten: Ein Erlebnisbericht aus den Jahren 1942–43* (Hanover, 1965), 91–92.

72. NA microcopy T-84, roll 120, frames 418563–564: "Unternehmungen der Metallbearbeitungs-Sektion der Abteilung für Industrie" (data compiled no later than January 1942); TsDAHOU, 1/22/6/25–26: D. S. Korotchenko to N. S. Khrushchev, "O sostoianii partizanskogo dvizheniia na pravoberezhnoi Ukraine," n.p., July 22, 1943; TsDAHOU, 1/22/123/29: "Razvedovat. [*sic*] svodka n. 29 po sostoianiiu na 16/XII. 42 g."; TsDAHOU, 166/3/244/2–3: Nadezhda Petrovna Konashko (Ukrainian born in 1913), Kiev, February 22, 1944; TsDAHOU, 1/23/633/32–33: Burdeniuk, Kiev obkom secretary, "Politinformatsiia na 10 hrudnia 1943 roku," [Kiev], December 15, 1943 (both on the Lenin Forge).

73. Riedel, "Bergbau und Eisenhüttenindustrie," 271–272; Dietrich Eichholtz, *Geschichte der deutschen Kriegswirtschaft, 1939–1945*, vol. 1: *1941–1943* (Berlin, 1985), 468; *Meldungen* 43 (February 26, 1943): 20.

74. Fevr, *Solntse*, 191–192.

75. TsDAVOV, 3206/1/111/28–29v: RKU "Anordnung zur Regelung der Lohn- und Arbeitsbedingungen gewerblicher Arbeitskräfte," Rivne, December 1, 1941 (on wages); TsDAVOV, 3676/4/475/473–474: Sipo-SD report on the Kiev GB in September 1942, Kiev, October 1, 1942; TsDAHOU, 166/3/244/2–3: Konashko. For the barter of nails and cutlery, see Riedel, "Bergbau und Eisenhüttenindustrie," 265–266.

76. TsDAHOU, 166/3/244/6: Koniushevskii.

77. Ibid., 7–7v.

78. On lack of direction by Germans, see TsDAHOU, 166/3/244/2v: Konashko. On insults and abuse, see NA microcopy T-120, roll 2533, frames E292537–538; Volodymyr Serhiichuk, [comp.], *OUN-UPA v roky viiny: Novi dokumenty i materialy* (Kiev, 1996), 335; HIA, B. I. Nicolaevsky collection, series no. 236, box 409, folder 19, fol. 47: Emigrant [pseud.], "Nemtsy v Kieve: (Iz vospominanii ochevidtsa)."

79. TsDAHOU, 166/3/244/2v: Konashko.

80. Ibid.; TsDAHOU, 166/3/244/7: Koniushevskii; Luk"ianova, "Zi shchodennyka," 60; Karmazin, *Nash khleb*, 217. Compare TsDAHOU, 166/3/246/3: Iablonskii.

81. TsDAHOU, 166/3/244/2–3: Konashko; TsDAHOU, 166/3/244/7v: Koniushevskii.

82. A. Anatoli (Kuznetsov) [Anatolii Kuznetsov], *Babi Yar: A Document in the Form of a Novel* (London, 1970), 363; Kuznetsov, *Babii iar*, 368. See also *Ereignismeldung UdSSR* 163 (February 2, 1942): 9–10.

83. TsDAHOU, 166/3/244/4–7v: Koniushevskii. See also TsDAHOU, 166/3/246/2v: Iablonskii; TsDAHOU, 1/22/87/72–73: A. V., "Spravka o nastroeniiakh naseleniia v okkupirovannykh nemetsko-fashistskimi zakhvatchikami raionakh Ukrainy," n.p., November 13, 1942.

84. *Meldungen* 43 (February 26, 1943): 17.

85. Riedel, "Bergbau und Eisenhüttenindustrie," 253; Eichholtz, *Geschichte der deutschen Kriegswirtschaft*, vol. 1, 470; *Meldungen* 43 (February 26, 1943): 17.

86. Riedel, "Bergbau und Eisenhüttenindustrie," 266; *Meldungen* 43 (February 26, 1943): 18, 20; TsDAVOV, 3206/5/15/640: RKU *Lagebericht* for January and February 1943, Rivne, March 14, 1943.

87. On the work at Nikopol', see Riedel, "Bergbau und Eisenhüttenindustrie," 272; Eichholtz, *Geschichte der deutschen Kriegswirtschaft*, vol. 1, 470. Compare Timothy Mulligan, *The Politics of Illusion and Empire: German Occupation Policy in the Soviet Union, 1942–1943* (New York, 1988), 109. For the Dniprohes dam, see *Meldungen* 32 (December 4, 1942): 24, and 43 (February 26, 1943): 17; Riedel, "Bergbau und Eisenhüttenindustrie," 273; Eichholtz, *Geschichte der deutschen Kriegswirtschaft*, vol. 1, 472; Dallin, *German Rule*, 379; Mulligan, *Politics of Illusion and Empire*, 109.

88. Pihido-Pravoberezhnyi, "*Velyka Vitchyzniana viina*," 153–154.

89. Ibid., 143–144, 155.

90. NA microcopy T-84, roll 120, frames 418565–570: "Unternehmungen der Metallbearbeitungs-Sektion der Abteilung für Industrie."

91. NA microcopy T-84, roll 120, frames 418576–581: "Unternehmungen der Nährmittel-Sektion."

92. Anatoli (Kuznetsov), *Babi Yar*, 288; Kuznetsov, *Babii iar*, 290.

93. *Ereignismeldung UdSSR* 183 (March 20, 1942): 10.

94. *Ereignismeldung UdSSR* 107 (October 8, 1941): 15. On the lack of natives by 1943, see Ortwin Buchbender, *Das tönende Erz: Deutsche Propaganda gegen die Rote Armee im Zweiten Weltkrieg* (Stuttgart, 1978), 318; *Ereignismeldung UdSSR* 107 (October 8, 1941): 14.

95. TsDAVOV, 3206/1/78/36: RKU *Lagebericht* for January 1942; [Sharandachenko], *Reiestratorka zahsu*, 14, 24, 43.

96. On the railroad, see TsDAHOU, 1/23/124/21: Savchenko, VRIO NKVD USSR, to Khrushchev, "Razvedsvodka No 11: O polozhenii v okkupirovannoi protivnikom Vinnitskoi oblasti po sostoianiiu na 30. 9. 42g.," Engel's, October 16, 1942; TsDAHOU, 1/23/124/85: Savchenko to Khrushchev, "Razvedsvodka No 33/68"; TsDAVOV, 3206/5/15/640: RKU *Lagebericht* for January and February 1943. For the highway, consult Christian Gerlach, *Kalkulierte Morde: Die deutsche Wirtschafts- und Vernichtungspolitik in Weißrußland 1941 bis 1944* (Hamburg, 1999), 389.

97. TsDAHOU, 1/23/124/21–22: Savchenko to Khrushchev, "Razvedsvodka no. 11";

TsDAHOU, 1/23/124/89: Savchenko to Khrushchev, "Razvedsvodka No 33/68"; Seleshko, *Vinnytsia*, 44–45; Maistrenko, *Istoriia moho pokolinnia*, 339; author's notes from I. Khoroshunova, "Kievskie zapiski" (unpublished manuscript), fol. 379; Gerstenfeld-Maltiel, *My Private War*, 212. On closure, see Kabaida, "1941," 50; Nartova diary, 9.

98. Nartova diary, 9; [Sharandachenko], *Reiestratorka zahsu*, 104; Emigrant, "Nemtsy v Kieve," 45; Dudin, "Velikii Mirazh," 110; TsDAVOV, 3676/4/474/ 573: Sipo-SD report on the Kiev GB in March and April 1942.

99. On visits by Germans and Hungarians, see Fevr, *Solntse*, 134–135. See also Kabaida, "1941," 50; Samchuk, *Na koni voronomu*, 84; [Sharandachenko], *Reiestratorka zahsu*, 40; Liubomyrenko, *Z Khrystom v Ukraïni*, 94; *Shchodennyk Arkadiia Liubchenka*, 103; Ternivs'kyi, "Spohady emigranta," 53. On the conversion of some stores to antique stores, see Dudin, "Velikii Mirazh," 100.

100. TsDAHOU, 1/23/685/72–73: Strokach and Martynov, "Dokladnaia zapiska 'O torgovle na okkupirovannoi territorii Ukrainy' po sostoianiiu na 29 ianvaria 1943 g.," Moscow, January 29, 1943; Seleshko, *Vinnytsia*, 44. For the production of Ukrainian shirts, see Fesenko, *Povest'*, 84.

101. Dallin, *German Rule*, 397–398.

102. TsDAVOV, 3206/1/72/24: "Besondere Anordnungen Nr. 47," March 9, 1942.

103. Seleshko, *Vinnytsia*, 76; *Ukraïns'kyi holos* (Proskuriv), March 28, 1943, 4; TsDAHOU, 166/3/243/43: Aleksei Mikhailovich Bashkulat (Ukrainian born in 1909), Kiev, February 28, 1944 (the quotation).

104. TsDAVOV, 4620/3/243a/57–58: Professor N. A. Shepelevskii, "Prebyvanie nemtsev v Kieve" (the quotation); TsDAVOV, 4620/3/243a/92–94: Iu. Iu. Kramarenko, "Politika nemetskikh okkupantov na Ukraine—v Kieve v oblasti zdravookhraneniia," Kiev, [1943]; *Shchodennyk Arkadiia Liubchenka*, 90–92; Kuznetsov, *Babii iar*, 229–230; Kravchenko, author interview.

105. T. S., "Working Conditions of Scientists and Specialists in Soviet Ukraine," *Ukrainian Quarterly* 5, no. 3 (New York, 1949): 261–271.

106. Ihor Verba, "Sproby vidnovlennia Ukraïns'koï Akademiï Nauk u Kyievi (kinets' 1941–seredyna 1942 rr.)," *Ukraïns'kyi istoryk* 32, nos. 1–4(124–127) (New York, 1995): 88–89.

107. Adolf Hitler, *Monologe im Führerhauptquartier 1941–1944: Die Aufzeichnungen Heinrich Heims herausgegeben von Werner Jochmann* (Hamburg, 1980), 311–312.

108. TsDAHOU, 166/3/243/16–18, 21: Vladimir Mikhailovich Artobolevskii (Russian born in 1874), Kiev, February 22 and 25, 1944; TsDAHOU, 166/3/244/8–11v: Novitskaia.

109. Blanka Jerabek, *Das Schulwesen und die Schulpolitik im Reichskommissariat Ukraine 1941–1944: Im Lichte deutscher Dokumente* (Munich, 1991), 108–109.

Examples of the senseless destruction are in *Trial of the Major War Criminals before the International Military Tribunal,* vol. 25 (Nuremberg, 1949), 344; TsDAVOV, 4620/3/243a/61: Shepelevskii, "Prebyvanie."

110. TsDAVOV, 3206/1/78/8: Acting General Commissar Quitzrau to Erich Koch, Kiev, January 21, 1942; TsDAHOU, 166/3/243/1–2: Grun'skii. See also TsDAVOV, 3206/2/23/6–7: East Ministry to Erich Koch, Berlin, January 21, 1942.

111. *Ereignismeldung UdSSR* 132 (November 12, 1941): 12–13; Otto Bräutigam, *Überblick über die besetzten Ostgebiete während des 2. Weltkrieges* (Tübingen, 1954), 74; Ivan Rozhin, "Iaroslav Samotovka," *Samostiina Ukraïna* 22, nos. 11–12(223–224)[sic; really 20, nos. 11–12(224–225)] (November–December 1967): 16–21.

112. Verba, "Sproby vidnovlennia," 90; TsDAHOU, 166/3/243/1–3: Grun'skii.

113. TsDAHOU, 166/3/244/16–16v: Iurii Mikhailovich Markovskii (Ukrainian born in 1904), Kiev, March 12, 1944.

114. DAKO, r-2356/8/7/76: Mykola Kuzmych Hruns'kyi to Mayor Forostivs'kyi, Kiev, April 22, 1942; TsDAVOV, 3206/1/78/8: Quitzrau to Koch, Kiev, January 21, 1942; Polons'ka-Vasylenko, *Ukraïns'ka Akademiia Nauk,* vol. 2, 64; TsDAHOU, 166/3/244/16v: Markovskii.

115. Nykon Nemyron [Mykola Andrusiak], "U zbudzhenii v ohni stolytsi Ukraïny (Slavnii pam"iati muchenykiv za Ukraïnu v Kyievi v 1941–42 rr.)," in Mykhailo H. Marunchak, ed., *V borot'bi za ukraïns'ku derzhavu: Eseï, spohady, svidchennia, litopysannia, dokumenty Druhoï svitovoï viiny* (Winnipeg, 1990), 812–813; DAKO, r-2356/8/7/76: Hruns'kyi to Forostivs'kyi.

116. Velychkivs'kyi, "Sumni chasy [. . .]," *Vyzvol'nyi shliakh* 12, no. 2 (1965): 153–154 and 12, no. 3 (1965): 299–301.

117. Bräutigam, *Überblick über die besetzten Ostgebiete,* 74–75.

118. Leontii Forostivs'kyi, *Kyïv pid vorozhymy okupatsiiamy* (Buenos Aires, 1952), 76; Kyslytsia, *Svite iasnyi,* 184, 202.

119. Kyslytsia, *Svite iasnyi,* 197; TsDAHOU, 166/3/243/4: Grun'skii; *Shchodennyk Arkadiia Liubchenka,* 75.

120. TsDAVOV, 3676/1/197/50–145: German-language essay by Shtepa; Liubomyr Vynar, "Oleksander Petrovych Ohloblyn (1899–1992): Korotkyi biohrafichnyi narys," *Ukraïns'kyi istoryk* 30, nos. 1–4(116–119) (New York, 1993): 33, n. 61; Patricia Kennedy Grimsted, "The Fate of Ukrainian Cultural Treasures during World War II: The Plunder of Archives, Libraries, and Museums under the Third Reich," *Jahrbücher für Geschichte Osteuropas* 39, no. 1 (1991): 67; TsDAVOV, 3676/1/226/121: Student Zahn, "Wochenbericht v. 4.10.–10.10.42" (both on Ohloblyn); TsDAHOU, 1/22/6/36–37: Korotchenko to Khrushchev, "O sostoianii [. . .]" (on Ohloblyn and Slobodianiuk).

121. Bogatyrchuk, *Moi zhiznennyi put',* 128, 132–133; Liudmyla Ivchenko, "Ukraïns'kyi Chervonyi Khrest u Kyievi (1941–1942)," in Modest Ripeckyj, ed.,

Medychna opika v UPA, which is *Litopys UPA*, vol. 23 (Toronto, 1992), 37–50; DAKO, r-2356/15/21/1–2v: "Dopovidna Zapyska pro robotu Komiteta [*sic*] Vzaiemodopomohy/kol. Chervonyi Khrest," March 15, 1942; TsDAHOU, 166/3/244/14v–15: Markovskii.

122. Samchuk, *Na koni voronomu*, 113; Pozhars'ka, "Lyst-podiaka z Kyieva," *Volyn'*, February 22, 1942, 3.

123. Kuznetsov, *Babii iar*, 163, 212; Malakov, *Oti dva roky*, 139.

124. Nemyron, "U zbudzhenii v ohni stolytsi Ukraïny," 809–810.

125. DAKO, r-2209/1/22/132: Professor Bohatyrchuk to district commissar in Khabne, letter in German, January 16, 1942; DAKO, r-2356/15/22/8: letter, March 20, 1942.

126. DAKO, r-2356/15/21/8–9; DAKO, r-2356/2/20/6–6v: Solodovnyk, Kerivnyk viddilu kul'tury i osvity, October 12, 1942; Nartova diary, 4; NA microcopy T-84, roll 120, frame 418938: report by Sipo-SD of the Kiev GB, July 30, 1942; TsDAVOV, 3676/4/474/574: Sipo-SD report on the Kiev GB in March and April 1942; TsDAVOV, 3676/4/475/448, 671: Sipo-SD reports on the Kiev GB in September and November 1942.

127. "Dopomoha naselenniu," *Nove ukraïns'ke slovo*, January 26, 1943, 4.

128. Ibid.; *Nove ukraïns'ke slovo*, January 27, 1943, 4 and January 29, 1943, 4; DAKO, r-2356/15/20/5: letter; Maliuzhenko, "Kyïv za 1942 r.," 179.

129. Armstrong, *Ukrainian Nationalism*, 168, citing *Nove ukraïns'ke slovo*, September 19, 1943.

130. DAKO, r-2356/8/7/57–58, 99: Professor Borys Bukreiev to deputy mayor Volkanovych, March 30, 1942, and audit record of May 15, 1942.

131. DAKO, r-2356/8/7/48; DAKO, r-2356/8/7/76: Hruns'kyi to Mayor Forostivs'kyi, Kiev, April 22, 1942; DAKO, r-2356/8/7/97: Nenadkevych and Pension Inspector Cheres to deputy mayor Volkanovych, June 17, 1942; TsDAHOU, 166/3/243/1–5v: Grun'skii.

132. *Shchodennyk Arkadiia Liubchenka*, 65; TsDAVOV, 3676/4/474/89–90: Sipo-SD report on the Kiev GB for April 2–18, 1943; TsDAHOU, 166/3/243/1–5v: Grun'skii; TsDAHOU, 166/3/243/35–36: Artobolevskii.

133. The name of the supplement to the paper *(Holos Poltavshchyny)* was *Nauka i mystetstvo*. On suicides in Kiev, see TsDAHOU, 166/3/248/25: V. Tverskoi, "Dorogie druzh'ia," Kiev, n.d. (before August 14, 1945); Nartova diary, 20.

134. Maistrenko, *Istoriia moho pokolinnia*, 365. On the general passivity of Soviet city dwellers during the 1930s, see Fitzpatrick, *Everyday Stalinism*, 221.

7. *Famine in Kiev*

1. Walther Hubatsch, ed., *Hitlers Weisungen für die Kriegsführung 1939–1945: Dokumente des Oberkommandos der Wehrmacht* (Frankfurt am Main, 1962), 148; H. R. Trevor-Roper, ed., *Hitler's War Directives 1939–1945: Texts from Wal-*

ter Hubatsch, *"Hitlers Weisungen für die Kriegsführung 1939–1945"* (London, 1964), 94.

2. Gerd R. Ueberschär, comp., "Ausgewählte Dokumente," in Gerd R. Ueberschär and Wolfram Wette, eds., *"Unternehmen Barbarossa": Der deutsche Überfall auf die Sowjetunion 1941. Berichte, Analysen, Dokumente* (Paderborn, Ger., 1984), 333.

3. Adolf Hitler, *Monologe im Führerhauptquartier 1941–1944: Die Aufzeichnungen Heinrich Heims herausgegeben von Werner Jochmann* (Hamburg, 1980), 334.

4. Christian Streit, *Die Wehrmacht und die sowjetischen Kriegsgefangenen 1941–1945* (Stuttgart, 1978), 145; Reinhard Rurüp, ed, *Der Krieg gegen die Sowjetunion 1941–1945: Eine Dokumentation* (Berlin, 1991), 84.

5. Richard Breitman, *The Architect of Genocide: Himmler and the Final Solution* (New York, 1991), 213.

6. On Himmler, see NA microcopy T-84, roll 387, frame 797: Hitler's personal secretary Koeppen, report of October 6, 1941; *Der Dienstkalender Heinrich Himmlers 1941/42*, ed. Peter Witte et al. (Hamburg, 1999), 224–225. For Jeckeln's impressions, see Hans-Heinrich Wilhelm, *Rassenpolitik und Kriegführung: Sicherheitspolizei und Wehrmacht in Polen und in der Sowjetunion 1939–1942* (Passau, Ger., 1991), 341. For the Sauckel quotation, see Rolf-Dieter Müller, ed., *Die deutsche Wirtschaftspolitik in den besetzten sowjetischen Gebieten 1941–1943: Der Abschlußbericht des Wirtschaftsstabes Ost und Aufzeichnungen eines Angehörigen des Wirtschaftskommandos Kiew* (Boppard am Rhein, Ger., 1991), 56, n. 63.

7. Otto Bräutigam, *So hat es sich zugetragen . . . : Ein Leben als Soldat und Diplomat* (Würzburg, Ger., 1968), 401.

8. NA microcopy T-120, roll 2533, frame E292711: "FHQ., den 18. Oktober 1941."

9. Streit, *Wehrmacht*, 162.

10. TsDAVOV, 3206/1/9/14–16v (also at 3206/4/9/24–26v): [Helmut] Körner of Wirtschaftsinspektion Süd, Chefgruppe Landwirtschaft, "An die Wirtschaftskommandos. Betr.: Lebensmittelzuteilung an die städtischen Zivilbevölkerung," n.p., September 5, 1941.

11. Partial text in Norbert Müller [et al.], ed., *Die faschistische Okkupationspolitik in den zeitweilig besetzten Gebieten der Sowjetunion (1941–1944)* (Berlin, 1991), 212–214. An original is at BA-Berlin, R 6/13, fols. 74–76.

12. Partial text in Norbert Müller, ed., *Okkupation, Raub, Vernichtung: Dokumente zur Besatzungspolitik der faschistischen Wehrmacht auf sowjetischem Territorium 1941–1944*, 2d ed. (Berlin, 1980), 193. Compare Truman Oliver Anderson III, "The Conduct of Reprisals by the German Army of Occupation in the Southern USSR, 1941–1943," Ph.D. diss., University of Chicago, 1995, 209.

13. Müller, *Okkupation, Raub, Vernichtung*, 192–194.

14. *Trial of the Major War Criminals before the International Military Tribunal* [TMWC], vol. 35 (Nuremberg, 1949), 85; Müller, *Die deutsche Wirtschaftspolitik*, 56, n. 63 (the quotation).

15. *TMWC*, vol. 32 (Nuremberg, 1949), 74. See also Rolf-Dieter Müller, "Das 'Unternehmen Barbarossa' als wirtschaftlicher Raubkrieg," in Ueberschär and Wette, "*Unternehmen Barbarossa*," 187–188.

16. Streit, *Wehrmacht*, 161–162, citing *TMWC*, vol. 34 (Nuremberg, 1949), 130.

17. Ueberschär, "Ausgewählte Dokumente," 385–388; Müller, *Die faschistische Okkupationspolitik*, 217–219.

18. Alexander Dallin, *German Rule in Russia, 1941–1945: A Study of Occupation Policies*, 2d ed. (Boulder, Colo., 1981), 123 (the quotation); Anderson, "Conduct of Reprisals," 210–211.

19. TsDAVOV, 3206/5/15/157: "Bericht über die Referentenbesprechung," Rivne, October 3, 1941.

20. TsDAVOV, 3206/1/65/17–18v: I.A. gez. Dr. [Friedrich] Ackermann KVACh, Der Reichskommissar für die Ukraine, Hauptabteilung III, Abteilung Ernährung u. Landwirtschaft, "Betrifft: Versorgung der städtischen Zivilbevölkerung mit Lebensmitteln," Rivne, February 20, 1942.

21. On the food supply, see HIA, B. I. Nicolaevsky collection, series no. 178, box 232, folder 10, fols. 28–29: [Lev Vladimirovich] Dudin, "Velikii Mirazh: Sobytiia 1941–1947 godov v ponimanii sovetskogo cheloveka," n.p., 1947. The nationalities of Kievans are my extrapolation, from the situation on January 1, 1940, mentioned in TsDAVOV, 4620/3/2a/3: Gosplan, "Pasport goroda (ekonomiko-statisticheskii spravochnik)" for Kiev.

22. See Table 1 in the Appendix.

23. BA-MA, RW 31/122, fol. 86: "Bericht über eine auf Anordnung des Herrn Amtschef durchgeführte Dienstreise des Obst. Dr. Petri nach Kiew vom 22. Bis 27.9.1941," Berlin, September 29, 1941.

24. Klaus Jochen Arnold, "Die Eroberung und Behandlung der Stadt Kiew durch die Wehrmacht im September 1941: Zur Radikalisierung der Besatzungspolitik," *Militärgeschichtliche Mitteilungen* 58, no. 1 (1999): 37.

25. Iaroslav Haivas, *Koly kinchalasia epokha* (n.p., 1964), 64–65.

26. Nina Mykhalevych, "Do Kyieva! Fragment zi spohadu," in Kost' Mel'nyk, Oleh Lashchenko, and Vasyl' Veryha, eds., *Na zov Kyieva: Ukraïns'kyi natsionalizm u II Svitovii Viini: Zbirnyk stattei, spohadiv i dokumentiv* (Toronto, 1985), 225. See also Hryhorii Kostiuk, *Zustrichi i proshchannia: Spohady. Knyha druha* (Edmonton, 1998), 30–31; TsDAVOV, 4620/3/243a/20: I. Zhitov, "Komisii po rassledovaniiu nemetskikh zverstv na Ukraine," Kiev, November 1943.

27. TsDAVOV, 3676/4/475/481: Sipo-SD report on the Kiev GB in September 1942, Kiev, October 1, 1942.

28. Haivas, *Koly kinchalasia epokha*, 65; Halyna Lashchenko, "Povorot," *Samostiina Ukraïna* 11, no. 11(119) (Chicago, November 1958): 12. Compare *OUN u viini 1939 1945* (n.p., n.d.), 61.

29. Dmytro Kyslytsia, *Svite iasnyi: Spohady. Vid r. Vovchi z Naddniprianshchyny do r. Sv. Lavrentiia na Ottavshchyni* (Ottawa, 1987), 193–194.

30. DAKO, r-2356/1/60/3–3v (the letter); *Ereignismeldung UdSSR* 191 (April 10, 1942): 39–40; Dudin, "Velikii Mirazh," 134.

31. Nykon Nemyron [Mykola Andrusiak], "U zbudzhenii v ohni stolytsi Ukraïny (Slavnii pam"iati muchenykiv za Ukraïnu v Kyievi v 1941–42 rr.)," in Mykhailo H. Marunchak, ed., *V borot'bi za ukraïns'ku derzhavu: Eseï, spohady, svidchennia, litopysannia, dokumenty Druhoï svitovoï viiny* (Winnipeg, 1990), 805; TsDAVOV, 3676/1/50/3. Compare Osyp Boidunyk, *Na perelomi: (Uryvky spohadiv)* (Paris, 1967), 104.

32. Richard Bidlack, *Workers at War: Factory Workers and Labor Policy in the Siege of Leningrad*, Carl Beck Papers in Russian and East European Studies, no. 902 (Pittsburgh, 1991), 44.

33. On the time from October 10, 1941, see DAKO, r-2356/1/60/3–3v: Bahazii to Stadtkommissar Muss, December 1941; Dudin, "Velikii Mirazh," 106; TsDAHOU, 1/22/347/3–4: "Iz dnevnika uchitel'nitsy gor. Kieva L. Nartovoi" (hereafter Nartova diary); Anatolii Kuznetsov (A. Anatolii), *Babii iar: Roman-dokument* (New York, 1986), 228; [O. P. Sharandachenko], *Reiestratorka zahsu: (Iz shchodennyka kyianky)* (Kiev, 1960), 21, 31, 33, 64. On the time from December 1941, see TsDAVOV, 3676/4/475/471: Sipo-SD report on the Kiev GB in September 1942; *Ereignismeldung UdSSR* 191 (April 10, 1942): 30; Ihor Kamenetsky, *Secret Nazi Plans for Eastern Europe: A Study of Lebensraum Policies* (New York, 1961), 147; [Sharandachenko], *Reiestratorka zahsu*, 64. On early 1942, see Hanna Luk"ianova, "Zi shchodennyka viiny 1941–1945 rokiv," *Rozbudova derzhavy*, no. 4 (Kiev, April 1995): 61. On the time from May 1942, see Luk"ianova, "Zi shchodennyka vinny"; NA microcopy T-84, roll 120, frame 418938: Sipo-SD of the Kiev GB, "Aktenvermerk," Kiev, July 30, 1942; TsDAVOV, 3676/4/475/471, 473: Sipo-SD report on the Kiev GB in September 1942. On the time from August 1942, see TsDAVOV, 3676/4/475/478–479: Sipo-SD report on the Kiev GB in September 1942; NA microcopy T-84, roll 120, frame 418941: Sipo-SD of the Kiev GB to Magunia, "Betr: Lebensmittellage der einheimischen Bevölkerung von Kiew," Kiev, February 24, 1943.

34. [Sharandachenko], *Reiestratorka zahsu*, 198, 220, 231.

35. Lashchenko, "Povorot," 9; Mykhalevych, "Do Kyieva!" 225; Kuznetsov, *Babii iar*, 228.

36. K. Ia. Hrynevych, author interview; TsDAHOU, 166/3/243/5v: Nikolai Kuz'mich Grun'skii [*sic*] (Ukrainian born in 1872), Kiev, February 19, 1944;

TsDAHOU, 166/3/244/2v: Nadezhda Petrovna Konashko (Ukrainian born in 1913), Kiev, February 22, 1944; [Sharandachenko], *Reiestratorka zahsu*, 65, 174, 226; Kuznetsov, *Babii iar*, 228; *Shchodennyk Arkadiia Liubchenka*, ed. Iurii Luts'kyi (Lviv, Ukr., 1999), 74–75; Tat'iana Fesenko, *Povest' krivykh let* (New York, 1963), 82.

37. Hrynevych and V. P. Kravchenko, author interviews; Ivan Maistrenko, *Istoriia moho pokolinnia: Spohady uchasnyka revoliutsiinykh podii v Ukraïni* (Edmonton, 1985), 338–339; Kuznetsov, *Babii iar*, 163; [Sharandachenko], *Reiestratorka zahsu*, 43; Fesenko, *Povest'*, 79.

38. [Sharandachenko], *Reiestratorka zahsu*, 174–175; Kuznetsov, *Babii iar*, 162.

39. Irina Khoroshunova, "Pervyi god voiny. Kievskie zapiski," *Iehupets'* 9 (Kiev, 2001): 61.

40. Author's notes from I. Khoroshunova, "Kievskie zapiski" (unpublished manuscript), fols. 70, 72. For Kievan memoirs, consult TsDAVOV, 4620/3/243a/21: Zhitov, "Komisii" (the quotation); Dudin, "Velikii Mirazh," 108. See also Paul Werner, *Ein Schweizer Journalist sieht Rußland: Auf den Spuren der deutschen Armee zwischen San und Dnjepr* (Olten, Switz., 1942), 104.

41. Fesenko, *Povest'*, 78; Hrynevych, author interview; TsDAHOU, 166/3/244/41v: Iurii Mikhailovich Markovskii (Ukrainian born in 1904), Kiev, March 12, 1944. The quotation is in TsDAHOU, 166/3/248/25: V. Tverskoi, "Dorogie druz'ia," Kiev, n.d. (before August 14, 1945).

42. DAKO, r-2356/8/7/92–95v: "Kopiia. Gospodinu Golove Gorodskoi Upravy g. Kiev. Ot invalidov, nakhodiashikhsia na izhdevenii v Dome Invalidov," Kiev, June 2, 1942.

43. Mikhail Iakovlevich Gerenrot, quoted in TsDAHOU, 1/22/11/3: Chepurnoi, "Informatsiia o sostoianii raboty kievskoi podpol'noi organizatsii KP/b/U," Starobil's'k, March 26, 1943.

44. Kuznetsov, *Babii iar*, 332; NA microcopy T-84, roll 120, frame 418722.

45. A. Anatoli (Kuznetsov), *Babi Yar: A Document in the Form of a Novel* (London, 1970), 221–222; Kuznetsov, *Babii iar*, 222–223.

46. Nartova diary, 3–4, note of December 26, 1941.

47. TsDAVOV, 3676/4/474/564: Sipo-SD report on the Kiev GB in March and April 1942.

48. Streit, *Wehrmacht*, 154, 362, n. 102.

49. Müller, *Die faschistische Okkupationspolitik*, 254.

50. TsDAVOV, 3676/4/474/353: Sipo-SD report on the Kiev GB in February 1942, Kiev, n.d.; Kamenetsky, *Secret Nazi Plans*, 147–148. Compare *Ereignismeldung UdSSR* 191 (April 10, 1942): 24, 30.

51. Kuznetsov, *Babii iar*, 250–251, 255.

52. *Meldungen* 13 (July 24, 1942): 11.

53. Julie Hessler, "A Postwar Perestroika? Toward a History of Private Enterprise in

the USSR," *Slavic Review* 57, no. 3 (1998): 520–522; Sheila Fitzpatrick, *Everyday Stalinism: Ordinary Life in Extraordinary Times. Soviet Russia in the 1930s* (New York, 1999), 57, 61.

54. TsDAHOU, 166/3/246/3: Vasilii Ivanovich Iablonskii (Ukrainian born in 1908), [Kiev], February 22, 1944.

55. A. Kabaida, "1941," *Kalendar-al'manakh Novoho Shliakhu*, 1991 (Toronto, n.d.): 50; Mykhailo Hartymiv, "Zemleiu ukraïns'koiu . . . ," in Mel'nyk, Lashchenko, and Veryha, *Na zov Kyieva*, 123–125.

56. For the list of things on sale, see Mykhalevych, "Do Kyieva!" 225. For "gluttony stalls" (original usage: *obzhorni riady*), see Dmytro Malakov, *Oti dva roky . . . : U Kyievi pry nimtsiakh* (Kiev, 2002), 112–113, 180, 183. On the participation of soldiers and policemen, see *Ereignismeldung UdSSR* 107 (October 8, 1941): 16; TsDAHOU, 166/3/245/6: Solomon Abramovich Peker (Jew born in 1884), Kiev, March 1, 1944; Dudin, "Velikii Mirazh," 94.

57. TsDAVOV, 4620/3/243a/60: N. A. Shepelevskii, "Prebyvanie nemtsev v Kieve," n.p., n.d.

58. Ie. M. Moskovs'ka, author interview (on pasties); Nartova diary, 9; Kuznetsov, *Babii iar*, 170, 252, 255; [Sharandachenko], *Reiestratorka zahsu* 104 (all three on teenagers); TsDAVOV, 4620/3/243a/60: Shepelevskii, "Prebyvanie" (on soldiers).

59. *Ereignismeldung UdSSR* 187 (March 30, 1942): 12–13; Dudin, "Velikii Mirazh," 112; HIA, B. I. Nicolaevsky collection, series no. 236, box 409, folder 19, fols. 30–31: Emigrant [pseud.] "Nemtsy v Kieve: (Iz vospominanii ochevidtsa)," n.p., n.d.; [Sharandachenko], *Reiestratorka zahsu*, 175.

60. TsDAVOV, 4620/3/243a/60: Shepelevskii, "Prebyvanie."

61. *Ereignismeldung UdSSR* 74 (September 5, 1941): 7, 107 (October 8, 1941): 16, *Ereignismeldung UdSSR* 135 (November 19, 1941): 15, and 191 (April 10, 1942): 29; TsDAVOV, 3206/5/15/343: RKU *Lagebericht* for March 1942, Rivne, April 15, 1942; Hrynevych, author interview; NA microcopy T-501, roll 5, frame 854: Bfh. rückw.H. Geb. Süd, Abt. VII/174/41, HQ, September 7, 1941.

62. *Ereignismeldung UdSSR* 125 (October 26, 1941): 6. See also TsDAHOU, 1/23/685/73–74: Strokach and Martynov to Korniiets' of the Central Committee of the CP(b)U, "Dokladnaia zapiska 'O torgovle na okkupirovannoi territorii Ukrainy'. Po sostoianiiu na 29 ianvaria 1943 g.," Moscow, January 29, 1943; Müller, *Die faschistische Okkupationspolitik*, 255; Rurüp, *Der Krieg*, 124. Examples of market prices in Kiev are in NA microcopy T-84, roll 120, frames 419074–078: Sipo-SD of the Kiev GB, "Die Geldentwertung im Generalbezirk Kiew," December 1, 1942; Kuznetsov, *Babii iar*, 211, 334; Ulas Samchuk, *Na koni voronomu: Spomyny i vrazhennia* (Winnipeg, 1975), 43, 60; L. Maliuzhenko, "Kyïv za 1942 r.," *Nashe mynule* 1(6) (Kiev, 1993): 177–178.

63. Fesenko, *Povest'*, 78 (on revenge); Khoroshunova, "Pervyi god voiny," 63–64; Khoroshunova, "Kievskie zapiski," 70, note of October 22, 1941.

64. *Meldungen* 13 (July 24, 1942): 10–11.

65. D. V. Malakov, *Kyïv 1941–1943: Fotoal'bom* (Kiev, 2000), 164–165; TsDAVOV, 3206/1/35/2: leaflet, "Uvaha ukraïntsi! Obminiuite vashi hroshi!"; *Vidrodzhennia* (Tarashcha), October 8, 1942, 4; *Vidrodzhennia*, October 11, 1942, 3.

66. *Shchodennyk Arkadiia Liubchenka*, 50; *Meldungen* 21 (September 18, 1942): 19; *Meldungen* 24 (October 9, 1942): 10 (about joy); Kuznetsov, *Babii iar*, 337; TsDAVOV, 3206/1/26/27, 30: "Teilbericht Politik über die Bereisung des Reichskommissariats mit Prof. v. Grünberg in der Zeit vom 13.8. bis 3.9.1942," Rivne, September 10, 1942.

67. *Ereignismeldung UdSSR* 191 (April 10, 1942): 24; Mykola Velychkivs'kyi, "Sumni chasy nimets'koï okupatsiï (1941–1944 roky)," *Vyzvol'nyi shliakh* 12, no. 3 (London, 1965): 303; Kuznetsov, *Babii iar*, 284; Khoroshunova, "Kievskie zapiski," 86, note of October 31, 1941. On the popularity of small-town markets, see TsDAVOV, 3676/4/476/222–223: Sipo-SD report on the Kiev GB in June 1942; *Meldungen* 21 (September 18, 1942): 11.

68. *Dzvin voli* (Bila Tserkva), November 6, 1942, 4; TsDAHOU, 166/3/246/2–2v: Iablonskii.

69. On back roads and vodka, see Hrynevych, author interview; for smuggling tricks, consult [Sharandachenko], *Reiestratorka zahsu*, 165.

70. Original usage: *Hungersnot*. TsDAVOV, 3676/4/476/190, 222: Sipo-SD reports on the Kiev GB in May and June 1942.

71. Khoroshunova, "Kievskie zapiski," 405, note of July 17, 1942.

72. Dudin, "Velikii Mirazh," 110–111.

73. Leonid Abramenko, ed., *Kyïvs'kyi protses: Dokumenty ta materialy* (Kiev, 1995), 44–45.

74. TsDAVOV, 3676/4/475/477, 482; Sipo-SD report on the Kiev GB in September 1942; *Nove ukraïns'ke slovo*, August 2, 1942, 4; NA microcopy T-84, roll 120, frame 418846.

75. [Sharandachenko], *Reiestratorka zahsu*, 120, 129 (the quotation); diary note by Hanna Luk"ianova on February 15, 1942, cited in Viktor Karmazin, *Nash khleb: Dokumental'noe povestvovanie o khlebe* (Moscow, 1986), 217. See also Irina Khoroshunova, "Vtoroi god voiny," *Iehupets'* 10 (Kiev, 2002): 10.

76. Kuznetsov, *Babii iar*, 268. See also TsDAVOV, 3676/4/474/169: SD report on the Kiev GB, Kiev, September 15, 1942.

77. Anatoli (Kuznetsov), *Babi Yar*, 284; Kuznetsov, *Babii iar*, 283–287. See also *Shchodennyk Arkadiia Liubchenka*, 73; Velychkivs'kyi, "Sumni chasy," 303; TsDAHOU, 1/22/6/25–26: D. S. Korotchenko to N. S. Khrushchev, "O sostoianii partizanskogo dvizheniia na pravoberezhnoi Ukraine," n.p., July 22, 1943.

78. *Nove ukraïns'ke slovo*, August 2, 1942, 4. Compare Dudin, "Velikii Mirazh," 111–112.

79. TsDAVOV, 3676/4/307/43: II/III B Mü, "Die deutsche Propaganda in der

Ukraine," n.p., n.d. See also "Povidomlennia," *Vasyl'kivs'ki visti*, August 6, 1942, 4.

80. Dudin, "Velikii Mirazh," 93; *Shchodennyk Arkadiia Liubchenka*, 54, 56–57, 63; DAKO, r-2356/8/7/112; Nartova diary, 13. On the situation after July 15, see NA microcopy T-120, roll 2533, frame E292536: findings by "a source who has returned from a business trip to the Ukraine," forwarded by the Foreign Office to the Foreign Office representative at the RKU, von Saucken, Berlin, December 31, 1942.

81. NA microcopy T-84, roll 120, frame 418940: Sipo-SD of the Kiev GB, "Aktenvermerk. Betr.: Anordnung über die Versorgung und den Verkehr mit Lebensmitteln in der Stadt Kiew vom 15.7.1942," Kiev, July 30, 1942.

82. NA microcopy T-84, roll 120, frames 418938–939. See also TsDAVOV, 3676/4/475/478: Sipo-SD report on the Kiev GB in September 1942.

83. On the Nazi perspective, see NA microcopy T-84, roll 120, frame 419196: "Auszug aus dem Lagebericht des Generalkommissars, Kiev, September 1, 1942. For the wartime Soviet authorities, see Iurii Nikolaiets', *Tsyvil'ne naselennia Ukraïny na pochatku viiny z nimets'ko-fashysts'kymy zaharbnykamy* (Kiev, 1998), 17–18.

84. TsDAVOV, 3676/4/475/476, 479–480: Sipo-SD report on the Kiev GB in September 1942.

85. NA microcopy T-84, roll 120, frame 419076: [Sipo-SD of the Kiev GB], "Die Geldentwertung im Generalbezirk Kiew," n.p., December 1, 1942; NA microcopy T-120, roll 2533, frame E292536.

86. TsDAHOU, 166/3/244/15–15v: Markovskii.

87. Nartova diary, 20; Kuznetsov, *Babii iar*, 352; TsDAVOV, 4620/3/243a/25–26: Zhitov, "Komisii."

88. *Shchodennyk Arkadiia Liubchenka*, 112–113.

89. TsDAHOU, 166/3/246/1–3: Iablonskii; TsDAVOV, 3676/4/474/537: Sipo-SD report on the Kiev GB in March and April 1942 (on homeless children); Hrynevych, author interview (the bedsheet incident); *Ereignismeldung UdSSR* 190 (April 8, 1942): 29 (on executions of "plunderers").

90. TsDAVOV, 3676/4/474/353, 537: Sipo-SD reports on the Kiev GB in February 1942 and in March–April 1942; *Ereignismeldung UdSSR* 191 (April 10, 1942): 24. For two examples, see *Nove ukraïns'ke slovo*, July 17, 1942, 1; *Shchodennyk Arkadiia Liubchenka*, 55.

91. NA microcopy T-84, roll 120, frame 419191: "Auszug aus dem Lagebericht des Generalkommissars," Kiev, September 1, 1942.

92. Kuznetsov, *Babii iar*, 340.

93. TsDAVOV, 3676/4/475/591: Sipo-SD report on the Kiev GB in October 1942, Kiev, November 1, 1942; *Meldungen* 41 (February 12, 1943): 17 (the quotation).

94. Dudin, "Velikii Mirazh," 71–72. See also *Shchodennyk Arkadiia Liubchenka*, 52; TsDAVOV, 3676/4/475/590: Sipo-SD report on the Kiev GB in October 1942, Kiev, November 1, 1942; TsDAVOV, 4620/3/243a/62: Shepelevskii, "Prebyvanie"; TsDAHOU, 166/3/246/3: Iablonskii; TsDAHOU, 166/3/243/40v: Aleksei Mikhailovich Bashkulat (Ukrainian born in 1909), Kiev, February 28, 1944.

95. TsDAVOV, 3206/1/99/20: ban, December 3, 1941.

96. Walther Bienert, *Russen und Deutsche: Was für Menschen sind das? Berichte, Bilder und Folgerungen aus dem Zweiten Weltkrieg* (Stein am Rhein, Switz., 1990), 38.

97. Samchuk, *Na koni voronomu*, 255.

98. TsDAVOV, 3676/4/307/113: "Auszug aus dem Lagebericht der A[ussen]stelle Poltawa vom 28.11.1942" (German report); M. Demydenko, author interview (on small-town girls); Christian Gerlach, *Kalkulierte Morde: Die deutsche Wirtschafts- und Vernichtungspolitik in Weißrußland 1941 bis 1944* (Hamburg, 1999), 1081 (on local children fathered by Germans).

99. Pavel Negretov, *Vse dorogi vedut na Vorkutu* (Benson, Vt., 1985), 50.

100. In the original: "Ne rugai menia mamasha / Chto ia Kiev razbombil / Moia zhena s nemtsem spala / Ia ee tol'ko razbudil." Mykhailo Seleshko, *Vinnytsia: Spomyny perekladacha Komisiï doslidiv zlochyniv NKVD v 1937–1938* (New York, 1991), 94, 152.

101. Nartova diary, 10; Fesenko, *Povest'*, 81–82.

102. H. Sova [Hryhorii Kariak], *Do istoriï bol'shevyts'koï diis'nosty: (25 rokiv zhyttia ukraïns'koho hromadianyna v SSSR)* (Munich, 1955), 76.

103. *Ereignismeldung UdSSR* 135 (November 19, 1941): 15, and 142 (December 5, 1941): 2.

104. *Ereignismeldung UdSSR* 142 (December 5, 1941): 2–3.

105. Nartova diary, 11, note of April 25, 1942.

106. Khoroshunova, "Kievskie zapiski," 390, note of July 4, 1942 (the first quotation), [Sharandachenko], *Reiestratorka zahsu*, 155; *Shchodennyk Arkadiia Liubchenka*, 63; Samchuk, *Na koni voronomu*, 263.

107. Nartova diary, 17 (the first quotation); *Meldungen* 21 (September 18, 1942): 12, 14.

108. [Sharandachenko], *Reiestratorka zahsu*, 47.

109. *Shchodennyk Arkadiia Liubchenka*, 87.

110. Ibid., 123; *Meldungen* 43 (February 26, 1943): 8. On salespeople demanding rubles, see *Meldungen* 47 (March 26, 1943): 14, 21; *Shchodennyk Arkadiia Liubchenka*, 116; TsDAHOU, 1/22/6/25–26: Korotchenko to Khrushchev, "O sostoianii."

111. Seleshko, *Vinnytsia*, 106, 139; Karmazin, *Nash khleb*, 221; Luk"ianova, "Zi shchodennyka," 61.

112. NA microcopy T-84, roll 120, frames 418941–943: Sipo-SD of the Kiev GB to Magunia, "Betr: Lebensmittellage der einheimischen Bevölkerung von Kiew," Kiev, February 24, 1943.

113. UCEC, Pavlo Ternivs'kyi [Ivan Zhyhadlo], "Spohady emigranta" (n.p., 1945), 53–54.

114. Ibid.

115. Fragment of an Auslandbriefprüfstelle report of July 10, 1943, in Müller, *Die faschistische Okkupationspolitik*, 453–455; also cited in Mulligan, *Politics of Illusion*, 31.

116. Fesenko, *Povest'*, 96, 98.

117. Seleshko, *Vinnytsia*, 47, 75, 83–84, 138–139.

118. See Table 1 in the Appendix.

8. *Popular Culture*

1. Hryhorii Kostiuk, *Zustrichi i proshchannia: Spohady. Knyha druha* (Edmonton, 1998), 115.

2. Norbert Müller et al., eds., *Die faschistische Okkupationspolitik in den zeitweilig besetzten Gebieten der Sowjetunion (1941–1944)* (Berlin, 1991), 321.

3. Sheila Fitzpatrick, *Everyday Stalinism: Ordinary Life in Extraordinary Times. Soviet Russia in the 1930s* (New York, 1999), 110.

4. Ivan R. Kostiuk, "Kremenchuk (Z bloknota kol. voiennoho zvitodavtsia)," *Visti kombatanta* 1, no. 13 (New York, 1964): 30.

5. TsDAVOV, 3206/1/26/33v, 37: "Teilbericht Politik über die Bereisung des Reichskommissariats mit Prof. v. Grünberg in der Zeit vom 13.8 bis 3.9.1942," Rivne, September 10, 1942; *Ivankivs'ki visti* (Ivankiv), December 27, 1942, 2.

6. Panas Khurtovyna [Mykhailo Podvorniak], *Pid nebom Volyni: (Voienni spomyny khrystyianyna)* (Winnipeg, 1952), 107–108.

7. M. I. Syn'ohub, author interview. See also *Zvil'nena Ukraïna* (Bohuslav), October 22, 1941. Compare Volodymyr Pokotylo, "Lytsari zolotoho tryzuba," *Slovo i chas*, no. 9 (Kiev, September 1992): 52.

8. *Ereignismeldung UdSSR* 47 (August 9, 1941): 13, and 81 (September 12, 1941): 11 (the quotation).

9. BA-MA, RW 2/149, fols. 276–277: Field Command 675, "Betr.: Leichenfund im Gefängnishof Winnica," Vinnytsia, August 28, 1941. A description of the events in 1943 is in Chapter 12.

10. Leontii Forostivs'kyi, *Kyïv pid vorozhymy okupatsiiamy* (Buenos Aires, 1952), 75–78; HIA, B. I. Nicolaevsky collection, series no. 236, box 409, folder 19, fol. 23: Emigrant, "Nemtsy v Kieve: (Iz vospominanii ochevidtsa)," n.p., n.d.

11. On the first anniversary of Kiev's "liberation," see TsDAVOV, 3676/4/307/66–68: K. Shtepa to Sipo-SD officer Hüber, n.p., September 21, 1942. For the other

celebrations, see D. M. Malakov, ed., *Kyïv 1941–1943: Fotoal'bom* (Kiev, 2000), 190–191; Friedrich Heyer, *Die orthodoxe Kirche in der Ukraine von 1917 bis 1945* (Cologne, 1953), 196; *Ukraïns'kyi holos* (Proskuriv), March 21, 1943, 4; *Dzvin voli* (Bila Tserkva), March 7, 1943, 4; TsDAHOU, 166/3/246/8–8v: Mitrofan Vasil'evich Reutovskii (Ukrainian born in 1896), [Kiev?], February 28, 1944.

12. Ivan Vlasovs'kyi, *Narys istoriï Ukraïns'koï Pravoslavnoï Tserkvy*, vol. 9: (*XX st.*), part 2 (New York, 1966), 239 (requiem for Kotliarevs'kyi). For commemorations of Ukraïnka, see *Shchodennyk Arkadiia Liubchenka*, ed. Iurii Luts'kyi (Lviv, Ukr., 1999), 68–69; Ulas Samchuk, *Na koni voronomu: Spomyny i vrazhennia* (Winnipeg, 1975), 269; Halyna Lashchenko, "Povorot," *Samostiina Ukraïna* 11, no. 10(118) (Chicago, October 1958): 11; Valerii Haidabura, *Teatr, zakhovanyi v arkhivakh: Stsenichne mystetsvo v Ukraïni periodu nimets'ko-fashysts'koï okupatsiï (1941–1944)* (Kiev, 1998), 82. On tributes to Hrushevs'kyi, see TsDAHOU, 166/3/243/4: Nikolai Kuz'mich Grun'skii [*sic*] (Ukrainian born in 1872), Kiev, February 19, 1944; *Shchodennyk Arkadiia Liubchenka*, 101, 114.

13. Hanna Luk"ianova, "Zi shchodennyka viiny 1941–1945 rokiv," *Rozbudova derzhavy*, no. 4 (Kiev, April 1995): 61–62; Malakov, *Kyïv*, 222; Forostivs'kyi, *Kyïv*, 33–36; Forostivs'kyi, "Do hromadian m. Kyieva," *Nove ukraïns'ke slovo*, May 14, 1943, 1; *Nove ukraïns'ke slovo*, May 16, 1943, 3; TsDAHOU, 1/22/6/30: D. S. Korotchenko to N. S. Khrushchev, "O sostoianii partizanskogo dvizheniia na pravoberezhnoi Ukraine," n.p., July 22, 1943; Tatiana Fesenko, *Povest' krivykh let* (New York, 1963), 88–89; Anatolii Kuznetsov (A. Anatolii), *Babii iar: Roman-dokument* (New York, 1986), 374; A. Dublians'kyi, *Ternystym shliakhom: Zhyttia Mytropolyta Nikanora Abramovycha. Do 20-littia arkhypastyrs'koho sluzhinnia, 1942–1962* (London, 1962), 49.

14. An example is in *Ukraïns'kyi holos*, February 1, 1942, 4.

15. TsDAVOV, 3676/4/476/243: Sipo-SD report on the Kiev GB in June 1942; TsDAVOV, 3676/4/307/107–108: Sipo-SD report on the Kiev GB, October 1, 1942; *Meldungen* 21 (September 18, 1942): 17–18; *Meldungen* 25 (October 16, 1942): 12–13.

16. For the psychologists' perspective, see, for instance, Robert B. Cialdini, *Influence: The Psychology of Persuasion*, rev. ed. (New York, 1993), 57–84.

17. Mykhailo Seleshko, *Vinnytsia: Spomyny perekladacha Komisiï doslidiv zlochyniv NKVD v 1937–1938* (New York, 1991), 101–102, 122–123, 129; TsDAVOV, 3676/4/307/124: commissar of Bila Tserkva district, June 19, 1943; *Ukraïns'kyi holos*, May 6, 1943, 1.

18. TsDAVOV, 3676/4/307/103–104: Sipo-SD report on the Kiev GB, October 1, 1942.

19. See Cialdini, *Influence*, 57–84.

20. Samchuk, *Na koni voronomu*, 109; Ulas Samchuk, *Na bilomu koni: Spomyny i*

vrazhennia (Winnipeg, 1972), 188; Ievhen Stakhiv, "Kryvyi Rih v 1941–1943 rr.," *Suchasna Ukraïna* (Munich), January 22, 1956, 10; Seleshko, *Vinnytsia*, 156–157; HIA-HURIP, box 23, no. 548 AD, B-6, fol. 6: editor of *Vinnyts'ki visti* [Mykhailo Zerov?], n.p., April 24, 1951.

21. On Liubchenko's "blacklisting," see *Shchodennyk Arkadiia Liubchenka*, 39–40, 83–84. On confiscations and bans of book imports, see Seleshko, *Vinnytsia*, 98.

22. Nikolai Fevr, *Solntse voskhodit na zapade* (Buenos Aires, 1950), 135; Fesenko, *Povest'*, 86; TsDAHOU, 1/22/347/19: "Iz dnevnika uchitel'nitsy gor. Kieva L. Nartovoi" (hereafter Nartova diary). On looted and purged libraries, see M. V. Koval', "Dolia ukraïns'koï kul'tury za 'novoho poriadku' (1941–1944 rr.)," *Ukraïns'kyi istorychnyi zhurnal*, nos. 11–12 (Kiev, November–December 1993): 32; DAKO, r-2412/2/37/2: school inspector of the Illintsi district, to all school inspectors, March 29, 1942; TsDAVOV, 4620/3/243a/61: professor N. A. Shepelevskii, "Prebyvanie nemtsev v Kieve," n.p., n.d.

23. TsDAVOV, 3206/1/78/31: RKU *Lagebericht* for January 1942, Rivne, February 14, 1942. The later total is my calculation from TsDAVOV, 3676/4/97/63–80: "Die Fremdsprachige Zeitungen und Zeitschriften im Reichskommissariat Ukraine," n.p., n.d.

24. *Meldungen* 24 (October 9, 1942): 13; *Meldungen* 32 (December 4, 1942): 12; TsDAVOV, 3676/1/307/110: commissar of Bila Tserkva district, October 28, 1942.

25. *Ereignismeldung UdSSR* 187 (March 30, 1942): 8.

26. Seleshko, *Vinnytsia*, 78–79; HIA, B. I. Nicolaevsky collection, series no. 178, box 232, folder 10, fol. 137: [Lev Vladimirovich] Dudin, "Velikii Mirazh: Sobytiia 1941–1947 godov v ponimanii sovetskogo cheloveka," n.p., 1947.

27. Seleshko, *Vinnytsia*, 138; *Shchodennyk Arkadiia Liubchenka*, 63 (availability of Ukrainian newspapers). On *Novoe slovo*, see Fevr, *Solntse*, 76; Pavel Negretov, *Vse dorogi vedut na Vorkutu* (Benson, Vt., 1985), 47; TsDAHOU, 166/3/243/40: Aleksei Mikhailovich Bashkulat (Ukrainian born in 1909), Kiev, February 28, 1944; *Shchodennyk Arkadiia Liubchenka*, 101.

28. TsDAVOV, 3676/4/307/93–97: Sipo-SD of Kiev GB, report, October 1, 1942.

29. "Rozsharuvannia ukraïns'koho suspil'stva," *Ukraïns'kyi holos*, October 25, 1942, 3, probably by Ulas Samchuk given information in Samchuk, *Na koni voronomu*, 71.

30. *Vidrodzhennia* (Tarashcha), December 6, 1942, 4.

31. Samchuk, *Na bilomu koni*, 181.

32. F. H. (Fedir Haiovych), "Kyïv u zhovtni 1941," in Kost' Mel'nyk, Oleh Lashchenko, and Vasyl' Veryha, eds, *Na zov Kyieva: Ukraïns'kyi natsionalizm u II Svitovii Viini. Zbirnyk stattei, spohadiv i dokumentiv* (Toronto, 1985), 164.

33. Fesenko, *Povest'*, 72, 77; F. P. Bogatyrchuk, *Moi zhiznennyi put' k Vlasovu i Prazhkomu manifestu* (San Francisco, 1978), 137; Lashchenko, "Povorot,"

Samostiina Ukraïna 11, no. 7(115) (New York, July 1958): 12. On peasants' reading and circulating papers, see TsDAVOV, 3206/2/27/4: RKU *Lagebericht* for December 1941, Rivne, January 14, 1942; TsDAVOV, 3206/1/78/31: RKU *Lagebericht* for January 1942; *Meldungen* 32 (December 4, 1942): 12; O. M. Kutsenko, author interview.

34. Sheila Fitzpatrick, *Stalin's Peasants: Resistance and Survival in the Russian Village after Collectivization* (New York, 1994), 271; Fitzpatrick, *Everyday Stalinism*, 165, 176, 187–188.

35. Samchuk, *Na bilomu koni*, 218; Samchuk, *Na koni voronomu*, 145–146.

36. Fevr, *Solntse*, 265.

37. Lashchenko, "Povorot," *Samostiina Ukraïna* [11], nos. 15–17[sic; really 3–4](111–113) (New York, March–May 1958): 12; Lashchenko, "Povorot" 11, no. 11(119) (Chicago, November 1958): 13; George Y. Shevelov, *The Ukrainian Language in the First Half of the Twentieth Century (1900–1941): Its State and Status* (Cambridge, Mass., 1989), 152–153.

38. Dudin, "Velikii Mirazh," 116, 126–127, 133, 135; K. Radzevych [Osyp Vynnyts'kyi], "U sorokarichchia Kyïvs'koï pokhidnoï hrupy OUN," *Kalendar-al'manakh Novoho Shliakhu, 1982* (Toronto, n.d.): 78–79; O. Dniprova, "O. Ol'zhych u Kyievi: Spohad," in Mel'nyk, Lashchenko, and Veryha, *Na zov Kyieva*, 167; Kuznetsov, *Babii iar*, 218; *Ereignismeldung UdSSR* 125 (October 26, 1941): 4.

39. Iurii Shevel'ov, "Iurii Sherekh (1941–1956) (Materiialy dlia biohrafiï)," in Iurii Sherekh [Iurii Shevel'ov], *Ne dlia ditei: Literaturno-krytychni statti i eseï* (New York, 1964), 11. See also *Shchodennyk Arkadiia Liubchenka*, 48, 58; Ivan Maistrenko, *Istoriia moho pokolinnia: Spohady uchasnyka revoliutsiinykh podii v Ukraïni* (Edmonton, 1985), 339, 341; Forostivs'kyi, *Kyïv*, 52; Samchuk, *Na koni voronomu*, 35, 205.

40. UCEC, Pavlo Ternivs'kyi [Ivan Zhyhadlo], "Spohady emigranta" (n.p., 1945), 58–60.

41. Samchuk, *Na koni voronomu*, 71.

42. Volodymyr Serhiichuk, [ed.], *OUN-UPA: Novi dokumenty i materialy* (Kiev, 1996), 338.

43. Seleshko, *Vinnytsia*, 45, 85, 155, 160.

44. *Ukraïns'kyi holos*, November 5, 1941, 3; Ternivs'kyi, "Spohady emigranta," 28; John A. Armstrong, *Ukrainian Nationalism*, 3d ed. (Englewood, Colo., 1990), 181.

45. Dudin, "Velikii Mirazh," 120 (on Soviet practice); Nikolas Laskovsky, "Practicing Law in the Occupied Ukraine," *American Slavic and East European Review* 10, no. 2 (New York, 1952): 126.

46. Blanka Jerabek, *Das Schulwesen und die Schulpolitik im Reichskommissariat Ukraine 1941–1944: Im Lichte deutscher Dokumente* (Munich, 1991), 208–209;

TsDAHOU, 1/23/41/62–63: RKU to various offices, "Sprachengebrauch in der Ukraine," Rivne, February 2, 1942.

47. TsDAVOV, 3206/5/15/350–351: RKU *Lagebericht* for April 1942, Rivne, May 15, 1942.
48. Shevelov, *Ukrainian Language*, 186–188; Fevr, *Solntse*, 265; *Meldungen* 21 (September 18, 1942), 18; TsDAVOV, 3206/1/26/36: "Teilbericht Politik."
49. Volodymyr Kubiiovych, *Meni 85* (Munich, 1985), 102.
50. Armstrong, *Ukrainian Nationalism*, 193; Illia Chaikovs'kyi, *Ukraïns'ki periodychni vydannia v druhii svitovii viini, 1939–1945*, ed. and expanded by M. Kravchuk (Philadelphia, 1976), 17; Illia Vytanovych, *Istoriia ukraïns'koho kooperatyvnoho rukhu* (New York, 1964), 512.
51. *Orlenia: Chasopys dlia ditei* 2, no. 11 (Rivne, November 1942): 16.
52. TsDAHOU, 1/22/123/62–63: Petr Timofeevich Berdnik, "Kharakteristika polozhenii na okkupirovannoi territorii," n.p., n.d.; TsDAVOV, 3676/4/307/105–106, 109, 134: Sipo-SD report on the Kiev GB, October 1, 1942, Sipo-SD Außenstelle Poltava, October 27, 1942, and commissar of the Smila district, June 18, 1943.
53. Volodymyr Kosyk, "Nimets'ka shkil'na polityka v Raikhskomisariiati Ukraïna (1941–1944)," *Vyzvol'nyi shliakh* 47, no. 3(352) (London, March 1994): 354; Dmytro Kyslytsia, *Svite iasnyi: Spohady. Vid r. Vovchi z Naddniprianshchyny do r. Sv. Lavrentiia na Ottavshchyni* (Ottawa, 1987), 207–214, 216; Iaroslav Haivas, *Koly kinchalasia epokha* (n.p., 1964), 71 (both on nonimplementation).
54. Kosyk, "Nimets'ka shkil'na polityka," 358; H. D. Handrack, *Das Reichskommissariat Ostland: Die Kulturpolitik der deutschen Verwaltung zwischen Autonomie und Gleichschaltung 1941–1944* (Hann. Münden, Ger., 1981), 185–186; Bernhard Chiari, *Alltag hinter der Front: Besatzung, Kollaboration und Widerstand in Weißrußland 1941–1944* (Düsseldorf, 1998), 220–230.
55. Mykola Velychkivs'kyi, "Sumni chasy nimets'koï okupatsiï (1941–1944 roky)," *Vyzvol'nyi shliakh* 12, no. 2 (London, 1965): 155. Compare, about the town of Korosten', TsDAHOU, 166/3/245/53: Ol'ga Sergeevna Pominchuk ([Ukrainian?], Kiev, January 20, 1946.
56. TsDAHOU, 166/3/243/46: Ol'ga Sergeevna Gudzenko-Tyshkova (Ukrainian born in 1901), Kiev, March 14, 1944, report signed on June 5, 1944; TsDAHOU, 1/23/124/93: Savchenko, VRIO NKVD USSR, to N. S. Khrushchev, "Razvedsvodka No 33/68 o polozhenii v okkupirovannom protivnikom g. Dnepropetrovske. Po sostoianiiu na 20. 10. 42g.," Engel's, October 21, 1942.
57. *Meldungen* 13 (July 24, 1942): 8; TsDAHOU, 1/22/123/60: Berdnik, "Kharakteristika polozhenii"; *Ukraïns'kyi holos*, June 4, 1942, 3; Serhiichuk, *OUN-UPA*, 344; DAKO, r-2209/1/50/10: Okhrimenko, chief of the Khabne raion, letter, April 30, 1942.

58. TsDAHOU, 166/3/243/46v: Gudzenko-Tyshkova (the quotation); Kyslytsia, *Svite iasnyi*, 219.

59. TsDAHOU, 1/22/123/60: Berdnik, "Kharakteristika polozhenii." Original usage: "*Breshesh!*"

60. Nartova diary, 12–13, 17; Ternivs'kyi, "Spohady emigranta," 27; Serhiichuk, *OUN-UPA*, 326.

61. TsDAHOU, 166/3/246/92: Nikolai Makarovich Kharchenko (born in 1906), [Melitopol'?], January 22, 1946.

62. TsDAVOV, 3206/5/15/262: RKU *Lagebericht* for February 1942, Rivne, March 15, 1942.

63. TsDAVOV, 3206/2/27/5–6: RKU *Lagebericht* for December 1941; *Meldungen* 25 (October 16, 1942, 15); TsDAVOV, 3676/4/307/54, 110: "Auszug aus dem Lagebericht des Gend. Postens in Smela von 26.6.42" and "Auszug aus dem Lagebericht der Außenstelle Bila-Cerkwa vom 28.10.1942."

64. TsDAVOV, 3206/1/26/33v: "Teilbericht Politik"; BA-Berlin, R 6/305, fol. 45: Der Generalkommissar, "Lagebericht für die Monate November-Dezember 1942," Dnipropetrovs'k, January 7, 1943.

65. Seleshko, *Vinnytsia*, 45; TsDAVOV, 3206/2/27/5–6: RKU *Lagebericht* for December 1941; TsDAVOV, 3206/5/78/30: RKU *Lagebericht* for February 1942; "Rik pratsi fil'movoho t-va v Ukraïni," *Dzvin voli*, November 27, 1942, 3; *Dzvin voli*, August 26, 1943, 4; *Ukraïns'kyi holos*, March 26, 1942, 4; V. P. Kravchenko, author interview.

66. *Meldungen* 25 (October 16, 1942): 14–15, evidently using TsDAVOV, 3676/4/307/100: Sipo-SD of the Kiev GB, report, Kiev, October 1, 1942 (the quotation); TsDAHOU, 1/22/123/61: Berdnik, "Kharakteristika polozhenii" (on return of Soviet movies).

67. TsDAHOU, 1/23/115/54: Savchenko, VRIO NKVD USSR, to N. S. Khrushchev, "Razvedsvodka No 32/67. O deiatel'nosti ukrainskikh natsionalistov na okkupirovannoi nemetsko-fashistskimi zakhvatchikami territorii USSR. Po sostoianiiu 1. 9. 42g.," Engel's, September 19, 1942; Samchuk, *Na bilomu koni*, 230; Kostiuk, "Kremenchuk," 29–30.

68. TsDAVOV, 3206/1/26/32: "Teilbericht Politik." See also TsDAVOV, 3206/1/26/30v and TsDAVOV, 3676/4/307/50: "Aus dem Lagebericht Gebietskommissar Iwankow v. 15.5.–15.6.42."

69. TsDAVOV, 3676/4/307/134: "Auszug aus dem Lagebericht des Geb.Komm. in Smela v. 18.6.43" (on satisfying Germans); TsDAVOV, 3676/4/307/128: "Auszug aus dem Lagebericht des Geb.Komm. Kiew-Land v. 18.6.43" (on technical difficulties).

70. Fitzpatrick, *Stalin's Peasants*, 271–272.

71. IMFE, Prytula collection, 14–3/24/35. Original text (apparently heard in Berdychiv in 1942): "Buly soviety / To davaly nam kino i khliba po kilo /

Pryishov vyzvolytel' / To dav Bozhyi khram i khliba po sto hram." Compare IMFE, T. Krasyts'ka collection, 14–3/20/111, 216; Nartova diary, 20.

72. NA microcopy T-120, roll 2533, frame E292536: report by Auswärtiges Amt citing a "Gewährsmann," Berlin, December 31, 1942; TsDAHOU, 166/3/243/37–43v: Bashkulat; Bogatyrchuk, *Moi zhizhnennyi put'*, 136; Nartova diary, 18.

73. TsDAHOU, 166/3/243/43: Bashkulat; TsDAVOV, 3676/4/101/1–8: Sipo-SD of the Kiev GB, report, Kiev, January 29, 1943.

74. TsDAHOU, 166/3/243/40: Bashkulat; *Nove ukraïns'ke slovo*, September 4, 1942, 4; *Poslednie novosti*, January 2, 1942, 6, and January 8, 1942, 6; Haidabura, *Teatr*, 24–25.

75. Seleshko, *Vinnytsia*, 154.

76. Haidabura, *Teatr*, 22, 72; NDB, collection "Afishy ta plakaty okupatsiinoho periodu," 316sa: "Vidkryttia kyïvs'koho teatru 'Var"iete'"; *Shchodennyk Arkadiia Liubchenka*, 37, 71.

77. TsDAVOV, 3206/1/78/30: RKU *Lagebericht* for January 1942; TsDAVOV, 3206/5/15/262: RKU *Lagebericht* for February 1942; Haidabura, *Teatr*, 84, 10–60.

78. Otto Bräutigam, *Überblick über die besetzten Ostgebiete während des 2. Weltkrieges* (Tübingen, Ger., 1954), 76 (on the guideline); TsDAHOU, 166/3/243/40: Bashkulat (on the persistence of some Russian culture).

79. TsDAHOU, 1/23/115/48, 50: Savchenko to Khrushchev, "Razvedsvodka No 32/67"; Armstrong, *Ukrainian Nationalism*, 172.

80. TsDAHOU, 1/22/123/60: Berdnik, "Kharakteristika polozhenii"; TsDAHOU, 1/23/115/46: Savchenko to Khrushchev, "Razvedsvodka No 32/67"; TsDAHOU, 1/22/122/33: Iakov Fedorovich Nosenko, komissar partizanskogo otriada Kanevskogo raiona Kievskoi oblasti, to Zam. nach. 4-go Otdela NKVD USSR, "Dokladnaia zapiska," n.p., January 3, 1942.

81. Kostiuk, *Zustrichi i proshchannia*, 51.

82. Haidabura, *Teatr*, 112, quotation on 110.

83. Ibid., 94, 102, 129, 136; *Ukraïns'kyi holos*, January 22, 1942, 4 (the quotation); Haidabura, *Teatr*, 109 (on melodramatic acting).

84. Seleshko, *Vinnytsia*, 151.

85. M. Demydenko, author interview; HIA-HURIP, box 32, no. 121 AD, B-6, fol. 13: electrician from Kherson, n.p., November 28–29, 1950.

86. Samchuk, *Na koni voronomu*, 197 (Lysenko birthday celebration); Ternivs'kyi, "Spohady emigranta," 56; *Shchodennyk Arkadiia Liubchenka*, 114–115.

87. Haidabura, *Teatr*, 112–113.

88. Boris Polevoi, *Sobranie sochinenii v deviati tomakh*, vol. 7 (Moscow, 1984), 444, 450–451, partly quoted in O. A. Pravdiuk, "Skhidnoslov"ians'ki patriotychni pisni u roky Velykoï Vitchyznianoï viiny," in O. K. Fedoruk et al., eds., *Khudozhnia kul'tura kraïn skhidnoï ta pivdennoï Ievropy v borot'bi proty fashyzmu: Zbirnyk naukovykh prats'* (Kiev, 1990), 26. Compare TsDAHOU, 1/

22/391/12: Mikhail Mikh. Skirda [et al.], "Otchet o podpol'noi partiinoi rabote i partizanskoi bor'be v Kirovogradskoi oblasti (avgust 1941 goda–mart 1944 goda)," n.d.

89. F. I. Lavrov, "Radians'ki ukraïns'ki narodni spivtsi-kobzari (Portrety i kharakterystyky)," *Mystetstvo. Fol'klor. Etnohrafiia: Naukovi zapysky* 1–2 (Kiev, 1947): 163–165.

90. Seleshko, *Vinnytsia*, 139, 151.

91. Amnon Ajzensztadt, *Endurance: Chronicles of Jewish Resistance* (Oakville, N.Y., 1987), 63.

92. Kyslytsia, *Svite iasnyi*, 216.

93. Dudin, "Velikii Mirazh," 103; Iur. Semenko, "Pam"iati Mykhaila Pronchenka," *Novi dni* 4, no. 39 (Toronto, April 1953): 11.

94. Samchuk, *Na koni voronomu*, 255.

95. Handrack, *Das Reichskommissariat Ostland*, 204–205.

96. Samchuk, *Na koni voronomu*, 197–198; Maistrenko, *Istoriia moho pokolinnia*, 341, 344–345; *Shchodennyk Arkadiia Liubchenka*, 51; TsDAVOV, 3206/5/15/262: RKU *Lagebericht* for February 1942.

97. TsDAVOV, 3206/5/15/262: RKU *Lagebericht* for February 1942; TsDAVOV, 3676/4/474/244–245: Sipo-SD report on the Kiev GB, September 15, 1942; Samchuk, *Na koni voronomu*, 210, 266; *Shchodennyk Arkadiia Liubchenka*, 68.

98. DAKO, r-2329/2/2/118: Ukrainian-language leaflet from General Commissar Magunia, September 6, 1942; *Vidrodzhennia*, November 26, 1942, and December 3, 1942, 2.

99. Ihor Verba, "Sproby vidnovlennia Ukraïns'koï Akademiï Nauk u Kyievi (Kinets' 1941–seredyna 1942 rr.)," *Ukraïns'kyi istoryk* 32, nos. 1–4(124–127) (New York, 1995): 98; TsDAVOV, 3676/4/307/67–68: Shtepa to Hüber.

100. On the Sich, see *OUN u viini 1939 1945* (n.p., n.d.), 62–63; TsDAHOU, 166/3/246/9–14: Mikhail Nikolaevich Sviridovskii (born in 1908), Kiev, March 3, 1944. On boxing in Kiev, see NDB, collection "Afishy ta plakaty okupatsiinoh periodu," 299sa, 302sa, 307sa. On swimming in the Dnieper, see *Nove ukraïns'ke slovo*, September 4, 1942, 4.

101. TsDAVOV, 3676/4/307/120: "Auszug aus dem Lagebericht des Geb.Komm. Kobeljaki v. 17.6.43."

102. NDB, collection "Afishy ta plakaty okupatsiinoho periodu," 297–298sa, 300–301sa, 303–306sa, 308–310sa, 729–732sa; *Nove ukraïns'ke slovo*, August 18, 1942, 4; TsDAHOU, 166/3/246/9–14: Sviridovskii; Malakov, *Kyïv*, 173; Oleksander Skotsen', *Z futbolom u svit: Spomyny* (Toronto, 1985), 258, 277–280.

103. Evgeniia Dimer, *Ogliadivaias' nazad* (New York, 1987), 35–36 (on dancing); Kostiuk, "Kremenchuk," 33 (on record players); Serhiichuk, *OUN-UPA*, 301 (on accordions and record players); Jacob Gerstenfeld-Maltiel, *My Private War: One Man's Struggle to Survive the Soviets and the Nazis* (London, 1993), 219

(on card games); Walther Bienert, *Russen und Deutsche: Was für Menschen sind das? Berichte, Bilder und Folgerungen aus dem Zweiten Weltkrieg* (Stein am Rhein, Switz., 1990), 70 (on dominoes); Fesenko, *Povest'*, 87 (on charades); Kravchenko, author interview.

104. Seleshko, *Vinnytsia*, 154.
105. Fevr, *Solntse*, 160–161.
106. *Nove ukraïns'ke slovo*, August 12, 1942, 4.
107. N. S. Zozulia, author interview.
108. *Meldungen* 54 (May 14, 1943): 15–16.
109. Fitzpatrick, *Everyday Stalinism*, 23, 225.
110. TsDAVOV, 3676/4/307/91: Sipo-SD on the Kiev GB, "Die deutsche Propaganda im Generalbezirk Kiew," Kiev, October 1, 1942.
111. Dudin, "Velikii Mirazh," 176; Emigrant, "Nemtsy v Kieve," 58–59; *Shchodennyk Arkadiia Liubchenka*, 50.

9. Ethnic Identity and Political Loyalties

1. Hiroaki Kuromiya, *Freedom and Terror in the Donbas: A Ukrainian-Russian Borderland, 1870s–1990s* (Cambridge, Eng., 1998), 277 (the first quotation); Amir Weiner, *Making Sense of War: The Second World War and the Fate of the Bolshevik Revolution* (Princeton, N.J., 2001), 298.
2. Weiner, *Making Sense of War*, 305, 330–331.
3. Yuri Slezkine, "The USSR as a Communal Apartment, or How a Socialist State Promoted Ethnic Particularism," *Slavic Review* 53, no. 2 (1994): 414–452; George O. Liber, *Soviet Nationality Policy, Urban Growth, and Identity Change in the Ukrainian SSR, 1923–1934* (Cambridge, Eng., 1992).
4. Francine Hirsch, "The Soviet Union as a Work-in-Progress: Ethnographers and the Category *Nationality* in the 1926, 1937, and 1939 censuses," *Slavic Review* 56, no. 2 (1997): 251–278; HIA, B. I. Nicolaevsky collection, series no. 178, box 232, folder 10, fol. 73: [Lev Vladimirovich] Dudin, "Velikii Mirazh: Sobytiia 1941–1947 godov v ponimanii sovetskogo cheloveka," n.p., 1947; HIA-HURIP, box 23, no. 441 AD, B-6, fol. 3: [Konstantyn Shtepa], n.p., February 12, 1951.
5. Mykhailo Seleshko, *Vinnytsia: Spomyny perekladacha Komisiï doslidiv zlochyniv NKVD v 1937–1938* (New York, 1991), 132; Mstyslav Z. Chubai, *Reid orhanizatoriv OUN vid Popradu po Chorne More: (Iz zapysnyka roiovoho)* (Munich, 1952), 33. Varying interpretations of the term "ours" may be found in Andrei Sinyavsky, *Soviet Civilization: A Cultural History* (New York, 1990), 260–264; Andrew Rossos, "Macedonianism and Macedonian Nationalism on the Left," in Ivo Banac and Katherine Verdery, eds., *National Character and National Ideology in Interwar Eastern Europe* (New Haven, Conn., 1995), 229,

231–232; Kuromiya, *Freedom and Terror*, 281; Weiner, *Making Sense of War*, 250. See also Sarah Davies, "'Us against Them': Social Identity in Soviet Russia, 1934–41," *Russian Review* 56, no. 1 (1997): 70–89.

6. N. F. Bondarenko, author interview.

7. Seleshko, *Vinnytsia*, 150, 152, cited in Karel Cornelis Berkhoff, "Hitler's Clean Slate: Everyday Life in the Reichskommissariat Ukraine, 1941–1944," Ph.D. diss., University of Toronto, 1998, 306–307 and in Weiner, *Making Sense of War*, 250. On the 1930s, see Terry Martin, *The Affirmative Action Empire: Nations and Nationalism in the Soviet Union, 1923–1939* (Ithaca, N.Y., 2001), 103–104. For the term *rus'ki*, see Josef Winkler, *Die Verschleppung: Njetotschka Iljaschenko erzählt über ihre russische Kindheit* (Frankfurt am Main, 1984), 204.

8. Compare John A. Armstrong, *Ukrainian Nationalism*, 3d ed. (Englewood, Colo., 1990), 91, 215, 218, with Bohdan Krawchenko, "Soviet Ukraine under Nazi Occupation, 1941–4," in Yury Boshyk, ed., *Ukraine during World War II: History and Its Aftermath. A Symposium* (Edmonton, 1986), 17–18, 21, 29, and Serhy Yekelchyk, "Stalinist Patriotism as Imperial Discourse: Reconciling the Ukrainian and Russian 'Heroic Pasts,' 1939–1945," *Kritika* 3, no. 1 (Winter 2002): 51–80. On Russian-speaking Soviet civilians, see David Brandenberger, *National Bolshevism: Stalinist Mass Culture and the Formation of Modern Russian National Identity, 1931–1956* (Cambridge, Mass., 2002), 160–180.

9. Pavel Negretov, *Vse dorogi vedut na Vorkutu* (Benson, Vt., 1985), 27. See also Iurii Nikolaiets', *Tsyvil'ne naselennia Ukraïny na pochatku viiny z nimets'ko-fashysts'kymy zaharbnykamy* (Kiev, 1998), 23. On deserters, see TsDAHOU, 1/22/122/101: "Deiatel'nost' partizanskikh otriadov v tylu vraga i v kakoi pomoshchi oni nuzhdaiutsia," n.p., n.d.

10. Mykola Velychkivs'kyi, "Sumni chasy nimets'koï okupatsiï (1941–1944 roky)," *Vyzvol'nyi shliakh* 12, no. 1 (London, 1965): 44. See also Irina Khoroshunova, "Pervyi god voiny: Kievskie zapiski," *Iehupets'* 9 (Kiev, 2001): 47–48; M. S., "Krov na Kvitakh," *Samostiina Ukraïna* 1, nos. 1–2 (Chicago, February–March 1948): 19–20.

11. Mykhailo Hartymiv, "Zemleiu ukraïns'koiu . . . ," in Kost' Mel'nyk, Oleh Lashchenko, and Vasyl' Veryha, eds., *Na zov Kyieva: Ukraïns'kyi natsionalizm u II Svitovii Viini. Zbirnyk stattei, spohadiv i dokumentiv* (Toronto, 1985), 125, 147; Kost' Pan'kivs'kyi, *Vid derzhavy do komitetu* (New York, 1957), 106; F. Pihido-Pravoberezhnyi, "*Velyka Vitchyzniana viina*" (Winnipeg, 1954), 45; Halyna Lashchenko, "Povorot," *Samostiina Ukraïna* [11], nos. 15–17[sic; should be 3–4](111–113) (New York, March–May 1958): 14; O. Horodys'kyi, "Iurii Klen—voiakom (Prodovzhennia)," *Kyïv* 4, no. 3 (Philadelphia, May–June 1953): 151 (on the army).

12. *Ereignismeldung UdSSR* 52 (August 14, 1941): 11; Hryhorii Stetsiuk, *Nepostavlenyi pam"iatnyk: (Spohady)* (Winnipeg, 1988), 33.

13. UCEC, Pavlo Ternivs'kyi [Ivan Zhyhadlo], "Spohady emigranta" (n.p., 1945), 22.

14. Khoroshunova, "Pervyi god voiny," 64; Hartymiv, "Zemleiu ukraïns'koiu," 147.

15. On intelligentsia, see TsDAVOV, 3206/1/78/29–30: RKU *Lagebericht* for January 1942, Rivne, February 14, 1942, Seleshko, *Vinnytsia*, 164; *Shchodennyk Arkadiia Liubchenka*, ed. Iurii Luts'kyi (Lviv, Ukr., 1999), 19–20.

16. TsDAVOV, 3206/2/26/10, 17: Hptm. [Hauptmann] Prof. Hans Koch, "Der Sowjet-Nachlass in der Ukraine. Stimmungs- und Erfahrungsbericht. Abgeschlossen 30. 9. 1941." See also NA microcopy T-501, roll 33, frame 570: Sicherungs-Division 444, Abt. VII, Nr. 125/41, "Lagebericht," [Kryvyi Rih?], August 28, 1941. For the SD quotation, consult *Ereignismeldung UdSSR* 81 (September 12, 1941): 17, and see 40 (August 1, 1941): 18, 52 (August 14, 1941): 9, and 191 (April 10, 1942): 20–21.

17. NA microcopy T-501, roll 33, frame 1104: "Tätigkeitsbericht der Abteilung VII [of Bfh.rückw.H.Geb.Süd] von 1.–30.11.1941," n.p., n.d. (the quotations); NA microcopy T-501, roll 33, frame 389: Feldkommandantur (V)239, Abt. VII Az. 029, "Monatsbericht der Abteilung VII für die Zeit vom 15.9.–15.10.41," [Kremenchuk], October 24, 1941; *Ereignismeldung UdSSR* 135 (November 19, 1941): 17.

18. *Ereignismeldung UdSSR* 187 (March 30, 1942): 9 (the quotation); *Meldungen* 13 (July 24, 1942): 9.

19. *Meldungen* 24 (October 9, 1942): 15. Compare *Meldungen* 25 (October 16, 1942): 9, and 54 (May 14, 1943): 11.

20. P. T. Duma (Dmytro Maïvs'kyi) in *Litopys UPA*, vol. 24 (Toronto, 1995), 188–189 and in Weiner, *Making Sense of War*, 333. See also Volodymyr Serhiichuk, [comp.], *OUN-UPA v roky viiny: Novi dokumenty i materialy* (Kiev, 1996), 295–296, 304.

21. On wartime folklore see, for example, TsDAHOU, 1/23/601/97–105: "Nadpysy radian'skykh hromadian, iakykh nimtsi vidpravlialy, pidchas okupatsiï Ukraïny[,] v Nimechchynu." For Seleshko's observations, see his *Vinnytsia*, 132, 144, 153.

22. O. Iaroslavs'kyi, O. [Lev Chaikovs'kyi?], "Vid Sianu po Dinets' (z spohadiv perekladacha)," *Visti Bratstva kol. Voiakiv I UD UNA* 7, nos. 7–8(69–70) (Munich, July–August 1956): 19, 21; Pihido-Pravoberezhnyi, "Velyka Vitchyzniana viina," 161.

23. Bohdan Liubomyrenko, *Z Khrystom v Ukraïni: Zapysky viruiuchoho za roky 1941–1943* (Winnipeg, 1973), 97. See also Mykola Klymyshyn, *V pokhodi do voli: Spomyny*, vol. 1 (Toronto, 1975), 324; Zynovii Matla, *Pivdenna pokhidna hrupa* (Munich, 1952), 27; Iaroslavs'kyi, "Vid Sianu," 19; Hartymiv, "Zemleiu ukraïns'koiu," 128–129, 144; A. Kabaida, "1941," *Kalendar-al'manakh Novoho Shliakhu*, 1991 (Toronto, n.d.): 53.

24. Koch, "Der Sowjet-Nachlass," 6; Olexa Woropay, *The Ninth Circle: In Commemoration of the Victims of the Famine of 1933* (Cambridge, Mass., 1983), 16.
25. Koch, "Der Sowjet-Nachlass," 16. Compare *Ereignismeldung UdSSR* 45 (August 7, 1941): 6.
26. Nikolai Fevr, *Solntse voskhodit na zapade* (Buenos Aires, 1950), 170–171.
27. Ulas Samchuk, *Na koni voronomu: Spomyny i vrazhennia* (Winnipeg, 1975), 260–261.
28. Klymyshyn, *V pokhodi do voli*, 350–351, cites a woman who reasoned this way.
29. Koch, "Der Sowjet-Nachlass," 14; Seleshko, *Vinnytsia*, 146; Serhiichuk, *OUN-UPA*, 296; Liubomyrenko, *Z Khrystom v Ukraïni*, 13, 18 (on persecution of Christians).
30. Serhiichuk, *OUN-UPA*, 327.
31. Meir Buchsweiler, *Volksdeutsche in der Ukraine am Vorabend und Beginn des Zweiten Weltkriegs—ein Fall doppelter Loyalität?* (Gerlingen, Ger., 1984), 287. Compare Benjamin Pinkus and Ingeborg Fleischhauer, *Die Deutschen in der Sowjetunion: Geschichte einer nationalen Minderheit im 20. Jahrhundert* (Baden-Baden, Ger., 1987), 306.
32. Ingeborg Fleischhauer, *Das Dritte Reich und die Deutschen in der Sowjetunion* (Stuttgart, 1983), 109; *Ereignismeldung UdSSR* 187 (March 30, 1942): 9; Buchsweiler, *Volksdeutsche*, 373. On taxes, see M. V. Koval' and P. V. Medvedok, "Fol'ksdoiche v Ukraïni (1941–1944 rr.)," *Ukraïns'kyi istorychnyi zhurnal*, no. 5 (1992): 22.
33. Fleischhauer, *Das Dritte Reich*, 180; Otto Bräutigam, *Überblick über die besetzten Ostgebiete während des 2. Weltkrieges* (Tübingen, 1954), 79.
34. TsDAHOU, 166/3/245/45: Ol'ga Sergeevna Pominchuk [Ukrainian?], Kiev, January 20, 1946 (on Korosten').
35. On food rations, see Fleischhauer, *Das Dritte Reich*, 183; TsDAVOV, 3206/1/26/37v: "Teilbericht Politik über die Bereisung des Reichskommissariats mit Prof. v. Grünberg in der Zeit vom 13.8. bis 3.9.1942," Rivne, September 10, 1942. On Germans Only stores, see Pinkus and Fleischhauer, *Die Deutschen*, 268.
36. See, for example, TsDAVOV, 3206/1/26/37: "Teilbericht Politik."
37. TsDAVOV, 3206/5/15/266: RKU *Lagebericht* for February 1942, Rivne, March 15, 1942; TsDAVOV, 3676/4/97/60: "Auszug aus dem Lagebericht des Generalkommissars in Kiew für den Monat Mai 1942"; Fleischhauer, *Das Dritte Reich*, 165, 173; Buchsweiler, *Volksdeutsche*, 322.
38. Fleischhauer, *Das Dritte Reich*, 88–89.
39. Ibid., 185; "Natsional'na spravedlyvist'," *Vasyl'kivs'ki visti*, October 18, 1942.
40. Fleischhauer, *Das Dritte Reich*, 162–163, 166, 186–187; Buchsweiler, *Volksdeutsche*, 367.
41. Fleischhauer, *Das Dritte Reich*, 188–189 (on altering of names), 188 (on all becoming citizens at once).

42. TsDAVOV, 4620/3/243a/62: professor N. A. Shepelevskii, "Prebyvanie nemtsev v Kieve," n.p., n.d.

43. TsDAHOU, 166/3/243/43: Aleksei Mikhailovich Bashkulat (Ukrainian born in 1909), Kiev, February 28, 1944.

44. TsDAHOU, 166/3/243/5: Nikolai Kuz'mich Grun'skii [sic] (Ukrainian born in 1872), Kiev, February 19, 1944; Anatolii Kuznetsov (A. Anatoli), *Babii iar: Roman-dokument* (New York, 1986), 164–165; Fleischhauer, *Das Dritte Reich*, 89. On administrators, see Pinkus and Fleischhauer, *Die Deutschen*, 268–269; Fleischhauer, *Das Dritte Reich*, 164.

45. Pihido-Pravoberezhnyi, "*Velyka Vitchyzniana viina*," 131.

46. Seleshko, *Vinnytsia*, 124, 133.

47. Fleischhauer, *Das Dritte Reich*, 168.

48. Ibid., 90, 92–93, 106–108, 105–106 (about fear); Pinkus and Fleischhauer, *Die Deutschen*, 251; Buchsweiler, *Volksdeutsche*, 345.

49. Chubai, *Reid*, 41.

50. Fleischhauer, *Das Dritte Reich*, 181; TsDAVOV, 3206/1/26/35v: "Teilbericht Politik."

51. Fleischhauer, *Das Dritte Reich*, 123, 180.

52. Pinkus and Fleischhauer, *Die Deutschen*, 271–272 (Zviahel' commissar); TsDAVOV, 4620/3/243a/62: Shepelevskii, "Prebyvanie" (Kiev); TsDAVOV, 3206/1/26/29v: "Teilbericht Politik" (the figure). Compare *Ereignismeldung UdSSR* 125 (October 26, 1941): 5 (figure of 3,000).

53. NDB, collection "Afishy ta plakaty okupatsiinoho periodu," 489sp: "Stina vpala."

54. Leo Meter, *Briefe an Barbara: Mit einem Nachwort von Barbara Meter* (Cologne, 1988), unnumbered page; K. Ia. Hrynevych, author interview.

55. Koch, "Der Sowjet-Nachlass," 12; Khoroshunova, "Pervyi god voiny," 47; Dudin, "Velikii Mirazh," 70–71.

56. Tatiana Fesenko, *Povest' krivykh let* (New York, 1963), 77. See also Dudin, "Velikii Mirazh," 72.

57. L. S. Khmilevs'ka, author interview.

58. TsDAVOV, 3206/1/78/49: RKU *Lagebericht* for January 1942.

59. Ernst Benz, *Die religiöse Lage in der Ukraine: Erlebnisbericht eines Divisionspfarrers. Als Manuskript gedruckt* (Marburg, Ger., 1942), 19 (the quotations); Kuznetsov, *Babii iar*, 298.

60. *Meldungen* 55 (May 21, 1943): 9–10.

61. NA microcopy T-120, roll 2533, frame E292538: Auswärtiges Amt, report based on an informant, Berlin, December 31, 1942; BA-Berlin, R 6/70, fols. 105–106: Zentralinformation to Otto Bräutigam, "Auszug aus dem vertraulichen Bericht eines russischen Berichterstatters über eine Reise in der Ukraine," Berlin, April

9, 1943; HIA-HURIP, box 23, no. 548 AD, B-6, fol. 4: editor of *Vinnyts'ki visti* [Mykhailo Zerov?], n.p., April 24, 1951.

62. Fleischhauer, *Das Dritte Reich*, 173.

63. TsDAHOU, 1/22/347/6: "Iz dnevnika uchitel'nitsy gor. Kieva L. Nartovoi" (hereafter Nartova diary), note of March 21, 1942.

64. NA microcopy T-120, roll 2533, frame E292538.

65. TsDAHOU, 1/22/11/10: Chepurnoi, zam. zav. orginstruktorskim otdelom TsK KP(b)U, "Informatsiia o sostoianii raboty kievskoi podpol'noi organizatsii KP(b)U," Starobil's'k, March 26, 1943. On hatred by city dwellers, see also Ivan R. Kostiuk, "Kremenchuk (Z bloknota kol. voiennoho zvitodavtsia)," *Visti kombatanta*, no. 1(13) (New York, 1964): 34; Chubai, *Reid*, 39; TsDAHOU, 166/3/248/24: V. Tverskoi, "Dorogie druz'ia," Kiev, n.d.; *Litopys UPA*, vol. 5 (Toronto, 1984), 22.

66. Kuznetsov, *Babii iar*, 369–371.

67. In the original: "Sovist' u tebe nimets'ka." "Posiiav, nimets' bere / Ne posiiav, nimets' dere / Khai ïkh chort zabere!" IMFE, 14–3/56: M. T. Ryl's'kyi, ed., "Fol'klor Velykoï Vitchyznianoï viiny" (typed manuscript, Kiev, 1945), fols. 491, 488, citing IMFE, Krasyts'ka collection, 14–3/20/125, 227 and 14–3/108/216. See also *Meldungen* 47 (March 26, 1943): 12; Serhiichuk, *OUN-UPA*, 340, 364.

68. TsDAVOV, 3676/4/161/31–31v: Auslandbriefprüfstelle Berlin, "Stimmungsbericht auf Grund von Briefen, die im April und Mai 1943 ausgewertet sind, über: Ostarbeiter (Post aus und nach der Ukraine)," Berlin, June 18, 1943.

69. "V kliatykh nimtsiv tovsti huby / Nakopycheni / Pro nas kazhut', shcho my hrubi / Neosvicheni." "My uden' na lanakh / Pasem vnochi koni / Lyshe kliatyi nimchura / Hra na patefoni." "U hrazhdans'komu ukraïntsi / Burzhuïv prohnaly / A z"iavylys' kliati nimtsi / I panamy staly." IMFE, K. Tolchennikova collection, 14–3/25/41, 44, 49.

70. Serhiichuk, *OUN-UPA*, 327 (*byty nimtsiv*); NA microcopy T-78, roll 565, frames 262–263, 257, 254: "Notatky pro pokhodzhennia i poshyrennia partyzanshchyny," n.p., n.d., with German translation and a summary by the Amt-Ausland/Abwehr dated May 18, 1943; NA microcopy T-120, roll 2533, frame E292538 (the quotations); P. Vershigora, *Men with a Clear Conscience* (Moscow, 1949), 294–297; *Shchodennyk Arkadiia Liubchenka*, 95; HIA-HURIP, box 20, no. 206 HD, B-General, fol. 3: anonymous informant, n.p., n.d.; HIA-HURIP, box 23, no. 182 AD, B-6, fols. 7–8: anonymous informant, Munich, December 5, 1950.

71. Dudin, "Velikii Mirazh," 43.

72. *Ereignismeldung UdSSR* 74 (September 5, 1941): 9; BA-Berlin, R 6/15, fol. 115: Heinz v. Homeyer to Reich Minister Alfred Rosenberg, Wolfsberg, October 15,

1943; TsDAVOV, 3206/5/15/351: RKU *Lagebericht* for April 1942, Rivne, May 15, 1942.

73. TsDAVOV, 3206/1/26/31v, 33v: "Teilbericht Politik"; Pihido-Pravoberezhnyi, "*Velyka Vitchyzniana viina*," 162 (the quotations).

74. "Tsar v Rosiï skasuvav / Vzhe davno kripatstvo / A ot Hitler nakazav / Vstanovyty rabstvo." IMFE, Tolchennikova collection, 14–3/25/20 (peasant women in the Kiev region); "Dumaie Hitler vsim svitom keruvaty / To pryidet'sia iomu sobakoiu zdykhaty." IMFE, Ie. I. Prytula collection, 14–3/24/30 (people in Berdychiv); "Het' Hitler-vyzvolytelia, khai zhyve Stalin-hnobytel'." TsDAHOU, 1/22/10/74: S. Oleksenko, obkom secretary, "Doklad o Kamenets-Podol'skikh partizanakh," n.p. [1943] (Kam"ianets'-Podil's'kyi region); "Durnyi iak Hitler." "Fol'klor Velykoï Vitchyznianoï viiny," 490, citing IMFE, Krasyts'ka collection, 14–3/20/40 (Dnipropetrovs'k area).

75. BA-Berlin, R 6/15, fol. 86: district commissar, "Stimmungsbericht des Gebiets Berdjansk lt. Verfügung vom 28.6.1943," Berdians'k, July 15, 1943; BA-Berlin, R 6/70, fol. 102: Der Vertreter des Auswärtigen Amts beim Reichskommissar f.d. Ukraine, "Haltung der ukrainischen Bevölkerung während der Winterschlacht 1942/43," Rivne, March 13, 1943; NA microcopy T-175, roll 81, frame 2601569: Reichskommissar Koch to Rosenberg, "Betr.: Derzeitiger Stand der Bandenlage," Rivne, June 25, 1943; Serhiichuk, *OUN-UPA*, 344.

76. V. G. Safronov, *Ital'ianskie voiska na sovetsko-germanskom fronte, 1941–1943* (Moscow, 1990), 41, quoted in B. N. Petrov, "Kak delili Ukrainu Gitler i Musso-lini," *Voenno-istoricheskii zhurnal*, no. 8 (1993): 15.

77. For the behavior of the Italians, see Dudin, "Velikii Mirazh," 95; Vershigora, *Men with a Clear Conscience*, 272; BA-Berlin, R 6/15, fol. 88: "Sonderbericht über die Februarereignisse im Gebiet Nowo-Moskowsk," n.p., n.d.; Walther Hubatsch, ed., *Kriegstagebuch des Oberkommandos der Wehrmacht (Wehrmachtführungsstab), 1940–1945*, vol. 3, part 2 (Frankfurt am Main, 1963), 1424. For their reception by city dwellers, see Jacob Gerstenfeld-Maltiel, *My Private War: One Man's Struggle to Survive the Soviets and the Nazis* (London, 1993), 222–223; *Shchodennyk Arkadiia Liubchenka*, 118; NA microcopy T-84, roll 120, frame 419260: general commissar, report, Kiev, March 4, 1943; F. P. Bogatyrchuk, *Moi zhiznennyi put' k Vlasovu i Prazhkomu manifestu* (San Francisco, 1978), 153–154.

78. Pihido-Pravoberezhnyi, "*Velyka Vitchyzniana viina*," 145. See also Lashchenko, "Povorot," *Samostiina Ukraïna* 9, no. 7(115) (New York, July 1958): 9.

79. Fevr, *Solntse*, 171.

80. Samchuk, *Na koni voronomu*, 254–255; Hartymiv, "Zemleiu ukraïns'koiu," 129, 138; Orest Zovenko, *Bezimenni: Spohad uchasnyka novitnikh vyzvol'nykh zmahan'* (n.p., 1946), 65; Serhiichuk, *OUN-UPA*, 248; Matla, *Pivdenna pokhidna hrupa*, 17; Chubai, *Reid*, 29; Mykola S.-Chartoryis'kyi, *Vid Sianu po*

Krym: (Spomyny uchasnyka III Pokhidnoï Grupy-Pivden') (New York, 1951), 166; Klymyshyn, *V pokhodi do voli*, 326, 361.

81. S.-Chartoryis'kyi, *Vid Sianu*, 112–114.
82. *Ereignismeldung UdSSR* 112 (October 13, 1941): 4–5. Compare *Ereignismeldung UdSSR* 129 (November 5, 1941): 15. On the eventual shunning of Galicians, see Seleshko, *Vinnytsia*, 90.
83. Koch, "Der Sowjet-Nachlass," 12–13.
84. Pihido-Pravoberezhnyi, *"Velyka Vitchyzniana viina,"* 81–82.
85. Fevr, *Solntse*, 177.
86. Koch, "Der Sowjet-Nachlass," 9. See also *Ereignismeldung UdSSR* 47 (August 9, 1941): 15; Serhiichuk, *OUN-UPA*, 252. Compare Pan'kivs'kyi, *Vid derzhavy do komitetu*, 104.
87. Khoroshunova, "Pervyi god voiny," 61. See also *Ereignismeldung UdSSR* 106 (October 7, 1941): 14. For the quotation, see TsDAHOU, 166/3/243/22: V. M. Artobolevskii (Russian born in 1874), Kiev, February 22 and 25, 1944.
88. *Ereignismeldung UdSSR* 135 (November 19, 1941): 17.
89. TsDAVOV, 3206/2/27/4: RKU *Lagebericht* for December 1941, Rivne, January 14, 1942.
90. TsDAVOV, 3206/5/15/260: RKU *Lagebericht* for February 1942; *Ereignismeldung UdSSR* 177 (March 6, 1942): 2–3; Nartova diary, 5, 8.
91. Nartova diary, 15; *Shchodennyk Arkadiia Liubchenka*, 70; NA microcopy T-120, roll 2533, frame E292549/17: Auslandbriefprüfstelle Berlin, "Stimmungsbericht," Berlin, November 11, 1942; *Meldungen* 25 (October 16, 1942): 8, evidently using TsDAVOV, 3676/4/474/170: Sipo-SD report on Kiev GB, September 14, 1942.
92. *Meldungen* 25 (October 17, 1942): 12, and 32 (December 4, 1942): 9.
93. Compare *Meldungen* 47 (March 26, 1943): 12, 14, 16.
94. Gerstenfeld-Maltiel, *My Private War*, 218.
95. Kuznetsov, *Babii iar*, 174; *Shchodennyk Arkadiia Liubchenka*, 40, 43, 95; *Meldungen* 47 (March 26, 1943): 12; "Fol'klor Velykoï Vitchyznianoï viiny," 489, citing IMFE, Krasyts'ka collection, 14–3/20/46 ("Za nimtsiv do vorozhky / Znov proterly dorozhky").
96. "Nemtsam gut / evreiam kaput / tsyganam tozhe / ukraintsam pozzhe." TsDAVOV, 4620/3/243a/14: I. N. Zhitov, "Komissii po rassledovaniiu nemetskikh zverstv na Ukraine," Kiev, November 1943. For slightly different versions, see Kuznetsov, *Babii iar*, 157; "Fol'klor Velykoï Vitchyznianoï viiny," 488, 623. On the July–August rumors, see TsDAVOV, 3676/4/474/414: Sipo-SD report on the Kiev GB, September 25, 1942.
97. NA microcopy T-84, roll 120, frame 419083: "Misstände und Schwierigkeiten in der Wohnungsfrage in Kiew. Lagebericht Material," n.p., n.d.
98. For German complaints, see TsDAVOV, 3206/5/15/191, 204, 212, 236, and

TsDAVOV, 3206/1/78/30: RKU *Lageberichte* for October 1941 through January 1942. On alcoholism, see Serhiichuk, *OUN-UPA*, 327; HIA-HURIP, box 32, no. 121 AD, B-6, fol. 14: anonymous informant from Kherson, n.p., November 28–29, 1950.

99. Khoroshunova, "Pervyi god voiny," 61.

100. TsDAVOV, 3206/5/15/260: RKU *Lagebericht* for February 1942.

101. TsDAVOV, 3676/4/476/180: Sipo-SD report on the Kiev GB in May 1942, June 2, 1942.

102. *Shchodennyk Arkadiia Liubchenka*, 110, 112; *Meldungen* 47 (March 26, 1943): 12, 17; Kuznetsov, *Babii iar*, 369; NA microcopy T-84, roll 120, frame 419253: general commissar, report, Kiev, March 1, 1943.

103. *Meldungen* 47 (March 26, 1943): 18.

104. Kuznetsov, *Babii iar*, 315 (the quotation); NDB, collection "Afishy ta plakaty okupatsiinoho periodu," 396sp: "Novyi grandioznyi obman."

105. *Shchodennyk Arkadiia Liubchenka*, 117.

106. *Dzvin voli* (Bila Tserkva), July 11, 1943, 3; Alexander Werth, *Russia at War, 1941–1945* (New York, 1965), 567; Larissa Kotyeva, *Three Worlds of Larissa: A Story of Survival* (Brunswick, Maine, 1993), 127 (on stories). For fears of hanging, see TsDAHOU, 166/3/244/18: Iu. M. Markovskii (Ukrainian born in 1904), Kiev, March 12, 1944. See also HIA-HURIP, box 22, no. 64 AD, B-6, fols. 2–3: anonymous Red Army veteran, n.p., November 1, 1950.

107. TsDAHOU, 1/22/122/31: Nosenko, "Dokladnaia zapiska." See also, on the Donbas, Kuromiya, *Freedom and Terror*, 281.

108. Pihido-Pravoberezhnyi, "*Velyka Vitchyzniana viina*," 45.

109. Original usage: *ti*; in Russian, *te*. Koch, "Der Sowjet-Nachlass," 9; Kuznetsov, *Babii iar*, 279.

110. Benz, *Die religiöse Lage*, 47; Nartova diary, 5, 8; S.-Chartoryis'kyi, *Vid Sianu*, 117, 146–147, 149, 182, 194; TsDAHOU, 166/3/244/11: M. A. Novitskaia (Ukrainian born in 1896), Kiev, February 22, 1944; IMFE, 14–3/56: "Fol'klor Velykoï Vitchyznianoï viiny," 496.

111. Kuznetsov, *Babii iar*, 28 (on *bosiaki*). On "devil's reign," see Chapter 10.

112. Fesenko, *Povest'*, 86.

113. Oleksander Bykovets' in James E. Mace and Leonid Heretz, eds., *Oral History Project of the Commission on the Ukraine Famine*, vol. 1 (Washington, 1990), 409.

114. The Ukrainian women and men whom I interviewed in Ukraine in 1995 consistently used the word *nashi*.

115. *Meldungen* 43 (February 26, 1943): 11, a report written before the end of the Battle of Stalingrad.

116. NA microcopy T-501, roll 28, frame 46: Der Kommandierende General der Sicherungstruppen und Befehlshaber im Heeresgeb.Süd Nr. 1454/43, I. V. Generalmajor Graf Stolberg, to Heeresgruppe Süd, "Monatsbericht (1.–

30.9.43)," Headquarters, October 6, 1943. See also *Litopys UPA*, vol. 2, 2d ed. (Toronto, 1985), 142.

117. TsDAHOU, 1/22/6/28–29: D. S. Korotchenko to N. S. Khrushchev, "O sostoianii partizanskogo dvizheniia na pravoberezhnoi Ukraine," n.p., July 22, 1943.

118. Ortwin Buchbender, *Das tönende Erz: Deutsche Propaganda gegen die Rote Armee im Zweiten Weltkrieg* (Stuttgart, 1978), 329.

119. Negretov, *Vse dorogi*, 50 (the quotation); Emigrant, "Nemtsy v Kieve," 59.

120. Gerstenfeld-Maltiel, *My Private War*, 228. For the Banderite report, see Serhiichuk, *OUN-UPA*, 327.

121. Dudin, "Velikii Mirazh," 110, 174, 186, 188.

122. NA microcopy T-120, roll 2533, frame E292538.

123. Buchbender, *Das tönende Erz*, 329.

124. Sheila Fitzpatrick, *Everyday Stalinism: Ordinary Life in Extraordinary Times. Soviet Russia in the 1930s* (New York, 1999), 138.

125. Armstrong, *Ukrainian Nationalism*, 87; HIA-HURIP, box 22, no. 32 AD, B-6, fol. 6: former Gulag inmate, n.p., October 7, 1950 (the last quotation). See also HIA-HURIP, box 23, no. 548 AD, B-6, fol. 5: editor of *Vinnyts'ki visti* [Mykhailo Zerov?].

126. "Okh, okh, iak zhe nam / Bez radvlady zhyt'? / Khto v Hestapo pobuvav / V toho tilo vse bolyt'." IMFE, Tolchennikova collection, 14–3/25/26.

127. "Khoch sukhari z vodoiu, aby vlast' iz zvizdoiu." "Iak Stalin namy keruvav, to kolhosp bidy ne znav. A nimets'ka vlast' znaishlasia, v kolhospi triastia zavelasia." "Fol'klor Velykoï Vitchyznianoï viiny," 486, citing IMFE, Prytula collection, no folio mentioned.

128. Serhiichuk, *OUN-UPA*, 343, 340.

129. Werth, *Russia at War*, 728.

130. Stephen Kotkin, review of Sarah Davies, *Popular Opinion in Stalin's Russia: Terror, Propaganda, and Dissent, 1934–1941*, in *Europe-Asia Studies* 50, no. 4 (1998): 741; Stephen Kotkin, *Magnetic Mountain: Stalinism as a Civilization* (Berkeley, Calif., 1995), esp. chapter 5; Weiner, *Making Sense of War*, 366; Kuromiya, *Freedom and Terror*, 312.

131. Orlando Figes, "The Russian Revolution of 1917 and Its Language in the Village," *Russian Review* 56, no. 3 (1997): 331–334.

132. I. Tolanenko, "Sushchaia pravda vo vremia germanskoi okkupatsii na Ukraine," *Vozrozhdenie*, no. 53 (Paris, May 1956): 78–88; Serhiichuk, *OUN-UPA*, 351 (confirmation of such polls). Similar evidence on the Donbas is documented in Kuromiya, *Freedom and Terror*, 280.

133. Gerhard Lorenz, *The Lost Generation and Other Stories* (Steinbach, Manitoba, 1982), 46, citing anonymously a grandson of "a well known leader among the Mennonites of Russia."

134. Ibid., 48. See also Fleischhauer, *Das Dritte Reich*, 183.

135. Lohrenz, *Lost Generation*, 48, 52.

136. Negretov, *Vse dorogi*, 24–25. See also Ternivs'kyi, "Spohady emigranta," 7. Similar comments about Soviet Russia are in Fitzpatrick, *Everyday Stalinism*, 68, 212, 224.

137. *Ereignismeldung UdSSR* 112 (October 13, 1941): 2.

138. H. Sova [Hryhorii Kariak], *Do istoriï bol'shevyts'koï diis'nosty: (25 rokiv zhyttia ukraïns'koho hromadianyna v SSSR)* (Munich, 1955), 95–96.

139. *La Stampa* (Turin), May 25, 1942, cited in Ievhen Onats'kyi, "Ukraïna ochyma italiis'kykh korespondentiv u druhii svitovii viini," *Samostiina Ukraïna* 18, no. 8(198) (New York, August 1965): 24.

140. *Ereignismeldung UdSSR* 45 (August 7, 1941): 10 (SD quotation); TsDAVOV, 3206/1/26/27v: "Teilbericht Politik."

141. Seleshko, *Vinnytsia*, 146, 164.

142. Ibid., 150.

143. Lashchenko, "Povorot," *Samostiina Ukraïna* 11, no. 10(118) (Chicago, October 1958): 11–12.

144. See Iaroslavs'kyi, "Vid Sianu," 21.

145. Onats'kyi, "Ukraïna," 23–24.

146. Seleshko, *Vinnytsia*, 146, 164.

147. *Meldungen* 54 (May 14, 1943): 16 (the quotations); Buchbender, *Das tönende Erz*, 268.

148. Nartova diary, 21 (the first quotation); *Shchodennyk Arkadiia Liubchenka*, 118.

149. *Meldungen* 54 (May 14, 1943): 16.

150. Seleshko, *Vinnytsia*, 146. Compare *Litopys UPA*, vol. 24, 198, 203. According to Pihido, "*Velyka Vitchyzniana viina*," 191, the gap also existed among the Soviet forced laborers in the Reich.

151. John Barber and Mark Harrison, *The Soviet Home Front, 1941–1945: A Social and Economic History of the USSR in World War II* (London, 1991), 72–73, 208.

152. Krawchenko, "Soviet Ukraine under Nazi Occupation."

153. Kuromiya, *Freedom and Terror*, 71, argues the same about the Donbas during the revolutionary period.

154. Shelley E. Taylor, Letitia Anne Peplau, and David O. Sears, *Social Psychology*, 10th ed. (Upper Saddle River, N.J., 2000), 455.

155. O. Iatsenko, author interview.

10. Religion and Popular Piety

1. See, for example, Hartmut Lehmann, ed., *Säkularisierung, Dechristianisierung, Rechristianisierung im neuzeitlichen Europa: Bilanz und Perspektiven der Forschung* (Göttingen, Ger., 1997).

2. Bohdan R. Bociurkiw, "The Renovationist Church in the Soviet Ukraine, 1922–1939," *Annals of the Ukrainian Academy of Arts and Sciences in the U.S.* 9, nos. 1–2(27–28) (New York, 1961): 52, 62–67.

3. Bohdan R. Bociurkiw, "The Soviet Destruction of the Ukrainian Orthodox Church, 1929–1936," *Journal of Ukrainian Studies* 12, no. 1 (1987): 5–12, 14; Friedrich Heyer, *Die orthodoxe Kirche in der Ukraine von 1917 bis 1945* (Cologne, 1953), 114.

4. Heyer, *Die orthodoxe Kirche*, 115–116, 118–120, 125.

5. Ibid., 126; Bociurkiw, "Renovationist Church," 72.

6. Heyer, *Die orthodoxe Kirche*, 144; DAKO, r-2412/2/199/75: Dionysii, letter, Warsaw, November 13, 1941.

7. NDB, collection "Afishy ta plakaty okupatsiinoho periodu," 764sp: "Doba stalins'koho bezbozhnytstva mynula."

8. Heyer, *Die orthodoxe Kirche*, 171; Harvey Fireside, *Icon and Swastika: The Russian Orthodox Church under Nazi and Soviet Control* (Cambridge, Mass., 1971), 118; O. Iaroslavs'kyi [Lev Chaikovs'kyi?], "Vid Sianu po Dinets' (Z spohadiv perekladacha)," *Visti Bratstva kol. Voiakiv I UD UNA* 7, nos. 7–8 (69–70) (Munich, July–August 1956): 21.

9. TsDAVOV, 3676/1/50/27: "Erklärung des orthodoxen Kirchenrates von Cherson, abgegeben am 21.10.41 auf Veranlassung des Kreislandwirtschaftführers, Sonderführer Linke," n.p., n.d. On churches as stables, see Mykhailo Hartymiv, "Zemleiu ukraïns'koiu . . . ," in Kost' Mel'nyk, Oleh Lashchenko, and Vasyl' Veryha, eds., *Na zov Kyieva: Ukraïns'kyi natsionalizm u II Svitovii Viini. Zbirnyk stattei, spohadiv i dokumentiv* (Toronto, 1985), 146.

10. Fireside, *Icon and Swastika*, 118; Walther Bienert, *Russen und Deutsche: Was für Menschen sind das? Berichte, Bilder und Folgerungen aus dem Zweiten Weltkrieg* (Stein am Rhein, Switz., 1990), 92.

11. DAKO, r-2412/2/199/19–20: Mykola Rybachuk, "Vidrodzhennia tserkovno-relihiinoho zhyttia v zvil'nomu nimets'kym viis'kom Zolotoverkhnomu Kyievi i oblasty," n.p., n.d.

12. DAKO, r-2292/1/2/23v. For bans on weekday services, see V. V. Hordiienko, "Nimets'ko-fashysts'kyi okupatsiinyi rezhym i pravoslavni konfesiï v Ukraïni," *Ukraïns'kyi istorychnyi zhurnal*, no. 3 (1998): 114–115.

13. Heyer, *Die orthodoxe Kirche*, 189, 199–200; Ivan Vlasovs'kyi, *Narys istoriï Ukraïns'koï Pravoslavnoï Tserkvy*, vol. 9: (*XX st.*), part 2 (New York, 1966), 239.

14. Vlasovs'kyi, *Narys istoriï*, 235–236; Heyer, *Die orthodoxe Kirche*, 197–199, 205; A. Dublians'kyi, *Ternystym shliakhom: Zhyttia Mytropolyta Nikanora Abramovycha. Do 20-littia arkhypastyrs'koho sluzhinnia, 1942–1962* (London, 1962), 40.

15. DAKO, r-2412/2/199/6–7, 16: Rybachuk; Heyer, *Die orthodoxe Kirche*, 127, 172.

16. John A. Armstrong, *Ukrainian Nationalism*, 3d ed. (Englewood, Colo., 1990), 155; Heyer, *Die orthodoxe Kirche*, 212–213, 217–218.

17. Vlasovs'kyi, *Narys istoriï*, 227–228; S. Haiuk, "Vodokhreshchi," *Litopys Volyni* 1 (Winnipeg, 1953): 85–86; HIA, Alexander Dallin collection, box 2, folder 14, fol. 9: AD G-20, Professor Hans Koch, Salzburg, Austria, June 1, 1951 (hereafter Koch interview). (The first page of the transcript is in box 7, folder 6, fol. 9.)

18. Dublians'kyi, *Ternystym shliakhom*, 40; Vlasovs'kyi, *Narys istoriï*, 236–237; Hans-Heinrich Wilhelm, "Der SD und die Kirchen in den besetzten Ostgebieten 1941/42," *Militärgeschichtliche Mitteilungen* 55, no. 1 (1981): 86.

19. A. I. Kishkovskii, untitled review of an article by W. Alexeev, *Vestnik Instituta po izucheniiu SSSR*, no. 2(27) (Munich, May–August 1958): 130–131; Osyp Zinkevych and Oleksander Voronyn, eds., *Martyrolohiia ukraïns'kykh tserkov u chotyr'okh tomakh*, vol. 1: *Ukraïns'ka pravoslavna tserkva* (Toronto, 1987), 677–678, 731.

20. Vlasovs'kyi, *Narys istoriï*, 211–212.

21. *Russkaia pravoslavnaia tserkov' i Velikaia Otechestvennaia voina: Sbornik tserkovnykh dokumentov* (Moscow, [1943]), 67; "Pershe zasidannia Ukraïns'koï Rady Dovir"ia na Volyni," *Volyn'* (Rivne), September 7, 1941, 2.

22. Zinkevych and Voronyn, *Martyrolohiia*, 737; Vlasovs'kyi, *Narys istoriï*, 210, 228; I. Vlasovs'kyi, "Iak bulo z obranniam na kyïvs'ku katedru Arkhyiepyskopa Ilariona (Ohiienka) roku 1941," *Tserkva i narid* ([Winnipeg], April–May 1949): 21, 24–26.

23. Vlasovs'kyi, "Iak bulo," 26; Heyer, *Die orthodoxe Kirche*, 174; TsDAHOU, 1/23/41/47–47v: "Aus dem Schreiben des Herrn Matzjuk," n.d., n.p.; "Pershe zasidannia"; Fedir Dudko, "Interv"iu z vladykoiu Polikarpom (vid vlasnoho korespondenta)," *Volyn'*, February 26, 1942, 3.

24. "Iedyna Pravoslavna Tserkva v Ukraïni," *Volyn'*, February 19, 1942, 1.

25. DAKO, r-2412/2/199/68: document from the May 1942 Synod in Kiev, May 17, 1942; DAKO, r-2412/2/199/74: letter to Hitler, Kiev, June 22, 1942; Vlasovs'kyi, *Narys istoriï*, 177, 226, 229–230.

26. Vlasovs'kyi, "Iak bulo," 23; A. Nesterenko, *Mytropolyt Ilarion: Sluzhytel' Bohovi i narodovi. Biohrafichna monohrafiia* (Winnipeg, 1958), 78.

27. TsDAVOV, 3206/1/78/34: RKU *Lagebericht* for January 1942, Rivne, February 14, 1942 (on a visa request by Aleksii).

28. Vlasovs'kyi, *Narys istoriï*, 221.

29. Ibid., 222. A list of the seven new bishops is in Karel C. Berkhoff, "Was There a Religious Revival in Soviet Ukraine under the Nazi Regime?" *Slavonic and East European Review* 78, no. 3 (2000): 544, n. 32.

30. Zinkevych and Voronyn, *Martyrolohiia*, 747–748. See also *Ukraïns'kyi holos* (Proskuriv), June 28, 1942, 4.

31. Vlasovs'kyi, *Narys istoriï*, 238; Armstrong, *Ukrainian Nationalism*, 155; Zinkevych and Voronyn, *Martyrolohiia*, 750.

32. Vlasovs'kyi, *Narys istoriï*, 241–243; Armstrong, *Ukrainian Nationalism*, 154–155; Zinkevych and Voronyn, *Martyrolohiia*, 729–731; Dublians'kyi, *Ternystym shliakhom*, 46–47. For German opposition, see Vlasovs'kyi, *Narys istoriï*, 243, 248.

33. Vlasovs'kyi, *Narys istoriï*, 246; Zinkevych and Voronyn, *Martyrolohiia*, 731–733, 735.

34. Vlasovs'kyi, *Narys istoriï*, 249, 252–253; Zinkevych and Voronyn, *Martyrolohiia*, 751–754; Dublians'kyi, *Ternystym shliakhom*, 43.

35. Christoph Kleßmann, "Nationalsozialistische Kirchenpolitik und Nationalitätenfrage im Generalgouvernement (1939–1945)," *Jahrbücher für Geschichte Osteuropas* 18, no. 4 (1970): 575.

36. Heyer, *Die orthodoxe Kirche*, 213–216; Vlasovs'kyi, *Narys istoriï*, 230, 250–252.

37. Heyer, *Die orthodoxe Kirche*, 216–217.

38. Zinkevych and Voronyn, *Martyrolohiia*, 745–746; Panas Khurtovyna [Mykhailo Podvorniak], *Pid nebom Volyni: (Voienni spomyny khrystyianyna)* (Winnipeg, 1952), 102–104.

39. Bohdan Liubomyrenko, *Z Khrystom v Ukraïni: Zapysky viruiuchoho za roky 1941–1943* (Winnipeg, 1973), esp. 76, 81, 90, 101–102; Stepan Nyshchyk, *Shliakh viry* (Winnipeg, 1975), 85; DAKO, r-2412/2/199/64: I. Korovyts'kyi, "Vidrodzhennia Tserkvy v Ukraïni ta Kyievi," Kiev, July 22, 1942. On Islam, see DAKO, r-2412/2/199/64: Korovyts'kyi, "Vidrodzhennia Tserkvy"; L. Maliuzhenko, "Kyïv za 1942 r.," *Nashe mynule* 1(6) (Kiev, 1993): 163–164."

40. Zinkevych and Voronyn, *Martyrolohiia*, 745–746; Heyer, *Die orthodoxe Kirche*, 179.

41. TsDAVOV, 3206/1/26/30v, 33v–34, 37: "Teilbericht Politik über die Bereisung des Reichskommissariats mit Prof. v. Grünberg in der Zeit vom 13.8 bis 3.9.1942," Rivne, September 10, 1942; NA microcopy T-84, roll 120, frame 419181: "Auszug aus dem Lagebericht des Generalkommissars," Kiev, September 1, 1942; Ingeborg Fleischhauer, *Das Dritte Reich und die Deutschen in der Sowjetunion* (Stuttgart, 1983), 164; Armstrong, *Ukrainian Nationalism*, 153; Zygmunt Zieliński, ed., *Życie religijne w Polsce pod okupacją 1939–1945* (Katowice, Pol., 1992), 502 (the figure); *Ereignismeldung UdSSR* 128 (November 3, 1941): 5–6; *Meldungen* 5 (May 29, 1942): 12, and 11 (July 10, 1942): 2.

42. TsDAVOV, 3206/1/26/28: "Teilbericht Politik."

43. Kleßmann, "Nationalsozialistische Kirchenpolitik," 582, 596, n. 91, 598.

44. Heyer, *Die orthodoxe Kirche*, 171; TsDAHOU, 166/3/259/9v: diary of F. K. Kushnir; *Ereignismeldung UdSSR* 120 (October 21, 1941): 10.

45. Bienert, *Russen und Deutsche*, 93 (on Vasylivka); *Ereignismeldung UdSSR* 81 (September 12, 1941): 15; F. Pihido-Pravoberezhnyi, *"Velyka Vitchyzniana viina"* (Winnipeg, 1954), 120; Osyp Zhaloba [Osyp Zales'kyi], "U sorokalittia 'pokhodu na skhid' (spomyny perekladacha)," *Kalendar-al'manakh Novoho Shliakhu, 1982* (Toronto, n.d.): 93; Nina Mykhalevych, "Do Kyieva! Fragment zi spohadu," in Mel'nyk, Lashchenko, and Veryha, *Na zov Kyieva*, 225–226; Vlasovs'kyi, *Narys istoriï*, 232–233; Heyer, *Die orthodoxe Kirche*, 172.

46. Heyer, *Die orthodoxe Kirche*, 170–171; Pihido-Pravoberezhnyi, *"Velyka Vitchyzniana viina,"* 149.

47. Pihido-Pravoberezhnyi, *"Velyka Vitchyzniana viina,"* 120. See also Khurtovyna, *Pid nebom Volyni*, 88.

48. Kost' Pan'kivs'kyi, *Vid derzhavy do komitetu* (New York, 1957), 104; *Ukraïns'kyi holos*, March 12, 1942, 4; Vlasovs'kyi, *Narys istoriï*, 232–233; Zinkevych and Voronyn, *Martyrolohiia*, 744; Heyer, *Die orthodoxe Kirche*, 171.

49. Wilhelm, "Der SD," 84; Ievhen Onats'kyi, "Ukraïna ochyma italiis'kykh korespondentiv u druhii svitovii viini," *Samostiina Ukraïna* 18, no. 8(198) (New York, August 1965): 23. On the illegality of burials without a priest, see TsDAHOU, 1/22/122/99: "Deiatel'nost' partizanskikh otriadov v tylu vraga i v kakoi pomoshchi oni nuzhdaiutsia," n.p., n.d.

50. Leonid D—s'kyi, "Pokhoron u Luts'ku," *Litopys Volyni* 1 (1953): 71–74.

51. Ulas Samchuk, *Na bilomu koni: Spomyny i vrazhennia* (Winnipeg, 1972), 183.

52. TsDAHOU, 1/23/41/26–27: Abteilung IIa, "Betr. Bericht ueber eine Kundgebung," Rivne, September 15, 1941.

53. DAKO, r-2210/1/3/112: raion chief Okhrymenko, note, January 1, 1942.

54. DAKO, r-2412/2/2/72: mayoral decree no. 252, December 12, 1941; *Ukraïns'kyi holos*, December 25, 1941, 1.

55. See, for example, DAKO, r-2418/1/13/3–3v: Ortskommandant in Iahotyn to raion chief, January 8, 1942; UCEC, Pavlo Ternivs'kyi [Ivan Zhyhadlo], "Spohady emigranta" (n.p., 1945), 57 (the quotation).

56. K. Ia. Hrynevych, author interview; DAKO, r-2505/1/5/14–15, 25, 27, 29–30, 34 and r-2505/1/8/11, 24: elementary school in Pliskachivka, Smila raion.

57. Heyer, *Die orthodoxe Kirche*, 200–201; Halyna V"iun, *Pid znakom Chervonoho Khresta v Poltavi 1941–42 rr.: Spohad-zvit dlia istoriï* ([Neu-Ulm, Ger.], 1973), 29.

58. Maliuzhenko, "Kyïv za 1942 r.," 163–164.

59. Pihido-Pravoberezhnyi, *"Velyka Vitchyzniana viina,"* 56–57 (the long quotation about Pilate's Empire—*tsarstvo Ïhemona*); Khurtovyna, *Pid nebom Volyni*, 96; K. T. Turkalo, *Tortury: (Avtobiohrafiia za bol'shevyts'kykh chasiv)* (New York, 1963), 192.

60. Ernst Benz, *Die religiöse Lage in der Ukraine: Erlebnisbericht eines Divisionspfarrers. Als Manuskript gedruckt* (Marburg, 1942), 15–16 (the quotation); Vlasovs'kyi, *Narys istoriï*, 232 (on participation by young people);

61. Koch interview, 8.

62. TsDAHOU, 1/22/123/64: Petr Timofeevich Berdnik, "Kharakteristika polozhenii na okkupirovannoi territorii," n.p., n.d.

63. TsDAHOU, 1/22/123/97: "Informatsiia tov. Matsko o polozhenii na territorii, vremenno okkupirovannoi nemetskimi voiskami," n.p., n.d. (deals with the middle of 1942).

64. Koch interview, 11; on the many requests for priests, see Heyer, *Die orthodoxe Kirche*, 206; Vlasovs'kyi, *Narys istoriï*, 218.

65. *Ereignismeldung UdSSR* 117 (October 18, 1941): 8.

66. DAKO, r-2412/2/199/18: Rybachuk, "Vidrodzhennia."

67. DAKO, r-2412/2/199/33: Korovyts'kyi, "Vidrodzhennia Tserkvy."

68. Zinkevych and Voronyn, *Martyrolohiia*, 711 (the quotation); Heyer, *Die orthodoxe Kirche*, 189 (Poltava); BA-Berlin, R 6/15, fol. 105: "Lagebericht über das Gebiet Kriwoi Rog-Land," Kryvyi Rih, June 30, 1943.

69. NA microcopy T-84, roll 120, frame 419181: "Auszug aus dem Lagebericht des Generalkommissars," Kiev, September 1, 1942.

70. TsDAVOV, 3206/1/26/30v, 31v, 37, 38: "Teilbericht Politik." Compare TSDAVOV 3206/1/26/28, 32v, 33v, 36.

71. Vlasovs'kyi, *Narys istoriï*, 261.

72. Zinkevych and Voronyn, *Martyrolohiia*, 698; Heyer, *Die orthodoxe Kirche*, 193–194; Mykola Velychkivs'kyi, "Sumni chasy," *Vyzvol'nyi shliakh* 12, no. 6 (London, 1965): 801.

73. Compare Armstrong, *Ukrainian Nationalism*, 191.

74. On Sviatoshyn, see DAKO, r-2412/2/199/21–22: Rybachuk, "Vidrodzhennia," who used DAKO, r-2412/2/199/107–108. For Kiev, see Zinkevych and Voronyn, *Martyrolohiia*, 711. For Dnipropetrovs'k, see M. P. Kostiuk, author interview; Vlasovs'kyi, *Narys istoriï*, 233; Heyer, *Die orthodoxe Kirche*, 218; Armstrong, *Ukrainian Nationalism*, 157.

75. TsDAVOV, 3676/1/50/12–20, "Protokoll Nr. 1 des kirchlichen Organisations-Sobor im Kiewer Bezirk, der am 20. November 1941 in der Peter-Paul-Kirche im Dorf Butscha-Lisna stattfand."

76. DAKO, r-2412/2/199/52: Korovyts'kyi, "Vidrodzhennia tserkvy."

77. Khurtovyna, *Pid nebom Volyni*, 99.

78. TsDAVOV, 3206/1/26/40v: "Teilbericht Politik"; Heyer, *Die orthodoxe Kirche*, 189.

79. DAKO, r-2412/2/199/62–63: Korovyts'kyi, "Vidrodzhennia tserkvy"; Mykola Velychkivs'kyi, "Sumni chasy," *Vyzvol'nyi shliakh* 12, no. 4 (1965): 399; Nykon Nemyron [Mykola Andrusiak], "U zbudzhenii v ohni stolytsi Ukraïny (Slavnii pam"iati muchenykiv za Ukraïnu v Kyievi v 1941–42 rr.)," in Mykhailo H. Marunchak, ed., *V borot'bi za ukraïns'ku derzhavu: Eseï, spohady, svidchennia, litopysannia, dokumenty Druhoï svitovoï viiny* (Winnipeg, 1990), 811, 817.

80. Zinkevych and Voronyn, *Martyrolohiia*, 714; Dublians'kyi, *Ternystym shliakhom*, 41, n. 32.

81. See, for example, DAKO, r-2292/1/2/13–15: "Reiestratsiia pravoslavnykh parafii Rokytnians'koho r-nu" (which also mentions Protestants).

82. Vlasovs'kyi, *Narys istoriï*, 234; Dublians'kyi, *Ternystym shliakhom*, 43, 45.

83. Heyer, *Die orthodoxe Kirche*, 206–208.

84. The calculation is based on Heyer, *Die orthodoxe Kirche*, 189, 206–208; Armstrong, *Ukrainian Nationalism*, 196, 200; Protopresviter A. Teodorovych, "Preosviashchennyi Platon, Iepyskop Rivens'kyi (V Sviti Pavlo Artemiuk) (Spohad)," *Litopys Volyni* 4 (1958): 22; Dublians'kyi, *Ternystym shliakhom*, 44–45; Vlasovs'kyi, *Narys istoriï*, 234–235. See also the table of eparchies and bishops in Berkhoff, "Was There a Religious Revival?" 558–559.

85. See the list in Berkhoff, "Was There a Religious Revival?" 558, n. 97.

86. TsDAVOV, 3206/2/231/45: "Uebersicht über die Verwaltungseinteilung des Reichskommissariats Ukraine nach dem Stand vom 1. Januar 1943."

87. *Ideia i chyn: Orhan Provodu OUN, 1942–1946. Peredruk pidpil'noho zhurnalu*, Iurii Maïvs'kyi and Ievhen Shtendera, eds., which is *Litopys UPA*, vol. 24 (Toronto, 1995), 124; Zinkevych and Voronyn, *Martyrolohiia*, 739; Wilhelm, "Der SD," 88 (on the Dormition Cathedral).

88. Vlasovs'kyi, *Narys istoriï*, 233.

89. Heyer, *Die orthodoxe Kirche*, 209. Compare Zinkevych and Voronyn, *Martyrolohiia*, 711. On St. Volodymyr's Cathedral, see Zinkevych and Voronyn, *Martyrolohiia*, 716; Heyer, *Die orthodoxe Kirche*, 209; Dublians'kyi, *Ternystym shliakhom*, 51; Tat'iana Fesenko, *Povest' krivykh let* (New York, 1963), 90.

90. Heyer, *Die orthodoxe Kirche*, 207–208.

91. Ibid., 171, 208.

92. DAKO, r-2418/1/13/64 (on the Baryshivka raion in 1942); Ortwin Buchbender, *Das tönende Erz: Deutsche Propaganda gegen die Rote Armee im Zweiten Weltkrieg* (Stuttgart, 1978), 278; Heyer, *Die orthodoxe Kirche*, 172 (on Spas).

93. See also, on Belarus, Wilhelm, "Der SD," 91.

94. Koch interview, 9.

95. Siegfried von Vegesack, *Als Dolmetscher im Osten: Ein Erlebnisbericht aus den Jahren 1942–43. Mit 12 Bildern nach Aufnahmen des Verfassers* (Hannover-Döhren, 1965), 121.

96. Heyer, *Die orthodoxe Kirche*, 207.

97. TsDAVOV, 3676/4/161/55: report based on Ukrainian propagandists, Berlin, November 30, 1943.

98. TsDAHOU, 1/22/123/97: "Informatsiia tov. Matsko"; N. Salata, author interview.

99. Zinkevych and Voronyn, *Martyrolohiia*, 717. See also Hartymiv, "Zemleiu ukraïns'koiu," 126; F. H. (Fedir Haiovych), "Kyïv u zhovtni 1941," in Mel'nyk, Lashchenko, and Veryha, *Na zov Kyieva*, 163; Dublians'kyi, *Ternystym shliakhom*, 36; Onats'kyi, "Ukraïna," *Samostiina Ukraïna* 18, no. 2(192) (Febru-

ary 1965): 20; Paul Werner, *Ein Schweizer Journalist sieht Rußland: Auf den Spuren der deutschen Armee zwischen San und Dnjepr* (Olten, Switz., 1942), 98–99.

100. Heyer, *Die orthodoxe Kirche*, 209; TsDAHOU, 1/23/124/97: Savchenko, VRIO NKVD USSR, to N. S. Khrushchev, "Razvedsvodka No 33/68 o polozhenii v okkupirovannom protivnikom g. Dnepropetrovske. Po sostoianiiu na 20. 10. 42g.," Engel's, October 21, 1942.

101. Mykhailo Seleshko, *Vinnytsia: Spomyny perekladacha Komisiï doslidiv zlochyniv NKVD v 1937–1938* (New York, 1991), 102.

102. Examples from early 1943 are in Heyer, *Die orthodoxe Kirche*, 209; Volodymyr Serhiichuk, *OUN-UPA v roky viiny: Novi dokumenty i materialy* (Kiev, 1996), 329. On priests, see Vlasovs'kyi, *Narys istoriï*, 237–238; TsDAHOU, 1/22/123/64: Berdnik, "Kharakteristika polozhenii." For the fear of deportation, see HIA-HURIP, box 22, no. 96 AD, B-6, fol. 21: anonymous Orthodox priest, n.p., November 5, 1950.

103. Seleshko, *Vinnytsia*, 103.

104. TsDAHOU, 1/22/391/24: Mikhail Mikh. Skirda et al., "Otchet o podpol'noi partiinoi rabote i partizanskoi bor'be v Kirovogradskoi oblasti (avgust 1941 goda–mart 1944 goda)," n.d.

105. TsDAVOV, 3206/1/26/28: "Teilbericht Politik"; TsDAVOV, 3676/1/50/27: "Erklärung des orthodoxen Kirchenrates von Cherson" (on inciting parishioners); *Poslednie novosti* (Kiev), April 20, 1942, 4; Fireside, *Icon and Swastika*, 112 (the quotation).

106. TsDAHOU, 1/22/391/24: Skirda, "Otchet"; TsDAHOU, 1/22/123/64: Berdnik, "Kharakteristika polozhenii."

107. Irina Khoroshunova, "Pervyi god voiny. Kievskie zapiski," *Iehupets'* 9 (Kiev, 2001): 63.

108. TsDAHOU, 1/22/391/24: Skirda, "Otchet." See also TsDAHOU, 1/22/123/64: Berdnik, "Kharakteristika polozhenii."

109. Mikhail Koriakov, *Osvobozhdenie dushi* (New York, 1952), 197.

110. *Ereignismeldung UdSSR* 37 (July 29, 1941): 6, and 81 (September 12, 1941): 15, as well as 120 (October 21, 1941): 10 (the estimate). See also Armstrong, *Ukrainian Nationalism*, 156, 189.

111. Seleshko, *Vinnytsia*, 102. See also *Ereignismeldung UdSSR* 52 (August 14, 1941): 14; TsDAVOV, 3206/1/26/31v: "Teilbericht Politik"; Buchbender, *Das tönende Erz*, 319; Serhiichuk, *OUN-UPA*, 345.

112. Heyer, *Die orthodoxe Kirche*, 201; Autocephalous Archpriest Demyd Burko, quoted in Vlasovs'kyi, *Narys istoriï*, 232.

113. Benz, *Die religiöse Lage*, 36–37. See also "Suchasne ukraïns'ke selo (Vid vlasnoho korespondenta)," *Ukraïns'kyi visnyk* (Berlin), April 4, 1943, 6–7; TsDAVOV, 3206/1/26/30v, 32v, 33v: "Teilbericht Politik."

114. *Ereignismeldung UdSSR* 45 (August 7, 1941): 6.

115. TsDAHOU, 1/22/122/32–33: Iakov Fedorovich Nosenko, komissar partizanskogo otriada Kanevskogo raiona Kievskoi oblasti, to Zam. nach. 4-go Otdela NKVD USSR, "Dokladnaia zapiska," n.p., January 3, 1942.

116. TsDAHOU, 1/22/122/99: "Deiatel'nost' partizanskikh otriadov" (Soviet report); *Ereignismeldung UdSSR* 81 (September 12, 1941): 15 (SD's observation).

117. Heyer, *Die orthodoxe Kirche*, 218.

118. Liubomyrenko, *Z Khrystom v Ukraïni*, 40, 49 (the last two quotations); TsDAHOU, 1/22/123/64: Berdnik, "Kharakteristika polozhenii."

119. TsDAVOV, 3676/4/161/51, 53: report, Berlin, November 30, 1943.

120. TsDAVOV, 3206/1/26/40v: "Teilbericht Politik."

121. Stefan Plaggenborg, *Revolutionskultur: Menschenbilder und kulturelle Praxis in Sowjetrussland zwischen Oktoberrevolution und Stalinismus* (Cologne, 1996), 289–314; Stefan Plaggenborg, "Säkularisierung und Konversion in Rußland und der Sowjetunion," in Lehmann, *Säkularisierung*, 275–290; Heather J. Coleman, "Atheism versus Secularization? Religion in Soviet Russia, 1917–61," *Kritika* 1, no. 3 (Bloomington, Ind., 2000): 547–558.

11. Deportations and Forced Migrations

1. Alexander Dallin, *German Rule in Russia, 1941–1945: A Study of Occupation Policies*, 2d ed. (Boulder, Colo., 1981), 428.

2. TsDAVOV, 3206/2/27/8: RKU *Lagebericht* for December 1941, Rivne, January 14, 1942 (workers from Kryvyi Rih); Rolf-Dieter Müller, "Die Rekrutierung sowjetischer Zwangsarbeiter für die deutsche Kriegswirtschaft," in Ulrich Herbert, ed., *Europa und der "Reichseinsatz": Ausländische Zivilarbeiter, Kriegsgefangene und KZ-Häftlinge in Deutschland 1938–1945* (Essen, Ger., 1991), 237 (workers from Zaporizhzhia).

3. An example is Nina Kaliuzhna, "Divchata ïdut' do Raikhu," *Dzvin voli* (Bila Tserkva), December 17, 1942, 3; on the film, see Anatolii Kuznetsov (A. Anatolii), *Babii iar: Roman-dokument* (New York, 1986), 338–339; TsDAHOU, 166/3/244/85: Vera Filippovna Kal'nitskaia, [Kiev?], n.d.

4. Ortwin Buchbender, *Das tönende Erz: Deutsche Propaganda gegen die Rote Armee im Zweiten Weltkrieg* (Stuttgart, 1978), 280; "Ukraïns'ki robitnyky z Nimechchyny vidviduiut' Ukraïnu," *Ukraïns'kyi holos* (Proskuriv), October 29, 1942, 4; *Ukraïns'kyi holos*, November 1, 1942, 1, 4; *Meldungen* 32 (December 4, 1942): 24, and 43 (February 26, 1943): 22–23.

5. NDB, collection "Afishy ta plakaty okupatsiinoho periodu," 591sp.

6. NBU, Filiia 1, Viddil starodrukiv, poster 1484: "Reikhskomisar Ukraïny Erikh Kokh do ukraïns'kykh selian," n.p., n.d. Compare *Ukraïns'kyi holos*, March 26, 1942, 4.

7. Buchbender, *Das tönende Erz*, 281; NDB, "Afishy ta plakaty okupatsiinoho periodu," 87sp, 235sp, 310sp, 590sp.

8. NDB, "Afishy ta plakaty okupatsiinoho periodu," 244sp (the first quotation), 180sp; DAKO, r-2519/1/80/250v: fragment of a poster.

9. Buchbender, *Das tönende Erz*, 282–283 (the quotations); Kuznetsov, *Babii iar*, 258.

10. TsDAVOV, 3833/2/75/9: brochure, *Stvorennia novoho zhyttia bez zhydiv.*

11. NDB, "Afishy ta plakaty okupatsiinoho periodu," 575sp (the quotation), 576sp, 756sp.

12. "Sviatyi oboviazok ukraïns'koho narodu," *Ukraïns'kyi holos*, June 21, 1942, 3.

13. *Dzvin voli*, November 27, 1942, 4. Compare *Ukraïns'kyi holos*, March 14, 1943, 3 (Metropolitan Aleksii).

14. HIA, B. I. Nicolaevsky collection, series no. 178, box 232, folder 10, fol. 175: [Lev Vladimirovich] Dudin, "Velikii Mirazh: Sobytiia 1941–1947 v ponimanii sovetskogo cheloveka," n.p., 1947.

15. HIA-HURIP, box 23, no. 441 AD, B-6, fol. 5: [Konstantyn Shtepa], n.p., February 12, 1951; HIA, B. I. Nicolaevsky collection, series no. 236, box 409, folder 19, fol. 42: Emigrant, "Nemtsy v Kieve: (Iz vospominanii ochevidtsa)," n.p., n.d.; *Poslednie novosti* (Kiev), January 12, 1942, 4; TsDAVOV, 3206/1/78/35: RKU *Lagebericht* for January 1942, Rivne, February 14, 1942; Antonina Khelemendyk-Kokot, *Kolhospne dytynstvo i nimets'ka nevolia: Spohady* (Toronto, 1989), 145.

16. Tat'iana Fesenko, *Povest' krivykh let* (New York, 1963), 82; Kuznetsov, *Babii iar*, 258; TsDAHOU, 166/3/244/85: Kal'nitskaia.

17. Khelemendyk-Kokot, *Kolhospne dytynstvo*, 143 (the quotation); Julia Alexandrow with Tommy French, *Flight from Novaa Salow: Autobiography of a Ukrainian Who Escaped Starvation in the 1930s under the Russians and Then Suffered Nazi Enslavement* (Jefferson, N.C., 1995), 58–59.

18. Khelemendyk-Kokot, *Kolhospne dytynstvo*, 143. See also Mykola Klymyshyn, *V pokhodi do voli: Spomyny*, vol. 1 (Toronto, 1975), 378.

19. Norbert Müller [et al.], ed., *Die faschistische Okkupationspolitik in den zeitweilig besetzten Gebieten der Sowjetunion (1941–1944)* (Berlin, 1991), 314, 366–367. Compare also *Ereignismeldung UdSSR* 191 (April 10, 1942): 31; *Meldungen* 7 (June 12, 1942): 12 (both optimistic), with *Meldungen* 13 (July 24, 1942): 12, and 32 (December 4, 1942): 10, as well as 47 (March 26, 1943): 22, and 54 (May 14, 1943): 13. On the decline in the Kiev general district, see Müller, "Die Rekrutierung," 240.

20. *Meldungen* 21 (September 18, 1942): 19–20; Müller, *Die faschistische Okkupationspolitik*, 313; TsDAVOV, 3676/4/476/401: Sipo-SD report on the Kiev GB, Kiev, September 15, 1942.

21. See, for example, Ulrich Herbert, *Hitler's Foreign Workers: Enforced Foreign Labor in Germany under the Third Reich* (Cambridge, Eng., 1997); *Meldungen* 43 (February 26, 1943): 25; John A. Armstrong, *Ukrainian Nationalism*, 3d ed. (Englewood, Colo., 1990), 88–89; Dallin, *German Rule*, 444–445; Dudin, "Velikii Mirazh," 177.

22. Ia. N. Vasylenko, author interview; Dudin, "Velikii Mirazh," 185; *Meldungen* 7 (June 12, 1942): 14.

23. Timothy Mulligan, *The Politics of Illusion and Empire: German Occupation Policy in the Soviet Union, 1942–1943* (New York, 1988), 114, 116; Müller, *Die faschistische Okkupationspolitik,* 462.

24. Bernd Bonwetsch, "Sowjetische Zwangsarbeiter vor und nach 1945: Ein doppelter Leidensweg," *Jahrbücher für Geschichte Osteuropas* 41, no. 4 (1993): 545.

25. F. Pihido-Pravoberezhnyi, "*Velyka Vitchyzniana viina*" (Winnipeg, 1954), 186–187.

26. *Ukraïns'kyi holos,* August 29, 1943, 4, referring to an order of February 19, 1942; for the form and amount, consult DAKO, r-2356/8/7/68: Kiev city commissar, letter in Ukrainian translation, n.p., March 31, 1942. See also DAKO, r-2356/8/7/60–62.

27. DAKO, r-2356/8/9/25–26: deputy mayor Volkanovych to city commissar, Kiev, June 4, 1942.

28. *Meldungen* 43 (February 26, 1943): 25; DAKO, r-2457/1/16/64–66, 80; DAKO, r-2457/1/80/208, 219, 233–234; DAKO, r-2519/1/8/5; on the increase in 1943, see *Ukraïns'kyi holos,* September 2, 1943, 4.

29. *Meldungen* 7 (June 12, 1942): 13; on postcards, see *Ukraïns'kyi holos,* September 17, 1942, 3, and October 11, 1942, 3; "Poshta dlia tykh, shcho ïdut' do Nimechchyny," *Dzvin voli,* November 27, 1942, 3; DAKO, r-2356/17/1/87: postcard.

30. *Meldungen* 21 (September 18, 1942): 12, and 43 (February 26, 1943): 22 (on the lack of official mail); Müller, *Die faschistische Okkupationspolitik,* 307 (on censors and the long wait for mail).

31. Marliese Fuhrmann, *Schneebruch: Geschichte einer Verschleppung* (Landau, Ger., 1993), 64; *Shchodennyk Arkadiia Liubchenka,* ed. Iurii Luts'kyi (Lviv, Ukr., 1999), 174.

32. *Meldungen* 24 (October 9, 1942): 22.

33. *Meldungen* 43 (February 26, 1943): 24; H. Sova [Hryhorii Kariak], *Do istoriï bol'shevyts'koï diis'nosty: (25 rokiv zhyttia ukraïns'koho hromadianyna v SSSR)* (Munich, 1955), 87–88; TsDAHOU, 1/22/391/18: Mikhail Mikh. Skirda [et al.], "Otchet o podpol'noi partiinoi rabote i partizanskoi bor'be v Kirovogradskoi oblasti (avgust 1941 goda–mart 1944 goda)," n.p., n.d.; F. P. Bogatyrchuk, *Moi zhiznennyi put' k Vlasovu i Prazhkomu manifestu* (San Francisco, 1978), 142; *Meldungen* 7 (June 12, 1942): 13, and 21 (September 18, 1942): 12.

34. TsDAHOU, 166/3/245/74: Tetiana Ivanivna Pyskovets' (Ukrainian), Borodianka, Kiev oblast, January 22, 1946; B. I. Chistova and K. V. Chistov, eds., *Preodolenie rabstva: Fol'klor i iazyk ostarbaiterov, 1942–1944* (Moscow, 1998), 27.

35. TsDAVOV, 3676/4/161/13v: Auslandbriefprüfstelle Berlin, "Stimmungsbericht

auf Grund von Briefen, die im April und Mai 1943 ausgewertet sind, über: Ostarbeiter (Post aus und nach der Ukraine)," Berlin, June 18, 1943; "Poshta dlia tykh, shcho ïdut' do Nimechchyny," *Dzvin voli*, November 27, 1942, 3; N. S. Zozulia, author interview.

36. *Meldungen* 21 (September 18, 1942): 22 (on Germans); TsDAVOV, 3676/4/161/ 49: Der Sonderbeauftragte f.d. Arbeitskräfte aus den besetzten Ostgebieten, report (based on Ukrainian propagandists traveling in Ukraine from June to August 1943), Berlin, November 30, 1943.

37. Müller, *Die faschistische Okkupationspolitik*, 315 (about women who died); *Meldungen* 21 (September 18, 1942): 23–24; *Meldungen* 24 (October 9, 1942): 22, and 43 (February 26, 1943): 24; TsDAHOU, 1/22/347/13, 15: "Iz dnevnika uchitel'nitsy gor. Kieva L. Nartovoi" (hereafter Nartova diary), notes of July 18 and October 4, 1942; TsDAHOU, 1/22/123/67–68: Petr Timofeevich Berdnik, "Kharakteristika polozhenii na okkupirovannoi territorii," n.p., n.d.; Ernst Klee and Willi Dreßen, *"Gott mit uns": Der deutsche Vernichtungskrieg im Osten 1939–1945* (Frankfurt, 1989), 174; Iaroslav Haivas, *Koly kinchalasia epokha* (n.p., 1964), 86–87.

38. *Meldungen* 21 (September 18, 1942): 15; DAKO, r-2209/1/85/4v: Russian-language leaflet (denies the rumor); NBU, Filiia 1, Viddil starodrukiv, poster 1402: "Ukraïntsi! Zholoshuites' do pratsi v Nimechchyni!"

39. *Meldungen* 32 (December 4, 1942): 10; Kuznetsov, *Babii iar*, 260.

40. *Meldungen* 7 (June 12, 1942): 13; *Meldungen* 21 (September 18, 1942): 22, and 43 (February 26, 1943): 24; Kuznetsov, *Babii iar*, 260; TsDAVOV, 3676/4/476/180: Sipo-SD report on the Kiev GB in May 1942, n.p., June 2, 1942 (on sterilization).

41. TsDAVOV, 3206/1/26/28v: "Teilbericht Politik über die Bereisung des Reichskommissariats mit Prof. v. Grünberg in der Zeit vom 13.8. bis 3.9.1942," Rivne, September 20, 1942 (the hanging); *Meldungen* 32 (December 4, 1942): 10; Müller, *Die faschistische Okkupationspolitik*, 432; TsDAHOU, 1/23/688/35: *Informatsiina sluzhba dlia kraievoho pravlinnia v Heneral'nii Okruzi Volyni i Podillia* (monthly, printed in Rivne), August 1943.

42. Mykhailo Seleshko, *Vinnytsia: Spomyny perekladacha Komisiï doslidiv zlochyniv NKVD v 1937–1938* (New York, 1991), 115; TsDAHOU, 166/3/246/16–17: Tat'iana Makarovna Selinchuk, [Kiev?], n.d. (typed on January 11, 1946); *Meldungen* 24 (October 9, 1942): 13 (Berdychiv rumor).

43. TsDAHOU, 1/23/601/99: "Nadpysy radian'skykh hromadian, iakykh nimtsi vidpravlialy, pidchas okupatsiï Ukraïny v Nimechchynu." See also TsDAHOU, 1/23/601/110: "Kopii zapisei. Peresyl'nyi punkt po otpravke v Germaniiu shkola-38 po Nekrasovskoi ul. 2," n.p., n.d.

44. Alexandrow, *Flight from Novaa Salow*, 72, 79; *Meldungen* 21 (September 18, 1942): 15.

45. "Shkolu ia pokynu . . . / Nashcho meni vchytyts'? / Dovedet'sia na chuzhyni /

Raboiu zrobytys'." IMFE, K. Tolchennikova collection, 14–3/25/27, recorded from peasant women in the Kiev region in late 1942 or early 1943. See also IMFE, Ie. I. Prytula collection, 14–3/24/5: "Vid zbyracha."

46. Müller, *Die faschistische Okkupationspolitik*, 337–338; Klee and Dreßen, *"Gott mit uns,"* 176–177.

47. Otto Bräutigam, *Überblick über die besetzten Ostgebiete während des 2. Weltkrieges* (Tübingen, 1954), 92–93; Fesenko, *Povest'*, 82; Müller, "Die Rekrutierung," 239.

48. Müller, "Die Rekrutierung," 242–243; NDB, collection "Lystivky okupatsiinoho periodu," 662lf and 3781lf: "Do naselennia Raikhskomisariatu Ukraïny!" n.p., n.d.

49. DAKO, r-2294/1/2/5: Rokytne Raion Chief (Bila Tserkva District) to the elder of Romashky, May 29, 1942.

50. DAKO, [r-]2215/1/5/21, 29: Maksymovychy administration, protocols 12 and 17, April 7 and June 3, 1942.

51. M. O. Vasylenko, author interview; T. Iakovkevych, "1939–1943 rr. na Volodymyrshchyni (Spohady)," *Litopys Volyni* 3 (Winnipeg, 1956): 115.

52. Pihido-Pravoberezhnyi, *"Velyka Vitchyzniana viina,"* 155; TsDAHOU, 166/3/246/9–14: Mikhail Nikolaevich Sviridovskii (born in 1908), Kiev, March 3, 1944.

53. Pihido-Pravoberezhnyi, *"Velyka Vitchyzniana viina,"* 156, 162–163; Mykhailo Lebid', "Chasy nimets'koï okupatsiï v Matiïvs'komu raioni na Volyni (Spohady kol. holovy raionovoï upravy)," *Litopys UPA*, vol. 5 (Toronto, 1985), 211; Jerzy Dębski and Leon Popek, eds., *Okrutna przestroga* (Lublin, Pol., 1997), 168, 321, 323.

54. TsDAVOV, 3206/5/15/369: RKU *Lagebericht* for April 1942, Rivne, May 15, 1942.

55. *Meldungen* 7 (June 12, 1942): 13.

56. TsDAHOU, 166/3/246/35–37: Mikhail Ivanovich Sokolov, [Vinnytsia?], January 20, 1946. Another example is in DAKO, r-2356/15/22/60–61v: H. A. Lahs to deputy mayor Volkanovych, n.p., September 23, 1942. On Communists reporting neighbors, see *Meldungen* 7 (June 12, 1942): 13.

57. Sova, *Do istoriï*, 88.

58. Lebid', "Chasy nimets'koï okupatsiï," 211–212.

59. Bräutigam, *Überblick über die besetzten Ostgebiete*, 93.

60. DAKO, r-2356/1/107/21–24: district administrator Bokii to Forostivs'kyi, n.p., April 12, 1942, and response, April 15, 1942. Compare NA microcopy T-175, roll 250, frame 2742722: Sipo-SD of the Kiev GB to Ukraine Sipo-SD, n.p., May 25, 1942.

61. Alexander Berkman, *The Bolshevik Myth: (Diary 1920–1922)* (New York, 1925), 232–233.

62. Nartova diary, 10–11, notes of April 21 and 28, 1942.

63. TsDAHOU, 166/3/244/85: Kal'nitskaia. See also *Meldungen* 24 (October 9, 1942): 22 (a case in Berdychiv). On the one woman's escapes, see TsDAHOU, 166/3/246/16: Selinchuk.

64. Müller, *Die faschistische Okkupationspolitik*, 302–304, a report used in *Meldungen* 21 (September 18, 1942): 21.

65. Fesenko, *Povest'*, 82–83 (the quotation); Kuznetsov, *Babii iar*, 337.

66. Nartova diary, 11–12; TsDAHOU, 166/3/243/150: Vanda Antonovna Volovskaia (Pole born in 1923), [Dniprodzerzhyns'k?], n.d.; TsDAVOV, 3676/4/476/403: Sipo-SD report on the Kiev GB, September 15, 1942; Dudin, "Velikii Mirazh," 177.

67. TsDAHOU, 166/3/244/85: Kal'nitskaia. See also *Nove ukraïns'ke slovo*, January 10, 1943, 4, April 9, 1943, 4, and April 22, 1943, 4 (requests for information about disappeared relatives).

68. TsDAHOU, 1/22/6/32–33: D. S. Korotchenko to N. S. Khrushchev, "O sostoianii partizanskogo dvizheniia na pravoberezhnoi Ukraine," n.p., July 22, 1943.

69. TsDAHOU, 1/22/391/19: Skirda, "Otchet," quoting F. M. Antonenko.

70. Nartova diary, 16.

71. Another deportation site in Kiev was 2 Nekrasov Street. Nartova diary, 22; TsDAHOU, 166/3/244/85: Kal'nitskaia; TsDAHOU, 166/3/246/17: Selinchuk; Dudin, "Velikii Mirazh," 178–179; Fesenko, *Povest'*, 82; Bogatyrchuk, *Moi zhiznennyi put'*, 143.

72. UCEC, Pavlo Ternivs'kyi [Ivan Zhyhadlo], "Spohady emigranta" (n.p., 1945), 55–56.

73. TsDAVOV, 3206/1/78/30: RKU *Lagebericht* for January 1942; TsDAVOV, 3206/5/15/268: RKU *Lagebericht* for February 1942, Rivne, March 15, 1942; DAKO, r-2107/1/131/24: letter by a peasant to the "Bohuslavs'ka Volost'" [sic], February 12, 1942.

74. TsDAVOV, 3206/2/27/21: RKU *Lagebericht* for December 1941; TsDAVOV, 3206/1/78/36: RKU *Lagebericht* for January 1942; TsDAVOV, 3206/2/121/1a–2: RKU Hauptabteilung III to the Kiev General Commissar, Kiev, January 22, 1942.

75. *Meldungen* 43 (February 26, 1943): 20.

76. V. P. Kravchenko, author interview; TsDAVOV, 3676/4/474/235–238: Sipo-SD report on the Kiev GB, Kiev, September 15, 1942; Blanka Jerabek, *Das Schulwesen und die Schulpolitik im Reichskommissariat Ukraine 1941–1944: Im Lichte deutscher Dokumente* (Munich, 1991), 114.

77. Jerabek, *Das Schulwesen*, 114; *Nove ukraïns'ke slovo*, November 12, 1942, 4, and November 15, 1942, 4; *Shchodennyk Arkadiia Liubchenka*, 93.

78. Nartova diary, 19; *Shchodennyk Arkadiia Liubchenka*, 94; NA microcopy T-120, roll 2533, frame E292536: report based on a source ("Gewährsmann") who visited Kiev; Jerabek, *Das Schulwesen*, 114–115.

79. Adolf Hitler, *Monologe im Führerhauptquartier 1941–1944: Die Aufzeichnungen Heinrich Heims herausgegeben von Werner Jochmann* (Hamburg, 1980), 331; Bräutigam, *Überblick über die besetzten Ostgebiete*, 93.

80. "Ukraïns'ki divchata v nimets'kykh domashnikh hospodarstvakh," *Dzvin voli*, November 27, 1942, 4; NDB, "Afishy ta plakaty okupatsiinoho periodu," 300sp: "Divchata i zhinky!"; Herbert, *Hitler's Foreign Workers*, 187–189, 439, n. 209. On scientists and technical specialists, see Müller, "Die Rekrutierung," 242; TsDAHOU, 166/3/243/1–5v: Nikolai Kuz'mich Grun'skii [sic] (Ukrainian born in 1872), Kiev, February 19, 1944. Compare Mykola Velychkivs'kyi, "Sumni chasy nimets'koï okupatsiï (1941–1944 roky)," *Vyzvol'nyi shliakh* 12, no. 3 (London, 1965): 297–298.

81. Fuhrmann, *Schneebruch*, 53 (the quotation); IMFE, K. Tolchennikova collection, 14–3/25/34: peasant women's song from the Kiev region; Kuznetsov, *Babii iar*, 273; TsDAHOU, 1/22/391/19: Skirda, "Otchet."

82. Kuznetsov, *Babii iar*, 274.

83. Ie. M. Moskovs'ka, author interview.

84. TsDAHOU, 166/3/249/7v: Valentina [Valentyna] Maksymivna Liashenko, (Ukrainian born in 1916), Zarubyntsi, Kiev oblast, August 8, 1946.

85. TsDAHOU, 166/3/249/7v–8 (on Zarubyntsi); M. Kh. Hohulia, author interview (on working harder); TsDAHOU, 1/22/123/67: Berdnik, "Kharakteristika polozhenii" (on movie theaters).

86. TsDAHOU, 166/3/245/72–74: Pyskovets'; NA microcopy T-120, roll 2533, frame E292556: Auslandsbriefprüfstelle, "Stimmungsbericht," Berlin, September 11, 1942; Müller, *Die faschistische Okkupationspolitik*, 313–315.

87. *Trial of the Major War Criminals before the International Military Tribunal* (hereafter TMWC), vol. 25 (Nuremberg, 1949), 331. Compare Herbert, *Hitler's Foreign Workers*, 280.

88. Letter by Antonina Sidel'nyk, quoted in NA microcopy T-120, roll 2533, frames E292549/12–15: Auslandbriefprüfstelle, "Stimmungsbericht," Berlin, November 11, 1942; also in *TMWC*, vol. 25 (Nuremberg, 1949), 78–79.

89. *TMWC*, vol. 25, 313–314; Müller, *Die faschistische Okkupationspolitik*, 367.

90. Nartova diary, 10.

91. TsDAHOU, 1/22/123/67–68: Berdnik, "Kharakteristika polozhenii."

92. TsDAHOU, 166/3/246/128–131: Vera Petrovna Rukosueva (born in 1892), [Melitopol'?], n.d.

93. Nartova diary, 17.

94. TsDAHOU, 166/3/246/128–131: Rukosueva.

95. O. M. Kutsenko, author interview (on scabies); IMFE, T. Krasyts'ka collection, 14–3/20/61, 493 ("Korosty dostala / V Germaniiu ne popala"); Moskovs'ka, author interview (on swelling); TsDAHOU, 166/3/246/92: Nikolai Makarovich Kharchenko (born in 1906), [Melitopol'?], January 22, 1946 (on soda); Kuznetsov, *Babii iar*, 260 (on brushes).

96. TsDAHOU, 166/3/249/28–28v: interview with Fydosia Zakharovna Masyna, [Velykyi Bukryn,] August 10, 1946. See also *Meldungen* 21 (September 18, 1942): 6.

97. On self-poisoning, see TsDAHOU, 166/3/245/30: Evgeniia Dosifeevna Ponizovskaia (born in 1899), n.p., n.d., signed by her on January 19, 1946; TsDAHOU, 166/3/246/92: Kharchenko; for pouring substances into one's eyes, see TsDAHOU, 166/3/246/128–131: Rukosueva; M. Vasylenko, author interview.

98. TsDAHOU, 166/3/246/128–131: Rukosueva (on legs); TsDAHOU, 1/22/391/38: Skirda, "Otchet" (on burnings and bites); Kuznetsov, *Babii iar*, 260; Hohulia, author interview (both on chopping); Nartova diary, 16 (on operations); M. V. Koval', *Bor'ba naseleniia Ukrainy protiv fashistskogo rabstva* (Kiev, 1979), 72–73 (on burnings); Volodymyr Serhiichuk, *OUN-UPA v roky viiny: Novi dokumenty i materialy* (Kiev, 1996), 333.

99. TsDAHOU, 1/22/391/38: Skirda, "Otchet" (on self-mutilation in Znam''ianka); NA microcopy T-120, roll 2533, frames E292556–557: Auslandsbriefprüfstelle (for prevalence among females). For the dangers of self-mutilation, see TsDAHOU, 166/3/246/128–131: Rukosueva; TsDAHOU, 166/3/246/92: Kharchenko (on deaths); TsDAHOU, 1/22/391/38: Skirda, "Otchet" (also on deaths); Kutsenko, author interview. On suicide, see TsDAHOU, 166/3/246/138: Viktor Ivanovich Iaremchenko, n.p., n.d.; HIA-HURIP, box 23, no. 548 AD, B-6, fol. 4: editor of *Vinnyts'ki visti* [Mykhailo Zerov?], n.p., April 24, 1951.

100. Kutsenko, author interview.

101. Bogatyrchuk, *Moi zhiznennyi put'*, 126–127, 129–130.

102. Koval', *Bor'ba naseleniia*, 75 (on Fastiv); Iu. N. Kvitnitskii-Ryzhov, "Iz istorii zdravookhraneniia v Kieve vo vremia Velikoi Otechestvennoi voiny 1941–1945," *Sovetskoe zdravookhranenie*, no. 5 (Moscow, 1990): 64; TsDAHOU, 166/3/245/65: Trofim Ivanovich Panchenko (born in 1899), [Novomoskovs'k?], January 22, 1946.

103. TsDAHOU, 166/3/243/117: Vera Fedorovna Bogdanova (born in 1911), n.p., January 20, 1946.

104. *Meldungen* 44 (March 5, 1943): 8 (on arrests); *Meldungen* 17 (August 20, 1942): 10–11, and 21 (September 18, 1942): 6 (on compensation).

105. See *Meldungen* 43 (February 26, 1943): 25.

106. Maksym Skorups'kyi (Maks-Kurinnyi UPA), *U nastupakh i vidstupakh: (Spohady)* (Chicago, 1961), 59; Oksana O. Sarapuka (born in 1927 in Medvyn), unrecorded personal communication to author, Medvyn, July 17, 1995. On girls trying to become pregnant, see Skorups'kyi, *U nastupakh*, 59; M. P. Kostiuk, author interview.

107. TsDAVOV, 3676/4/161/13: Auslandbriefprüfstelle Berlin; Dallin, *German Rule*, 458 (on the June 1943 report).

108. Nartova diary, 16 (on adoption); Kuznetsov, *Babii iar*, 260.

109. *Meldungen* 17 (August 20, 1942): 6; TsDAVOV, 3676/4/476/401: Sipo-SD report on the Kiev GB, Kiev, September 15, 1942.

110. On bribes to mediators, see Nikolas Laskovsky, "Practicing Law in the Occupied Ukraine," *American Slavic and East European Review* 10, no. 2 (New York, 1952): 137. On bribes to house custodians, see Kravchenko, comment on tape recording of author interview with K. Ia. Hrynevych; *Meldungen* 7 (June 12, 1942): 13.

111. TsDAHOU, 166/3/244/18: Iurii Mikhailovich Markovskii (Ukrainian born in 1904), Kiev, March 12, 1944; TsDAHOU, 166/3/244/84: Kal'nitskaia; Nartova diary, 16; Kuznetsov, *Babii iar,* 261.

112. NA microcopy T-120, roll 2533, frame E292557: Auslandsbriefprüfstelle; Seleshko, *Vinnytsia,* 116.

113. Serhiichuk, *OUN-UPA,* 325, 333; compare 328, 332, 349.

114. *Meldungen* 43 (February 26, 1943): 23, and 47 (March 24, 1943): 8–9.

115. *Meldungen* 43 (February 26, 1943): 23 (leaflet); *Meldungen* 7 (June 12, 1942): 12–13 (the last quotation).

116. Herbert, *Hitler's Foreign Workers,* 280; Pihido-Pravoberezhnyi, "*Velyka Vitchyzniana viina,*" 163.

117. Müller, "Die Rekrutierung," 243, revised version in *Meldungen* 47 (March 26, 1943): 22; Serhiichuk, *OUN-UPA,* 341.

118. Muzei istoriï Bohuslavshchyny im B. M. Levchenko Archives (Bohuslav, Ukraine): Grigorii M. Levchenko, "Dnevnik: Puteshestvie v Germaniiu" (manuscript, Medvyn, 1945), 1–2.

119. Müller, *Die faschistische Okkupationspolitik,* 463–464.

120. Dudin, "Velikii Mirazh," 180–181 mentions one case of beating; Dallin, *German Rule,* 435 (on the situation in Kiev).

121. Alexandrow, *Flight from Novaa Salow,* 68, 70, 72–73, slightly revised.

122. Buchbender, *Das tönende Erz,* 329.

123. Hrynevych, author interview; O. Sarapuka, author interview.

124. *Meldungen* 43 (February 26, 1943): 24.

125. Müller, *Die faschistische Okkupationspolitik,* 399–400.

126. See *Meldungen* 43 (February 26, 1943): 23, and 47 (March 26, 1943): 22.

127. For the August 1942 figure, see *TMWC,* vol. 39 (Nuremberg, 1949), 401; also "Aktual'ni pytannia ukraïns'koï polityky. Svidchennia Raikhkomisar Erikha Kokha," *Dzvin voli,* August 30, 1942, 3. For the June 1943 figure, see TsDAVOV, 3206/5/15/666: RKU *Lagebericht* for May and June 1943, Rivne, July 15, 1943.

128. Estimate of one in forty by Sauckel, in Armstrong, *Ukrainian Nationalism,* 89; see page 90 for the 1.5 million figure.

129. Dallin, *German Rule,* 431, n. 1. Compare Mulligan, *Politics of Illusion,* 113.

130. *Meldungen* 21 (September 18, 1942): 12, 15, and 43 (February 26, 1943): 10.

131. See, for example, Alexander Werth, *Russia at War, 1941–1945* (New York, 1965), 717, 719.

132. Fesenko, *Povest'*, 82; Ternivs'kyi, "Spohady emigranta," 37. See also Emigrant, "Nemtsy v Kieve," 43, 55; Dudin, "Velikii Mirazh," 98.

12. Toward the End of Nazi Rule

1. A. S. Kniaz'kov et al., comps., *Velikaia Otechestvennaia*, vol. 9 (Moscow, 1999), 115; V. I. Klokov, *O strategii i taktike sovetskikh partizan v bor'be protiv fashistskikh okkupantov na Ukraine (1941–1944)* (Kiev 1994), 40–41, 65; A. S. Chaikovs'kyi, *Nevidoma viina: (Partyzans'kyi rukh v Ukraïni 1941–1944 rr. movoiu dokumentiv, ochyma istoryka)* (Kiev, 1994), 108, 126, 131, 136, 139, 165.

2. Chaikovs'kyi, *Nevidoma viina*, 94–95, 97.

3. Kniaz'kov et al., *Velikaia Otechestvennaia*, vol. 9, 133–134, 149 (the "illegal CC CP(b)U"), 277–278, 281–282 (Stalin's actions in spring 1943).

4. Beria to Stalin, report, August 8, 1941, in "Iz istorii Velikoi Otechestvennoi voiny," *Izvestiia TsK KPSS*, no. 9 (September 1990): 197–198.

5. NA microcopy T-501, roll 33, frames 1098–1099: Army Group South, "Tätigkeitsbericht der Abt. VII vom 1.–30.10.1941," n.p., n.d.; NA microcopy T-501, roll 349, frames 586–592: Gruppe Geheime Feldpolizei 725, "Betrifft: Partisanen, Erfahrungsbericht," n.p., January 22, 1942; TsDAHOU, 1/22/118/5: "Donesenie komandira partizanskogo otriada Nechaeva," n.p., December 3, 1941; TsDAHOU, 1/22/122/27: Iakov Fedorovich Nosenko, komissar partizanskogo otriada Kanevskogo raiona Kievskoi oblasti, to Zam. nach. 4-go Otdela NKVD USSR, "Dokladnaia zapiska," n.p., January 3, 1942. Compare V. A. Perezhogin, "Partizany i naselenie (1941–1945 gg.)," *Otechestvennaia istoriia*, no. 6 (1997): 152.

6. John A. Armstrong, "The Dnepr Bend Area," in John A. Armstrong, ed., *Soviet Partisans in World War II* (Madison, Wisc., 1964), 646; BA-Berlin, R 6/305, fol. 45: general district *Lagebericht* for November and December 1942, Dnipropetrovs'k, January 7, 1943 (the quotation).

7. TsDAVOV, 3676/4/161/13: Auslandbriefprüfstelle Berlin, "Stimmungsbericht," June 18, 1943.

8. Ibid.; NA microcopy T-78, roll 565, frames 259–266, 254–258: Anon. [informant of the Amt Ausland/Abwehr], "Notatky pro pokhodzhennia i poshyrennia partyzanshchyny," n.p., n.d., and German translation and summary dated May 18, 1943; Chaikovs'kyi, *Nevidoma viina*, 111.

9. Kniaz'kov et al., *Velikaia Otechestvennaia*, vol. 9, 354.

10. Ibid., 354–355; P. Vershigora, *Men with a Clear Conscience* (Moscow, 1949), 118, 204–205; John A. Armstrong, *Ukrainian Nationalism*, 3d ed. (Englewood, Colo., 1990), 105–106; NA microcopy T-175, roll 81, frame 2601547: General

Commissar Leyser to Rosenberg, via Reichskommissar Koch, "Betr.: Bandenbekämpfung im Generalbezirk Shitomir," Zhytomyr, February 12, 1943; Chaikovs'kyi, *Nevidoma viina*, 83 (on Kovpak's arrest).

11. TsDAVOV, 3676/4/161/13: Auslandbriefprüfstelle Berlin, "Stimmungsbericht," Berlin, June 18, 1943.

12. Norbert Müller et al., eds., *Die faschistische Okkupationspolitik in den zeitweilig besetzten Gebieten der Sowjetunion (1941–1944)* (Berlin, 1991), 431. See also V. I. Kucher, *Partyzans'ki kraï i zony na Ukraïni v roky Velykoï Vitchyznianoï viiny (1941–1944)* (Kiev, 1974); Armstrong, *Ukrainian Nationalism*, 97–101.

13. Chaikovs'kyi, *Nevidoma viina*, 137; Alexander Werth, *Russia at War, 1941–1945* (New York, 1965), 720.

14. Kniaz'kov et al., *Velikaia Otechestvennaia*, vol. 9, 355.

15. Ibid.; Klokov, *O strategii i taktike sovetskikh partizan*, 47.

16. NA microcopy T-78, roll 589, frames 510, 517–518: Fremde Heere Ost, "Vermutliche Bandengliederung zur Bandenlage Ost," n.p., n.d.

17. TsDAHOU, 1/22/6/12: D. S. Korotchenko to N. S. Khrushchev, "O sostoianii partizanskogo dvizheniia na pravoberezhnoi Ukraine," n.p., July 22, 1943 (the estimate). The percentage is my conclusion; Chaikovs'kyi, *Nevidoma viina*, 51 arrives at it on the basis of other sources.

18. Werth, *Russia at War*, 721; NA microcopy T-501, roll 349, frame 588: Gruppe Geheime Feldpolizei 725, report about Soviet partisans in Ukraine, n.p., January 22, 1942 (the quotation); Kenneth D. Slepyan, "'The People's Avengers': Soviet Partisans, Stalinist Society and the Politics of Resistance, 1941–1944," Ph.D. diss., University of Michigan, 1994, 372.

19. Chaikovs'kyi, *Nevidoma viina*, 61, 83; Leo Heiman, *I Was a Soviet Guerrilla* (London, 1959), 92, 122 (on drunkenness and illness); NA microcopy T-501, roll 27, frame 1196: Kavallerie-Regiment Mitte, "Erfahrungsbericht über die Kampftaktik der Partisanen und Möglichkeiten unsererseits, die Bandengefahr zu beschränken," n.p., June 23, 1943 (on sleeping and plunder among the partisans in Belarus); Vershigora, *Men with a Clear Conscience*, 308–309 (on plunder); Maksym Skorups'kyi, *U nastupakh i vidstupakh: (Spohady)* (Chicago, 1961), 170–171 (on theft among UPA members).

20. Heiman, *I Was a Soviet Guerrilla*, 90–91; Slepyan, "People's Avengers," 252–257. On lack of medical knowledge, see Kniaz'kov et al., *Velikaia Otechestvennaia*, vol. 9, 356. For the harsh conditions endured, see D. Karov [Dmitrii Petrovich Kandaurov], *Partizanskoe dvizhenie v SSSR v 1941–1945 gg.* (Munich, 1954), 75–78; M. V. Koval', "Material'nyi byt partizan Ukrainy (1941–1944 gg.)," *Sovetskaia etnografiia*, no. 2 (March–April 1985): 14–23.

21. Chaikovs'kyi, *Nevidoma viina*, 122–123 (on attacks in 1942).

22. This is also evident from Chaikovs'kyi, *Nevidoma viina*, 134–135, 181.

23. M. V. Koval', *Bor'ba naseleniia Ukrainy protiv fashistskogo rabstva* (Kiev, 1979), 47.

24. V. P. Iampols'kii et al., comps., *Organy gosudarstvennoi bezopasnosti SSSR v Velikoi Otechestvennoi voine: Sbornik dokumentov*, vol. 2, book 2: *Nachalo. 1 sentiabria–31 dekabria 1941 goda* (Moscow, 2000), 371–372.

25. Kniaz'kov et al., *Velikaia Otechestvennaia*, vol. 9, 133 (the September 1942 order). For the sanctioned killing of family members, see Timothy Mulligan, *The Politics of Illusion and Empire: German Occupation Policy in the Soviet Union, 1942–1943* (New York, 1988), 137; Heiman, *I Was a Soviet Guerilla*, 167.

26. TsDAVOV, 3676/4/161/13–14: Auslandbriefprüfstelle Berlin, "Stimmungsbericht," June 18, 1943.

27. NA microcopy T-175, roll 81, frame 2601567: Reichskommissar Koch to Rosenberg, "Betr.: Derzeitiger Stand der Bandenlage," Rivne, June 25, 1943; TsDAHOU, 1/22/6/53: D. S. Korotchenko, "Ukrainskie partizany v bor'be protiv nemetskikh okkupantov," March 25, 1942 (refers to 1,205; 238; and 11,896).

28. Kniaz'kov et al., *Velikaia Otechestvennaia*, vol. 9, 457 (documents 58,685 and 946).

29. On the area east of the pre-1939 border, see Armstrong, *Ukrainian Nationalism*, 108, 113, 188; Volodymyr Serhiichuk, *OUN-UPA v roky viiny: Novi dokumenty i materialy* (Kiev, 1996), 306.

30. TsDAHOU, 1/22/227/136: "Otchet o deiatel'nosti podpol'noi partiinoi organizatsii i partizanskikh otriadov Zhitomirskoi oblasti," Zhytomyr, 1945; TsDAHOU, 1/22/6/19–20: Korotchenko to Khrushchev, "O sostoianii partizanskogo dvizheniia"; TsDAHOU, 1/23/530/3: Robert Satanovskii to Khrushchev, n.p., October 5, 1943.

31. Müller, *Die faschistische Okkupationspolitik*, 336.

32. TsDAHOU, 1/22/227/139–140: "Otchet o deiatel'nosti podpol'noi partiinoi organizatsii i partizanskikh otriadov Zhitomirskoi oblasti," Zhytomyr, 1945.

33. Amir Weiner, *Making Sense of War: The Second World War and the Fate of the Bolshevik Revolution* (Princeton, N.J., 2001), 160; Karov, *Partizanskoe dvizhenie*, 83.

34. On identification tags, see TsDAHOU, 1/22/391/41: Mikhail Mikh. Skirda [et al.], "Otchet o podpol'noi partiinoi rabote i partizanskoi bor'be v Kirovogradskoi oblasti (avgust 1941 goda–mart 1944 goda)," n.d.; Müller, *Die faschistische Okkupationspolitik*, 335. On the reinforced bases, see Müller, *Die faschistische Okkupationspolitik*, 335; DAKO, r-2292/1/3/51: order by District Commissar Dr. Stelzer, Bila Tserkva, April 12, 1943; NA microcopy T-84, roll 120, frame 419211: Boryspil' District Commisar to the General Commissar, Boryspil', December 16, 1942; Serhiichuk, *OUN-UPA*, 331.

35. The following account derives from O. F. Fedorov and V. A. Maniuk et al., *Vinok bezsmertia: Knyha-memorial* (Kiev, 1987), 222–229 (includes the account

by A. Korneliuk); *Istoriia mist i sil Ukraïns'koï RSR: Volyns'ka oblast'* (Kiev, 1970), 595–596; Polishchuk [pseud.], "Trahediia sela Kortelis," *Litopys Volyni* 7 (Winnipeg, 1964): 86–89; Paul Kohl, *Der Krieg der deutschen Wehrmacht und der Polizei 1941–1944: Sowjetische Überlebende berichten* (Frankfurt am Main, 1995), 45–50. The assault was part of a larger campaign that primarily struck villages in present-day Belarus; see Christian Gerlach, *Kalkulierte Morde: Die deutsche Wirtschafts- und Vernichtungspolitik in Weißrußland 1941 bis 1944* (Hamburg, 1999), 938–941, 967–968.

36. TsDAHOU, 166/3/243/164: Ol'ha Vasyl'evych [Vasyl'ovych] Buhai (Ukrainian), Borodianka, Kiev oblast, January 22, 1946. See also Ruth Bettina Birn, *Die Höheren SS- und Polizeiführer: Himmlers Vertreter im Reich und in den besetzten Gebieten* (Düsseldorf, 1986), 229.

37. NA microcopy T-175, roll 81, frames 2601544–546: Hellwig, Der SS- und Polizeiführer in Shitomir, "Betr.: Bandenbekämpfung," Zhytomyr, January 27, 1943; NA microcopy T-175, roll 81, frames 2601547–551: General Commissar Leyser to Rosenberg, via Reichskommissar Koch, "Betr.: Bandenbekämpfung im Generalbezirk Shitomir," Zhytomyr, February 12, 1943, also in Müller, *Die faschistische Okkupationspolitik*, 388–389.

38. TsDAHOU, 1/22/391/20/30/38: Skirda, "Otchet" (events in Buda); the similarity to the earlier massacres is also noted in Dieter Pohl, "Die Holocaust-Forschung und Goldhagens Thesen," *Vierteljahrshefte für Zeitgeschichte* 45, no. 1 (1997): 29.

39. Ulas Samchuk, *Na koni voronomu: Spomyny i vrazhennia* (Winnipeg, 1975), 296.

40. NA microcopy T-175, roll 81, frame 2601654: order by Himmler regarding the area of the Höhere SS- und Polizeiführer Ukraine–Russland-Süd, n.p., June 21, 1943.

41. Original usage: *Ansiedlung* and *Umsiedlung*. Müller, *Die faschistische Okkupationspolitik*, 471. See also NA microcopy T-175, roll 140, frame 2668022.

42. TsDAHOU, 1/23/585/12: Behma and Timofeev to Khrushchev and Strokach, "Dokladnaia zapiska," n.p., n.d. (mentions shootings in the Volhynian town of Liubeshiv).

43. SD officer Wilhelm W. Hellerfort, cited in Leonid Abramenko, ed., *Kyïvs'kyi protses: Dokumenty i materialy* (Kiev, 1995), 57.

44. F. Pihido-Pravoberezhnyi, *"Velyka Vitchyzniana viina"* (Winnipeg, 1954), 168–170.

45. Samchuk, *Na koni voronomu*, 351–352; Ivan Vlasovs'kyi, *Narys istoriï Ukraïns'koï Pravoslavnoï Tserkvy*, vol. 9: (XX st.), part 2 (New York, 1966), 265, 268–269.

46. See, for example, *Ivankivs'ki visti*, July 18, 1943.

47. NDB, collection "Afishy ta plakaty okupatsiinoho periodu," 481sp: "Chy ruïnu ta holod, shcho ïkh nesut' Tobi soviets'ki bandy?"

48. Ivan Khmel'nyts'kyi [Konstantyn Kospiruk], "V kraïni rabstva i smerty," *Samostiina Ukraïna* 4, no. 2(37) (Chicago, February 1951): 2; Mykhailo Seleshko, *Vinnytsia: Spomyny perekladacha Komisiï doslidiv zlochyniv NKVD v 1937–1938* (New York, 1991), 67.

49. Alfred M. De Zayas, *The Wehrmacht War Crimes Bureau, 1939–1945* (Lincoln, Neb., 1989), 240–244.

50. Khmel'nyts'kyi, "V kraïni rabstva i smerty," 2; Seleshko, *Vinnytsia*, 71, 79–80; Tatiana Fesenko, *Povest' krivykh let* (New York, 1963), 97–98; HIA-HURIP, box 23, no. 548 AD, B-6, fol. 7: editor of *Vinnyts'ki visti* [Mykhailo Zerov?], n.p., April 24, 1951.

51. For an example of a press announcement, see *Dzvin voli*, July 29, 1943, 3. For delegate trips, consult Seleshko, *Vinnytsia*, 110; Hryhorii Kostiuk, *Zustrichi i proshchannia: Spohady. Knyha druha* (Edmonton, 1998), 102; *Dzvin voli*, August 19, 1943, 4.

52. Seleshko, *Vinnytsia*, 50–51, 59–60; HIA-HURIP, box 23, no. 548 AD, B-6, fol. 5; TsDAHOU, 1/22/10/11: Burchenko to N. S. Khrushchev and D. S. Korotchenko, "Kratkaia informatsiia o Vinnitskoi oblast," n.p., August 31, 1943; Weiner, *Making Sense of War*, 67.

53. Khmel'nyts'kyi, "V kraïni rabstva," 7.

54. TsDAHOU, 1/23/1062/153–155: Vinnytsia Obkom secretary Mishchenko and Oblast Soviet Chairman Godov, untitled report, n.p., [1944].

55. The following account derives from Leon Popek et al., eds., *Wołyński testament* (Lublin, Pol., 1997).

56. TsDAVOV, 3206/2/231/45–46: "Uebersicht über die Verwaltungseinteilung des Reichskommissariats Ukraine nach dem Stand vom 1. Januar 1943" (general figures). The estimate of 250,000 Poles is mine; compare Mikołaj Siwicki, [ed.], *Dzieje konfliktów polsko-ukraińskich*, vol. 2 (Warsaw, 1992), 85; Wolodymyr Kosyk, *L'Allemagne national-socialiste et l'Ukraine* (Paris, 1986), 235.

57. Siwicki, *Dzieje konfliktów*, 130, 210 (Polish reports from 1943 mentioning "over 15,000")—compare to Siwicki's estimate of "at most 20,000" on page 27; Timothy Snyder, "The Causes of Ukrainian-Polish Ethnic Cleansing, 1943," *Past and Present*, no. 179 (May 2003): 202 ("about 50,000").

58. The best entry in this historiography is Snyder, "Causes," 197–234. For the term "provocation" see, for example, Andrzej Leon Sowa, *Stosunki polsko-ukraińskie 1939–1947: Zarys problematyki* (Cracow, 1998), 155, 217.

59. Siwicki, *Dzieje konfliktów*, 20; Serhiichuk, *OUN-UPA*, 233.

60. See, for example, Snyder, "Causes"; Alexander V. Prusin, "Revolution and

Ethnic Cleansing in Western Ukraine: The OUN-UPA Assault against Polish Settlements in Volhynia and Eastern Galicia, 1943–1944," in Steven Bela Vardy and T. Hunt Tooley, eds., *Ethnic Cleansing in Twentieth Century Europe* (Boulder, Colo., 2003), 517–535. See also the dicussion of the term in Norman M. Naimark, *Fires of Hatred: Ethnic Cleansing in Twentieth-Century Europe* (Cambridge, Mass., 2001), 2–5.

61. Miriam Berger, "The War," in Haim Dan, comp. and Yosef Kariv, ed., *Horchiv Memorial Book/Sefer Horochow* (Tel Aviv, 1966), 50–51. See also Sonya Tesler-Gyraph, "Memories from the Nazi Period," 63–64.

62. Taras Bul'ba-Borovets', *Armiia bez derzhavy: Slava i trahediia ukraïns'koho povstans'koho rukhu. Spohady* (Winnipeg, 1981), 255.

63. NA microcopy T-175, roll 81, frame 2601567: Reichskommissar Koch to Rosenberg, "Betr.: Derzeitiger Stand der Bandenlage," Rivne, June 25, 1943. In publishing this document, *Litopys UPA*, vol. 6 (Toronto, 1983), 81–83 replaces this passage with ellipses.

64. The quotation is from NA microcopy T-78, roll 565, frame 230: Amt Ausland/Abwehr, "Feststellungen zur Bandenlage. Banden und Widerstandbewegungen in der Nordwestukraine," n.p., July 13, 1943; also in *Litopys UPA*, vol. 6, 84. For events in late 1944, see NA microcopy T-78, roll 562, frame 460: Fremde Heere Ost, report, November 1, 1944 (refers to an *Ausrottungsfeldzug* in western Ukraine).

65. TsDAHOU, 1/23/523/44: Strokach and Martynov to N. S. Khrushchev, "Spetssoobshchenie o deiatel'nosti ukr. natsionalistov na okk. territorii Ukrainskoi SSR," Moscow, April 21, 1943. Compare Serhiichuk, *OUN-UPA*, 62, 86–87.

66. Serhiichuk, *OUN-UPA*, 66, citing TsDAHOU, 1/22/75/37–43. The original document is at TsDAHOU, 1/23/523/80–83.

67. TsDAHOU, 1/23/585/29, 40: Behma and Timofeev to Khrushchev and Strokach, "Dokladnaia zapiska," n.p., n.d. (not before September 20, 1943). For reports from eastern Volhynia, see Serhiichuk, *OUN-UPA*, 31 (the first quotation); Władysław Filar, *"Burza" na Wołyniu: Z dziejów 27 Wołyńskiej Dywizji Piechoty Armii Krajowej. Studium historyczno-wojskowe* (Warsaw, 1997), 54, citing TsDAHOU, 57/4/191/118.

68. *Litopys UPA*, vol. 2, corrected 2d ed. (Toronto, 1985), 44.

69. *Litopys UPA. Nova seriia*, vol. 2 (Kiev, 1999), 310.

70. See Sowa, *Stosunki*, 197. For a leaflet, see Siwicki, *Dzieje konfliktów*, 174–177.

71. Leon Żur, *Mój wołyński epos* (Suwałki, Pol., 1997), 53; Jerzy Dębski and Leon Popek, eds., *Okrutna przestroga* (Lublin, Pol., 1997), 68–69, 138, 219, 274, 284, 287, 301–302, 321–322.

72. On the deterioration after the Soviet invasion, see Dębski and Popek, *Okrutna przestroga*, 62, 137, 248, 267, 285, 291, 293, 305, 313, 321, 331–332. On activities af-

ter the Germans' arrival, see O. Shuliak, [Oleh Shtul'], *V im"ia pravdy: (Do istoriï povstanchoho rukhu v Ukraïni)* (Rotterdam, 1947), 31.

73. Siwicki, *Dzieje konfliktów*, 139; *Ereignismeldung UdSSR* 191 (April 10, 1942): 18; *Meldungen* 13 (July 24, 1942): 4–5; compare *Meldungen* 24 (October 9, 1942): 15.

74. Armstrong, *Ukrainian Nationalism*, 129; Oleksander Hrytsenko [Taras Borovets'?], "Armiia bez derzhavy," in Vasyl' Mykhal'chuk, ed., *Tudy de bii za voliu: Zbirnyk viis'kovo-politychnykh materiialiv u pam"iat' Maksyma Skorups'koho-Maksa, Kurinnoho UPA* (London, 1989), 412–414; Hryhorii Stetsiuk, *Nepostavlenyi pam"iatnyk: (Spohady)* ([Winnipeg], 1988), 43.

75. Petro Mirchuk, *Narys istoriï Orhanizatsiï Ukraïns'kykh Natsionalistiv* (Munich, 1968), 579, quoted in Viktor Polishchuk, *Hirka pravda: Zlochynnist' OUN-UPA. (Spovid' ukraïntsia)* (Toronto, 1995), 119; Roy F. Baumeister, *Evil: Inside Human Cruelty and Violence* (New York, 1999), 183.

76. For the planned boundaries, see NA microcopy T-78, roll 562, frame 459: Fremde Heere Ost, report, November 1, 1944. On evicting "enemies and foreigners," see Mirchuk, *Narys istoriï*, 93, 98, 581, quoted in Polishchuk, *Hirka pravda*, 109, 119; Weiner, *Making Sense of War*, 241; Dieter Pohl, *Nationalsozialistische Judenverfolgung in Ostgalizien 1941–1944: Organisation und Durchführung eines staatlichen Massenverbrechens* (Munich, 1996), 325.

77. Mstyslav Z. Chubai, *Reid orhanizatoriv OUN vid Popradu po Chorne More: (Iz zapysnyka roiovoho)* (Munich, 1952), 38 (the quotation); Karel C. Berkhoff and Marco Carynnyk, "The Organization of Ukrainian Nationalists and Its Attitude toward Germans and Jews: Iaroslav Stets'ko's 1941 *Zhyttiepys*," *Harvard Ukrainian Studies* 23, nos. 3–4 (1999): 149–184.

78. Panas Khurtovyna [Mykhailo Podvorniak], *Pid nebom Volyni: (Voienni spomyny khrystyianyna)* (Winnipeg, 1952), 150.

79. Mykola S.-Chartoryis'kyi, *Vid Sianu po Krym: (Spomyny uchasnyka III Pokhidnoï Grupy-Pivden'* (New York, 1951), 127–128; Armstrong, *Ukrainian Nationalism*, 25.

80. TsDAVOV, 3833/2/1/38: "Borot'ba i diial'nist' OUN pidchas viiny. Napriamni OUN," quoted in Berkhoff and Carynnyk, "Organization of Ukrainian Nationalists," 154.

81. TsDAVOV, 3833/1/63/10, quoted in Berkhoff and Carynnyk, "Organization of Ukrainian Nationalists," 154. See also Dębski and Popek, *Okrutna przestroga*, 79, 243; Erhard Roy Wiehn, comp., *Die Schoáh von Babij Jar: Das Massaker deutscher Sonderkommandos an der jüdischen Bevölkerung von Kiew 1941 fünfzig Jahre danach zum Gedenken* (Konstanz, Ger., 1991), 277; Anatolii Kuznetsov (A. Anatolii), *Babii iar: Roman-dokument* (New York, 1986), 68; HIA, B. I. Nicolaevsky collection, box 232, folder 10, fol. 115: [Lev Vladimirovich] Dudin, "Velikii Mirazh: Sobytiia 1941–1947 godov v ponimanii

sovetskogo cheloveka," n.p., 1947. For the marching chant, see Dębski and Popek, *Okrutna przestroga*, 233; Sowa, *Stosunki*, 198.

82. John-Paul Himka, "Ukrainian Collaboration in the Extermination of the Jews during the Second World War: Sorting Out the Long-Term and Conjunctural Factors," *Studies in Contemporary Jewry: An Annual* 13 (New York, 1997): 176, 179. On zealous Greek Catholics, see Khurtovyna, *Pid nebom Volyni*, 141–142, 144, 147, 166.

83. Skorups'kyi, *U nastupakh i vidstupakh*, 148; Mykhailo Karkots'-Vovk, *Vid Voronizha do Ukraïns'koho Legionu Samooborony* (Minneapolis, Minn., 1995), 52.

84. Mykola Behesh and Ivan Korol' with L. Ikavchuk, "Z istoriï diial'nosti UPA: 'Polis'ka Sich'," in Mykola Behesh and Ivan Korol', *Bilia dzherel povstans'koï armiï: (Istorychni narysy)* (Uzhhorod, Ukr., 1996), 27–29. For the dissolution of the Sich, compare Karkots'-Vovk, *Vid Voronizha*, 45; Bul'ba, *Armiia*, 170; Maksym Boiko, *Bibliohrafichnyi ohliad zbroinoï borot'by Volyni* (Toronto, 1976), 127; Iaroslav Haivas, *Koly kinchalasia epokha* (n.p., 1964), 83.

85. Bul'ba, *Armiia*, 195; Armstrong, *Ukrainian Nationalism*, 102–103.

86. Haivas, *Koly kinchalasia epokha*, 116.

87. Żur, *Mój wołyński epos*, 56–57.

88. For the agreement to merge, see Bul'ba, *Armiia*, 252. On subsequent events, consult Jan Lukaszów [Tadeusz Andrzej Olszański], "Walki polsko-ukraińskie 1943–1947," *Zeszyty historyczne*, no. 90 (Paris, 1989): 166–167; Siwicki, *Dzieje konfliktów*, 135; Ryszard Torzecki, *Polacy i Ukraińcy: Sprawa ukraińska w czasie II wojny światowej na terenie II Rzeczypospolitej* (Warsaw, 1993), 258; Serhiichuk, *OUN-UPA*, 31, 51 (on arrival from the General Government).

89. Dębski and Popek, *Okrutna przestroga*, 267; Khurtovyna, *Pid nebom Volhyni*, 128.

90. Siwicki, *Dzieje konfliktów*, 111–112. Examples of such shootings are in Ivan Soika, "Kharakterystyka chasu nimets'koï okupatsiï 1941–44 rr. na tli okremykh faktiv," *Litopys Volyni* 6 (1962): 73; Bul'ba, *Armiia*, 262; Serhiichuk, *OUN-UPA*, 291.

91. On the shootings, see Stetsiuk, *Nepostavlenyi pam"iatnyk*; Skorups'kyi, *U nastupakh i vidstupakh*; Shuliak, *V im"ia pravdy*, 25–26. See also Khurtovyna, *Pid nebom Volyni*, 144–145. On the Schuma unit, see Karkots'-Vovk, *Vid Voronizha*, 72, 74, 76–77, 92–96; Taras Hunchak [Hunczak], *U mundyrakh voroha* (Kiev, 1993), 143.

92. NA microcopy T-78, roll 562, appendix, frame 468: Fremde Heere Ost, report, November 1, 1944; *Litopys UPA*, vol. 27 (Toronto, 1997), 97, 115–116, 147. On the groups and their commanders, see *Litopys UPA*, vol. 6, 99; *Litopys UPA*, vol. 27, 116, 118, 156, 163.

93. NA microcopy T-78, roll 589, frame 518: "Vermutliche Bandengliederung zur Bandenlage Ost." Compare Bul'ba, *Armiia*, 272; *Litopys UPA*, vol. 6, 96–97;

NA microcopy T-78, roll 565, frames 224–226: O[tto] A. Bräutigam, Dienststelle Walli I (Dienststelle Baun) I/Bd. [of the Abwehr] to Fremde Heere Ost (I/Bd.), "Betr.: Bandenabwehrmeldungen Ost. Ukrainische Aufstands-Armee ("Bandera")," n.p., December 5, 1943; NA microcopy T-78, roll 565, frame 243: "Bericht über die gegenwärtige Bandenlage und die politische Stimmung in der Westukraine," n.p., [late 1943]. For the percentage of UPA members connected to the OUN, see Shuliak, *V im"ia pravdy*, 28.

94. Serhiichuk, *OUN-UPA*, 263; compare *Ideia i chyn: Orhan Provodu OUN, 1942–1946. Peredruk pidpil'noho zhurnalu*, ed. Iurii Maivs'kyi and Ievhen Shtendera, which is *Litopys UPA*, vol. 24 (Toronto, 1995), 170 (on greeting); Shuliak, *V im"ia pravdy*, 29.

95. On Ukrainian usage, see *Litopys UPA*, vol. 5 (Toronto, 1984), 21, 171, 178, 253; Khurtovyna, *Pid nebom Volyni*, 156–157; Skorups'kyi, *U nastupakh i vidstupakh*, 150.

96. Bul'ba, *Armiia*, 251, 253, 272. See also his earlier memoir in Boiko, *Bibliohrafichnyi ohliad*, 134.

97. Dębski and Popek, *Okrutna przestroga* (in particular the maps in the back); Sowa, *Stosunki*, 180. See also *Litopys UPA*, vol. 6, 87; Prusin, "Revolution and Ethnic Cleansing," 528 (on Battle of Kursk).

98. See Filar, *"Burza" na Wołyniu*, 50, which cites State Archives of the Security Service of Ukraine for the Volhynia Oblast, sprava 11315, tom I, ch. II/16; Popek, *Wołyński testament*, 167, and Dębski and Popek, *Okrutna przestroga*, 343–344, which both cite Vladyslav Nakonechnyi, "Mertvy zaklykaiut' zhyvykh," *Volyn'* (Luts'k), August 4, 1994.

99. Dębski and Popek, *Okrutna przestroga*, 231; Żur, *Mój wołyński epos*, 58; Dębski and Popek, *Okrutna przestroga*, 138, 291.

100. Dębski and Popek, *Okrutna przestroga*, 320, compare 175, 178, 331 (Ukrainians not talking to Poles); 22–23 (Ukrainians unaware of assault plan); 51, 53 (crosses on Polish homes); 172, 258 (flares); 138, 253 (attackers' clothing); 110, 134 (ruse); 58, 315 (waves of attackers).

101. Ibid., 131, 234; Serhiichuk, *OUN-UPA*, 66.

102. Dębski and Popek, *Okrutna przestroga*, 45, 335 (recitation of Lord's Prayer); 276, 297, 299 (fate of Polish children); 97, 296 (dynamiting of churches); 65, 189, 321 (burying of bodies).

103. *Ideia i chyn: Orhan Provodu OUN, 1942–1946*, 211.

104. Siwicki, *Dzieje konfliktów*, 171–173. At this time, only one Polish political orientation, the Stronnictwo Narodowe in Galicia, wanted to expel the Ukrainians from what it considered Poland; see 231, 233–240.

105. Facsimile in Mykola Lebed', *UPA: Ukraïns'ka Povstans'ka Armiia. Ïi heneza, rist i diï u vyzvol'nii borot'bi ukraïns'koho narodu za ukraïns'ku samostiinu sobornu derzhavu, I chastyna: Nimets'ka okupatsiia Ukraïny* (n.p., 1946), 116.

106. Siwicki, *Dzieje konfliktów*, 174–177.

107. Danylo Shumuk, *Life Sentence: Memoirs of a Ukrainian Political Prisoner* (Edmonton, 1984), 73.

108. Ibid., 83.

109. Baumeister, *Evil*, 57. See also, on aggressors' self-concept of being victims, and on desensitization, 94, 285–290.

110. Sowa, *Stosunki*, 158–159, 161; Bruno Wasser, "Die 'Germanisierung' im Distrikt Lublin als Generalprobe und erste Realisierungsphase des 'Generalplans Ost,'" in Mechtild Rössler and Sabine Schleiermacher, eds., *Der 'Generalplan Ost': Hauptlinien der nationalsozialistischen Planungs- und Vernichtungspolitik* (Berlin, 1993), 271–293.

111. Dębski and Popek, *Okrutna przestroga*, 50, 52, 75, 101, 131, 137, 172, 175, 177–179, 226, 268; Żur, *Mój wołyński epos*, 62 (the quotation). On Poles' awaiting their murder, see V. N. Evstigneev et al., comps., *V tylu vraga: Listovki partiinykh organizatsii i partizan perioda Velikoi Otechestvennoi voiny 1941–1945 gg.* (Moscow, 1962), 189.

112. Sowa, *Stosunki*, 211–212; Żur, *Mój wołyński epos*, 56; Serhiichuk, *OUN-UPA*, 31, 82; TsDAHOU, 1/23/585/16: Behma and Timofeev, "Dokladnaia zapiska." Compare Serhiichuk, *OUN-UPA*, 68–69 (also at TsDAHOU, 1/23/523/79).

113. Sowa, *Stosunki*, 186–191.

114. Soviet sources on this are Serhiichuk, *OUN-UPA*, 30, 54, 67–70; TsDAHOU, 1/23/585/36: Behma and Timofeev, "Dokladnaia zapiska." Polish sources are Siwicki, *Dzieje konfliktów*, 88–89, 136; Dębski and Popek, *Okrutna przestroga*, 51, 80, 178, 201, 234, 321, 324, 333. Ukrainian and Jewish sources are Khurtovyna, *Pid nebom Volyni*, 129, 152, 154, 157; Gershon Zik, ed., *Rozyszcze: My Old Home* ([Tel Aviv], 1976), 47.

115. Dębski and Popek, *Okrutna przestroga*, 68, 88; Serhiichuk, *OUN-UPA*, 81; Khurtovyna, *Pid nebom Volyni*, 136. Compare Torzecki, *Polacy i Ukraińcy*, 260.

116. Filar, *"Burza" na Wołyniu*, 90; Sowa, *Stosunki*, 187–188; *Litopys UPA*, vol. 6, 174 (on arrests). On Poles enlisting for work in Germany, see Siwicki, *Dzieje konfliktów*, 173; Dębski and Popek, *Okrutna przestroga*, 232.

117. TsDAHOU, 57/4/344/19: "Dennyk Povshuka Oleksandra vid 17.IX 1939 r."; Himka, "Ukrainian Collaboration," 176–177 (on nationalism).

118. Jan T. Gross, *Revolution from Abroad: The Soviet Conquest of Poland's Western Ukraine and Western Belorussia* (Princeton, N.J., 1988), 35–45. Himka, "Ukrainian Collaboration," 175, also points at desensitization during the prewar decades.

119. Michael Diment, *The Lone Survivor: A Diary of the Lukacze Ghetto and Svyniukhy, Ukraine* (New York, 1992), 201; Zik, *Rozyszcze*, 43. See also Dębski and Popek, *Okrutna przestroga*, 93, 318, 320; Shmuel Spector, *The Holocaust of Volhynian Jews, 1941–1944* (Jerusalem, 1990), 270–271; TsDAHOU, 1/22/16/30:

Behma of the Rivne obkom and others to Khrushchev, kh. Shugalets, May 25, 1943; Weiner, *Making Sense of War*, 263–264 (cites NKVD interrogation records). Compare Leo Heiman, "We Fought for Ukraine! The Story of Jews with the UPA," *Ukrainian Quarterly* 20, no. 1 (1964): 35–36 (an atypical account of a Jewish woman who survived in a UPA unit).

120. Dębski and Popek, *Okrutna przestroga*, 50, 69, 247, 289, 319.

121. Ibid., 103–104.

122. Popek, *Wołyński testament*, 108, 141.

123. Dębski and Popek, *Okrutna przestroga*, 77–78, 178, 209, 249, 265, 291, 314, 320. On the seventeen-year-old, see 119–120.

124. Skorups'kyi, *U nastupakh i vidstupakh*, 86–88; Khurtovyna, *Pid nebom Volyni*, 147–148; Armstrong, *Ukrainian Nationalism*, 158.

125. Sowa, *Stosunki*, 210.

126. Friedrich Heyer, *Die orthodoxe Kirche in der Ukraine von 1917 bis 1945* (Cologne, 1953), 220–221.

127. Ibid., 220; T. Iakovkevych, "1939–1943 rr. na Volodymyrshchyny (Spohady)," *Litopys Volyni* 3 (Winnipeg, 1956): 115–116; Armstrong, *Ukrainian Nationalism*, 158–159; Stetsiuk, *Nepostavlenyi pam"iatnyk*, 69–70.

128. On prior warnings, see Dębski and Popek, *Okrutna przestroga*, 16, 22, 43, 101, 121, 192, 207, 216, 226, 245, 258, 268, 289, 291, 296, 313, 323, 333.

129. Ibid., 119, 131.

130. Ibid., 104, see also 38, 50, 52, 63–64, 75, 92–93, 100, 119, 123, 131, 135, 216, 230–231, 234–234, 269–270, 273, 287, 291, 301, 324–325. On Czech saviors, see 226. On saviors identified as Ukrainian Baptists, see 120, 284, 321; Khurtovyna, *Pid nebom Volyni*, 161–163.

131. TsDAVOV, 3833/2/1/39: "Borot'ba i diial'nist' OUN pidchas viiny. Napriamni OUN."

132. Dębski and Popek, *Okrutna przestroga*, 96; see also 50, 63–64, 288, 335, and, on beatings, 111, 231, 288.

133. TsDAHOU, 1/23/585/40: Behma and Timofeev, "Dokladnaia zapiska."

134. Skorups'kyi, *U nastupakh i vidstupakh*, 68–69, 148; Stetsiuk, *Nepostavlenyi pam"iatnyk*, esp. 118–120.

135. Skorups'kyi, *U nastupakh i vidstupakh*, 146, 163–164, 226; Shuliak, *V im"ia pravdy*, 30; Khurtovyna, *Pid nebom Volyni*, 146; TsDAHOU, 1/23/585/12: Behma and Timofeev, "Dokladnaia zapiska" (on forced mobilization).

136. Armstrong, *Ukrainian Nationalism*, 118–123; NA microcopy T-501, roll 28, frames 192–199: Abwehrstelle Ukraine report, Zdolbuniv, September 15, 1943, also in *Litopys UPA*, vol. 6, 94–96; M. V. Koval' [et al.], comps., "OUN i UPA u druhii svitovii viini," *Ukraïns'kyi istorychnyi zhurnal*, no. 4 (Kiev, July–August 1994): 104 (Klym Savur order).

137. NA microcopy T-78, roll 565, frames 195–196: Klym Savur, order, German

translation, n.p., August 31, 1943, also in *Litopys UPA*, vol. 6, 93–94; Serhiichuk, *OUN-UPA*, 95; Khurtovyna, *Pid nebom Volyni*, 158.

138. Khurtovyna, *Pid nebom Volyni*, 132, 134–135. On the new UPA raid, see TsDAHOU, 1/23/530/2: V. Sokolov, I.O. Nachal'nika Ukrainskogo Shtaba Partizanskogo Dvizheniia, to N. S. Khrushchev, "Spetssoobshchenie o deatel'nosti ukrainskikh natsionalistov," n.p., September 30, 1943.

139. Khurtovyna, *Pid nebom Volyni*, 140; Serhiichuk, *OUN-UPA*, 87–88.

140. Serhiichuk, *OUN-UPA*, 120.

141. Khurtovyna, *Pid nebom Volyni*, 144–145, 150; Skorups'kyi, *U nastupakh i vidstupakh*, 148, 213; Stetsiuk, *Nepostavlenyi pam"iatnyk*, 75; Siwicki, *Dzieje konfliktów*, 139.

142. NA microcopy T-501, roll 217, frame 830: "Auszug aus dem Lagebericht einer Kreishauptmannschaft des Distriktes Galizien für die Monate Oktober u. November 1943."

143. NA microcopy T-78, roll 562, frame 470: Fremde Heere Ost, "Die national-ukrainische Widerstandsbewegung UPA. Anlage 2," n.p., November 1, 1944. For the OUN communiqué, see fascimile in Lebed', *UPA*, 117.

144. NA microcopy T-78, roll 565, frames 252–253: Fremde Heere Ost, "Vortragsnotiz," n.p., May 19, 1943 (also in *Litopys UPA*, vol. 6, 73–75); NA microcopy T-175, roll 81, frame 2601567: Koch, "Betr.: Derzeitiger Stand der Bandenlage" (a passage omitted from *Litopys UPA*, vol. 6, 81–83); Polishchuk, *Hirka pravda*, 258; Dębski and Popek, *Okrutna przestroga*, 318.

145. *Litopys UPA*, vol. 27, 204; A. V. Kentii, ed., "Poranennia i smert' M. F. Vatutina," *Ukraïns'kyi istorychnyi zhurnal*, no. 11 (November 1991): 79–88.

146. Samchuk, *Na koni voronomu*, 160.

147. A. V. Kentii, *Ukraïns'ka Povstans'ka Armiia v 1942–1943 rr.* (Kiev, 1999), 155.

148. Naimark, *Fires of Hatred*, 185–199.

149. NA microcopy T-78, roll 565, frames 200–203: German translation of an article in the August 1, 1943, issue of the newspaper *Oborona Ukraïny*; Bul'ba, *Armiia*, 263; Serhiichuk, *OUN-UPA*, 291. See also Baumeister, *Evil*, 349.

150. Leon Żur, comp. and ed., *Polacy i Ukraińcy: Zabliźnić rany* (Suwałki, Pol., 2001), 203–206.

151. I. Ia. Omel'ianenko, "Povstannia v Pavlohradi u liutomu 1943 r.," *Ukraïns'kyi istorychnyi zhurnal* 9, no. 2 (February 1965): 91–94.

152. Jacob Gerstenfeld-Maltiel, *My Private War: One Man's Struggle to Survive the Soviets and the Nazis* (London, 1993), 226–227; *Meldungen* 54 (May 14, 1943): 19–20 (on trench digging).

153. NA microcopy T-84, roll 120, frame 419259: General Commissar Magunia, report, Kiev, March 4, 1943.

154. TsDAVOV, 3676/4/105/133–134: RKU *Lagebericht*, Rivne, November 13, 1943 (the figure and the quotation); Benjamin Pinkus and Ingeborg Fleischhauer,

Die Deutschen in der Sowjetunion: Geschichte einer nationalen Minderheit im
20. Jahrhundert (Baden-Baden, Ger., 1987), 284–286; Ingeborg Fleischhauer,
Das Dritte Reich und die Deutschen in der Sowjetunion (Stuttgart, 1983), 206–
222, 231, 242.

155. Müller, Die faschistische Okkupationspolitik, 474; TsDAVOV, 3676/4/105/135–
136: RKU Lagebericht, Rivne, November 13, 1943.

156. Reinhard Rürup, ed., Der Krieg gegen die Sowjetunion 1941–1945: Eine
Dokumentation (Berlin, 1991), 102, 232.

157. TsDAHOU, 1/23/599/29: "Akt," [Obolon'], October 3, 1943; TSDAHOU, 1/23/
558/68: "Vypiska iz akta o zverstvakh nemetskikh fashistov v sele Bol'shie
Lipniagi, Semenovskogo raiona Poltavskoi oblasti," n.d.

158. TsDAHOU, 1/23/588/63: "Vypiska iz akta o zlodeianiiakh nemetskikh fashistov
v g. Poltave," n.d. For evidence regarding the Melitopol' region, see
TsDAHOU, 166/3/246/98–99, 130: Vladimir Ivanovich Tikhonovich (b. 1879),
n.p., January 23, 1946, and Vera Petrovna Rukosueva (b. 1892), [Melitopol'?],
n.d.; Abramenko, Kyïvs'kyi protses, 21–22. For the evacuation of the Left Bank,
see Müller, Die faschistische Okkupationspolitik, 520–521.

159. Serhiichuk, OUN-UPA, 364: Seleshko, Vinnytsia, 113; Pihido-Pravoberezhnyi,
"Velyka Vitchyzniana viina," 170–171.

160. TsDAHOU, 1/23/1064/50: "Akt 25 marta 1944 goda." For other examples, see
TsDAHOU, 1/23/1064/24, 28: "Akt o zverstvakh nemetsko-fashistskikh
razboinikov v sele Kislin Bugskogo raiona Kievskoi oblasti," n.d., and "Akt 13
marta 1944 goda," Kitaihorod, Dashiv raion, Vinnytsia oblast.

161. Werth, Russia at War, 720 (on events in Uman'). Examples of plunder are in
TsDAHOU, 1/23/1064/25: "Akt 12 marta 1944 goda," Rossokhvata, Dashiv raion,
Vinnytsia oblast; NA microcopy T-84, roll 120, frame 419211: Boryspil' District
Commissar to General Commissar, December 16, 1942. On rapes, see
TsDAHOU, 1/23/1064/24: "Akt o zverstvakh," Kislin; TsDAHOU, 1/23/1064/30:
"Akt 15 marta 1944 goda"; Marliese Fuhrmann, Schneebruch: Geschichte einer
Verschleppung (Landau, Ger., 1993), 64–65.

162. NA microcopy T-501, roll 28, frames 47–48: Der Kommandierende General der
Sicherungstruppen und Befehlshaber im Heeresgeb.Süd Nr. 1454/43, I. V.
Generalmajor Graf Stolberg, to Heeresgruppe Süd, "Monatsbericht (1.–
30.9.43)," Headquarters, October 6, 1943. For announcements in Kiev, see
Fesenko, Povest', 90, 92–93.

163. TsDAHOU, 166/3/243/25–26: V. M. Artobolevskii (Russian born in 1874), Kiev,
February 22 and 25, 1944.

164. TsDAVOV, 4620/3/243a/11: N. A. Prakhov, "Chto bylo v Kieve pri nemtsakh,"
Kiev, May 21, 1941 [sic]; Fesenko, Povest', 91.

165. TsDAHOU, 166/3/248/31–34: V. Tverskoi, "Dorogie druz'ia," Kiev, n.d. (before
August 14, 1945). On those who fled, see Fesenko, Povest', 93.

166. Wiehn, *Die Schoáh*, 372, 539, 557, 560, 564. The survivors' estimates are "about 70,000," "over 100,000," "about 120,000," "120,000 to 125,000," and "over 125,000."

167. Ibid., 372, 539, 545, 560, 564; David Budnik and Iakov Kaper, *Nichto ne zabyto: Evreiskie sud'by v Kieve, 1941–1943* (Konstanz, Ger., 1993), 165; M. V. Panasyk, quoted in "Babyn Iar (veresen' 1941–veresen' 1943 rr.)," *Ukraïns'kyi istorychnyi zhurnal*, no. 12 (1991): 63–64. For the young women, see Wiehn, *Die Schoáh*, 372; Budnik and Kaper, *Nichto ne zabyto*, 37–38, 166.

168. "Babyn Iar," 63–64; K. Ia. Hrynevych, author interview (including recorded confirmation of the random roundups by V. P. Kravchenko); Zakhar Trubakov, *Taina Bab'ego Iara: Dokumental'naia povest'-khronika* (Tel-Aviv, 1997), 155.

169. Müller, *Die faschistische Okkupationspolitik*, 498; D. M. Malakov, ed., *Kyïv, 1941–1943: Fotoal'bom* (Kiev, 2000), 228–229.

170. Bernhard Chiari, "Deutsche Zivilverwaltung in Weißrußland 1941–1944: Die lokale Perspektive der Besatzungsgeschichte," *Militärgeschichtliche Mitteilungen* 52, no. 1 (1993): 75. On the Red Army's reception, see TsDAHOU, 166/3/249/10: Valentina [Valentyna] Maksymivna Liashenko (Ukrainian born in 1916), Zarubyntsi, Kiev oblast, August 8, 1946.

171. Serhiichuk, *OUN-UPA*, 135. Compare Khurtovyna, *Pid nebom Volyni*, 179; Siwicki, *Dzieje konfliktów*, 139.

Conclusion

1. Amir Weiner, *Making Sense of War: The Second World War and the Fate of the Bolshevik Revolution* (Princeton, N.J., 2001), 171–182. Studies tend to focus on eastern Galicia; see, for example, Jeffrey Burds, "Gender and Policing in Soviet West Ukraine, 1944–1948," *Cahiers du Monde russe* 42, nos. 2–4 (2001): 279–320.

2. Gerald Reitlinger, *The House Built on Sand: The Conflicts of German Policy in Russia, 1939–1945* (London, 1960), 225–227.

3. Alfred E. Frauenfeld, *Und trage keine Reu': Vom Wiener Gauleiter zum Generalkommissar der Krim. Erinnerungen und Aufzeichnungen* (Leoni am Starnberger See, Ger., 1978).

4. Weiner, *Making Sense of War*, 160; Tony Judt, "The Past Is Another Country: Myth and Memory in Postwar Europe," in István Deák, Jan T. Gross, and Tony Judt, eds., *The Politics of Retribution in Europe: World War II and Its Aftermath* (Princeton, N.J., 2000), 293–323.

5. Aleksandr Saburov, cited in A. S. Chaikovs'kyi, *Nevidoma viina: (Partyzans'kyi rukh v Ukraïni 1941–1944 rr. movoiu dokumentiv, ochyma istoryka)* (Kiev, 1994), 91.

6. Karel C. Berkhoff, "Ukraine under Nazi Rule (1941–1944): Sources and Finding Aids. Part II," *Jahrbücher für Geschichte Osteuropas* 45, no. 2 (1997): 291.

7. Michail Semirjaga, "Der Grosse Vaterländische Krieg im Bewusstsein des

Sowjetvolkes in der Zeit von Perestrojka und Glasnost," in Walter Leimgruber, ed., *1.9.39: Europäer erinnern sich an den Zweiten Weltkrieg* (Zürich, 1990), 178.

8. Mykola Patsera, "Iak na kontstabirnomu platsu trymaiut' kolyshnikh v"iazniv i ostarbaiteriv kyïvs'ki chynovnyky," *Kyïv'ski vidimosti*, January 5, 1996, 1, 6; Lev Bakal, "The Long, Dusty Road to Nazi Compensation," *Moscow Times*, April 16, 2002, 12–13.

9. [V. F. Shevchenko], "Okupatsiinyi rezhym v Ukraïni—henotsyd narodu," in I. O. Herasymov et al., eds., *Bezsmertia: Knyha pam"iati Ukraïny, 1941–1945* (Kiev, 2000), 174, 181, writes of a "genocide of the people," the "main object" of which was the Ukrainians. M. V. Koval', *Ukraïna v Druhii svitovii i Velykii Vitchyznianii viinakh (1939–1945)* (Kiev, 1999), 158, refers to a "total war for the destruction of the population." Compare the title of Christian Gerlach, *Kalkulierte Morde: Die deutsche Wirtschafts- und Vernichtungspolitik in Weißrußland 1941 bis 1944* (Hamburg, 1999). On the discriminate nature of Nazi terror in the Reich, see Eric A. Johnson, *Nazi Terror: The Gestapo, Jews, and Ordinary Germans* (New York, 1999), esp. 485.

10. Gerlach, *Kalkulierte Morde*, 1111.

11. Michael Ellman and S. Maksudov, "Soviet Deaths in the Great Patriotic War: A Note," *Europe-Asia Studies* 46, no. 4 (1994): 676–677.

12. See, for example, Hiroaki Kuromiya, *Freedom and Terror in the Donbas: A Ukrainian-Russian Borderland, 1870s–1990s* (Cambridge, Eng., 1998), 190–191, 193–194.

13. As testified, for example, in *Shchodennyk Arkadiia Liubchenka*, ed. Iurii Luts'kyi (Lviv, Ukr., 1999), 50, quoting another person.

14. TsDAHOU, 1/22/347/14: "Iz dnevnika uchitel'nitsy gor. Kieva L. Nartovoi," note of July 30, 1942.

15. Orlando Patterson, *Slavery and Social Death: A Comparative Study* (Cambridge, Mass., 1982), 198, 205.

16. Compare Bernhard Chiari, *Alltag hinter der Front: Besatzung, Kollaboration und Widerstand im Weißrußland 1941–1944* (Düsseldorf, 1998), esp. 3.

17. The word "egoism" appears in Mykhailo Seleshko, *Vinnytsia: spomyny perekladacha Komisiï doslidiv zlochyniv NKVD v 1937–1938* (Toronto, 1991), 81.

18. Michael Geyer, "Resistance as Ongoing Project: Voices of Order, Obligations to Strangers, and Struggles for Civil Society, 1933–1990," in Michael Geyer and John W. Boyer, eds., *Resistance against the Third Reich, 1933–1990* (Chicago, 1994), 340–341.

19. Bob Moore, "Comparing Resistance and Resistance Movements," in Bob Moore, ed., *Resistance in Western Europe* (Oxford, 2000), 262. See also Tim Kirk and Anthony McElligott, "Introduction: Community, Authority and Resistance to Fascism," in Tim Kirk and Anthony McElligott, eds., *Opposing Fascism: Community, Authority and Resistance in Europe* (Cambridge, Eng., 1999), 1–11.

20. The quotation is from Andrei Sinyavsky, *Soviet Civilization: A Cultural History* (New York, 1990), 163.

21. See, for example, David A. Kideckel, *The Solitude of Collectivism: Romanian Villagers to the Revolution and Beyond* (Ithaca, N.Y., 1993).

22. Mykhailo Hartymiv, "Zemleiu ukraïns'koiu . . . ," in Kost' Mel'nyk, Oleh Lashchenko, and Vasyl' Veryha, eds., *Na zov Kyieva: Ukraïns'kyi natsionalizm u II Svitovii Viini. Zbirnyk stattei, spohadiv i dokumentiv* (Toronto, 1985), 147.

23. At least this tendency prevailed in Russia's countryside. See Jeffrey Burds, *Peasant Dreams and Market Politics: Labor Migration and the Russian Village, 1861–1905* (Pittsburgh, 1998), cited in Kuromiya, *Freedom and Terror*, 146–147.

24. John Barber and Mark Harrison, *The Soviet Home Front, 1941–1945: A Social and Economic History of the USSR in World War II* (London, 1991), 72–73, 208.

25. See, for example and respectively, Richard Stites, "Introduction: Russia's Holy War," in Richard Stites, ed., *Culture and Entertainment in Wartime Russia* (Bloomington, Ind., 1995), 5; Bohdan Krawchenko, "Soviet Ukraine under Nazi Occupation, 1941–4," in Yury Boshyk, ed., *Ukraine during World War II: History and Its Aftermath. A Symposium* (Edmonton, 1986), 15–37. Historians of countries such as Greece, Poland, and Czechoslovakia have also argued that World War II made significant changes in political attitudes. See, in particular, Mark Mazower, *Inside Hitler's Greece: The Experience of Occupation, 1941–44* (New Haven, Conn., 1993), 52; Bradley F. Abrams, "The Second World War and the East European Revolution," *East European Politics and Societies* 16, no. 3 (2003): 623–664.

26. Weiner, *Making Sense of War*.

SOURCES

BA-Berlin

Bundesarchiv-Berlin (Federal Archives of Germany, Berlin branch)
   R 6. Reichsministerium für die besetzten Osgebiete

BA-MA

Bundesarchiv-Militärarchiv (Military Archives, Koblenz, Germany)
   RH 24–48. Army Corps 48 of the Sixth Army
   RH 26–454. Infantry Division 454 of Army Corps 49 of the Seventeenth Army
   RW 2. Chief of Supreme Command of the Wehrmacht and directly subordinate
offices
   RW 31. Wirtschaftsrüstungsamt

DAKO

Derzhavnyi arkhiv Kÿïvs'koï oblasti (State Archives of the Kiev oblast, Kiev)
   f. r-2275, op. 1. Kievskaia shkola n. 5/7 (Kurenevskaia)
   f. r-2329, op. 1–2. Editors of *Vasyl'kivs'ki visti*
   f. r-2356, op. 1–18. Kÿïvs'ka Mis'ka Uprava
   f. r-2412, op. 1–2. Muzei-Arkhiv perekhodnogo perioda
   f. r-2505, op. 1. Elementary school in Pliskachivka (Smila raion)
Raion administrations:
   f. r-2107, op. 1. Bohuslav
   f. r-2209, op. 1–2. Khabne
   f. r-2292, op. 1. Rokytne
   f. r-2418, op. 1. Baryshivka
   f. r-2457, op. 1. Ivankiv
   f. r-2509, op. 2. Skvyra
   f. r-3110, op. 1. Borodianka
Village administrations:
   f. r-2097, op. 1. Dmytrenky (Bohuslav raion)
   f. r-2145, op. 1. Nemishaieve (Borodianka raion)

f. r-2160, op. 1. Nova Buda (Borodianka raion)

f. r-2167, op. 1. Druzhnia (Borodianka raion)

f. r-2210, op. 1. Khabne (Khabne raion)

f. r-2212, op. 1. Steshchyna (Khabne raion)

f. r-2215, op. 1. Maksymovychy (Khabne raion)

f. r-2293, op. 1. Teleshivka (Rokytne raion)

f. r-2294, op. 1. Romashky (Rokytne raion)

f. r-2295, op. 1. Ol'shanytsia (Rokytne raion)

f. r-2519, op. 1. Kam"iana Hreblia (Skvyra raion)

f. r-2679, op. 1. Sloboda (Kaharlyk raion)

HIA

Archives of the Hoover Institution on War, Revolution and Peace, Stanford University, Stanford, California

Alexander Dallin collection

Box 2, folder 14; box 4, folder 7; box 7, folder 6; box 8, folder 2: transcripts of three interviews from the Harvard University Refugee Interview Project

B. I. Nicolaevsky collection

Series no. 178, box 232, folders 10–11: [Lev Vladimirovich] Dudin, "Velikii Mirazh: Sobytiia 1941–1947 godov v ponimanii sovetskogo cheloveka" (n.p., 1947)

Series no. 236, box 409, folder 19: Emigrant, "Nemtsy v Kieve: (Iz vospominanii ochevidtsa)" (n.p., n.d.)

Russian Research Center, Harvard University. Interview transcripts, 1950–1951, of the Harvard University Refugee Interview Project (abbreviated in the notes as HIA-HURIP)

IMFE

Instytut Mystetstvoznavstva, Fol'kloru ta Etnohrafiï im. M. T. Ryl's'koho (M. T. Rylsky Institute of Art Science, Folklore, and Ethnography, National Academy of Sciences of Ukraine, Kiev)

Viddil rukopysnykh fondiv (Manuscripts Department)

f. 14–3

International Court of Justice, The Hague, the Netherlands

Nuremberg Trial archives. Document 053-PS, Hptm Dr. Dr. [Hans] Koch, "Bericht 10. (abgeschlossen am 5. Oktober 1941)"

Muzei istoriï Bohuslavshchyny im B. M. Levchenko, Archives, Bohuslav, Ukraine

Grigorii M. Levchenko, "Dnevnik: Puteshestvie v Germaniiu" (manuscript, Medvyn, 1945)

NA

National Archives of the United States (Washington, D.C.)
Microcopies
T-78. Fremde Heere Ost
T-84. Miscellaneous German Records Collection, 1892–1945
T-120. Records of the German Foreign Office Received by the Department of State
T-175. Records of the Reich Leader of the SS and Chief of the German Police. Include, on rolls 233–236, the Security Police and Security Service mimeographs, *Ereignismeldung UdSSR* and *Meldungen aus den besetzten Ostgebieten*
T-501. Records of German Field Commands: Rear Areas, Occupied Territories, and others

NBU, Filiia 1

Natsional'na biblioteka Ukraïny im. V. I. Vernads'koho, Filiia 1 (V. I. Vernadsky National Library of Ukraine, branch 1, Kiev)
Viddil starodrukiv ta ridkisnykh vydan' (Old Imprints and Rarities Department)—posters, leaflets, and magazines from the Nazi period
Hazetnyi viddil (Newspaper Department)

NDB

Naukovo-dovidkova biblioteka tsentral'nykh derzhavnykh arkhiviv Ukraïny (Scholarly Reference Library of the Central State Archives of Ukraine, Kiev)
Collection "Afishy ta plakaty okupatsiinoho periodu"
Collection "Lystivky okupatsiinoho periodu"

Private archives

Karel C. Berkhoff, Amsterdam—Tape recordings of interviews by Karel C. Berkhoff. All of the informants were Ukrainian, and unless otherwise indicated, the interviews were conducted in Ukrainian.
Bondarenko, Nadiia Fedorovna [Fedorivna] (b. 1930, Bohuslav), July 20, 1995, Bohuslav, Kiev oblast, Ukraine
Demydenko, Mykhailo (b. 1928, Trusivtsi), July 18, 1995, Bohuslav
Hohulia, Mariia Khtodosiïvna (b. 1927, Medvyn), July 22, 1995, Medvyn, Bohuslav raion
Hrynevych, Klavdiia Iakivna (b. 1930, Klyntsi), August 10, 1995, Kiev (in Russian)
Iatsenko, Oksana (b. 1919, Mysailivka), July 21, 1995, Mysailivka, Bohuslav raion
Khmilev'ska, Liudmyla Stanyslavivna (b. 1923, Kiev), July 13, 1995, Kiev (in Russian)

Kostiuk, Mykola Pavlovych (b. 1915, Dnipropetrovs'k, d. 1997), March 1, 1996, Downsview, Ontario, Canada

Kravchenko, Valentyna Pavlivna (b. 1922, Kiev), August 10, 1995, Kiev (in Russian)

Kutsenko, Ol'ha Mykolaïvna (b. 1926, Poberezhka), July 18, 1995, Bohuslav

Moskovs'ka, Ievheniia Makarivna (b. Stari Bezradychy, 1930), July 29, 1995, Kiev

Prylipko, Mariia (b. 1913, Medvyn), July 17, 1995, Medvyn

Salata, Hryts'ko Hryts'kovych (b. 1909, Medvyn), July 17, 1995, Medvyn

Salata, Nikolai [Mykola] (b. 1914, Medvyn), July 17, 1995, Medvyn

Sarapuka, Oksana (b. 1927, Medvyn), July 17, 1995, Medvyn

Syn'ohub, Mykola Iosypovych (b. 1924, Medvyn), July 22, 1995, Medvyn

Vasylenko, Iakiv Nesterovych (b. 1924, Medvyn), July 22, 1995, Medvyn

Vasylenko, Mariia Oleksandrivna (b. 1931, Huta), July 22, 1995, Medvyn

Zozulia, Nina Serhiïvna (b. 1929, Oksaverivka), July 21, 1995, Bohuslav

Miron Semenovich Petrovskii, Kiev

Vladimir Alekseevich Ponsov, Moscow

RGASPI

Rossiiskii gosudarstvennyi arkhiv sotsial'no-politicheskoi istorii (Russian State Archives of Sociopolitical History, Moscow)

f. 17, op. 3. Records *(protokoly)* of the Politburo of the Central Committee of the All-Union Communist Party (Bolshevik)

f. 17, op. 125. Otdel Propagandy i Agitatsii

Robarts Library, University of Toronto, Canada

Volyn' (Rivne), newspaper

TsDAHOU

Tsentral'nyi derzhavnyi arkhiv hromads'kykh ob"iednan' Ukraïny (Central State Archives of Civic Organizations of Ukraine, Kiev)

f. 1, op. 22. Tsentral'nyi Komitet Kommunisticheskoi Partii Ukrainy, Osobyi Sektor i organizatsionno-instruktorskii otdel. Dokumenty o podpol'no partizanskom dvizhenii v period Velikoi Otechestvennoi voiny 1941–1945 gg.

f. 1, op. 23. Tsentral'nyi Komitet Kommunisticheskoi Partii Ukrainy (Osobyi sektor—sekretnaia chast')

f. 1, op. 70. Tsentral'nyi Komitet Kommunisticheskoi Partii Ukrainy, Viddil propahandy i ahitatsii

f. 57, op. 4. Kollektsiia dokumentov po istorii kompartii Ukrainy: Period otechestvennoi voiny 1941–1945 gg.

f. 166, op. 2–3. Komisiia z pytan' istoriï velykoï vitchyznianoï viiny pry akademiï nauk URSR. Obshchaia chast'

TsDAVOV

Tsentral'nyi derzhavnyi arkhiv vyshchykh orhaniv vlady ta upravlinnia Ukraïny (Central State Archives of the Higher Agencies of Power and Administration of Ukraine, Kiev)

f. 3206, op. 1–6. Reikhskomissariat Ukrainy, g. Rovno

f. 3676, op. 1–5. Shtab imperskogo rukovoditelia (reikhsliaitera) Rozenberga dlia okkupirovannykh vostochnykh oblastei, g. Berlin, g. Kiev

f. 3833, op. 1–3. Kraiovyi Provid Orhanizatsiï Ukraïns'kykh Natsionalistiv (OUN) na Zakhidnoukraïns'kykh Zemliakh

f. 4620, op. 3. Kolektsiia dokumentiv z istoriï Velykoï Vitchyznianoï viiny 1941–1945 r.r.

UCEC

Ukrainian Cultural and Educational Centre, Winnipeg, Manitoba, Canada
Collection of manuscripts:

[Mykola Balanchuk], "Kyïv za nimets'koï okupatsiï 1941–43 rr." (n.p., n.d.)

Pavlo Ternivs'kyi [Ivan Zhyhadlo], "Spohady emigranta" (n.p., 1945)

ACKNOWLEDGMENTS

A t the end of the long road to this book I take pleasure in thanking the people who helped to make it possible and enjoyable. They included the directors and staff members of four repositories in Kiev: Larysa V. Iakovlieva and Larysa A. Pykhtina of the Central State Archives of the Higher Agencies of Power and Administration of Ukraine (TsDAVOV), Ruslan Ia. Pyrih and Iryna L. Komarova of the Central State Archives of Civic Organizations of Ukraine (TsDAHOU), Nionila P. Voitsekhivska, Liubov F. Velychko, Olga I. Primas, and Ekaterina I. Dotsenko of the State Archives of the Kiev Oblast (DAKO), and Halyna V. Porokhniuk of the Scholarly Reference Library of the Central State Archives of Ukraine (NDB). The staff of the V. I. Vernadsky National Library of Ukraine and the M. T. Rylsky Institute of Art Science, Folklore, and Ethnography also need special mention in this context. I wish to mention these citizens of Ukraine first because in spite of trying material conditions, they were very forthcoming to me, a foreign visitor, who moreover wanted to find out about a painful part of their country's all too recent past.

The book also draws from materials that I gathered elsewhere and the staff of those other places—in particular the library of the University of Toronto, the German Federal Archives, the Hoover Institution on War, Revolution and Peace, and the repositories mentioned in the photo credits—all were helpful. I began to conduct oral history interviews in 1995. The benefits were immediate and I am deeply grateful to my interviewees. To find people who were willing to give their recollections, allowed me to record them on tape, and never asked to remain anonymous (their names are in the notes), would have been impossible without Eileen Consey-Heywood, Petro Hohulia, Vladyslav Hrynevych, Maryna Kravets, Iurii Maniichuk, and Svetlana Vasilevna Petrovskaia. Svetlana Vasilevna and her husband, Miron Semenovich Petrovskii, warmly hosted me during two summers in Kiev and tirelessly helped me in many ways without my even asking.

I owe a debt of special gratitude to the readers of the various versions of the manuscript. They included Paul Robert Magocsi, who supervised the dissertation at the University of Toronto that laid the groundwork for this book and who has been and remains inspiring to me. In the best tradition of German scholarship, Dieter Pohl generously gave me many useful comments. Other readers were Amir Weiner (who also supported my research in many other ways), Robert Austin, Jacques Kornberg, Hiroaki Kuromiya, Michael R.

Marrus, Andrew Rossos, Peter H. Solomon, Jr., Mark von Hagen, and two scholars approached by Harvard University Press, one of whom turned out to be Norman M. Naimark. (After completing his review, he asked the press to reveal his name.) The editors of *Holocaust and Genocide Studies* and the *Slavonic and East European Review*, as well as the reviewers they asked to read my work, improved the arguments set forth in Chapters 4 and 10. Valuable comments on individual chapters, as well as references, advice, and photocopies, came from other friends and colleagues. At the risk of omitting someone I mention here Nanci Adler, Ray Brandon, Jane Burbank, Marco Carynnyk, Erich Haberer, Johannes Houwink ten Cate, Vladyslav Hrynevych, Liudmyla Hrynevych, Andrij Makuch, Dmytro Malakov, Roman Senkus, Timothy Snyder, and R. J. Tyndorf. I also benefited from those attending presentations of findings in Europe and North America. In the end, of course, I alone assume responsibility for my statements of fact or opinion.

In the early stages, the research received financial support from the Department of History, the Travel Grant Fund of the School of Graduate Studies, and the Centre for Russian and East European Studies at the University of Toronto, and from the Government of Ontario, Canada. My colleagues at the Netherlands Institute for War Documentation, led by Hans Blom, and the Center for Holocaust and Genocide Studies in Amsterdam, led by Johannes Houwink ten Cate, provided a congenial working environment. Cora Rijks and Lucie de Vries of the Netherlands Institute for War Documentation helped with the typing. Oxford University Press and the University of London's School of Slavonic and East European Studies allowed me to include slightly revised versions of articles from their journals.

Kathleen McDermott at Harvard University Press courageously took on the long manuscript; Julie Carlson was the manuscript editor. Their suggestions vastly improved the text. My sincere thanks go to them, to Kathleen Drummy, Christine Thorsteinsson, and Nicholas Koenig, who made the index. I am deeply grateful to the Wiener Library in London for awarding the manuscript the Fraenkel Prize in Contemporary History, Category A, for 2001. Finally, I thank my parents: Iet Scheers and Egbert Berkhoff. The wait for them has been long, but they never lost patience.

INDEX

Academy Institute of Economics, Statistics, and Geography, 159

Alcohol consumption, 136, 203–204, 221, 278

Aleksii (Hromadsky), archbishop, 235–238, 242, 296

All-Ukrainian Cooperative Society, 129, 195

Andrusiak, Mykola, 170–171

Apostolove, conservatory in, 201

Arsenovych, 296

Autocephalous Orthodox church, 55, 189–190, 194, 232–233, 235–238, 243–248, 250, 296, 308; Archbishop Polikarp, 83–84, 235–238, 241, 244, 246–247, 255; anti-Semitism in, 83–84, 255

Autonomous Orthodox church, 190, 232, 235–238, 243–244, 246–247, 255, 284, 295–296, 308; anti-Semitism in, 84; Archbishop Aleksii, 235–238, 242, 296

Babi Yar, 52, 147, 203, 302–303; massacre of Jews at, xi, 33, 58, 65–69, 75–77, 86, 98, 165, 169, 250, 306–307

Backe, Herbert, 45, 165

Bahazii, Volodymyr, 51–52, 108, 151, 158–159, 170, 242

Baltic states, 10, 227, 299

Bandera, Stepan, 10, 241, 288

Banderites, x, 23, 56, 117, 119, 193, 207–208, 210, 212, 218–219, 224–225, 228, 241; origin of, 10; Lviv statehood proclamation, 20, 25, 103; German executions of, 52; relations with Melnykites, 53, 290–291; in Kiev, 55; as anti-Semitic, 83–84, 288–289; and deportations to Germany, 271; Banderite Security Service (SB), 287, 289, 291, 293, 297–298; massacres of Poles by, 287–300, 310; *Ideiia i chyn*, 292. *See also* Melnykites; Organization of Ukrainian Nationalists

Banderite Security Service (SB), 287, 289, 291, 293, 297–298

Baptisms, 85, 241, 243, 250

Baptists, 87, 238–239, 252, 308

Baratz, Barbara, 81, 86

Barter, 175–176, 183, 185–186

Batasheva, G. A., 67–68

Baumeister, Roy F., 5

Bazar, 52

Beatings, 132–133, 135, 249–250, 263, 272

Behma, Vasyl, 287

Belarus, 37, 43, 45, 92, 138, 173, 196, 201, 238, 304; Soviet partisans in, 275–276, 278–279

Berdiansk, 91; massacre of Jews in, 76, 256

Berdychiv, town of, 217; NKVD massacre in, 16; looting in, 23; massacre of Jews from, 62, 75; anti-Semitism in, 73, 75; death march of Jews in, 75; POW camp in, 105–106

Berdychiv district, 118, 126

Berdychiv raion, 139

Berdychiv region, 225, 258–259

Berndt (Kiev City Commissar), 177, 202

Bessarabia, southern, 10, 37

Białystok district, 36

Białystok region, 305

Bila Tserkva, town of, 11, 209–210, 218, 303; POW camp in, 103; market in, 176

Bila Tserkva district, 118

Bilozirka, 267

Bohatyrchuk, Fedir, 66, 77, 108, 160, 269

Bohuslav, 86, 119, 138, 206, 271

Bondarenko, Liudmyla, 86

Borodianka, village of, 58, 131–132, 282

Borodianka raion, 127, 246

Borove, 290

Borovets, Taras "Bulba," 286, 289–291, 299

Boryspil, 104, 234

Bräutigam, Otto, 165

Brest district, 304

Brest-Litovsk, 37

Bribes, 110, 180, 185–186, 212, 270

Brothels, 114–115, 148, 182, 303

Brückner, Wolfgang, 198

Bucha, 245

Buda: German massacre of natives in, 282

Bukovina, northern, 2, 10, 37, 42, 53

Bukovinian Battalion, 52, 68

Bykivnia: NKVD mass graves in, 16, 188

Cannibalism, 8, 103, 181, 209

Carpatho-Ukraine, 9

Central Trade Corporation East (ZHO), 41, 211

Chełm (Kholm) region, 10, 288, 293

Chemerivtsi raion, 266

Cherkasy, 11; scorched-earth policy in, 21

Chernihiv, town of, 2

Chernihiv oblast, 37

Chernihiv region, 94, 276

Chervony Iar, 133

Children: attitudes toward Germans among, 13, 196; evacuated from Kiev, 26; killed by parents, 181–182; fathered by Germans, 182; magazines for, 195; schools for, 195–196, 229, 234, 242, 308; deported to Germany, 229, 260, 262, 264–266, 268, 271–272. See also Young generation

Chudniv region, 225

Church Slavonic, 234, 245–246

Chyhyryn, 50, 134, 282; NKVD massacre in, 16; school in, 196

Cinema. See Motion pictures

City dwellers, 141–163; attitudes of Nazis toward, 3, 35–36, 45–46, 137, 149, 154, 162, 164–169, 177, 186, 307–308; starvation of, 3, 45–46, 164–186, 221, 253, 255, 306, 308; attitudes toward Germans, 28–29, 62, 164, 182–184, 186, 198, 215–216, 221; relations with peasants, 131, 169–170, 176–177, 180, 185–186; social fragmentation among, 141–142; solidarity among, 141–142, 162–163, 309; as hostages, 142, 147; relations with house custodians, 142, 260–261, 270; housing for, 142–144; Germans as, 144, 149–151, 156–157, 199–200; working conditions for, 144–160, 162; wages for, 145–146, 150, 152, 153; transportation for, 146; curfews for, 146–147, 200, 203; executions of, 147–148; dress of, 148–149; private businesses among, 156–157, 162; medical doctors among, 157, 309; scientists and scholars among, 157–160, 162; relations with German soldiers, 182–183, 202; private gatherings of, 203; attitudes toward Soviet rule among, 224, 225; church attendance among, 249; deported to Germany, 260–266, 268, 270, 273

Clothing, 50, 131, 148–149

Collaboration: concept of, 4–5

Commissar Order, 91–93

Communist Party members, 12, 80, 137, 172, 176, 230, 269–271, 310; Jews as, 7, 72–73, 83–84; prewar purges of, 8; Khrushchev, 8, 18, 52, 278, 304; treatment by Germans of, 54, 57–58, 115, 118, 144, 152–153, 212, 260, 283; as informers, 78, 261; among POWs, 90–93, 106; and partisans, 275, 278–279. See also Komsomol members; NKVD

Communist Youth League. See Komsomol members

Crimea, general district of, 39

Crimean peninsula, 2, 6, 37; Kerch, 91

Czechoslovakia, 9

Dachau concentration camp, 309

Damaskyn (Maliuta), bishop, 296, 299

Dargel, Paul, 47, 135, 195, 283

Darnytsia, Kiev district of, 151; POW camp in, 101, 111

Dashkevich, Raisa, 86

Death marches: of Mennonites, 17; of Jews, 75, 94, 98; of Soviet POWs, 93–99, 112

Denunciations, 54–57, 77–78, 81, 85, 222, 251, 312

Deportations to Germany, 155, 175, 183–184, 186, 196, 215, 224, 259–264, 282–283, 306–307, 311; resistance to, 4, 182, 253, 261, 268–271, 279, 298, 310; Jews and, 71; number of, 112,

253, 259, 264–266, 273; of children, 229, 260, 262, 264–266, 268, 271–272; role of Schuma in, 259, 261–268, 270–273; medical exams related to, 268–270

Diment, Mechel, 60, 69–71, 82

Dionysii (Valedynsky), Metropolitan, archbishop of Warsaw, 233, 235–237

Dnieper Hydroelectric Station, 22–23, 155

Dnieper Ukraine: defined, 4; Right Bank, 4, 19, 91, 99, 106–107, 112, 118–119, 126, 223–224, 252, 302; Left Bank, 4, 36, 48–49, 93, 101–102, 106, 109–110, 114, 119–120, 226, 270, 300–301; Germans welcomed in, 20–21; Dnieper bend, 41, 72–73; fugitive Jews in, 70–71, 78, 149; anti-Semitism in, 71–73, 77–78, 80–81, 250–251; return of Red Army to, 80–81, 88, 205, 220–221, 223–224, 229–230, 300, 303–306, 312; 1941 harvest in, 112–113, 119–120

Dniprodzerzhynsk. See Kamianske

Dniprohes, 22–23, 155

Dnipropetrovsk, city of, 11, 49, 71, 221, 224, 271, 303; industrialization in, 7; scorched-earth policy in, 21; looting in, 23; German administration of, 39, 45, 149–150, 152–153, 162; massacre of Jews in, 68–69; anti-Semitism in, 80; housing in, 143–144; working conditions in, 146, 150–151, 153, 162; Comintern Metallurgical Factory in, 153; H. Petrovsky Metallurgical Factory in, 153; mining industry in, 154; research institutes in, 158; Polytechnical Institute in, 159; movie theater in, 197; Orthodox Christianity in, 245, 248–249; German massacre of civilians in, 300. See also City dwellers

Dnipropetrovsk, general district of, 39, 103, 131, 139

Dnipropetrovsk oblast, 36; ethnic Germans in, 17; scorched-earth policy in, 18

Dnipropetrovsk region, 73, 103, 131, 217, 226, 228

Dominopol: UPA massacre of Poles at, 293

Donbas/Donets River Basin, 37, 226; industrialization in, 7; ethnic Germans in, 17; private German corporations in, 41

Donetsk, 2

Doshne, 295–296

Drama theaters, 199–200

Dubno, 294; NKVD massacre in, 15, 56–57; anti-Jewish pogrom in, 57; Jewish ghetto in, 69

Dubodil, Demyd, 135–136

Dubrovytsia: Jewish ghetto in, 69

Dudin, Lev, 13, 65, 89, 177, 182–183, 224

Dutchmen, 41, 139, 282

Dynamit Nobel AG, 153

Dynamo Kiev, 202–203

Eastern Galicia. See Galicia, eastern

Eastern Volhynia. See Volhynia, eastern

Eastern Workers. See Deportations to Germany

East Prussia, 35–36

Eberhard, Kurt, 85, 147

Economy Inspectorate Center, 138

Economy Inspectorate South, 41, 166–167, 169, 174

Economy Staff East, 41, 45, 125–126, 165–166, 168, 173

Egorycheva-Minkina, Izabella, 85

Einsatzgruppen (Operational Groups), 41–42, 52, 54, 62; Einsatzgruppe C, 64, 68, 72–73, 92, 158

Einsatzstab Reichsleiter Rosenberg, 160, 170–171

Employee canteens, 150–153

Enlightenment societies, 199

Evangelical Christianity, 87, 238–239, 252, 308

Famine: in Kiev, 3, 164–186, 221, 253, 255, 306, 308; Great Famine of 1932–1933, 8, 83, 176, 180, 186, 192, 209, 227, 311; in Athens, 164; in Jewish ghettoes, 164; in Kharkiv, 164; in Netherlands, 164

Feichtmeier, Josef, 108–109

Felshtyn, 218–219

Fesenko, Tatiana, 262

Fevr, Nikolai, 131, 143, 148, 153, 203, 209–210, 219

First Ethnic German Cavalry Regiment, 226

Fomenko, Vitold, 86

Football teams, 202–203

Forced labor, 62, 175, 183, 224, 253, 282, 307; working conditions, 155–156, 162, 306. See also Deportations to Germany

Forced migration, 264–266; Soviet, 17, 94; of ethnic Germans, 45, 211, 264; to southern Ukraine, 254, 264

Forostivsky, Leontii, 151, 161, 190, 203, 261–262

Fotii (Tymoshchuk), bishop, 238, 296

Frank, Anne, 85
Frank, Hans, 187
Franko, Ivan, 54
Frauenfeld, Alfred, 39, 48, 305
Free Cossacks, 107

Galicia, eastern, 10, 73, 292; Lviv, x, 2, 6, 11, 20, 25, 103, 149, 163, 187, 201; Stanislav, 6; Ternopil, 6; Ukrainians in, 6, 8–9, 37, 187, 208, 289, 311; OUN activities in, 8–9; Ukrainians coming from, 12, 42, 53, 109, 149, 193, 207–209, 218–220, 230, 289, 311; and General Government, 37; Orthodox Christianity in, 233, 246; Polish population of, 298
Gas vans, 4, 147, 302–303
General Government: Ukrainians in, x, 10, 51, 53, 187, 195, 290; vs. Reichskommissariat Ukraine, 10, 51, 53, 136, 149, 163, 187, 195, 201, 204, 239, 308, 310; Ukrainian Central Committee in, 10, 51, 195; and eastern Galicia, 37; Jews in, 71, 149; Poles in, 136, 163; underground society in, 141, 310; Holy Orthodox Autocephalous church in, 233, 235–236; Greek Catholic church in, 239; Kholm/Zamość region, 293; Lublin district, 293
German Army, 145, 174–175, 207–208, 273; invasion of Soviet Union, 2, 10–13, 24–34, 62, 117, 213, 215, 230, 234–235, 239–240; Army Group South, 11–12, 35, 48–49, 91, 120, 167, 173, 302; Sixth Army, 26–27, 33, 49, 94, 167; Rear Army Area South, 37, 42, 167–168; Secret Field Police, 41, 49, 57–58; defeated at Stalingrad, 47, 83–84, 98–99, 138–139, 183–184, 190, 217, 221, 225, 271–272, 276–277, 289–290, 300; reprisals for partisan activity, 48–49; attitudes toward "Russian" prisoners of war, 89–92, 99–100, 108–109, 112–113; "Guidelines for the Conduct of the Army in Russia," 92; policies regarding POW camps, 99–100; Eleventh Army, 100, 168; recruitment of Hiwis, 107; rapes by, 114–115, 302; relations with peasants, 114–117; Army Group North, 124; Army Group Center, 124, 173; attitudes toward starvation in Kiev, 166–168; relations with city dwellers, 182–183, 202; and Eastern Workers, 258, 272; retreat from Ukraine, 300–304
German Nationality List, 211–212
German News Agency, 192

German police, 33, 42, 216, 262–263, 267, 270, 273, 282, 298
Germans: defined, x; attitudes toward natives, 1–3, 44–46, 149, 154, 162, 164–169, 177, 182–183, 186, 204, 210–213, 221, 300, 307–309; attitudes toward "Russian" prisoners of war, 3, 89, 99–100, 105–110; private corporations, 41; attitudes toward ethnic Germans, 44–45, 210–213, 300, 309; attitudes toward Ukrainian prisoners of war, 90, 92, 106, 110, 206; social fragmentation among, 141; as city dwellers, 144, 149–151, 156–157, 199–200. See also German Army; German police; Germans, ethnic; Landwirts; Nazis; SS
Germans, ethnic, x, 129, 144, 157; Nazi policies toward, 1, 44–45, 114, 142, 168, 210–213, 300, 309; forced migrations of, 17, 44–45, 211, 264; Mennonites, 17, 45, 212, 226–227, 300, 312; population, 17, 210; and Jewish Holocaust, 44, 87; as prisoners of war, 106; as house custodians, 142; standard of living, 210–211; relations with Reich Germans, 211–213, 242, 300; attitudes toward Nazism among, 212, 226–227, 231, 312; young vs. older generation, 212–213; Catholics among, 239
Germany: annexation of Austria, 9; annexation of Czech lands, 9; relations with France, 9; relations with Slovakia, 9; relations with Great Britain, 9, 11; invasion of Poland, 9–10; relations with Soviet Union, 9–10, 17, 61, 169; relations with Romania, 37; volunteers for work in, 253–258; working conditions for Eastern Workers in, 256–259
Gerstenfeld-Maltiel, Jacob, 78, 80, 149–150
Gestapo. See SS
Ghettoes, 69–71, 82, 88; Order Service in, 42, 69–70; Jewish councils in, 69–70
Glagolev, Fr. Aleksei, 85
Gnadenfeld, 17
Göring, Hermann, 99–100, 106, 165, 168
Great Britain, 9, 11
Greek Catholic church, 2, 6, 8, 83, 206, 238–239, 246, 289, 308
"Guidelines for the Conduct of the Army in Russia," 92
Guralnik, Evgeniia (Zhenia), 62, 64, 74, 86–87
Gypsies. See Roma

Hadiach raion, 138

Haivas, Iaroslav, 169–170

Halbstadt district, 45

Halder, Franz, 35, 164

Hegewald district, 45, 264

Heydekampf, Hans Stieler von, 167

Heyer, Friedrich, 247–249

Himmler, Heinrich: relationship with
Prützmann, 42, 300–301; policies toward ethnic Germans, 44–45, 211–212; germanization
policies, 44–47; Second Sweep against the
Jews, 46–47, 69, 73; policies toward Kiev, 165;
relationship with Hitler, 165, 282; policies toward Soviet partisans, 280, 282–283. *See also*
Hitler, Adolf; Nazis; SS

Hitler, Adolf, 126, 250; attitudes toward Ukrainian raw materials, 1; attitudes toward
Ukraine as source of food, 1, 35, 45–46; attitudes toward rural lifestyle, 1–2; racist ideology of, 1–2; attitudes regarding Lebensraum,
1–2, 44–46, 306; attitudes of natives toward,
27, 216–217, 224; attitudes toward "Russian"
cities, 35–36, 164–166, 169, 186, 308; attitudes
toward Slavs, 35–36, 266; relationship with
Koch, 37–38, 47–48, 187, 308; relationship
with Rosenberg, 47–48; in German propaganda, 50–51, 120, 241–242; attitudes toward
Jews, 72, 82–83; and Commissar Order, 93;
attitudes toward Soviet prisoners of war, 93,
106–107; attitudes toward university in Kiev,
158; relationship with Himmler, 165, 282; attitudes toward deportations to Germany, 265–
266, 282–283. *See also* Himmler, Heinrich;
Nazis

Hiwis, 107

Hladun, Mykola, 115

Hnivan, 239

Holocaust, 59–62, 64–88, 243; Babi Yar massacre, xi, 33, 58, 65–69, 75–77, 86, 98, 165, 169,
250, 306–307; massacres of Jews, 3, 41, 44, 46–
48, 57, 59, 62, 64–69, 92, 99, 105, 253, 255–
257, 259–260, 282, 289, 295, 297, 299, 306–
307, 310–311, 313; massacres of Roma, 3, 41,
44, 48, 59–60, 253, 255–256, 259–260, 282,
299, 306, 311, 313; role of SS in, 32–33, 46–48,
57, 64, 69, 73–74, 77, 83, 113, 212; and ethnic
Germans, 44, 87; Second Sweep, 46–47, 69,
73; in eastern Volhynia, 62, 64; role of

Schuma in, 64, 68–69, 82–83, 113, 295; in
western Volhynia, 64–65, 81–83;
Dnipropetrovsk massacre, 68–69

Holy Orthodox Autocephalous church in the
General Government, 233, 235–237

Holy Orthodox Autocephalous church in the
Liberated Lands of Ukraine. *See*
Autocephalous Orthodox church

Horokhiv, 65, 286

Hostage taking, 49, 142, 147, 282–283

Hrushevsky, Mykhailo, 7, 189

Hryhorii (Ohiichuk), bishop, 84, 238

Hungarian army, 2, 97, 112, 114–115, 150, 157,
174–175, 182, 202, 217, 276, 302

Hungary: as ally of Germany, 9; annexation of
Carpatho-Ukraine by, 9

Huta, 54

Iablonsky, Vasyl, 176, 181

Iakivska, M. A., 98

Iakovets, 135–136

Iakymivka, 158

Ianiuk, Stepan, 15–16

Iatsenko, Oksana, 134, 231

Ieremishchuk, Sava, 290

Ievlohii (Markovsky), bishop, 284

Ilarion (Ohiienko), archbishop, 235–236

Irpin, 123

Islam, 92, 239

Italian army, 2, 11, 112, 217

Ivanivka, 19–20

Ivchenko, Liudmyla, 108–109

Jeckeln, Friedrich, 165

Jews, x, 10, 80–81, 188, 206, 211–212; Babi Yar
massacre of, xi, 33, 58, 65–69, 75–77, 86, 98,
165, 169, 250, 306–307; anti-Semitism, 3, 30,
42, 52, 56–57, 59–62, 65–66, 71–73, 77–78,
80–85, 190–192, 203, 222–223, 250–251, 255,
288, 295, 310–311; massacres of, 3, 41, 44, 46–
48, 57, 59, 62, 64–69, 92, 99, 105, 253, 255–
257, 259–260, 282, 289, 295, 297, 299, 306–
307, 310–311, 313; in Soviet Ukraine, 7, 10,
60–61; as Communist Party members, 7, 72–
73, 83–84; homes looted, 23, 78, 80, 116; in
Kherson, 24; in Kiev, 29–30, 32–33, 49, 61–62,
65–68, 70–71, 75, 77, 81, 85–86, 169; in Order
Service, 42, 69–70; ghettoes for, 42, 69–71, 82,

Jews (continued)

88; in western Volhynia, 56–57, 62; number in Soviet Ukraine, 60; helped by natives, 60, 65, 77, 84–86, 88, 309; relations with peasants, 60, 82–83; anti-Communism among, 61–62; as fugitives, 70–71, 78, 149; in General Government, 71, 149; death marches of, 75, 94, 98; informers on, 77–78, 81; baptism of, 85; adoption by non-Jews, 86; as prisoners of war, 92, 98–99; curfews for, 146; artisans among, 157

Kaharlyk region, 59
Kalashnikov (mythical partisan), 216
Kamianets-Podilsky, town of, 192, 201, 269
Kamianets-Podilsky oblast, 21
Kamianets-Podilsky region, 217
Kamianske (Dniprodzerzhynsk), 146, 154; German administration of, 39
Kaminka: massacre of peasants in, 134
Kandyba, Oleh, 51
Kaniv, town of, 55
Kaniv raion, 114, 133
Kariak, Hryhorii, 57, 261
Kassner (Kovel District Commissar), 281
Katyn forest, 283
Kegel, Gerhard, 96–97
Keitel, Wilhelm, 49, 94, 99–100, 105, 164
Kerch, 91
Khabne (Poliske), 123, 127
Khabne raion, 135–136
Khaniv (Pidhaine), 115
Kharkiv, city of, 2, 190, 193, 222–223, 226, 300; famine in, 164
Kharkiv oblast, 37
Kharkiv region, 226
Khazhyn, 105–106
Kherson, 11, 234, 304; looting in, 23–24; anti-Communism in, 24; Germans welcomed in, 24; Jews in, 24; research institutes in, 158
Khmelnytsky. See Proskuriv
Khorol: POW camp in, 102–103
Khoroshunova, Iryna, 27–28, 144–145, 220; on Babi Yar massacre, 75–76; on POWs, 96–98, 107; on famine in Kiev, 172, 183
Khortytsia district, 45, 212
Khrushchev, Nikita, 8, 18, 52, 278, 304
Kiev, city of, 53–54, 195, 207; Babi Yar, xi, 33, 52, 58, 65–69, 75–77, 86, 98, 147, 165, 169, 203, 250, 302–303, 306–307; famine in, 3, 130, 151–152, 164–186, 221, 249, 253, 255, 306, 308; gassing of civilians in, 4, 147, 302–303; during Soviet rule, 6, 16, 24–34, 61–62, 91; German capture of, 11–12, 24–34; NKVD in, 16, 25–26, 30–33; Soviet scorched-earth policy in, 25–27, 30–33; children evacuated from, 26; draft evasion in, 27; looting in, 27, 29, 153, 302; attitudes toward Germans in, 28–29, 62, 164, 182–184, 186, 198, 215–216, 221; anti-Communism in, 28–29, 73, 191, 220, 222; the Khreshchatyk in, 28–32, 53, 65, 78; Jews in, 29–30, 32–33, 49, 61–62, 65–68, 70–71, 75, 77, 81, 85–86, 169; Great Fire in, 29–33, 65, 78, 142; Dormition Cathedral, 32, 247–248; German administration in, 39, 41–42; Ukrainian National Council in, 51–52; Melnykites in, 51–52, 58; St. Sophia's Cathedral, 53, 247; Banderites in, 55; informers in, 55, 77–78; Roma in, 59; anti-Semitism in, 66, 73, 77–78, 84; Lukianivka Cemetery, 67, 75, 190; Poslednie novosti, 89, 151, 177, 193; death marches of POWs through, 96–97; Soviet POWs in, 96–97, 105; Darnytsia district, 101, 111, 151; Red Cross in, 107–109, 160–162; hostage taking in, 142, 147; housing in, 142–144, 147; electricity in, 144; working conditions in, 144–146, 153–156; curfews in, 147, 203; executions in, 147–148, 156; Nove ukraïnske slovo, 151, 171–172, 179, 192–193; Deutsche Ukraine-Zeitung, 151, 191–192; Lukianivka Prison, 153–154; Lenin Forge in, 153–154, 162; factories in, 153–156, 162; Sport Factory, 154; Ukrainian Ship and Machine Factory in, 154; Mukomol factory, 155; Vilna Ukraïna factory, 155; Vlasna pomich factory, 155; Polytechnical Institute, 155, 159; commission stores in, 156–157; Ukrainian Agricultural Office in, 158; University of Kiev, 158; academy of sciences in, 158–159; Medical Institute in, 159, 265; Pedagogical Institute, 159–160; Commission of Ukrainian Civic and Cultural Leaders, 161; Kiev Mutual Aid Committee, 161; House of Scientists, 161, 189; suicides in, 162; vs. Leningrad, 168, 171; population of, 169, 186, 317; bread in, 171–172, 174, 176, 180, 184, 249; mar-

kets in, 174–177, 179–181, 183–186, 262–263; barter in, 175–176, 183, 185–186; cannibalism in, 181; crime in, 181–182; prostitution in, 182; popular culture in, 188–190, 200; *Ukraïnske slovo*, 192–193; St. Andrew's Cathedral, 194, 248–249; Large Opera Theater in, 198; drama theaters in, 199; conservatory in, 201; Ensemble of Bandurists from, 201; painting academy in, 201; Museum of Ukrainian Art, 201–202; Museum-Archive of the Transition Period, 202; ethnic Germans in, 213; Muslims in, 239; Orthodox Christianity in, 244–249; St. Volodymyr's Cathedral, 248; Labor Office in, 255, 260–261, 268, 270; deportations to Germany from, 260–266, 268, 270; German retreat from, 302–303. *See also* City dwellers

Kiev, general district of, 39, 101, 221, 277; peasants in, 122, 125, 130–131, 139; Orthodox Christianity in, 244–249; deportations to Germany from, 256, 260–266, 268, 270

Kiev oblast, 36; Kiev Oblast Administration, 52

Kiev region, 73, 91, 94, 217, 228, 241, 243, 247, 252

Kirovohrad, city of, 11, 54, 114, 130, 133, 137, 183, 200; Red Star factory in, 23, 153; scorched-earth policy in, 23, 153; POW camp in, 103

Kirovohrad region, 130, 207, 243–244

Kitzinger, Karl, 49, 102–103, 111, 157, 241

Kivertsi, 294

Klemm, Kurt, 39

Kliachkivsky, Dmytro, 291–292, 298

Klyntsi, 130, 137

Kobeliaky, 49

Kobryn district, 304

Koch, Erich, x, 36–39, 42, 168, 198, 279, 300–301, 305; attitudes toward native population, 1, 37–38, 45, 47–48, 186, 308; policies toward agriculture/peasants, 1, 124, 126–127, 132, 135–136, 138; relationship with Rosenberg, 36, 47–48, 196, 286–287; relationship with Hitler, 37–38, 47–48, 187, 308; policies toward ethnic Germans, 45, 211–212, 300; policies toward educational institutions, 48; policies toward Ukrainian nationalists, 51–52; policies toward Jews, 62, 69; policies toward POWs, 106, 111; policies toward hiring system, 145; policies toward Ukrainian cultural life, 187, 194; policies toward Ukrainian language, 194–195, 308; policies toward religious organizations, 211, 234–237; policies toward Eastern Workers, 254, 257; policies toward Ukrainian cities, 308

Koch, Hans, 32, 52, 209; on public manners of natives, 50; on Babi Yar massacre, 76; and POWs, 97, 110; on political thinking of natives, 115, 208; on peasants, 115–117; on religiosity, 243, 248

Komsomol members, 11–12, 14, 19, 62, 115, 152–153. *See also* Communist Party members; NKVD

Konashko, Nadiia, 154

Konovalets, Ievhen, 53

Korets: anti-Jewish pogrom in, 57

Korneliuk, Anastasiia, 281

Korosten district, 211

Korostyshiv district, 124

Korsun: battle at, 304

Kortelisy: German massacre of population of, 280–281

Kostiuk, Hryhorii, 187, 199, 201

Kostiuk, Fr. Iurii, 246

Kostiuk, Mykola, 150–151

Kostopil, town of, 195

Kostopil raion, 297

Kotliarevsky, Ivan, 189

Kotsiubynsky, Mykhailo, 54

Kovali, 93

Kovel, town of: Jewish ghetto in, 69

Kovel district, 280–281

Kovel region, 291, 296

Kovpak, Sydir, 276–277, 298, 305

Kraków, x, 10, 195

Kremenchuk: scorched-earth policy in, 21; Secret Field Police in, 49; anti-Jewish pogrom in, 57; Jewish ghetto in, 70; baptism of Jews in, 85; POW camp in, 103–104; deportations to Germany from, 269–270

Kremenets, town of, 73–74; NKVD massacre in, 16, 57; anti-Jewish pogrom in, 57; seminary in, 235

Kremenets region, 267, 291

Krychevsky, Fedir, 201

Kryvy Rih, city of, xi, 11, 201, 224, 304; industrialization in, 7; scorched-earth policy in, 21–22, 152–153; German administration of, 39, 45,

Kryvy Rih (*continued*)
162; mining industry in, 154–155, 253; popular culture in, 200; volunteers for labor in Germany from, 253
Kryvy Rih region, 103, 244
Kube, Wilhelm, 48
Kubiiovych, Volodymyr, 195
Kulaks, 7–8, 136–137
Kuntseve, 50
Kursk, Battle of, 291
Kursk region, 288
Kuznetsov, Anatolii, 28–29, 149, 155–156, 222, 266; and Jews, 65–66, 78; and famine in Kiev, 171–174, 179
Kuznetsov, Nikolai, 283
Kytasty, Hryhorii, 201

Labor Offices, 144–145, 255, 259–261, 268, 270
Landwirts, 40–41, 115, 118, 120, 122–126; treatment of peasants by, 128, 131–133, 137–139, 249
Lanivtsi raion, 267
Lashchenko, Halyna, 171
Lazorenko, Oleksii, 159
Lebed, Mykola, 289, 291, 298
Lebid, Mykhailo, 261
Left Bank, 36, 114, 226, 270; defined, 4; German civilian rule in, 48–49; Soviet POWs in, 93, 101–102, 106, 109–110; 1941 harvest in, 119–120; German retreat from, 300–301
Lelchitsy, 276
Lemko region, 10
Lenin, Vladimir, 7, 228
Leningrad, 51, 168, 171, 220
Levko, Uncle, 200
Leykauf, Hans, 167–168
Leyser, Ernst, 39, 238
Liakhiv, 84
Liubchenko, Arkadii, 183–184, 191
Liubeshiv: Jewish ghetto in, 70
Liuboml region, 285–286, 291
Lokachi raion, 60; Jewish ghetto in, 69–71, 82
Looting, 23–24, 34; of Jewish homes, 23, 78, 80, 116; in Kiev, 27, 29, 153, 302; by Germans, 114, 215
Lubny, town of, 21, 194, 255
Lubny region, massacre of Jews in, 78
Luhyny raion, 87

Lutheran church, 212
Lutsk, town of, 6, 11, 39, 62, 86, 289, 296, 303–304; NKVD massacres in, 14–15, 241
Lutsk region, 290–291
Lviv, x, 2, 6, 11, 149, 163, 187, 201; Banderite proclamation of statehood in, 20, 25, 103
Lychansk, 245
Lypkivsky, Metropolitan Vasyl, 232, 244
Lysenko, Mykola, 200
Lytvynivka, 119

Magazines: bulletin of All-Ukrainian Cooperative Society, 195; *Orlenia*, 195; *Shkoliar*, 195; *Silsky hospodar*, 195; *Ukraïnka*, 195; *Ukraïnska dytyna*, 195; *Ukraïnsky khliborob*, 195
Magunia, Waldemar, 39, 131, 143, 177, 181, 184–185, 244, 265
Main Office for Reich Security, 41, 248
Maistrenko, Ivan, 163
Makar, Vasyl, 287
Makariv, 20
Manstein, Fritz von, 100, 168
Manuïl (Tarnavsky), bishop, 296
Marriages, 85–86, 105, 211–212, 241, 270
Massacres: of Jews, 3, 41, 44, 46–48, 57, 62, 64–69, 92, 99, 105, 253, 255–257, 259–260, 282, 289, 295, 297, 299, 306–307, 310–311, 313; of Roma, 3, 41, 44, 48, 59–60, 253, 255–256, 259–260, 282, 299, 306, 311, 313; of Soviet POWs, 3, 44, 89–93, 96–97, 105–106, 111–113; by NKVD, 7–8, 13–17, 19–20, 56–57, 76, 81, 84, 188, 210, 241, 279, 283–285; of Poles, 287–299, 310. *See also* Reichskommissariat Ukraine, death penalty in
Matiïv (Lukiv) raion, 261
May, Karl, 116
Mazyr, 37
Medvyn, 119, 127, 130, 133–135, 137, 188, 271
Melitopol, 12, 39, 48, 91, 196
Melnyk, Andrii, 10, 288
Melnykites, x, 107, 160, 169–170, 192, 206, 294–295; origin of, 10; in Kiev, 51–52, 58; German executions of, 52; relations with Banderites, 53, 290–291; at Babi Yar, 68; as anti-Semitic, 83; and Sich sporting organization, 202. *See also* Banderites; Organization of Ukrainian Nationalists (OUN)

Mennonites, 17, 45, 212, 226–227, 300, 312

Merkulov, Vsevolod N., 14, 16

Mining and Metallurgical Corporation East, 41

Mining industry, 154–155

Minstrels, blind, 200

Mizoch: Jewish ghetto in, 70

Moldavian Autonomous Soviet Socialist Republic, 6, 10

Molotov, Viacheslav, 11, 18, 24, 51, 216–217, 222; Molotov-Ribbentrop pact, 9, 17, 61, 169

Moscow, 34–36, 51, 168, 220

Motion pictures, 197–198, 253; *The Jews and the NKVD*, 197; *The Life of the German Farmer and Worker and the Life of the People under Stalin's Yoke*, 197; *Süß the Jew*, 197

Mstyslav (Skrypnyk), bishop. *See* Skrypnyk, Stepan

Muslims, 92, 239

Muss (Kiev City Commissar), 170

Mykhalevych, Nina, 170

Mykolaïv, city of, 11, 45, 146, 239, 270–271, 304

Mykolaïv, general district of, 39, 45, 273

Mykolaïv oblast, 36–37; ethnic Germans in, 17

Mykolaïv region, 223, 225, 244

Myrhorod, 49, 130

Nartova, L., 105, 215; on Babi Yar massacre, 65–66, 76; on famine in Kiev, 173, 183–184; on deportations to Germany, 262–263, 268

Natives of Reichskommissariat Ukraine: defined, ix-x; Koch's attitudes toward, 1, 37–38, 45, 47–48, 186, 308; anti-Semitism among, 3, 30, 42, 52, 56–57, 59–62, 65–66, 71–73, 75, 77–78, 80–85, 87–88, 190–192, 203, 222–223, 250–251, 255, 288, 295, 310–311; attitudes toward prisoners of war, 3, 89, 91, 95–98, 100–101, 104–105, 107–111, 113; attitudes toward Soviet rule, 3, 204–205, 207, 209–210, 220–231, 242–243, 257, 286, 299, 308–309, 311–312; attitudes toward Roma, 3, 313; attitudes toward Germans, 3–4, 20–21, 28–29, 34, 62, 114–117, 120–122, 130, 133–134, 139–140, 164, 182–184, 186, 196, 198, 204, 213, 215–217, 220–221, 223–227, 229–231, 239–242, 274–275, 308–309, 311–313; attitudes toward ethnic identity/nationality, 4–5, 206–213, 228, 230, 311; anti-Commu-nism among, 20, 24, 28–29, 52, 54–58, 61, 64, 73, 83–84, 115, 117, 134, 191, 203–204, 220, 222–223, 225–226, 242–243, 255, 288; attitudes toward Hitler, 27, 216–217, 224; fear among, 32, 74–75, 77, 85, 88, 134, 136, 140, 150–151, 221, 224–225, 228–230, 249–251, 257–259, 261–262, 266–267, 273–274, 295–297, 310; as administrators, 39–41, 43, 51–52, 64–65, 118, 126, 129, 135–136, 151, 158–159, 161, 170, 190, 203, 242, 259–262, 271, 279, 283, 309–310; informers among, 54–57, 77–78, 134–135, 142, 250–251; Jews helped by, 60, 65, 76–77, 84–86, 309; prisoners of war helped by, 89, 95–98, 100–101, 104, 107–111, 113, 309; solidarity among, 141–142, 162–163, 190, 309–313; scientists and scholars among, 157–160, 162, 170, 172–173, 185, 265–266; attitudes toward Ukrainian nationalism, 205, 207–210, 218–219, 228, 230–231, 288–289, 294, 298–299, 312; attitudes toward Russians, 206–207, 209–210, 230, 288; use of *svoï/nashi* among, 206–207, 223, 228, 230–231, 304, 311–312; attitudes toward tsarist period, 209–210, 226, 230, 312; attitudes toward Stalin, 217, 221–222, 224–225, 228, 230–231, 312. *See also* City dwellers; Deportations to Germany; Germans, ethnic; Partisans, Soviet; Peasants; Ukrainian Insurgent Army; Young generation

Nazis: defined, x; attitudes toward Ukraine as source of food, 1, 35, 45–46, 99–100, 122, 125, 166; attitudes toward Ukrainian raw materials, 1, 44; policies toward ethnic Germans, 1, 44–45, 114, 142, 168, 210–213, 300, 309; attitudes toward rural lifestyle, 1–2; Lebensraum ethos of, 1–2, 44–47, 306; racist ideology of, 1–3, 44–47, 59–61, 72, 89–90, 113, 165, 187, 211, 266, 306; attitudes toward native city dwellers, 3, 35–36, 45–46, 137, 149, 154, 162, 164–169, 177, 186, 306–308; attitudes toward "Russian" prisoners of war, 3, 44, 89, 99–100, 105–110; attitudes toward Ukrainian culture, 4, 187–191, 194–196, 204; relations with OUN, 20, 41–42, 103, 110; policies toward Ukrainian prisoners of war, 90, 92, 106, 110, 206; attitudes toward non-Slavs, 92; attitudes toward Ukrainian science and scholarship, 158; policies toward religious organizations, 232–239, 241–242, 250, 308; policies toward partisans,

Nazis (*continued*)
280–285. *See also* Himmler, Heinrich; Koch, Erich; SS
Nazi-Soviet pact of 1939, 9, 17, 61, 169
Negretov, Pavlo, 207, 227–228
Nenadkevych, Mykhailo, 161
Newspapers, 191–194; *Poslednie novosti*, 89, 151, 177, 193; *Nove ukraïnske slovo*, 151, 171–172, 179, 192–193; *Deutsche Ukraine-Zeitung*, 151, 191–192; *Novoe slovo*, 192; *Podolianyn*, 192; *Volyn*, 192, 241; *Ukraïnske slovo*, 192–193; underground press, 204
Newsreels, 197
Nikanor (Abramovych), bishop, 55, 84, 190, 244
Nikolai (Avtonomov), bishop, 238
Nikopol, 154–155
NKVD, 91, 103, 118, 158, 162, 202–203, 227–228, 257, 286, 297; massacres by, 7–8, 13–17, 19–20, 56–57, 76, 81, 84, 188, 210, 241, 279, 283–285; extermination battalions of, 14–15, 27, 276; in Kiev, 16, 25–26, 30–33; informers for, 54, 78, 142, 222, 312; and Soviet partisans, 275, 278–279, 283. *See also* Communist Party members; Komsomol members
Northern Bukovina. *See* Bukovina, northern
Nosach, Pavlo, 200
Nova Praha, town of, 271
Nova Praha raion, 272
Nove Selo, 272
Novi Sanzhary raion, 50, 56–58, 129, 136–139, 281
Novy Hai, 296

Oberländer, Theodor, 48
Obolon: German massacre in 1941 in, 115; German massacre in 1943 in, 301
Obukhiv raion, 58, 267
Odessa, city of, 201, 221
Odessa oblast, 17, 37
Ohloblyn, Oleksander, 51, 85, 160, 202
Older generation: vs. young generation, 212–213, 228–230, 250–252; church attendance among, 249–251; and deportation to Germany, 268
Oleksander (Inozemtsev), archbishop, 236
Oleksandriia, town of: death march through, 98; butter factory in, 134, 229; deportation to Germany from, 263
Oleksandriia district: motion pictures in, 197

Oleksandrivka, small town of, 114, 250
Oleksandrivka, village of: UPA massacre of Poles at, 296
Oleksandrivka district: anti-Semitism in, 73
Oleksiienko, Stepan, 123
Onufriïvka, 101
Oppermann, Ewald, 39
Order Police, 41–43, 62, 106. *See also* Schuma
Order Service, 69–70
Organisation Todt, 211, 218, 273
Organization of Ukrainian Nationalists (OUN): in eastern Galicia, 8–9, 20; and Carpatho-Ukraine, 9; relations with Nazis, 20, 41–42, 103, 110; in Kiev, 51–52; as anti-Semitic, 52, 83–84, 288–289, 310; and Ukrainian national symbols, 53; and Soviet prisoners of war, 103, 111; relations with Red Cross, 109–110, 160; and deportations to Germany, 270–271. *See also* Banderites; Melnykites
Orikhiv, 61
Orthodox Autocephalous Synodal church, 232–233
Orthodox Christianity, 2, 4, 6, 55, 82–84; Autocephalous Orthodox church, 55, 83–84, 189–190, 194, 232–233, 235–238, 243–248, 250, 255, 296, 308; and anti-Semitism, 83–84, 255, 310; Autonomous Orthodox church, 84, 190, 232, 235–238, 243–244, 246–247, 255, 284, 295–296, 308; Renovationism, 232; Orthodox Autocephalous Synodal church, 232–233; Russian Orthodox church, 232–233, 235–236; Ukrainian Autocephalous Orthodox church, 232–233, 236; German policies toward, 232–238, 241–243; in eastern Galicia, 233; in Poland, 233; in western Volhynia, 233; taught in schools, 234, 243; Church Slavonic language in, 234, 245; Ukrainian language in, 234–235; Oblasny Sobor of 1941, 235; popular piety, 239–243, 252; in Kiev, 244–249; numbers of parishes, 246–248; church attendance, 248–252; and massacres of Poles, 292, 296
Ostrivky: UPA massacre of Poles at, 285–286, 295
OUN. *See* Organization of Ukrainian Nationalists

Panteleimon (Rudyk), bishop, 84, 190
Partisans, Polish, 293–294

Partisans, Soviet, 107, 111, 131, 224, 287, 293, 298; and deportations, 4, 273–274, 279, 282–283, 310; reprisals for activity of, 48–49, 115, 132, 134, 147, 280–281, 283; anti-Semitism among, 83; numbers of, 83, 276–278; Kalashnikov (mythical partisan), 216; Central Staff for, 275; Stalin's policies toward, 275, 278–279; after Stalingrad, 276–277; railroads attacked by, 278–279; fighting with Ukrainian nationalists, 279–280; relations with Polish partisans, 294

Partisans, Ukrainian nationalist. *See* Polissian Sich; Ukrainian Insurgent Army

Pasichna, Tetiana, 85

Patriarchal church. *See* Russian Orthodox church

Pavlohrad, 154, 300

Pavlovychi, 87; massacres of Jews in, 62, 64, 74, 86–87

Peasants, 114–140; attitudes toward Germans, 3–4, 20–21, 34, 114–117, 120–122, 130, 133–134, 139–140, 213, 215–217, 225, 239–240; working conditions for, 3–4, 122–125, 131–132, 138–139, 145, 154; and collectivization, 7–8, 71–72, 117, 119, 121–126, 131, 138–140, 307–308; *kulaks*, 7–8, 136–137; and scorched-earth policy, 19–20; attitudes toward Communism, 20, 115, 117, 134, 220, 225–226, 242–243; relations with landwirts, 40–41, 115, 118, 120, 122, 124–126, 128, 131–133, 137–139, 249; relations with Jews, 60, 82–83; rape of, 114–115, 217; relations with German Army, 114–117; killing of, 116; food available to, 116–117, 127–131, 135–136, 138–140; poverty of, 116–117, 131; in Red Army, 117–118; women among, 117–118, 134; curfews for, 118; identification documents for, 118; and 1941 harvest, 119–120; wages for, 120–121, 123, 125; food confiscated from, 122, 125, 127–130, 138, 170–171, 177, 179, 186; taxation of, 122–123, 125–127, 138; forced labor of, 123, 134–135; and cooperatives, 124–125, 129, 211–212; livestock of, 125, 127, 131, 138; and "tenth" system, 125, 128; gardens of, 125–127, 131, 139–140, 307; alcohol consumption among, 131, 136, 203–204; relations with city dwellers, 131, 169–170, 176–177, 180, 185–186; floggings of, 132–133, 135, 249; collective punishment of, 134–135; and privatization of land, 139–140; and motion pictures, 197–198; private gather-

ings of, 203–204; attitudes toward tsarist period, 226, 230; church attendance among, 248–252; deported to Germany, 263–264, 266–268, 273

People's Commissariat of Internal Affairs. *See* NKVD

Pereiaslav raion, 128

Pervomaisk, 130

Petersburg, 51

Petliura, Symon, 53, 80, 199, 207, 210, 219, 226

Petrenko, Valentyna, 15

Petrusenko, Liza, 86

Pihido, Fedir, 25, 155, 212; on Red Army, 12–13; on POWs, 12–13, 94; on Babi Yar massacre, 65–66; on Jews as fugitives, 70–71; on peasants, 115, 130–131, 136, 209, 219, 241; on Eastern Workers, 256–257, 406n150; on Operation Lightning, 283

Pinsk, town of, 37, 236

Pinsk district, 304

Pisky, 268

Plotnikov, V. O., 158

Poberezhka, 54

Pochaïv monastery, 235, 241–242

Pochapyntsi, 266

Podlachia, 10, 235–236

Podolia, 37, 85, 130, 192, 218–219, 247, 258, 302; NKVD killings in, 8; anti-Communism in, 20; Soviet partisans in, 111, 277; deportations from, 266, 272

Podvorniak, Mykhailo, 54, 298

Pohrebyshche raion, 279–280

Poland: Ukrainian population of, 6, 8–10; German invasion of, 9–10; Soviet invasion of, 9–10, 288, 295; social solidarity in, 141, 163, 310; Orthodox Christianity in, 233; Home Army, 294. *See also* General Government

Poles: in western Volhynia, x, 4, 208–209, 212, 239, 285–297, 299–300, 310; massacred by UPA, 4, 285–297, 299–300, 310; as "guest workers," 150, 258; helped by Ukrainians, 296–297

Police, auxiliary. *See* Schuma

Polikarp (Sikorsky), archbishop, 83–84, 235–238, 241, 244, 246–247, 255

Polissia, 37, 53, 130, 236, 238; attitudes toward Germans in, 20; massacres of Jews in, 64, 74; Soviet partisans in, 276–277, 280–281

Polissian Sich, 64, 286, 289

Politsai. *See* Schuma

Poltava, city of, 78, 130, 162, 182; NKVD massacre in, 16; Hitler's visit near, 35; POW camp in, 102, 109–111; popular culture in, 188–189, 201; Orthodox Christianity in, 248–249, 255

Poltava district, 242

Poltava oblast, 36, 210

Poltava region, 21, 49, 53, 73, 115, 138, 223, 228, 244

Ponomarenko, Panteleimon, 275

Popular culture, 4, 187–204; commemorations, 188–190; reading and writing, 190–195; schools, 195–196, 229, 234, 243, 308; movies, 197–198; performances and exhibitions, 198–202; *Hetman Doroshenko*, 199; *Marusia Bohuslavka*, 199; *They Were Duped*, 199; blind minstrels, 200; sports, 202–203; private gatherings, 203–204

Porytsk, 84

Potapenko, Ivan, 245

Povshuk, Oleksander, 294–295

Prisoners of war, German, 112

Prisoners of war, Soviet, 89–113; "Russians" among, 3, 44, 89–92, 99–100, 105–110; massacres of, 3, 44, 89–93, 96–97, 105–106, 111–113; numbers of, 11–12, 89, 91, 99; starvation of, 44, 95–96, 99–103, 108–113, 168, 253, 255–256, 307, 311; helped by natives, 89, 95–98, 100–101, 104, 107–111, 113, 309; Ukrainians among, 90, 92, 106, 110, 206; Communists among, 90–93, 106; Commissar Order regarding, 91–93; and "Guidelines for the Conduct of the Army in Russia," 92; non-Slavs among, 92; Jews among, 92, 98–99; Belarusans among, 92, 106; death marches of, 93–99, 112; as members of camp police (Lagerpolizei), 99, 101–103, 113; camps for, 99–113; and Red Cross, 100, 102, 105, 107–111; anti-Communism among, 103; cannibalism among, 103; escapes of, 103, 110–112; work performed by, 104–105; ethnic Germans among, 106; releases of, 106–110, 260; and "people's mail," 107; as "voluntary helpers" (Hiwis), 107

Privatization of land, 138–140, 298

Produbiïvka, 280

Pronicheva, Dina, 67–68

Propaganda, German, 120, 126–127, 138, 166, 188, 190–191, 222, 283–284; effectiveness of, 27, 50–51, 81, 88, 204, 309; Hitler in, 50–51, 120, 241–242; as anti-Semitic, 72, 81, 88; regarding POWs, 90–91; movies, 197, 253; for labor in Germany, 253–255

Propaganda, Soviet, 10–11, 120, 204, 207, 216–217, 222, 229, 254, 270–271, 308–309

Proskuriv (Khmelnytsky), 11, 55, 194, 304; NKVD massacre in, 16

Prostitution, 114–115, 182

Prosvita societies, 199

Protestantism, 4; Mennonites, 17, 45, 212, 226–227, 300, 312; Baptists, 87, 238–239, 252, 308; Evangelical Christianity, 87, 238–239, 252, 308; Lutherans, 212

Prützmann, Hans-Adolf, 42, 300

Prykhodko, Mykola, 16

Pshebrazhe, 294

Quitzrau, I., 159

Raba, Khyma, 19–20

Radio broadcasts: Soviet, 24–26, 222, 275; Nazi, 61, 96, 120, 221, 254, 265, 284, 302; neglected, 190

Radomyshl: massacre of Jews in, 64

Raions: administration of, 39–41, 43, 129, 260–262

Rape, 114–115, 217, 222, 302

Ratne, 280–281, 295–296

Red Army: purged by Stalin, 9; during German invasion, 11–13, 207, 210, 220, 289–290; morale in, 12–13, 91, 103, 207, 210; in Kiev, 27, 303; victory at Stalingrad, 47, 83–84, 98–99, 138–139, 183–184, 190, 217, 221, 225, 271–272, 276–277, 289–290, 300; return to Dnieper Ukraine, 80–81, 88, 145, 205, 220–221, 223–224, 229–230, 300, 303–306, 312; commissars in, 90–92, 103; fugitives from, 91–92, 103, 110–113; peasants in, 117–118; in Kharkiv, 222; opposed by UPA, 286, 299, 305; First Ukrainian Front, 299. *See also* Prisoners of war, Soviet

Red Cross, 138, 170; and POWs, 100, 102, 105, 107–110, 111; in Kiev, 107–109, 160–162; relations with OUN, 109–110, 160

Reichenau, Walter von, 48–49, 94, 167

Reich Ministry for the Fortification of Germandom, 44

Reich Ministry for the Occupied Eastern Territories, 36, 48, 72, 160; decollectivization banned by, 117, 120

Reich Security, Main Office for, 41, 248

Reichskommissariat Ostland, 36, 43, 48, 196, 201, 304

Reichskommissariat Ukraine, ix-xi; administration of, x, 3, 39–48, 52–53, 126, 144–146, 149–152, 157, 166, 187, 211, 234–238, 242, 259–260, 298, 305, 309–310; death penalty in, 3, 77, 85, 88, 111, 127, 133–134, 147–148, 156, 181, 259, 263, 265, 267–268, 271–273, 283, 295–298, 302, 309; vs. General Government, 10, 51, 53, 136, 149, 163, 187, 195, 201, 204, 239, 308, 310; origins of, 36–37; population of, 36–37; vs. Soviet Ukraine, 39–40, 76, 94, 117, 119–123, 125, 131, 139–140, 145–146, 153, 180, 186, 192–193, 197–198, 231, 251–252, 254, 258, 262, 308, 310–311; raion administration in, 39–41, 43, 129, 173, 260–262; armament commands in, 41; private German corporations in, 41; collective farms in, 41, 45, 121–123, 126, 131, 139–140, 169, 307–308; economy commands in, 41, 166, 174; vs. Reichskommissariat Ostland, 43, 48, 196, 201; judicial system in, 43, 126, 132, 135–137, 182, 194, 270; state farms in, 45, 123, 265; concentration/labor camps in, 58, 156, 203; cooperatives in, 120, 124–125, 129, 139, 155, 174, 195, 211–212; Labor Offices in, 144–145, 255, 260–261, 268, 270; currency in, 146, 176

Reprisals: for partisan activity, 48–49, 134, 280–281; for sabotage, 48–49, 147

Resistance: to German deportation, 4, 182, 253, 261, 268–271, 279, 298, 310; concept of, 5, 310; by Jews, 69–70; in Pavlohrad in 1943, 300. See also Partisans, Soviet; Ukrainian Insurgent Army

Right Bank, 118, 223–224, 252; defined, 4; Soviet scorched-earth policy in, 19; Soviet POWs in, 91, 99, 106–107; Red Army fugitives in, 112; 1941 harvest in, 119; peasant gardens in, 126; German retreat from, 302

Rivne, town of, xi, 6, 11, 20, 42, 45, 62, 160, 303; as capital of Reichskommissariat Ukraine, 39, 166, 168–169; massacre of Jews in, 81, 86; POW camps in, 101, 103, 108; Volyn, 151; publishing in, 151, 192, 195; popular culture in, 200–201; NKVD massacre in, 241; deportation to Germany from, 263; killing of prison inmates by Security Police in, 282

Rivne region, 287, 291

Rivno: German massacre of civilians in, 302

Rogausch (Kiev City Commissar), 159–161, 177, 202, 262

Rokytne raion, 118

Rokytne region, 299–300

Roma, x; massacres of, 3, 41, 44, 48, 59–60, 253, 255–256, 259–260, 282, 299, 306, 311, 313; attitudes of natives toward, 3, 313; in Sarny, 70

Roman Catholic church, 206, 211–212, 238–239, 308

Romania, 221, 226; relations with Soviet Union, 10; and northern Bukovina, 10, 37; and southern Bessarabia, 10, 37; relations with Germany, 37; and Transnistria, 37, 201

Romanian army, 2, 11, 97, 112, 114–115, 217

Romashky, 118

Roques, Karl von, 167

Rosenberg, Alfred, 42, 44, 168, 176–177, 194; relationship with Koch, 36, 47–48, 196, 286–287; relationship with Hitler, 47–48; attitudes toward Ukraine, 47–48, 306; attitudes toward Soviet prisoners of war, 94, 100–101; relationship with Keitel, 94, 100–101; policies toward schools, 195–196

Rukh (football team), 202

Rumors, 27, 51, 120, 220–222, 243, 255, 258–259, 284

Russian language, 7, 193–195, 198, 288, 311

Russian Liberation Army (ROA), 53, 190

Russian Orthodox church, 232–233, 235–236

Russians, x, 2, 7, 42, 153, 312; as prisoners of war, 3, 44, 89–92, 99–100, 105–110; attitudes of Ukrainians toward, 206–207, 209–210, 230, 288

Russo-Japanese war of 1905, 12

Rykun, 266

Rzhyshchiv, 269

Samchuk, Ulas, 151, 182, 201, 299, 390n29; Mariia, 191

Samoilenko, Hrytsko, 135–136

Sarny, town of: NKVD massacre in, 16; Jewish ghetto in, 69–70; massacre of Roma in, 70; research institute in, 158

Sarny region, 290–291

Sauckel, Fritz, 165, 259, 261, 273

Savchenko, Mariia, 19–20

SB. *See* Banderite Security Service

Scheer, Paul Albert, 46

Schöne, Heinrich, 39, 267–268

Schools, 195–196, 229, 234, 242, 308

Schuma, 42–43, 55–56, 87, 105, 118, 135, 146, 175, 202–203, 216; Gendarmerie, 42, 46, 51, 133–134, 176; Protective Police (Schutzpolizei), 42, 46, 179; Poles as, 42, 294; Jews killed by, 64, 68–69, 76, 82–83, 113, 295; at Babi Yar massacre, 68; peasants executed by, 133–134; food confiscated by, 177, 179–180; role in deportations to Germany, 259, 261–268, 270–273; and Soviet partisans, 278–283; and Ukrainian nationalists, 290–291; and UPA, 295, 298

Schwarzman, Getzel, 70

SD (Security Service), 41, 48, 55, 151, 257; reports by, 57, 64, 130, 143–144, 152–153, 170, 174, 197, 204, 208, 220, 223, 230, 244, 251, 261, 271; and Kiev famine, 130, 170, 173–174, 177, 180–184; Operation Lightning, 283

Secret Field Police, 41, 49, 57–58

Security Police, 41, 48, 92–93, 109, 151, 156, 159, 188, 202, 282, 284, 287, 291, 302–303; Jews killed by, 99; and Kiev famine, 170, 180–181, 184–185; and Orthodox church, 235; and Baptists, 238–239; and Catholics, 238–239; and Evangelical Christians, 238–239; and reburials, 241; and deportations to Germany, 262, 271; Operation Lightning, 283; school in Zakopane, 289, 298

Seleshko, Mykhailo, 203, 206, 208, 212, 228–230, 249–251

Selzner, Claus, 39

Semenivka, village of, 115

Semenivka raion, 301

Senytsia (Mayor of Kremenchuk), 85

Sergii (Stragorodskii), Metropolitan, 233

Sevastianov, Aleksandr, 97–98

Shaposhnikov, Boris, 222

Sharivka, 271–272

Shepetivka: POW camp in, 103

Sheptytsky, Metropolitan Andrei, 83, 239

Shevchenko, Taras, 55, 188, 199–200

Sheveleva, Evgeniia, 85

Shtepa, Konstantyn, 151, 160

Shukhevych, Roman, 298

Shumsk: anti-Jewish pogrom in, 57

Shumuk, Danylo, 293

Shybene, 246

Shytov, Ivan, 287

Skrypnyk, Stepan, 51, 84, 237

Slavuta: POW camp in, 111

Slobodianiuk, Mykhailo, 160

Slovak army, 2, 11, 112, 219

Slovakia, 9

Social cohesion, 141–142, 162–163, 190, 309–313

Sokil, 285

Sosnove: Jewish ghetto in, 69

Sovietization, 4, 10, 204–205, 219–220, 227–230, 308–312

Soviet Ukraine, 6–34, 194; Stalin's policies toward, 3, 7–8, 10, 12, 17–27, 30–34; anti-Semitism in, 3, 30, 32–33, 60–61, 71–72; sovietization in, 4, 10, 204–205, 219–220, 227–230, 308–312; administration of, 6–7, 39–40; industrialization in, 7; Jews in, 7, 10, 60–61; collectivization in, 7–8, 71–72, 117, 119–122, 124, 126, 131, 133–135; Great Famine in, 8, 83, 176, 180, 186, 192, 209, 227, 311; Belarusan population of, 10; Poles in, 10; Soviet scorched-earth policy in, 17–27, 29–34, 117, 119–120, 152–153, 155; anti-Communism in, 20, 24, 28–29, 33; looting in, 23–24, 27, 29, 34, 116; paranoia about spies in, 23–25, 34; draft evasion in, 27, 34; raions in, 39–40; vs. Reichskommissariat Ukraine, 39–40, 76, 94, 117, 119, 120–123, 125, 131, 139–140, 145–146, 153, 180, 186, 192–193, 197–198, 231, 251–252, 254, 258, 262, 308, 310–311; Great Terror of 1930s in, 77; state farms in, 123; newspapers in, 192–193; football teams in, 202–203; religion in, 232–233, 236. *See also* Communist Party members; Komsomol members; NKVD

Soviet Union, x; German invasion of, 2, 11–13, 24–34, 207, 210, 213, 215, 220, 230, 234–235, 239–240, 289–290; invasion of Poland by, 9–10; relations with Germany, 9–10, 17, 61, 169; annexation of Baltic states by, 10; relations with Finland, 10; relations with Romania, 10

Spies, Soviet, 238, 249, 297

Sports, 202–203

SS, 28, 43–47, 105–106, 135, 282–283, 298; gas vans operated by, 4, 147, 302–303; reputation of, 21; Jews killed by, 32–33, 46–48, 57, 64, 69, 73–74, 77, 83, 113, 212; and Babi Yar, 33, 77, 302–303; Main Office for Reich Security, 41, 248; *Einsatzgruppen* (Operational Groups), 41–42, 52, 54, 62, 64, 68, 72–73, 92, 158; Himmler, 42, 44–47, 69, 73, 165, 211–212, 280, 282–283, 300–301; and Soviet partisans, 48–49, 276; POWs killed by, 91–93; Waffen-SS, 270, 301. *See also* Order Police; Schuma; SD (Security Service); Security Police

Staiky, 19, 115, 241, 283

Stalin, Joseph: policies toward Ukraine, 3, 7–8, 10, 12, 17–27, 30–34; attitudes of natives toward, 3, 217, 221–222, 224–225, 228, 230–231, 312; policies of collectivization, 7–8; relationship with Khrushchev, 8, 18, 304; Red Army purged by, 9; policies toward ethnic Germans, 17; scorched-earth policies, 17–27, 29–34, 117, 119–120, 152–153, 155; policies toward partisans, 275, 278–279; after Stalingrad, 300

Stalingrad, 37; German defeat at, 47, 83–84, 98–99, 138–139, 183–184, 190, 217, 221, 225, 271–272, 276–277, 289–290, 300

Stanislav, 6

Stanovyshche, 123

Stari Bezradychy, 54, 58, 267

Start (football team), 202–203

Starvation: of city dwellers, 3, 45–46, 164–186, 221, 253, 255, 306, 308; of POWs, 44, 95–96, 99–103, 108–113, 168, 253, 255–256, 307, 311

Stavyshche, 116

Stoianka, 123

Strokach, Tymofii, 275, 278, 287

Stryzhivka, 124

Stukalo, Fr. N. P., 250

Subcarpathian Rus (Transcarpathia), 2, 9, 42

Sukhenko, Iasha, 86

Sumy oblast, 37

Sumy region, 226, 276

Svitnytska, Olha, 86

Svyniukhy (Pryvitne), 82

Sylvestr (Haievsky), bishop, 84, 189

Syrets concentration camp, 58, 203

Tahancha, 133

Tarashcha, town of, 54

Tarashcha region, 134–135, 170

Tatars, 2

Ternopil, 6

Timoshenko, Semen, 51

Torchyn, 56

Transnistria, 37, 201

Trubakov, Zakhar, 303

Tuchyn: anti-Jewish pogrom in, 57; Jewish ghetto in, 70

Ukraine, Reichskommissariat. *See* Reichskommissariat Ukraine

Ukraine, Soviet. *See* Soviet Ukraine

Ukrainian Autocephalous Orthodox church, 232–233, 236

Ukrainian Central Committee, 10, 51, 195

Ukrainian Council of Trust in Volhynia, 51, 237

Ukrainian Insurgent Army (UPA), 277, 285–300; massacres of Polish civilians by, 4, 285–297, 299–300, 309–310; relations with Autonomous Orthodox church, 244; fighting against Soviet partisans, 279–280; opposing Red Army, 286, 299, 305; fighting against Germans, 287, 298; number of members, 291; as anti-Semitic, 295; Schuma deserters in, 295, 298

Ukrainian language, 7–8, 60, 193–195, 198, 234, 245–246, 308, 311

Ukrainian National Council, 51–52, 159, 246

Ukrainian National Democratic Alliance, 9

Ukrainian National Republic, 28, 210

Ukraïnka, Lesia, 189

Ukraïnska Korespondentsiia, 192

Uman, town of, 11, 86, 91, 194; NKVD massacre in, 16, 20; research institute in, 158; deportations to Germany from, 271; German massacre in, 302

Uman region, 127–128, 225, 244

Uniate church. *See* Greek Catholic church

Union for the Liberation of Ukraine, 207

Union of Belarusan Youth, 196

UPA. *See* Ukrainian Insurgent Army

Vasylkiv, town of, 139, 195

Vasylkiv district, 124

Vasylkivka, 240

Vatutin, Nikolai, 299

Velychkivsky, Mykola, 51, 159, 246

Velyka Bahachka raion, 130, 138

Velyki Lypniahy: German massacre of civilians in, 301

Velykopolovetske raion, 139

Velyky Stydyn, 297

Veniiamyn (Novytsky), bishop, 255

Verbivka, 87

Verkhovskoi (Mayor of Kremenchuk), 85

Vershyhora, Petro, 305–306

Vilna Tarasivka, 139

Vinnytsia, city of, 11, 45, 146, 152, 157, 183, 185–186, 194, 208, 230, 238, 304; NKVD killings in, 16, 84, 188, 283–285; anti-Semitism in, 73; Jewish ghetto in, 88; POWs marching through, 97–99; POW camp in, 101; housing in, 144; popular culture in, 198–200, 203; drama theater in, 199; Orthodox Christianity in, 248–250; deportations to Germany from, 261; Labor Office in, 270. See also City dwellers

Vinnytsia district, 239

Vinnytsia oblast, 37; scorched-earth policy in, 21

Vinnytsia region, 107, 206–207, 212, 228, 247, 251–252

Viun, Halyna Ivanivna, 109–110

Vlasov, Andrei, 53, 190

Volhynia, eastern, 6, 51; Pavlovychi, 62, 64, 74; Holocaust in, 62, 64, 86–87; partisans in, 287

Volhynia, western, 2, 6, 10, 36, 50–51, 54, 193–194, 277; Polish population of, x, 4, 208–209, 212, 239, 260, 285–297, 299, 309–310; UPA massacres in, 4, 285–297, 299, 309–310; Ukrainian population of, 6, 12, 208–209, 218–219, 260; NKVD massacres in, 14–16, 57, 188; Soviet scorched-earth policy in, 18–19, 21; Germans welcomed in, 20; anti-Communism in, 20, 56, 64; peasants in, 20, 119; German administration of, 53; Jews in, 56–57, 62, 69–70; anti-Semitism in, 57, 81–83; and Polissian Sich, 64; Holocaust in, 64–65, 81–84, 87; collective farms in, 117; state farms in, 123; alcohol consumption in, 136; popular culture in, 200–201; Orthodox Christianity in, 233–235, 244–245, 250; Roman Catholic church in, 239; deportations to Germany from, 259; hostage taking in, 283; return of Red Army to, 304

Volhynia-Podolia, general district of, 39, 130, 267–268

Volia Ostrovetska: UPA massacre of Poles at, 285–286

Volodymyrets, Jewish ghetto in, 69

Volodymyr-Volynsky, 296; NKVD massacre in, 15–16; POW camp in, 103, 111

Volynsky, Leonid, 93–95

Voroshilov, Kliment, 51

Vynnychenko, Volodymyr, 207, 210

Vysotsk: anti-Jewish pogrom in, 84

Wages: for peasants, 120–121, 123, 125; for city dwellers, 145–146, 150, 152–153. See also Working conditions

Wagner, Eduard, 100

Warsaw, 62

Weiner, Amir, 312

Western Volhynia. See Volhynia, western

West Ukrainian National Republic, 6

Wochenschauen, 197

Women: NKVD massacre in Dubno, 15, 56; Soviet scorched-earth policy and, 19–20; looting, 23–24; kill NKVD informant, 56; living with former POWs, 105, 112; peasant, 117–118, 122, 134, 243; as employees in cities, 146, 150, 158; German, 149; friendships with German soldiers, 182–183, 198, 258; selling at Kiev markets, 185–186; in Germany as Eastern Workers, 256, 266. See also Brothels; Rape

Working conditions: for peasants, 3–4, 122–125, 131–132, 138–139, 145, 154; for Soviet POWs, 104–105; for city dwellers, 144–160, 162; for Eastern Workers, 256–259. See also Wages

World War I, 12

Yiddish, 60

Young generation: vs. older generation, 13, 212–213, 228–230, 250–252; among ethnic Germans, 226–227, 312; as pro-Communist, 227–230, 312; religion among, 250–252; and deportation to Germany, 260–262, 264–266, 268, 271–272; partisan activity, 282. See also Children

Zaporizhzhia, city of, xi, 146, 153, 182, 228–229, 240, 303; industrialization in, 7; Soviet scorched-earth policy in, 21–23; German administration of, 39, 45; volunteers for labor in Germany from, 253

Zaporizhzhia oblast, 36; ethnic Germans in, 17

Zaporizhzhia region, 130, 265

Zarubyntsi, 128, 267

Zbytyn, 294–295

Zhukov, Georgii, 222

Zhyhadlo, Ivan, 78, 263–264

Zhytomyr, city of, 11, 146, 235, 238, 303; Soviet scorched-earth policy in, 21; looting in, 23; Melnykites executed in, 52; death march of Jews through, 75; death march of POWs through, 98; POW camp in, 99–102, 106–107

Zhytomyr, general district of, 39, 238; forced migration in, 45, 211, 264; peasants in, 124, 126–127, 137; Soviet partisans in, 276–277, 279–280, 282

Zhytomyr oblast, 6, 11; ethnic Germans in, 17; Soviet scorched-earth policy in, 21

Zhytomyr region, 45, 72, 208, 233, 247, 252, 264, 276

Zinkiv raion, 138

Znamianka, 269

Żur, Leon, 290, 293, 299–300

Zvenyhorodka region, 244

Zviahel (Novohrad-Volynsky), 213